aboard	탑승하여, 배 위로	**abroad**	해외에(서)
access	접근[접속]하다, 접근	**assess**	평가하다, 재다
adapt	적응시키다, 적응하다	**adopt**	채택하다, 입양하다
addiction	중독	**addition**	추가, 덧셈
aesthetic	미학의, 미(美)의	**authentic**	진짜의, 진정한
affect	영향을 미치다, 감정	**effect**	가져오다, 결과, 영향, 효과
alley	골목	**ally**	동맹국, 협력자, 지지하다
annual	매년의, 연간의	**annul**	취소하다
appeal	매력, 간청	**appear**	나타나다, ~인 것 같다
arise	생기다, 발생하다	**arouse**	불러일으키다
artificial	인공의, 인위적인	**artistic**	예술적인
assault	폭행, 공격, 괴롭히다	**assort**	분류하다, 구분하다
bald	대머리인	**bold**	대담한, 용감한
barrel	통, 배럴	**barren**	척박한, 황량한
beat	이기다, 때리다	**bit**	조금, 약간
beside	~의 옆에	**besides**	게다가, ~이외에도
borrow	빌리다, 차용하다	**burrow**	굴을 파다
breadth	폭, 넓이	**breath**	숨, 호흡
bribe	뇌물, 뇌물을 주다	**bride**	신부
cancel	취소하다, 무효화하다	**cancer**	암
cite	인용하다, 예로 들다	**site**	장소, (인터넷) 사이트
cloth	옷감, 직물, 천	**clothes**	옷, 의복
clown	광대	**crown**	왕관, 왕위에 앉히다
coast	해안, 해변, 연안	**cost**	값, (값·비용이) ~이다
collect	모으다, 수집하다	**correct**	맞는, 옳은, 바로잡다
command	명령, 명령하다	**commend**	칭찬하다, 추천하다
competent	유능한, 적격인	**competitive**	경쟁의
complement	보충하다, 보충	**compliment**	칭찬하다, 칭찬
confident	자신 있는	**confidential**	비밀의, 기밀의
confirm	확인하다, 승인하다	**conform**	따르다, 순응하다
conscience	양심	**conscious**	의식하는
considerable	상당한, 중요한	**considerate**	사려 깊은
council	의회, 협의회	**counsel**	조언, 상담을 하다
curb	억제하다, 억제	**curve**	곡선, 곡선을 이루다
daily	매일 일어나는, 일일	**dairy**	낙농업, 유제품의
dedicate	바치다, 헌신하다	**delicate**	연약한, 섬세한
deep	깊은, 깊이	**dip**	살짝 담그다, 내려가다
deprive	빼앗다	**derive**	끌어내다, 얻다, 유래하다
desert	사막, 버리다	**dessert**	디저트, 후식
devote	바치다, 헌신하다	**devout**	독실한
die	죽다, 사망하다	**dye**	염색하다
discreet	신중한, 분별 있는	**discrete**	분리된, 별개의
distinct	별개의, 뚜렷한	**instinct**	본능, 직감
emigrate	이주하다, 이민	**immigrate**	이민 오다, 와서 살다
emphasize	강조하다, 역설하다	**empathize**	공감하다, 감정 이입하다
ethical	윤리[도덕]의	**ethnic(al)**	민족의
expand	확장하다, 확대되다	**expend**	(돈·시간을) 쏟다
extend	확장하다, 연장하다	**extent**	정도, 크기
fail	실패하다, ~하지 못하다	**fair**	타당한, 공정하게, 박람회
fertile	비옥한, 다산의	**futile**	헛된, 쓸데없는
find	찾다, 발견하다	**found**	설립하다, 기초를 쌓다
firm	회사, 딱딱한	**form**	종류, 유형, 형성되다
flesh	살, 과육	**fresh**	신선한, 생생한
fury	분노, 격분	**furry**	털로 덮인, 털 같은
garage	차고, 주차장	**garbage**	쓰레기(장)
greed	탐욕, 식탐	**grid**	격자무늬, 격자판
imaginable	상상할 수 있는	**imaginary**	가상적인
immense	엄청난, 어마어마한	**immerse**	담그다, ~에 몰두하다
imply	암시하다, 내포하다	**infer**	추론하다, 유추하다
industrial	산업의, 공업의	**industrious**	근면한, 부지런한

ingenious	독창적인, 정교한	ingenuous	솔직한, 숨김없는	personal	개인의, 개인적인	personnel	직원의, 직원
inhabit	살다, 거주하다	inhibit	억제하다, ~하지 못하게 하다	phase	단계, 시기	phrase	구, 구절
instigate	선동하다, 부추기다	investigate	조사하다, 수사하다	poem	시	poet	시인
intend	의도하다, 의미하다	intent	몰두하는, 의도	pole	막대기, 극	pore	구멍
invaluable	매우 귀중한	valueless	하찮은, 가치 없는	politic	현명한, 신중한	political	정치적인, 정당의
invent	발명하다	invert	뒤집다, 도치시키다	pray	기도하다	prey	먹이, 사냥감
irrigate	물을 대다, 관개하다	irritate	짜증나게 하다, 자극하다	principal	주요한, (단체의) 장	principle	원리, 원칙
label	표, 라벨을 붙이다	labo(u)r	노동, 노동의	probe	조사하다, 조사	prove	입증하다, 증명하다
lay	놓다, (알을) 낳다	lie	눕다, 거짓말하다, 거짓말	propel	나아가게 하다	proper	적절한, 정당한
lead	이끌다, 납	lid	뚜껑	qualify	자격을 얻다, 자격을 주다	quantify	양을 나타내다, 수량화하다
lessen	줄이다, 줄다	lesson	수업, 교훈	quota	한도, 몫	quote	인용하다
level	정도, 수준, 평평한	lever	지레, 지렛대로 움직이다	raise	올리다, 일으키다	rise	오르다, 증가
literal	문자 그대로의	literate	글을 읽고 쓸 줄 아는	real	진짜의, 현실적인	rear	뒤쪽, 뒤쪽의
literary	문학의, 문학적인	literacy	글을 읽고 쓸 줄 아는 능력	reality	현실, 실재	realty	부동산, 물적 재산
loose	느슨한, 헐렁한	lose	잃다, 지다	require	필요하다, 요구하다	inquire	묻다, 조사하다
mass	덩어리, 대규모의	mess	엉망진창인 상태	respectable	존경할 만한, 훌륭한	respective	각자의, 각각의
mean	뜻하다, 비열한	means	수단, 방법	responsible	책임이 있는	responsive	즉각 반응하는
mediation	조정, 중재	meditation	명상, 심사숙고	role	역할	roll	통, 구르다
meld	섞이다, 섞다	melt	녹다, 녹이다	rot	썩다, 썩히다	rote	암기
miner	광부	minor	적은, 미성년자, 부전공	royal	왕실의, 왕의	loyal	충성스러운
momentary	순간적인, 잠깐의	momentous	중대한	sail	항해하다, 돛	sale	판매, 매출, 영업
moss	이끼	moth	나방	sand	모래, 모래사장	send	보내다, 발송하다
mound	언덕, 무더기	mount	오르다, 증가하다	saw	톱, 톱질하다	sew	바느질하다, (바느질로) 만들다
neural	신경(계통)의	neutral	중립의	scrap	조각, 폐기하다	scrape	긁다, 긁기
noble	고결한, 귀족	novel	소설, 새로운	sensible	분별 있는, 합리적인	sensitive	민감한, 예민한
numeral	숫자, 수사	numerous	많은	sole	유일한, 단 하나의	sore	아픈, 상처
objective	목적, 객관적인	objection	이의, 반대	soul	영혼, 정신, 마음	sour	신, 상하다
odd	이상한, 홀수의	odds	가능성, 역경	successful	성공한, 성공적인	successive	연속하는
own	소유하다, 자신의	owe	빚지고 있다	sympathy	동정, 연민, 공감	empathy	감정 이입, 공감
pare	벗기다, 깎다	pear	배	vague	모호한, 애매한	vogue	유행
peak	절정, 정점, 봉우리	peek	훔쳐 보다	vain	헛된, 하찮은	vein	정맥, 혈관
peel	벗기다, 껍질	pill	알약	virtual	사실상의, 가상의	virtue	미덕, 덕
persevere	버티다, 이겨내다	preserve	보존하다	wonder	궁금해하다, 놀라움	wander	돌아다니다

목차

모바일로 교재 MP3 이용하기

마더텅의 교재 MP3는 모바일
스트리밍/다운로드를 지원합니다.

이용방법 1
스마트폰으로 QR 코드 스캔!

이용방법 2
① 주소창에 **www.toptutor.co.kr**
　또는 포털에서 | 마더텅 | 검색
② 상단 메뉴 학습자료실
　→ **[무료동영상강의]** 클릭
③ 무료 동영상 강의에서
　[학년], [시리즈], [과목], [교재]
　선택 후 원하는 동영상 강의 수강

특별 제공

① 다양한 빠르기의 MP3 파일 지원!
난이도를 조절하여 듣기 실력을 향상시켜 보세요!

MP3 ① 원배속 ② 1.1배속 ③ 1.25배속 ④ 1.5배속

② 문항별 분할 MP3 파일 지원!
효율적인 학습을 위해 모든 회차의 각 문항별
MP3 파일 다운로드를 지원합니다.

영어 듣기 MP3 파일 다운로드 안내

한국교육과정평가원 홈페이지
www.suneung.re.kr
자료마당 〉 기출문제 〉 해당 모의평가 및
수능 MP3 파일 다운로드

서울특별시교육청 홈페이지
www.sen.go.kr
교육정보 〉 학력평가 자료 〉 해당
학력평가 MP3 파일 다운로드

* 또는 마더텅 홈페이지(www.toptutor.co.kr)
　'고등-교재자료실'에서 해당 교재 게시글의
　링크 확인 후 클릭하시면 다운로드 페이지로
　연결됩니다.

* 다운로드 과정에서 어려움을 겪으신 분들은,
　마더텅 고객센터(1661-1064)로 연락 바랍니다.

01

2018년 11월
학력평가

MP3
2SBL1_A01

동영상 강의
2SBL1_L01

1번부터 17번까지는 듣고 답하는 문제입니다. 1번부터 15번까지는 한 번만 들려주고, 16번부터 17번까지는 두 번 들려줍니다. 방송을 잘 듣고 답을 하시기 바랍니다.

01

고1 2018년 11월 3번

다음을 듣고, 여자가 하는 말의 목적으로 가장 적절한 것을 고르시오.

① 강의 일정 변경을 공지하려고
② 감사 일기 쓰는 것을 권장하려고
③ 건강 관리의 중요성을 강조하려고
④ 자기소개서 작성 요령을 설명하려고
⑤ 효과적인 시간 활용법을 안내하려고

02

고1 2018년 11월 4번

대화를 듣고, 남자의 의견으로 가장 적절한 것을 고르시오.

① 집중력 향상을 위해서는 충분한 휴식이 필요하다.
② 정돈된 학습 공간은 집중력을 높이는 데 도움이 된다.
③ 효율적인 학습을 위해서 학습 계획표를 작성해야 한다.
④ 많은 과제는 학생에게 학습에 대한 스트레스를 줄 수 있다.
⑤ 책임감을 기르기 위해서는 자녀도 집안일을 분담해야 한다.

03

고1 2018년 11월 5번

대화를 듣고, 두 사람의 관계를 가장 잘 나타낸 것을 고르시오.

① 안과 의사 - 환자
② 보건 교사 - 학생
③ 프로젝트 팀장 - 팀원
④ 컴퓨터 판매원 - 구매자
⑤ 약사 - 제약 회사 직원

04

고1 2018년 11월 6번

대화를 듣고, 그림에서 대화의 내용과 일치하지 않는 것을 고르시오.

05

고1 2018년 11월 7번

대화를 듣고, 남자가 여자를 위해 할 일로 가장 적절한 것을 고르시오.

① 감자 사 오기
② 케이크 만들기
③ 장학금 신청하기
④ 스테이크 주문하기
⑤ 식료품점 위치 검색하기

06

고1 2018년 11월 9번

대화를 듣고, 남자가 지불할 금액을 고르시오.

① $45
② $50
③ $63
④ $70
⑤ $72

07

고1 2018년 11월 8번

대화를 듣고, 여자가 거리 공연을 보러 갈 수 <u>없는</u> 이유를 고르시오.

① 학교 축제를 위한 부스를 만들어야 해서
② 좋아하는 밴드의 팬 사인회에 가야 해서
③ 동아리 부원들과 기타 연습을 해야 해서
④ 학급 친구들과 합창 대회 준비를 해야 해서
⑤ 과학 프로젝트를 위해 조원들을 만나야 해서

08

고1 2018년 11월 10번

대화를 듣고, Moonlight Palace Tour에 관해 언급되지 <u>않은</u> 것을 고르시오.

① 시작 시간　　② 참가비　　③ 인원 제한
④ 관람 시 유의점　　⑤ 예약 방법

09

고1 2018년 11월 11번

Forest Concert에 관한 다음 내용을 듣고, 일치하지 <u>않는</u> 것을 고르시오.

① 10월 7일에 열린다.
② 주제는 '꿈을 찾아서'이다.
③ 무료로 입장할 수 있다.
④ 사전 예약이 필요하다.
⑤ 집에서 TV로 시청할 수 있다.

10

고1 2018년 11월 12번

다음 표를 보면서 대화를 듣고, 두 사람이 선택할 수업을 고르시오.

Rainbow Community Center Evening Classes

	Class	Day	Time (p.m.)	Monthly Fee
①	Pottery	Mon.	7:00 ~ 9:00	$110
②	Drawing	Tue.	6:30 ~ 8:00	$80
③	French Baking	Wed.	6:30 ~ 8:00	$90
④	Yoga	Thu.	6:30 ~ 8:00	$70
⑤	Photography	Fri.	7:00 ~ 9:00	$80

11

고1 2018년 11월 1번

대화를 듣고, 여자의 마지막 말에 대한 남자의 응답으로 가장 적절한 것을 고르시오.

① You should be honest about your ideas.
② I can help to choose the right class for you.
③ I already took the career counseling program.
④ I'm thinking of making an English debate club.
⑤ You'll get all the academic advice as you need.

12

고1 2018년 11월 2번

대화를 듣고, 남자의 마지막 말에 대한 여자의 응답으로 가장 적절한 것을 고르시오.

① Of course. I bought it online.
② Not at all. It was fun to make a hat.
③ Okay. Let's go there together next time.
④ Was that you? I didn't know you went there.
⑤ It's true. I've never been to the local market.

13

대화를 듣고, 여자의 마지막 말에 대한 남자의 응답으로 가장 적절한 것을 고르시오. 3점

Man:

① Come on. You'll do fine if you volunteer with a kind heart.

② Okay, will you search for volunteer opportunities for me?

③ Sure. Let's check the list of art schools you could attend.

④ Yeah, you'd better plan your trip to Africa in advance.

⑤ You're right. We should have watched that movie.

14

대화를 듣고, 남자의 마지막 말에 대한 여자의 응답으로 가장 적절한 것을 고르시오. 3점

Woman:

① Sure. You can win the election with those strategies.

② Yeah, I'll support your effort to make a better school.

③ No way. It's impossible to satisfy everyone around you.

④ Thanks. I appreciate you for encouraging me to be positive.

⑤ Right. We need to talk more to understand one another better.

15

다음 상황 설명을 듣고, Sophia가 John에게 할 말로 가장 적절한 것을 고르시오. 3점

Sophia:

① Let's preview what we'll learn next class.

② How about applying math theory to the real life?

③ Could you tell me your secret to improving math skills?

④ You should read the directions of the questions carefully.

⑤ Why don't you practice less challenging math questions first?

[16~17] 다음을 듣고, 물음에 답하시오.

16

남자가 하는 말의 주제로 가장 적절한 것은?

① the best souvenirs to bring home from travel

② popular places in the world to photograph nature

③ tips on how to save money on souvenir shopping

④ the variety of cultural environments around the world

⑤ the most important travel safety rules to keep in mind

17

언급된 지역이 아닌 것은?

① Beijing　　② Paris　　③ Sydney
④ Hawaii　　⑤ Venice

※ 최신 영어 영역 시험의 듣기 문항 순서 변경에 따라 회차 내 문항 순서를 재배치하였습니다.

02 2019년 3월 학력평가

MP3   동영상 강의

2SBL1_A02   2SBL1_L02

😊 1번부터 17번까지는 듣고 답하는 문제입니다. 1번부터 15번까지는 한 번만 들려주고, 16번부터 17번까지는 두 번 들려줍니다. 방송을 잘 듣고 답을 하시기 바랍니다.

01
고1 2019년 3월 3번

다음을 듣고, 남자가 하는 말의 목적으로 가장 적절한 것을 고르시오.

① 파손된 사물함 신고 절차를 안내하려고
② 사물함에 이름표를 부착할 것을 독려하려고
③ 사물함을 반드시 잠그고 다녀야 함을 강조하려고
④ 사물함 교체를 위해 사물함을 비울 것을 당부하려고
⑤ 사물함 사용에 대한 학생 설문 조사 참여를 요청하려고

02
고1 2019년 3월 4번

대화를 듣고, 여자의 의견으로 가장 적절한 것을 고르시오.

① 무리한 여행 계획은 여행을 망칠 수 있다.
② 관광지에서 자연환경을 훼손하지 말아야 한다.
③ 여행할 지역의 문화를 미리 조사해 보는 것이 필요하다.
④ 남들이 추천하는 음식점에 꼭 가 볼 필요는 없다.
⑤ 여행을 가면 현지 음식을 먹어 보는 것이 좋다.

03
고1 2019년 3월 5번

대화를 듣고, 두 사람의 관계를 가장 잘 나타낸 것을 고르시오.

① 미용사 - 고객   ② 화방 점원 - 화가
③ 미술관장 - 방문객   ④ 패션 디자이너 - 모델
⑤ 모자 가게 주인 - 손님

04
고1 2019년 3월 6번

대화를 듣고, 그림에서 대화의 내용과 일치하지 않는 것을 고르시오.

05
고1 2019년 3월 7번

대화를 듣고, 여자가 남자를 위해 할 일로 가장 적절한 것을 고르시오.

① 악기 빌려다 주기
② 해변에 데려다 주기
③ 음악회에 함께 가기
④ 해양 스포츠 예약하기
⑤ 오디션 일정 확인해 주기

06
고1 2019년 3월 9번

대화를 듣고, 두 사람이 지불할 금액을 고르시오. [3점]

① $75   ② $80   ③ $85
④ $105   ⑤ $110

07

고1 2019년 3월 8번

대화를 듣고, 남자가 발표 자료를 수정해야 하는 이유를 고르시오.

① 최신 자료가 아니어서
② 발표 일정이 바뀌어서
③ 명칭 표기에 오류가 있어서
④ 그림 자료가 선명하지 않아서
⑤ 발표할 내용의 순서가 틀려서

08

고1 2019년 3월 10번

대화를 듣고, Royal Botanic Garden에 관해 언급되지 <u>않은</u> 것을 고르시오.

① 위치   ② 크기   ③ 프로그램
④ 입장료   ⑤ 개관 시간

09

고1 2019년 3월 11번

2019 Riverside High School Musical에 관한 다음 내용을 듣고, 일치하지 <u>않는</u> 것을 고르시오.

① 공연작은 *Shrek*이다.
② 공연을 위한 오디션은 작년 12월에 있었다.
③ 공연은 사흘간 진행된다.
④ 입장권은 1인당 8달러이다.
⑤ 입장권은 연극 동아리실에서 구입할 수 있다.

10

고1 2019년 3월 12번

다음 표를 보면서 대화를 듣고, 남자가 구입할 운동 매트를 고르시오.

Exercise Mats

	Model	Thickness	Price	Non-slip Surface
①	A	4mm	$24	×
②	B	6mm	$33	○
③	C	8mm	$38	×
④	D	8mm	$45	○
⑤	E	10mm	$55	○

11

고1 2019년 3월 1번

대화를 듣고, 여자의 마지막 말에 대한 남자의 응답으로 가장 적절한 것을 고르시오.

① Sorry, but I'd rather go to Spain by myself.
② No, I'm taking a class in the community center.
③ Yes, you need to eat healthy food for your brain.
④ Yeah, you don't have to worry about your brain.
⑤ Well, I'm not interested in learning Spanish.

12

고1 2019년 3월 2번

대화를 듣고, 남자의 마지막 말에 대한 여자의 응답으로 가장 적절한 것을 고르시오.

① That's right. I'll go there and see.
② Let's hurry. The P.E. class starts soon.
③ Good idea. It's important to clean the gym.
④ Thanks. I'll go to the lost and found now.
⑤ Okay. I'll return it tomorrow.

정답과 해설 : 07~12 8~9

13

고1 2019년 3월 13번

대화를 듣고, 여자의 마지막 말에 대한 남자의 응답으로 가장 적절한 것을 고르시오. [3점]

Man: _____

① There's no room for a new member in our club.

② I'm sorry that you didn't pass the club interview.

③ That's true. We can't trust all the information there.

④ Thanks, but I don't want to take the drone class again.

⑤ Right. I'll post an ad for a drone club I'm going to make.

14

고1 2019년 3월 14번

대화를 듣고, 남자의 마지막 말에 대한 여자의 응답으로 가장 적절한 것을 고르시오.

Woman: _____

① You're right. That's why I chose this book.

② That makes sense. I'll switch to an easier book.

③ Okay. I'll choose one from the bestseller list next time.

④ Don't worry. It's not too difficult for me to read.

⑤ Yeah. I'll join the book club to read more books.

15

고1 2019년 3월 15번

다음 상황 설명을 듣고, Becky가 Clara에게 할 말로 가장 적절한 것을 고르시오. [3점]

Becky: _____

① Why don't we find a camp on different dates?

② You should check the camp dates on this flyer first.

③ You need your parents' permission to join the camp.

④ How about signing up for the camp right now?

⑤ Let's not go to camp this year.

[16~17] 다음을 듣고, 물음에 답하시오.

16

고1 2019년 3월 16번

여자가 하는 말의 주제로 가장 적절한 것은?

① proverbs that have animals in them

② different proverbs in various cultures

③ why proverbs are difficult to understand

④ importance of studying animals' behavior

⑤ advantages of teaching values through proverbs

17

고1 2019년 3월 17번

언급된 동물이 아닌 것은?

① birds   ② mice   ③ cows
④ chickens   ⑤ dogs

02

19년 3월 학력평가

03 2019년 6월 학력평가

MP3   동영상 강의

😊 1번부터 17번까지는 듣고 답하는 문제입니다. 1번부터 15번까지는 한 번만 들려주고, 16번부터 17번까지는 두 번 들려줍니다. 방송을 잘 듣고 답을 하시기 바랍니다.

01
고1 2019년 6월 3번

다음을 듣고, 여자가 하는 말의 목적으로 가장 적절한 것을 고르시오.

① 자선 행사 개최를 공지하려고
② 경제 특강 참가자를 모집하려고
③ 물자 절약의 중요성을 강조하려고
④ 학생 회장 선거 후보자를 소개하려고
⑤ 학교 체육관 이용 방법을 안내하려고

02
고1 2019년 6월 4번

대화를 듣고, 남자의 의견으로 가장 적절한 것을 고르시오.

① 다양한 영양소의 섭취는 성장에 필수적이다.
② 식품 구매 시 영양 성분의 확인이 필요하다.
③ 새우를 섭취하는 것은 건강에 도움이 된다.
④ 체중 관리는 균형 잡힌 식단에서 비롯된다.
⑤ 음식을 조리할 때 위생 관리가 중요하다.

03
고1 2019년 6월 5번

대화를 듣고, 두 사람의 관계를 가장 잘 나타낸 것을 고르시오.

① 호텔 직원 - 투숙객
② 식당 지배인 - 요리사
③ 여행 가이드 - 여행객
④ 열쇠 수리공 - 집주인
⑤ 부동산 중개인 - 세입자

04
고1 2019년 6월 6번

대화를 듣고, 그림에서 대화의 내용과 일치하지 <u>않는</u> 것을 고르시오.

05
고1 2019년 6월 7번

대화를 듣고, 남자가 할 일로 가장 적절한 것을 고르시오.

① 감사 편지 쓰기
② 풍선 장식하기
③ 파스타 요리하기
④ 케이크 구매하기
⑤ 카네이션 만들기

06
고1 2019년 6월 9번

대화를 듣고, 남자가 지불할 금액을 고르시오.

① $15
② $30
③ $48
④ $54
⑤ $60

07

고1 2019년 6월 8번

대화를 듣고, 여자가 토론 대회에 참가할 수 <u>없는</u> 이유를 고르시오.

① 남들 앞에서 말하는 것이 힘들어서

② 뮤지컬 공연 준비를 해야 해서

③ 수행평가 일정이 연기되어서

④ 글쓰기 과제를 해야 해서

⑤ 토론 주제가 어려워서

08

고1 2019년 6월 10번

대화를 듣고, Career Vision Camp에 관해 언급되지 <u>않은</u> 것을 고르시오.

① 참가 대상   ② 등록 비용   ③ 지원 마감일

④ 기념품   ⑤ 행사 장소

09

고1 2019년 6월 11번

Children's Book Fair에 관한 다음 내용을 듣고, 일치하지 <u>않는</u> 것을 고르시오. [3점]

① 3일 동안 진행된다.

② 만화책을 포함한 아동용 도서를 전시한다.

③ 50% 할인된 가격으로 책을 살 수 있다.

④ 행사 첫 날에 유명 작가를 만날 수 있다.

⑤ 방문하는 모든 어린이는 책갈피를 선물로 받는다.

10

고1 2019년 6월 12번

다음 표를 보면서 대화를 듣고, 여자가 구입할 전기면도기를 고르시오.

Electric Shaver

	Model	Price	Battery Life	Waterproof	Color
①	A	$55	20 minutes	×	black
②	B	$70	40 minutes	×	white
③	C	$85	60 minutes	○	black
④	D	$90	70 minutes	○	white
⑤	E	$110	80 minutes	○	black

11

고1 2019년 6월 1번

대화를 듣고, 여자의 마지막 말에 대한 남자의 응답으로 가장 적절한 것을 고르시오.

① Yes. My car is broken.

② Sure. Let's go together.

③ No way. The show is over.

④ Right. I'll join the study club.

⑤ Sorry. I couldn't find the ticket.

12

고1 2019년 6월 2번

대화를 듣고, 남자의 마지막 말에 대한 여자의 응답으로 가장 적절한 것을 고르시오.

① Okay. I'll take the subway then.

② No. I didn't take your umbrella.

③ Right. It was too much work.

④ Yes. It will rain tomorrow.

⑤ Sorry. I can't drive a car.

13

대화를 듣고, 남자의 마지막 말에 대한 여자의 응답으로 가장 적절한 것을 고르시오. 3점

Woman: _____

① No problem. I've already handed it in.

② All right. Thank you for understanding.

③ Of course. I hope you'll get better soon.

④ Never mind. I'll take you to the hospital.

⑤ Sorry. The meeting hasn't been canceled yet.

14

대화를 듣고, 여자의 마지막 말에 대한 남자의 응답으로 가장 적절한 것을 고르시오. 3점

Man: _____

① You're welcome. I'm glad that you really enjoyed the gift.

② Don't worry about that. Everyone can learn from mistakes.

③ Yeah, I've sung the song. I want to sing in harmony now.

④ Okay, I'll sing for you. I hope you won't expect too much.

⑤ I don't think so. It's not easy to choose a wedding ring.

15

다음 상황 설명을 듣고, Alex가 Olivia에게 할 말로 가장 적절한 것을 고르시오.

Alex: _____

① You're very lucky to have a new job.

② I'll tell you where you should transfer to.

③ Let's keep in touch even after we part.

④ I was deeply touched by your kind words.

⑤ I hope you'll get used to your new school.

[16~17] 다음을 듣고, 물음에 답하시오.

16

남자가 하는 말의 주제로 가장 적절한 것은?

① foods at risk due to climate change

② reasons why sea temperatures rise

③ animals and plants in the water

④ requirements of growing crops

⑤ ways to solve global warming

17

언급된 음식이 아닌 것은?

① coffee   ② avocados

③ apples   ④ strawberries

⑤ coconuts

04 2019년 9월 학력평가

MP3   동영상 강의

2SBL1_A04   2SBL1_L04

※ 최신 영어 영역 시험의 듣기 문항 순서 변경에 따라 회차 내 문항 순서를 재배치하였습니다.

😊 1번부터 17번까지는 듣고 답하는 문제입니다. 1번부터 15번까지는 한 번만 들려주고, 16번부터 17번까지는 두 번 들려줍니다. 방송을 잘 듣고 답을 하시기 바랍니다.

01
고1 2019년 9월 3번

다음을 듣고, 여자가 하는 말의 목적으로 가장 적절한 것을 고르시오.

① 오디션 준비 요령을 알려주려고
② 학교 행사 아이디어를 공모하려고
③ 축제 홍보 활동 참여를 독려하려고
④ 공연 관람 규칙 준수를 당부하려고
⑤ 공연 리허설 장소 변경을 공지하려고

02
고1 2019년 9월 4번

대화를 듣고, 두 사람이 하는 말의 주제로 가장 적절한 것을 고르시오.

① 감자의 전파 과정
② 감자의 다양한 효능
③ 감자를 보관하는 방법
④ 감자를 이용한 요리법
⑤ 감자 재배 시 유의사항

03
고1 2019년 9월 5번

대화를 듣고, 두 사람의 관계를 가장 잘 나타낸 것을 고르시오.

① 신문 기자 — 작가
② 녹음 기사 — 성우
③ 영화감독 — 배우
④ 매니저 — 가수
⑤ 의사 — 환자

04
고1 2019년 9월 6번

대화를 듣고, 그림에서 대화의 내용과 일치하지 않는 것을 고르시오.

05
고1 2019년 9월 7번

대화를 듣고, 남자가 할 일로 가장 적절한 것을 고르시오.

① 배낭 빌려주기
② 항공권 예매하기
③ 은행에서 환전하기
④ 여행 안내 책자 주문하기
⑤ 호텔 숙박비 비교 앱 알려 주기

06
고1 2019년 9월 9번

대화를 듣고, 남자가 지불할 금액을 고르시오. [3점]

① $27   ② $36   ③ $40
④ $45   ⑤ $63

정답과 해설 : 01~06 15~17

07

고1 2019년 9월 8번

대화를 듣고, 여자가 El Bistro 레스토랑을 선택한 이유를 고르시오.

① 호텔에서 가까워서
② 오랜 전통이 있어서
③ 프랑스 요리로 유명해서
④ TV 프로그램에 소개되어서
⑤ 지역 주민에게 인기가 많아서

08

고1 2019년 9월 10번

대화를 듣고, Stress Free Program에 관해 언급되지 않은 것을 고르시오.

① 활동 종류　　② 등록 방법　　③ 운영 장소
④ 참가비　　　 ⑤ 운영 시간

09

고1 2019년 9월 11번

Show Me Your Dishes에 관한 다음 내용을 듣고, 일치하지 않는 것을 고르시오.

① 참가 대상은 15세부터 18세의 청소년이다.
② 2004년부터 매년 열리는 대회이다.
③ 참가하려면 조리법을 대회 웹 사이트에 업로드해야 한다.
④ 참가자에게 90분의 요리 시간이 주어진다.
⑤ 심사의 기준은 맛과 창의성이다.

10

고1 2019년 9월 12번

다음 표를 보면서 대화를 듣고, 여자가 주문할 블루투스 키보드를 고르시오.

Bluetooth Keyboards

	Model	Price	Weight	Battery Life	Foldable
①	A	$45	160g	100 hours	×
②	B	$38	250g	82 hours	○
③	C	$30	280g	48 hours	×
④	D	$26	350g	10 hours	○
⑤	E	$15	420g	24 hours	×

11

고1 2019년 9월 1번

대화를 듣고, 여자의 마지막 말에 대한 남자의 응답으로 가장 적절한 것을 고르시오.

① Well, the project was successful.
② Great! You can buy a new cell phone.
③ Absolutely. You can contact me anytime.
④ Luckily, fixing the phone wasn't expensive.
⑤ No worries. I'll get my phone back after school.

12

고1 2019년 9월 2번

대화를 듣고, 남자의 마지막 말에 대한 여자의 응답으로 가장 적절한 것을 고르시오.

① All right. Either day is fine with me.
② I'm sorry. You can't choose the date.
③ Really? I didn't know about the change.
④ Thanks. I enjoyed the volunteer program.
⑤ Good. I'm looking forward to this weekend.

정답과 해설 : 07~12 17~19

13

고1 2019년 9월 13번

대화를 듣고, 남자의 마지막 말에 대한 여자의 응답으로 가장 적절한 것을 고르시오. [3점]

Woman:

① I know. Studying psychology is fun.
② Really? Please ask him if I can visit him.
③ Right. It's not easy to decide on your career.
④ Well, I think the counseling job is right for you.
⑤ Okay. I'll tell your uncle how to apply for the job.

14

고1 2019년 9월 14번

대화를 듣고, 여자의 마지막 말에 대한 남자의 응답으로 가장 적절한 것을 고르시오. [3점]

Man:

① We can post the notice on social media.
② Let's move our instruments indoors, then.
③ I've already cancelled our outdoor concert.
④ We'd better change the location right away.
⑤ We can check the weather forecast using an app.

15

고1 2019년 9월 15번

다음 상황 설명을 듣고, Jina가 어머니에게 할 말로 가장 적절한 것을 고르시오.

Jina:

① Please help me choose a nice flower pot.
② Would you come with me to the Market Day?
③ Can I take this flower pot for a school event?
④ I'm not sure if I can plant my flowers in this pot.
⑤ Why don't we look for an item to sell at the market?

[16~17] 다음을 듣고, 물음에 답하시오.

16

고1 2019년 9월 16번

여자가 하는 말의 주제로 가장 적절한 것은?

① benefits of sharing things
② ways to sell used stuff online
③ steps in the recycling process
④ necessity of sharing information
⑤ problems caused by online markets

17

고1 2019년 9월 17번

언급된 물품이 아닌 것은?

① a dress   ② toys   ③ a car
④ books   ⑤ a bicycle

05 2019년 11월 학력평가

MP3
동영상 강의

2SBL1_A05
2SBL1_L05

😊 1번부터 17번까지는 듣고 답하는 문제입니다. 1번부터 15번까지는 한 번만 들려주고, 16번부터 17번까지는 두 번 들려줍니다. 방송을 잘 듣고 답을 하시기 바랍니다.

01
고1 2019년 11월 3번

다음을 듣고, 남자가 하는 말의 목적으로 가장 적절한 것을 고르시오.

① 유행성 독감 예방 접종을 권고하려고
② 열탕 목욕의 화상 위험성을 경고하려고
③ 겨울철 피부 건강 관리법을 소개하려고
④ 겨울철 체온 유지의 중요성을 강조하려고
⑤ 피부 트러블을 진정시키는 제품을 홍보하려고

02
고1 2019년 11월 4번

대화를 듣고, 여자의 의견으로 가장 적절한 것을 고르시오.

① 에너지 음료의 과잉 섭취를 주의해야 한다.
② 적당량의 카페인은 긴장 완화에 효과적이다.
③ 어지럼증에는 충분한 수분을 공급하는 것이 좋다.
④ 명상은 일상의 불안감을 해소하는 데 도움이 된다.
⑤ 균형 잡힌 식단은 성적 향상에 긍정적인 영향을 준다.

03
고1 2019년 11월 5번

대화를 듣고, 두 사람의 관계를 가장 잘 나타낸 것을 고르시오.

① 호텔 직원 — 투숙객
② 식당 주인 — 종업원
③ 가구 제작자 — 의뢰인
④ 박람회장 안내원 — 방문객
⑤ 전시 기획자 — 실내 디자이너

04
고1 2019년 11월 6번

대화를 듣고, 그림에서 대화의 내용과 일치하지 <u>않는</u> 것을 고르시오.

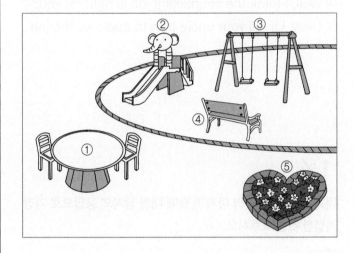

05
고1 2019년 11월 7번

대화를 듣고, 남자가 여자에게 부탁한 일로 가장 적절한 것을 고르시오.

① 회의실 예약 확인하기
② 일정 알림 문자 보내기
③ 차에서 간식 가져오기
④ 참석자 이름표 만들기
⑤ 회의 자료 출력하기

06
고1 2019년 11월 9번

대화를 듣고, 남자가 지불할 금액을 고르시오. 3점

① $40   ② $45   ③ $50
④ $54   ⑤ $60

07

고1 2019년 11월 8번

대화를 듣고, 여자가 가족 여행을 갈 수 없는 이유를 고르시오.

① 발목 상태가 좋지 않아서

② 항공권을 구입하지 못해서

③ 요리 대회에 참가해야 해서

④ 해외 봉사 활동을 가야 해서

⑤ 부모님께 다른 일정이 생겨서

08

고1 2019년 11월 10번

대화를 듣고, Junior Badminton Competition에 관해 언급되지 않은 것을 고르시오.

① 대회 일시   ② 참가비   ③ 준비물

④ 우승 상품   ⑤ 신청 방법

09

고1 2019년 11월 11번

Dream Children's Library에 관한 다음 내용을 듣고, 일치하지 않는 것을 고르시오.

① 6학년까지의 어린이를 대상으로 한다.

② 도서뿐 아니라 다양한 장난감이 있다.

③ 특별 독서 토론 프로그램을 운영한다.

④ 주말에 어린이들을 위해 영화를 상영한다.

⑤ 개관일에 만화 캐릭터 엽서를 제공한다.

10

고1 2019년 11월 12번

다음 표를 보면서 대화를 듣고, 여자가 선택할 미술용품 세트를 고르시오.

Art Supplies Set for Children

	Model	Price	Coloring Tool	Number of Colors	Sketchbook
①	A	$12	Crayons	24	×
②	B	$16	Crayons	32	○
③	C	$17	Watercolors	28	○
④	D	$18	Markers	32	×
⑤	E	$22	Markers	36	○

11

고1 2019년 11월 1번

대화를 듣고, 남자의 마지막 말에 대한 여자의 응답으로 가장 적절한 것을 고르시오.

① The building is too far from here.

② We don't need to bring umbrellas.

③ We can buy one on the first floor.

④ I don't know where your umbrella is.

⑤ You'd better check the weather forecast.

12

고1 2019년 11월 2번

대화를 듣고, 여자의 마지막 말에 대한 남자의 응답으로 가장 적절한 것을 고르시오.

① Actually, I couldn't find your essay.

② Don't worry. I can make a copy for you.

③ Too bad. I can't remember the deadline.

④ Not at all. I didn't start writing my essay.

⑤ Congratulations! I knew you could make it.

13

대화를 듣고, 여자의 마지막 말에 대한 남자의 응답으로 가장 적절한 것을 고르시오. 3점

Man: _____

① No kidding. I'm not interested in a yoga club.

② Too late. I can't lend you my registration card.

③ As you know, swimming isn't my favorite sport.

④ In that case, I'd better go and see if I can join the club.

⑤ Trust me. I bet you can be an excellent sports club leader.

14

대화를 듣고, 남자의 마지막 말에 대한 여자의 응답으로 가장 적절한 것을 고르시오. 3점

Woman: _____

① Great. I should try to keep a weekly budget.

② Good luck. I hope you can find a part-time job.

③ Come on. You can coach me on my eating habits.

④ No way. You can't spend so much money shopping.

⑤ I know. I need to spend more time with my friends.

15

다음 상황 설명을 듣고, Ted가 Linda에게 할 말로 가장 적절한 것을 고르시오.

Ted: _____

① Why don't you use a calendar app as a reminder?

② I recommend you ask your friends for some help.

③ Do you prefer a wall calendar or a desk calendar?

④ I wonder why you didn't submit your paper on time.

⑤ Could you tell me how you overcame your bad habit?

[16~17] 다음을 듣고, 물음에 답하시오.

16

여자가 하는 말의 주제로 가장 적절한 것은?

① limits to producing energy-saving products

② importance of teaching recycling to teenagers

③ creative ways of turning waste into new items

④ useful tips for making household furniture easily

⑤ various reasons for using eco-friendly materials

17

언급된 물건이 <u>아닌</u> 것은?

① plastic bottles   ② cardboard boxes

③ glasses   ④ cans

⑤ newspapers

06 2020년 3월 학력평가

1번부터 17번까지는 듣고 답하는 문제입니다. 1번부터 15번까지는 한 번만 들려주고, 16번부터 17번까지는 두 번 들려줍니다. 방송을 잘 듣고 답을 하시기 바랍니다.

01
고1 2020년 3월 3번

다음을 듣고, 남자가 하는 말의 목적으로 가장 적절한 것을 고르시오.

① 미세 먼지 수치가 높을 때 대처 요령을 안내하려고
② 교실 내 공기 정화기 설치 일정을 알리려고
③ 체육 실기 시험 준비 방법을 설명하려고
④ 미세 먼지 방지용 마스크 배부 행사를 홍보하려고
⑤ 미세 먼지 감축을 위해 대중교통 이용을 독려하려고

02
고1 2020년 3월 4번

대화를 듣고, 여자의 의견으로 가장 적절한 것을 고르시오.

① 받는 사람에게 필요한 것을 선물해야 한다.
② 정성 어린 선물 포장은 선물의 가치를 높인다.
③ 선물 포장을 위해 다양한 재료를 활용해야 한다.
④ 선물을 받으면 적절한 감사 인사를 하는 것이 좋다.
⑤ 환경을 위해 선물 포장을 간소하게 할 필요가 있다.

03
고1 2020년 3월 5번

대화를 듣고, 두 사람의 관계를 가장 잘 나타낸 것을 고르시오.

① 정원사 ― 집주인
② 출판사 직원 ― 작가
③ 가구 판매원 ― 손님
④ 관광 가이드 ― 관광객
⑤ 인테리어 디자이너 ― 잡지 기자

04
고1 2020년 3월 6번

대화를 듣고, 그림에서 대화의 내용과 일치하지 <u>않는</u> 것을 고르시오.

05
고1 2020년 3월 7번

대화를 듣고, 여자가 할 일로 가장 적절한 것을 고르시오.

① 악기 점검하기
② 연습 시간 확인하기
③ 단원들에게 연락하기
④ 관객용 의자 배치하기
⑤ 콘서트 포스터 붙이기

06
고1 2020년 3월 9번

대화를 듣고, 여자가 지불할 금액을 고르시오. 3점

① $140   ② $180   ③ $200
④ $220   ⑤ $280

07

고1 2020년 3월 8번

대화를 듣고, 남자가 이번 주말에 캠핑하러 갈 수 <u>없는</u> 이유를 고르시오.

① 계단을 수리해야 해서

② 캠프장을 예약할 수 없어서

③ 폭우로 인해 캠프장이 폐쇄되어서

④ 프로젝트를 마무리해야 해서

⑤ 어머니를 돌봐야 해서

08

고1 2020년 3월 10번

대화를 듣고, Pinewood Bake Sale에 관해 언급되지 <u>않은</u> 것을 고르시오.

① 개최 요일　　② 시작 시간　　③ 판매 제품

④ 수익금 기부처　　⑤ 개최 장소

09

고1 2020년 3월 11번

2020 Global Village Festival에 관한 다음 내용을 듣고, 일치하지 <u>않는</u> 것을 고르시오. [3점]

① 이틀간 Green City Park에서 열린다.

② 음악 공연과 미술 전시회를 포함한다.

③ 현금이나 신용 카드로 음식을 구입할 수 있다.

④ 선착순 100명에게 특별 선물을 준다.

⑤ 차량당 주차비는 10달러이다.

10

고1 2020년 3월 12번

다음 표를 보면서 대화를 듣고, 두 사람이 예약할 방을 고르시오.

Wayne Island Hotel Rooms

	Room	View	Breakfast	Price
①	A	City	×	$70
②	B	Mountain	×	$80
③	C	Mountain	○	$95
④	D	Ocean	×	$105
⑤	E	Ocean	○	$120

11

고1 2020년 3월 1번

대화를 듣고, 남자의 마지막 말에 대한 여자의 응답으로 가장 적절한 것을 고르시오.

① No thanks. I'm already full.

② Sure. The onion soup is great here.

③ No idea. I've never been here before.

④ Yes. I recommend you be there on time.

⑤ I agree. Let's go to a Mexican restaurant.

12

고1 2020년 3월 2번

대화를 듣고, 여자의 마지막 말에 대한 남자의 응답으로 가장 적절한 것을 고르시오.

① I see. Thank you for letting me know.

② Unfortunately, I got caught in the rain.

③ Well, it's been raining since yesterday.

④ You're right. It'll be sunny this afternoon.

⑤ Yeah. These umbrellas are available online.

13

고1 2020년 3월 13번

대화를 듣고, 여자의 마지막 말에 대한 남자의 응답으로 가장 적절한 것을 고르시오. 3점

Man: _____

① I have, but he didn't take it seriously.
② Don't worry. I have no problem with him.
③ Well, he always keeps the bathroom clean.
④ Sorry. I delayed moving out of the apartment.
⑤ Of course. I'll help you move into a new apartment.

14

고1 2020년 3월 14번

대화를 듣고, 남자의 마지막 말에 대한 여자의 응답으로 가장 적절한 것을 고르시오.

Woman: _____

① I'll text you how much it costs to fix the floor.
② Right. I don't think you can enter the competition.
③ Okay. I'll let you know as soon as the date is set.
④ But the auditorium was already repaired last week.
⑤ The competition will be held in the school gym instead.

15

고1 2020년 3월 15번

다음 상황 설명을 듣고, Billy의 어머니가 Billy에게 할 말로 가장 적절한 것을 고르시오.

Billy's mother: _____

① Make sure to answer the letters.
② Try to participate in school events often.
③ I'm sure you can make some good friends.
④ You need to prepare for the meeting.
⑤ Don't forget to bring me the letters.

[16~17] 다음을 듣고, 물음에 답하시오.

16

고1 2020년 3월 16번

여자가 하는 말의 주제로 가장 적절한 것은?

① major exporting countries of dairy products
② health benefits of drinking milk regularly
③ unique food cultures around the world
④ suitable environments for dairy animals
⑤ various milk sources in different countries

17

고1 2020년 3월 17번

언급된 나라가 아닌 것은?

① Canada　　② India　　③ Finland
④ Norway　　⑤ Romania

07

2020년 6월
학력평가

MP3
동영상 강의

25BL1_A07   25BL1_L07

1번부터 17번까지는 듣고 답하는 문제입니다. 1번부터 15번까지는 한 번만 들려주고, 16번부터 17번까지는 두 번 들려줍니다. 방송을 잘 듣고 답을 하시기 바랍니다.

01

고1 2020년 6월 3번

다음을 듣고, 여자가 하는 말의 목적으로 가장 적절한 것을 고르시오.

① 축제 관련자 안전 교육 참석을 공지하려고
② 정해진 장소에서 활동할 것을 요청하려고
③ 다양한 공연을 준비할 것을 독려하려고
④ 동아리 담당 교사 변경을 안내하려고
⑤ 적극적인 동아리 활동을 부탁하려고

02

고1 2020년 6월 4번

대화를 듣고, 남자의 의견으로 가장 적절한 것을 고르시오.

① 땀을 많이 흘린 후에는 수분 보충이 중요하다.
② 운동 전 음식 섭취가 운동을 위한 힘을 준다.
③ 운동은 땀을 흘릴 만큼 충분히 해야 한다.
④ 달리기 전 충분한 준비 운동을 해야 한다.
⑤ 꾸준한 운동이 건강한 신체를 만든다.

03

고1 2020년 6월 5번

대화를 듣고, 두 사람의 관계를 가장 잘 나타낸 것을 고르시오.

① 구직자 ― 채용 담당 직원
② 소설가 ― 영화감독
③ 배우 ― 방송 작가
④ 서점 직원 ― 출판업자
⑤ 뮤지컬 배우 ― 무대 감독

04

고1 2020년 6월 6번

대화를 듣고, 그림에서 대화의 내용과 일치하지 않는 것을 고르시오.

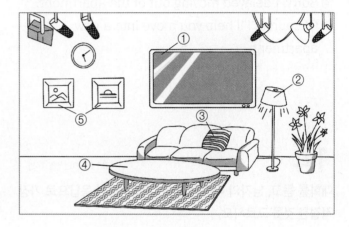

05

고1 2020년 6월 7번

대화를 듣고, 여자가 할 일로 가장 적절한 것을 고르시오.

① 사진 앨범 만들기
② 파티 초대장 보내기
③ 생일 케이크 만들기
④ 풍선으로 거실 장식하기
⑤ TV로 사진 영상 재생하기

06

고1 2020년 6월 9번

대화를 듣고, 여자가 지불할 금액을 고르시오. 3점

① $15   ② $23   ③ $27
④ $30   ⑤ $33

정답과 해설 : 01~06 30~32

07

고1 2020년 6월 8번

대화를 듣고, 남자가 수영장에 갈 수 없는 이유로 가장 적절한 것을 고르시오.

① 감기에 걸려서
② 취업 면접이 있어서
③ 친구와 약속이 있어서
④ 봉사 활동을 가야 해서
⑤ 저녁에 일을 해야 해서

08

고1 2020년 6월 10번

대화를 듣고, Rock Music Festival에 관해 언급되지 않은 것을 고르시오.

① 개최 일시　　　② 입장료　　　③ 개최 장소
④ 주차 요금　　　⑤ 참여 음악가

09

고1 2020년 6월 11번

Westbank High School Science Fair에 관한 다음 내용을 듣고, 일치하지 않는 것을 고르시오.

① 7월 21일에 열린다.
② 평가자와 방문객 앞에서 과제 발표가 이루어진다.
③ 각 팀에게 피드백이 주어진다.
④ 세 분야에 상이 주어진다.
⑤ 모든 방문객에게 무료로 티셔츠를 준다.

10

고1 2020년 6월 12번

다음 표를 보면서 대화를 듣고, 여자가 수강할 수업을 고르시오.

Summer Program Time Table

	Class	Day	Time	Monthly Fee
①	English Conversation	Mon.	9:00 a.m.	$50
②	Cartoon Creating	Tue.	10:00 a.m.	$60
③	Aquarobics	Wed.	10:00 a.m.	$75
④	Soccer	Thu.	6:00 p.m.	$80
⑤	Drawing	Fri.	3:00 p.m.	$75

11

고1 2020년 6월 1번

대화를 듣고, 여자의 마지막 말에 대한 남자의 응답으로 가장 적절한 것을 고르시오.

① I already did, but I couldn't find it.
② Okay, I'll wait in the living room.
③ You need to fix the cellphone.
④ I called the Lost and Found.
⑤ Wi-Fi is not available here.

12

고1 2020년 6월 2번

대화를 듣고, 남자의 마지막 말에 대한 여자의 응답으로 가장 적절한 것을 고르시오.

① Visiting a sunflower festival would be nice.
② You can't send her a birthday card.
③ Your kindness is always repaid.
④ I'll wrap the flowers for free.
⑤ White roses are nice at this time of year.

13

고1 2020년 6월 13번

대화를 듣고, 여자의 마지막 말에 대한 남자의 응답으로 가장 적절한 것을 고르시오.

Man: _____

① No. Just once a week.

② Sure. Drink it every day.

③ Sorry. I'm afraid I can't.

④ Yes. Not far from here.

⑤ Exactly. You'll join the trip.

14

고1 2020년 6월 14번

대화를 듣고, 남자의 마지막 말에 대한 여자의 응답으로 가장 적절한 것을 고르시오. 3점

Woman: _____

① Sure. You should submit your homework on time.

② Right. Students should have proper Internet etiquette.

③ Good idea. It will introduce Korean culture to the world.

④ Thanks. I really appreciate your inviting us to Korea.

⑤ Okay. I'll go and buy some tickets for them.

15

고1 2020년 6월 15번

다음 상황 설명을 듣고, Olivia가 온라인 쇼핑몰 고객센터 직원에게 할 말로 가장 적절한 것을 고르시오. 3점

Olivia: _____

① I'd like to send the pants back and get a refund.

② Could you deliver the pants by tomorrow?

③ Let me know when you have blue pants.

④ Can I exchange them for blue pants?

⑤ I want to check the delivery status.

[16~17] 다음을 듣고, 물음에 답하시오.

16

고1 2020년 6월 16번

남자가 하는 말의 주제로 가장 적절한 것은?

① various aerobic workouts for losing weight

② effective exercises for reducing back pain

③ activities to make your body flexible

④ importance of having correct posture

⑤ common symptoms of muscle pain

17

고1 2020년 6월 17번

언급된 운동이 아닌 것은?

① biking   ② swimming   ③ yoga

④ climbing   ⑤ walking

정답과 해설 : 13~17 33~34

08   2020년 9월 학력평가

※ 최신 영어 영역 시험의 듣기 문항 순서 변경에 따라 회차 내 문항 순서를 재배치하였습니다.

😊 1번부터 17번까지는 듣고 답하는 문제입니다. 1번부터 15번까지는 한 번만 들려주고, 16번부터 17번까지는 두 번 들려줍니다. 방송을 잘 듣고 답을 하시기 바랍니다.

01
고1 2020년 9월 3번

다음을 듣고, 여자가 하는 말의 목적으로 가장 적절한 것을 고르시오.

① 놀이공원의 개장을 홍보하려고
② 어린이 뮤지컬 배우를 모집하려고
③ 뮤지컬 시상식 일정을 공지하려고
④ 어린이 안전사고 예방을 당부하려고
⑤ 어린이 뮤지컬 특별 공연을 안내하려고

02
고1 2020년 9월 4번

대화를 듣고, 두 사람이 하는 말의 주제로 가장 적절한 것을 고르시오.

① 코딩 학습의 이점
② 코딩 시 주의할 점
③ 코딩 기술이 필요한 직업
④ 조기 코딩 교육의 문제점
⑤ 코딩 초보자를 위한 학습법

03
고1 2020년 9월 5번

대화를 듣고, 두 사람의 관계를 가장 잘 나타낸 것을 고르시오.

① 출판사 직원 — 번역가
② 여행 가이드 — 관광객
③ 도서관 사서 — 학생
④ 서점 직원 — 고객
⑤ 잡지 기자 — 배우

04
고1 2020년 9월 6번

대화를 듣고, 그림에서 대화의 내용과 일치하지 <u>않는</u> 것을 고르시오.

Magic Show
October 15th, 3:00 p.m.

05
고1 2020년 9월 7번

대화를 듣고, 여자가 할 일로 가장 적절한 것을 고르시오.

① Tom에게 전화하기
② 화학 과제 제출하기
③ 인터뷰 사진 촬영하기
④ Cindy와 발표 준비하기
⑤ 인터뷰 질문지 작성하기

06
고1 2020년 9월 9번

대화를 듣고, 여자가 지불할 금액을 고르시오. 3점

① $40   ② $45   ③ $50
④ $56   ⑤ $63

07

고1 2020년 9월 8번

대화를 듣고, 남자가 Winter Sports Camp에 참가할 수 없는 이유를 고르시오.

① 다른 캠프 일정과 겹쳐서
② 발목 통증이 낫지 않아서
③ 가족 여행이 예정되어 있어서
④ 과학 보고서를 제출하지 못해서
⑤ 전국 과학 대회 참가를 준비해야 해서

08

고1 2020년 9월 10번

대화를 듣고, Mind-Up Program에 관해 언급되지 않은 것을 고르시오.

① 목적　　② 특별 강연　　③ 개최 장소
④ 시작 시간　　⑤ 입장료

09

고1 2020년 9월 11번

Plata Tea Festival에 관한 다음 내용을 듣고, 일치하지 않는 것을 고르시오.

① 시청에서 개최되는 행사이다.
② 20개가 넘는 차 회사가 참여할 것이다.
③ 전문가로부터 차 예절을 배울 수 있다.
④ 5세 미만 어린이의 입장료는 무료이다.
⑤ 예약을 해야만 참가할 수 있다.

10

고1 2020년 9월 12번

다음 표를 보면서 대화를 듣고, 여자가 구입할 휴대용 선풍기를 고르시오.

Handheld Fans

	Model	Price	Battery Run Time	Fan Speed Level	Foldable
①	A	$20	6 hours	2	×
②	B	$23	9 hours	3	×
③	C	$25	9 hours	3	○
④	D	$28	12 hours	4	○
⑤	E	$33	12 hours	4	○

11

고1 2020년 9월 1번

대화를 듣고, 여자의 마지막 말에 대한 남자의 응답으로 가장 적절한 것을 고르시오.

① Really? I should have seen her.
② No way. I'm going to miss you a lot.
③ No. I didn't go to the bookstore that day.
④ I'm sorry. I'm not interested in her writing.
⑤ Yes. I can't believe I'm going to see her in person.

12

고1 2020년 9월 2번

대화를 듣고, 남자의 마지막 말에 대한 여자의 응답으로 가장 적절한 것을 고르시오.

① Good idea! I'll look for some videos online.
② Great! Teach me how to make a video clip.
③ Wow! You're good at controlling the drone.
④ Okay. Let's go buy a new drone together.
⑤ Right. I should read the instructions.

13

고1 2020년 9월 13번

대화를 듣고, 여자의 마지막 말에 대한 남자의 응답으로 가장 적절한 것을 고르시오. 3점

Man: _____

① Your sister had difficulty booking them.

② I'm sure the construction will be done soon.

③ The community center will be available tomorrow.

④ I hope I can reserve a court to continue practicing.

⑤ I don't think they'll allow us to practice in the gym.

14

고1 2020년 9월 14번

대화를 듣고, 남자의 마지막 말에 대한 여자의 응답으로 가장 적절한 것을 고르시오. 3점

Woman: _____

① Sure. Write as many activities as possible.

② Of course. The more specific, the better.

③ Thanks. But I'll do it my way this time.

④ Great. You've finally made it to college.

⑤ That's right. First come, first served.

15

고1 2020년 9월 15번

다음 상황 설명을 듣고, Cathy가 Brian에게 할 말로 가장 적절한 것을 고르시오.

Cathy: _____

① Let me show you how to play better.

② You should practice more after school.

③ Will you come to the concert with me?

④ You need to follow the doctor's instructions.

⑤ Why don't you try yoga for your back pain?

[16~17] 다음을 듣고, 물음에 답하시오.

16

고1 2020년 9월 16번

여자가 하는 말의 주제로 가장 적절한 것은?

① benefits of using LEDs

② how the LED was invented

③ misunderstandings about LEDs

④ competition in the LED market

⑤ ways to advance LED technology

17

고1 2020년 9월 17번

언급된 물건이 아닌 것은?

① lamps   ② clocks   ③ a television

④ traffic lights   ⑤ a computer keyboard

09 2020년 11월 학력평가

MP3

동영상 강의

2SBL1_A09

2SBL1_L09

1번부터 17번까지는 듣고 답하는 문제입니다. 1번부터 15번까지는 한 번만 들려주고, 16번부터 17번까지는 두 번 들려줍니다. 방송을 잘 듣고 답을 하시기 바랍니다.

01

다음을 듣고, 남자가 하는 말의 목적으로 가장 적절한 것을 고르시오.

① 교통사고 발생 시 대처 요령을 안내하려고
② 자전거 투어 시 안전 규칙을 설명하려고
③ 자전거 전용 도로 확충을 요청하려고
④ 단체 관광 일정 변경을 공지하려고
⑤ 자전거 대회 참가를 독려하려고

02

대화를 듣고, 여자의 의견으로 가장 적절한 것을 고르시오.

① 잠들기 직전의 운동은 수면을 방해할 수 있다.
② 운동은 규칙적으로 하는 것이 효과적이다.
③ 과격한 운동은 심장에 무리를 줄 수 있다.
④ 충분한 수면은 건강 관리에 도움이 된다.
⑤ 지나친 스트레스는 건강을 해친다.

03

대화를 듣고, 두 사람의 관계를 가장 잘 나타낸 것을 고르시오.

① 구급 대원 - 간호사
② 피부과 의사 - 환자
③ 화장품 판매원 - 손님
④ 제약 회사 직원 - 약사
⑤ 물리 치료사 - 운동선수

04

대화를 듣고, 그림에서 대화의 내용과 일치하지 <u>않는</u> 것을 고르시오.

05

대화를 듣고, 여자가 할 일로 가장 적절한 것을 고르시오.

① 모금함 만들기
② 물품 배치하기
③ 가격표 붙이기
④ 스피커 점검하기
⑤ 동영상 제작하기

06

대화를 듣고, 남자가 지불할 금액을 고르시오. 3점

① $41
② $45
③ $46
④ $50
⑤ $54

07

대화를 듣고, 남자가 학생 패션쇼에 갈 수 <u>없는</u> 이유를 고르시오.

① 친구 생일 선물을 사야 해서
② 가족과 식사를 하기로 해서
③ 집수리를 도와줘야 해서
④ 회의에 참석해야 해서
⑤ 콘서트에 가기로 해서

08

대화를 듣고, World Dinosaur Exhibition에 관해 언급되지 <u>않은</u> 것을 고르시오.

① 장소　　　② 프로그램　　　③ 운영 시간
④ 입장료　　　⑤ 교통편

09

Greenville Animation Film Festival에 관한 다음 내용을 듣고, 일치하지 <u>않는</u> 것을 고르시오.

① 1995년에 시작된 행사이다.
② 일주일 동안 열린다.
③ 올해의 주제는 우정이다.
④ 영화 스케줄은 웹사이트에 게시될 것이다.
⑤ 근처에 주차장이 있다.

10

다음 표를 보면서 대화를 듣고, 여자가 등록할 그리기 강좌를 고르시오.

One-day Drawing Lessons

	Class	Material	Lesson Type	Day	Time
①	A	Oil paint	Group	Monday	11 a.m.
②	B	Acrylic paint	Private	Wednesday	11 a.m.
③	C	Crayon	Group	Wednesday	6 p.m.
④	D	Colored pencil	Group	Friday	11 a.m.
⑤	E	Pastel	Private	Friday	6 p.m.

11

대화를 듣고, 남자의 마지막 말에 대한 여자의 응답으로 가장 적절한 것을 고르시오.

① *Bulgogi* is already sold out.
② You can choose what to eat.
③ We'll meet at the restaurant.
④ I'll order the food for tomorrow.
⑤ I got the recipe from the Internet.

12

대화를 듣고, 여자의 마지막 말에 대한 남자의 응답으로 가장 적절한 것을 고르시오.

① No problem. Your car is repaired.
② Sorry. I can't go camping with you.
③ Of course. You can borrow my tent.
④ Okay. I'll bring you the speakers now.
⑤ Don't worry. I already turned them off.

13

대화를 듣고, 남자의 마지막 말에 대한 여자의 응답으로 가장 적절한 것을 고르시오.

Woman: _____

① Then, you should sell the items using this app.
② Good. Let's buy a sweater in the marketplace.
③ All right. It's easy to order this bag online.
④ No worries. I'll lend you some money.
⑤ Well, you'd better buy new clothes.

14

대화를 듣고, 여자의 마지막 말에 대한 남자의 응답으로 가장 적절한 것을 고르시오. [3점]

Man: _____

① Don't worry. I'll send you a notice by email.
② Great. Let me know how to use your services.
③ I don't agree. You can get a refund without a receipt.
④ Good. I'm looking forward to watching a movie tonight.
⑤ Okay. I'll call customer service to cancel the membership.

15

다음 상황 설명을 듣고, Ms. Brown이 Chris에게 할 말로 가장 적절한 것을 고르시오. [3점]

Ms. Brown: _____

① You should stop worrying about your major.
② You'd better read an English book every day.
③ Why don't you start writing a diary in English?
④ I think you need to learn a lot of English words.
⑤ How about having conversations with foreigners?

[16~17] 다음을 듣고, 물음에 답하시오.

16

여자가 하는 말의 주제로 가장 적절한 것은?

① positive effects of raising animals
② useful tips for recording animal behavior
③ common characteristics sea animals have
④ different ways animals use to communicate
⑤ importance of protecting endangered species

17

언급된 동물이 아닌 것은?

① 개   ② 돌고래   ③ 고릴라
④ 코끼리   ⑤ 기린

※ 고1 2021년 3월 학력평가 시험지와 문항 순서가 동일합니다.

10 | 2021년 3월 학력평가

😊 1번부터 17번까지는 듣고 답하는 문제입니다. 1번부터 15번까지는 한 번만 들려주고, 16번부터 17번까지는 두 번 들려줍니다. 방송을 잘 듣고 답을 하시기 바랍니다.

01

다음을 듣고, 남자가 하는 말의 목적으로 가장 적절한 것을 고르시오.

① 교내 청소 일정을 공지하려고
② 학교 시설 공사의 지연에 대해 사과하려고
③ 하교 시 교실 창문을 닫을 것을 요청하려고
④ 교내의 젖은 바닥을 걸을 때 조심하도록 당부하려고
⑤ 깨끗한 교실 환경 조성을 위한 아이디어를 공모하려고

02

대화를 듣고, 여자의 의견으로 가장 적절한 것을 고르시오.

① 짧은 낮잠은 업무 효율을 높인다.
② 야식은 숙면에 방해가 될 수 있다.
③ 사람마다 최적의 수면 시간이 다르다.
④ 베개를 바꾸면 숙면에 도움이 될 수 있다.
⑤ 숙면을 위해 침실을 서늘하게 하는 것이 좋다.

03

대화를 듣고, 두 사람의 관계를 가장 잘 나타낸 것을 고르시오.

① 파티 주최자 ― 요리사
② 슈퍼마켓 점원 ― 손님
③ 배달 기사 ― 음식점 주인
④ 영양학자 ― 식품 제조업자
⑤ 인테리어 디자이너 ― 의뢰인

04

대화를 듣고, 그림에서 대화의 내용과 일치하지 <u>않는</u> 것을 고르시오.

05

대화를 듣고, 남자가 할 일로 가장 적절한 것을 고르시오.

① 영화 예매하기
② 지갑 가져오기
③ 시간표 출력하기
④ 학생증 재발급받기
⑤ 영화 감상문 제출하기

06

대화를 듣고, 여자가 지불할 금액을 고르시오. 3점

① $72
② $80
③ $90
④ $100
⑤ $110

07

대화를 듣고, 남자가 보고서를 완성하지 <u>못한</u> 이유를 고르시오.

① 실험을 다시 해서
② 제출일을 착각해서
③ 주제가 변경되어서
④ 컴퓨터가 고장 나서
⑤ 심한 감기에 걸려서

08

대화를 듣고, Spring Virtual Run에 관해 언급되지 <u>않은</u> 것을 고르시오.

① 달리는 거리   ② 참가 인원   ③ 달리는 장소
④ 참가비   ⑤ 기념품

09

Family Night at the Museum에 관한 다음 내용을 듣고, 일치하지 <u>않는</u> 것을 고르시오.

① 박물관 정규 운영 시간 종료 후에 열린다.
② 행성과 별 모형 아래에서 잠을 잔다.
③ 참가자들에게 침낭이 제공된다.
④ 6세부터 13세까지를 위한 프로그램이다.
⑤ 사전 등록 없이 현장에서 참가할 수 있다.

10

다음 표를 보면서 대화를 듣고, 여자가 구매할 스마트 워치를 고르시오.

Smart Watches

	Model	Waterproof	Warranty	Price
①	A	×	2 years	$90
②	B	○	3 years	$110
③	C	○	1 year	$115
④	D	×	2 years	$120
⑤	E	○	4 years	$125

11

대화를 듣고, 여자의 마지막 말에 대한 남자의 응답으로 가장 적절한 것을 고르시오.

① Oh, I should get it exchanged.
② Sure. I'll order a shirt for you.
③ Well, it's too expensive for me.
④ No. Please find me a smaller size.
⑤ Sorry, but this shirt is not on sale.

12

대화를 듣고, 남자의 마지막 말에 대한 여자의 응답으로 가장 적절한 것을 고르시오.

① Good. Let's meet around six.
② That's okay. I don't like donuts.
③ I want to open my own donut shop.
④ Don't worry. I can do that by myself.
⑤ Thanks for sharing your donut recipe.

정답과 해설 : 07~12 45~47

13

대화를 듣고, 여자의 마지막 말에 대한 남자의 응답으로 가장 적절한 것을 고르시오. [3점]

Man: _____

① This coffee place is very popular.
② You can stop using plastic straws.
③ I'll order drinks when you're ready.
④ Your drink will be ready in a minute.
⑤ The cups come in various colors and shapes.

14

대화를 듣고, 남자의 마지막 말에 대한 여자의 응답으로 가장 적절한 것을 고르시오. [3점]

Woman: _____

① Luckily, I didn't get hurt in the accident.
② I have enough money to get a new bike.
③ You really need one for your own safety.
④ You may feel sleepy after biking to school.
⑤ We can put our bikes in the school parking lot.

15

다음 상황 설명을 듣고, Jasper가 Mary에게 할 말로 가장 적절한 것을 고르시오.

Jasper: _____

① Where is the audition being held?
② How about writing your own song?
③ Let's play a different song this time.
④ I think you should be our lead singer.
⑤ Don't you think we need more practice?

[16~17] 다음을 듣고, 물음에 답하시오.

16

남자가 하는 말의 주제로 가장 적절한 것은?

① eco-friendly toys for pets
② roles of toys in pets' well-being
③ types of pets' unusual behaviors
④ foods that are dangerous to pets
⑤ difficulties in raising children with pets

17

언급된 동물이 아닌 것은?

① cat　　② hamster　　③ dog
④ turtle　　⑤ parrot

11

2021년 6월
학력평가

MP3

25BL1_A11

동영상 강의

25BL1_L11

1번부터 17번까지는 듣고 답하는 문제입니다. 1번부터 15번까지는 한 번만 들려주고, 16번부터 17번까지는 두 번 들려줍니다. 방송을 잘 듣고 답을 하시기 바랍니다.

01

다음을 듣고, 남자가 하는 말의 목적으로 가장 적절한 것을 고르시오.

① 건강 검진 일정을 공지하려고
② 독감 예방 접종을 권장하려고
③ 개인 위생 관리를 당부하려고
④ 보건소 운영 기간을 안내하려고
⑤ 독감 예방 접종 부작용을 경고하려고

02

대화를 듣고, 여자의 의견으로 가장 적절한 것을 고르시오.

① 독서 습관을 기르자.
② 지역 서점을 이용하자.
③ 지역 특산품을 애용하자.
④ 중고 서점을 활성화시키자.
⑤ 온라인을 통한 도서 구입을 늘리자.

03

대화를 듣고, 두 사람의 관계를 가장 잘 나타낸 것을 고르시오.

① 호텔 직원 - 투숙객
② 열쇠 수리공 - 집주인
③ 경비원 - 입주민
④ 은행원 - 고객
⑤ 치과의사 - 환자

04

대화를 듣고, 그림에서 대화의 내용과 일치하지 <u>않는</u> 것을 고르시오.

05

대화를 듣고, 남자가 여자를 위해 할 일로 가장 적절한 것을 고르시오. [3점]

① 부엌 청소하기
② 점심 준비하기
③ 카메라 구매하기
④ 딸 데리러 가기
⑤ 요리법 검색하기

06

대화를 듣고, 여자가 지불할 금액을 고르시오.

① $30
② $50
③ $63
④ $65
⑤ $70

07

대화를 듣고, 남자가 공연장에 갈 수 없는 이유로 가장 적절한 것을 고르시오.

① 출장을 가야 해서
② 숙제를 끝내야 해서
③ 조카를 돌봐야 해서
④ 이사 준비를 해야 해서
⑤ 친구와 만날 약속을 해서

08

대화를 듣고, 강아지 키우기에 관해 언급되지 <u>않은</u> 것을 고르시오.

① 산책시키기
② 먹이 주기
③ 목욕시키기
④ 배변 훈련시키기
⑤ 소변 패드 치우기

09

Sharing Friday Movement에 관한 다음 내용을 듣고, 일치하지 <u>않는</u> 것을 고르시오. [3점]

① 매주 금요일에 2달러씩 기부하는 운동이다.
② 2001년 핀란드에서 시작되었다.
③ 기부금은 가난한 지역에 깨끗한 물을 공급하는 데 쓰인다.
④ 올해 20명의 학생에게 장학금을 지급했다.
⑤ 추가 정보는 홈페이지를 통해 얻을 수 있다.

10

다음 표를 보면서 대화를 듣고, 여자가 구입할 모델을 고르시오.

Selfie Sticks

	Model	Weight	Maximum Length	Bluetooth Remote Control	Price
①	A	150g	60cm	×	$10
②	B	150g	80cm	○	$30
③	C	180g	80cm	○	$20
④	D	180g	100cm	×	$15
⑤	E	230g	100cm	○	$25

11

대화를 듣고, 남자의 마지막 말에 대한 여자의 응답으로 가장 적절한 것을 고르시오.

① Again? You've lost your bag twice.
② You're right. I'll take a warm jacket.
③ Why? I know you prefer cold weather.
④ What? I finished packing a present for you.
⑤ Sorry. But you can't join the trip at this point.

12

대화를 듣고, 여자의 마지막 말에 대한 남자의 응답으로 가장 적절한 것을 고르시오.

① No thank you. I've had enough.
② Great. I'll book for five people at six.
③ That's a good choice. The food is wonderful.
④ Okay. I'll set a place and time for the meeting.
⑤ Sorry to hear that. I'll cancel the reservation now.

13

대화를 듣고, 남자의 마지막 말에 대한 여자의 응답으로 가장 적절한 것을 고르시오.

Woman: _____

① I'm in charge of giving the presentation.
② I think you're the right person for that role.
③ It's important to choose your team carefully.
④ The assignment is due the day after tomorrow.
⑤ I hope we don't stay up late to finish the project.

14

대화를 듣고, 여자의 마지막 말에 대한 남자의 응답으로 가장 적절한 것을 고르시오.

Man: _____

① I'm good at public speaking.
② I'm sorry for forgetting my assignment.
③ Unfortunately, my alarm doesn't wake me up.
④ The speech contest is just around the corner.
⑤ It helps me keep deadlines to complete specific tasks.

15

다음 상황 설명을 듣고, Harold가 Kate에게 할 말로 가장 적절한 것을 고르시오. 3점

Harold: _____

① Okay. You'd better put your best effort into the match.
② I see. You should play the match instead of her.
③ Take it easy. Take good care of yourself first.
④ You deserve it. Practice makes perfect.
⑤ Don't worry. You'll win this match.

[16~17] 다음을 듣고, 물음에 답하시오.

16

여자가 하는 말의 주제로 가장 적절한 것은?

① problems with illegal hunting
② characteristics of migrating animals
③ effects of light pollution on wild animals
④ various ways to save endangered animals
⑤ animal habitat change due to water pollution

17

언급된 동물이 아닌 것은?

① sea turtles   ② fireflies   ③ salmon
④ honey bees   ⑤ tree frogs

※ 고1 2021년 9월 학력평가 시험지와 문항 순서가 동일합니다.

12 2021년 9월 학력평가

MP3
25BL1_A12

동영상 강의
25BL1_L12

😊 1번부터 17번까지는 듣고 답하는 문제입니다. 1번부터 15번까지는 한 번만 들려주고, 16번부터 17번까지는 두 번 들려줍니다. 방송을 잘 듣고 답을 하시기 바랍니다.

01

다음을 듣고, 남자가 하는 말의 목적으로 가장 적절한 것을 고르시오.

① 시민 자율 방범 단원을 모집하려고
② 어린이 안전 교육 장소를 안내하려고
③ 초등학교 개교 기념행사를 홍보하려고
④ 학교 주변 제한 속도 준수를 독려하려고
⑤ 시청에서 열리는 공청회 일정을 공지하려고

02

대화를 듣고, 남자의 의견으로 가장 적절한 것을 고르시오.

① 고민이 있을 때는 가족이나 친구와 대화해야 한다.
② 가까운 사람일수록 말을 신중하게 하는 것이 좋다.
③ 사과를 받아들일 수 있는 넓은 마음이 필요하다.
④ 일어나지 않은 일을 미리 걱정할 필요는 없다.
⑤ 가족이라도 개인 공간을 존중해야 한다.

03

대화를 듣고, 두 사람의 관계를 가장 잘 나타낸 것을 고르시오.

① 교사 - 학생
② 방송 작가 - 배우
③ 라디오 진행자 - 청취자
④ 이벤트 업체 직원 - 고객
⑤ 설문 조사원 - 설문 응답자

04

대화를 듣고, 그림에서 대화의 내용과 일치하지 않는 것을 고르시오.

05

대화를 듣고, 남자가 할 일로 가장 적절한 것을 고르시오.

① 생일 카드 쓰기
② 스웨터 구매하기
③ 거실 장식하기
④ 케이크 찾아오기
⑤ 샌드위치 재료 주문하기

06

대화를 듣고, 여자가 지불할 금액을 고르시오. 3점

① $16
② $20
③ $21
④ $23
⑤ $26

07

대화를 듣고, 남자가 헬스장 회원권을 연장하지 <u>않은</u> 이유를 고르시오.

① 어깨 부상이 회복되지 않아서
② 운동에 흥미를 잃어서
③ 샤워 시설이 낡고 좁아서
④ 가격이 인상되어서
⑤ 방과후 수업에 참여해야 해서

08

대화를 듣고, Tour of Liberty University에 관해 언급되지 <u>않은</u> 것을 고르시오.

① 날짜　　　② 활동 내용　　　③ 참가 가능 인원수
④ 기념품　　　⑤ 신청 방법

09

Green Action Photo Contest에 관한 다음 내용을 듣고, 일치하지 <u>않는</u> 것을 고르시오.

① 9월 한 달간 사진을 업로드 할 수 있다.
② 정해진 해시태그를 붙이면 자동으로 참가하게 된다.
③ 사진은 5장까지 올릴 수 있다.
④ 우승 상품은 10월 11일까지 직접 찾아가야 한다.
⑤ 우승 사진은 연말까지 마을 웹 사이트에 게시된다.

10

다음 표를 보면서 대화를 듣고, 여자가 주문할 Rolling Cart를 고르시오.

Rolling Cart

	Model	Material	Number of Shelf	Lockable Wheel	Price
①	A	Metal	2	○	$80
②	B	Metal	3	○	$95
③	C	Wood	3	○	$105
④	D	Wood	4	×	$110
⑤	E	Plastic	4	×	$75

11

대화를 듣고, 여자의 마지막 말에 대한 남자의 응답으로 가장 적절한 것을 고르시오.

① Okay. Then let's ask them if they lost their dog.
② Take it easy. This dog is not dangerous at all.
③ Sorry. I tried my best, but I couldn't find it.
④ What a relief! I thought I had lost my dog forever.
⑤ Right! Dog owners must walk their pets twice a day.

12

대화를 듣고, 남자의 마지막 말에 대한 여자의 응답으로 가장 적절한 것을 고르시오.

① We're open from 11 o'clock in the morning.
② Sorry, but all the tables are full right now.
③ Our special for today is barbecue chicken.
④ Thank you for visiting our restaurant.
⑤ I don't have enough time to cook.

13

대화를 듣고, 여자의 마지막 말에 대한 남자의 응답으로 가장 적절한 것을 고르시오. [3점]

Man: _____

① Don't worry. You can book another hotel.
② That's right. You have already paid your bill.
③ Yes. But you don't have to pay for a full day.
④ Sorry. You should have cancelled your reservation.
⑤ Of course. You can stay in the lobby till the afternoon.

14

대화를 듣고, 남자의 마지막 말에 대한 여자의 응답으로 가장 적절한 것을 고르시오. [3점]

Woman: _____

① Oh, no! I can come over today to help you clear it out.
② Never mind. Everyone needs time to make a decision.
③ Okay. We can go to the basement if we're in danger.
④ Yes. Why don't you water your trees more often?
⑤ Sorry. I don't know how to change a light bulb.

15

다음 상황 설명을 듣고, Emily가 Chris에게 할 말로 가장 적절한 것을 고르시오.

Emily: _____

① Luckily, I have finished my homework.
② May I watch the movie with my brother?
③ Thanks, and I'll gratefully enjoy your cookies.
④ I'm sorry, but I need to take care of my brother.
⑤ Will you watch over my brother for just a minute?

[16~17] 다음을 듣고, 물음에 답하시오.

16

여자가 하는 말의 주제로 가장 적절한 것은?

① different animals that are popular in different cultures
② unique sleeping habits that animals use for survival
③ wild animals that are becoming endangered species
④ how animals have changed their ways of eating
⑤ animals that bring people good luck

17

언급된 동물이 아닌 것은?

① bats   ② ducks   ③ chimpanzees
④ giraffes   ⑤ dolphins

13 2021년 11월
학력평가

1번부터 17번까지는 듣고 답하는 문제입니다. 1번부터 15번까지는 한 번만 들려주고, 16번부터 17번까지는 두 번 들려줍니다. 방송을 잘 듣고 답을 하시기 바랍니다.

01

다음을 듣고, 남자가 하는 말의 목적으로 가장 적절한 것을 고르시오.

① 지하철 앱 출시를 홍보하려고
② 지하철 연장 운행을 안내하려고
③ 지하철 운행 지연에 대해 사과하려고
④ 지하철 시설 보수 공사 일정을 공지하려고
⑤ 지하철 내 영화 촬영에 대한 양해를 구하려고

02

대화를 듣고, 여자의 의견으로 가장 적절한 것을 고르시오.

① 날씨가 더울수록 수분 보충이 중요하다.
② 적당한 준비 운동이 부상 위험을 줄인다.
③ 흐린 날에도 자외선 차단제를 발라야 한다.
④ 햇빛이 강한 날에는 야외 활동을 자제해야 한다.
⑤ 화상을 입었을 때 신속하게 응급 처치를 해야 한다.

03

대화를 듣고, 두 사람의 관계를 가장 잘 나타낸 것을 고르시오.

① 세차장 직원 - 고객
② 청소 업체 직원 - 집주인
③ 중고차 판매원 - 구매자
④ 분실물 센터 직원 - 방문자
⑤ 액세서리 디자이너 - 의뢰인

04

대화를 듣고, 그림에서 대화의 내용과 일치하지 <u>않는</u> 것을 고르시오.

05

대화를 듣고, 남자가 할 일로 가장 적절한 것을 고르시오.

① 가방 준비하기
② 배지 가져오기
③ 스크린 점검하기
④ 동영상 편집하기
⑤ 포스터 업로드하기

06

대화를 듣고, 여자가 지불할 금액을 고르시오. [3점]

① $45
② $50
③ $54
④ $55
⑤ $60

07

대화를 듣고, 남자가 London Walking Tour에 참여하지 **못한** 이유를 고르시오.

① 발목에 통증이 있어서

② 뮤지컬을 관람해야 해서

③ 투어 예약을 하지 못해서

④ 기념품을 사러 가야 해서

⑤ 날씨로 인해 투어가 취소되어서

08

대화를 듣고, Winter Lake Festival에 관해 언급되지 **않은** 것을 고르시오.

① 기간　　　② 장소　　　③ 입장료

④ 기념품　　　⑤ 활동 종류

09

Mascot Design Contest에 관한 다음 내용을 듣고, 일치하지 **않는** 것을 고르시오.

① 팀을 사랑하는 누구든 참여할 수 있다.

② 디자인은 팀 슬로건과 관련되어야 한다.

③ 수상작은 팬 투표로 선정될 것이다.

④ 수상자는 상으로 시즌 티켓을 받게 될 것이다.

⑤ 참가 희망자는 디자인을 이메일로 보내야 한다.

10

다음 표를 보면서 대화를 듣고, 두 사람이 예약할 캠핑장을 고르시오.

2021 Best Campsites

	Campsite	Location	Price (per night)	Type	Kids' Playground
①	A	Seaside	$65	tent	×
②	B	Jungle Hut	$70	tent	○
③	C	Rose Valley	$85	camping car	○
④	D	Blue Forest	$90	camping car	×
⑤	E	Pine Island	$110	camping car	○

11

대화를 듣고, 남자의 마지막 말에 대한 여자의 응답으로 가장 적절한 것을 고르시오.

① It takes an hour by bus.

② It's bigger than your office.

③ You should've left home earlier.

④ The company moved last month.

⑤ I had a hard time getting the job.

12

대화를 듣고, 여자의 마지막 말에 대한 남자의 응답으로 가장 적절한 것을 고르시오.

① Okay. I'll order a shrimp pizza.

② Thanks. You're good at cooking.

③ No. The pizza isn't delivered yet.

④ Sure. You can come over anytime.

⑤ Yes. Skipping meals is bad for your health.

13

대화를 듣고, 남자의 마지막 말에 대한 여자의 응답으로 가장 적절한 것을 고르시오.

Woman: _____

① Too late. The meeting is already over.

② Sure. There are lots of French cookbooks.

③ I agree. You spend too much time reading.

④ No. We're not allowed to eat in the library.

⑤ You're right. I'll change the reservation now.

14

대화를 듣고, 여자의 마지막 말에 대한 남자의 응답으로 가장 적절한 것을 고르시오. 3점

Man: _____

① Sorry. I forgot to bring my laptop.

② Then, I'd like to replace the battery.

③ Well, the screen still doesn't work well.

④ Good. A new repair shop opened yesterday.

⑤ Actually, I don't have a receipt for a refund.

15

다음 상황 설명을 듣고, Amy가 Terry에게 할 말로 가장 적절한 것을 고르시오. 3점

Amy: _____

① How about using a colorful font on the poster?

② You'd better inform your friends of the concert.

③ Can you make the letter size bigger on the poster?

④ Why don't we hold a concert in the school festival?

⑤ You should put important information on the poster.

[16~17] 다음을 듣고, 물음에 답하시오.

16

여자가 하는 말의 주제로 가장 적절한 것은?

① ways to prevent plant diseases

② factors that affect plant growth

③ benefits of growing plants at home

④ plants that can grow in shaded areas

⑤ materials that help plants grow in shade

17

언급된 식물이 아닌 것은?

① lemon balm　　② ivy　　③ mint

④ camellia　　⑤ lavender

14 | 2022년 3월 학력평가

MP3   동영상 강의
2SBL1_A14   2SBL1_L14

※ 고1 2022년 3월 학력평가 시험지와 문항 순서가 동일합니다.

😊 1번부터 17번까지는 듣고 답하는 문제입니다. 1번부터 15번까지는 한 번만 들려주고, 16번부터 17번까지는 두 번 들려줍니다. 방송을 잘 듣고 답을 하시기 바랍니다.

01

다음을 듣고, 남자가 하는 말의 목적으로 가장 적절한 것을 고르시오.

① 농구 리그 참가 등록 방법의 변경을 알리려고
② 확정된 농구 리그 시합 일정을 발표하려고
③ 농구 리그의 심판을 추가 모집하려고
④ 농구 리그 경기 관람을 권장하려고
⑤ 농구 리그 우승 상품을 안내하려고

02

대화를 듣고, 여자의 의견으로 가장 적절한 것을 고르시오.

① 평소에 피부 상태를 잘 관찰할 필요가 있다.
② 여드름을 치료하려면 피부과 병원에 가야 한다.
③ 얼굴을 손으로 만지는 것은 얼굴 피부에 해롭다.
④ 지성 피부를 가진 사람은 자주 세수를 해야 한다.
⑤ 손을 자주 씻는 것은 감염병 예방에 도움이 된다.

03

대화를 듣고, 두 사람의 관계를 가장 잘 나타낸 것을 고르시오.

① 방송 작가 - 연출자
② 만화가 - 환경 운동가
③ 촬영 감독 - 동화 작가
④ 토크쇼 진행자 - 기후학자
⑤ 제품 디자이너 - 영업 사원

04

대화를 듣고, 그림에서 대화의 내용과 일치하지 <u>않는</u> 것을 고르시오.

05

대화를 듣고, 여자가 남자에게 부탁한 일로 가장 적절한 것을 고르시오.

① 장난감 사 오기
② 풍선 달기
③ 케이크 가져오기
④ 탁자 옮기기
⑤ 아이들 데려오기

06

대화를 듣고, 남자가 지불할 금액을 고르시오. 3점

① $14
② $16
③ $18
④ $20
⑤ $22

07

대화를 듣고, 두 사람이 오늘 실험을 할 수 <u>없는</u> 이유를 고르시오.

① 실험용 키트가 배달되지 않아서
② 실험 주제를 변경해야 해서
③ 과학실을 예약하지 못해서
④ 보고서를 작성해야 해서
⑤ 남자가 감기에 걸려서

08

대화를 듣고, Stanville Free-cycle에 관해 언급되지 <u>않은</u> 것을 고르시오.

① 참가 대상　　② 행사 장소　　③ 주차 가능 여부
④ 행사 시작일　　⑤ 금지 품목

09

River Valley Music Camp에 관한 다음 내용을 듣고, 일치하지 <u>않는</u> 것을 고르시오.

① 4월 11일부터 5일 동안 진행된다.
② 학교 오케스트라 단원이 아니어도 참가할 수 있다.
③ 자신의 악기를 가져오거나 학교에서 빌릴 수 있다.
④ 마지막 날에 공연을 촬영한다.
⑤ 참가 인원에는 제한이 없다.

10

다음 표를 보면서 대화를 듣고, 여자가 주문할 소형 진공청소기를 고르시오.

Handheld Vacuum Cleaners

	Model	Price	Working Time	Weight	Washable Filter
①	A	$50	8 minutes	2.5 kg	×
②	B	$80	12 minutes	2.0 kg	○
③	C	$100	15 minutes	1.8 kg	○
④	D	$120	20 minutes	1.8 kg	×
⑤	E	$150	25 minutes	1.6 kg	○

11

대화를 듣고, 남자의 마지막 말에 대한 여자의 응답으로 가장 적절한 것을 고르시오.

① Why don't you rinse your eyes with clean water?
② Can you explain more about the air pollution?
③ I need to get myself a new pair of glasses.
④ I agree that fine dust is a serious problem.
⑤ We should go outside and take a walk.

12

대화를 듣고, 여자의 마지막 말에 대한 남자의 응답으로 가장 적절한 것을 고르시오.

① That's not fair. I booked this seat first.
② Thank you. My friend will be glad to know it.
③ You're welcome. Feel free to ask me anything.
④ Not at all. I don't mind changing seats with you.
⑤ That's okay. I think the seat next to it is available.

13

대화를 듣고, 남자의 마지막 말에 대한 여자의 응답으로 가장 적절한 것을 고르시오.

Woman: _____

① Smells good. Can I try the pizza?
② Great. I'll bring chips and popcorn.
③ No problem. I'll cancel the tickets.
④ Sorry. I don't like watching baseball.
⑤ Sure. Here's the hammer I borrowed.

14

대화를 듣고, 여자의 마지막 말에 대한 남자의 응답으로 가장 적절한 것을 고르시오. 3점

Man: _____

① Exactly. This is a best-selling novel.
② Sounds cool. I'll join a book club, too.
③ Not really. Books make good presents.
④ New year's resolutions are hard to keep.
⑤ Let's buy some books for your book club.

15

다음 상황 설명을 듣고, Brian이 Sally에게 할 말로 가장 적절한 것을 고르시오. 3점

Brian: _____

① You shouldn't touch a guide dog without permission.
② The dog would be happy if we give it some food.
③ I'm sure it's smart enough to be a guide dog.
④ I suggest that you walk your dog every day.
⑤ I'm afraid that dogs are not allowed in here.

[16~17] 다음을 듣고, 물음에 답하시오.

16

여자가 하는 말의 주제로 가장 적절한 것은?

① activities that help build muscles
② ways to control stress in daily life
③ types of joint problems in elderly people
④ low-impact exercises for people with bad joints
⑤ importance of daily exercise for controlling weight

17

언급된 운동이 아닌 것은?

① swimming   ② cycling
③ horseback riding   ④ bowling
⑤ walking

15 2022년 6월 학력평가

MP3

동영상 강의

1번부터 17번까지는 듣고 답하는 문제입니다. 1번부터 15번까지는 한 번만 들려주고, 16번부터 17번까지는 두 번 들려줍니다. 방송을 잘 듣고 답을 하시기 바랍니다.

01

다음을 듣고, 남자가 하는 말의 목적으로 가장 적절한 것을 고르시오.

① 사생활 보호의 중요성을 강조하려고
② 건물 벽 페인트 작업을 공지하려고
③ 회사 근무시간 변경을 안내하려고
④ 새로운 직원 채용을 공고하려고
⑤ 친환경 제품 출시를 홍보하려고

02

대화를 듣고, 여자의 의견으로 가장 적절한 것을 고르시오.

① 운전자는 제한 속도를 지켜야 한다.
② 교통경찰을 더 많이 배치해야 한다.
③ 보행자의 부주의가 교통사고를 유발한다.
④ 교통사고를 목격하면 즉시 신고해야 한다.
⑤ 대중교통을 이용하면 이동시간을 줄일 수 있다.

03

대화를 듣고, 두 사람의 관계를 가장 잘 나타낸 것을 고르시오.

① 작가 - 출판사 직원
② 관람객 - 박물관 해설사
③ 손님 - 주방장
④ 탑승객 - 항공 승무원
⑤ 학생 - 사서

04

대화를 듣고, 그림에서 대화의 내용과 일치하지 <u>않는</u> 것을 고르시오.

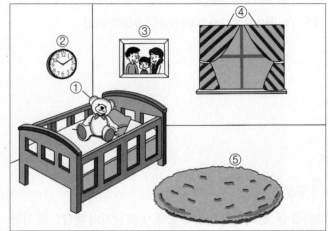

05

대화를 듣고, 남자가 할 일로 가장 적절한 것을 고르시오.

① 보고서 제출하기
② 티켓 예매하기
③ 자전거 수리하기
④ 축구 연습하기
⑤ 팝콘 구입하기

06

대화를 듣고, 여자가 지불할 금액을 고르시오. 3점

① $40
② $60
③ $80
④ $100
⑤ $120

07

대화를 듣고, 남자가 음식 부스에 갈 수 <u>없는</u> 이유로 가장 적절한 것을 고르시오.

① 밴드 오디션 연습을 해야 해서
② 보드게임 부스를 설치해야 해서
③ 영어 프로젝트를 끝내야 해서
④ 샌드위치를 준비해야 해서
⑤ 친구를 만나러 가야 해서

08

대화를 듣고, Spanish culture class에 관해 언급되지 <u>않은</u> 것을 고르시오.

① 강사   ② 활동 종류   ③ 수업 요일
④ 준비물   ⑤ 수강료

09

Summer Flea Market에 관한 다음 내용을 듣고, 일치하지 <u>않는</u> 것을 고르시오. [3점]

① 일주일 동안 진행된다.
② 학교 주차장에서 열린다.
③ 장난감, 양초와 같은 물품을 살 수 있다.
④ 상태가 좋은 중고 물품을 판매할 수 있다.
⑤ 첫날 방문하면 할인 쿠폰을 선물로 받는다.

10

다음 표를 보면서 대화를 듣고, 여자가 구입할 운동화를 고르시오.

Sneakers

	Model	Price	Style	Waterproof	Color
①	A	$50	casual	×	black
②	B	$60	active	×	white
③	C	$65	casual	○	black
④	D	$70	casual	○	white
⑤	E	$85	active	○	white

11

대화를 듣고, 여자의 마지막 말에 대한 남자의 응답으로 가장 적절한 것을 고르시오.

① All children's books are 20% off.
② It takes time to write a good article.
③ I like to read action adventure books.
④ There are too many advertisements on TV.
⑤ The store has been closed since last month.

12

대화를 듣고, 남자의 마지막 말에 대한 여자의 응답으로 가장 적절한 것을 고르시오.

① You're welcome. I'm happy to help you.
② That's not true. I made it with your help.
③ Okay. Good food always makes me feel better.
④ Really? You should definitely visit the theater later.
⑤ Never mind. You'll do better on the next presentation.

13

대화를 듣고, 여자의 마지막 말에 대한 남자의 응답으로 가장 적절한 것을 고르시오.

Man: _____

① I'm excited to buy a new guitar.
② Summer vacation starts on Friday.
③ You can find it on the school website.
④ Let's go to the school festival together.
⑤ You can get some rest during the vacation.

14

대화를 듣고, 남자의 마지막 말에 대한 여자의 응답으로 가장 적절한 것을 고르시오.

Woman: _____

① I agree. There are many benefits of exercising at the gym.
② You're right. Not all exercise is helpful for your brain.
③ Don't worry. It's not too difficult for me to exercise.
④ That sounds great. Can I join the course, too?
⑤ That's too bad. I hope you get well soon.

15

다음 상황 설명을 듣고, Ted가 Monica에게 할 말로 가장 적절한 것을 고르시오. 3점

Ted: _____

① Can I draw your club members on the poster?
② Are you interested in joining my drawing club?
③ Could you tell me how to vote in the election?
④ Can you help me make posters for the election?
⑤ Would you run in the next school president election?

[16~17] 다음을 듣고, 물음에 답하시오.

16

여자가 하는 말의 주제로 가장 적절한 것은?

① downsides of fatty food
② healthy foods for breakfast
③ ways to avoid eating snacks
④ easy foods to cook in 5 minutes
⑤ the importance of a balanced diet

17

언급된 음식이 <u>아닌</u> 것은?

① eggs   ② cheese   ③ potatoes
④ yogurt   ⑤ berries

※ 고1 2022년 9월 학력평가 시험지와 문항 순서가 동일합니다.

16 2022년 9월 학력평가

MP3   동영상 강의

25BL1_A16   25BL1_L16

😊 1번부터 17번까지는 듣고 답하는 문제입니다. 1번부터 15번까지는 한 번만 들려주고, 16번부터 17번까지는 두 번 들려줍니다. 방송을 잘 듣고 답을 하시기 바랍니다.

01

다음을 듣고, 여자가 하는 말의 목적으로 가장 적절한 것을 고르시오.

① 도서관 확장 이전을 공지하려고
② 도서관 이용 안내 영상을 소개하려고
③ 독서 습관 형성 프로그램을 홍보하려고
④ 독해력 향상 방안에 대한 의견을 구하려고
⑤ 독서 프로그램 만족도 조사 참여를 요청하려고

02

대화를 듣고, 남자의 의견으로 가장 적절한 것을 고르시오.

① 중고품은 직접 만나서 거래해야 한다.
② 물품 구매 시 여러 제품을 비교해야 한다.
③ 계획적으로 예산을 세워 물품을 구매해야 한다.
④ 온라인 거래 시 개인 정보 유출에 유의해야 한다.
⑤ 중고품 구매 시 세부 사항을 꼼꼼히 확인해야 한다.

03

대화를 듣고, 두 사람의 관계를 가장 잘 나타낸 것을 고르시오.

① 의사 - 간호사
② 안경사 - 고객
③ 보건 교사 - 학부모
④ 사진사 - 모델
⑤ 앱 개발자 - 의뢰인

04

대화를 듣고, 그림에서 대화의 내용과 일치하지 않는 것을 고르시오.

05

대화를 듣고, 여자가 할 일로 가장 적절한 것을 고르시오.

① 식료품 주문하기
② 자동차 수리 맡기기
③ 보고서 제출하기
④ 고객 센터에 전화하기
⑤ 냉장고에 식료품 넣기

06

대화를 듣고, 남자가 지불할 금액을 고르시오. [3점]

① $27
② $30
③ $36
④ $40
⑤ $45

정답과 해설 : 01~06 71~73

07

대화를 듣고, 여자가 가방을 구입한 이유를 고르시오.

① 유명 연예인들이 착용해서
② 재활용 소재를 사용해서
③ 많은 친구들이 추천해서
④ 디자인이 독특해서
⑤ 가격이 저렴해서

08

대화를 듣고, Youth Street Dance Contest에 관해 언급되지 않은 것을 고르시오.

① 신청 마감일　　② 심사 기준　　③ 우승 상금액
④ 참가 부문　　⑤ 신청 방법

09

Lakewoods Plogging에 관한 다음 내용을 듣고, 일치하지 않는 것을 고르시오.

① 참가자는 운동복과 운동화를 착용해야 한다.
② 쓰레기를 담을 봉투가 배부된다.
③ 10월 1일 오전 7시부터 진행될 것이다.
④ 학교 웹사이트에서 신청할 수 있다.
⑤ 참가자 모두 스포츠 양말을 받을 것이다.

10

다음 표를 보면서 대화를 듣고, 두 사람이 주문할 휴대용 캠핑 히터를 고르시오.

Portable Camping Heater

	Model	Weight (kg)	Price	Energy Source	Customer Rating
①	A	4.2	$85	Oil	★★★
②	B	3.6	$90	Oil	★★★★
③	C	3.4	$92	Electricity	★★★★★
④	D	3.2	$95	Electricity	★★★★
⑤	E	2.8	$115	Electricity	★★★★★

11

대화를 듣고, 여자의 마지막 말에 대한 남자의 응답으로 가장 적절한 것을 고르시오.

① You can join the tour, too.
② The bike wasn't that expensive.
③ I haven't decided the place, yet.
④ I'm going to rent a bike in the park.
⑤ Autumn is the best season for the tour.

12

대화를 듣고, 남자의 마지막 말에 대한 여자의 응답으로 가장 적절한 것을 고르시오.

① Great. I'll be there at that time.
② Okay. I'll change my toothbrush.
③ Too bad. I hope you get well soon.
④ No worries. Your painkillers work well.
⑤ Sure. Let me know when he's available.

정답과 해설 : 07~12 73~74

13

대화를 듣고, 여자의 마지막 말에 대한 남자의 응답으로 가장 적절한 것을 고르시오.

Man: _____

① Fantastic! We'll be a really good team.
② Sorry. I don't understand why you like it.
③ Good idea! I'll find another partner for you.
④ No problem. I can use my racket to practice.
⑤ I know. Everyone loves watching sports competitions.

14

대화를 듣고, 남자의 마지막 말에 대한 여자의 응답으로 가장 적절한 것을 고르시오. [3점]

Woman: _____

① Nice! I'm curious about what you'll ask.
② Sure. You should study hard for the quiz.
③ Okay. I'll make some questions right away.
④ All right. I'll see if I can add more pictures.
⑤ Don't worry. It won't take too long to answer.

15

다음 상황 설명을 듣고, Ms. Olson이 Steven에게 할 말로 가장 적절한 것을 고르시오. [3점]

Ms. Olson: _____

① You can come see me any time you want.
② I'm happy to hear that you've met the CEO.
③ Why do you want to run a gaming company?
④ How about going to your role model's book-signing?
⑤ You should buy more books written by your role model.

[16~17] 다음을 듣고, 물음에 답하시오.

16

남자가 하는 말의 주제로 가장 적절한 것은?

① tips for caring for musical instruments
② ways to choose a good musical instrument
③ effects of the weather on musical instruments
④ benefits of learning musical instruments as a child
⑤ difficulties of making your own musical instruments

17

언급된 악기가 아닌 것은?

① flutes   ② trumpets   ③ pianos
④ drums   ⑤ guitars

17

2022년 11월
학력평가

MP3

2SBL1_A17

동영상 강의

2SBL1_L17

1번부터 17번까지는 듣고 답하는 문제입니다. 1번부터 15번까지는 한 번만 들려주고, 16번부터 17번까지는 두 번 들려줍니다. 방송을 잘 듣고 답을 하시기 바랍니다.

01

다음을 듣고, 남자가 하는 말의 목적으로 가장 적절한 것을 고르시오.

① 얼음으로 덮인 일부 등산로 폐쇄를 공지하려고
② 등산객에게 야간 산행의 위험성을 경고하려고
③ 겨울 산행을 위한 안전 장비를 안내하려고
④ 긴급 제설에 필요한 작업자를 모집하려고
⑤ 일출 명소인 전망대를 소개하려고

02

대화를 듣고, 남자의 의견으로 가장 적절한 것을 고르시오.

① 조리법을 있는 그대로 따를 필요는 없다.
② 요리 도구를 정기적으로 소독해야 한다.
③ 설탕 섭취는 단기 기억력을 향상시킨다.
④ 열량이 높은 음식은 건강에 좋지 않다.
⑤ 신선한 재료는 요리의 풍미를 높인다.

03

대화를 듣고, 두 사람의 관계를 가장 잘 나타낸 것을 고르시오.

① 음악 평론가 — 방송 연출가
② 작곡가 — 게임 제작자
③ 독자 — 웹툰 작가
④ 삽화가 — 소설가
⑤ 영화감독 — 배우

04

대화를 듣고, 그림에서 대화의 내용과 일치하지 않는 것을 고르시오.

05

대화를 듣고, 남자가 할 일로 가장 적절한 것을 고르시오.

① 음료 구매하기
② 연필 준비하기
③ 의자 설치하기
④ 마이크 점검하기
⑤ 스케치북 가져오기

06

대화를 듣고, 여자가 지불할 금액을 고르시오. 3점

① $17
② $22
③ $35
④ $37
⑤ $39

07

대화를 듣고, 남자가 얼음낚시를 갈 수 없는 이유를 고르시오.

① 손목을 다쳐서
② 병원에 입원해야 해서
③ 직장에 출근해야 해서
④ 기상 여건이 나빠져서
⑤ 친구와 농구를 해야 해서

08

대화를 듣고, Kids' Pottery Class에 관해 언급되지 않은 것을 고르시오.

① 날짜　　　　　② 장소
③ 수강 인원　　　④ 수강료
⑤ 등록 방법

09

2022 Online Whistling Championship에 관한 다음 내용을 듣고, 일치하지 않는 것을 고르시오.

① 좋아하는 어떤 노래든 선택할 수 있다.
② 12월 4일까지 동영상을 업로드해야 한다.
③ 녹음 시 마이크의 에코 효과를 반드시 꺼야 한다.
④ 운영진의 심사에 의해 수상자들이 결정될 것이다.
⑤ 결과는 웹사이트에 발표될 것이다.

10

다음 표를 보면서 대화를 듣고, 두 사람이 선택할 커튼을 고르시오.

Curtains

	Product	Price	Care Instruction	Blackout	Color
①	A	$70	machine washable	✕	navy
②	B	$80	machine washable	○	brown
③	C	$90	dry cleaning only	○	ivory
④	D	$95	machine washable	○	gray
⑤	E	$110	dry cleaning only	✕	white

11

대화를 듣고, 남자의 마지막 말에 대한 여자의 응답으로 가장 적절한 것을 고르시오.

① I've been waiting for 30 minutes.
② I've enjoyed this ride very much.
③ You're standing in the correct line.
④ I have enough time to wait for you.
⑤ You may end the construction in a year.

12

대화를 듣고, 여자의 마지막 말에 대한 남자의 응답으로 가장 적절한 것을 고르시오.

① No way. I don't know who's lost.
② Okay. Let's see if he needs our help.
③ Exactly. Just stop crying like a child.
④ Sure. He loves walking around the park.
⑤ Thanks. We were worried about our son.

13

대화를 듣고, 남자의 마지막 말에 대한 여자의 응답으로 가장 적절한 것을 고르시오. 3점

Woman: _____

① Great. I believe my previous offer will benefit your company.

② I'm sorry. Your interview has been delayed to next Wednesday.

③ Good. Your effort will give a good impression on the interviewer.

④ Excellent. The second candidate's work experience caught my eye.

⑤ No worries. You can purchase nice clothes for the upcoming party.

14

대화를 듣고, 여자의 마지막 말에 대한 남자의 응답으로 가장 적절한 것을 고르시오.

Man: _____

① Please wait. I'll be back with the shoes in a minute.

② Hurry up. You don't have enough time to do this.

③ Of course. You can get a refund for these shoes.

④ Don't worry. The color doesn't matter to me.

⑤ Sorry. The red ones are already sold out.

15

다음 상황 설명을 듣고, Amelia가 Jacob 교수에게 할 말로 가장 적절한 것을 고르시오. 3점

Amelia: _____

① Could you extend the deadline for the assignment?

② Would it be possible to change our appointment?

③ Why don't you join my final psychology project?

④ Do you want to meet at the information center?

⑤ How about visiting the doctor for a checkup?

[16~17] 다음을 듣고, 물음에 답하시오.

16

여자가 하는 말의 주제로 가장 적절한 것은?

① ways to stop the spread of false information

② methods of delivering messages in the past

③ modes of communication in modern times

④ types of speeches according to purposes

⑤ means to survive in prehistoric times

17

언급된 수단이 아닌 것은?

① drum　　　　② smoke

③ pigeon　　　④ flag

⑤ horse

18 2023년 3월 학력평가

MP3

동영상 강의

25BL1_A18   25BL1_L18

🗣 1번부터 17번까지는 듣고 답하는 문제입니다. 1번부터 15번까지는 한 번만 들려주고, 16번부터 17번까지는 두 번 들려줍니다. 방송을 잘 듣고 답을 하시기 바랍니다.

01

다음을 듣고, 남자가 하는 말의 목적으로 가장 적절한 것을 고르시오.

① 아이스하키부의 우승을 알리려고
② 아이스하키부 훈련 일정을 공지하려고
③ 아이스하키부 신임 감독을 소개하려고
④ 아이스하키부 선수 모집을 안내하려고
⑤ 아이스하키부 경기의 관람을 독려하려고

02

대화를 듣고, 여자의 의견으로 가장 적절한 것을 고르시오.

① 과다한 항생제 복용을 자제해야 한다.
② 오래된 약을 함부로 폐기해서는 안 된다.
③ 약을 복용할 때는 정해진 시간을 지켜야 한다.
④ 진료 전에 자신의 증상을 정확히 확인해야 한다.
⑤ 다른 사람에게 처방된 약을 복용해서는 안 된다.

03

대화를 듣고, 두 사람의 관계를 가장 잘 나타낸 것을 고르시오.

① 관람객 — 박물관 관장
② 세입자 — 건물 관리인
③ 화가 — 미술관 직원
④ 고객 — 전기 기사
⑤ 의뢰인 — 건축사

04

대화를 듣고, 그림에서 대화의 내용과 일치하지 않는 것을 고르시오.

05

대화를 듣고, 남자가 할 일로 가장 적절한 것을 고르시오.

① 티켓 디자인하기
② 포스터 게시하기
③ 블로그 개설하기
④ 밴드부원 모집하기
⑤ 콘서트 장소 대여하기

06

대화를 듣고, 여자가 지불할 금액을 고르시오. 3점

① $70   ② $90
③ $100   ④ $110
⑤ $120

07

대화를 듣고, 남자가 지갑을 구매하지 <u>못한</u> 이유를 고르시오.

① 해당 상품이 다 팔려서
② 브랜드명을 잊어버려서
③ 계산대의 줄이 길어서
④ 공항에 늦게 도착해서
⑤ 면세점이 문을 닫아서

08

대화를 듣고, Youth Choir Audition에 관해 언급되지 <u>않은</u> 것을 고르시오.

① 지원 가능 연령
② 날짜
③ 심사 기준
④ 참가비
⑤ 지원 방법

09

2023 Career Week에 관한 다음 내용을 듣고, 일치하지 <u>않는</u> 것을 고르시오.

① 5일 동안 열릴 것이다.
② 미래 직업 탐색을 돕는 프로그램이 있을 것이다.
③ 프로그램 참가 인원에 제한이 있다.
④ 특별 강연이 마지막 날에 있을 것이다.
⑤ 등록은 5월 10일에 시작된다.

10

다음 표를 보면서 대화를 듣고, 여자가 구입할 프라이팬을 고르시오.

Frying Pans

	Model	Price	Size (inches)	Material	Lid
①	A	$30	8	Aluminum	○
②	B	$32	9.5	Aluminum	○
③	C	$35	10	Stainless Steel	×
④	D	$40	11	Aluminum	×
⑤	E	$70	12.5	Stainless Steel	○

11

대화를 듣고, 남자의 마지막 말에 대한 여자의 응답으로 가장 적절한 것을 고르시오.

① I don't think I can finish editing it by then.
② I learned it by myself through books.
③ This short movie is very interesting.
④ You should make another video clip.
⑤ I got an A⁺ on the team project.

12

대화를 듣고, 여자의 마지막 말에 대한 남자의 응답으로 가장 적절한 것을 고르시오.

① All right. I'll come pick you up now.
② I'm sorry. The library is closed today.
③ No problem. You can borrow my book.
④ Thank you so much. I'll drop you off now.
⑤ Right. I've changed the interior of my office.

13

대화를 듣고, 남자의 마지막 말에 대한 여자의 응답으로 가장 적절한 것을 고르시오.

Woman: _____

① Try these tomatoes and cucumbers.

② I didn't know peppers are good for skin.

③ Just wear comfortable clothes and shoes.

④ You can pick tomatoes when they are red.

⑤ I'll help you grow vegetables on your farm.

14

대화를 듣고, 여자의 마지막 말에 대한 남자의 응답으로 가장 적절한 것을 고르시오. [3점]

Man: _____

① You're right. I'll meet her and apologize.

② I agree with you. That's why I did it.

③ Thank you. I appreciate your apology.

④ Don't worry. I don't think it's your fault.

⑤ Too bad. I hope the two of you get along.

15

다음 상황 설명을 듣고, John이 Ted에게 할 말로 가장 적절한 것을 고르시오. [3점]

John: _____

① How can we find the best sunrise spot?

② Why do you go mountain climbing so often?

③ What time should we get up tomorrow morning?

④ When should we come down from the mountain top?

⑤ Where do we have to stay in the mountain at night?

[16~17] 다음을 듣고, 물음에 답하시오.

16

여자가 하는 말의 주제로 가장 적절한 것은?

① indoor sports good for the elderly

② importance of learning rules in sports

③ best sports for families to enjoy together

④ useful tips for winning a sports game

⑤ history of traditional family sports

17

언급된 스포츠가 아닌 것은?

① badminton

② basketball

③ table tennis

④ soccer

⑤ bowling

19 2023년 6월
학력평가

1번부터 17번까지는 듣고 답하는 문제입니다. 1번부터 15번까지는 한 번만 들려주고, 16번부터 17번까지는 두 번 들려줍니다. 방송을 잘 듣고 답을 하시기 바랍니다.

01

다음을 듣고, 여자가 하는 말의 목적으로 가장 적절한 것을 고르시오.

① 체육대회 종목을 소개하려고
② 대회 자원봉사자를 모집하려고
③ 학생 회장 선거 일정을 공지하려고
④ 경기 관람 규칙 준수를 당부하려고
⑤ 학교 홈페이지 주소 변경을 안내하려고

02

대화를 듣고, 남자의 의견으로 가장 적절한 것을 고르시오.

① 산책은 창의적인 생각을 할 수 있게 돕는다.
② 식사 후 과격한 운동은 소화를 방해한다.
③ 지나친 스트레스는 집중력을 감소시킨다.
④ 독서를 통해 창의력을 증진할 수 있다.
⑤ 꾸준한 운동은 기초체력을 향상시킨다.

03

대화를 듣고, 두 사람의 관계를 가장 잘 나타낸 것을 고르시오.

① 고객 — 우체국 직원
② 투숙객 — 호텔 지배인
③ 여행객 — 여행 가이드
④ 아파트 주민 — 경비원
⑤ 손님 — 옷가게 주인

04

대화를 듣고, 그림에서 대화의 내용과 일치하지 않는 것을 고르시오.

05

대화를 듣고, 남자가 할 일로 가장 적절한 것을 고르시오.

① 초대장 보내기
② 피자 주문하기
③ 거실 청소하기
④ 꽃다발 준비하기
⑤ 스마트폰 사러 가기

06

대화를 듣고, 여자가 지불할 금액을 고르시오. 3점

① $54   ② $60
③ $72   ④ $76
⑤ $80

07

대화를 듣고, 남자가 록 콘서트에 갈 수 <u>없는</u> 이유를 고르시오.

① 일을 하러 가야 해서
② 피아노 연습을 해야 해서
③ 할머니를 뵈러 가야 해서
④ 친구의 개를 돌봐야 해서
⑤ 과제를 아직 끝내지 못해서

08

대화를 듣고, Eco Day에 관해 언급되지 <u>않은</u> 것을 고르시오.

① 행사 시간　　　② 행사 장소
③ 참가비　　　　④ 준비물
⑤ 등록 방법

09

Eastville Dance Contest에 관한 다음 내용을 듣고, 일치하지 <u>않는</u> 것을 고르시오.

① 처음으로 개최되는 경연이다.
② 모든 종류의 춤이 허용된다.
③ 춤 영상을 8월 15일까지 업로드 해야 한다.
④ 학생들은 가장 좋아하는 영상에 투표할 수 있다.
⑤ 우승팀은 상으로 상품권을 받게 될 것이다.

10

다음 표를 보면서 대화를 듣고, 두 사람이 구입할 정수기를 고르시오.

Water Purifiers

	Model	Price	Water Tank Capacity (liters)	Power-saving Mode	Warranty
①	A	$570	4	×	1 year
②	B	$650	5	○	1 year
③	C	$680	5	×	3 years
④	D	$740	5	○	3 years
⑤	E	$830	6	○	3 years

11

대화를 듣고, 남자의 마지막 말에 대한 여자의 응답으로 가장 적절한 것을 고르시오.

① Great. We don't have to wait in line.
② All right. We can come back later.
③ Good job. Let's buy the tickets.
④ No worries. I will stand in line.
⑤ Too bad. I can't buy that car.

12

대화를 듣고, 여자의 마지막 말에 대한 남자의 응답으로 가장 적절한 것을 고르시오.

① Yes. You can register online.
② Sorry. I can't see you next week.
③ Right. I should go to his office now.
④ Fantastic! I'll take the test tomorrow.
⑤ Of course. I can help him if he needs my help.

13

대화를 듣고, 여자의 마지막 말에 대한 남자의 응답으로 가장 적절한 것을 고르시오. [3점]

Man: _____

① I agree. You can save a lot by buying secondhand.
② Great idea! Our message would make others smile.
③ Sorry. I forgot to write a message in the book.
④ Exactly. Taking notes during class is important.
⑤ Okay. We can arrive on time if we leave now.

14

대화를 듣고, 남자의 마지막 말에 대한 여자의 응답으로 가장 적절한 것을 고르시오. [3점]

Woman: _____

① Why not? I can bring some food when we go camping.
② I'm sorry. That fishing equipment is not for sale.
③ I don't think so. The price is most important.
④ Really? I'd love to meet your family.
⑤ No problem. You can use my equipment.

15

다음 상황 설명을 듣고, Violet이 Peter에게 할 말로 가장 적절한 것을 고르시오.

Violet: _____

① Will you join the science club together?
② Is it okay to use a card to pay for the drinks?
③ Why don't we donate our books to the library?
④ How about going to the cafeteria to have lunch?
⑤ Can you borrow the books for me with your card?

[16~17] 다음을 듣고, 물음에 답하시오.

16

남자가 하는 말의 주제로 가장 적절한 것은?

① different causes of sleep disorders
② various ways to keep foods fresh
③ foods to improve quality of sleep
④ reasons for organic foods' popularity
⑤ origins of popular foods around the world

17

언급된 음식이 아닌 것은?

① kiwi fruits   ② milk
③ nuts   ④ tomatoes
⑤ honey

20 | 2023년 9월 학력평가

MP3   동영상 강의

2SBL1_A20   2SBL1_L20

😊 1번부터 17번까지는 듣고 답하는 문제입니다. 1번부터 15번까지는 한 번만 들려주고, 16번부터 17번까지는 두 번 들려줍니다. 방송을 잘 듣고 답을 하시기 바랍니다.

01

다음을 듣고, 남자가 하는 말의 목적으로 가장 적절한 것을 고르시오.

① 강당의 천장 수리 기간을 공지하려고
② 콘서트 관람 규칙 준수를 요청하려고
③ 학교 축제에서 공연할 동아리를 모집하려고
④ 폭우에 대비한 교실 시설 관리를 당부하려고
⑤ 학교 록 밴드 공연의 장소 변경을 안내하려고

02

대화를 듣고, 여자의 의견으로 가장 적절한 것을 고르시오.

① 달리기를 할 때 적합한 신발을 신어야 한다.
② 운동을 한 후에 충분한 물을 섭취해야 한다.
③ 야외 활동 전에 일기예보를 확인하는 것이 좋다.
④ 달리기 전 스트레칭은 통증과 부상을 예방해 준다.
⑤ 초보자의 경우 달리는 거리를 점진적으로 늘려야 한다.

03

대화를 듣고, 두 사람의 관계를 가장 잘 나타낸 것을 고르시오.

① 관객 — 영화감독
② 연극 배우 — 시나리오 작가
③ 잡지 기자 — 의상 디자이너
④ 토크쇼 진행자 — 영화 평론가
⑤ 배우 지망생 — 연기 학원 강사

04

대화를 듣고, 그림에서 대화의 내용과 일치하지 <u>않는</u> 것을 고르시오.

05

대화를 듣고, 여자가 할 일로 가장 적절한 것을 고르시오.

① 관객용 의자 배치하기
② 마이크 음향 점검하기
③ 공연 포스터 붙이기
④ 무대 조명 설치하기
⑤ 배터리 구매하기

06

대화를 듣고, 남자가 지불할 금액을 고르시오. [3점]

① $37   ② $45
③ $55   ④ $60
⑤ $80

07

대화를 듣고, 여자가 스키 여행을 갈 수 <u>없는</u> 이유를 고르시오.

① 카페에서 일해야 해서
② 숙소를 예약하지 못해서
③ 역사 시험 공부를 해야 해서
④ 수술받은 고양이를 돌봐야 해서
⑤ 캐나다에 사는 친척을 방문해야 해서

08

대화를 듣고, Street Photography Contest에 관해 언급되지 <u>않은</u> 것을 고르시오.

① 참가 대상   ② 주제
③ 심사 기준   ④ 제출 마감일
⑤ 우승 상품

09

Twin Stars Chocolate Day에 관한 다음 내용을 듣고, 일치하지 <u>않는</u> 것을 고르시오.

① 11월 12일 오후에 열린다.
② 초콜릿의 역사에 관한 강의가 진행된다.
③ 초콜릿 5개를 만든다.
④ 사전 등록 없이 참가할 수 있다.
⑤ 등록비에 재료비가 포함된다.

10

다음 표를 보면서 대화를 듣고, 두 사람이 주문할 실내 사이클링 자전거를 고르시오.

Indoor Cycling Bikes

	Model	Price	Color	Foldable	Customer Rating
①	A	$100	White	✕	★★★★
②	B	$150	Black	✕	★★★
③	C	$190	Black	○	★★★★
④	D	$250	Black	○	★★★★★
⑤	E	$320	White	✕	★★★★★

11

대화를 듣고, 여자의 마지막 말에 대한 남자의 응답으로 가장 적절한 것을 고르시오.

① Sure. I'll send you a link to the website.
② It would look better in a different color.
③ Sorry. I forgot to bring your sweater.
④ You need your receipt to return it.
⑤ My brother bought it on sale, too.

12

대화를 듣고, 남자의 마지막 말에 대한 여자의 응답으로 가장 적절한 것을 고르시오.

① Let's take the leftovers home.
② I prefer fried chicken over pizza.
③ I don't want to go out for lunch today.
④ I'll call the restaurant and check our order.
⑤ The letter was delivered to the wrong address.

정답과 해설 : 07~12 91~93

13

대화를 듣고, 여자의 마지막 말에 대한 남자의 응답으로 가장 적절한 것을 고르시오.

Man: _____

① You're right. I won't skip meals anymore.
② Thank you for the lunch you prepared for me.
③ You need to check when the cafeteria is open.
④ Trust me. I can teach you good table manners.
⑤ No problem. We'll finish the science project on time.

14

대화를 듣고, 남자의 마지막 말에 대한 여자의 응답으로 가장 적절한 것을 고르시오. 3점

Woman: _____

① No. It isn't difficult for me to learn Spanish.
② I'm glad you finally passed the vocabulary test.
③ Exactly. Learning a language starts with repetition.
④ It's very helpful to use a dictionary while writing.
⑤ You should turn in your homework by this afternoon.

15

다음 상황 설명을 듣고, Brian이 Melissa에게 할 말로 가장 적절한 것을 고르시오. 3점

Brian: _____

① Let's clean the classroom after art class.
② Did you remove the stickers from the board?
③ Please turn off the heater when you leave the room.
④ When is the final date to sign up for the design class?
⑤ Will you design stickers that encourage energy saving?

[16~17] 다음을 듣고, 물음에 답하시오.

16

남자가 하는 말의 주제로 가장 적절한 것은?

① advantages of renting houses in cities
② reasons tourists prefer visiting old cities
③ ways cities deal with overtourism problems
④ correlation between cities' sizes and overtourism
⑤ how cities face their aging transportation systems

17

언급된 도시가 아닌 것은?

① Barcelona   ② Amsterdam
③ London   ④ Venice
⑤ Paris

1번부터 17번까지는 듣고 답하는 문제입니다. 1번부터 15번까지는 한 번만 들려주고, 16번부터 17번까지는 두 번 들려줍니다. 방송을 잘 듣고 답을 하시기 바랍니다.

01

다음을 듣고, 남자가 하는 말의 목적으로 가장 적절한 것을 고르시오.

① 로봇 프로그램 만족도 조사 참여를 독려하려고
② 관람객을 위한 안내 로봇 서비스를 소개하려고
③ 전시 작품 해설 서비스 중단을 안내하려고
④ 오디오 가이드 대여 장소를 공지하려고
⑤ 전시관 온라인 예약 방법을 설명하려고

02

대화를 듣고, 여자의 의견으로 가장 적절한 것을 고르시오.

① 번역 프로그램으로 번역한 글은 검토가 필요하다.
② 읽기 학습을 통해 쓰기 능력을 향상시킬 수 있다.
③ 글을 인용할 때는 출처를 명확히 밝혀야 한다.
④ 예상 독자를 고려하여 글을 작성해야 한다.
⑤ 번역기 사용은 외국어 학습에 효과적이다.

03

대화를 듣고, 두 사람의 관계를 가장 잘 나타낸 것을 고르시오.

① 광고 제작자 — 사진작가
② 이사업체 직원 — 의뢰인
③ 고객 — 에어컨 설치 기사
④ 트럭 운전사 — 물류 창고 직원
⑤ 구매자 — 중고 물품 개인 판매자

04

대화를 듣고, 그림에서 대화의 내용과 일치하지 않는 것을 고르시오.

05

대화를 듣고, 남자가 할 일로 가장 적절한 것을 고르시오.

① 스티커 준비하기
② 안내문 게시하기
③ 급식 메뉴 선정하기
④ 설문 조사 실시하기
⑤ 우수 학급 시상하기

06

대화를 듣고, 남자가 매달 지불할 금액을 고르시오.

① $20　　　　② $27
③ $30　　　　④ $36
⑤ $40

07

대화를 듣고, 여자가 토크 쇼를 방청하러 갈 수 없는 이유를 고르시오.

① 가족 모임에 가야 해서
② 아르바이트를 해야 해서
③ 책 사인회를 준비해야 해서
④ 화학 프로젝트를 해야 해서
⑤ 친구 결혼식에 참석해야 해서

08

대화를 듣고, Polar Bear Swim에 관해 언급되지 않은 것을 고르시오.

① 행사 날짜   ② 제출 서류
③ 최대 참가 인원   ④ 기념품
⑤ 참가비

09

Walk in the Snow에 관한 다음 내용을 듣고, 일치하지 않는 것을 고르시오.

① 1일 투어 프로그램이다.
② 하이킹에 관심이 있는 누구든 참여할 수 있다.
③ 장비를 무료로 대여할 수 있다.
④ 학생에게 등록비 할인을 해 준다.
⑤ 참여하려면 사전에 등록해야 한다.

10

다음 표를 보면서 대화를 듣고, 두 사람이 선택할 달력을 고르시오.

Calendar

	Product	Price	Format	Recyclable Paper	Theme
①	A	$8	standing desk	×	modern art
②	B	$10	standing desk	○	classic art
③	C	$12	standing desk	○	movie
④	D	$16	wall	○	nature
⑤	E	$22	wall	×	animal

11

대화를 듣고, 여자의 마지막 말에 대한 남자의 응답으로 가장 적절한 것을 고르시오.

① I covered the worrying state of marine life.
② I sent an article to the biology department.
③ Whatever you did, let's not speak about it.
④ I spent lots of time preparing the speech.
⑤ The article was mainly read by students.

12

대화를 듣고, 남자의 마지막 말에 대한 여자의 응답으로 가장 적절한 것을 고르시오.

① Take care. The weather is freezing cold.
② Good news. Thanks for letting me know.
③ Hurry up. The bus is leaving very soon.
④ Seriously? I'd better try walking, then.
⑤ Really? I was on the shuttle bus, too.

13

대화를 듣고, 여자의 마지막 말에 대한 남자의 응답으로 가장 적절한 것을 고르시오. [3점]

Man: _____

① Definitely. That's why I got a refund for the app.

② Sorry. I should have repaired my tablet PC earlier.

③ Exactly. Documents were filed in alphabetical order.

④ I see. I'll give it some thought before buying this app.

⑤ Don't worry. I still have a few more days for the free trial.

14

대화를 듣고, 남자의 마지막 말에 대한 여자의 응답으로 가장 적절한 것을 고르시오. [3점]

Woman: _____

① Good idea. Let's learn how to read sign language.

② You're right. That's because I wanted to help him.

③ Okay. Wish me luck in getting this volunteer work.

④ Trust me. I bet you'll be selected as a note-taker.

⑤ Wonderful. Thank you for taking notes for me in class.

15

다음 상황 설명을 듣고, Tony가 Kate에게 할 말로 가장 적절한 것을 고르시오. [3점]

Tony: _____

① Why don't we post a review of this bakery?

② Let's give her the baker of the month award.

③ We'd better check if we're on the waiting list.

④ We should come later when the repairs are done.

⑤ How about finding a different bakery for the list?

[16~17] 다음을 듣고, 물음에 답하시오.

16

여자가 하는 말의 주제로 가장 적절한 것은?

① fruits that can pose a risk to dogs' health

② ways to help dogs develop a taste for fruits

③ tips for protecting garden fruits from animals

④ reasons fruits should be included in dogs' diets

⑤ stories that use fruits and vegetables as characters

17

언급된 과일이 아닌 것은?

① grapes   ② cherries

③ avocados   ④ grapefruits

⑤ cranberries

정답과 해설 : 13~17 97~99

22 2024년 3월 학력평가

1번부터 17번까지는 듣고 답하는 문제입니다. 1번부터 15번까지는 한 번만 들려주고, 16번부터 17번까지는 두 번 들려줍니다. 방송을 잘 듣고 답을 하시기 바랍니다.

01

다음을 듣고, 남자가 하는 말의 목적으로 가장 적절한 것을 고르시오.

① 학교 체육관 공사 일정을 알리려고
② 학교 수업 시간표 조정을 안내하려고
③ 학교 통학 시 대중교통 이용을 권장하려고
④ 학교 방과 후 수업 신청 방식을 설명하려고
⑤ 학교 셔틀버스 운행 시간 변경을 공지하려고

02

대화를 듣고, 여자의 의견으로 가장 적절한 것을 고르시오.

① 전기 자전거 이용 전에 배터리 상태를 점검하여야 한다.
② 전기 자전거 운행에 관한 규정이 더 엄격해야 한다.
③ 전기 자전거의 속도 규정에 대한 논의가 필요하다.
④ 전기 자전거 구입 시 가격을 고려해야 한다.
⑤ 전기 자전거 이용 시 헬멧을 착용해야 한다.

03

다음을 듣고, 여자가 하는 말의 요지로 가장 적절한 것을 고르시오.

① 학업 목표를 분명히 설정하는 것이 필요하다.
② 친구와의 협력은 학교생활의 중요한 덕목이다.
③ 과제 제출 마감 기한을 확인하고 준수해야 한다.
④ 적절한 휴식은 성공적인 과업 수행의 핵심 요소이다.
⑤ 할 일의 목록을 활용하는 것이 시간 관리에 유용하다.

04

대화를 듣고, 그림에서 대화의 내용과 일치하지 않는 것을 고르시오.

05

대화를 듣고, 남자가 할 일로 가장 적절한 것을 고르시오.

① 따뜻한 옷 챙기기
② 체스 세트 가져가기
③ 읽을 책 고르기
④ 간편식 구매하기
⑤ 침낭 준비하기

06

대화를 듣고, 여자가 지불할 금액을 고르시오. 3점

① $15   ② $20
③ $27   ④ $30
⑤ $33

07

대화를 듣고, 남자가 체육 대회 연습을 할 수 없는 이유를 고르시오.

① 시험공부를 해야 해서
② 동아리 면접이 있어서
③ 축구화를 가져오지 않아서
④ 다리가 완전히 회복되지 않아서
⑤ 가족 식사 모임에 참석해야 해서

08

대화를 듣고, Science Open Lab Program에 관해 언급되지 않은 것을 고르시오.

① 지원 가능 학년
② 실험 재료 구입 필요성
③ 지원서 제출 기한
④ 참가 인원수
⑤ 시상 여부

09

Triwood High School Volunteer Program에 관한 다음 내용을 듣고, 일치하지 않는 것을 고르시오.

① 노인을 도와주는 봉사 활동이다.
② 봉사자는 대면으로 활동한다.
③ 스마트폰 사용 방법 교육을 한다.
④ 봉사자는 매주 토요일에 세 시간씩 참여한다.
⑤ 지원자는 이메일로 참가 신청서를 보내야 한다.

10

다음 표를 보면서 대화를 듣고, 여자가 주문할 휴대용 선풍기를 고르시오.

Portable Fan

	Model	Number of Speed Options	Color	LED Display	Price
①	A	1	blue	✕	$15
②	B	3	white	○	$26
③	C	3	yellow	✕	$31
④	D	4	pink	✕	$37
⑤	E	5	green	○	$42

11

대화를 듣고, 남자의 마지막 말에 대한 여자의 응답으로 가장 적절한 것을 고르시오.

① I can help you find it.
② I already bought a new one.
③ I had it before biology class.
④ You should report it to the police.
⑤ It was a birthday gift from my dad.

12

대화를 듣고, 여자의 마지막 말에 대한 남자의 응답으로 가장 적절한 것을 고르시오.

① Thank you. Everything looks delicious.
② Yes. I have an appointment this Saturday.
③ You're welcome. I made it with my dad's recipe.
④ Sounds good. What time did you make a reservation?
⑤ That's too bad. Why don't we try another restaurant?

13

대화를 듣고, 남자의 마지막 말에 대한 여자의 응답으로 가장 적절한 것을 고르시오. [3점]

Woman: _____

① No problem. You can find other projects at the organization.
② Sure. Let's choose one from your old children's books.
③ Congratulations. You finally made your first audiobook.
④ I hope so. You're going to be a wonderful writer.
⑤ Exactly. Kids grow faster than you think.

14

대화를 듣고, 여자의 마지막 말에 대한 남자의 응답으로 가장 적절한 것을 고르시오.

Man: _____

① Well, let's do the presentation together.
② Cheer up! I know you did your best.
③ Yes, I got a good grade on science.
④ Wow! It was a really nice presentation.
⑤ Right. I have already finished the project.

15

다음 상황 설명을 듣고, Robert가 Michelle에게 할 말로 가장 적절한 것을 고르시오. [3점]

Robert: _____

① When can I use the library?
② Where can I find the library?
③ How can I join the reading club?
④ Why do you want to go to the library?
⑤ What time does the lost and found open?

[16~17] 다음을 듣고, 물음에 답하시오.

16

남자가 하는 말의 주제로 가장 적절한 것은?

① useful foods to relieve coughs
② importance of proper food recipes
③ various causes of cough symptoms
④ traditional home remedies for fever
⑤ connection between weather and cough

17

언급된 음식 재료가 <u>아닌</u> 것은?

① ginger
② lemon
③ pineapple
④ honey
⑤ banana

23

2024년 6월
학력평가

MP3

동영상 강의

25BL1_A23   25BL1_L23

1번부터 17번까지는 듣고 답하는 문제입니다. 1번부터 15번까지는 한 번만 들려주고, 16번부터 17번까지는 두 번 들려줍니다. 방송을 잘 듣고 답을 하시기 바랍니다.

01

다음을 듣고, 여자가 하는 말의 목적으로 가장 적절한 것을 고르시오.

① 친환경 제품 사용을 홍보하려고
② 음식 대접에 대한 감사를 표하려고
③ 간식이 마련되어 있음을 안내하려고
④ 휴식 시간이 변경되었음을 공지하려고
⑤ 구내식당 메뉴에 관한 의견을 구하려고

02

대화를 듣고, 남자의 의견으로 가장 적절한 것을 고르시오.

① 인공 지능에서 얻은 정보를 맹목적으로 믿어서는 안 된다.
② 출처를 밝히지 않고 타인의 표현을 인용해서는 안 된다.
③ 인공 지능의 도움을 통해 과제물의 질을 높일 수 있다.
④ 과제를 할 때 본인의 생각이 들어가는 것이 중요하다.
⑤ 기술의 변화에 맞추어 작업 방식을 바꿀 필요가 있다.

03

다음을 듣고, 여자가 하는 말의 요지로 가장 적절한 것을 고르시오.

① 소셜 미디어는 원만한 대인관계 유지에 도움이 된다.
② 온라인에서는 자아가 다양한 모습으로 표출될 수 있다.
③ 소셜 미디어는 자존감에 부정적인 영향을 줄 수 있다.
④ 친밀한 관계일수록 상대의 언행에 쉽게 영향을 받는다.
⑤ 유명인 사생활 보호의 중요성은 종종 간과된다.

04

대화를 듣고, 그림에서 대화의 내용과 일치하지 <u>않는</u> 것을 고르시오.

05

대화를 듣고, 남자가 할 일로 가장 적절한 것을 고르시오.

① 과학 캠프 지원하기
② 참가 실험 결정하기
③ 체크리스트 작성하기
④ 실험 계획서 보여주기
⑤ 자기 소개 영상 촬영하기

06

대화를 듣고, 여자가 지불할 금액을 고르시오. [3점]

① $50   ② $55
③ $60   ④ $65
⑤ $70

정답과 해설 : 01~06 103~105

07

대화를 듣고, 남자가 마술쇼에 갈 수 없는 이유를 고르시오.

① 록 콘서트에 가야 해서
② 다른 학교 축제에 가야 해서
③ 가족 중 아픈 사람이 있어서
④ 동아리 축제를 준비해야 해서
⑤ 삼촌 생일 파티에 참석해야 해서

08

대화를 듣고, Victory Marathon에 관해 언급되지 않은 것을 고르시오.

① 행사 날짜
② 신청 방법
③ 출발 지점
④ 참가비
⑤ 예상 참가 인원

09

Violet Hill Mentorship에 관한 다음 내용을 듣고, 일치하지 않는 것을 고르시오.

① 다음 주 금요일에 개최될 예정이다.
② 대학 생활에 관한 조언이 제공된다.
③ 신청 시 질문을 미리 제출해야 한다.
④ 신청 마감일은 다음 주 화요일이다.
⑤ 전공별 참가 가능한 인원은 20명이다.

10

다음 표를 보면서 대화를 듣고, 두 사람이 구입할 무선 진공청소기를 고르시오.

Cordless Vacuum Cleaner

	Model	Battery Life	Price	Wet Cleaning	Color
①	A	1 hour	$300	×	Red
②	B	2 hours	$330	×	White
③	C	2 hours	$370	○	Red
④	D	3 hours	$390	○	White
⑤	E	3 hours	$410	○	Black

11

대화를 듣고, 남자의 마지막 말에 대한 여자의 응답으로 가장 적절한 것을 고르시오.

① Fine. Let's talk about it over dinner.
② Okay. Be more responsible next time.
③ Great. I already ordered some pet food.
④ Too bad. I hope your cat gets well soon.
⑤ Sorry. I can't take care of your cat tonight.

12

대화를 듣고, 여자의 마지막 말에 대한 남자의 응답으로 가장 적절한 것을 고르시오.

① I can't accept late assignments.
② You did an excellent job this time.
③ Upload your work to our school website.
④ Try to do your homework by yourself.
⑤ We can finish it before the next class.

23
24년 6월 학력평가

13

대화를 듣고, 남자의 마지막 말에 대한 여자의 응답으로 가장 적절한 것을 고르시오. 3점

Woman: _____

① Yes. I can give you the phone number of the clinic I visited.

② I agree. Last evening's badminton match was awesome.

③ No problem. I'll teach you how to serve this time.

④ Too bad. I hope you recover from your knee injury soon.

⑤ You're right. Maybe I should start taking badminton lessons.

14

대화를 듣고, 여자의 마지막 말에 대한 남자의 응답으로 가장 적절한 것을 고르시오. 3점

Man: _____

① Sure. It seems like a perfect place for bears.

② Great. Let's think about the club name first.

③ My pleasure. I can always give you a ride.

④ I agree. It's hard to give up using plastics.

⑤ No worries. I'll get my bike repaired.

15

다음 상황 설명을 듣고, Laura가 Tony에게 할 말로 가장 적절한 것을 고르시오.

Laura: _____

① I don't like visiting a hospital for medical checkups.

② I appreciate you taking me to the doctor today.

③ You'd better take a break for a few days.

④ You should finish your work before the deadline.

⑤ I'm afraid I can't reduce your workload right now.

[16~17] 다음을 듣고, 물음에 답하시오.

16

남자가 하는 말의 주제로 가장 적절한 것은?

① relationships between media and voters

② common ways of promoting school policy

③ guidelines for student election campaigns

④ requirements for becoming a candidate

⑤ useful tips for winning school debates

17

언급된 매체가 아닌 것은?

① social media   ② poster

③ pamphlet   ④ school newspaper

⑤ school website

24

2024년 9월
학력평가

※ 고1 2024년 9월 학력평가 시험지와 문항 순서가 동일합니다.

1번부터 17번까지는 듣고 답하는 문제입니다. 1번부터 15번까지는 한 번만 들려주고, 16번부터 17번까지는 두 번 들려줍니다. 방송을 잘 듣고 답을 하시기 바랍니다.

01

다음을 듣고, 여자가 하는 말의 목적으로 가장 적절한 것을 고르시오.

① 축제 기간 연장을 요청하려고
② 신설된 지하철 노선을 홍보하려고
③ 축제 당일의 지하철 연장 운행을 안내하려고
④ 축제 방문객에게 안전 수칙 준수를 당부하려고
⑤ 축제 기간 중 도심 교통 통제 구간을 공지하려고

02

대화를 듣고, 남자의 의견으로 가장 적절한 것을 고르시오.

① 불규칙한 수면 습관은 청소년의 뇌 발달을 방해한다.
② 스마트폰의 화면 밝기를 조절하여 눈을 보호해야 한다.
③ 취침 전 스마트폰 사용을 줄여야 수면의 질이 높아진다.
④ 집중력 향상을 위해 디지털 기기 사용을 최소화해야 한다.
⑤ 일정한 시간에 취침하는 것이 생체 리듬 유지에 도움을 준다.

03

다음을 듣고, 남자가 하는 말의 요지로 가장 적절한 것을 고르시오.

① 과도한 컴퓨터 사용은 스트레스 지수를 증가시킨다.
② 컴퓨터 관련 취미 활동은 IT 활용 능력을 향상시킨다.
③ 직업을 선택할 때 자신의 흥미와 적성을 고려해야 한다.
④ 다양한 악기 연주를 배우는 것은 인생을 풍요롭게 만든다.
⑤ 직업과 관련 없는 취미 활동이 스트레스 감소에 도움이 된다.

04

대화를 듣고, 그림에서 대화의 내용과 일치하지 <u>않는</u> 것을 고르시오.

05

대화를 듣고, 여자가 할 일로 가장 적절한 것을 고르시오.

① 선물 준비하기
② 온라인 초대장 보내기
③ 음식 주문하기
④ 초대 손님 명단 확인하기
⑤ 전시 부스 설치하기

06

대화를 듣고, 남자가 지불할 금액을 고르시오. [3점]

① $63   ② $70
③ $81   ④ $86
⑤ $90

07

대화를 듣고, 여자가 이번 주말에 등산을 갈 수 없는 이유를 고르시오.

① 아르바이트를 해야 해서
② 학교 시험공부를 해야 해서
③ 폭우로 인해 등산로가 폐쇄되어서
④ 경연을 위한 춤 연습을 해야 해서
⑤ 주문한 등산 장비가 도착하지 않아서

08

대화를 듣고, Lakestate Apartment Yoga Program에 관해 언급되지 않은 것을 고르시오.

① 대상 연령　　　　　② 운영 요일
③ 모집 인원　　　　　④ 등록 방법
⑤ 등록 준비물

09

Global Food Market에 관한 다음 내용을 듣고, 일치하지 않는 것을 고르시오.

① 학교 주차장에서 열린다.
② 이틀간 진행된다.
③ 8개 국가의 음식을 즐길 수 있다.
④ 음식마다 가격이 다르다.
⑤ 채식주의자를 위한 메뉴가 있다.

10

다음 표를 보면서 대화를 듣고, 남자가 주문할 디지털 텀블러를 고르시오.

Digital Tumblers

	Model	Price	Size	Water Intake Display	Color
①	A	$35	350ml	×	White
②	B	$40	470ml	×	Gold
③	C	$45	470ml	○	Black
④	D	$55	550ml	○	White
⑤	E	$65	550ml	○	Gold

11

대화를 듣고, 여자의 마지막 말에 대한 남자의 응답으로 가장 적절한 것을 고르시오.

① If it's too dry inside, you can easily get a cold.
② When you cough, you should cover your mouth.
③ You need to wash your hands not to get a cold.
④ It's really important to keep yourself warm.
⑤ Drinking water can make your skin soft.

12

대화를 듣고, 남자의 마지막 말에 대한 여자의 응답으로 가장 적절한 것을 고르시오.

① Awesome. The new bookshelf looks good in your room.
② Right. Then, shall we sell them at a used bookstore?
③ I see. Can you borrow them from the library?
④ Okay. I'll buy you books in a good condition.
⑤ I'm sorry. I haven't finished the book yet.

정답과 해설 : 07~12 110~111

13

대화를 듣고, 여자의 마지막 말에 대한 남자의 응답으로 가장 적절한 것을 고르시오. 3점

Man: _____

① I'll clarify each group member's specific role.

② I'll collect more data for our group research.

③ I should challenge myself for the competition.

④ I need to change the topic of our group project.

⑤ I'll let you know how to analyze data effectively.

14

대화를 듣고, 남자의 마지막 말에 대한 여자의 응답으로 가장 적절한 것을 고르시오. 3점

Woman: _____

① Trust me. When we eat makes a big difference.

② Okay. I'll check my meals to get in better shape.

③ Thank you for your tip. But I don't think I can do it.

④ Of course. I'll make sure to follow your workout routine.

⑤ Sure. That's why I didn't succeed at keeping a balanced diet.

15

다음 상황 설명을 듣고, Julia가 Sophie에게 할 말로 가장 적절한 것을 고르시오.

Julia: _____

① Could you help me assemble my desk?

② Can you share where you bought your desk?

③ How about choosing a new computer together?

④ Why don't you repair the furniture by yourself?

⑤ Do you have any ideas for decorating my room?

[16~17] 다음을 듣고, 물음에 답하시오.

16

여자가 하는 말의 주제로 가장 적절한 것은?

① material trends in the fashion industry

② benefits of making clothes from nature

③ tips to purchase natural material clothes

④ development of clothes washing methods

⑤ proper ways to wash natural material clothes

17

언급된 소재가 아닌 것은?

① cotton   ② silk

③ leather   ④ linen

⑤ wool

01 2018년 11월 학력평가
딕테이션

MP3

2SBL1_A01

😊 녹음을 듣고, 빈칸에 알맞은 말을 쓰시기 바랍니다. 빈칸은 문제풀이에 핵심이 되는 키워드와 헷갈리기 쉬운 발음에 표시되어 있으니 이 점에 유의하여 듣기 바랍니다.

01
고1 2018년 11월 3번

W: Hello and welcome back to 'Happy Life.' I'm Christine Brown, _____ life coach. When was the last time you sat down and thought about the good things in your life? With our busy schedules, we easily _____ _____ _____ the blessings we already have. However, according to a recent study, people who are more _____ for what they have are more hopeful and physically healthier. So here is today's tip. _____ _____ _____ _____. A gratitude journal is a diary in which you can express all the things you're thankful for. Just invest five to ten minutes each day in the journal. You'll feel more _____ and stay healthier.

02
고1 2018년 11월 4번

M: What are you doing, Jennifer? Mom wants us to study now.

W: I'm getting ready to go to the library to study.

M: _____ _____ the library takes so much time. Why don't you study at home?

W: Strangely, I can't focus on my studies here. I don't know why.

M: Hmm, how about _____ _____ your study space?

W: Tidying up my study space? Why?

M: When I organized my study place, I could _____ _____ and focus better.

W: Do you really think it'll work for me as well?

M: Sure. A disorganized desk leads to a disorganized mind. _____ spaces can even create stress.

W: That makes sense. I often get anxious looking at my messy desk.

M: Right. I think an _____ _____ _____ can help to improve your focus.

W: I guess it's worth trying out.

03
고1 2018년 11월 5번

[Door knocks.]

W: Come on in. [Pause] Have a seat, please.

M: Thanks!

W: What has been troubling you, Mr. Williams?

M: My _____ _____ _____ and sore, and I can't see things clearly.

W: Okay. Let me check your eyes first. Put your chin on the machine and don't move.

M: Alright.

W: [Pause] Oh, you have _____ eyes. Have you been using your computer more than usual?

M: Yes, I've been working all week on an important project.

W: You should _____ your eyes and blink more frequently.

M: I see. I was worried I got an eye infection.

W: No, you didn't. Just put some eyedrops in your eyes. I'll give you a _____.

M: Okay. Do I have to come again?

W: I recommend you have your eyes checked again

next week. The nurse will help you make an appointment.

M: All right. Thank you.

04

M: What do you think of this new office lounge, Ms. Jones?

W: It's really nice. You must have worked hard to decorate this place.

M: I enjoyed it. As you asked, _____ _____ _____ have been placed in front of the window.

W: Thanks! Our colleagues can browse the web in their free time.

M: Good. Look at the letter M on the wall. I hung it yesterday. It's your company's logo, right?

W: Yeah, I like it. Oh, there is a _____ oven below the logo.

M: Yes, you can use it conveniently for meals. I put the _____ _____ _____ _____.

W: Thanks! I love this picture. It was taken at our company's second anniversary party.

M: Great! There is a _____ _____, so you can read some books and enjoy coffee time here.

W: Thank you. Our colleagues will love this place.

05

[Cellphone rings.]

W: Benjamin, I'm sorry to call you during work, but I have great _____ _____

_____.

M: No problem, Mom. I'm about to leave my office. What's up?

W: Your brother Wilson got the football scholarship! Let's _____ a party tonight to celebrate.

M: Wow, wonderful. I'll buy a cake for him on my way home.

W: Good! I'll cook his favorite steak.

M: Oh, he'll love it!

W: Yeah, I hope so. But I think something is _____ from the meal. How about adding mashed potatoes as a side dish?

M: Great, it goes well with steak.

W: Right, but we're _____ _____

_____.

M: Don't worry. I'll buy some for you. The grocery store is near the bakery. I'll be at home in an hour.

W: Thanks. _____ _____. We still have some time.

06

W: Welcome to Springwood Farm Land. How may I help you?

M: Hi, I'd like to buy tickets for a farm _____ program.

W: We're sorry, but most of the programs are sold out except for two programs, the _____ _____ program and the cheese making program.

M: Hmm, my children might want to try something new, so we'll join the _____ _____ program. How much is it?

W: The price for the cheese making program is $20 per adult and $15 per child.

M: I'd like to buy _____ _____ tickets and two child tickets.

W: Okay. You want to buy tickets for two adults and two children, right?

M: Yes, and I have the coupon from your website. Can I use this?

W: Sure, then you'll get _____% off the total price.

M: Good! I'll pay by credit card.

07

고1 2018년 11월 8번

M: Hi, Charlotte, long time no see!

W: Hi, Andrew. Are you doing well at your new school?

M: I think I'm _____ well. All of my new classmates are nice.

W: Good to hear that. Are you still playing the guitar? I loved your _____ at the school festival last year.

M: Yeah, I joined my new school's rock band. _____ _____ _____ hard with the other members.

W: Great! I'd like to listen to your band play.

M: Actually, our band will have a street performance at Union Square. Will you come and watch?

W: Sure, I'd love to. _____ _____ will it be?

M: Next Saturday at 2 o'clock. Can you make it?

W: Oh, sorry but unfortunately not. I have to _____ _____ _____ next Saturday afternoon for the science project.

M: Okay. There should be another performance soon.

W: I'll try to make it then!

08

고1 2018년 11월 10번

M: Honey, how about going to the Moonlight Palace Tour this Friday night?

W: I heard about the tour. It'll be wonderful to walk through the palace under the night sky.

M: I agree. The tour _____ _____ 8 p.m. and takes two hours.

W: Then we can join it after dinner.

M: Sure! A tour guide tells us _____ _____ about the royal family.

W: That could be fun. How much is a ticket for the tour?

M: It's $30. It seems expensive but the tour includes watching a traditional dance and _____ traditional tea and snacks.

W: I think it's reasonable. We could have a wonderful night.

M: Right. It's said that only _____ _____ _____ _____ per day. Let's hurry up and make a reservation.

W: Okay. How can we do that?

M: We have to _____ on the website. I'll do it.

W: Thanks. I can't wait.

09

고1 2018년 11월 11번

W: Hello, listeners! We have some good news for music lovers. The Grand Philharmonic will hold the Forest Concert in Central Park on October 7th. The _____ Russian conductor, Alexander Ivanov, will lead the orchestra with the theme of 'In Search of a Dream.' This concert is a gift from the Grand Philharmonic to all music lovers so everyone can enjoy _____ _____ to this 90-minute musical treat. Seats are on a first come first serve basis, so prior reservation is _____

_____. You can also watch it live on

TV at home, but _____ _____

_____ at the park could be a once in a

lifetime experience.

10

고1 2018년 11월 12번

M: Hey, Julia. How about learning something

exciting after work?

W: Sure. I'd love to spend my _____ doing

something more interesting.

M: I have a time table for evening classes in our

community center. Let's look at it.

W: Hmm, they all look good, but I do _____

_____ _____ at home, so

except for that, the others are fine.

M: Okay. Oh, Wednesday _____

_____ for me. I have my regular

badminton club meeting then.

W: I see. I think we need a little break after work, so

how about a class starting at _____?

M: Alright. Then we're left with two options. Which

one do you prefer?

W: Actually, I'm on a tight budget these days, so I

don't want to spend more than $_____.

M: Me, neither. Let's sign up for the cheaper one.

11

고1 2018년 11월 1번

W: Hey, James, did you _____ which club

you're going to join?

M: Not yet. To be honest, I'd like to create a new

academic club.

W: Great idea! _____ _____

_____ _____ do you want to

make?

M: (I'm thinking of making an English debate club.)

12

고1 2018년 11월 2번

M: What a nice hat, Kelly. It looks perfect on you.

W: Thanks. I got it from a _____

_____. You can find many good

hand-made items there.

M: Really? I'd love to _____ _____

_____ _____ the market.

W: (Okay. Let's go there together next time.)

13

고1 2018년 11월 13번

W: That was a great documentary film, wasn't it,

David?

M: Yeah, I was really _____ _____

the Korean man, devoting his life to helping the

poorest people of Africa.

W: Right, his life was so beautiful. Living one's life

for others is _____ _____.

M: I think so, too. Evelyn, would you like to volunteer

with me?

W: Great! What kind of volunteer work are you

thinking about?

M: Actually, I've been working at the children's

hospital as a volunteer teacher.

W: Volunteer teacher?

M: Yeah, I teach children _____

_____ _____. The hospital is

now looking for more teachers.

W: I'd like to, but can I be helpful?

M: Sure, your major is art, so you might be a good

fit.

W: I've never taught anyone before, so I'm

_____ _____ I can teach them

well.

M: (Come on. You'll do fine if you volunteer with a

kind heart.)

14

M: You look so down these days. What's the matter, Alice?

W: Do I look down? Actually, I am _____ _____ in myself, Dad.

M: Oh, are you still discouraged about the school election results?

W: Yeah, I worked so hard to become the student president, but I failed.

M: You _____ _____ president, but challenging yourself was very brave.

W: Everyone around me keeps telling me the same thing. But I can't stop feeling like a failure.

M: I understand it's hard to get over, but you _____ yourself capable.

W: You really think so?

M: Sure, there were so many students who supported you.

W: You're right. I hadn't thought about it that way.

M: Cheer up, Alice! This experience will help you _____ _____ _____ _____ in the end.

W: (Thanks. I appreciate you for encouraging me to be positive.)

15

W: Sophia and John are classmates and they study math together in a study group. John spends lots of time studying math but his _____ _____ _____ _____ much. Sophia is good at math so John asks her to help him as a mentor. Sophia finds out that John always tries to solve difficult questions without practicing _____ ones. Sophia thinks that in order to get a good grade, John has to go from easy questions to _____ _____ step by step. So she wants to suggest to John that he should solve easy math questions _____ _____ _____ _____ challenging ones. In this situation, what would Sophia most likely say to John?

Sophia: (Why don't you practice less challenging math questions first?)

16~17

M: Welcome to 'Smart Traveler.' I'm your host, Brian Lewis. _____ _____ _____, shopping for souvenirs is one of the greatest pleasures, and many people enjoy bringing small souvenirs back home. Today I'll _____ some of the best souvenirs from around the world! First, when you travel to Beijing, jasmine tea is a great souvenir. _____ tea in the morning will become a wonderful reminder of all those memories there. Second, in _____, Eiffel Tower keychains are popular. With this little metal item hanging on your keys, you can remember the _____ _____ _____ _____ at the top of the Eiffel Tower. Third, when visiting Hawaii, bring back a Hawaiian dancing doll. _____ _____ you of the intense sun, crystal clear water, and amazing beaches. Last, in Venice, you can buy a traditional Venetian mask. Hanging the mask on the wall as a decoration, you can feel the _____ of Venice at home long afterwards. I hope these tips will help you in your souvenir shopping.

MP3

25BL1_A02

02 2019년 3월 학력평가
딕테이션

녹음을 듣고, 빈칸에 알맞은 말을 쓰시기 바랍니다. 빈칸은 문제풀이에 핵심이 되는 키워드와 헷갈리기 쉬운 발음에 표시되어 있으니 이 점에 유의하여 듣기 바랍니다.

01

고1 2019년 3월 3번

M: Hello, students. This is your vice principal Mike Westwood. I have an important announcement today. As the student _____ are getting old, we've been receiving complaints from many of you. _____ _____ _____ _____ _____ the lockers over the weekend. We ask that you empty your lockers and _____ _____ _____ by this Friday, March 22nd. Make sure to take all the items from your lockers and leave nothing behind. Any items that are _____ _____ will be thrown away. Thank you for your cooperation.

02

고1 2019년 3월 4번

W: Hey, Daniel. How are you _____ _____ for your trip to Seoul?

M: Hi, Claire. Everything is going great, but I'm worried about food.

W: Why?

M: I heard that Korean food is very _____ _____ _____. I think I should bring some food with me.

W: Oh, aren't you going to try any Korean food?

M: Well, I don't like trying new food. I feel comfortable with what I'm used to.

W: But _____ _____

_____ is the beauty of travel. It's the best way to get to the heart of the _____.

M: Maybe you're right. I'll give it a try during my travels.

W: Good thinking. You can find some good Korean restaurants on the web.

M: Okay. Thanks.

03

고1 2019년 3월 5번

M: Hello, Ally! Long time no see.

W: Hi, Robert. It's been a long time since I came to _____ _____.

M: You must have been busy.

W: Yeah. Did I tell you that I had to _____ _____ an exhibition?

M: Oh, yeah. I remember. How did it go?

W: It went well. It was finally over last week.

M: Good. So _____ _____ _____ _____ are you looking for today?

W: Actually I've changed my hair style, so I'm not sure which hat will _____ me.

M: Oh, you cut your hair short! Why don't you try this hat? It _____ _____ with short hair.

W: Let me try. [Pause] I love it!

M: It looks great on you.

W: Thanks. I'll take it.

04

M: What are you looking at, Sumi?

W: Hi, David. I'm looking at the picture I took on my middle school graduation day.

M: Let me see it. [Pause] Wow! There are _____ balloons above the blackboard.

W: Yeah. My friends and I put them there.

M: How nice! I also like the "Thank You" _____ below the balloons.

W: We really wanted to express our thanks to our homeroom teacher, Mr. Kim. I took this picture with him.

M: Oh, he's wearing a _____ tie.

W: Right. He usually doesn't wear a tie, but it was a special day.

M: I see. What is it in your hand?

W: It's the _____ _____.

M: And you're making a V-sign with your fingers.

W: Yes. I was very happy and proud that day.

05

W: Freddie, what are you doing on the computer?

M: I'm working on my music _____, Mom.

W: What is it about?

M: I have to write a song, but I can't think of a good melody.

W: When is the _____ _____?

M: I only have a week to finish. I feel pressed for time.

W: _____ _____ _____. Is there anything I can do for you?

M: I think I need to get some fresh air.

W: Why don't you _____ _____ _____ _____? I can take you there.

M: Great. It'll help me come up with some ideas. Thanks.

06

M: Honey, I think Paul needs new shoes.

W: You're right. His shoes are _____ _____ _____ for his feet.

M: Let's buy a pair online. I know a good store. [Clicking sound] Have a look.

W: Oh, how about these shoes? They're originally $100 a pair, but they're _____% off now.

M: That's a good deal. Let's buy a pair.

W: Oh, there are shoe bags, too. Why don't we buy one?

M: Okay. There are _____ _____, a $10 bag and a $15 bag. Which one do you like?

W: The $10 one looks good enough.

M: Then let's take it. Is that all we need?

W: Yes. Oh, here it says that if you're a member of this online store, _____ _____ $5 off.

M: That's good. I'm a member. Let's buy them now.

W: Okay.

07

W: Tony, are you ready for your _____ presentation tomorrow?

M: Yes, Ms. Woods, thanks to your help. I've already printed out the presentation material.

W: Can I take a look at it? Hmm. I'm afraid you need to _____ _____ _____.

M: Why? Are there any errors in the date or the names? I've checked them twice.

W: No, they're _____.

M: Did I use old data?

W: No, you used the latest data. But this picture of the planets is _____ _____.

M: Oh, my! I'll change it to a clearer picture.

W: Okay. I'm sure you'll do well tomorrow.

M: Thank you, Ms. Woods.

08

고1 2019년 3월 10번

W: Honey, it's spring. How about visiting the new botanic garden this weekend?

M: Do you mean the Royal Botanic Garden _____ _____ Redwood Valley?

W: Yes, it's not far from here. It's one of the biggest botanic gardens in the country.

M: That's right. I heard its size is about

_____ _____ _____

than a soccer field.

W: Yeah. You know, they offer interesting programs such as _____ _____ and guided tours.

M: Sounds great. Our kids will love planting trees.

W: Definitely. Let's go this Saturday. What time shall we leave?

M: How about 9 in the morning? The botanic garden is _____ _____ 10 a.m. to 6 p.m.

W: Okay. It'll be fun.

09

고1 2019년 3월 11번

W: Hello, students. This is Janice Hawkins, your drama teacher. I'm happy to invite you and your family to the 2019 Riverside High School Musical. This year we're _____ *Shrek*, based on the famous animated film. It's full of singing, dancing, romance and lots of fun. The _____ for the show were in December last year. The cast and crew have been

_____ _____ _____

to perfect their performance. The musical will be held in the auditorium for _____

_____ _____ _____

15th and 16th. Tickets are $8 per person. You can buy tickets in the drama club room. For more details, visit the school website. Thank you.

10

고1 2019년 3월 12번

W: Good morning. How may I help you?

M: I'm looking for an _____ mat for home training.

W: Okay. Here are our best-selling models.

M: They all look nice. Are thicker mats better?

W: Not really. But I think it _____

_____ _____ _____

5mm for home trainers.

M: I see. Then I have to choose from these four.

W: How about this one? It's the most popular.

M: It's too expensive. _____ _____

_____ _____ _____

more than $40.

W: Out of these two options left, I recommend this model with a non-slip _____. It keeps you from sliding around.

M: Okay. Safety is important. I'll take it.

11

W: Grandpa, is that a Spanish book you're reading?

M: Yes, I just _____ _____ _____ Spanish. You know learning a foreign language is good for your brain.

W: Sounds great. Are you learning it _____ _____?

M: (No, I'm taking a class in the community center.)

12

M: Sally, what are you _____ _____?

W: I can't find my jacket. I don't remember where I put it.

M: Why don't you _____ _____ _____? You were wearing it in P.E. class.

W: (That's right. I'll go there and see.)

13

W: Hi, David. What are you looking at?

M: School club _____.

W: Is there any club you want to join?

M: I'm interested in drones, but there's no drone club.

W: That's too bad. Why don't you _____ _____ _____ club yourself?

M: Oh, I haven't thought about it. What do I have to do first?

W: You'll need at least five people to _____ a club.

M: Then I have to find people who are interested in drones.

W: How about _____ _____ _____? It's an easy way to attract people.

M: (Right. I'll post an ad for a drone club I'm going to make.)

14

M: What are you reading, Lily?

W: It's a book for my English class, Dad. We have to read a book and _____ _____ _____.

M: Do you like the book?

W: Well, I'm not sure. Frankly it's too difficult for me.

M: Why did you _____ to read that book then?

W: It was on the bestseller list and it looked interesting. It's very _____, though.

M: Maybe you should try another book that suits your level.

W: I know what you mean, but wouldn't I learn more from reading a difficult book?

M: Well, what's _____ _____ _____ _____ it if you can't understand it?

W: (That makes sense. I'll switch to an easier book.)

15

고1 2019년 3월 15번

M: Clara and Becky go to summer camp together every year. They are _____ _____ _____ one this year, too. Today Clara gets a flyer for an interesting camp at the community center. She shows Becky the flyer and asks her to _____ _____ for the camp together. Checking the dates, Becky finds out that she has a family vacation _____ _____ _____. When Becky tells Clara that she won't be able to join the camp, Clara is very disappointed. So Becky wants to suggest to Clara that they _____ _____ _____ camp. In this situation, what would Becky most likely say to Clara?

Becky: (Why don't we find a camp on different dates?)

16~17

고1 2019년 3월 16번~17번

W: Hello, class. You must have heard of the proverb, '_____ _____ _____ _____ flock together.' We all know what this proverb means because it's commonly used. Like this, there are many proverbs in which _____ _____. Let's talk about them today. First one is, 'When the cat's away, the _____ will play.' It is using the fun relationship between the two animals. We can easily _____ the meaning of this proverb: the weaker do whatever they want when the stronger are not around. The next one is, 'Don't _____ _____ _____ before they're hatched.' It's using a chicken's life cycle. From this proverb, we can learn the lesson that we should not make _____ decisions. Now it's your turn to talk about a few proverbs like these. You may have already thought about _____ _____ _____, like 'Every dog has its day.' Let's talk about some together.

03

2019년 6월 학력평가
딕테이션

MP3

25BL1_A03

녹음을 듣고, 빈칸에 알맞은 말을 쓰시기 바랍니다. 빈칸은 문제풀이에 핵심이 되는 키워드와 헷갈리기 쉬운 발음에 표시되어 있으니 이 점에 유의하여 듣기 바랍니다.

01

고1 2019년 6월 3번

W: Good morning, everyone. This is Rachel Adams, your student president. As you know, the student union is _____ _____ _____ from next Monday until Wednesday. Thank you to those who have already donated _____ _____ _____ useful items. We're selling all of those items for five dollars or less, and all of the money will be donated to a _____ charity. The event will be held in the school gym from 3 p.m. to 5 p.m. I hope many students will _____ in this event for charity. Thank you for listening.

02

고1 2019년 6월 4번

M: Brenda, my uncle bought a shrimp pizza. Help yourself.

W: Oh! But I don't like shrimp.

M: Really? Do you have an _____ to shrimp?

W: No. I've heard shrimp is a little high in cholesterol. So, I think it isn't good for our health.

M: Hmm, that's a misunderstanding about shrimp.

W: You mean eating shrimp has a _____ _____ on health?

M: Of course. It can increase your level of good cholesterol.

W: Oh, I didn't know that.

M: Eating shrimp can give us _____ and minerals. Plus, shrimp is low-calorie.

W: Then it might be good to add shrimp to my diet.

M: Sure. It would be _____ _____ your health.

W: I guess I didn't know much about shrimp. I'll give it a try.

03

고1 2019년 6월 5번

W: Good afternoon. How may I help you?

M: I made a _____ _____. It's under the name of Stennis.

W: Could you spell it, sir?

M: Sure. S-T-E-N-N-I-S.

W: All right. You've booked _____ _____ _____ with an ocean view for two nights. Is that correct?

M: Yes. And I want to stay on a higher floor if possible.

W: Let me check. [Typing sound] We have rooms _____ on the 15th and 19th floors. Which one would you prefer?

M: 19th is better.

W: Okay. You'll be staying in Room 1911. Here are your key and breakfast coupons.

M: Thanks. When does the morning _____ begin?

W: You can have breakfast from 7 to 9 a.m. at the restaurant on the first floor. Have a nice stay.

04

M: Mom, this is a picture from Science Day.

W: Let me see. The woman _____

_____ must be your science teacher.

M: Yes, she is. She helped me a lot. Do you see the

rocket next to the _____ _____?

W: Oh, it looks fantastic! Who made it?

M: I made it myself. I received a lot of good

_____ about it.

W: Good job. What are the two pictures on the wall?

M: They are pictures of _____

_____.

W: I see. And there is a robot in front of the window.

M: Yeah, my class put all the parts of the robot

together.

W: Sounds great. I can see a _____

_____ on the table, too.

M: My teacher showed us how to make it with a

3D-printer, and it was very exciting.

W: You must've had a great time.

05

W: Brian, Mom and Dad are coming home

_____ an hour.

M: I hope they will like this surprise party for

Parents' Day.

W: Of course they will. [Pause] Good. We

_____ _____ the party table.

M: I love the balloons on the wall. They're cute.

W: I like them, too. And Dad will love this paper

carnation. You did a good job.

M: Thanks. Where is the cake for the party?

W: It's in the refrigerator. Let me take it out.

M: _____ _____ do we need?

W: We have two more things to do, cooking pasta

for dinner and writing a thank-you letter.

M: Mom does like your cooking, so you do the

pasta. And _____ _____ the

letter.

W: Okay, I'll do that. Let's hurry.

06

W: Hello. Can I help you?

M: Yes. I want to buy a baseball bat for my son. He

is 11 years old.

W: How about this baseball bat? It's the most

popular. It's _____ dollars.

M: Okay. I'll take one bat. Do you also have baseball

gloves?

W: Sure. How about this glove? It's soft and

comfortable.

M: How much is it?

W: It's _____ dollars.

M: Hmm... That's reasonable. I'll buy two gloves.

W: Okay. Don't you need any safety balls for

children? They are _____ and soft.

M: I think I've got all I need. Can I use this coupon?

W: Of course. Then you can get 10% _____

_____ _____ _____.

M: Great. I'll use the coupon and pay by credit card.

07

M: Linda, there'll be a team _____ _____ next week. The topic is Social Network Services.

W: Sounds interesting. Are you going to sign up?

M: Yes. I'm interested in debating. Do you want to be my teammate?

W: _____ _____ _____, but I can't.

M: Right. You said you're busy doing your writing assignment.

W: No, I've already finished it.

M: Well, do you find it hard to _____ in front of others?

W: Not really. Actually, I'm preparing for a school _____ _____. It's next Thursday.

M: Oh, I see. You don't have enough time to join me this time.

W: Right. I hope you will find someone good to be your teammate.

08

[Door knocks.]

M: Can I come in, Ms. Wilson?

W: Sure, come on in. [Pause] Oh, Peter. I was waiting for you to come. How's your career _____ going?

M: I'm still trying to find some information about my future career.

W: Good. So I'd like to _____ the Career

Vision Camp to you.

M: Okay. I heard that the camp is only for high school students. Is that right?

W: Yes. It'll be helpful. Plus, there's _____ _____ _____.

M: Great. Hmm, can you tell me when the application deadline is?

W: It's _____ _____. You should hurry since it's first come, first served.

M: I see. I will apply for the camp as soon as possible.

W: It'll be held at the Lincoln Center _____ school. You can get there easily.

M: Okay. Thank you.

09

W: Good morning, residents. This is the librarian of the Jacksonville Community Center. We're holding the Children's Book Fair for three days, from _____ 21st to the 23rd. It will offer your children an opportunity to feel the joy of reading books. We'll _____ a wide variety of children's books including comic books, picture books, and fairy tales. In addition, you will be able to buy all books at 50% off their _____ _____. On the first day of the fair, you will be able to meet and talk with the famous writer, Andy Murphy. Also, every child visiting the fair will get a _____ _____ _____ _____. I hope you will enjoy the fair. Thank you.

10

M: Katie, what are you doing with your smartphone?

W: I'm searching for an _____ shaver for my dad's birthday. Will you help me find a good one?

M: Sure. Let me see... *[Pause]* How about this one?

W: Well, that's too expensive. I _____ _____ more than $100.

M: Okay. And I think a 20-minute battery life is _____ _____ to use conveniently.

W: I think so, too. It needs frequent charging.

M: You're right. Does it need to be _____?

W: Of course. He shaves in the shower every morning.

M: Then we have only two options left. _____ _____ do you think is better?

W: Dad likes black, so I'll buy the black one.

M: I think it's a nice choice.

11

W: Jason, I'm going to a _____ _____ this Friday. Can you join me?

M: I'd love to. But we have classes until 3 p.m. on that day.

W: No worries. The show is open until 8 p.m. _____ _____ _____ after school?

M: (Sure. Let's go together.)

12

M: Honey, look out the window. It's _____ a lot.

W: Yeah, I think it might be dangerous to drive to work.

M: You're right. You'd better use _____ _____ today.

W: (Okay. I'll take the subway then.)

13

[Cellphone rings.]

W: Hello, this is Claire.

M: Hi, what's up?

W: I have something to tell you about the _____ _____ _____ economics assignment.

M: What happened? Is there a problem?

W: Actually, my mom broke her ankle this morning. She can't walk because of the pain.

M: I'm sorry to hear that. That must be hard for her.

W: It is. So I will have to _____ _____ _____ her this weekend.

M: Then we can't have our meeting this Saturday.

W: That's right. I'm terribly sorry, but I have to _____ the meeting.

M: Don't worry about that. So, when will you have time?

W: I guess any day next week is good for me.

M: Okay, then _____ _____ _____ _____ next Monday?

W: (All right. Thank you for understanding.)

14

M: Hi, Emily! How are your wedding _____ going?

W: They're going well so far. I reserved a wedding hall and ordered invitation cards.

M: Good. Everything's almost _____. It's on the first Saturday of July, right?

W: Yes. Can you come?

M: Of course. Is there anything that I can help you with?

W: Actually, I _____ _____ who'll sing at the wedding. So, would you sing for me?

M: I'd love to, but I've never done anything like that before.

W: I heard you singing at the college song festival, so I know you're a good singer.

M: Thanks, but I'm afraid I may not sing well enough to do so at a wedding.

W: Oh, please! I'm sure it would be the best wedding gift. I'd _____ _____ _____ it.

M: (Okay, I'll sing for you. I hope you won't expect too much.)

15

W: Alex and Olivia have been close friends since they were children. They _____ _____ in the same town, and they attend the same high school. One day, Alex tells Olivia that his father got a new job so his family has to move to another city. That's why he's going to _____ _____ a new school next week. Olivia feels sad because they have been friends for _____ a long time. Alex also hopes to keep his friendship with her. So, Alex wants to suggest that they

_____ _____ _____ _____ even after he leaves the city. In this situation, what would Alex most likely say to Olivia?

Alex: (Let's keep in touch even after we part.)

16~17

M: Hello, everyone. Last class we learned about the dangers of climate change. Today, I'll tell you about some foods that _____ _____ because of climate change. First of all, 70 percent of the world's _____ could disappear by 2080 due to climate change. In Africa, the amount of coffee produced _____ _____ by more than 50 percent. Secondly, avocados are also in danger. It usually takes 72 gallons of water to make just one pound of avocados. Climate change in California _____ _____ _____ a lack of water, so the avocado plants aren't producing enough fruit. Thirdly, warmer temperatures _____ _____ _____, too. To grow properly, apple trees need a certain period of cold weather. Lack of cold weather time leads to _____ apple production. Finally, the unstable climatic conditions through crop season are causing a decrease in _____ _____ in Florida. Specifically, hotter-than-normal weather has delayed the flowering and production of strawberries. Now, let me show you some slides about this issue.

04 2019년 9월 학력평가
딕테이션

MP3

25BL1_A04

녹음을 듣고, 빈칸에 알맞은 말을 쓰시기 바랍니다. 빈칸은 문제풀이에 핵심이 되는 키워드와 헷갈리기 쉬운 발음에 표시되어 있으니 이 점에 유의하여 듣기 바랍니다.

01

고1 2019년 9월 3번

W: Hello, students. Our _____ school talent show is coming soon. I'm glad that so many talented students signed up for the audition. Now, I'd like to give you some tips on _____ _____ _____ _____ it. First, practice your lines, your dance moves, or your songs over and over until you _____ them perfectly. After that, rehearse with your friends or in front of a mirror. Practicing again and again will help you feel _____ _____ _____. Finally, wear clothes you'll feel comfortable in. You can bring your own costumes if you want. I wish all of you good luck and hope you _____ on the stage. Thank you.

02

고1 2019년 9월 4번

M: Honey, where did you get all these potatoes?

W: My friend Jennifer runs a potato farm, so she gave me some.

M: This is a lot! Let's put them in the refrigerator.

W: Oh, no. _____ potatoes in a refrigerator gives them an unpleasant taste.

M: Okay. Where should we keep them?

W: They should be stored in a _____ _____ _____ place.

M: Then the basement would be good.

W: That's perfect, but we also need to take the potatoes out of the plastic bag. Potatoes _____ _____ in plastic bags.

M: I see. And I remember reading an article saying that storing potatoes with an apple _____ _____ _____ sprouting.

W: Really? That's good to know.

M: I'll bring an apple, and we can keep them together.

03

고1 2019년 9월 5번

M: Hi, Kate. How do you feel today?

W: I feel better, but I still have a sore throat. How does my _____ sound?

M: It sounds fine, so don't worry about it.

W: Thanks. Did you hear about one of the _____ _____ _____ _____ in this studio last year?

M: You mean "The Dreaming Tree?" I heard it was the best-selling audio book of the year.

W: It was. The sound _____ _____ _____ made the story feel alive.

M: Thank you. Most of all, your voice acting was great in the various roles.

W: I'm flattered. Okay, I think I'm ready now. Is this the _____ for the radio drama we're working on today?

M: Yes. We can begin once you step into the _____ _____. I'll check the microphone.

W: All right. I'll start when you give me the signal.

04

M: Ms. Morgan, how's the preparation for the
   school talk show going?

W: I've finished setting up the stage. How do you
   like it?

M: Great! I like the banner for the talk show
   _____ _____ _____
   _____ the curtains.

W: Thanks. What do you think about the picture
   under the banner?

M: I think the image of the laptop computer and
   _____ _____ is perfect for the
   talk show on "Information Security."

W: I think the picture shows the topic clearly.

M: It does. You put _____ _____
   _____ below the picture.

W: Yes. They're the ones we bought recently for the
   show.

M: Okay. The students will sit and talk on those
   chairs on the _____ _____,
   right?

W: Exactly. I also put a white board next to the
   standing microphone. Students have asked me
   to set that up.

M: Great! I'll be looking forward to the event.

05

M: Hey, Lucy! Where are you going?

W: Hi, Steve. I'm on my way to the bank to
   _____ some money.

M: Oh, is it for your trip to Europe? You must be
   excited. Did you buy the big backpack you
   needed?

W: No, but I borrowed a nice one from my cousin.
   And I ordered the guide book you recommended.

M: That's good. It'll be very useful. You seem to be
   _____ _____ for your trip.

W: Almost. I've renewed my passport and booked
   the flight. But I _____ _____
   _____ a hotel yet.

M: How come?

W: Because there are so many different options. It's
   difficult to find the right deal.

M: Why don't you use mobile _____
   _____ _____ the hotel prices?
   It'll save you time and money.

W: Mobile apps? Do you know of any good ones?

M: Yes, I know a few. I'll _____ you and let
   you know their names.

W: Thanks. I'll try them out.

06

W: Hello, sir. How can I help you?

M: I'm looking for a teapot for my mother. She
   _____ _____ tea with her
   friends.

W: Okay. How about this teapot with a simple
   and classic design? It'll never _____
   _____ _____ style.

M: I think she'll like it. How much is it?

W: It's $20. But if you like this design, we also have
   this teapot set that comes with the cups. It's
   only $_____.

M: Great! I'll take the set. Can you recommend
   some tea as well?

W: Sure. How about this lavender tea? It's definitely
   good for _____, and it's $10 a package.

M: Sounds good. I'll take two packages. Can I use
   this discount coupon?

W: Absolutely. You'll get a _____% discount
   from the total price.

M: Great. Here's my credit card.

07

M: Agnes, what are you doing?

W: I'm _____ the Internet to find a nice restaurant for my trip this weekend.

M: All the places on the website look nice.

W: Yes, but I've finally decided where to go. It's this French restaurant _____ El Bistro.

M: Oh, I've watched a travel TV show about that restaurant.

W: Have you?

M: Yes. It said it's so popular among the local people that they have to _____ _____ a long line to get in.

W: I know. I don't like crowded places, but I think it'll be worth the wait because of _____ _____ _____. The family's been running it since 1890.

M: Wow, that long?

W: Yes. I like old places that maintain their tradition. It's far from my hotel, but I'm _____ _____ go anyway.

M: I'm sure you'll enjoy the meal there.

08

W: Hey, Ryan, did you hear about the Stress Free Program?

M: Stress Free Program? No, what is it?

W: It's a new school program for students. You might want to join it. You look really _____ _____ these days.

M: Yeah, I really need to relax. What do I do there?

W: You can take part in _____ _____ like coloring, e-sports, and board games.

M: Sounds interesting! How can I register for the program?

W: You can register _____ _____ or on the school website.

M: Where's the program held?

W: It's held on the second floor of the Student Union building.

M: All right. Is the program _____ _____?

W: No, it runs from 3 to 7 p.m. There's a schedule for each activity.

M: Okay, I'll check the schedule first.

W: Great. I hope you can _____ your mind there.

09

M: Hello, listeners. I'm Nick Adams from Healthy Cooking. I'm pleased to make this announcement about the _____ cooking contest, Show Me Your Dishes. It's open to young adults aged 15 to 18 who want to become chefs. This contest is an annual event which _____ _____ _____ every October since 2004. If you'd like to participate, please upload your recipe to our contest website by September 6th. The participants will have _____ _____ to cook up their best dishes. Their dishes will be judged based on _____ _____ _____ _____ by chefs from some of the most famous local restaurants. Don't miss this great opportunity to show off your cooking skills!

10

M: Jessica, what are you doing on the computer?

W: I'm looking for a bluetooth keyboard that works with my smartphone.

M: What do you need it for?

W: I need to _____ during meetings at work. Can you help me choose one?

M: Sure. How about this model? It looks great and is the cheapest.

W: I already have that model, but it's too _____ to carry around.

M: Then, why don't you get something that _____ _____ _____ 300 grams?

W: Yeah. That makes sense.

M: You can get this one. It also has a _____ _____ of 100 hours.

W: It's nice, but it's not foldable. I want to buy that one, instead.

M: You mean this foldable keyboard?

W: Yeah, it'll _____ _____ much less space in my bag. I think I'll order it now.

11

W: Mike, I couldn't _____ _____ _____ your cell phone yesterday.

M: My cell phone wasn't working, so I took it to the repair shop.

W: Really? We need to discuss our science project tonight. How can I _____ you?

M: (No worries. I'll get my phone back after school.)

12

[Telephone rings.]

M: Hello. This is the Youth Volunteer Center. What can I do for you?

W: I'm supposed to _____ the volunteer program tomorrow, but can I change my volunteering schedule?

M: Sure. You can _____ _____ Thursday or Friday.

W: (All right. Either day is fine with me.)

13

M: Hi, Amy. What are you watching on your tablet?

W: Hi, Dan. It's a _____ _____ on psychology. This lecture is really great!

M: I didn't know you were interested in psychology.

W: Actually, I'm thinking of becoming a _____.

M: Great! I think it'll suit you. You're a good listener and you give good advice to others.

W: Thanks. I'd like to get some _____ _____ in counseling, but it's not easy to find opportunities.

M: How about checking the school's volunteer center? You might find something.

W: I've already checked it, but it didn't help much.

M: Oh, _____ _____ works at a local counseling center. Maybe he can help you.

W: (Really? Please ask him if I can visit him.)

14

고1 2019년 9월 14번

W: Chris, did you hear the ＿＿＿＿＿＿ forecast?

M: No, what did it say?

W: It said there would be heavy rain and strong winds this afternoon.

M: Oh, no! Our outdoor concert is supposed to start at 4 p.m. What should we do?

W: The teacher said we have to ＿＿＿＿＿＿ ＿＿＿＿＿＿ ＿＿＿＿＿＿ of the concert to the school auditorium.

M: Okay. We still have several hours to set up the stage. But how can we ＿＿＿＿＿＿ people of the change?

W: I'll make a notice and put it up on the notice board at the outdoor concert hall.

M: Good. I'll go and ask the school ＿＿＿＿＿＿ ＿＿＿＿＿＿ to make an announcement about it.

W: Good idea. Is there any other way for us to ＿＿＿＿＿＿ ＿＿＿＿＿＿ ＿＿＿＿＿＿ to more people quickly?

M: (We can post the notice on social media.)

15

고1 2019년 9월 15번

M: Jina is a high school student. Her school is ＿＿＿＿＿＿ a Market Day to raise money for the homeless in the neighborhood. Jina's teacher says that students who want to

＿＿＿＿＿＿ ＿＿＿＿＿＿ ＿＿＿＿＿＿ the event should bring their own items to school. Jina wants to participate in the school market, so as soon as she gets home, she starts looking for ＿＿＿＿＿＿ she can sell at the school Market Day. Finally, she finds her mother's old flower pot in the basement. Now, she wants to ask her mother for ＿＿＿＿＿＿ to take the flower pot to school. In this situation, what would Jina be most likely to say to her mother?

Jina: (Can I take this flower pot for a school event?)

16~17

고1 2019년 9월 16~17번

W: Hello, everyone! Today, I want you to consider this: do you have something you're not using in your home? Then, how about ＿＿＿＿＿＿ ＿＿＿＿＿＿ ＿＿＿＿＿＿ others? It enables products to be recycled and reused, reducing the negative effects on the ＿＿＿＿＿＿. For example, if you have a nice dress for a party, lend it to others who need it. Then the ＿＿＿＿＿＿ used in making a new dress can be saved. The same thing with toys. Every year, millions of toys that children no longer play with are ＿＿＿＿＿＿ ＿＿＿＿＿＿. By sharing things with others, you can reduce waste. Also, you can benefit ＿＿＿＿＿＿ by sharing your goods. If you have books you've finished reading, register them on online sharing systems. Then, someone who wants to read your books can ＿＿＿＿＿＿ them and you can make money by sharing. Similarly, if you need a ＿＿＿＿＿＿, you can find some people who share theirs on bike-sharing systems and save money. Why don't you awaken your "sleeping" goods?

05 2019년 11월 학력평가 딕테이션

MP3

25BL1_A05

😊 녹음을 듣고, 빈칸에 알맞은 말을 쓰시기 바랍니다. 빈칸은 문제풀이에 핵심이 되는 키워드와 헷갈리기 쉬운 발음에 표시되어 있으니 이 점에 유의하여 듣기 바랍니다.

01

고1 2019년 11월 3번

M: Hello, everyone. Welcome back to our show, 'Secrets to a Healthy Life.' I'm your _____ _____ _____ _____, Eric Bolton. You might have heard that many people suffer from dry skin as the weather gets colder. Let me _____ _____ _____ to keep your skin healthy in the winter. When you take a bath, use water that is not very hot. A long hot bath in cold weather can make your skin dry and _____ _____ skin trouble. And one more tip for your skin in the winter: Put lotion or oil on your skin as often as possible. I hope you can make use of these tips to _____ _____ _____ _____ even in the winter.

02

고1 2019년 11월 4번

W: Hello, Jake. Is studying for the final exams going well?

M: Not really, Ms. Baker. I've been drinking energy drinks to stay awake.

W: Well, I think _____ _____ _____ drink too many of them.

M: Why? Do they have harmful effects?

W: Energy drinks have a lot of caffeine, so drinking them too much can _____ your sleep and make you feel dizzy.

M: That explains why I can't sleep well at night.

W: Right. Also, drinking them can _____ _____ _____.

M: Really? I thought it would relieve my stress instead.

W: That's not true. And the more you drink energy drinks, the more you become _____ _____ them.

M: Do you mean I can become addicted to them?

W: That's right. So you should be _____ _____ _____ drink too many of them.

M: Okay. I'll keep that in mind. Thanks, Ms. Baker.

03

고1 2019년 11월 5번

W: Hello. How can I help you?

M: Hi, I made an online reservation. Do I get the _____ _____?

W: You don't have to get tickets if you have a reservation number. Just _____ _____ at the entrance and you can enjoy the whole camping expo.

M: That's great. I heard there is a _____ _____ camping tables and chairs in the expo. Where can I find it?

W: When you go inside, you'll see it on your right. Look for camping _____ on display.

M: Thanks. Is there a cafeteria around here?

W: Yes, we have one on the second floor.

M: Thank you so much for your help.

W: My pleasure. _____ _____ _____ in our camping expo.

04

M: What are you looking at, honey?

W: It's the picture Sally sent to me. She recommended that we go to the new community park near her house.

M: Let me see it. *[Pause]* I like this _____ _____ _____ on the left. We can have some sandwiches and talk there.

W: Sounds great. Look at the elephant face at the top of the _____. It looks cute.

M: Yeah, there are also swings next to it. Our son would like this park, too.

W: He sure would. Oh, there is a _____ in front of the swings.

M: Wow, this park has everything a child could want.

W: It's great to find a place where parents and children can have a good time together.

M: It really is. Take a look at these flowers _____ _____ _____ _____ of a heart!

W: They're beautiful. How about going there this weekend?

M: Terrific! I can't wait to go there.

05

W: David, how are the preparations going for your meeting tomorrow?

M: Hi, Jennifer. They're almost done. I'm _____ _____ _____ if everything is ready.

W: Sounds good. Since I finished my own work today, I can help you.

M: That's very kind of you. I confirmed the reservation for the meeting room and _____ _____ _____ informing the participants of tomorrow's schedule.

W: What about snacks for the meeting?

M: They're in my car. I'll get them tomorrow morning.

W: And, is there anything else left to do?

M: Let me see... I need to make name tags to give to the _____.

W: Do you want me to help you with that?

M: No, thanks. I can handle it. Could you _____ _____ _____ _____ for the meeting instead?

W: Sure. I'll do that for you.

M: I'll send you the file to print out right now. Thank you.

06

W: Welcome to Good Aroma Candle. How may I help you?

M: Hi. I'm looking for _____ candles for my parents. They like flower scents.

W: Come over here and try this flower scent.

M: Thanks. *[Pause]* I like this rose scented candle. How much is it?

W: Large candles and medium ones are on sale now. Large ones are $_____ and medium ones are $10 each.

M: Well then, I'll take two large candles.

W: If you buy _____ _____ candles, we give you a soap for free.

M: Great. Then I'll have a medium one with the same scent as well. Did you say they're $10?

W: Exactly. You're getting two large candles and one medium candle.

M: That's right. Can I also use this _____ _____?

W: Of course, you get 10% off the total price with that.

M: Thank you. I'll pay by credit card.

07

고1 2019년 11월 8번

[Cell phone rings.]

M: Hello. Janis! What's up?

W: Hi, Chris. How are you spending your vacation?

M: _____ _____ _____ a lot of cooking. How about you? You said you're going on a family trip.

W: Yeah, I was supposed to, but I can't.

M: Really? Aren't there flight tickets _____?

W: Well, it's not about tickets.

M: Then why? Oh, is there still a problem with your ankle?

W: No, I'm okay now. Actually I _____ _____ _____ _____ volunteering program earlier and I was accepted.

M: What a great chance! So you can't go on that family trip.

W: You're right. _____ _____ _____ for a month. I wanted to say goodbye to you before I leave.

M: Take good care of yourself. I'm sure you'll have a meaningful experience.

W: Thank you for supporting me. Have a nice vacation!

08

고1 2019년 11월 10번

M: Kelly, did you see this Junior Badminton Competition leaflet?

W: No, not yet. Let me see. The competition is on _____ 21st, at 10 a.m.

M: It's after the midterm exams. Why don't we sign up for the competition as a team?

W: Sounds exciting. It would be an unforgettable event before graduating.

M: Exactly. The _____ _____ is only $8.

W: That's reasonable. Oh, look at this. They provide lunch for free.

M: But here it says we have to _____ _____ _____ _____.

W: Then, we should bring ours. How can we apply for the competition?

M: It says we can _____ _____ _____. Let's do it together now.

W: Okay. I'm really looking forward to it.

09

고1 2019년 11월 11번

W: Hello, listeners! I'm happy to introduce you to the first children's library in our town. It's the Dream Children's Library. Our library is for children in the _____ _____ and younger. We have a variety of toys as well as books for _____ _____ of children. There are special reading discussion programs for your children. Also, we offer _____ _____ for children every weekend. We're excited to tell you our library is now ready to open. Our opening day is November 24th. On opening day, we'll provide _____ _____ _____ to all the visitors. Don't miss it! For more information, visit our website www.dreamchildrenslibrary.org.

10

고1 2019년 11월 12번

M: Hey, Cathy! What are you looking at?

W: Hi, Steve. I was searching for an _____ _____ set. I'm thinking about sending it as a Christmas gift to children in need.

M: You're so kind. Do you need help choosing one?

W: Yeah, thank you. I want it to be _____ $20.

M: All right. Let me see. Which type of coloring tool would be good for them?

W: Hmm... I think watercolors are _____ _____ _____. The kids would need extra things like brushes.

M: I agree. The other tools would be better.

W: Right. How about the number of colors?

M: They'll need _____ _____ _____ colors to express what they want.

W: You're right. Then, there are two choices left.

M: Yeah. Oh, there is a model which _____ _____ _____.

W: Perfect! They might need it in their art classes. I'll choose that one.

11

고1 2019년 11월 1번

M: Mom, look! It's raining outside. But we don't have _____.

W: I think we need to buy one in this building.

M: Okay. _____ _____ _____ buy one?

W: (We can buy one on the first floor.)

12

고1 2019년 11월 2번

W: Mr. Smith, can you give me advice on how to edit my essay?

M: Sure. First, take a look at the _____ I gave you last class. It has helpful examples.

W: Really? Oh, I'm sorry. I'm _____ _____ _____ it.

M: (Don't worry. I can make a copy for you.)

13

고1 2019년 11월 13번

W: Brian, you look so tired today.

M: Yeah, even though I get enough rest, I feel _____ these days.

W: Hmm... maybe you need some exercise. You like swimming, don't you?

M: I do, but I often feel lazy.

W: That's true for me, too. So, I _____ _____ _____ a sports club at school.

M: What kind of sports club?

W: I exercise in a yoga club. I find it very helpful to work out with other people at a fixed time.

M: I guess exercising with others can help you _____ _____.

W: Exactly. Why don't you join a sports club, too?

M: Actually, I'm interested in the swimming club, but as far as I know, the _____ _____ ended.

W: It's too early to give up! I saw a notice that all the clubs _____ their registration period to this Friday.

M: (In that case, I'd better go and see if I can join the club.)

14

M: Bonnie, what are you doing?

W: I'm checking my _____ _____.
I'm running out of money again.

M: Haven't you gotten paid for your part-time job yet?

W: I have, but I already spent most of the money hanging out with my friends. At the end of month, _____ _____ _____.

M: Then, how about setting a weekly budget?

W: A weekly budget? What do you mean by that?

M: I usually set a budget for each week, and don't spend more than it allows. So I've _____ _____ _____ everyday spending on chips and soda.

W: Good for you. Can I save money if I make it a habit, too?

M: Of course, you can. If you _____ your budget, you'll think twice before you spend money.

W: That makes sense. Keeping a weekly budget seems advantageous.

M: Now that I keep a weekly budget, I spend money _____ _____ _____ _____ it. I bet it'll work for you, too.

W: (Great. I should try to keep a weekly budget.)

15

M: Ted and Linda are classmates. Linda has some trouble with her friends because she often _____ _____ _____ with them. In contrast, Ted is always on time and the other classmates think he's very _____ _____ _____.
Today, Linda even forgets to submit an important paper. She knows what she has to do, but it's not easy for her to _____ everything. Disappointed in herself, she asks Ted for some help on how she can _____ _____ _____ _____ forgetting. He thinks using a calendar app could help break her bad habit. So Ted wants to advise Linda to try using a calendar app to _____ _____ _____ important things. In this situation, what would Ted most likely say to Linda?

Ted: (Why don't you use a calendar app as a reminder?)

16~17

W: Hello, students! Last class we learned about recycling. Today, I'll introduce you to something better than recycling. It's the _____ _____ _____ waste into new items in a creative way. Let me show you some examples. First, one creative way is to make _____ _____ into vases for your home. Second, you can turn old cardboard boxes into fun chairs. All you need is just a little time and some paint. Third, an easy way to use _____ _____ creatively is turning them into fancy pencil holders for your desk. Lastly, when old newspapers pile up in your home, you can use them to _____ any present. It'll make your gift unique and memorable. In this way, you can create something new out of waste on your own. There are _____ _____ _____ ideas you can come up with if you use your imagination. Let's do something wonderful for our _____ by this process, upcycling.

06 2020년 3월 학력평가 딕테이션

녹음을 듣고, 빈칸에 알맞은 말을 쓰시기 바랍니다. 빈칸은 문제풀이에 핵심이 되는 키워드와 헷갈리기 쉬운 발음에 표시되어 있으니 이 점에 유의하여 듣기 바랍니다.

01
고1 2020년 3월 3번

M: Hello, students. This is Mike Smith, your P.E. teacher. These days, the fine dust problem is getting serious. So, I'd like to explain

_____ _____ _____

_____ when the fine dust level is high. First, close all the classroom windows to _____ _____ the dust. Second, turn on the air purifier in the classroom. The air purifier will help keep the air _____. Third, drink water and wash your hands as often as possible. Last, it's important to

_____ _____ _____

when you're outside. Thank you for listening.

02
고1 2020년 3월 4번

W: Look at all the shiny paper and ribbons! What are you doing, Tom?

M: I'm _____ a birthday present for my friend Laura.

W: What are you going to give her?

M: A key chain. I hope she likes it.

W: That's a pretty big box for a key chain, isn't it?

M: Yes, I _____ _____

_____ paper flowers. Now I'm going to wrap the box with shiny paper and decorate it with ribbons.

W: I think it's a little too much. Most of the paper and ribbons will _____ _____ in

the trash can.

M: Hmm.... You're right. My packaging will produce a lot of trash.

W: Yeah. We need to make gift packaging

_____ _____ _____

_____.

M: I agree. I'll try to reduce the packaging then.

W: Good thinking.

03
고1 2020년 3월 5번

M: Come on in, Ms. Miller. It's been a while

_____ _____ _____

_____.

W: Good morning, Mr. Stevens. I've been in Europe for the last two months.

M: Wow. Are you preparing for your _____ book?

W: Yes, I'm working on it.

M: I'm looking forward to it. So, what brings you here today?

W: I'd like to _____ _____

_____ _____.

M: I see. Do you have a particular design in mind?

W: Just a plain rectangular one would be great.

M: Okay. What color would you like?

W: I was thinking dark brown.

M: Great. We have a perfect one for you

_____. Come this way.

W: All right.

04

W: James, have you been to our new club room?

M: _____, I haven't.

W: I have a picture of it. Do you want to take a look?

M: Sure. *[Pause]* Wow, I see lockers on the _____ _____ of the picture.

W: Yes. We finally have our own lockers. Do you see the trophies on the lockers?

M: Yeah. There are two trophies. Are they the ones we won in the National School Band Contest?

W: Right. We won two years _____ _____ _____. I'm so proud of our band.

M: Me, too. And the drums are under the clock.

W: Yes. And on the right side of the picture is a _____ _____ with chairs.

M: Looks great. I also love the star-shaped _____ in front of the drums.

W: I like it, too. We're really going to enjoy our new club room.

05

M: Ellie, the school orchestra's concert is just three days away. How's the preparation _____ _____?

W: Great, Mr. Brown. All of our orchestra members are very excited.

M: Good. Did everyone check their _____?

W: Of course. Everything sounded fine in practice today.

M: I heard the posters were ready.

W: Yes. Here they are. One of the orchestra

members designed them.

M: They look pretty nice. When are you going to _____ _____ _____ _____ in the hallway?

W: I'm going to do that now.

M: You're doing a great job as the leader of the school orchestra. Have you _____ the chairs for the audience?

W: I already did it with some of the members.

M: Perfect.

06

M: Good afternoon. How can I help you?

W: I'd like to buy some _____ _____ for my children. How much is this pair?

M: It's $60 for a pair. It's a very popular model.

W: Great. I'll take _____ _____.

M: I see. Is there anything else you need?

W: Oh, I also need a portable speaker.

M: These two are the latest models.

W: How much are they?

M: This black one is $_____ and the pink one is $100.

W: I'll take the black one.

M: Okay. Is that all you need?

W: Yes. Oh, I have this discount coupon. Can I use it?

M: Sure. You can get 10% off the _____ _____ with this coupon.

W: Great. Here's the coupon and here's my credit card.

07

W: Jason, you're going camping this weekend, right?

M: I _____ _____ _____, but I'm afraid I can't go.

W: Why not? Is it going to rain?

M: No. It'll be sunny this weekend.

W: Then do you have to work this weekend? You said you're busy with your project.

M: No, I _____ the project last week.

W: Then why can't you go camping?

M: My mother fell down the stairs and _____ her arm.

W: Oh, no. Is she all right?

M: Well, she had surgery. So I have to _____ _____ _____ _____ in the hospital this weekend.

W: I see. I hope she'll get better soon.

M: Thanks.

08

W: Hi, Ross. What's on the _____?

M: The Pinewood Bake Sale is this Friday. Would you like to go with me?

W: A bake sale? What's that?

M: In a bake sale, people raise money _____ _____ _____ _____. At the Pinewood Bake Sale, people will be selling doughnuts and cupcakes.

W: Sounds delicious. So all profits go to people in need, right?

M: That's right. The flyer says the profits will be _____ _____ Pinewood Children's Hospital.

W: I'd like to join you. Where is it going to be held?

M: In the Pinewood High School _____.

W: Okay. Let's go together.

09

W: Hello, Green City residents. This is Rachel White, the _____ of the Community Services Department. Are you ready to enjoy the 2020 Global Village Festival? It'll be held on March 28th and 29th at Green City Park. This two-day festival _____ _____ _____ and art exhibitions. Samples of food from around the world will be served. Prices of the food _____ from $2 to $5 and you can pay by cash or credit card. _____ _____ _____ _____ will get special gifts. Parking will be available for $10 a car. For more information, visit the festival website. Thank you.

10

M: Honey, what are you doing on your computer?

W: I'm trying to _____ _____ _____ at Wayne Island Hotel for our summer vacation.

M: Our summer vacation? Isn't it a bit early?

W: We can get a room much cheaper if we book early.

M: I see. Which room do you _____ _____ _____?

W: I was thinking a room with a city view. What do you think?

M: Well, a room with a _____ view or an ocean view would be better.

W: I agree. Shall we have _____ in the hotel?

M: I don't think we need to. I heard there are some good restaurants near the hotel.

W: Okay. Then we have two options left. I'd like to go with the _____ one.

M: Sounds good. Let's book this room then.

11

고1 2020년 3월 1번

M: _____ _____ looks great. Have you been here before?

W: Yeah, it's one of my favorite restaurants. Let's see the menu.

M: Everything looks so good. Can you _____ anything?

W: (Sure. The onion soup is great here.)

12

고1 2020년 3월 2번

W: Honey, don't _____ _____ _____ your umbrella to work today.

M: Umbrella? The sky is clear now.

W: The weather forecast said _____ _____ this afternoon.

M: (I see. Thank you for letting me know.)

13

고1 2020년 3월 13번

W: Hey, Chris. What are you looking at on your cell phone?

M: I'm looking for an apartment _____ _____.

W: Aren't you sharing an apartment with William?

M: Yeah, but I'm thinking about moving out.

W: Why? I thought you two _____ _____ _____ with each other.

M: There have been a lot of problems between us. One thing especially _____ me.

W: Oh, what is it?

M: Actually, he never cleans up. The kitchen and the bathroom are always messy.

W: That's awful. _____ _____ _____ about this issue with him?

M: (I have, but he didn't take it seriously.)

14

고1 2020년 3월 14번

M: Ms. Peterson! I heard you were looking for me.

W: Yes, Louis. I need to tell you about the science competition _____ _____ next week.

M: Okay. What's it about?

W: As you know, it'll be held in the school auditorium, but part of the floor _____ _____.

M: Then is it going to be held somewhere else?

W: No, but the competition will be delayed.

M: Then when is it going to be held?

W: The _____ hasn't been decided yet, but it'll take at least two weeks to repair the floor. I'll _____ _____ the exact date later.

M: I see. I'll wait for your text message.

W: (Okay. I'll let you know as soon as the date is set.)

15

고1 2020년 3월 15번

M: Billy entered high school this year. In Billy's school, _____ _____ _____ are given to the students. The letters include a lot of information about school events such as parent-teacher meetings. Students have to _____ them to their parents, but Billy often forgets to bring them to his mother. Billy's mother is worried that she may not get important information about school events. She _____ _____ some of them because she didn't get the letters. So she wants to tell Billy that he _____

_____ _____ _____ her. In this situation, what would Billy's mother most likely say to Billy?

Billy's mother: (Don't forget to bring me the letters.)

16~17

W: Good morning, class. What did you have for breakfast? I guess some of you had your favorite cereal with milk. Have you ever wondered

_____ _____ _____

_____? Most people would say it's from cows, and they're right. Around ninety percent of milk in Canada and the U.S. comes from cows. But cows are not the only _____ of milk. People around the world get milk from _____ _____. Water buffalos are the main source of milk in India. They produce half the milk _____ in the country. Some people in the northern part of Finland drink reindeer milk because they are the only dairy animals that can _____ such a cold environment. People in Romania get milk from sheep and use it to make cheese. It has

_____ _____ _____

content of cow milk. Now let's watch a video about these animals.

07 2020년 6월 학력평가
딕테이션

MP3

😊 녹음을 듣고, 빈칸에 알맞은 말을 쓰시기 바랍니다. 빈칸은 문제풀이에 핵심이 되는 키워드와 헷갈리기 쉬운 발음에 표시되어 있으니 이 점에 유의하여 듣기 바랍니다.

01
고1 2020년 6월 3번

W: Hello, students. This is vice principal Susan Lee. I know all of you are _____ _____ for the upcoming school festival. There are club activities going on in every part of our school building. You may want to _____ between places during activities. But I'd like to ask you to work in the place _____ _____ _____ _____ to be. Your teachers want to make your safety the top priority. Once again, make sure to prepare for the festival in your _____ places. Thank you for your cooperation.

02
고1 2020년 6월 4번

W: Hello, Chris. Why are you _____ like that?

M: Hi, Helen. I've just jogged for an hour.

W: For an hour? But, you don't _____ _____ at all.

M: That's because I had a banana before jogging.

W: What do you mean?

M: If you _____ _____ _____ _____ running, you will get more energy.

W: Really? Does it work?

M: Yes! It gives your body more _____ _____ _____.

W: That's why you look so energetic even after running for a long time.

M: Yeah. You should try it.

W: Okay, I will.

03
고1 2020년 6월 5번

[Telephone rings.]

M: Hello, this is Daniel Johnson.

W: Hello, Mr. Johnson. It's Elena Roberts. Have you thought about my proposal?

M: Yes. You said you wanted to _____ _____ _____ _____ a movie, right?

W: That's right. I loved your novel, and it would make a great movie.

M: I'm glad to hear that. And _____ _____ _____ the movie, it would be a great honor for me.

W: Thank you for _____ my offer. I'd like us to speak about the details of the story _____ _____.

M: Then, shall I go to your office?

W: That would be great. Can you come tomorrow?

M: Sure. I'll be there by 10 a.m.

04
고1 2020년 6월 6번

W: Eugene, the stage is ready. Why don't you check it out?

M: Okay. Did you _____ _____ _____ the TV I asked for?

W: Yeah, I put it on the wall above the sofa.

M: Great. I need to play video clips during the talk show.

W: And I placed the _____ _____ between the sofa and the flower pot. Do you like it?

M: Absolutely. It's simple but looks cool. Oh, I like

the cushion with the striped pattern on the sofa.

W: So do I. How about the _____ _____ on the rug? Isn't it too big?

M: It looks fine. But those two pictures below the clock don't seem to _____ _____ there.

W: Then, I'll take them away.

M: Thank you, Rebecca.

05

M: Honey, Nathan's birthday is tomorrow.

W: I can't believe he's almost ONE!

M: _____ can I. He's already learning to walk.

W: I made a digital photo album for his birthday party.

M: Wow! That's great! How do you _____ _____ _____ it?

W: How about showing the photos on the TV in the living room?

M: Sounds good. _____ _____ do we need?

W: Every birthday party needs balloons and a cake.

M: Okay. I'll decorate the living room with balloons.

W: Then, _____ _____ the cake.

M: Great! He'll love it.

06

[Telephone rings.]

M: Good evening, John's Food Delivery. How may I help you?

W: Hi. _____ _____ _____

_____ some dinners.

M: Okay. What would you like?

W: How much is a cheeseburger set?

M: It's _____ dollars. How many would you like?

W: I need two sets. Is there anything else you can recommend?

M: Yes, our _____ _____, the avocado sandwich, is very delicious. It's seven dollars.

W: Good. _____ two avocado sandwiches to my order, please.

M: So two cheeseburger sets and two avocado sandwiches, right?

W: Yes. And I have a discount coupon for new customers.

M: Okay, then you'll get _____% off the total. Where would you like your food delivered?

W: 101 Fifth St., please.

07

W: Hey, Patrick. I have good news.

M: Hi, Jennifer. What is it?

W: The _____ _____ _____ at the community center opened last weekend.

M: I heard that. You know it is _____ _____ at night.

W: Cool! Let's go swimming tonight, then.

M: Well. I really want to, but I can't.

W: Do you have other plans?

M: Do you remember I had an _____ for a part-time job yesterday?

W: Sure, how did it go?

M: I got the job. So I have to _____ _____ this evening.

W: Oh well, we can go swimming some other day. Good luck!

08

고1 2020년 6월 10번

W: Mike, did you see the poster for the Rock Music Festival in our town?

M: No, I didn't. Please give me some details. When will it be?

W: On _____ 13th at 8 p.m. Can you come with me?

M: Sure, I'd love to. How much are the tickets for the festival?

W: They're only ten dollars _____ _____ _____ us.

M: Wonderful! Where is the event taking place?

W: It'll be held _____, at Central Stadium.

M: That's good. We can get there on foot. Who will be playing?

W: _____ _____ _____ Garcia and Martin will perform.

M: Wow! I can't wait to see them.

09

고1 2020년 6월 11번

M: Hello, students. This is Kyle Evans, your _____ teacher. I'm very glad to tell you about the Westbank High School Science Fair. It'll be held on July 21st in the school auditorium. You'll _____ _____ _____ in front of judges and visitors. The judges will be professors and teachers from other schools. They'll all _____ _____ _____ _____ to each team. Awards will be given in three areas: Physics, Chemistry, and Biology. Also, _____ _____ _____ _____ will get T-shirts for free. Spread the word and please invite your friends and parents to come. I hope you enjoy the fair.

10

고1 2020년 6월 12번

M: Linda, what are you looking at?

W: Hi, James. I'm _____ _____ taking one of the summer programs on this time table.

M: Let me see. What program would you like to take?

W: Well, I took English Conversation last year. This time I want to take _____ _____.

M: If I were you, I would take this class.

W: I'd love to, but I plan to volunteer on _____ this summer.

M: I see. Then, how about this one?

W: Sounds good, but I have to be home _____ _____ for dinner with my family.

M: Then, you're left with two options. Which one do you prefer?

W: Well, _____ my budget, I'll take the cheaper one.

11

고1 2020년 6월 1번

W: Jimmy, what are you _____ _____?

M: My cellphone. I forgot where I left it.

W: Why don't you look for it _____ _____ _____ first?

M: (I already did, but I couldn't find it.)

12

고1 2020년 6월 2번

M: Excuse me. I'd like to _____ some flowers for my wife.

W: Do you have any kind in mind?

M: Not really. _____ _____

_____ _____?

W: (White roses are nice at this time of year.)

13

W: Hi, Thomas. Are you okay? You look worried.

M: Cindy, may I _____ _____

_____ _____?

W: Sure! Just tell me what you need.

M: As you know, I'm going on a family trip for three weeks.

W: To Europe this Sunday, right?

M: Yes. Can you _____ _____

_____ _____ while I'm away?

W: I'd love to, but I don't know how to take care of them.

M: No worries. It's really easy. You just need to remember one thing: Water them regularly.

W: I can do that. Do I have to _____

_____ _____ _____?

M: (No. Just once a week.)

14

M: Ms. White, you look so busy tonight.

W: I am. I have to check my students' homework.

M: Wow, I can't believe students made these.

W: Yeah, I was surprised how _____ they

were when making their videos.

M: By making videos, students could learn

_____ _____ of Korean culture

and share them in a fun way.

W: You're right. That's why I _____ them

this homework.

M: I see. Which is your favorite one?

W: I think this one is the best, because it shows 'Ganggangsullae' performed by many students in harmony.

M: It would be excellent _____

_____ _____ _____ on

the Internet.

W: (Good idea. It will introduce Korean culture to the world.)

15

W: Olivia likes to shop online. She ordered

_____ _____ _____

blue pants from a famous online shopping mall a few days ago. When they are _____, she finds out that the pants are not blue, but black. So she calls the customer service center. When she _____ her situation, the employee who answers her call apologizes for their mistake and tells her that the blue pants are sold out. So, Olivia wants to return the black pants and _____ _____

_____ _____. In this situation what would Olivia most likely say to the customer service employee?

Olivia: (I'd like to send the pants back and get a refund.)

16~17

M: Good morning, listeners. This is Dr. Cooper of Daily HealthLine Radio. These days, you can see many people around you who ＿＿＿＿＿＿＿ ＿＿＿＿＿＿＿ ＿＿＿＿＿＿＿ ＿＿＿＿＿＿＿.

Any incorrect positioning of your body or lifting of heavy objects may cause it. So, today, I'll share some ＿＿＿＿＿＿＿ ＿＿＿＿＿＿＿ ＿＿＿＿＿＿＿ ＿＿＿＿＿＿＿ to help reduce your own back pain. First, biking can ＿＿＿＿＿＿＿ back pain by building your core muscles. Second, swimming is good because you can do it without much stress on your back muscles. Also, ＿＿＿＿＿＿＿ is a helpful way to stretch safely and strengthen your back as well. Finally, ＿＿＿＿＿＿＿ is the easiest exercise to keep your spine in a natural position to ＿＿＿＿＿＿＿ back pain. I hope this will be helpful information for you and allow you to be fit again.

08 2020년 9월 학력평가
딕테이션

MP3
25BL1_A08

녹음을 듣고, 빈칸에 알맞은 말을 쓰시기 바랍니다. 빈칸은 문제풀이에 핵심이 되는 키워드와 헷갈리기 쉬운 발음에 표시되어 있으니 이 점에 유의하여 듣기 바랍니다.

01

고1 2020년 9월 3번

W: Hello, everyone. Thank you for visiting Dream Amusement Park. To celebrate our 20th anniversary, we have a _____ _____ _____ for children, *The Winter Princess*, all through this week. It was awarded the Best Children's Musical last year and _____ many famous musical artists that you love. Today, the performance will start at 4 p.m. at the Rainbow Theater. If _____ _____ to join the show, you need to make a reservation at any information center _____. We hope you all have a wonderful time with us. Thank you.

02

고1 2020년 9월 4번

M: Hey, Sarah. What are you going to _____ _____ your after-school activity?

W: I'm not sure, Dad.

M: What about taking a coding course?

W: A coding course? Why should I do that?

M: I think learning to code can give you _____ _____ for the future.

W: Oh, I remember my teacher saying that coding is a skill that can increase the _____ _____ getting a job. But it sounds difficult.

M: It might be, but it can help you learn how to plan and organize your thoughts.

W: Good to know. And I heard coding helps with math. Right?

M: Definitely. Plus, it _____ your problem-solving skills.

W: Cool! I think I'm going to take the course.

03

고1 2020년 9월 5번

W: Hello, Mr. Williams.

M: Please come on in, Ms. Jackson. How are you doing?

W: I'm good. Recently _____ _____ _____ several books, so I've been really busy.

M: Oh, I hope you get some time off soon.

W: I hope so, too. Well, I've read your work, *The Great Man*. I think you _____ _____ the feeling of the original book.

M: Thank you. Which book _____ _____ _____ this time?

W: It is a novel written by a Spanish writer, Isabel Martinez.

M: Sounds good. I'm so happy to translate the book.

W: My boss said that the book needs to be _____ by December. So, is it possible to get the first draft by the end of October?

M: No problem.

04

고1 2020년 9월 6번

M: Lisa, how's the poster for our magic show going?

W: I have changed a few things. Take a look.

M: Oh, I like the _____ _____ at the top.

W: And I wrote the date and the time under the title, Magic Show.

M: Nice choice. It's more _____.

W: What do you think of the rabbit in the hat?

M: I really like it. It's so cute. And you put the _____ _____ _____ _____ the square one.

W: Yes, but I'm still not sure about the shape of the table.

M: I think the round one looks much better.

W: Okay. And as you suggested, I drew a magician _____ _____ _____ _____.

M: Nice. I think it's perfect now.

W: Yeah, finally. Thanks for your help.

05

고1 2020년 9월 7번

W: Chris, what are you doing?

M: I'm writing interview questions for the feature story of our next school _____.

W: Who are you interviewing?

M: The new English teacher. I'm going to interview him tomorrow.

W: Do you need any help with the interview questions?

M: No, I'm almost done. But I'm still looking for _____ _____ _____ during the interview.

W: Why don't you ask Cindy? She's good at taking photos.

M: I already asked her, but she said she has an important _____ tomorrow.

W: Well, how about Tom? He's a member of the photo club.

M: You mean the one in our chemistry class?

W: Yes. I think he's the right person. Do you want me to _____ _____ _____ _____ if he's available tomorrow?

M: That would be great. Thanks.

06

고1 2020년 9월 9번

M: Hello, ma'am. Welcome to the Aerospace Exhibition.

W: Hi, I'd like to get tickets for the exhibition.

M: Sure. We have two options, a _____ ticket and a half-day ticket.

W: I'll take the half-day ticket. How much is it?

M: It's $_____ for adults and $20 for children. How many tickets do you need?

W: One adult and two children's tickets, please. I have a membership card. Do you _____ _____ _____?

M: Yes. Gold membership holders get 20% off the total, and silver membership holders get 10% off the total.

W: Great. I have a _____ _____.

M: Okay. May I have your membership card?

W: Here it is. And I'll be paying with cash.

07

고1 2020년 9월 8번

W: James, check out the poster. It's about this year's Winter Sports Camp.

M: I remember we had a great time at last year's camp.

W: Yes, we did. Let's go to the camp together again.

M: _____ _____ _____

_____.

W: Why not? Do you still have ankle pain?

M: I'm still taking my pills, but don't worry. I'm fine.

W: Ah, you must have another family trip scheduled.

M: No, not this time. Actually, it's because of my

_____ _____.

W: Haven't you finished it yet?

M: I've already handed in the final report for

the project, but Mr. Miller said that I have to

_____ _____ the National

Science Contest with it.

W: That's great. You should definitely spend

your whole winter vacation _____

_____ it, then.

M: I'm going to do my best. Have fun for me.

08

고1 2020년 9월 10번

W: Hey, Sam. Have you heard about the Mind-Up
Program?

M: No, I haven't. What is it?

W: It's a program for high school students.

_____ _____ is to encourage

us to build a positive mindset. You should come.

M: It sounds interesting. Please tell me more about
it.

W: There will be a lot of _____

_____ _____ _____

stress. Also, we'll get to listen to special lectures

from successful young CEOs.

M: _____! I should sign up. When is it?

W: This Friday. It starts at 6 p.m.

M: Cool. How much is the admission fee?

W: It's free for all students. You can _____

for the program on our school website.

M: Great. I'll do it now.

09

고1 2020년 9월 11번

M: Hello, listeners. I'm Ted Potter, the manager of

the Plata Community Center. I'd like to tell you

about the _____ Plata Tea Festival.

It's an annual tea festival held at City Hall.

This year it'll _____ _____

_____ September 5th and 6th. More

than 20 tea companies will participate in this

festival. During the festival, you can enjoy

_____ _____ _____

and food pairing events. Also, you can learn

tea etiquette from experts. The admission fee

is $10 and children under 5 enter for free.

_____ are not necessary. Come to this

festival and share a cup of tea with your friends

and family.

10

고1 2020년 9월 12번

M: Julie, what are you looking at?

W: I'm thinking of buying a new handheld fan. Can

you help me pick one?

M: Sure. Hmm, how about this one?

W: It looks good, but I _____ _____

_____ _____ more than $30.

M: Okay. And I think you should get one with a

battery that _____ more than 8 hours.

W: I think so, too. I usually spend more than 8 hours

outside.

M: What about the fan speed levels? Do you need a

fan with 4 levels?

W: No. _____ _____ will be

enough for me.

M: Then you have two models left. I recommend the

_____ one.

W: What's special about it?

M: If you fold the handle, it'll easily fit into your

handbag. It can also stand up on your desk.

W: That sounds convenient. I'll buy that one.

11

W: Did you hear that Golden Bookstore will hold a
_____ _____ event for Lora
Johnson?

M: Oh, she is one of my favorite writers. I've read all
of her novels. When is it?

W: This Sunday afternoon. Do you _____
_____ _____ with me?

M: (Yes. I can't believe I'm going to see her in
person.)

12

M: Jane, are you almost done _____
_____ your drone?

W: Not yet. I'm having a hard time understanding
the instructions.

M: _____ _____ _____
_____ might be helpful. I'm sure you'll
find some showing you how to do it.

W: (Good idea! I'll look for some videos online.)

13

W: Hi, Andrew. I heard that your tennis club is
_____ in the City Tennis Tournament.

M: Yes. We've been practicing a lot these days.

W: I'm sure you'll do well.

M: Thanks. But our school tennis court is going to
be _____ _____ starting next
week, so we won't have a place to practice.

W: What about the community center? It has
several tennis courts.

M: We already checked. But all the courts are
_____ _____.

W: That's too bad. Oh, wait! My sister told me her
school tennis courts would be open to the public
starting this Saturday.

M: Really? That's great news. Do I need a
reservation?

W: Yes. I remember she said that reservations
_____ _____ at 9 a.m.
tomorrow.

M: (I hope I can reserve a court to continue
practicing.)

14

W: Hey, Minho. What are you doing?

M: Hi, Mrs. Sharon. I'm writing an _____
_____ for college.

W: Can I take a look at it?

M: Of course. Please give me some advice after
you're finished reading it.

W: Hmm.... You only listed the activities you've done
_____ _____ _____.

M: Yeah. Isn't it good to include as many activities
as possible?

W: No. If you do that, your application letter won't
be memorable.

M: But I thought if I wrote down a lot of activities, I
would stand out.

W: It's actually the _____. You should focus
on a few things and write about them in detail.

M: I never thought about that. Do you really think
_____ _____?

W: (Of course. The more specific, the better.)

15

M: Cathy and Brian are members of the same orchestra. They are _____ together for the upcoming concert. Lately, Brian doesn't look so good and seems to be _____ _____ _____ during practice. When Cathy asks why, he tells her that it's because of his back pain. He sits for _____ _____ _____ _____ preparing for the concert, so his back hurts. Cathy understands his pain because she had the same problem last year. However, after she started yoga, her back pain disappeared. She wants to suggest to Brian _____ _____ _____ yoga. In this situation, what would Cathy most likely say to Brian?

Cathy: (Why don't you try yoga for your back pain?)

16~17

W: Hello, class! Last time we learned about LED technology. I hope all of you have a _____ _____ of what an LED is now. Today, I'll talk about how LEDs _____ _____ _____ _____. First, one of the advantages of LEDs is the long lifespan. LED bulbs are used in _____ and last for over 17 years before you need to change them. Second, LEDs use very _____ _____ of power. For example, a television using LEDs in its backlight saves a lot of energy. Next, LEDs are brighter than traditional bulbs. So, they make _____ _____ more visible in foggy conditions. Finally, thanks to their small size, LEDs can be used in various small devices. Any light you see on a computer keyboard is an LED light. Now, let's think about other products that use LEDs.

09 2020년 11월 학력평가
딕테이션

MP3
25BL1_A09

녹음을 듣고, 빈칸에 알맞은 말을 쓰시기 바랍니다. 빈칸은 문제풀이에 핵심이 되는 키워드와 헷갈리기 쉬운 발음에 표시되어 있으니 이 점에 유의하여 듣기 바랍니다.

01

M: Hello, welcome to Fun Bike Touring. I'm Harry Wilson, your tour guide. Before starting the tour, let me tell you the ＿＿＿＿＿ ＿＿＿＿＿. First, always keep your helmet on. Wearing a helmet protects you from serious injuries ＿＿＿＿＿ ＿＿＿＿＿ ＿＿＿＿＿ an accident. Second, you should use bicycle-only lanes. If you ride ＿＿＿＿＿ ＿＿＿＿＿ ＿＿＿＿＿ ＿＿＿＿＿, there is a chance that you could be hit by a car. Lastly, don't use your cell phone while riding. Taking pictures or talking on the phone ＿＿＿＿＿ ＿＿＿＿＿ can be really dangerous to you and others. Now, are you ready to start? Let's go!

02

M: Good morning, Rosa.

W: Hi, Tony. You look tired. Are you all right?

M: Yeah, I'm okay. I'm just ＿＿＿＿＿ ＿＿＿＿＿ ＿＿＿＿＿ ＿＿＿＿＿ falling asleep these days.

W: Why? Are you worried about something?

M: No. Since I started exercising late at night, it's been hard to fall asleep.

W: What time do you exercise?

M: I usually go to the gym around 10 p.m. When I come back, it's ＿＿＿＿＿ ＿＿＿＿＿.

W: Hmm, I think that's why you can't sleep well.

M: Really?

W: As far as I know, when you exercise, your heart rate and temperature go up, which makes you ＿＿＿＿＿ ＿＿＿＿＿. These can disturb your sleep.

M: Oh, that makes sense.

W: So, it's ＿＿＿＿＿ ＿＿＿＿＿ ＿＿＿＿＿ ＿＿＿＿＿ to exercise right before going to bed.

M: I'll keep that in mind. Thanks for your advice.

03

[Door knocks.]

W: Hello, Mr. Cooper. Come on in. Have a seat, please.

M: Thank you.

W: You came here last week because of a ＿＿＿＿＿. How are the symptoms now?

M: Much better.

W: Great. Let me look at the sunburn. [Pause] The redness is ＿＿＿＿＿ ＿＿＿＿＿.

M: Yeah. The cream you prescribed was really helpful.

W: Good. Do you still have any pain?

M: Not anymore.

W: I'm glad to hear that. If you put the cream on for a few days more, your ＿＿＿＿＿ ＿＿＿＿＿ ＿＿＿＿＿ ＿＿＿＿＿.

M: Okay. But I don't have any more cream. Could you write me another ＿＿＿＿＿?

W: Sure. [Typing sound] If you have any problems, please come back.

M: Thank you.

04

M: Hi, Claire. What did you do yesterday?

W: Hi, Henry. I set up an exercise room in my house. Look at this picture.

M: Cool! The _____ _____ under the clock looks nice.

W: Thanks. I bought the bike a few days ago.

M: Good. Is that a hula-hoop _____ _____ _____?

W: Yes. I exercise with it for 30 minutes every day. What do you think of the _____ _____ _____ _____ pattern on the floor?

M: I love it. By the way, what's the big ball next to the door?

W: It's a gym ball. I use it for back stretches.

M: Good. Oh, I know that T-shirt on the wall.

W: Yeah. It's from the marathon we ran together.

M: Great. It _____ _____ with your room.

W: Thanks. Next time, come over and we'll exercise together.

05

W: Simon, I think we're ready for the _____ event.

M: Right. Let's do one last check.

W: Okay. We're going to play a short video clip for the event. Is the screen working?

M: Yes. I checked the screen and there's no problem at all.

W: Great. What about the speakers?

M: I already tried using them, and _____ _____ _____. Did you bring the

donation box?

W: Yes. Look. I made it by myself.

M: Wow! It looks nice.

W: Thanks. All the items we're going to sell are _____ set up on the table.

M: Okay. The only thing left is to put the price tags on. I'll do that later because I have to go to my part-time job now.

W: Oh, don't worry. I'll _____ _____ _____ _____ on.

M: Really? Thanks.

06

M: Good afternoon.

W: Hello. Welcome to Happy Pet World. How can I help you?

M: I'm looking for a _____ _____ _____ _____.

W: Okay, how about these? These are the most popular models.

M: The pink one looks cute. How much is it?

W: Originally, it was $_____. But due to a special promotion, you can get a 10 percent _____ _____ cushions.

M: Great. I'll buy one cushion, then.

W: Sure. Anything else?

M: Do you have dog biscuits?

W: Of course. They're right over here. _____ _____ of biscuits is $5.

M: I'll buy two boxes of biscuits. Do I get a discount on the biscuits, too?

W: I'm sorry. We _____ _____ a discount on biscuits.

M: Okay, then. Here's my credit card.

07

[Cell phone rings.]

W: Hello.

M: Hi, Linda. Did you _____ _____ _____? I was in my book club meeting. What's up?

W: I called you to make sure you can come to the student fashion show. The _____ has changed.

M: Really? When is the show now?

W: It has changed to 6 p.m. next Friday. The place we were going to use is _____ _____ this week.

M: I see. I'm afraid I can't go then.

W: Oh, didn't you say you're going to a concert next Friday?

M: No, that's next Saturday.

W: Then, why can't you come?

M: It's my mom's birthday. So, I'm going to _____ _____ _____ my family.

W: Oh, I understand. Have a good time.

M: Thanks.

08

M: Honey, what are you reading?

W: Look at this article. There will be a World Dinosaur Exhibition this Saturday. Why don't we bring the kids?

M: That sounds great! _____ the exhibition held?

W: At the Redstone Science Museum.

M: Good. I know where that is.

W: There are _____ _____ _____ _____ like making dinosaur toys and watching a 3D dinosaur movie.

M: Our kids will love them. What time shall we go?

W: Since the exhibition _____ from 10 a.m. to 5 p.m., how about going there in the afternoon?

M: Okay. How much is the _____ _____?

W: It's $10 for an adult and $5 for a child and if we register online, we can get a discount.

M: Really? Let's register now.

W: Okay.

09

W: Hello, listeners! Are you excited for the Greenville Animation Film Festival? This festival, one of Greenville's largest events, _____ in 1995. This year, it'll start on December 5th and _____ _____ one week. The theme for this year is friendship. Throughout the festival, visitors can watch different animation movies _____ _____ the theme every night. The movie schedule will be posted on our website. Remember, there's _____ _____ _____ _____. So, please use public transportation. For more information, visit www.GAFF.com. Thank you.

10

M: Jane, what are you doing?

W: Dad, I'm searching for a one-day drawing lesson, but it's not easy to choose one. Can you help me?

M: Sure. Is there any _____ _____

_____ you want to use?

W: I've done pastel drawing before. So, this time

I want to try a new material, _____

_____.

M: Okay. Do you want to have a private lesson?

W: No, I want to learn _____

_____ _____ _____.

M: Okay. You have piano lessons Monday mornings,

right?

W: Yes. So I should choose a lesson on

_____ _____ _____.

M: That leaves you two choices.

W: Let me think. *[Pause]* I'd rather take a lesson in

the morning.

M: There's only one left then.

W: Yes. I'll register for that lesson. Thank you, Dad.

11

M: Emma, it _____ good in here. What's

that you're cooking?

W: I cooked some *Bulgogi*. Try some.

M: Okay. Wow, it's really delicious. Where did you

_____ _____ _____?

W: (I got the recipe from the Internet.)

12

W: Honey, where are the _____ we used

when we went camping?

M: Oh, I just left them in my car.

W: Really? I need to _____ _____

tomorrow.

M: (Okay. I'll bring you the speakers now.)

13

M: Kelly, what are you doing?

W: Hey, Paul. I'm trying to sell my _____

_____ using the Local Market app.

M: Local Market app? What's that?

W: It's a kind of online _____

_____ _____ _____.

I can buy or sell items with this app.

M: Interesting! How do you use it?

W: If I upload pictures of my sweater, somebody

who needs a sweater will see and buy it.

M: That's great. Have you ever _____

_____ _____ the app?

W: Sure. Look at this bag. I bought it for only $5.

M: Wow, that's a good deal! I also have a lot of

_____ _____ _____.

W: (Then, you should sell the items using this app.)

14

W: Honey, look at this bill. Have you been using a

_____ _____ service?

M: No. But a few months ago, I used a one-month

free trial.

W: Look. A $15 membership _____

_____ _____ _____ for

three months.

M: Oh, no! There must be something wrong.

W: Did you get any notice about that?

M: Well, I did, but I didn't _____

_____ _____ to it when I

signed up for it.

W: Let's check it now.

M: Wait. *[Clicking sound]* Hmm, it says the

membership fee will be charged if I don't cancel

it after the free trial.

W: Well, one of my friends was in the same

situation and she tried to get a refund but she couldn't.

M: Then, what should I do?

W: Hmm, the only thing you can do is _____ _____ the membership.

M: (Okay. I'll call customer service to cancel the membership.)

15

M: Ms. Brown teaches English in high school. Chris is one of the students who takes her class. Since he wants to major in English _____ _____ _____, he thinks English writing skills are important. To get advice, Chris visits Ms. Brown and asks _____ _____ _____ his English writing skills. Ms. Brown thinks that writing in English _____ is important. So she wants to suggest that Chris _____ _____ _____ for his English writing skills. In this situation, what would Ms. Brown most likely say to Chris?

Ms. Brown: (Why don't you start writing a diary in English?)

16~17

W: Hello, everyone. I'm Monica Dale from Blue River Animal Center. Today, let's talk about the different ways _____ _____. First, smell is probably the most basic type of animal communication. For example, _____ _____ _____

_____ with their smell to send a clear message to others to stay away. Second, when animals make sounds, those usually _____ _____ _____. For instance, dolphins get the attention of others in the area by using various sounds. Sometimes, they sing to their mates. Third, _____ _____ are widely used by many animals. Gorillas stick out their tongues to show anger. Lastly, many animals _____ _____ _____ to communicate their feelings to others. Giraffes press their necks together when they're attracted to each other. Now, let's take a look at a video clip that _____ interesting animal communication.

10 2021년 3월 학력평가
딕테이션

녹음을 듣고, 빈칸에 알맞은 말을 쓰시기 바랍니다. 빈칸은 문제풀이에 핵심이 되는 키워드와 헷갈리기 쉬운 발음에 표시되어 있으니 이 점에 유의하여 듣기 바랍니다.

01

M: Good morning, students. This is Mr. Lewis from the school administration office. Last night there was a _____ _____.
The pouring rain left some of the school's hallways wet and _____. The first floor hallway and the central stairway are especially dangerous to walk on. Please _____ _____ _____ when you walk through these areas. You could get seriously hurt if you _____ _____ the wet floor. We're doing our best to take care of the situation. Thank you.

02

W: Mike, you look very tired today.
M: I am. I'm _____ _____ _____ at night these days.
W: What's the matter?
M: I don't know. I just can't fall asleep until late at night.
W: I feel bad for you.
M: I need to find a way to sleep better.
W: Can I share how I _____ my sleeping problem?
M: Sure.
W: After I changed my pillow, I was able to sleep much better. _____ _____ _____ can help you with your sleeping problem.
M: Thanks for the tip. I hope that _____ _____ me, too.

03

M: Hi, I'm Daniel Jones. I'm glad to _____ meet you.
W: Welcome. Mr. Harvey told me you're coming.
M: He told me nice things about you.
W: Thanks. I hear that you're _____ _____ _____ at your house in two weeks.
M: That's right. I'm hoping you could take charge of the food for my party.
W: Sure. You can always _____ _____ _____ _____ like me.
M: Great. Is there anything I need to prepare for you?
W: No need. I'll be taking care of the party food _____ _____ to finish.
M: Sounds fantastic.
W: Now let's talk about the menu.

04

W: Is that the photo of our school's new studio?
M: Yes. We can _____ _____ _____ here.
W: Can I have a look?
M: Sure. Do you see that camera facing the chair? It's the latest model.
W: I see. What is that _____ _____ _____ next to the camera?
M: That's the lighting. It's to brighten the teacher's face.

W: Hmm.... The _____ _____ on the wall looks simple and modern.

M: Teachers can check the time on the clock while shooting.

W: The microphone on the table looks very professional.

M: It really does. Also, I like the tree _____ _____ _____. It goes well with the studio.

05

M: Hi, Jamie. You remember we're going to the movies later today, right?

W: Of course. I'll see you after class.

M: Didn't you say there's a student _____ _____ the movie ticket?

W: Yes, I did. Don't forget to bring your student ID card.

M: But _____ _____ my ID. Is there any other way to get the discount?

W: Probably not. Why don't you go _____ _____ _____ _____ card from the school office?

M: Do you know where the office is?

W: Yes. It's on the first floor.

M: Okay. _____ _____ _____ right away.

06

W: Hi, I'm looking for camping chairs. Can you recommend one?

M: Good morning. This is our bestselling chair. They're $_____ _____.

W: That sounds good. I'll take it.

M: How many do you need?

W: I _____ _____ chairs.

M: Okay. Is there anything else you need?

W: I also need a camping _____.

M: How about this one? It's $20.

W: That looks convenient. I'll buy one. Do you offer any discounts?

M: Yes. Since your _____ _____ _____ _____ $80, we'll give you a 10% discount on the total amount.

W: That sounds nice. I'll pay with my credit card.

07

M: Hi, Rebecca. What's up?

W: Hey, Tom. Can I _____ your laptop today?

M: Yes, but I have to finish my science report first.

W: Really? Wasn't the science report _____ last week?

M: Yes, it was. But I couldn't finish it.

W: What happened? I thought your _____ _____ _____.

M: Actually, it didn't. I made a mistake in the experimental process.

W: Oh, no. Did you have to do the experiment _____ _____ _____ _____?

M: Yes, it took a lot of time. So I haven't finished my report yet.

W: I see. Let me know when you're done.

08

W: Hi, Asher. What are you doing on the computer?

M: I'm signing up for an event called the Spring Virtual Run.

W: The Spring Virtual... Run?

M: It's a race. Participants _____ _____ _____ after running either a three-mile race or a ten-mile race.

W: Can you run at any location?

M: Yes. I can _____ _____ _____ in the city.

W: That sounds interesting. I want to participate, too.

M: Then you should sign up online and pay the _____ _____. It's twenty dollars.

W: Twenty dollars? That's pretty expensive.

M: But souvenirs are _____ in the fee. All participants will get a T-shirt and a water bottle.

W: That's reasonable. I'll sign up.

09

W: Do your children love adventures? Here's a great adventure for you and your children. The Museum of Natural History is starting a special program — Family Night at the Museum. When the _____ _____ _____ are over, you and your children get to walk around the museum with a flashlight. After your adventure is complete, you will sleep under the amazing _____ _____ _____ and stars. Sleeping bags, snacks, and water will be provided. This program is for children _____ 6 to 13. All those who want to join must register in advance. On-site registration is _____ _____. Why not call today and sign up?

10

M: Hi, how can I help you today?

W: Hi, I'm looking for a _____ _____.

M: Sure. We have these five models.

W: Hmm.... I want to wear it when I swim.

M: Then you're looking for _____ _____ _____.

W: That's right. Do you think a one-year warranty is too short?

M: Yes. I recommend one that has a warranty _____ _____ one year.

W: Okay. I'll take your advice.

M: That leaves you with these two options. I'd get the _____ one because it's as good as the other one.

W: I see. Then I'll go with the cheaper one.

M: Good choice.

11

W: Liam, how did your _____ go?

M: It was good, Mom. I got this shirt at a good price.

W: It looks nice. Wait! It's _____ _____ _____.

M: (Oh, I should get it exchanged.)

12

M: Alicia, these donuts are delicious. Can you tell me _____ _____ _____ them?

W: They're from a new donut shop. I can take you there if you want.

M: That'd be nice. How's _____ _____ _____?

W: (Good. Let's meet around six.)

13

W: Brandon, I'm sorry I'm late.

M: That's okay. Let's _____ our drinks. I'll get my coffee in my personal cup.

W: Oh, you brought your own cup?

M: Yes, it is a _____ cup. I'm trying to reduce my plastic footprint.

W: What is plastic footprint?

M: It is the total amount of plastic a person _____ _____ _____ _____.

W: You care a lot about the environment.

M: I do. Plastic waste is a huge environmental problem.

W: I should use a reusable cup, too. _____ _____ _____ _____ do to reduce my plastic footprint?

M: (You can stop using plastic straws.)

14

M: Good morning, Kathy. That's a cool helmet.

W: Hi, Alex. It's for biking. I _____ _____ _____ to school.

M: How often do you ride your bike to school?

W: I try to do it every day. It's very _____.

M: Sounds nice. I'm thinking of riding to school, too.

W: Good! We should ride together.

M: Let's do that, but I'm not very _____ _____ _____.

W: It's okay. We can go slowly. Also, remember to wear your helmet.

M: But I _____ _____ a helmet yet.

W: (You really need one for your own safety.)

15

W: Jasper and Mary are trying to form a _____ _____ for the school band competition. Mary plays the guitar, and Jasper is the drummer. They pick a keyboard player through an audition. Now, they need a lead singer. Although the band is not _____ _____, they begin their first practice today. Since they don't have a lead singer yet, Mary sings while playing the guitar. _____ her sing, the other members are amazed. Mary has the perfect voice for rock music! So Jasper wants to tell Mary to _____ _____ _____ _____ for their band. In this situation, what would Jasper most likely say to Mary?

Jasper: (I think you should be our lead singer.)

16~17

M: Good afternoon, everybody. Today, we'll talk about what our _____ _____ _____: Toys. How do toys help our pets? First, toys play a very important role in _____ your pet happy. A toy like a scratcher helps to reduce your _____ _____. Second, toys are a great tool for a pet to get exercise. For example, a hamster loves to _____ _____ _____ _____ toy. Third, toys build a bond between you and your pet. Playing with a small soft ball will give you and your dog a joyful experience. Lastly, toys help keep your pet _____. A small hiding tent will make your parrot feel less _____ when you are not around. Now let's watch a video of pets playing with their toys.

11 2021년 6월 학력평가
딕테이션

MP3

2SBL1_A11

녹음을 듣고, 빈칸에 알맞은 말을 쓰시기 바랍니다. 빈칸은 문제풀이에 핵심이 되는 키워드와 헷갈리기 쉬운 발음에 표시되어 있으니 이 점에 유의하여 듣기 바랍니다.

01

M: Hello, students. This is Allan, your school nurse. Many students get sick with seasonal influenza. Some cases can ＿＿＿＿＿＿＿ ＿＿＿＿＿＿＿ serious pain or even hospitalization. I would recommend you to ＿＿＿＿＿＿＿ ＿＿＿＿＿＿＿ ＿＿＿＿＿＿＿ ＿＿＿＿＿＿＿.

A flu shot can keep you from getting sick. Also, since flu viruses keep changing, flu vaccines are updated to ＿＿＿＿＿＿＿ ＿＿＿＿＿＿＿ such viruses. Please get a flu shot offered in doctors' offices or health departments ＿＿＿＿＿＿＿ ＿＿＿＿＿＿＿ ＿＿＿＿＿＿＿ of this month. Thank you.

02

M: Irene, where are you heading?

W: Hello, Mason. I'm going to the bookstore to buy some books.

M: The bookstore? Isn't it more ＿＿＿＿＿＿＿ to order books online?

W: Yes, but I like to flip through the pages at bookstores.

M: Yeah, but buying books online is cheaper.

W: Right. But we can ＿＿＿＿＿＿＿ ＿＿＿＿＿＿＿ ＿＿＿＿＿＿＿ when we buy books from them.

M: I guess you're right. The bookstore near my house shut down last month.

W: It's a pity to see local bookstores ＿＿＿＿＿＿＿ ＿＿＿＿＿＿＿ ＿＿＿＿＿＿＿ ＿＿＿＿＿＿＿ nowadays.

M: I agree. Next time I need a book, I'll try to go to a ＿＿＿＿＿＿＿ bookstore.

03

[Telephone rings.]

M: Hello. This is G-Solution. How may I help you?

W: Hello. I'm ＿＿＿＿＿＿＿ ＿＿＿＿＿＿＿ ＿＿＿＿＿＿＿ my home. The keypad on my door isn't responding.

M: It might be an electric problem. It's probably a ＿＿＿＿＿＿＿ ＿＿＿＿＿＿＿ and it won't cost much.

W: How much is it?

M: It's 30 dollars including the service charge. But you'll have to ＿＿＿＿＿＿＿ ＿＿＿＿＿＿＿ if there're any additional problems.

W: I got it. Can you come over right away?

M: I'm afraid not. I'm doing a job at the Capital Bank.

W: How long will it ＿＿＿＿＿＿＿ ＿＿＿＿＿＿＿ ＿＿＿＿＿＿＿ ＿＿＿＿＿＿＿?

M: Just one hour. I'll call you as soon as I'm done. Address, please?

W: 705 Cozy Street near Lee's Dental Clinic.

M: Okay. See you soon.

04

M: Grace, let me show you my _____ _____ room.

W: Wow, Jake! It's so cool.

M: Look at the monitor between the speakers. I changed my old monitor for this new one.

W: Looks nice. But isn't your desk too crowded to put your electric keyboard on it?

M: It's fine with me. I find it convenient there.

W: Is that a _____ in the corner? Do you sing?

M: Yes. Singing is my all-time favorite hobby.

W: What's that _____ _____ on the wall? Where did you get it?

M: I won that medal at a guitar contest with my dad.

W: Incredible! Do you often _____ the guitar with your dad?

M: Sure. That's why there're two guitars in the room.

05

W: _____ nice, Daniel. What did you make for lunch?

M: Creamy pasta. I found the recipe online.

W: Fantastic. But don't you think the kitchen is a little _____ _____?

M: Sorry. I'll clean it up later.

W: You promise?

M: Yes. Let's have lunch. [Pause] By the way, do you remember you have to _____

_____ _____ _____ from the library this afternoon?

W: Oh, my! I totally forgot. What should I do? My friend Amy is coming in an hour.

M: Don't worry. I planned to go camera shopping, but I'll pick up Betty, _____.

W: Thanks. How sweet of you! Then I'll clean the kitchen.

06

M: Good afternoon. May I help you?

W: Yes, please. I want to buy a bag for my laptop. Can you recommend one?

M: How about this one? It's only _____

_____ _____ _____.

The original price was 65 dollars.

W: Wow, more than 50% off?

M: It's a very good _____.

W: I like the design and color, but it's not big enough.

M: If you want something bigger, how about this one? It has a USB _____ _____, too.

W: I like it, but it looks expensive.

M: It's 70 dollars. But I can give you a 10% discount.

W: Well... It's still beyond my budget. Let me look at the _____ _____ again.

M: Here it is. 30 dollars is a bargain.

W: Okay. I'll take it.

07

W: Hi, Chris. How was your business trip?

M: It went fine. By the way, I heard Emma is _____ _____ this Saturday.

W: You're right. She's very busy preparing to move. So she gave me _____ _____ for a musical because she can't go.

M: Good for you. What's the name of the musical?

W: It's "Heroes."

M: Really? I heard it's popular. Who are you going with?

W: No one, yet. My sister _____ _____ _____ because she has to finish her homework.

M: Well, can I go with you instead?

W: Sure. Why not? The show is at 8 p.m. this Friday.

M: Friday? Oh, no! I promised to take care of _____ _____ at that time.

W: No problem. I'll ask Susan to go with me then.

08

W: Dad, I want to have a puppy just like my friend, Julie.

M: Why not? But do you know how hard it is to _____ a dog?

W: Yes, but I'm ready. I think I will name my puppy Toby.

M: Okay. But will you _____ Toby every day?

W: That'll be easy.

M: Also, you'll have to feed Toby three times a day.

W: No big deal. Anything else?

M: You'll have to _____ _____ Toby, too.

W: Really?

M: Of course. Plus, you'll need to clean up the dog's pee pads.

W: Hmm... Dad, you'll help me, right?

M: Sometimes. But remember having a dog _____ _____.

09

W: Good afternoon, listeners. Why don't you join the Sharing Friday Movement and _____ two dollars to our fund every Friday? This movement started in 2001 in Finland as an idea to _____ _____ _____ _____ good. Since then, this idea has grown into a global movement. Most of the donations go to poor areas across the world and help people get clean water. This year, scholarships were _____ _____ _____ _____ in these areas to celebrate our 20th anniversary. Please join us, and help _____ _____ _____. If you want to get more information, visit our homepage.

10

W: Kevin, I'm looking for a selfie stick. Can you help me?

M: Sure, Mom. You can buy ＿＿＿＿＿＿ ＿＿＿＿＿＿ your smart phone. [Pause] What kind of selfie stick do you want?

W: I'd prefer a light one.

M: Then I ＿＿＿＿＿＿ ＿＿＿＿＿＿ a selfie stick over 200 grams. How about the length?

W: I have no idea. What's your opinion?

M: Hmm... It should ＿＿＿＿＿＿ ＿＿＿＿＿＿ ＿＿＿＿＿＿ 80cm at least.

W: Okay. I also want a bluetooth remote control. I heard they're convenient to use.

M: Then you have two options left. Which one do you want?

W: I'll buy ＿＿＿＿＿＿ ＿＿＿＿＿＿ ＿＿＿＿＿＿.

M: Great choice.

11

M: Have you finished ＿＿＿＿＿＿ your bags for your trip to Mount Jiri?

W: I think so. Look! What else do I need?

M: You'd better prepare for the ＿＿＿＿＿＿ ＿＿＿＿＿＿ at night.

W: (You're right. I'll take a warm jacket.)

12

W: Honey, we ＿＿＿＿＿＿ ＿＿＿＿＿＿ ＿＿＿＿＿＿ tomorrow evening.

M: Why not? I've already booked a table at the restaurant.

W: I'm sorry. I have ＿＿＿＿＿＿ ＿＿＿＿＿＿ ＿＿＿＿＿＿ ＿＿＿＿＿＿ at that time.

M: (Sorry to hear that. I'll cancel the reservation now.)

13

M: Why do you look so ＿＿＿＿＿＿?

W: I'm working on a team project.

M: What's it about?

W: It's about 'Climate Change.'

M: Sounds interesting. ＿＿＿＿＿＿ ＿＿＿＿＿＿ your team?

W: You know Chris? He's the leader.

M: I know him very well. He's responsible and smart.

W: Jenny is ＿＿＿＿＿＿ ＿＿＿＿＿＿ ＿＿＿＿＿＿ and Alex is making the slides.

M: What a nice team! Then ＿＿＿＿＿＿ ＿＿＿＿＿＿ ＿＿＿＿＿＿?

W: (I'm in charge of giving the presentation.)

14

M: Hi, Diana. You look down. What's the problem?

W: Hi, Peter. I _____ _____ _____ for the speech contest. It was yesterday.

M: No way. You'd been waiting for it for a long time.

W: Yeah. It totally slipped my mind. I'm so _____.

M: Why don't you write notes to remember things?

W: I've tried, but it doesn't work. I even forget _____ _____ _____ the notes.

M: How about using a time management application like me?

W: Well... What's _____ _____ _____ _____?

M: (It helps me keep deadlines to complete specific tasks.)

15

M: Harold is a tennis coach. He's been teaching Kate, a _____ _____ _____ player, for years. While practicing for an upcoming match, Kate injured her elbow badly. Her doctor strongly recommends she stop playing tennis for a month. However, Kate _____ _____ playing the match. Harold knows how heart-broken she would be to miss the match. But he's _____ about her tennis career if her elbow doesn't recover. So he wants to persuade her to _____ _____ _____ _____ on her recovery. In this situation, what would Harold most likely say to Kate?

Harold: (Take it easy. Take good care of yourself first.)

16~17

W: This is Linda from "Life and Science." Did you know _____ _____ from bright lights at night can drive wildlife to death? For example, _____ _____ lay eggs on beaches and their babies find their way to the sea with the help of moonlight. But artificial lights can _____ them and cause them not to reach the sea and die. Fireflies have been disappearing across the globe. Male fireflies _____ _____ by artificial lights when they try to attract mates. This means less fireflies are born. Also, _____ _____ _____ when exposed to artificial lights at night. This threatens their chances of survival. Lastly, light pollution _____ _____ _____ _____ of tree frogs at night. As male frogs reduce the number of their mating calls, the females don't _____. So light pollution can be a matter of life and death for some animals.

12 2021년 9월 학력평가
딕테이션

MP3
25BL1_A12

녹음을 듣고, 빈칸에 알맞은 말을 쓰기 바랍니다. 빈칸은 문제풀이에 핵심이 되는 키워드와 헷갈리기 쉬운 발음에 표시되어 있으니 이 점에 유의하여 듣기 바랍니다.

01

M: Hello, citizens of Portland. This is Jerry Wilson, your Mayor. As you know, Port Elementary School has opened, and it is so nice to hear the kids playing. To _____ _____ _____ of the students at the school, we've been communicating with the New Jersey State Police and requested that they _____ speed limits in the area around the school. This is in response to the many _____ City Hall has received regarding excessive speeding, especially in front of the school. Please _____ _____ _____ for the safety of the kids and your fellow citizens. Thank you for your cooperation. Stay safe and healthy.

02

M: Lily, what's wrong? Are you all right?
W: Oh, it's nothing.
M: Are you sure? You look pretty worried.
W: Actually, I said something _____ to my sister and I feel really bad about it.
M: What did you say to her?
W: I said she's the worst sister because she wore my favorite jacket again!
M: Jeez! She must have been really hurt by that.
W: Yeah, but I told her not to wear my jacket a million times. She never listens.
M: Still, you should be _____ _____ when you talk to someone close to you.

W: I know, but I was so angry.
M: People _____ _____ more easily when someone close to them says mean things.
W: Yeah, you're right. I'll _____ _____ her when I get home.

03

W: Hi, listeners! Now we have one person on the line. He has something special to share with us. Hello, you're on the air!
M: Hello. Wow! I'm surprised that I _____ _____ _____ you. Thank you for taking my call.
W: Sure. Please introduce yourself.
M: I'm Jin, a high school student. I'm a big _____ _____ _____ _____.
W: Thank you, Jin. By the way, you left a message on our website, didn't you?
M: Yes. Today is my parents' 20th wedding anniversary. I wanted to honor them on the show.
W: I see. Are your parents _____ now?
M: Yes, they listen to your show every day.
W: That's great. What is your message to your parents?
M: Hmm... Mom and Dad, you're amazing parents. Happy Anniversary to you both!
W: What a lovely message! Thank you for _____ _____ today, Jin.
M: Thanks again for taking my call.

04

W: Hi, Tim. How's everything going with the festival?

M: Hey, Julie! It's going great. This is a picture of what our booth will look like.

W: What will people do at your booth?

M: They'll be asked to answer questions and be given snacks if they _____ _____.

W: Okay, that sounds good. I like the banner that says 'Guessing Time' in the center.

M: Thanks. What do you think about the photos that are under the clock?

W: Great idea! What are you using the _____ _____ for?

M: We're going to put the snacks on it.

W: That makes sense. Then, what about the _____ _____ _____ _____?

M: It's for choosing countries. We're going to ask people geography questions.

W: That should be interesting. What's that _____ on the left side?

M: That's a photo zone for all participants.

W: Cool. I can't wait for this year's festival!

05

M: Kasey, how's everything _____ _____ for grandma's birthday this Sunday?

W: Hey, Dad. I wrote a card for her and got some decorations yesterday.

M: That's good!

W: Have you gotten anything for her yet?

M: I already bought a sweater. Can I help _____ _____ the living room for the party?

W: Clara will take care of that. Also, she's picking up a birthday cake.

M: Awesome! Your grandma will be so happy because you guys are going to make her birthday so special.

W: I hope so. What about food? What can we make for her?

M: How about _____ _____ _____? She loves those!

W: Good idea, but I won't have time to handle that on my own.

M: Then, I'll _____ salmon and vegetables online today.

W: Thanks, Dad! That's a big help.

06

M: Hello. How can I help you?

W: Hi, how much is the ice cream?

M: It depends on the size. The small cup is $_____, the medium is $10, and the large is $15. What size would you like?

W: I'll take _____ _____ and one medium.

M: Okay. What flavor would you like?

W: I'll take chocolate for all three cups.

M: Sounds good. Do you want any _____ on your ice cream? We have chocolate chips and crunchy nuts. Toppings cost $1 each.

W: Oh, yes. I'll have crunchy nuts _____ _____ _____ _____ and nothing on the small cups.

M: Good choice. Do you need anything else?

W: No, that's it.

M: How would you like to pay? Cash or credit?

W: I'll pay with my credit card.

07

M: Mom, I'm home.

W: Hi. Did you go to the gym?

M: Yes. My membership _____ today, but I didn't renew it.

W: Why? Does your shoulder still hurt?

M: No, my shoulder _____ _____ _____.

W: So, what's the problem? I thought you were enjoying exercising.

M: I was. It's actually been fun.

W: Then why didn't you renew your membership?

M: Well, the shower facilities at the gym are too old, and there's _____ _____ _____ in the shower stalls.

W: I see. Why don't you check out the new health club nearby? It may be more expensive, but the facilities are _____ a lot better.

M: Okay. Maybe I should visit there tomorrow on my way home after school.

W: That sounds like a good plan!

08

W: Hey, Bruce! I'm going to take a tour of Liberty University. Do you want to come?

M: Absolutely! That's one of the schools that I'm interested in. When is the tour?

W: There's one on _____ _____ and another one on October 10th. They're both Saturdays. Which date is better for you?

M: October 10th is better for me. What will we do during the tour?

W: We'll get to _____ _____ _____ in the morning and then we'll meet with an admissions counselor in the afternoon. You can ask them questions about the _____ _____ when we see them.

M: Okay, then I should make a list of questions. I have a lot of things to ask them.

W: That's a good idea. Also, everyone who goes on the tour will get a free Liberty University T-shirt _____ _____ _____.

M: Really? That's cool. So how do I sign up for the tour?

W: You can sign up on their website.

M: Okay, I will do that. Thank you so much for telling me about it.

09

W: Are you taking actions to help the environment? Then, why don't you join our Green Action Photo Contest? As long as you are a resident of our town, you can be the winner! From September 1st until September 30th, 2021, you can upload photos of you participating in eco-friendly activities on social media. _____ _____ your photos with the hash tag #GreenAction, you can automatically participate in our contest. The _____ _____ of photos you can post is five. The winner will be announced on October 4th. The prize for the winner _____ _____ _____ by October 11th. The winning photos will be posted on the town's website until the _____ _____ _____ _____. Show us your green actions. No action is too small!

10

M: Hey, Jessica. What are you working on?

W: Hey! I'm trying to order a new rolling cart for our school's library. Do you want to help me?

M: Sure. Let's see. Hmm... How about this plastic one? It looks like it's easy to use.

W: Well, the cart we have now is plastic and it's not strong enough, so, I'd prefer to buy one that's made of _____ _____ _____.

M: That makes sense. Then, let's get one that's made of metal or wood. What about the number of shelves?

W: I think it would be nice to have a cart that has _____ _____ _____ shelves.

M: That's a good idea. I would also recommend one that has lockable wheels because that makes it _____ _____ _____.

W: You're right! The one we have now doesn't have lockable wheels, so it's really hard to control.

M: I understand. That leaves us with these two options.

W: Well, we don't have much left in our budget. I can't spend more than $_____.

M: All right. Then, this one would be the best choice.

W: Okay, then I'll order this one. Thanks for your help.

11

W: Hey, Sean! Is this your dog? He's adorable!

M: He's actually not my dog. I think _____ _____, but I don't know what to do.

W: Oh, really? [Pause] Look at the couple over there! It seems like they're _____ _____ something.

M: (Okay. Then let's ask them if they lost their dog.)

12

M: Hi, we just wanted to see if we could still sit and order dinner.

W: Umm... I'm sorry but the _____ _____ in five minutes, so we won't be able to serve you.

M: That's disappointing. What time do you _____ tomorrow?

W: (We're open from 11 o'clock in the morning.)

13

M: Good morning, ma'am. May I help you?

W: Yes, please. I just heard that my flight will be _____ for six hours.

M: Oh, I'm sorry to hear that. Is there anything I can do for you?

W: Well, I know I have to check out of my room by 11, but that means I would be waiting at the airport for almost eight hours.

M: I understand. That's a long time to sit around and wait.

W: Is it possible for me _____ _____ in my room for a couple more hours until I leave this afternoon?

M: Let me check to see if the room is _____. [Pause] Luckily, ma'am, the room hasn't been booked for today.

W: Okay, then if I stay for a couple more hours, do I have to pay _____ _____ _____?

M: (Yes. But you don't have to pay for a full day.)

14

W: Hi, James. Is everything okay? I heard there was a _____ _____ in your area last night.

M: Yeah, we had some really intense thunderstorms throughout the night. There was some damage.

W: Did anyone get hurt?

M: Thankfully, no, but there were a lot of fallen trees, and the roads were blocked.

W: Oh my! That must have been _____!

M: Yeah, it was. Then the electricity went out while the roads were being cleared.

W: So you didn't have any power last night?

M: No, I couldn't _____ _____ _____ _____ or use any electronic devices, but it's okay now.

W: That must have been so frustrating. Is there anything you need help with?

M: Well, my _____ _____ _____ _____. The water is up to my knees and all of my stuff down there is wet.

W: (Oh, no! I can come over today to help you clear it out.)

15

M: Emily and Chris are classmates. Emily is making cookies when she gets a call from Chris. He says he is going to _____ _____ _____ with his friends and asks if she can join them. She says that she would love to, but she can't go because her parents aren't home and she _____ _____ _____ her younger brother. Chris suggests that Emily bring her brother with her to the movie. Emily _____ to Chris that her little brother has homework to finish, so he can't go either. She wants to tell Chris that she has

to _____ _____ her brother. In this situation, what would Emily most likely say to Chris?

Emily: (I'm sorry, but I need to take care of my brother.)

16~17

W: Everyone loves a good night's sleep, but for wild animals, finding the _____ _____ _____ _____ can be difficult. Whether it's staying safe, keeping warm, or remembering to breathe, animals have a _____ _____ _____ before they go to bed. As a result, they've come up with some clever and interesting solutions. To start with, _____ _____ _____ _____ while hanging upside down. Doing that not only keeps them away from enemies but also means they are in the perfect position to _____ _____ if necessary. Meanwhile, ducks sleep side by side in rows. The ducks on the outside of the rows sleep _____ _____ _____ _____ to watch for danger, while the ducks on the inside sleep with both eyes closed. _____ require little rest, sleeping for only five minutes at a time or as little as 30 minutes a day. They sleep in _____ _____, sometimes sitting down or even standing up, so that they're ready to run. Finally, _____ have to consciously think in order to breathe, even when they're sleeping. They only let part of their _____ _____ and keep one eye open as they sleep.

13 2021년 11월 학력평가
딕테이션

MP3
25BL1_A13

🙂 녹음을 듣고, 빈칸에 알맞은 말을 쓰시기 바랍니다. 빈칸은 문제풀이에 핵심이 되는 키워드와 헷갈리기 쉬운 발음에 표시되어 있으니 이 점에 유의하여 듣기 바랍니다.

01

[Chime bell rings.]

M: Hello, passengers. I'm James Walker from the Greenville Subway System. As you know, the _____ _____ festival will be held in our city next month. Throughout the festival, some movies will _____ _____ _____ at night. So, for our citizens' convenience, the Greenville City Council has decided to _____ _____ subway service hours during the festival. All Greenville subway lines will run extra hours while the festival is going on. You can easily check the _____ _____ _____ using the Greenville Subway App. I hope you can make the most of the festival experience with our services. Thank you.

02

W: Good morning, Jason. It's sports day today. Do you have everything you need?

M: Yes, Mom. I put a water bottle, some snacks, and a _____ in my bag. Is there anything I forgot?

W: What about sunblock? Did you put it on?

M: Sunblock? It's not sunny outside.

W: Jason, you should wear sunblock _____ _____ day.

M: But I don't feel the sun in weather like this.

W: Even if you don't feel the sun on your skin, the _____ _____ from the sun can damage your skin because the clouds don't block it.

M: Really? You mean I can still _____ _____ _____ even on a cloudy day?

W: Yes. That's why you shouldn't forget to wear sunblock even if it's not sunny outside.

M: I didn't know that. I'll put it on now.

03

M: Hello, Ms. Green. You came just on time.

W: Really? I thought I was early.

M: No. Your car is over there. Follow me, please.

W: Wow. _____ _____ _____ is gone. It looks like a new car.

M: Yeah. But some stains were difficult to remove. It's better to have your car washed right after it gets dirty.

W: I went on a business trip for a month, so I didn't have time. I'll keep that in mind.

M: Anyway, _____ _____ _____ _____, we found this earring under the driver's seat.

W: Really? I thought I had lost that. Thank you.

M: You're welcome. Would you like to pay _____ credit card or in cash?

W: I'll pay in cash. Here you are.

M: Okay. *[Pause]* Here is your receipt. And this is a discount coupon for our _____ _____ _____. You can use it on your next visit.

W: That's nice. Thank you.

04

W: Hi, Harry. Congratulations on your wedding. Did you finish _____ the new house?

M: I just finished the living room. Look at this picture, Linda.

W: Wow. I love the _____ _____ on the window.

M: Thanks. Do you see those two cushions on the sofa? My sister made them as wedding gifts.

W: That's lovely. Oh, you put a _____ _____ on the rug.

M: Yeah. We spend time reading books around the table. What do you think of the clock on the bookshelf?

W: It looks good in that room. By the way, is that a plant _____ _____ _____?

M: Yes. I placed it there because the plant helps to clean the air.

W: You decorated your house really well.

M: Thanks. I'll invite you over when we have the housewarming party.

05

M: Jane, the Stop Using Plastic _____ starts tomorrow. Let's do a final check.

W: Okay, Robin. I just finished editing a video clip about plastic waste.

M: Then, I'm going to check the screen that we'll use for the video.

W: No worries. I've already done it, and it works well.

M: That's nice. I _____ a campaign poster on our organization's website.

W: Yeah. Some of my friends saw it and texted me

they're coming.

M: My friends, too. They showed a huge interest in the _____ _____ decorating activity. The bags are ready in that box.

W: Good. By the way, where are the badges you ordered for visitors?

M: Oh, I left the badges in my car. I'll _____ _____ _____ _____.

W: Great. It seems that everything is prepared.

06

M: Welcome to Kids Clothing Club. How may I help you?

W: I'm looking for a muffler for my son. He's 5 years old.

M: Okay. Follow me. [Pause] This red muffler is one of the _____ _____ in our shop.

W: I love the color. How much is it?

M: It's $_____. This one is popular because of the cartoon character here.

W: Oh, that's my son's favorite character. I'll buy one red muffler, then.

M: Great. Anything else?

W: How much are these winter socks?

M: _____ _____ _____ socks is $5.

W: All right. I'll buy two pairs.

M: So, one red muffler and two pairs of winter socks, right?

W: Yes. Can I use this discount coupon?

M: Of course. With that coupon, you can get 10% _____ _____ _____ _____.

W: Good. Here's my credit card.

07

W: Hi, Jeremy. How was your trip to London?

M: It was _____, Julia. I watched the musical you recommended.

W: Good. What about the London Walking Tour? Did you enjoy it?

M: Unfortunately, I couldn't join the tour.

W: Why? Didn't you say you _____ _____?

M: Yes. I made a reservation for the tour in advance.

W: Oh, was the tour canceled because of the weather?

M: No. The weather was no problem at all.

W: Then, why couldn't you join the tour?

M: Actually, I fell down the day before the tour, so I had some _____ _____ _____ _____. That's why I couldn't make it.

W: I'm sorry to hear that. Is it okay, now?

M: Yes. It's _____ _____ now. Oh, I forgot to bring the souvenir I bought for you. I'll bring it tomorrow.

W: That's so sweet. Thanks.

08

M: What are you doing, Laura?

W: Hi, Tim. I'm looking for winter festivals to visit during _____.

M: Is there anything good?

W: Yes, look at this. There is a new local event called the Winter Lake Festival.

M: Awesome. When does it start?

W: _____ _____ and it'll be held for two weeks.

M: Cool. Oh, it'll take place in Stevenson Park.

W: Great. It's near our school. If you don't have any plans during vacation, let's go together.

M: Of course. Is there _____ _____ _____?

W: Yes. Here, it says $3. It's not expensive.

M: Good. Look! There are so many kinds of _____ _____ _____.

W: Yeah, there is ice skating, ice fishing, and a snowball fight.

M: They all sound exciting. Let's have fun there.

09

W: Hello, supporters! I'm Christine Miller, manager of Western Football Club. This year, we're holding a Mascot Design Contest to _____ our team's 1st championship. Anyone who loves our team can participate in this contest. The mascot design should be _____ _____ our team's slogan "One team, one spirit." The winning design will be chosen through a fan vote. And the winner will _____ _____ as a prize. People who want to participate should send their design by email by December 5th. Show your creativity and love for our team _____ _____ _____. For more information, please visit our website. Thank you.

10

W: Honey, what are you looking at?

M: This is a list of the best campsites in 2021. How about going to one of them next month?

W: Sounds great. Let me see. *[Pause]* There are five different campsites.

M: Yeah. Since we went to _____ campsite last time, let's choose among the other four.

W: Good. Hmm, I don't want to spend more than $100 _____ _____. It's too expensive.

M: I agree with that. What do you think of staying in a _____ _____?

W: Oh, I want to try it. It'll be a special experience.

M: Then, we can choose between these two.

W: What about going to this campsite? Since this has a _____ _____, our children can have more fun.

M: Cool! I'll make a reservation for this campsite.

11

M: Kate, I heard your company _____ to a new office. How is it?

W: It's all good except one thing. It's far from my house.

M: Oh, really? _____ _____ does it take to get there?

W: (It takes an hour by bus.)

12

W: Honey, you know my _____ is coming over this evening. How about ordering pizza for dinner?

M: Sure. Which topping does he prefer, grilled beef or shrimp?

W: Oh, he doesn't like beef. He _____ _____.

M: (Okay. I'll order a shrimp pizza.)

13

M: Honey, did you read this leaflet on the table?

W: Not yet. What's it about?

M: It says the local children's library is going to hold some events to celebrate their _____.

W: Is there anything good?

M: Let me see. *[Pause]* There will be a Meet-the-Author event. Rebecca Moore is coming.

W: Oh, she's one of our son's _____ _____.

M: Yes. He'll be excited if he can meet her _____ _____.

W: Let's take him to that event. When is it?

M: It's next Saturday, 1 p.m.

W: But we have a lunch reservation at the French restaurant at that time.

M: Oh, I forgot. Then how about _____ lunch? It's a rare chance to meet the author.

W: (You're right. I'll change the reservation now.)

14

[Cell phone rings.]

W: This is Fairview Laptop Repair. How may I help you?

M: Hello, this is David Brown. I _____ _____ _____ this morning.

W: Oh, Mr. Brown. You requested the screen repair yesterday, right?

M: Yes. Is there any problem?

W: The screen is all repaired. But we found another problem with your laptop. You need to _____ the battery.

M: Oh, I didn't know that. How bad is it?

W: Even when the battery is fully charged, it won't last longer than an hour.

M: Really? How much does it cost to change the battery?

W: It's $70. It's on sale now.

M: That sounds great. But, I'm worried it'll _____ the laptop pick-up time, 5 p.m. today.

W: Don't worry. You can still pick it up _____ _____ _____.

M: (Then, I'd like to replace the battery.)

15

M: Amy is the leader of a high school band and Terry is one of the band members. The band is going to hold a mini concert in the school festival, and Terry is _____ _____ making a concert poster. When he completes the poster, he shows it to the band members. Even though the poster has all the _____ _____, it's hard to read it because the size of the letters is too small. Amy thinks if Terry changes the font size to a _____ one, it could be easier to notice. So, Amy wants to suggest that Terry _____ _____ _____ of the letters on the poster. In this situation, what would Amy most likely say to Terry?

Amy: (Can you make the letter size bigger on the poster?)

16~17

W: Hello, students. Previously, we discussed why _____ is a great hobby. But not everyone has a sunny front yard. So, today we'll learn about plants that _____ _____ _____ _____. First, lemon balm survives in full shade. So if your place is _____, it's the plant you should choose. Next, ivy is the ultimate shade-loving plant. Its ability to grow in shade makes it survive under trees where most plants can't. Also, there's mint. It lives well under _____ _____, so you can grow it in a small pot indoors. Lastly, camellia grows better in _____ shade. Especially when it's a young plant, it needs protection from the sun. Many plants like these can live even in the shade. Isn't it _____? Now, let's watch a video clip about how to grow these plants.

14 2022년 3월 학력평가
딕테이션

녹음을 듣고, 빈칸에 알맞은 말을 쓰시기 바랍니다. 빈칸은 문제풀이에 핵심이 되는 키워드와 헷갈리기 쉬운 발음에 표시되어 있으니 이 점에 유의하여 듣기 바랍니다.

01

M: Good afternoon, everybody. This is Student President Sam Wilson. As you know, the _____ _____ _____ will begin soon. Many students are interested in joining the league and waiting for the _____ _____ to be handed out at the gym. For easier access, we've decided to _____ _____ _____ _____. Instead of going to the gym to register, simply log into the school website and _____ _____ the registration form online. Thank you for listening and let's have a good league.

02

W: Daniel, what are you doing in front of the mirror?

M: I have _____ _____ these days. I'm trying to pop these pimples on my face.

W: Pimples are really annoying, but I wouldn't do that.

M: Why not?

W: When you pop them _____ _____ _____, you're touching your face.

M: Are you saying that I shouldn't touch my face?

W: Exactly. You know our hands are covered with bacteria, right?

M: So?

W: You'll be _____ bacteria all over your face with your hands. It could worsen your skin problems.

M: Oh, I didn't know that.

W: _____ _____ _____ with your hands is bad for your skin.

M: Okay, I got it.

03

M: Excuse me. You're Chloe Jones, aren't you?

W: Yes, I am. Have we met before?

M: No, but I'm a big fan of yours. I've watched your _____ _____ _____ _____, and they're very inspiring.

W: Thank you. I'm so glad to hear that.

M: And, I also think your campaign about plastic pollution has been very successful.

W: As _____ _____ _____, that means a lot to me.

M: May I make a suggestion? I thought it'd be nice if more children could hear your ideas.

W: That's what I was thinking. Do you have any good ideas?

M: Actually, I'm a _____. Perhaps I can make comic books based on your work.

W: That is a wonderful idea. Can I contact you later to _____ it more?

M: Sure. By the way, my name is Jack Perse. Here's my business card.

04

W: Yesterday, I decorated my fish tank
_____ _____ _____.

M: I'd like to see it. Do you have a picture?

W: Sure. Here. [Pause] Do you _____
_____ _____ in the bottom left
corner?

M: Yes. It's the one I gave you, isn't it?

W: Right. It looks good in the fish tank, doesn't it?

M: It does. I love the beach _____
_____ _____ _____.

W: Yeah. I like it, too.

M: I see a starfish next to the chair.

W: Isn't it cute? And do you see these
_____ _____ _____ on
the right side of the picture?

M: Yeah. I like how you put both of them side by
side.

W: I thought that'd look cool.

M: Your fish in the top left corner looks happy with
its new home.

W: I hope so.

05

[Cell phone rings.]

M: Hello, honey. I'm on the way home. How's setting
up Mike's birthday party going?

W: Good, but I still have _____
_____ _____. Mike and his
friends will get here soon.

M: Should I pick up the birthday cake?

W: No, that's okay. I already did that.

M: Then, do you want me to put up the balloons
around the doorway when I get there?

W: I'll take care of it. Can you _____
_____ _____ out to the front
yard?

M: Sure. Are we having the party outside?

W: Yes. The weather is beautiful so I made a
_____ _____ _____.

M: Great. The kids can play with water guns in the
front yard.

W: Good idea. I'll go to the garage and
_____ the water guns.

06

W: Welcome to Green Eco Shop. How can I help
you?

M: Hi, do you sell _____ toothbrushes?

W: Yes, we have a few types over here. Which do
you like?

M: Hmm.... How much are these?

W: They're $2 each. They are _____
_____ _____.

M: All right. I'll take four of them.

W: Excellent choice. Anything else?

M: I also need bath sponges.

W: They're right behind you. They're plastic-free and
only $_____ each.

M: Okay. I'll also take four of them. That'll be all.

W: If you have a store membership, you can get a
10% discount _____ _____
_____.

M: Great. I'm a member. Here are my credit and
membership cards.

07

[Cell phone rings.]

M: Hey, Suji. Where are you?

W: I'm in the library checking out books. I'll be

_____ _____ _____

the science lab for our experiment in a couple of

minutes.

M: I guess you haven't checked my _____

yet. We can't do the experiment today.

W: Really? Isn't the lab available today?

M: Yes, it is, but I canceled our reservation.

W: Why? Are you still _____ _____

your cold?

M: No, I'm fine now.

W: That's good. Then why aren't we doing the

experiment today? We need to hand in the

science report by next Monday.

M: Unfortunately, the experiment _____

_____ _____ _____

yet. It'll arrive tomorrow.

W: Oh, well. The experiment has to wait one more

day, then.

08

W: Honey, did you see the poster about the Stanville

Free-cycle?

M: Free-cycle? What is that?

W: It's _____ _____

_____ _____. You give away

items you don't need and anybody can take

them for free.

M: Oh, it's like _____ _____

_____ is another man's treasure. Who

can participate?

W: It's open to everyone _____

_____ Stanville.

M: Great. Where is it taking place?

W: At Rose Park on Second Street.

M: When does the event start?

W: It starts on April 12th and runs for a week.

M: Let's see what we can free-cycle, starting from

the cupboard.

W: Okay. But _____ _____ like

glass dishes or cups won't be accepted.

M: I see. I'll keep that in mind.

09

M: Hello, River Valley High School students. This is

your music teacher, Mr. Stailor. _____

_____ April 11th, we are going to

have the River Valley Music Camp for five

days. You don't need to be a member of the

school orchestra to join the camp. You may

_____ _____ _____

_____ or you can borrow one from

the school. On the last day of camp, we

are going to _____ _____

_____ and play it on screen at the

school summer festival. Please keep in mind

the camp is _____ _____

50 students. Sign-ups start this Friday, on a

first-come-first-served basis. Come and make

music together!

10

W: Ben, do you have a minute?

M: Sure. What is it?

W: I'm trying to buy a handheld vacuum cleaner among these five models. Could you help me choose one?

M: Okay. How much are you willing to spend?

W: _____ _____ _____ $130.

M: Then we can cross this one out. What about the _____ _____?

W: I think it should be longer than 10 minutes.

M: Then that narrows it down to these three.

W: Should I go with one of the lighter ones?

M: Yes. Lighter ones are easier to _____ _____ _____.

W: All right. What about the filter?

M: The one with a washable filter would be a _____ _____.

W: I got it. Then I'll order this one.

11

M: My eyes are sore today.

W: Too bad. Maybe some _____ _____ _____ your eyes.

M: You're probably right. What should I do?

W: (Why don't you rinse your eyes with clean water?)

12

W: Excuse me. Would you _____ if I sit here?

M: I'm sorry, but it's my friend's seat. He'll be back in a minute.

W: Oh, I didn't know that. Sorry for _____ you.

M: (That's okay. I think the seat next to it is available.)

13

M: Hey, Jasmine.

W: Hi, Kurt. Are you going to be at home tomorrow afternoon?

M: Yeah, I'm going to watch the baseball game with my friends at home.

W: Good. Can I _____ _____ your house and give you back the hammer I borrowed?

M: Sure. _____ _____ _____ _____. By the way, why don't you join us and watch the game?

W: I'd love to. Which teams are playing?

M: Green Thunders and Black Dragons.

W: That'll be _____. What time should I come?

M: Come at five. We'll have pizza before the game.

W: Perfect. Do you want me to bring anything?

M: _____ _____ _____ to eat while watching the game.

W: (Great. I'll bring chips and popcorn.)

14

W: Hi, Tom.

M: Hi, Jane. What are you reading?

W: It's a novel by Charles Dickens. I'm going to

_____ _____ _____
with my book club members this weekend.

M: Oh, you're in a book club?

W: Yes. I joined it a few months ago. And now I read much more than before.

M: Really? Actually one of my _____ _____ _____ is to read more books.

W: Then, joining a book club will surely help.

M: Hmm…. What other _____ can I get if I join one?

W: You can also share your reading experiences with others.

M: That'd be nice.

W: Yeah, it really broadens your mind. I really _____ _____ _____ _____ a book club.

M: (Sounds cool. I'll join a book club, too.)

15

M: Brian and Sally are walking down the street together. A blind man and his guide dog are walking towards them. Sally likes dogs very much, so she _____ _____ _____ _____ the guide dog. Brian doesn't think that Sally should do that. The guide dog needs to _____ on guiding the blind person. If someone touches the dog, the dog can _____ its focus. So Brian wants to tell Sally not to touch the guide dog _____ _____ _____ of the dog owner. In this situation, what would Brian most likely say to Sally?

Brian: (You shouldn't touch a guide dog without permission.)

16~17

W: Hello, everybody. Welcome to the health _____. I'm Alanna Reyes, the head trainer from Eastwood Fitness Center. As you know, joints are body parts that _____ _____ together. And doing certain physical activities puts stress on the joints. But the good news is that people with bad joints can still _____ _____ _____. They have relatively low impact on the joints. Here are some examples. The first is swimming. While swimming, the water _____ _____ _____ _____. The second is cycling. You put almost no stress on the knee joints when you pedal smoothly. _____ _____ is another exercise that puts very little stress on your knees. Lastly, walking is great because it's low-impact, _____ running. If you have bad joints, don't give up exercising. Instead, stay active and stay healthy!

14

22년 3월 딕테이션

15 2022년 6월 학력평가
딕테이션

MP3
25BL1_A15

🗣 녹음을 듣고, 빈칸에 알맞은 말을 쓰시기 바랍니다. 빈칸은 문제풀이에 핵심이 되는 키워드와 헷갈리기 쉬운 발음에 표시되어 있으니 이 점에 유의하여 듣기 바랍니다.

01

M: Good afternoon, this is the building manager, Richard Carson. We are planning to

_____ _____ _____

_____ on our building next week. The working hours will be from 9 a.m. to 6 p.m. Don't be surprised to see _____

_____ your windows. Please keep your windows closed while they are painting. There

_____ _____ _____

_____ from the paint. But don't worry. It is totally safe and eco-friendly. Sorry for any inconvenience and thank you for your

_____.

02

M: Hello, Veronica.

W: Hi, Jason. I heard that you are trying to get a

_____ _____ these days. How is it going?

M: You know what? I already got it. Look!

W: Oh, good for you! How was the driving test?

M: Well, _____ _____ the driving test, I was very nervous because some people were driving so fast.

W: But there are _____ _____

_____ everywhere.

M: Right, there are. But so many drivers ignore

speed limits these days.

W: That's terrible. Those drivers could cause serious car accidents.

M: That's true. Driving too fast can be dangerous for everybody.

W: Exactly. In my opinion, all drivers _____

_____ the speed limits.

M: I totally agree with you.

03

W: Excuse me. Can you _____

_____ _____ some books for my homework?

M: Sure. What is your homework about?

W: It's for my history class. The topic is the

_____ between France and Germany.

M: What about this world history book?

W: It looks good. Do you have any other books?

M: I can also recommend this European history book.

W: Great. How many books can I _____

_____ _____ _____?

M: You can borrow up to four books for three weeks each.

W: Okay. I'll take these two books, then.

M: All right. *[Beep sound]* Don't forget to

_____ _____ _____

_____.

04

M: Honey, come to Lucy's room. Look at what I did for her.

W: It looks great. Is that a toy bear on the bed?

M: Yes. That's right. She can sleep with the toy bear.

W: It's cute. Oh, and I like the round clock on the wall.

M: The round clock _____ _____ _____ the room, doesn't it? How do you like the family picture next to the window?

W: That's so sweet. I also love the _____ _____ on the window.

M: I'm happy you like them. What do you think of the _____ rug on the floor?

W: It is lovely. Lucy will feel safe and _____ on the rug.

M: Looks like everything's prepared.

W: Thanks, honey. You've done a great job.

05

W: David, did you fix your bicycle yesterday?

M: Yes. Luckily, I was able to fix it _____ _____. How was your soccer practice, Christine?

W: A new coach came to our soccer club and we _____ very hard.

M: You must be so tired. Do you still want to see a movie this afternoon?

W: Of course, I booked the tickets two weeks ago.

M: All right. Let's get going.

W: Wait, did you email your science report to Mr. Smith? _____ _____ today.

M: [Pause] Oh, no! I finished it but forgot to send it.

What should I do?

W: Why don't you send it before meeting me at the movie theater?

M: Good idea. I'll go home quickly and _____ _____ _____, but can you buy some popcorn for me before I get there?

W: No problem. See you there.

06

M: Good morning. Welcome to Happy Land.

W: Hello. I'd like to buy some tickets. How much are they?

M: $_____ for the amusement park and $10 for the water park. How many tickets do you need?

W: We're five people in total, and we only want to go to the amusement park.

M: Okay. Do you have _____ _____ coupons?

W: I printed out a birthday coupon from your website. It's my birthday today.

M: It's your birthday? Just let me check your ID, please.

W: Here you are.

M: Oh, happy birthday! With your birthday coupon, _____ _____ _____ _____.

W: That's great. Please give me five tickets including my ticket.

M: Let me see. That'll be four people _____ _____ _____ _____, and one person with a birthday coupon.

W: Right. Here is my credit card.

07

W: Hi, Alex. How is it going?

M: I'm good. Thanks. I've just finished my English project. How about you, Tracy?

W: I'm a little _____ _____ for my food booth.

M: A food booth? What for?

W: My school festival is next Tuesday. I'm _____ a food booth that day.

M: That is so cool. What is on the menu?

W: We're making sandwiches. You should come.

M: I'd love to, but I can't.

W: You can't? I was really _____ _____ _____ seeing you at my school.

M: I'm terribly sorry. I have to practice _____ _____ _____ _____.

W: Oh, I see. Well, good luck with your audition.

M: Thank you.

08

[Telephone rings.]

W: Hello, this is the World Culture Center. How can I help you?

M: Hi, I'm calling about a Spanish culture class for my _____ son.

W: Okay. We have an interesting class for teenagers.

M: Great. Who teaches it?

W: A Korean teacher and a _____ _____ teach it together.

M: What kind of activities are there in the class?

W: Students can _____ _____ _____, learn new words, and try on traditional clothing.

M: On what day is the class?

W: It's on Wednesday and Friday afternoons.

M: I see. Is there anything my son should prepare before the class?

W: He just needs to bring a pen and a notebook. The center provides all the other _____ _____.

M: Perfect. Thanks for the information.

09

W: Good afternoon, residents. This is the _____ of the Pineville Community Center. We're holding the Summer Flea Market for one week. It'll be held in the _____ _____ of Pineville Middle School. You can get many different kinds of items such as toys and candles at reasonable prices. You can also sell any of _____ _____ _____ _____ if they are in good condition. On the first day, every resident visiting the market will _____ _____ _____ _____ as a gift. For more information, please check out the community center's website.

10

W: Kyle, I'm looking for some sneakers. Can you help me find some good ones?

M: Of course. Let me see... [Pause] Look. These are the five best-selling ones.

W: Wow, they all look so cool. It's hard to choose among them.

M: Well, _____ _____

_____?

W: I don't want to spend more than 80 dollars.

M: All right. Which style do you want, active or casual?

W: I _____ casual ones. I think they match my clothes better.

M: Good. And I'd like to recommend _____ shoes for rainy days.

W: Okay, I will take your advice.

M: So you have two options left. Which color do you prefer?

W: Most of my shoes are black, so I'll buy _____ _____ this time.

M: You made a good choice.

11

W: Justin, what are you reading?

M: An advertisement. There's a special event at Will's Bookstore downtown.

W: _____ _____ _____

_____ is it?

M: (All children's books are 20% off.)

12

M: You look so _____. What's wrong, Liz?

W: I didn't do well on my presentation yesterday.

M: Sorry about that. To help _____

_____ _____ _____ of

it, how about having a nice meal?

W: (Okay. Good food always makes me feel better.)

13

M: Jenny, what class do you want to take this summer vacation?

W: Well, [Pause] I'm _____ _____ the guitar class.

M: Cool! I'm interested in playing the guitar, too.

W: Really? It would be exciting if we _____

_____ _____ _____.

M: I know, but I am thinking of taking a math class instead. I didn't do well on the final exam.

W: Oh, there is a math class? I didn't know that.

M: Yes. Mrs. Kim said she is _____ a math class for first graders.

W: That might be a good chance to improve my skills, too. _____ _____

_____ _____ the schedule for

the math class?

M: (You can find it on the school website.)

14

M: Hi, Claire! How are you doing?

W: I'm good. You're looking great!

M: Thanks. _____ _____

_____ _____ these days.

W: I need to start working out, too. What kind of exercise do you do?

M: I do yoga and some _____ at home.

W: At home? Do you exercise alone?

M: Yes and no. I exercise online _____

_____ _____.

W: Exercising online with others? What do you mean by that?

M: I'm taking an online _____

_____. We work out together on the

Internet every evening at 7.

W: (That sounds great. Can I join the course, too?)

15

M: Ted is a high school student. He is _____ _____ _____ _____ school president this year. He really wants to win the election. He thinks using posters is _____ _____ _____ to make a strong impression on his schoolmates. But he is not good at _____. His friend, Monica, is a member of a drawing club and she is good at drawing. So, he wants to ask her to _____ _____ _____ _____. In this situation, what would Ted most likely say to Monica?

Ted: (Can you help me make posters for the election?)

16~17

W: Good morning, _____. This is your host Rachel at the Morning Radio Show. What do you eat for breakfast? Today I will introduce a _____ _____ _____ _____. Eggs are an excellent choice because they are high in protein. High-protein foods such as eggs provide energy for the brain. _____ is another good option. It reduces hunger so it supports _____ _____. Yogurt is also great to eat in the morning. It contains probiotics that can improve digestion. _____ _____ such as blueberries or strawberries is another perfect way to start the morning. They are _____ _____ _____ than most other fruits, but higher in fiber. Add them to yogurt for a tasty breakfast. Start every day with a healthy meal. Thank you.

16

2022년 9월 학력평가
딕테이션

MP3

2SBL1_A16

😊 녹음을 듣고, 빈칸에 알맞은 말을 쓰시기 바랍니다. 빈칸은 문제풀이에 핵심이 되는 키워드와 헷갈리기 쉬운 발음에 표시되어 있으니 이 점에 유의하여 듣기 바랍니다.

01

W: Good evening, Vermont citizens. I'm Elizabeth Bowen, the _____ of the Vermont City Library. I'd like to tell you about our online 15-Minute Book Reading program. This program is designed to help your children _____ _____ _____ _____ at home. Every day, individual tutoring is provided for 15 minutes. It's _____ _____ to your child's reading level! Don't hesitate to sign up your children for this amazing opportunity to _____ their reading habits! For more information, please visit the Vermont City Library. Thank you.

02

M: Clara, why the _____ _____?

W: Aw, Dad, I bought this hair dryer, but the cool air mode doesn't work.

M: Where did you get it?

W: I bought it second-hand online.

M: Did you check the condition before you ordered it?

W: I did, but I _____ _____ _____ _____ that said the cool air mode doesn't work.

M: Oh dear. It's important to check all the details when you buy second-hand items.

W: You're right. I was just so excited because it was _____ _____ than other hair dryers.

M: Some second-hand items are almost like new, but others are not. So, you should _____ _____ _____ of the item carefully.

W: Thanks, Dad. I'll keep that in mind.

03

M: Hello, Ms. Adams! It's been a while since you were here.

W: Last time I came, you told me I should _____ _____ _____ every year.

M: That's right. When did you last visit us?

W: I guess I came here last October.

M: Okay. Then, let me check your vision. Please sit here. [Pause] Hmm... your _____ got a little worse.

W: Yeah, maybe it's because I've been working on a computer for too long.

M: Actually, the blue light from computers and smartphones makes your eyes tired.

W: Really? Is there a lens that _____ _____ _____?

M: Sure. You can wear these blue light blocking lenses.

W: That sounds perfect. But I'd like to _____ _____ _____ again.

M: No problem, you can just change the lenses. You can come pick them up in a week.

W: Okay, thank you so much. See you then.

04

W: Carl, what are you looking at?

M: Oh, hi, Amy. Come take a look. It's a picture of my grandparents' house. I was there last weekend.

W: What a beautiful house! There's even a

_____ _____

_____!

M: Yes, my grandfather dug it himself. And how about that flower-patterned tablecloth?

W: I love it. It makes the table look cozy.

M: Did you see the _____ _____

_____ _____ on the door?

W: Oh! Did you paint that?

M: Yeah, I did it when I was 8 years old.

W: It's cute. And there are two windows

_____ _____ _____.

M: Right, we get a lot of sunlight through the windows.

W: I like that! And can you still _____

_____ _____ next to the house?

M: Of course. That's the best spot to see the sunset.

W: Wow, your grandparents' house looks like a nice place!

05

M: Honey, there's a box in the doorway. What is it?

W: I _____ _____ _____ online. Would you bring it in?

M: Sure. Is this for the house-warming party today?

W: Yeah. Since I had to have my car repaired, I couldn't go shopping yesterday.

M: Sorry, I _____ _____ you to the market.

W: That's okay. You worked late to meet the deadline for your report. Would you open the box for me?

M: Sure. [Pause] Oh no, some eggs are broken! Have a look.

W: Ah... that's never happened before.

M: Why don't we _____ _____

_____ _____ about it?

W: Okay. I'll do it right now.

M: While you do that, I'll put the other

_____ _____ _____

_____.

W: Thanks.

06

W: Hello, welcome to Kelly's Bake Shop. How can I help you?

M: Hi, I'd like to order a carrot cake.

W: Okay, we have two sizes. A small one is $25 and a large one is $_____. Which one would you like?

M: Well, we're four people, so _____

_____ _____ would be good.

W: Great. Do you need candles?

M: No thanks, but can you write on the cake?

W: We can. It costs $5. What would you like the

_____ _____ _____?

M: Please write "Thank You Mom" on it.

W: Sure. It takes about half an hour. Is that okay?

M: No problem. Can I use this 10% off coupon?

W: Certainly. You get 10% _____

_____ _____.

M: Thanks. Here's my credit card.

07

M: Anna, I haven't seen you use this bag before. Did you buy a new one?

W: Hi, Jason. Yeah, I _____ _____ _____ last week.

M: I saw some celebrities posting about it on their _____ _____.

W: Really? I didn't know that, but this bag seems to be popular.

M: It does, but its design isn't that unique. It's _____ _____.

W: Yeah, and it's a little expensive compared to other bags.

M: Well, then why did you buy it?

W: I bought it because it's _____ _____ _____ _____.

M: Oh, you're a responsible consumer.

W: Exactly. So, I'm recommending it to all my friends.

M: Good idea. I'll check the website for more information.

08

W: Jimmy, what are you doing with your smartphone?

M: I'm _____ _____ _____ _____ about the Youth Street Dance Contest.

W: Oh, isn't it a street dance contest for high school students?

M: Yeah. Why don't you enter? I know you're good at dancing.

W: Hmm... when is it?

M: The competition is October 22nd, but the _____ _____ _____ is September 30th.

W: Okay, good. I have a few months to practice.

M: And look! The _____ _____ $2,000!

W: That's amazing! What types of dancing are there?

M: It says participants should choose one of these three types: hip-hop, locking, and breakdancing.

W: I'm really into breakdancing lately, so I'll enter with that. How do I apply?

M: You just _____ _____ _____ form from the website and submit it by email.

W: Okay! It'll be a great experience for me to try out.

09

M: Hello, Lakewoods High School students! I'm Lawrence Cho, president of the student council. I'm happy to _____ a special new event to reduce waste around our school: Lakewoods Plogging! Since plogging is the activity of _____ _____ _____ while running, all participants should wear workout clothes and sneakers. We provide eco-friendly bags for the trash, so you don't _____ _____ _____ _____. The event will be held on October 1st from 7 a.m. to 9 a.m. You can sign up for the event on the school website starting tomorrow. The _____ _____ _____ will get a pair of sports socks. For more information, please visit our school website. Don't miss this fun opportunity!

10

M: Honey, what are you doing?

W: I'm looking at a website to order a _____ heater for winter camping. Would you like to choose one together?

M: Sure, let me see.

W: We should be able to carry it easily, so _____ _____ is important. I think we should get one of these under 4kg.

M: Good point. Oh, this one is pretty expensive.

W: I know. Let's choose one of these for less than $100.

M: Okay. And I think _____ _____ _____ would be good. What do you think?

W: I agree. It's safer to use.

M: Now we have these two models left.

W: I'd like the one with a five-star _____ _____.

M: All right. Let's order this one.

11

W: Kevin, is this bike yours?

M: Yes, I bought it for my bike tour.

W: Really? _____ _____ _____ _____ to go?

M: (I haven't decided the place, yet.)

12

[Telephone rings.]

M: Hello, this is Ashley's Dental Clinic. How may I help you?

W: Hello, this is Emily Gibson. _____ _____ _____ the dentist today? I have a terrible toothache.

M: Just a second. Let me check. [Pause] He's _____ at 4:30 this afternoon.

W: (Great. I'll be there at that time.)

13

W: Hey, Justin. Do you know where those students are going?

M: They're probably _____ _____ _____ _____ to practice badminton.

W: Why are so many students practicing badminton?

M: Haven't you heard about the School Badminton Tournament? Many of the students have already signed up for it.

W: Really? Why is it so popular?

M: The winners will get a big scholarship and there are _____ _____ _____ _____ as well.

W: That's nice! Why don't you sign up for it, too?

M: I'd like to, but only _____ can participate. And I haven't found a partner, yet.

W: Actually, I used to be a badminton player in my elementary school.

M: Wow! I have a top expert right here! How about _____ _____ _____?

W: Sure. Not an expert, but I can try.

M: (Fantastic! We'll be a really good team.)

14

M: Hey, Natalie. What are you doing on your computer?

W: Hi, Dave. I'm working on my presentation for social studies class. It's about _____ games in Asia.

M: Sounds interesting. Can I see it?

W: Sure. I'll introduce some games with these pictures.

M: That's a great idea, but I think you have too many words on the slides.

W: You're right. I'm worried it might be boring.

M: Then, how about _____ _____ _____ and using some questions? It would make your presentation more interesting.

W: Great idea! What do you think about _____ _____?

M: That's good. Your audience will be able to focus on your presentation while thinking about the answers.

W: But... what if they don't know the answers?

M: It doesn't matter. They'll _____ _____ just doing it.

W: (Okay. I'll make some questions right away.)

15

W: Steven is a high school student and Ms. Olson is a _____ _____ at his school. Steven has much interest in the video game industry. A few days ago, Ms. Olson recommended a book written by a CEO who runs a famous gaming company. After reading the book, Steven told her that the CEO is his _____ _____. This morning, Ms. Olson hears the news that the CEO is going to have a _____ at a bookstore nearby. She thinks Steven would love to meet his role model _____ _____. So, Ms. Olson wants to tell Steven that he should go see the CEO at the event. In this situation, what would Ms. Olson most likely say to Steven?

Ms. Olson: (How about going to your role model's book-signing?)

16~17

M: Hello, students. Last class, we took a brief look at how to tune your musical instruments. Today, we're going to talk a bit about how to _____ _____ _____ and maintain your instruments. First, let's take flutes. They may have moisture from the _____ _____ _____ them, so you should clean and wipe the mouth piece before and after playing. Next are _____. They can be taken apart, so you should air dry the parts in a cool dry place, _____ _____ _____ sunlight. And as for pianos, they don't need everyday care, but it's _____ to protect the keys by covering them with a protective pad when not in use. The last ones are string instruments like _____. Their strings need replacement. When you replace the strings, it's good to do it gradually, one at a time. Proper care can _____ _____ _____ of your musical instruments. I hope this lesson helps you to keep your musical instruments safe from damage.

17

2022년 11월 학력평가
딕테이션

MP3

🔊 녹음을 듣고, 빈칸에 알맞은 말을 쓰시기 바랍니다. 빈칸은 문제풀이에 핵심이 되는 키워드와 헷갈리기 쉬운 발음에 표시되어 있으니 이 점에 유의하여 듣기 바랍니다.

01

[Chime bell rings.]

M: Good morning. This is Ethan Cooper from the Reindeer Mountain maintenance office. Last night, we had 20cm of _____ _____. Most of the snow melted away with the sun out in the morning, but some of it froze in the shade. For hikers' safety, _____ _____ some of the trails covered with ice. At this moment, Sunrise Trail and Lakeview Trail are _____ _____ hikers. I'll make an announcement later when the trails are _____ _____ _____ _____. Until then, keep in mind that Sunrise Trail and Lakeview Trail are closed. Thank you.

02

M: Honey, what are you doing?

W: I'm looking for the _____ _____. Do you know where they are?

M: They're in the first drawer. Why do you need them?

W: The recipe says four teaspoons of sugar.

M: Dear, you don't have to follow the recipe _____ _____ _____.

W: What do you mean?

M: A recipe is just an example. You don't need to add the same amount of ingredients as stated in the recipe.

W: Hmm. Right. Sometimes the food is _____ _____ when I cook based on the recipe instructions.

M: See? You don't need to _____ _____ the recipe.

W: Okay. I'll remember that.

03

[Door knocks.]

W: Can I come in?

M: Yes. Oh, Ms. Smith. Did you read the email I sent?

W: I did. I liked your _____ _____. The characters exploring space were very mysterious. How did you create the characters?

M: Actually, old science fiction movies _____ _____ _____ _____ those characters.

W: Interesting. Now, could you describe the main character more specifically? It'll be helpful _____ _____ _____ the theme song for the character.

M: Well, he's a thrill seeker. So, a strong, bold, and rhythmic sound would suit him.

W: Okay. Do you need anything else?

M: I also want you to make some _____ _____.

W: Of course. When do you need them?

M: By December 21st. I'd like to start putting the music into the game by then.

W: All right. Then I'll talk to you later.

04

M: Hi, Chelsea. Did you finish your _____ _____?

W: Oh, my dream room drawing? Yes. Here's the picture.

M: Wow, it's so creative. There is a staircase next to the door.

W: Yes. I've always dreamed of a room with two floors. Look at the three _____ _____ above the staircase.

M: They look very stylish. And I like the flower picture above the sofa. It'll bring warmth to your room.

W: Thanks. Check out the _____ _____ on the floor.

M: It goes well with this place. Oh, there is a bookshelf by the sofa.

W: You're right. I want to keep my favorite books _____.

M: That's a good idea.

05

W: Jamie, is the cartoon artist on her way?

M: Yes. She'll arrive at our studio in an hour.

W: Perfect. Let's check if we have everything ready for our talk show.

M: Okay. I _____ _____ _____ _____ for our guest yesterday.

W: Great. And I bought a drink and put it on the table.

M: Good. Did you prepare a pencil? The artist said she'll _____ caricatures of us during the live show.

W: Oh, she told me that she'll bring her own pencil.

M: She did? Then we don't need it.

W: Yeah. By the way, _____ _____ _____?

M: Oops. I left it in my car. I'll go get it right now.

W: Fine. Then _____ _____ the microphones.

M: Thanks.

06

M: Welcome to Crispy Fried Chicken. What would you like to order?

W: What kind of chicken do you have?

M: We only have two kinds. Fried chicken is $_____ and barbecue chicken is $20.

W: I'll have one fried and one barbecue chicken.

M: Okay. Would you like some _____ _____ with your order? They're our most popular side dish.

W: How much are they?

M: _____ _____ of potato chips is $2.

W: Then I'll get one basket.

M: Will that be all?

W: Yes. And can I use this coupon for a free soda?

M: Of course. You can _____ _____ soda from the fridge.

W: Great. Here's my credit card.

07

[Cell phone rings.]

W: Leo, I'm sorry I _____ your call. What's up?

M: Well, I just called to tell you that I can't go ice fishing with you this weekend.

W: Oh, no. I heard the weather will be perfect this weekend.

M: I'm sorry. I really wish I could go.

W: Didn't you say you're off from work this weekend?

M: I am. It's not because of work. Actually, I _____ _____ _____.

W: That's terrible. Are you okay?

M: Don't worry. I'll be fine.

W: How did you _____ _____?

M: I was playing basketball with a friend and sprained my wrist.

W: Did you go to the hospital?

M: I did. The _____ _____ _____ that it'll be better in a month.

W: That's good. I hope you feel better soon.

08

M: Honey, look at this flyer about Kids' Pottery Class.

W: Okay. Let's take a look.

M: I think our little Austin would love to _____ _____ _____ cereal bowl.

W: I think so, too. It says that the class is held on _____ _____. We can take him there on that day.

M: Great. And it's held in Pottery Village. It's a 10-minute drive from our home.

W: That's so close. And check out the price. The class _____ _____ $15.

M: That's reasonable. We should sign up. How can we register for the class?

W: It says you can simply scan the QR code to _____ online.

M: Okay. Let's do it right away.

09

W: Hello, listeners. The most interesting music _____ is back! You can now sign up for the 2022 Online Whistling Championship. You can select any song that you like, but note that the length of your whistling video is _____ _____ three minutes. To enter the competition, you must upload your video on our website by December 4th. When recording your whistling, be sure to turn off the echo effect on the microphone. _____ _____ _____ by public online voting. The result will be announced on our website. We look forward to your _____ participation.

10

M: Honey, I'm looking at a shopping site to choose curtains for our bedroom. But there are too many options to consider.

W: Okay. Let's pick one together.

M: I don't think we _____ _____ more than $100.

W: I agree. Let's drop this one. And some of them are _____ _____ at home.

M: Fantastic. We won't have to pay for dry cleaning all the time.

W: Good for us. Let's cross out this one then. What about a blackout option?

M: We definitely need it. It'll _____ _____ _____, so we won't be disturbed. And which color do you like?

W: I don't mind any color _____ _____ _____.

M: Okay. Then we narrowed it down to one.

W: Well then, let's choose this one.

11

M: Excuse me. Is this really the line for the rollercoaster?

W: Yes. This is the line for the _____.

M: Oh, no. I can't believe it. There are so many people standing in line. _____ _____ _____ _____ been waiting here?

W: (I've been waiting for 30 minutes.)

12

W: Chris, what are you looking at?

M: A little boy is crying and _____ around the park. He's all by himself.

W: Oh, I see him, too. We should ask him _____ _____ _____.

M: (Okay. Let's see if he needs our help.)

13

M: Hi, Ava.

W: Hi, Samuel. Are you all set for the job interview?

M: I'm still working on it. _____ _____ _____ _____ a list of questions the interviewer might ask.

W: Good job. Preparing answers to those questions will help you for the interview.

M: But I think I'm not ready.

W: Hmm. Have you thought about how you'll make a _____ _____ _____?

M: Could you be more specific?

W: You know a smile makes you look confident. Also, people usually _____ _____ to give a favorable impression.

M: That's a good point.

W: I believe you'll get a good interview result with a proper presentation of yourself.

M: Okay. Then I'm going to _____ _____ and look for my best suit.

W: (Good. Your effort will give a good impression on the interviewer.)

14

W: Excuse me.

M: Yes, ma'am. How can I help you?

W: How much are those shoes?

M: They're $60. But today only, _____ _____ a 30% discount.

W: That's a good price. Do you have a size six?

M: Sure. Here they are. Take a seat here and try them on.

W: Thank you. *[Pause]* Well, these shoes are _____ _____ _____ for me. Can I get a size six and a half?

M: I'm sorry. That size in this color is _____ _____.

W: Do you have these shoes in a different color?

M: Let me check. *[Typing sounds]* We have red and green in storage.

W: A green pair sounds good. I want to _____ _____ _____.

M: (Please wait. I'll be back with the shoes in a minute.)

15

M: Amelia is a high school student. She is working on a psychology project. She thinks that an interview with an _____ _____ _____ _____ will make her project even better. She emails Professor Jacob, who is a _____ psychology professor. Even though he's busy, she manages to set up an interview with him. Unfortunately, on that morning, she eats a sandwich and feels sick. She knows this interview is important, and _____ _____ _____ _____ again. But she can't go meet him because of a severe stomachache. So she wants to ask him if he can _____ their meeting. In this situation, what would Amelia most likely say to Professor Jacob?

Amelia: (Would it be possible to change our appointment?)

16~17

W: Good morning, students. These days we can _____ _____ _____ to each other using phones or computers. However, communication has not always been as simple as it is today. Here are _____ _____ _____ people in the past used to carry their messages. First, some tribes used a _____ _____. They were able to send warnings or important information by varying the pitch or beat. Next, other people used _____ to send messages over long distances. For example, our ancestors used smoke to signal attacks from enemies. Third, a pigeon was a _____ _____ of communication. It always found its way home with messages attached to its legs. Finally, a _____ was one of the most efficient ways to communicate. The horse with a messenger on its back _____ _____ more quickly than runners. Now you may understand the ways of sending messages back in the old days. Then let's take a look in detail at each communication method.

18 2023년 3월 학력평가
딕테이션

녹음을 듣고, 빈칸에 알맞은 말을 쓰시기 바랍니다. 빈칸은 문제풀이에 핵심이 되는 키워드와 헷갈리기 쉬운 발음에 표시되어 있으니 이 점에 유의하여 듣기 바랍니다.

01

M: Hello, Villeford High School students. This is principal Aaron Clark. _____

_____ _____ _____

of the Villeford ice hockey team, I'm very excited about the upcoming National High School Ice Hockey League. As you all know, the _____ _____ will be held in the Central Rink at 6 p.m. this Saturday. I want as many of you _____ _____

_____ _____ and cheer our team to victory. I've seen them put in _____ _____ _____

of effort to win the league. It will help them play better just to see you there cheering for them. I really hope to see you at the rink. Thank you.

02

W: Honey, are you okay?

M: I'm afraid _____ _____ a cold. I've got a sore throat.

W: Why don't you go see a doctor?

M: Well, I don't think it's necessary. I've found some medicine in the cabinet. I'll take it.

W: You shouldn't take that medicine. That's what I _____ _____ last week.

M: My symptoms are similar to yours.

W: Honey, you shouldn't take medicine prescribed _____ _____.

M: It's just a cold. I'll get better if I take your medicine.

W: It _____ _____ _____ to take someone else's prescription.

M: Okay. Then I'll go see a doctor this afternoon.

03

W: Hi, Mr. Thomson. How are your _____ going?

M: You arrived at the right time. I have something to tell you.

W: Okay. What is it?

M: Well, I'm afraid that we have to _____ _____ _____ _____ for your paintings.

W: May I ask why?

M: Sure. We have some electrical problems there.

W: I see. Then where are you going to exhibit _____ _____?

M: Our gallery is going to exhibit your paintings in the _____ _____.

W: Okay. Can I see the hall now?

M: Sure. Come with me.

04

M: Hi, Grace. What are you looking at on your phone?

W: Hi, James. It's a photo I took when I did some volunteer work. We painted pictures on a street wall.

M: Let me see. Wow, I like the whale with the _____ _____.

W: I like it, too. How do you like the house under the whale?

M: It's beautiful. What are these _____ _____ _____?

W: You can take a picture sitting there. The painting becomes the background.

M: Oh, I see. Look at this tree! It has _____ _____.

W: That's right. We named it the Love Tree.

M: The _____ _____ the tree branch is lovely, too.

W: I hope a lot of people enjoy the painting.

05

M: Hi, Stella. How are you doing these days?

W: Hi, Ryan. I've been _____ _____ my granddad with his concert. He made a rock band with his friends.

M: There must be a lot of things to do.

W: Yeah. I _____ _____ _____ for the concert yesterday.

M: What about posters and tickets?

W: Well, I've just finished designing a poster.

M: Then I think I can help you.

W: Really? How?

M: Actually, I have a music blog. I think I can _____ the poster there.

W: That's great!

M: Just send the poster to me, and I'll _____ _____ _____.

W: Thanks a lot.

06

M: Good morning. How may I help you?

W: Hi. I want to buy a coffee pot.

M: Okay. You can choose from these coffee pots.

W: I like this one. How much is it?

M: It was originally $60, but it's _____ _____ _____ $50.

W: Okay, I'll buy it. I'd also like to buy this _____ _____.

M: Actually, it comes in two sizes. This smaller one is $_____ and a bigger one is $30.

W: The smaller one would be easier to _____ _____. I'll buy two smaller ones.

M: All right. Is there anything else you need?

W: No, that's all. Thank you.

M: Okay. How would you like to pay?

W: I'll pay by credit card. Here you are.

07

[Cell phone rings.]

W: Hi, Brian.

M: Hi, Mom. I'm in line to get on the plane.

W: Okay. By the way, did you _____ _____ the duty free shop in the airport?

M: Yes, but I couldn't buy the wallet you asked me to buy.

W: Did you forget the _____ _____?

M: No. I remembered that. I took a memo.

W: Then did you arrive late at the airport?

M: No, I had enough time to shop.

W: Then why couldn't you buy the wallet?

M: Actually, because they were _____ _____ _____.

W: Oh, really?

M: Yeah. The wallet must be very popular.

W: Okay. _____ _____ _____ anyway.

08

M: Lucy, look at this.

W: Wow. It's about the Youth Choir Audition.

M: Yes. It's open to _____ _____ 13 to 18.

W: I'm interested in joining the choir. When is it?

M: April 2nd, from 9 a.m. to 5 p.m.

W: The place for the audition is the Youth Training Center. It's really _____ _____ here.

M: I think you should leave early in the morning.

W: That's no problem. Is there _____ _____ _____?

M: No, it's free.

W: Good. I'll apply for the audition.

M: Then you should _____ _____ _____ _____ form on this website.

W: All right. Thanks.

09

W: Hello, Rosehill High School students! I'm your school counselor, Ms. Lee. I'm so _____ _____ _____ a special event, the 2023 Career Week. It'll be held from May 22nd for five days. There will be many programs to help you explore various future jobs. Please kindly _____ that the number of participants for each program is limited to 20. A _____ _____ on future career choices will be presented on the first day. _____ _____ on May 10th. For more information, please visit our school website. I hope you can come and enjoy the 2023 Career Week!

10

M: Jessica, what are you doing?

W: I'm trying to buy one of these five frying pans.

M: Let me see. This frying pan seems pretty expensive.

W: Yeah. I don't want to spend more than $_____.

M: Okay. And I think 9 to 12-inch frying pans will work for most of your cooking.

W: I think so, too. An 8-inch frying pan _____ _____ _____ for me.

M: What about the material? Stainless steel pans are good for fast cooking.

W: I know, but they are _____. I'll buy an aluminum pan.

M: Then you have two options left. Do you _____ _____ _____?

W: Of course. A lid keeps the oil from splashing. I'll buy this one.

M: Good choice.

11

M: Have you finished your team's short-movie _____?

W: Not yet. I'm still editing the video clip.

M: Oh, you edit? _____ _____ _____ _____ to do that?

W: (I learned it by myself through books.)

12

[Cell phone rings.]

W: Daddy, are you still working now?

M: No, Emma. I'm _____ _____ get in my car and drive home.

W: Great. Can you _____ _____ _____ _____? I'm at the City Library near your office.

M: (All right. I'll come pick you up now.)

13

M: Claire, how's your farm doing?

W: Great! I _____ some cherry tomatoes and cucumbers last weekend. Do you want some?

M: Of course. I'd like some very much.

W: Okay. I'll bring you some tomorrow.

M: Thanks. Are you going to the farm this weekend too?

W: Yes. The peppers are _____ _____ to be picked.

M: Can I go with you? I'd like to look around your farm and _____ _____ _____ the peppers.

W: Sure. It would be fun to work on the farm together.

M: Sounds nice. Is there anything I _____ _____ _____?

W: (Just wear comfortable clothes and shoes.)

14

W: Daniel, what's wrong?

M: Hi, Leila. I _____ _____ _____ with Olivia.

W: Was it serious?

M: I'm not sure, but I think I made a mistake.

W: So that's why you have a long face.

M: Yeah. I want to get along with her, but she's still angry at me.

W: Did you say you're sorry to her?

M: Well, I _____ _____ _____ that I'm sorry.

W: I don't think it's a good idea to express your _____ _____ a text message.

M: Do you think so? Now I know why I haven't received any response from her yet.

W: I think it'd be best to go and talk to her _____ _____.

M: (You're right. I'll meet her and apologize.)

15

M: Ted and John are _____ _____. They are climbing Green Diamond Mountain together. Now they have reached the campsite near the mountain top. After climbing the mountain all day, they have a _____ time at the campsite. While drinking coffee, Ted suggests to John that they _____ _____ _____ at the mountain top the next morning. John thinks it's a good idea. So, now John wants to ask Ted how early they _____ _____ _____ to see the sunrise. In this situation, what would John most likely say to Ted?

John: (What time should we get up tomorrow morning?)

16~17

W: Good morning, everyone. Do you spend a lot of time with your family? One of the best ways to spend time with your family is to _____ _____ together. Today, I will share some of the best sports that _____ _____ _____ together. The first one is badminton. The whole family can enjoy the sport with _____ _____. The second one is basketball. You can easily find a basketball court near your house. The third one is _____ _____. It can be played indoors anytime. The last one is _____. Many families have a great time playing it together. When you go home today, how about playing one of these sports with your family?

19

2023년 6월 학력평가
딕테이션

MP3

2SBL1_A19

녹음을 듣고, 빈칸에 알맞은 말을 쓰기 바랍니다. 빈칸은 문제풀이에 핵심이 되는 키워드와 헷갈리기 쉬운 발음에 표시되어 있으니 이 점에 유의하여 듣기 바랍니다.

01

W: Good afternoon, everybody. This is your student council president, Monica Brown. Our school's _____ _____ _____ will be held on the last day of the semester. For the competition, we _____ _____ _____ to help set up computers. If you're interested in helping us make the competition successful, please _____ _____ the volunteer application form and email it to me. For more _____, please visit our school website. I hope many of you will join us. Thank you for listening.

02

M: Hannah, how's your design project going?

W: Hey, Aiden. I'm still working on it, but I'm not making much _____.

M: Can you tell me what the problem is?

W: Hmm... [Pause] It's hard to think of creative ideas. I feel like I'm wasting my time.

M: I understand. Why don't you _____ _____ _____?

W: How can that help me to improve my creativity?

M: It will actually make your brain more active. Then you'll _____ _____ _____.

W: But I don't have time for that.

M: You don't need a lot of time. Even a short walk will help you to _____ _____ _____ creative ideas.

W: Then I'll try it. Thanks for the tip.

03

W: Excuse me. Could you please tell me where I can put this box?

M: Right here on this counter. How can I help you today?

W: I'd like to send this to Jeju Island.

M: Sure. Are there any _____ _____ in the box?

W: No, there are only clothes in it.

M: Then, there should be no problem.

W: I see. What's the _____ _____ to send it?

M: You can send the package by express mail, but there's _____ _____ _____.

W: That's okay. I want it to be delivered as soon as possible. When will it arrive in Jeju if it goes out today?

M: If you send it today, it will be there by this Friday.

W: Oh, Friday will be great. I'll _____ _____ _____ _____.

04

M: Kayla, I heard you went busking on the street last weekend.

W: It was amazing! I've got a picture here. Look!

M: Oh, you're _____ _____ _____ I gave you.

W: Yeah, I really like it.

M: Looks great. This boy playing the _____ _____ _____ you must be your brother Kevin.

W: You're right. He played while I sang.

M: Cool. Why did you leave the guitar case open?

W: That's for the audience. If they like our performance, they give us some money.

M: Oh, and you _____ _____ _____ _____!

W: I did. I recently bought them.

M: I see. And did you design that _____ _____ _____ _____?

W: Yeah. My brother and I worked on it together.

M: It sounds like you really had a lot of fun!

05

W: Honey, are we ready for Jake's birthday party tomorrow?

M: I sent the _____ cards last week. What about other things?

W: I'm not sure. Let's check.

M: We are _____ a lot of guests. How about the dinner menu?

W: I haven't decided yet.

M: We won't have much time to cook, so let's just order pizza.

W: Okay. I'll do it tomorrow. What about the present?

M: Oh, you _____ _____ _____? I forgot to get it!

W: That's alright. Can you go to the electronics store and _____ _____ _____?

M: No problem. I'll do it right away.

W: Good. Then, I'll clean up the living room while you're out.

06

M: Good morning! How can I help you?

W: Hi. I'm looking for a blanket and some cushions _____ _____ _____.

M: Okay. We've got some on sale. Would you like to have a look?

W: Yes. How much is this green blanket?

M: That's $_____.

W: Oh, I love the color green. Can you also show me some cushions that _____ _____ _____ this blanket?

M: Sure! How about these?

W: They look good. I need two of them. How much are they?

M: The cushions are $20 each.

W: Okay. I'll take one green blanket and two cushions. Can I use this coupon?

M: Sure. _____ _____ _____ _____ 10% off the total.

W: Thanks! Here's my credit card.

07

W: Hello, Justin. What are you doing?

M: Hi, Ellie. I'm doing my _____ _____ _____ _____.

W: Can you go to a rock concert with me this Saturday? My sister gave me two tickets!

M: I'd love to! [Pause] But _____ _____ I can't.

W: Do you have to work that day?

M: No, I don't work on Saturdays.

W: Then, why not? I thought you really like rock music.

M: Of course I do. But I have to _____ _____ _____ my friend's dog this Saturday.

W: Oh, really? Is your friend going somewhere?

M: He's visiting his grandmother that day.

W: Okay, no problem. I'm sure I can find _____ _____ to go with me.

08

W: Scott, did you see this Eco Day poster?

M: No, not yet. Let me see. [Pause] It's an event for _____ _____ _____ while walking around a park.

W: Why don't we do it together? It's next Sunday from 10 a.m. to 5 p.m.

M: Sounds good. I've been thinking a lot about the environment lately.

W: Me, too. Also, the event will _____ _____ _____ Eastside Park.

You know, we often used to go there.

M: That's great. Oh, look at this. We have to _____ _____ _____ _____ and small bags for the trash.

W: No problem. I have extra. I can bring some for you as well.

M: Okay, thanks. Do we have to _____ _____ _____ the event?

W: Yes. The poster says we can do it online.

M: Let's do it right now. I'm looking forward to it.

09

M: Hello, Eastville High School students. This is your P.E. teacher, Mr. Wilson. I'm pleased to let you know that _____ _____ the first Eastville Dance Contest. Any Eastville students who love dancing can participate in the contest as a team. _____ _____ _____ dance are allowed. If you'd like to participate, please upload your team's dance video to our school website by August 15th. Students can _____ _____ their favorite video from August 16th to 20th. The winning team will _____ _____ _____ as a prize. Don't miss this great opportunity to show off your talents!

10

M: Honey, we need a water purifier for our new house.

W: You're right. Let's order one online.

M: Good idea. *[Clicking Sound]* Look! These are the five bestsellers.

W: I see. _____ _____ _____?

M: Well, I don't want to spend more than 800 dollars.

W: Okay, how about the water tank _____?

M: I think the five-liter tank would be perfect for us.

W: I think so, too. And I like the ones with a _____ _____.

M: Okay, then we can save electricity. Now, there are just two options left.

W: Let's look at the _____. The longer, the better.

M: I agree. We should order this model.

11

M: Let's get inside. I'm so excited to see this auto show.

W: Look over there. _____ _____ _____ are already standing in line to buy tickets.

M: Fortunately, I bought our tickets _____ _____.

W: (Great. We don't have to wait in line.)

12

W: Hi, Chris. Did you check your _____ for the history test we took last week?

M: Yes. But I think there's something wrong with my grade.

W: Don't you think you _____ _____ _____ Mr. Morgan about it?

M: (Right. I should go to his office now.)

13

M: Mom, did you write this note?

W: What's that?

M: I found this in the book you gave me.

W: Oh, the one I bought for you at the _____ _____ last week?

M: Yes. At first I thought it was a bookmark, but it wasn't. It's a note _____ _____ _____!

W: What does it say?

M: It says, "I hope you enjoy this book."

W: How sweet! That really _____ _____ _____ to my face.

M: Yeah, Mom. I love this message so much.

W: Well, then, why don't we _____ _____ _____ if we resell this book later?

M: (Great idea! Our message would make others smile.)

14

M: Do you have any plans for this weekend, Sandy?

W: Hey, Evan. I'm _____ to go camping with my family.

M: I've never gone before. Do you go camping often?

W: Yes. Two or three times a month at least.

M: That's cool. Why do you like it so much?

W: I like spending time in nature with my family. It makes me _____ _____ to them.

M: I understand. It's like a family hobby, right?

W: Yes, you're right. Camping _____ _____ _____ all my stress, too.

M: Sounds interesting. I'd love to try it.

W: If you go camping with your family, you'll see what I mean.

M: I wish I could, but I _____ _____ _____ _____ for it.

W: (No problem. You can use my equipment.)

15

W: Violet and Peter are classmates. They're doing their _____ _____ _____ together. On Saturday morning, they meet at the public library. They decide to find the books they need in _____ _____ of the library. Violet finds two useful books and tries to check them out. Unfortunately, she _____ _____ that she didn't bring her library card. At that moment, Peter walks up to Violet. So, Violet wants to ask Peter to _____ _____ the books for her because she knows he has his library card. In this situation, what would Violet most likely say to Peter?

Violet: (Can you borrow the books for me with your card?)

16~17

M: Hello, everyone. I'm Shawn Collins, a doctor at Collins Sleep Clinic. Sleep is one of the most essential parts of our daily lives. So today, I'm going to _____ _____ _____ _____ for helping you sleep better. First, kiwi fruits contain a _____ _____ _____ hormones that help you fall asleep more quickly, sleep longer, and wake up less during the night. Second, milk is rich in vitamin D and it _____ _____ _____ and nerves. If you drink a cup of milk before you go to bed, it will definitely help you get a good night's sleep. Third, _____ can help to produce the hormone that controls your internal body clock and _____ _____ for the body to sleep at the right time. The last one is honey. Honey helps you sleep well because it _____ the hormone that keeps the brain awake! Now, I'll show you some delicious diet plans using these foods.

20

2023년 9월 학력평가
딕테이션

MP3
2SBL1_A20

녹음을 듣고, 빈칸에 알맞은 말을 쓰시기 바랍니다. 빈칸은 문제풀이에 핵심이 되는 키워드와 헷갈리기 쉬운 발음에 표시되어 있으니 이 점에 유의하여 듣기 바랍니다.

01

M: Attention, Fargo High School students. This is your music teacher, Mr. Nelson. Our school rock band _____ _____ _____ _____ its concert in the auditorium today. I'm sure you've been looking forward to the concert. Unfortunately, the rain yesterday _____ _____ _____ in the ceiling of the auditorium. The ceiling needs to be fixed, so we decided to _____ _____ _____ of the concert. The rock band will now perform in the school theater. The time for the concert hasn't changed. I hope you'll _____ _____ _____.

02

W: Simon, are you doing anything after school?

M: Nothing special. What about you?

W: I'm planning to _____ _____ _____ _____ in the park. It's a five-kilometer route.

M: The weather is perfect for running. Can I go with you?

W: Why not? [Pause] Wait! You're wearing slippers. Those aren't good for running.

M: It's okay. I can run _____ slippers.

W: No way. Slippers aren't designed for running. You can _____ _____ if you run in them.

M: You mean I need to put on running shoes?

W: You got it. You need to _____ _____ _____ _____ for running.

M: All right. I'll go home and change.

03

M: Good morning, Ms. Clapton. It's nice to meet you.

W: Nice to meet you, too. I'm a _____ _____ _____ _____.

M: You won many awards at the film festival this year. Congratulations!

W: Thank you. I was lucky to work with a great director and talented actors.

M: The clothes and accessories in the movie are impressive. How do you _____ _____ _____ _____?

W: I read the script to fully understand the characters. Then I research the characters' backgrounds.

M: That sounds like a lot of work. Which of the costumes from this film is your favorite?

W: It's hard to _____ _____ _____ because I love all of my designs.

M: I totally understand. Thank you for sharing your story with the readers of _____ _____.

W: It was my pleasure.

04

W: Come look at the new reading room in the library.

M: Wow! It's much better than I thought.

W: Same here. I like the rug in the center of the room.

M: The _____ _____ of the rug makes the room feel warm.

W: I agree. I think putting the sofa _____ _____ _____ was a good idea.

M: Right. We can sit there and read for hours.

W: There's a _____ _____ on the wall.

M: I have the same clock at home. Oh, the bookshelf under the clock is full of books.

W: We can read the books at the long table.

M: Yeah, it looks like a good place to read. The _____ _____ on the table will make it easy to focus.

W: Good lighting is important for reading.

M: I can't wait to start using the reading room.

05

M: Kelly, the school musical is tomorrow. Shall we go over the final checklist together?

W: Let's do it. What's first? [Pause] Oh, the posters. We _____ _____ _____ _____ school last week.

M: Right. Do we have extra batteries for the wireless microphones?

W: Yeah. I bought them yesterday. We should check that the microphones work well with the sound system.

M: I did that this morning. They sound _____.

W: How about the stage _____?

M: They work perfectly. I think everyone will love the lighting design you made.

W: Really? Thanks. It looks like we've finished everything.

M: No, wait. The _____ _____ _____ _____ haven't been arranged yet.

W: You're right! I'll go take care of that now.

M: The musical is going to be fantastic.

06

W: Welcome to Libby's Flowers. How can I help you?

M: _____ _____ _____ _____ a rose basket for my parents' wedding anniversary.

W: All right. Our rose baskets come in two sizes.

M: What are the options?

W: The regular size is 30 dollars, and the _____ _____ _____ _____ dollars.

M: Hmm.... I think the bigger one is better.

W: Good choice. So, you'll get one rose basket in the large size. By the way, we're giving a 10-percent discount _____ _____ _____ this week.

M: Excellent! When will my order be ready?

W: It'll be ready around 11 a.m. If you can't pick it up, we offer a delivery service. It's 10 dollars.

M: Oh, great. I'd like it _____ _____ _____. Here's my credit card.

07

M: You _____ _____ this morning, Olivia.

W: I am. I had to see Professor Martin about my history test.

M: Oh, I see. Do you remember that our club's ski trip is this weekend?

W: Yeah. I heard that a nice ski resort _____ _____ _____ for the trip.

M: I didn't know that. I'm so excited to go skiing at a nice resort.

W: I bet it'll be great, but I don't think I can go this time.

M: Why? You don't work at the cafe on the weekends, do you?

W: No, I don't. But I need to _____ _____ _____ my cat. She's recovering from surgery.

M: Isn't there anyone else who can look after your cat?

W: No one but me. My parents are visiting relatives in Canada. They _____ _____ _____ _____ two weeks.

M: I'm sorry that you can't join us.

W: Me, too. Have fun this weekend.

08

W: What are you doing, Tim?

M: I'm looking at the Street Photography Contest website.

W: I've heard about that. It's a contest for college students, right?

M: Actually, it's _____ _____ high school students, too. Why don't you try it?

W: Really? Maybe I will. Does the contest have a theme?

M: Sure. _____ _____ _____ is Daily Life.

W: That sounds interesting. When is the _____?

M: You have to submit your photographs by September 15th.

W: That's sooner than I expected.

M: You should hurry and choose your photos. The _____ _____ _____ a laptop as a prize.

W: Okay! Wish me luck.

09

M: Hello, listeners. I'm Charlie Anderson from the Twin Stars Chocolate Museum. I'm happy to introduce the Twin Stars Chocolate Day, a special _____ _____ _____ your own delicious chocolates. It'll be held on November 12th from 1 p.m. to 4 p.m. First, you'll listen to a _____ _____ _____ _____ of chocolate. Then you'll have a chance to taste our most popular flavors. At the end of the event, you'll make five chocolates yourself. If you want to take part in the event, you must _____ _____ _____. You can sign up on our website until November 1st. The registration fee is 20 dollars, which _____ _____ _____ of ingredients. Don't miss this sweet opportunity!

10

M: Honey, what are you looking at?

W: I'm looking at indoor cycling bikes. Would you like to choose one together?

M: Sure, let me see. [Pause] The price differs by model.

W: I don't want to _____ _____ _____ _____ dollars. That's too expensive.

M: I agree. Which color do you like?

W: I prefer a dark color because it goes well with our living room.

M: Okay. Then we _____ _____ a white one. What do you think about the foldable one?

W: We definitely need that. It'll take up _____ _____ _____.

M: We have just two options left. Which one should we get?

W: I think we should go with the one with a higher customer rating. The _____ _____ _____ _____ actual customers' experiences.

M: Sounds good. Let's order this one.

11

W: Jason, is that a new sweater? It looks good on you.

M: Thanks. I _____ it online. It was on sale.

W: I'd love to buy the same one for my brother. Can you tell me _____ _____ _____ it?

M: (Sure. I'll send you a link to the website.)

12

M: Becky, did you order _____ _____ for dinner?

W: Yes. I ordered pizza about an hour ago.

M: An hour ago? Delivery usually takes _____ _____ _____ minutes.

W: (I'll call the restaurant and check our order.)

13

W: I _____ _____ _____ in the cafeteria this week. Where have you been?

M: I've been in the library working on my science project.

W: Does that mean you've been skipping lunch?

M: Yeah. This project is really _____ _____ _____ _____.

W: You shouldn't do that. It's not good for your health.

M: Don't worry. I always have a big dinner when I get home.

W: That's the problem. _____ _____ makes you overeat later.

M: I hadn't thought of that. Then what should I do?

W: It's simple. You should _____ _____ to stay healthy.

M: (You're right. I won't skip meals anymore.)

14

M: Excuse me, Ms. Lopez. Can I ask you something?

W: Sure, Tony. What can I do for you?

M: I want to do better in Spanish, but I don't know _____ _____ _____.

W: You seem to do well during class. Do you study when you're at home?

M: I do all my homework and try to learn 20 new words every day.

W: That's a good start. Do you also practice saying those words _____?

M: Do I need to do that? That sounds like it'll take a lot of time.

W: It does. But since you're still a beginner, you have to _____ _____ _____ _____ to get used to new words.

M: I see. So are you suggesting that I practice them _____ _____ _____?

W: (Exactly. Learning a language starts with repetition.)

15

W: Brian is a class leader. He is _____ _____ _____ _____ and saving energy. Recently, he's noticed that his classmates don't turn the lights off when they leave the classroom. Brian thinks this is very _____. He wants to make stickers that remind his classmates to save energy by turning off the lights. He tells this idea to his classmate Melissa, and she _____ it's a good idea. Brian knows Melissa is a great artist, so he wants to _____ _____ _____ _____ stickers that encourage their classmates to save energy. In this situation, what would Brian most likely say to Melissa?

Brian: (Will you design stickers that encourage energy saving?)

16~17

M: Good afternoon, everyone. Last time, we learned that _____ _____ when there are too many visitors to a particular destination. Today, we'll learn how cities _____ _____ caused by overtourism. First, some cities limit the number of hotels so there are _____ places for visitors to stay. In Barcelona, building new hotels is not allowed in the city center. Second, other cities _____ areas away from popular sites. For instance, Amsterdam encourages tourists to visit less-crowded areas. Third, many cities have tried to _____ _____. For example, Venice has tried to reduce tourism overall by stopping large cruise ships from _____ _____ the island. Similarly, Paris has focused on reducing tourism to certain parts of the city by having _____ areas. Now, let's watch some video clips.

MP3

21

2023년 11월 학력평가
딕테이션

2SBL1_A21

녹음을 듣고, 빈칸에 알맞은 말을 쓰시기 바랍니다. 빈칸은 문제풀이에 핵심이 되는 키워드와 헷갈리기 쉬운 발음에 표시되어 있으니 이 점에 유의하여 듣기 바랍니다.

01

[Chime bell rings.]

M: Hello, visitors. This is Scott Wolfman from the Edison Convention Center management office. We're doing our best to make sure that visitors have a _____ _____ in our convention center. As part of our effort, our center _____ a robot guide service. The robot offers guided-tours of our exhibitions. _____ _____, such as Chinese and Spanish, are available. And if you lose your way, the robot will _____ _____ _____ _____ you want to go. So, please feel free to ask our friendly robot guide, and it'll kindly help you. I hope this service makes your experience even better. Thank you.

02

W: Kevin, what are you doing?

M: Mom, I'm writing a letter to my sponsored child in Congo.

W: That's why you're writing in French. Your French has gotten better and better.

M: Actually, I got help from a translation program.

W: I see. *[Pause]* Did you check the _____ _____ _____ it?

M: No, I didn't. Do you think I have to?

W: Yes. You'd better check the translation.

M: Well, I think the translation program does a better job than I can.

W: Not exactly. The translation could have _____ _____ _____ what you intended.

M: Hmm, you may be right. The translated text often loses the meaning of my _____ _____.

W: See? When translating a text with a translation program, you need to check the _____.

M: Okay. Thanks for your advice.

03

[Cell phone rings.]

M: Hello. This is Johnny. We've been messaging each other on the _____ _____.

W: Oh, hi. You have more questions about the air conditioner, right?

M: Yes. Could you tell me how long _____ _____ _____ it?

W: I bought it a year ago. It works well and is like new as you can see from the photo.

M: Then why do you _____ _____ _____ it?

W: Because I don't need it anymore. I'm moving to a place with a built-in air conditioner.

M: I see. I'd like to buy it, then. It's $400, correct?

W: That's right. When can you _____ _____ _____?

M: Maybe tomorrow. I need to find a truck to load it on first.

W: Okay. Let me know when you're ready.

M: Thanks. I'll call you again.

21

23
년
11
월
딕
테
이
션

04

W: Hi, Benjamin. Did you finish your work for the student lounge design contest?

M: Yes. I'm confident that I'm going to win. Here's my design for it.

W: Awesome. Is that a _____ _____ in front of the window?

M: Yes. The plant will give a fresh feel to the lounge. What do you think about the banner on the wall?

W: I love it. The slogan "TO THE WORLD" goes well with the world map.

M: I hope this place helps students _____ _____.

W: That's cool. And the two cushions on the sofa make the atmosphere cozier.

M: You're right. Check out the _____ _____ as well.

W: Good. It can be useful. Most of all, students will love the _____ _____ under the clock.

M: You bet!

05

M: Ms. Kim, Empty Your Plate Day is coming. How's the preparation going?

W: I've finally decided on the lunch menu for that day.

M: You did! How did you do that?

W: I _____ _____ _____ of students' favorite foods.

M: Good idea! Can I help you with anything?

W: Actually, Mr. Han, I'm not sure how to _____ students to participate.

M: How about an award for the class with the _____ _____?

W: Sounds great. But how will we find that class?

M: You could give a sticker to the students who leave nothing on their plates. And then, you can find the class with the most stickers.

W: Excellent. _____ _____ _____ some stickers for me?

M: Sure. I'll do that for you.

W: Thanks. Then I'll put a notice on the bulletin board.

06

W: Welcome to Boom Telecom. How can I help you?

M: Hi. I'm thinking of changing my internet provider. What _____ _____ do you have?

W: Okay. We have the Economic plan that's $20 per month. And the Supreme plan, which is faster, is $_____ per month.

M: I prefer the faster one.

W: Alright. We also have an OTT service for an extra $10 per month. What do you think?

M: Awesome. _____ _____ _____ as well.

W: Excellent choice. Then you'll have the Supreme plan with the OTT service, right?

M: Correct. Can I get a discount?

W: I'm afraid that the 10% discount _____ _____ _____.

M: That's a shame. But I'll take it anyway.

W: Thank you. Please fill in this paper with your payment information.

M: Okay. [Writing sound] Here you are.

07

[Cell phone rings.]

M: Hi, Isabella.

W: Hi, Lorenzo. Did you finish your part-time job?

M: Yes. I'm on my way to a meeting for a _____ _____. What's up?

W: Your favorite talk show is *The Alice Mitchell Show*, right?

M: Yeah, I'm a big fan of hers. I even went to her _____ _____ event.

W: I knew it! I got two tickets for her talk show. It's next Saturday evening.

M: Whoa! Can you please take me with you?

W: Actually, I'm not available that day. The tickets are _____ _____.

M: Wait, why can't you go? Is it because of the family gathering you mentioned before?

W: No, that's in two weeks. Next Saturday I have to _____ _____ _____ _____.

M: Oh, I see. Then I'll take the tickets with pleasure. Thank you so much.

08

W: Michael, look at this poster. The Polar Bear Swim will be held soon.

M: I know! I've been really looking forward to it. *[Pause]* It's on _____ _____.

W: Yeah. We can enjoy winter sea-swimming.

M: How nice! To join this event, we must hand in a _____ _____ paper.

W: I think it's a good policy for everyone's health since the water is icy cold.

M: I agree. By the way, it says that there's _____ _____ _____ 100 people.

W: Oh, we must hurry. Look! Registration starts this Saturday.

M: I'll set a reminder on my phone.

W: Great idea. And the entry fee is just $15.

M: Yes. And all entry fees will be donated to charity.

W: Cool. Let's have some icy fun while _____ _____ _____ _____.

09

W: Hello, listeners! Are you a winter person? Then, Walk in the Snow might just be the adventure for you. It's a _____ tour program at Great White Mountain. Regardless of hiking experience, anyone who _____ _____ _____ hiking can participate in the tour. Participants are required to bring their own snowshoes and poles. But equipment is also available to rent _____ _____ _____ _____.

The registration fee is $10, and we offer discounts to students. Don't forget that you must _____ _____ _____ to participate. For more information, please visit our website, www.walkinthesnow.com. Thank you.

10

M: Honey, what are you looking at?

W: It's a brochure for a new calendar. Why don't we choose one together?

M: Great. How much do you want to spend?

W: I think more than $20 is _____ _____.

M: Agreed. How about trying a new format instead of a wall calendar? We've only used wall calendars so far.

W: Good idea. Let's pick the _____ _____ format, then.

M: Okay. And I prefer one that's made of _____ paper.

W: Me, too. It's more eco-friendly than those that cannot be recycled.

M: Then, let's cross this out. Now, we have two options left. Which one do you prefer?

W: I think the classic art theme _____ _____ our interior design.

M: Good point. Then, let's choose this one.

11

W: Congratulations, Lucas! I heard you were invited to speak at the National Assembly.

M: Thanks. It's a _____ _____. I think the article I wrote in the newspaper made a strong impression.

W: I'm so proud of you. What did you _____ _____ _____?

M: (I covered the worrying state of marine life.)

12

M: Claire, why are you sweating? It's pretty cold outside.

W: Hey, Jamie. I ran _____ _____ _____ _____ for class. It's too far to walk from the subway station to our college, don't you think?

M: Yes, but the _____ _____ began running last week. You can take it instead.

W: (Good news. Thanks for letting me know.)

13

W: Good morning, Pablo.

M: Hi, Eva. Look at my new tablet PC.

W: Wow. How do you like it?

M: It's _____ _____ _____ _____ world to me. But I have a small problem.

W: What is it? Maybe I can be of help.

M: This file works well on my laptop, but it won't open on my tablet.

W: Did you _____ a file-reading app? You need one to open the file on a tablet.

M: I already did that a week ago.

W: Then, I'll check a few things. [Tapping sound] I got it. The _____ _____ _____ of this app is over.

M: Oh, that's why it doesn't work. Do you think I should pay for this app?

W: Well, _____ _____ _____ _____. You can consider it if you need this app.

M: (I see. I'll give it some thought before buying this app.)

14

M: Hi, Naomi. What are you up to?

W: Hi. I'm looking for volunteer work. Didn't you say you're volunteering?

M: Yes. I'm working as a note-taker.

W: You mean helping students _____ _____ _____?

M: Right. It helps deaf students understand the class better.

W: Interesting. Could you tell me more?

M: I type everything during class, even jokes. _____ _____ _____, the more understandable.

W: It sounds like a unique and valuable experience.

M: Yeah. Are you thinking about joining?

W: Absolutely. But can I join in the _____ _____ _____ _____?

M: It could be possible. I heard one member quit a few days ago.

W: Lucky me. Is the _____ _____ available?

M: Hmm, I'm not sure, but if you ask the student volunteer center, you'll get an answer immediately.

W: (Okay. Wish me luck in getting this volunteer work.)

15

M: Tony and Kate are members of the bread lovers club. They plan to go on a bakery tour every month. To make a _____ _____ _____ to visit, they're sharing their ideas about must-visit bakeries. Kate proposes a bakery whose bread she thinks is _____ _____. However, Tony finds out that the baker there quit and since then there have been lots of _____ _____ about the bread quality getting worse. So, he wants to suggest that they _____ _____ _____ bakery for their where-to-go list. In this situation, what would Tony most likely say to Kate?

Tony: (How about finding a different bakery for the list?)

16~17

W: Hello, students. Last time, we learned why it's good for us to eat fruits and veggies. But what's good for us isn't always good for animals. Today, let's find out what fruits to _____ _____ _____ dogs. First, grapes are known to be highly toxic to dogs. You should be careful because even a _____ grape can cause severe health damage. Now, let's take a look at _____. If a dog swallows their seeds, the dog is likely to have difficulties breathing. Next, if your dog doesn't eat avocados, it would be for the best. That's because eating _____ _____ of avocados can make your dog sick. Finally, don't let your dog snack on grapefruits. The fruit _____ _____ _____ _____ that some dogs can develop stomach problems. Now, you may understand why some fruits are said to be _____ to dogs. I hope this information will help you and your dog in living a happy life.

22 2024년 3월 학력평가 딕테이션

MP3

2SBL1_A22

녹음을 듣고, 빈칸에 알맞은 말을 쓰시기 바랍니다. 빈칸은 문제풀이에 핵심이 되는 키워드와 헷갈리기 쉬운 발음에 표시되어 있으니 이 점에 유의하여 듣기 바랍니다.

01

M: Good afternoon, students! This is your vice principal, Jack Eliot. Due to the _____ _____ last night, there's some damage on the road and the road condition is not good. So we decided to _____ _____ _____ to the school shuttle bus schedule. From tomorrow, keep in mind that the bus schedule will be _____ _____ 15 minutes. We want to make sure all of you are safe. This bus schedule change will continue for one week. We _____ your understanding and cooperation. Thank you for your attention!

02

W: Brian, I heard that you are _____ _____ _____ an electric bicycle.

M: Yes, that's right.

W: That's good. But be careful when you ride it.

M: Yeah, I know what you mean. _____ _____ _____ _____ I saw a man riding an electric bicycle without wearing a helmet.

W: Some riders don't even follow _____ _____ _____.

M: What do you mean by that?

W: These days many people ride electric bicycles on sidewalks.

M: Yes, it's so dangerous.

W: Right. There should be _____ _____ about riding electric bicycles.

M: I totally agree with you.

03

W: Hello, this is your student counselor, Susan Smith. You might be _____ _____ your new school life as a freshman. You have a lot of things to do in the beginning of the year. Today, I'm going to give you a _____ _____ _____ _____. Make a to-do list! Write down the tasks you have to do on a list and check off what you finish, one by one. By doing this, you won't _____ _____ _____ you need to do. Using a to-do list will help you manage your time efficiently. Good luck to you and don't forget to start today.

04

M: Hi, Amy. I heard that you've joined the English Newspaper Club.

W: Yes, Tom. I went to the club room yesterday and took a picture of it. Look.

M: Wow, the place looks nice. I like the _____ _____ _____ _____.

W: Yes, they're good. We also have a star-shaped mirror on the wall.

M: It looks cool. What's that on the bookshelf?

W: Oh, that's the _____ my club won for 'Club of the Year'.

M: You must be very proud of it. There's also a computer on the _____ _____ of the room.

W: Yeah, we use the computer when we need it.

M: Great. I can see a _____ _____ _____ _____.

W: Yes, it was published last December.

05

W: Mike, I think we've got most of the camping _____ ready now.

M: Yeah, the tent, sleeping bags, and cooking tools are all set.

W: Perfect. I bought some easy-to-cook meals and snacks for us.

M: Great. What about some warm clothes? It might get cold at night.

W: I've packed some warm jackets for us, too. _____ _____ we need to consider?

M: We need something fun for the camping night. I already packed some books to read.

W: How about playing board games?

M: Nice. I have a _____ _____ at home.

W: Cool, can you bring it?

M: Of course! I'll _____ _____ _____ me.

06

M: Hello, what can I help you with today?

W: Hi! I want to buy some _____ _____ _____. What's fresh today?

M: We just got some apples in.

W: How much are they?

M: They are ten dollars for one bag.

W: Fantastic! I'll take _____ _____ _____ apples.

M: Okay, what else do you need?

W: I'd like to buy some carrots, too.

M: The carrots are _____ dollars for one bag. How many do you need?

W: I need two bags of carrots.

M: Okay, you need two bags of apples and two bags of carrots.

W: Right. And I have a coupon. I can _____ _____ _____ with this, right?

M: Yes. You can get a ten percent discount off the total price.

W: Good. Here's the coupon and my credit card.

07

W: Hey, Jake! How was your math test yesterday?

M: Better than I expected.

W: That's great. Let's go and _____ _____ Sports Day.

M: I'm so sorry but I can't make it.

W: Come on, Jake! Sports Day is just around the corner.

M: I know. That's why I _____ _____ _____ _____.

W: Then, why can't you practice today? Do you have a club interview?

M: No, I already had the interview last week.

W: Then, does your leg still hurt?

M: Not really, it's okay, now. Actually, I have to attend a _____ _____ _____ tonight for my mother's birthday.

W: Oh, that's important! Family always comes first. Are you available tomorrow, then?

M: Sure. Let's _____ _____ _____ the missed practice.

08

W: Hey, Chris. Have you heard about the Science Open Lab Program?

M: Yes, I heard about it. But I don't know what it is exactly.

W: In that program, we can design any science experiment we want.

M: That sounds pretty cool. Do you want to join the program?

W: Sure, it's _____ _____ _____ like us. Let's join it together.

M: Great! Do we need to buy some _____ for experiments?

W: No, they'll prepare everything for us. We just need to send the application form online.

M: When is the _____ _____ _____?

W: It's tomorrow. We need to hurry.

M: Oh, I see. Is there any special prize?

W: Yes. I heard they're _____ _____ _____ for the most creative projects.

M: Perfect! I'm so excited.

09

W: Hello, students! Are you looking for a chance to help others? Then, I recommend you to join Triwood High School Volunteer Program to help senior citizens. _____ _____ _____ help the senior citizens face-to-face. You teach them how to use their smartphones for things _____ _____ sending text messages or taking pictures. You will also teach seniors how to use various apps. The program will require volunteers to _____ _____ _____ every Saturday. If you are interested in joining our program, please send us an _____ _____ through email.

10

M: Sophie, what are you looking for?

W: I'm trying to choose one of these portable fans as a gift for my friend Cathy.

M: Oh, let me help you. How many _____ options do you think she would want?

W: She would like it if the fan has _____ _____ two options.

M: Okay, then, what color do you have in mind?

W: Cathy's old one was white. I want to choose a _____ color.

M: Good idea. Do you want an LED display to show the _____ _____ power?

W: Hmm, I don't think she will need it.

M: You're left with two options. Which one do you prefer?

W: Well, I'll take the cheaper one.

11

M: What's wrong, Jane? You look so upset.

W: I lost my _____! I have been searching for it for an hour, but I can't find it.

M: When did you _____ _____ it?

W: (I had it before biology class.)

12

W: Honey, what do you have in mind for _____ this Saturday?

M: I was thinking we should try the new Italian restaurant.

W: Hmm... I heard that _____ _____ to make a reservation there these days.

M: (That's too bad. Why don't we try another restaurant?)

13

M: Mom! I've started to record audiobooks for kids.

W: That's great! How did you _____ _____ _____ that?

M: My teacher told me that a local organization is looking for students to record audiobooks.

W: Fantastic! Are you having fun with it?

M: Well, actually, I'm _____ _____ my voice acting.

W: Oh? Is that so?

M: Yes, it's a bit challenging to get the _____ _____ for kids.

W: I'm sure you'll get better with practice soon.

M: Thanks. I'm trying my best.

W: That's wonderful. Anything I can help you with?

M: Can you _____ _____ _____ _____ for my audiobook recording?

W: (Sure. Let's choose one from your old children's books.)

14

W: Hi, Fred. What should we do for our history project?

M: Actually, I was thinking about it. Why don't we _____ _____ _____ for the project?

W: Okay. Good idea. We have the research part, the visual material part, and the presentation part.

M: Hmm, is there any part you want to _____ _____?

W: Well, I would like to do the research. I've been collecting news articles about history.

M: Excellent. You are good at gathering _____ information.

W: Thanks. Can you handle the visual material?

M: Okay. I'll take care of it. I have done it before.

W: All right. Then, the _____ _____ _____ is the presentation.

M: (Well, let's do the presentation together.)

15

W: Robert and Michelle are _____ their high school orientation. After short greetings, the teacher begins to explain student clubs, school activities, and school facilities. Robert is _____ on the explanation. However, while writing down important things about the school library, Robert _____ his pen. Trying to find his pen, Robert misses important information about the _____ _____ of the library, so

now, Robert wants to ask Michelle when the library is open. In this situation, what would Robert most likely say to Michelle?

Robert: (When can I use the library?)

16~17

M: Hello, listeners. Thank you for tuning in to our Happy Radio Show. Are you taking good care of your _____ in the early spring? Today, I want to recommend some foods that can _____ _____ _____ of a cough. Ginger is a popular home remedy for coughs. A cup of hot ginger tea can be helpful for reducing your cough. Lemon is a _____ _____ of vitamin C. Lemon tea can help you relieve your cough. Surprisingly, _____ is another excellent food to help relieve a cough. When you are suffering from a cough, _____ _____ also helps to get rid of the symptoms more easily. These foods are rich in vitamins and they are recommended for people _____ _____ a cough. I hope you have a healthy week.

23

2024년 6월 학력평가
딕테이션

MP3

2SBL1_A23

녹음을 듣고, 빈칸에 알맞은 말을 쓰시기 바랍니다. 빈칸은 문제풀이에 핵심이 되는 키워드와 헷갈리기 쉬운 발음에 표시되어 있으니 이 점에 유의하여 듣기 바랍니다.

01

[Chime bell rings.]

W: Attention, everyone! Our CEO, Mr. Wayne, has prepared a _____ _____ _____ _____ our success on last month's project. Please come down to the _____ and enjoy some delicious snacks. They'll be available until 4 p.m. You'll be _____ _____ the amazing variety, from crispy fries and hot dogs to fresh lemonade and coffee. It'd be great if you could bring your _____ _____ _____ for the drinks. See you there.

02

M: Hi, Pamela. Did you finish your history assignment?

W: Yes, Dad. I finished it quite easily with the help of AI.

M: Really? Do you mean you _____ _____ _____ website?

W: Yeah. I typed in the questions and AI gave me the answers right away.

M: Well, is it a good idea to do your homework that way?

W: Why not? It _____ a lot of time and gives me just the information I need.

M: I used to think so, too. But after trying it a couple of times, I found out AI sometimes uses _____ information as well.

W: Really? I didn't know that.

M: Yeah, you _____ _____ _____ the answers from AI.

W: Okay. I'll keep that in mind next time.

03

W: Hello, listeners. This is Kelly Watson's *Love Yourself*. Have you ever thought about your social media use? Social media lets you _____ _____ _____ others easily. However, it can make you compare yourself with others, too. For example, a celebrity's post about going on a luxurious trip may make you jealous. _____ _____ _____ stops you from looking at yourself the way you truly are. You might think, "Why can't I have a better life?" and _____ _____ about yourself. As you can see, social media can have a _____ _____ _____ your self-esteem. I'll be right back with some tips for healthy social media use.

04

W: Honey, I love this park!

M: Me, too. This park is so cool. But, oh, look! What's that in the tree?

W: It's just a _____ _____ in the tree's branches.

M: I guess some kids went home without their kite.

W: By the same tree, a woman is walking her dog. They look so lovely.

M: What about the little girl beside her?

W: You mean the girl _____ _____ in her hand?

M: Right. She's adorable. And look there! Did you notice a _____ _____ _____ flowers on the picnic mat?

W: Yes, right. It adds a touch of romance to the scene.

M: I think so, too. Oh, there's a fountain. Next to it, a man is _____ _____ _____.

W: The melody is beautiful. I'm glad we came here.

05

M: Hey, Alice. I _____ _____ the science camp next week. What about you?

W: Me, too. But I didn't know that there were so many things to do before the camp.

M: Right. Would you like to go over my checklist together?

W: Hmm, let's see. Did you _____ _____ _____ video to the website?

M: Yes, I tried to show my interest in science. Oh, hey, have you picked which experiment to work on?

W: Yes. I _____ _____ _____ _____ a biology experiment.

M: Me, too. Wasn't it difficult to make a plan for your experiment?

W: Actually, I haven't even started yet because I've never written a plan for a biology experiment before.

M: _____ _____ _____ _____ after class. Maybe you can get some ideas.

W: Really? That'd be great. See you soon.

06

W: Hi, I'm looking for a backpack for my niece. She's going on a camping trip this summer.

M: Great. We have this blue backpack that has multiple pockets.

W: It looks _____ _____ _____. How much is it?

M: It's $50, but we have a _____ _____ _____ _____ backpacks today. Every backpack is 10% off.

W: That's a great deal! I'll take it.

M: I'm sure your niece will love it. Do you need anything else?

W: Yes. I like this camping hat. How much is it?

M: It's $_____, not on sale, though.

W: That's okay. I'll take it as well.

M: Gift wrapping for them would be _____ _____ _____ $5. Would you like gift wrapping?

W: Yes, please. Here's my credit card.

07

W: Hi, Chris. How was your weekend?

M: Hello, Martha. I went to a _____ _____ and had fun. How about you?

W: I've been preparing for tomorrow's club festival.

M: Oh, what _____ _____ _____ are you preparing for the festival?

W: Our club members are presenting a magic show. _____ _____ _____ _____ at 4 p.m. tomorrow if you are available.

M: I'd love to, but I can't make it.

W: Why? It'd be nice to have you there.

M: I'm sorry, but I have to _____ _____ _____ _____ party.

W: Oh, I understand. I hope you have a wonderful time with your family.

M: Thank you, I will.

08

W: Hey, Alex. Have you seen the _____ for the Victory Marathon?

M: Not yet, but I'm curious about it. When's the event?

W: It's on Saturday, _____ _____.

M: Nice. Where will the race start?

W: It will start at William Stadium.

M: Oh, great. How _____ _____ _____ _____ to participate?

W: It costs $30.

M: That's reasonable. How many participants are they expecting?

W: Last year, there were around 5,000. They say they _____ _____ _____ _____ this year.

M: I didn't know that many people love marathons. I'm in!

W: Great. I look forward to running with you.

09

M: Good morning, students of Violet Hill High School. This is your principal speaking. I'm _____ _____ _____ that the annual Violet Hill Mentorship will be held next Friday. Our school graduates who are now majoring in English literature, _____, and theater and film will be giving some tips on university life. To register for this event, visit our school website and submit two questions you would like to ask them in advance. The _____ _____ _____ is next Tuesday, so don't wait too long. And remember, the maximum number of participants for each major is _____ _____. For more information, visit our school website.

10

M: Honey, look. This website's Summer Sale has just begun.

W: Oh, great. Why don't we buy a new cordless vacuum cleaner?

M: Sure. There are five bestsellers shown here.

W: Let's check the _____ _____ first.

M: I think it should be at least two hours so that we don't have to _____ _____ _____ _____ .

W: I agree. But let's not spend more than $400 on a vacuum cleaner.

M: Fine. Oh, some of these also have a _____ _____ function.

W: I'd love that. With that function, we can definitely save a lot of time.

M: Okay. What about the color? _____ _____ _____ looks better to me.

W: Right. It'll match the color tone of our living room.

M: Perfect. So, let's buy this one.

W: Great.

11

M: Mom, I want to have a cat. Have you ever thought about us _____ a cat?

W: Sweetie, having a pet requires a lot of responsibility.

M: I'm totally ready for it. Mom, we _____ _____ _____ _____ it.

W: (Fine. Let's talk about it over dinner.)

12

W: Jake, I _____ _____ about the math assignment. When's the deadline?

M: You need to submit it by next Tuesday.

W: Phew, I still have some time. _____ _____ _____ submit it?

M: (Upload your work to our school website.)

13

M: Hey, Cindy. Have you been playing a lot of badminton these days?

W: No, I've been experiencing some _____ _____ _____ _____ since a badminton match last weekend.

M: I'm sorry to hear that. Did you go see a doctor?

W: Yes, I visited a _____ _____ yesterday.

M: I hope you feel better soon. By the way, have you ever taken a badminton lesson?

W: No, I haven't. Why are you asking?

M: In my experience, that kind of injury can come from _____ _____ . A lesson might reduce the risk of any further injury.

W: Well, I thought I didn't need those lessons.

M: Cindy, if you want to keep playing badminton without any injuries, it's important to _____ _____ _____ to develop the right posture.

W: (You're right. Maybe I should start taking badminton lessons.)

14

W: Mike, don't you think _____

_____ is kind of scary?

M: Right. The temperature seems higher than ever.

W: I heard it's putting a number of _____

_____ _____ these days.

M: Right. Maybe one day we won't be able to see polar bears anymore.

W: That's not good. What can we do?

M: Use less plastic, plant more trees.

_____ _____ _____.

W: And maybe we can ride bikes instead of always asking for rides.

M: Yeah. Making a Tree-Planting Day at school can also be helpful.

W: Absolutely. Then, why don't we make our own _____ _____ to put it into action?

M: (Great. Let's think about the club name first.)

15

W: Laura and Tony are close coworkers. Laura notices that Tony has been looking

_____ _____ _____

_____ recently. One day, she asks Tony if he's not been feeling well lately, but Tony says he's just a bit tired from work. Laura knows that Tony sometimes works even on weekends

_____ _____ _____

_____ or getting any rest. However, this time, she is really worried about him and wants him to take at least a _____

_____ _____ _____.

In this situation, what would Laura most likely say to Tony?

Laura: (You'd better take a break for a few days.)

16~17

M: Hello, Lincoln High School. This is David Newman, your current student _____, and I'm speaking to you today to let you know about the _____ _____ for next year's student representative. Candidates can now begin their campaigns, _____ these instructions. First, they can share short promotional video clips on their _____ _____, but the video clips must not be longer than 3 minutes. Second, candidates can _____ _____ only in allowed areas, and it's important to keep the size to A3 or smaller, as larger posters will be removed without warning. Third, the _____ _____ _____ is allowed, but they must only be distributed within the school campus. Lastly, there will be an online debate broadcast on our school _____ _____ the candidates three days before the election. It's important to be respectful toward the other candidates during the debate. Let's make this election a success.

24 2024년 9월 학력평가
딕테이션

녹음을 듣고, 빈칸에 알맞은 말을 쓰시기 바랍니다. 빈칸은 문제풀이에 핵심이 되는 키워드와 헷갈리기 쉬운 발음에 표시되어 있으니 이 점에 유의하여 듣기 바랍니다.

01

W: Hello! I'm Olivia Parker from Pineview City Subway. I have an announcement for this Saturday's _____ festival. Many people are expected to visit and enjoy the festival late into the night. For smooth transportation and visitor safety, we're _____

_____ _____ _____

of the subway on the day of the festival. The subway will run for an extra two hours after the

_____ _____ _____

from the festival area stations. For a comfortable and safe journey from the event, we encourage you to take advantage of our extended subway services. We hope you enjoy this fantastic festival with _____. Thank you!

02

M: Hi, Emma. What's up? You look tired.

W: Hey, David. I always feel tired. Even though I sleep many hours, I guess I don't get any good sleep.

M: That's too bad. Is there anything you do before you go to bed?

W: I usually read webtoons on my smartphone for a few hours.

M: Ah, that's the problem. Having too much screen time _____ _____ is not good.

W: Really? But I'm so used to spending time on my phone at night!

M: _____ _____ _____ the screen light can make your brain stay awake.

W: I never knew using smartphones had a _____ _____ on sleep.

M: Reducing your smartphone use before going to bed will increase the _____ of your sleep.

W: Okay, I can give it a try.

03

M: Hello, listeners! Welcome to your *Daily Tips*. Today, I'll tell you a helpful way to relieve your stress. Recent research shows that having hobbies _____ _____ _____ your job can significantly reduce stress. For example, if you work in IT, consider _____ _____ that are far from the digital field. Playing the guitar might be a good option rather than playing computer games. Let's enjoy hobbies that are _____ _____ our work! That'll be the best way to get a refreshing break. Remember, a well-chosen hobby can be a _____ _____ for stress relief. Tune in tomorrow for more helpful daily tips!

04

M: Hey, Amy. Here is the new _____ _____ for our band. How do you like it?

W: Wow, these two speakers are impressive!

M: Yes, they are. The sound quality is excellent.

W: Also, the _____ _____ _____ the speakers looks great.

M: Yeah. And on the desk, there is a microphone. We can use it to give recording directions.

W: Nice. Oh, this _____ _____ _____. It could be helpful for long recordings.

M: Agreed. And the rug under the chair gives the room a cozy feeling, doesn't it?

W: Yes, and I like the _____ _____ on the rug.

M: I like it, too. How about the poster on the wall?

W: It's cool. This studio feels like where music truly comes alive!

M: I'm glad you like this place.

W: Absolutely. I can't wait to start recording here.

05

W: Tony, I'm so excited for our Go-Green event!

M: Me, too. The event is almost here. Why don't we go over our preparations together?

W: Okay. I think the _____ _____ are very important for our event. How are they going?

M: Almost ready. I'm working on the booth setup this afternoon. What about the _____ _____?

W: I've already prepared some eco-friendly bags.

M: Perfect! What's next?

W: We need to confirm the list of guests for the ceremony.

M: I double-checked the list. But I haven't sent the _____ _____ cards, yet.

W: No problem. I'll deal with it right away. How about the food and drinks?

M: I've scheduled food and drink services and I'll serve the guests with reusable dishes.

W: Nice! I'm _____ our event will be a great success.

06

W: Welcome to the Riverside Camping store. How can I help you?

M: I'm looking for a camping table for my family. Can you recommend one?

W: Sure. How about this one? It's _____ _____ _____ to fold, so it's our best-selling product.

M: It looks good. How much is it?

W: It comes in two sizes. The small one is 30 dollars and the large one is _____ dollars.

M: I'll buy the large one. Are there folding chairs, too?

W: Yep. These folding chairs might _____ _____ _____ the table. They're 10 dollars each.

M: Sounds good. I'll buy four of those chairs.

W: Okay. That's one large camping table and four chairs.

M: That's right. Can I _____ _____ _____ _____ now?

W: Of course. You can get a 10% discount on the total price.

M: Perfect. Here's my credit card.

07

W: Lately, the weather has been lovely. This is a perfect time for climbing.

M: Indeed. Oh, would you like to go mountain climbing together?

W: Sounds awesome. I have all the climbing _____.

M: Great. How about this upcoming weekend? I'll find a nice mountain for us.

W: Hold on, this weekend? I don't think I can make it then.

M: Really? All school _____ _____ _____ done, so I thought this weekend would be good for us.

W: Sorry, but I have something important to do this weekend.

M: Do you have a part-time job?

W: No. Actually, I need to _____ _____ for the entire weekend.

M: Ah, for the dance competition you mentioned before?

W: Yes. Surprisingly, I _____ _____ _____ the first round, and it's the finals next Monday.

M: That's fantastic! I wish you the best of luck.

08

W: Grandpa, take a look at this. It's a Lakestate Apartment Yoga Program poster.

M: Wow, a new program for the _____. I've always wanted to join a yoga program.

W: I know, and this one is only for those _____ _____ _____ _____.

M: That's perfect for me. [Pause] Oh, it says it's held at 8 a.m. every Tuesday and Friday.

W: It'll be a good time for you. You're an early bird.

M: Yes, I am. _____ _____ _____ _____?

W: You just need to fill out an application form at the apartment fitness center.

M: Okay, I think I'll go right now.

W: Good. But _____ _____ _____ _____ your ID card with you.

M: Oh, do I need that for the registration?

W: Yes. It says that on the poster. Would you like me to go with you?

M: That would be lovely.

09

W: Good morning! This is Allison from the student council. I'm happy to announce the Global Food Market right here at Westhill High School. Get ready for a _____ _____ around the world in the school parking lot. Our Global Food Market will take place for two days, on _____ 25th and 26th. You can enjoy food from eight different countries, including Mexico and France. And there's no need to worry about prices. _____ _____ _____ is only five dollars. Wait! You don't eat meat? No problem! We also have menus for vegetarians. So, join us at the Global Food Market. It's not just about food, but a _____ _____ _____ and diversity. Don't miss this chance to taste the world!

10

W: Honey, what are you looking at?

M: I'm looking at digital tumblers. They show the temperature on an LED screen. Would you like to help me choose one?

W: Sure, let me see. [Pause] The price differs by model.

M: Hmm, I don't want to _____ _____ _____ _____ dollars.

W: That sounds reasonable. Look, there are various sizes to choose from.

M: _____ _____ 400ml would be too small for me.

W: Alright. Oh, there's a new function. Do you need the _____ _____ display? It'll show you how much water you drink in a day.

M: That sounds smart. I'd love to have it. Then, I have just two options left.

W: What color do you like? You have too many black items and they're boring.

M: Okay. I'll go with the _____ _____ _____ black. Then, I'll order this one.

W: Great idea!

11

W: I easily catch a cold these days.

M: That's too bad. It's a good idea to keep some moisture in your room.

W: Oh, _____ _____ _____ _____ to a cold?

M: (If it's too dry inside, you can easily get a cold.)

12

M: Mom, the bookshelf in my room is full of books. There's no space for new ones.

W: Well, how about _____ away the books you don't read anymore?

M: But some of them are in too _____ _____ to throw away.

W: (Right. Then, shall we sell them at a used bookstore?)

13

W: Hey, Peter. How's your group project going?

M: Hello, Ms. Adams. It's my first time as a leader, so it's quite challenging.

W: I thought your group was working well together.

M: Yes. We're all _____ and working hard, but progress is slow.

W: Well, what are you all working on at this moment?

M: Everyone is focusing on gathering data as much as possible.

W: Hmm, did you _____ _____ _____ to each member?

M: Oh, we haven't discussed it yet. We're not exactly sure who does what.

W: That's crucial. Otherwise, it can _____ _____ _____ tasks in a group project.

M: That makes sense. That's why our progress is not that fast.

W: Then, as the leader, what do you think _____ _____ _____ now?

M: (I'll clarify each group member's specific role.)

14

M: Hey, Emily! You're looking great these days.

W: Thanks, Isaac. I've been trying _____ _____ _____ _____ better shape.

M: Good for you! I'm trying to get fit, too. But it's tough.

W: Haven't you been working out a lot lately?

M: Yeah, but I don't see a big difference. What's your secret?

W: Well, I started being _____ _____ _____ I eat.

M: You mean like not eating right before bed?

W: Kind of. I _____ I was eating a lot at night. So now I don't eat after 7 p.m.

M: Hmm... I don't know if _____ _____ to get me in better shape.

W: (Trust me. When we eat makes a big difference.)

15

M: Julia is a college student, living in the dormitory. Recently, she ordered a new computer desk. _____ _____ the desk, she realized that the desk was a DIY product. It means she needs to put the pieces together to build the desk. However, it was _____ to assemble it by herself. Julia knows that Sophie, her best friend, is _____ _____ assembling DIY furniture and enjoys it. So, Julia wants to ask Sophie to _____ _____ _____ the desk. In this situation, what would Julia most likely say to Sophie?

Julia: (Could you help me assemble my desk?)

16~17

W: Hello, *Family-Life* subscribers! These days, many people are looking for clothes _____ _____ _____ _____ for their family. Today, I'd like to introduce some tips for how to _____ _____ natural material clothes. First, for cotton, like 100% cotton t-shirts, you should hand-wash in cool water to _____ _____ or wrinkling. Second, silk should be washed separately and quickly to keep _____ _____ and color. Also, when you dry silk clothes such as blouses, avoid direct sunlight and dry them in the shade. Third, linen is a _____ material to wash. For example, to wash linen jackets, use vinegar instead of fabric softener. Lastly, for wool, the best way is to wash _____ _____ _____ possible. If you have to wash wool sweaters, use special wool washing soap. Apply these tips so you can keep and enjoy natural clothes for a longer time!

마더텅 전자책

마음껏 쓰고 지우는 자유로운 필기!
원하는 내용을 손쉽게 검색! 원하는 페이지로 간편하게 이동!

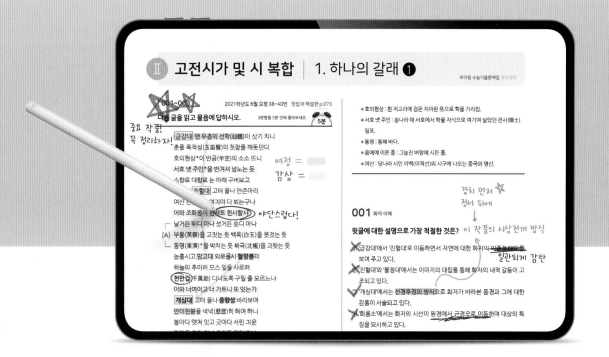

마더텅 전자책 지원 어플리케이션

노팅   스콘   교보eBook   meBOOK

Goodnotes   예스24 eBook   디북   EBS eBook

▶ 구글 플레이스토어 또는 🅰 애플 앱스토어 에서

원하는 **어플리케이션**을 **다운로드**해 주세요.

2025 마더텅
전국연합 학력평가 기출문제집
고1 영어 듣기
정답과 해설편

MOTHERTONGUE
마더텅출판사
since1999.4.1.

정답표

01회
2018년 11월 학력평가 · 문제편 p.2 해설편 p.1

01 ②	02 ②	03 ①	04 ④	05 ①
06 ③	07 ⑤	08 ④	09 ④	10 ⑤
11 ④	12 ①	13 ③	14 ④	15 ⑤
16 ①	17 ③			

02회
2019년 3월 학력평가 · 문제편 p.5 해설편 p.6

01 ④	02 ⑤	03 ⑤	04 ④	05 ②
06 ①	07 ④	08 ④	09 ③	10 ②
11 ④	12 ①	13 ⑤	14 ②	15 ①
16 ①	17 ③			

03회
2019년 6월 학력평가 · 문제편 p.8 해설편 p.10

01 ①	02 ③	03 ①	04 ⑤	05 ①
06 ④	07 ①	08 ④	09 ⑤	10 ③
11 ②	12 ①	13 ②	14 ④	15 ③
16 ①	17 ⑤			

04회
2019년 9월 학력평가 · 문제편 p.11 해설편 p.15

01 ①	02 ③	03 ②	04 ④	05 ⑤
06 ④	07 ②	08 ④	09 ⑤	10 ⑤
11 ⑤	12 ①	13 ②	14 ①	15 ③
16 ①	17 ③			

05회
2019년 11월 학력평가 · 문제편 p.14 해설편 p.20

01 ③	02 ①	03 ④	04 ④	05 ⑤
06 ②	07 ①	08 ④	09 ⑤	10 ②
11 ③	12 ②	13 ④	14 ①	15 ①
16 ③	17 ③			

06회
2020년 3월 학력평가 · 문제편 p.17 해설편 p.25

01 ①	02 ⑤	03 ③	04 ④	05 ⑤
06 ②	07 ⑤	08 ②	09 ④	10 ②
11 ②	12 ①	13 ①	14 ③	15 ⑤
16 ⑤	17 ④			

07회
2020년 6월 학력평가 · 문제편 p.20 해설편 p.30

01 ②	02 ②	03 ②	04 ④	05 ③
06 ⑤	07 ⑤	08 ④	09 ⑤	10 ②
11 ①	12 ⑤	13 ①	14 ③	15 ①
16 ②	17 ④			

08회
2020년 9월 학력평가 · 문제편 p.23 해설편 p.34

01 ⑤	02 ①	03 ①	04 ④	05 ①
06 ⑤	07 ⑤	08 ③	09 ⑤	10 ③
11 ⑤	12 ①	13 ④	14 ③	15 ⑤
16 ①	17 ②			

09회
2020년 11월 학력평가 · 문제편 p.26 해설편 p.39

01 ②	02 ①	03 ②	04 ③	05 ③
06 ③	07 ②	08 ⑤	09 ⑤	10 ④
11 ⑤	12 ④	13 ①	14 ⑤	15 ③
16 ④	17 ④			

10회
2021년 3월 학력평가 · 문제편 p.29 해설편 p.44

01 ④	02 ④	03 ①	04 ③	05 ④
06 ③	07 ①	08 ②	09 ⑤	10 ②
11 ①	12 ⑤	13 ⑤	14 ③	15 ④
16 ②	17 ④			

11회
2021년 6월 학력평가 · 문제편 p.32 해설편 p.48

01 ②	02 ②	03 ②	04 ⑤	05 ①
06 ①	07 ⑤	08 ④	09 ⑤	10 ③
11 ②	12 ⑤	13 ①	14 ⑤	15 ③
16 ③	17 ④			

12회
2021년 9월 학력평가 · 문제편 p.35 해설편 p.53

01 ④	02 ②	03 ③	04 ③	05 ⑤
06 ③	07 ③	08 ③	09 ④	10 ②
11 ①	12 ④	13 ①	14 ⑤	15 ③
16 ②	17 ③			

13회
2021년 11월 학력평가 · 문제편 p.38 해설편 p.58

01 ②	02 ③	03 ①	04 ⑤	05 ②
06 ③	07 ①	08 ④	09 ④	10 ③
11 ①	12 ①	13 ⑤	14 ②	15 ③
16 ④	17 ⑤			

14회
2022년 3월 학력평가 · 문제편 p.41 해설편 p.62

01 ①	02 ③	03 ②	04 ④	05 ④
06 ③	07 ①	08 ③	09 ⑤	10 ①
11 ④	12 ①	13 ②	14 ③	15 ①
16 ④	17 ④			

15회
2022년 6월 학력평가 · 문제편 p.44 해설편 p.67

01 ②	02 ①	03 ⑤	04 ④	05 ②
06 ③	07 ②	08 ②	09 ⑤	10 ④
11 ①	12 ③	13 ③	14 ④	15 ④
16 ②	17 ③			

16회
2022년 9월 학력평가 · 문제편 p.47 해설편 p.71

01 ②	02 ⑤	03 ②	04 ④	05 ④
06 ③	07 ②	08 ②	09 ⑤	10 ③
11 ④	12 ③	13 ①	14 ⑤	15 ⑤
16 ①	17 ④			

17회
2022년 11월 학력평가 · 문제편 p.50 해설편 p.76

01 ①	02 ②	03 ②	04 ④	05 ⑤
06 ④	07 ①	08 ②	09 ①	10 ②
11 ②	12 ①	13 ②	14 ①	15 ④
16 ②	17 ④			

18회
2023년 3월 학력평가 · 문제편 p.53 해설편 p.81

01 ⑤	02 ③	03 ③	04 ④	05 ②
06 ②	07 ①	08 ③	09 ④	10 ②
11 ⑤	12 ①	13 ③	14 ①	15 ④
16 ③	17 ④			

19회
2023년 6월 학력평가 · 문제편 p.56 해설편 p.85

01 ②	02 ①	03 ③	04 ④	05 ⑤
06 ③	07 ①	08 ⑤	09 ⑤	10 ①
11 ①	12 ③	13 ②	14 ⑤	15 ⑤
16 ①	17 ④			

20회
2023년 9월 학력평가 · 문제편 p.59 해설편 p.89

01 ⑤	02 ①	03 ③	04 ④	05 ①
06 ④	07 ①	08 ③	09 ④	10 ④
11 ①	12 ④	13 ①	14 ③	15 ①
16 ③	17 ③			

21회
2023년 11월 학력평가 · 문제편 p.62 해설편 p.94

01 ②	02 ①	03 ⑤	04 ④	05 ①
06 ⑤	07 ①	08 ④	09 ③	10 ②
11 ①	12 ②	13 ④	14 ①	15 ⑤
16 ①	17 ⑤			

22회
2024년 3월 학력평가 · 문제편 p.65 해설편 p.99

01 ①	02 ②	03 ④	04 ⑤	05 ②
06 ③	07 ②	08 ④	09 ④	10 ①
11 ②	12 ①	13 ②	14 ②	15 ①
16 ①	17 ④			

23회
2024년 6월 학력평가 · 문제편 p.68 해설편 p.103

01 ②	02 ①	03 ③	04 ⑤	05 ④
06 ⑤	07 ⑤	08 ②	09 ⑤	10 ④
11 ①	12 ③	13 ⑤	14 ②	15 ④
16 ③	17 ④			

24회
2024년 9월 학력평가 · 문제편 p.71 해설편 p.108

01 ③	02 ①	03 ⑤	04 ④	05 ②
06 ⑤	07 ④	08 ⑤	09 ④	10 ④
11 ⑤	12 ①	13 ④	14 ①	15 ②
16 ⑤	17 ③			

01 2018년 11월 학력평가

01	②	02	②	03	①	04	④	05	①
06	③	07	⑤	08	④	09	④	10	⑤
11	④	12	③	13	①	14	④	15	⑤
16	①	17	③						

01 여자가 하는 말의 목적

고1 2018년 11월 3번 | 정답률 75%
▶ 정답 ②

W: Hello and welcome back to 'Happy Life.' I'm Christine Brown, professional life coach. When was the last time you sat down and thought about the good things in your life? With our busy schedules, we easily forget to count the blessings we already have. However, according to a recent study, people who are more grateful for what they have are more hopeful and physically healthier. So here is today's tip. Write a gratitude journal. A gratitude journal is a diary in which you can express all the things you're thankful for. Just invest five to ten minutes each day in the journal. You'll feel more thankful and stay healthier.

해석
여: 안녕하세요, 'Happy Life(행복한 인생)'에 돌아오신 것을 환영합니다. 저는 전문 인생 상담사인 Christine Brown입니다. 마지막으로 앉아서 여러분의 삶에 있는 좋은 점들에 대해 생각해본 게 언제였나요? 바쁜 일정으로, 우리는 우리가 이미 가지고 있는 축복들을 세는 것을 쉽게 잊습니다. 하지만, 최근의 연구에 따르면, 자신들이 가진 것에 더 감사하는 사람들이 더 희망적이고 신체적으로 더 건강하다고 합니다. 그래서 오늘의 조언이 있습니다. 감사 일기를 쓰십시오. 감사 일기는 여러분이 감사하는 모든 것들을 표현할 수 있는 일기입니다. 매일 5분에서 10분 정도만 일기에 투자하십시오. 여러분은 더 감사하게 느끼고 더 건강해질 것입니다.

① 강의 일정 변경을 공지하려고
❷ 감사 일기 쓰는 것을 권장하려고
③ 건강 관리의 중요성을 강조하려고
④ 자기소개서 작성 요령을 설명하려고
⑤ 효과적인 시간 활용법을 안내하려고

02 남자의 의견

고1 2018년 11월 4번 | 정답률 90%
▶ 정답 ②

M: What are you doing, Jennifer? Mom wants us to study now.

W: I'm getting ready to go to the library to study.

M: Walking to the library takes so much time. Why don't you study at home?

W: Strangely, I can't focus on my studies here. I don't know why.

M: Hmm, how about tidying up your study space?

W: Tidying up my study space? Why?

M: When I organized my study place, I could avoid distractions and focus better.

W: Do you really think it'll work for me as well?

M: Sure. A disorganized desk leads to a disorganized mind. Messy spaces can even create stress.

W: That makes sense. I often get anxious looking at my messy desk.

M: Right. I think an organized study space can help to improve your focus.

W: I guess it's worth trying out.

해석
남: 무엇을 하고 있니, Jennifer? 엄마께서는 우리가 지금 공부하기를 바라셔.
여: 나는 공부하기 위해서 도서관에 갈 준비를 하고 있어.
남: 도서관에 걸어 가는 것은 시간이 너무 많이 걸려. 집에서 공부하는 게 어때?
여: 이상하게도, 나는 여기에서 공부에 집중할 수가 없어. 왜인지 모르겠어.
남: 흠, 네 학습 공간을 정리하는 게 어떠니?
여: 내 학습 공간을 정리하라고? 왜?
남: 나는 내 학습 공간을 정돈했을 때, 산만함을 피하고 더 잘 집중할 수 있었거든.
여: 정말 그것이 나에게도 효과가 있을 거라고 생각해?
남: 물론이지. 정돈되지 않은 책상은 정돈되지 않은 정신으로 이어지는 거야. 지저분한 공간은 스트레스마저 야기할 수 있어.
여: 그거 일리가 있네. 나는 종종 내 지저분한 책상을 보면 불안해지거든.
남: 맞아. 나는 정돈된 학습 공간이 네 집중력을 향상시키는 데 도움이 된다고 생각해.
여: 시도할 만한 가치가 있는 것 같아.

① 집중력 향상을 위해서는 충분한 휴식이 필요하다.
❷ 정돈된 학습 공간은 집중력을 높이는 데 도움이 된다.
③ 효율적인 학습을 위해서 학습 계획표를 작성해야 한다.
④ 많은 과제는 학생에게 학습에 대한 스트레스를 줄 수 있다.
⑤ 책임감을 기르기 위해서는 자녀도 집안일을 분담해야 한다.

03 두 사람의 관계

고1 2018년 11월 5번 | 정답률 95%
▶ 정답 ①

[Door knocks.]
W: Come on in. [Pause] Have a seat, please.
M: Thanks!
W: What has been troubling you, Mr. Williams?
M: My eyes are red and sore, and I can't see things clearly.
W: Okay. Let me check your eyes first. Put your chin on the machine and don't move.
M: Alright.
W: [Pause] Oh, you have dry eyes. Have you been using your computer more than usual?
M: Yes, I've been working all week on an important project.
W: You should rest your eyes and blink more frequently.
M: I see. I was worried I got an eye infection.
W: No, you didn't. Just put some eyedrops in your eyes. I'll give you a prescription.
M: Okay. Do I have to come again?
W: I recommend you have your eyes checked again next week. The nurse will help you make an appointment.
M: All right. Thank you.

해석
[문을 노크하는 소리]
여: 들어오세요. [잠시 후] 앉으세요.
남: 감사합니다!
여: 무슨 문제가 있으신가요, Williams 씨?
남: 눈이 빨갛고 아파요, 그리고 사물을 또렷하게 볼 수 없어요.
여: 알겠습니다. 눈을 먼저 검사해 볼게요. 턱을 기계 위에 올리고 움직이지 마세요.
남: 알겠습니다.
여: [잠시 후] 오, 안구건조증이 있으시네요. 컴퓨터를 평소보다 많이 사용하셨나요?
남: 네, 제가 일주일 내내 중요한 프로젝트를 하고 있어서요.
여: 눈을 쉬게 하고 더 자주 깜빡이셔야 해요.
남: 알겠습니다. 저는 눈이 감염되었을까 봐 걱정했어요.
여: 아니요, 감염되지 않았어요. 눈에 안약을 좀 넣어주세요. 처방전을 드릴게요.
남: 알겠습니다. 저 다시 와야 하나요?
여: 다음 주에 눈을 다시 검사해 보실 것을 권합니다. 간호사가 예약할 수 있도록 도와드릴 거예요.
남: 알겠습니다. 감사합니다.

❶ 안과 의사 — 환자
② 보건 교사 — 학생
③ 프로젝트 팀장 — 팀원
④ 컴퓨터 판매원 — 구매자
⑤ 약사 — 제약 회사 직원

04 그림에서 대화의 내용과 일치하지 않는 것

▶ 정답 ④

M: What do you think of this new office lounge, Ms. Jones?
직원 휴게실
W: It's really nice. You must have worked hard to decorate this place.
열심히 일했음에 틀림없다 (must have p.p.: ~했음에 틀림없다) 꾸미다
M: I enjoyed it. As you asked, two laptop computers have been placed
노트북 컴퓨터들
in front of the window.
~의 앞에
W: Thanks! Our colleagues can browse the web in their free time.
동료들 웹을 검색하다
M: Good. Look at the letter M on the wall. I hung it yesterday. It's your
걸었다(hang)
company's logo, right?
회사의 로고
W: Yeah, I like it. Oh, there is a microwave oven below the logo.
전자레인지
M: Yes, you can use it conveniently for meals. I put the photo on the
편리하게 사진
bookshelf.
책꽂이
W: Thanks! I love this picture. It was taken at our company's second
사진 우리 회사의 2주년 파티
anniversary party.
M: Great! There is a round table, so you can read some books and
원형 테이블
enjoy coffee time here.
W: Thank you. Our colleagues will love this place.

해석

남: 새로운 직원 휴게실에 대해 어떻게 생각해요, Jones 씨?
여: 정말 멋져요. 당신은 이곳을 꾸미기 위해서 열심히 일했음에 틀림없어요.
남: 저는 즐겁게 했어요. 당신이 부탁한 대로, 두 대의 노트북 컴퓨터는 창문 앞에 놓여 있어요.
여: 고마워요! 저희 동료들이 여가 시간에 웹을 검색할 수 있겠네요.
남: 좋아요. 벽에 있는 글자 M을 보세요. 제가 어제 그것을 걸었어요. 당신 회사의 로고잖아요, 맞죠?
여: 네, 마음에 들어요. 오, 로고 아래에 전자레인지가 있네요.
남: 네, 식사를 위해 그것을 편리하게 사용할 수 있어요. 책꽂이 위에는 사진을 놓았어요.
여: 고마워요! 저는 이 사진이 정말 마음에 들어요. 그것은 우리 회사의 2주년 파티에서 찍은 거예요.
남: 멋지네요! 원형 테이블이 있어서, 여기에서 책을 읽으면서 커피 타임을 즐길 수도 있어요.
여: 고마워요. 저희 동료들이 이곳을 정말 좋아할 거예요.

05 남자가 여자를 위해 할 일

▶ 정답 ①

[Cellphone rings.]
W: Benjamin, I'm sorry to call you during work, but I have great news
근무 시간에 전할 소식
to share.
M: No problem, Mom. I'm about to leave my office. What's up?
나는 막 퇴근하려는 참이다
(be about to V: 막 ~하려는 참이다, leave one's office: 퇴근하다)
W: Your brother Wilson got the football scholarship! Let's throw a
축구 장학금 파티를 열다
party tonight to celebrate.
축하하다
M: Wow, wonderful. I'll buy a cake for him on my way home.
집에 가는 길에
W: Good! I'll cook his favorite steak.
요리하다 (on one's way home)
M: Oh, he'll love it!
W: Yeah, I hope so. But I think something is missing from the meal.
빠지다(miss) 식사
How about adding mashed potatoes as a side dish?
으깬 감자 곁들임 요리로

M: Great, it goes well with steak.
~과 잘 어울리다
W: Right, but we're out of potatoes.
감자가 다 떨어진(out of A: A가 다 떨어진)
M: Don't worry. I'll buy some for you. The grocery store is near the
식료품점
bakery. I'll be at home in an hour.
빵집 한 시간 후에
W: Thanks. No rush. We still have some time.

해석

[휴대전화가 울린다.]
여: Benjamin, 근무 시간에 전화해서 미안한데, 전해야 할 좋은 소식이 있어.
남: 괜찮아요, 엄마. 저는 막 퇴근하려는 참이에요. 무슨 일이세요?
여: 네 동생 Wilson이 축구 장학금을 받았단다! 오늘 밤에 축하하기 위해 파티를 열자.
남: 와, 멋지네요. 제가 집에 가는 길에 그를 위해 케이크를 살게요.
여: 좋아! 나는 그 애가 가장 좋아하는 스테이크를 요리할게.
남: 오, 그가 정말 좋아할 거예요!
여: 그래, 그랬으면 좋겠구나. 그런데 식사에서 무언가 빠진 것 같아. 곁들임 요리로 으깬 감자를 추가하는 건 어떨까?
남: 좋아요, 그것은 스테이크와 잘 어울리잖아요.
여: 맞아, 그런데 감자가 다 떨어졌어.
남: 걱정하지 마세요. 제가 엄마를 위해서 좀 사 갈게요. 식료품점이 빵집 근처에 있어요. 한 시간 후엔 집에 있을 거예요.
여: 고맙구나. 서두르지는 말고. 아직 시간이 좀 있어.

✔① 감자 사 오기
② 케이크 만들기
③ 장학금 신청하기
④ 스테이크 주문하기
⑤ 식료품점 위치 검색하기

06 남자가 지불할 금액

▶ 정답 ③

W: Welcome to Springwood Farm Land. How may I help you?
스프링우드 농장
M: Hi, I'd like to buy tickets for a farm experience program.
농장 체험 프로그램
W: We're sorry, but most of the programs are sold out except for two
매진되었다 ~을 제외하고
(be sold out)
programs, the sheep feeding program and the cheese making
양 먹이 주기 프로그램 치즈 만들기 프로그램
program.
M: Hmm, my children might want to try something new, so we'll join
시도해 보고 싶어하다
(want to V: ~하고 싶어하다, try: 시도하다)
the cheese making program. How much is it?
W: The price for the cheese making program is $20 per adult and $15
가격 성인 한 명당
per child.
어린이 한 명당
M: I'd like to buy two adult tickets and two child tickets.
W: Okay. You want to buy tickets for two adults and two children, right?
M: Yes, and I have the coupon from your website. Can I use this?
쿠폰
W: Sure, then you'll get 10% off the total price.
총액에서 10% 할인을 받다
M: Good! I'll pay by credit card.
신용카드로 지불하다

해석

여: Springwood Farm Land(스프링우드 농장)에 오신 것을 환영합니다. 어떻게 도와드릴까요?
남: 안녕하세요, 저는 농장 체험 프로그램 티켓을 사고 싶어요.
여: 최송하지만, 양 먹이 주기 프로그램과 치즈 만들기 프로그램이라는 2개의 프로그램을 제외하고 대부분의 프로그램이 매진되었습니다.
남: 흠, 저희 아이들은 뭔가 새로운 것을 시도해 보고 싶어할 것 같으니까, 저희는 치즈 만들기 프로그램에 참여할게요. 얼마죠?
여: 치즈 만들기 프로그램 가격은 성인 한 명당 20달러이고 어린이 한 명당 15달러입니다.
남: 저는 성인 티켓 2장과 어린이 티켓 2장을 사고 싶어요.
여: 알겠습니다. 성인 2명과 어린이 2명의 티켓을 사고 싶으신 거죠, 맞습니까?
남: 네, 그리고 웹사이트에서 받은 쿠폰을 가지고 있어요. 이것을 쓸 수 있을까요?
여: 물론이죠, 그러면 총액에서 10% 할인을 받으실 거예요.
남: 잘됐네요! 신용카드로 지불할게요.

① $45　　　② $50　　　✔③ $63
④ $70　　　⑤ $72

문제 풀이

20달러짜리 성인 티켓 2장과 15달러짜리 어린이 티켓 2장을 사면 각각 40달러와 30달러로, 총 70달러이다. 남자가 총액에서 10퍼센트 할인해주는 쿠폰을 사용하기 때문에 70달러에서

7달러를 뺀 63달러, 즉 ③ '$63'가 답이다.

07 여자가 거리 공연을 보러 갈 수 없는 이유

▶ 정답 ⑤

M: Hi, Charlotte, long time no see!

W: Hi, Andrew. Are you doing well at your new school?

M: I think I'm adjusting well. All of my new classmates are nice.
적응하는(adjust)

W: Good to hear that. Are you still playing the guitar? I loved your
기타를 치는(play the guitar)
performance at the school festival last year.
공연   학교 축제

M: Yeah, I joined my new school's rock band. I've been practicing hard
새 학교의 록 밴드   연습하는(practice)
with the other members.

W: Great! I'd like to listen to your band play.

M: Actually, our band will have a street performance at Union Square.
거리 공연을 하다
Will you come and watch?

W: Sure, I'd love to. When exactly will it be?
정확히

M: Next Saturday at 2 o'clock. Can you make it?

W: Oh, sorry but unfortunately not. I have to meet my group members
유감스럽게도   만나야 하다   조원들
(have to V: ~해야 하다)
next Saturday afternoon for the science project.
과학 프로젝트

M: Okay. There should be another performance soon.

W: I'll try to make it then!

해석

남: 안녕, Charlotte, 오랜만이야!

여: 안녕, Andrew. 새 학교에는 잘 다니고 있니?

남: 잘 적응하고 있는 것 같아. 새로운 반 친구들이 모두 좋거든.

여: 다행이구나. 너는 아직도 기타를 치고 있니? 나는 작년 학교 축제에서의 네 공연이 정말 좋았어.

남: 응, 나는 새 학교의 록 밴드에 가입했어. 다른 멤버들과 열심히 연습하고 있어.

여: 잘됐다! 나는 네 밴드가 연주하는 것을 듣고 싶어.

남: 사실, 우리 밴드가 Union Square(유니언 스퀘어)에서 거리 공연을 할 거야. 와서 볼래?

여: 물론이지, 그리고 싶어. 정확히 언제 하는 거야?

남: 다음 주 토요일 2시. 올 수 있겠어?

여: 오, 미안하지만 유감스럽게도 안 되겠어. 과학 프로젝트를 위해 다음 주 토요일 오후에 조원들을 만나야 하거든.

남: 알겠어. 곧 또 공연이 있을 거야.

여: 그때는 가도록 노력할게!

① 학교 축제를 위한 부스를 만들어야 해서
② 좋아하는 밴드의 팬 사인회에 가야 해서
③ 동아리 부원들과 기타 연습을 해야 해서
④ 학급 친구들과 합창 대회 준비를 해야 해서
☑ 과학 프로젝트를 위해 조원들을 만나야 해서

08 Moonlight Palace Tour에 관해 언급되지 않은 것

▶ 정답 ④

M: Honey, how about going to the Moonlight Palace Tour this Friday
달빛 궁전 관광
night?

W: I heard about the tour. It'll be wonderful to walk through the palace
under the night sky.
밤하늘 아래에서

M: I agree. The tour starts at 8 p.m. and takes two hours.
2시간이 걸리다

W: Then we can join it after dinner.

M: Sure! A tour guide tells us historical tales about the royal family.
역사적인 이야기들   왕실

W: That could be fun. How much is a ticket for the tour?

M: It's $30. It seems expensive but the tour includes watching a
비싼   포함하다
traditional dance and tasting traditional tea and snacks.
전통춤   전통 차와 간식들

W: I think it's reasonable. We could have a wonderful night.
합리적인

M: Right. It's said that only 100 people are accepted per day. Let's
하루에
hurry up and make a reservation.
서두르다   예약하다

W: Okay. How can we do that?

M: We have to register on the website. I'll do it.
등록하다

W: Thanks. I can't wait.

해석

남: 여보, 이번 주 금요일 밤에 Moonlight Palace Tour(달빛 궁전 관광)에 가는 게 어때요?

여: 저는 그 관광에 대해 들었어요. 밤하늘 아래에서 궁전을 걸으면 멋질 거예요.

남: 동의해요. 관광은 오후 8시에 시작해서 2시간이 걸려요.

여: 그럼 저녁 식사 후에 그것에 참가해요.

남: 그래요! 관광 가이드가 왕실에 대한 역사적인 이야기들을 들려줘요.

여: 그거 재미있겠네요. 관광 티켓은 얼마예요?

남: 30달러예요. 비싸 보이지만 관광에 전통춤을 구경하고 전통 차와 간식들을 맛보는 것이 포함되어 있어요.

여: 제 생각에는 합리적인 것 같아요. 우리는 멋진 밤을 보낼 수 있겠어요.

남: 맞아요. 하루에 100명만 받는다고 하더라고요. 서둘러서 예약합시다.

여: 좋아요. 어떻게 하는 거예요?

남: 웹 사이트에서 등록해야 해요. 제가 할게요.

여: 고마워요. 너무 기대가 돼요.

① 시작 시간   ② 참가비   ③ 인원 제한
④ 관람 시 유의점   ⑤ 예약 방법

문제풀이

남자가 오후 8시에 관광이 시작된다고 말했으므로 시작 시간이 언급되었다. 또한 티켓 값이 30달러라는 대목에서 참가비도 언급되었다. 하루에 100명만 받는다는 부분에서 인원 제한을 알 수 있으며, 예약할 때는 웹 사이트에서 등록해야 한다고 했으니 예약 방법도 알 수 있다. 따라서 언급되지 않은 것으로 ④ '관람 시 유의점'이 답이 된다.

09 Forest Concert에 관한 내용과 일치하지 않는 것

▶ 정답 ④

W: Hello, listeners! We have some good news for music lovers. The
음악 애호가들
Grand Philharmonic will hold the Forest Concert in Central Park on
열다   숲속 음악회
October 7th. The legendary Russian conductor, Alexander Ivanov,
전설적인 러시아의 지휘자
will lead the orchestra with the theme of 'In Search of a Dream.'
오케스트라를 이끌다   주제   꿈을 찾아서
This concert is a gift from the Grand Philharmonic to all music
선물
lovers so everyone can enjoy free admission to this 90-minute
~에 무료 입장
musical treat. Seats are on a first come first serve basis, so prior
음악 선물   선착순으로
reservation is not required. You can also watch it live on TV at
사전 예약   그것을 생방송으로 시청하다
home, but seeing it live at the park could be a once in a lifetime
그것을 실황으로 보는 것(see it live)   평생에 한 번밖에 없는 경험
experience.

해석

여: 안녕하세요, 청취자 여러분! 음악 애호가들을 위한 좋은 소식이 있습니다. Grand Philharmonic(그랜드 필하모닉)이 10월 7일에 Central Park(센트럴 파크)에서 Forest Concert(숲속 음악회)를 엽니다. 전설적인 러시아의 지휘자, Alexander Ivanov(알렉산더 이바노프)가 'In Search of a Dream(꿈을 찾아서)'이라는 주제로 오케스트라를 이끌 것입니다. 이 음악회는 Grand Philharmonic이 모든 음악 애호가들에게 주는 선물이므로 모든 사람들이 이 90분짜리 음악 선물에 무료로 입장할 수 있습니다. 좌석은 선착순이므로, 사전 예약은 필요치 않습니다. 여러분은 집에서 TV로 그것을 생방송으로 시청할 수도 있지만, 공원에서 실황으로 보는 것은 평생에 한 번밖에 없는 경험일 수 있습니다.

① 10월 7일에 열린다.
② 주제는 '꿈을 찾아서'이다.
③ 무료로 입장할 수 있다.
④ 사전 예약이 필요하다.
⑤ 집에서 TV로 시청할 수 있다.

10 표에서 두 사람이 선택할 수업

▶ 정답 ⑤

M: Hey, Julia. How about learning something exciting after work?
퇴근 후에

W: Sure. I'd love to spend my evenings doing something more
더 흥미로운 일을 하는 데 내 저녁 시간을 보내다
interesting.
(spend A (on) V-ing: ~하는 데 A를 보내다, interesting: 흥미로운)

M: I have a time table for evening classes in our community center.
시간표   야간 수업들   지역 문화 센터
Let's look at it.

W: Hmm, they all look good, but I do yoga by myself at home, so
요가를 하다   혼자(by oneself)

except for that, the others are fine.
그것을 제외하면

M: Okay. Oh, Wednesday doesn't work for me. I have my regular
badminton club meeting then.
정기적인 배드민턴 클럽 모임

W: I see. I think we need a little break after work, so how about a class
조금 쉬어야 하다
starting at 7?

M: Alright. Then we're left with two options. Which one do you prefer?
선택들   선호하다

W: Actually, I'm on a tight budget these days, so I don't want to spend
예산이 빠듯한
more than $100.

M: Me, neither. Let's sign up for the cheaper one.
~에 등록하다

해석

남: 이봐, Julia. 퇴근 후에 신나는 것을 배우는 건 어때?
여: 좋아. 나는 더 흥미로운 일을 하는 데 내 저녁 시간을 보내고 싶어.
남: 나에게 우리 지역 문화 센터의 야간 수업 시간표가 있어. 그것을 보자.
여: 흠, 모두 좋아 보이지만, 내가 집에서 혼자 요가를 해서, 그것을 제외하면, 다른 것들은 괜
찮아.
남: 알겠어. 오, 나는 수요일은 안 되겠어. 그때 정기적인 배드민턴 클럽 모임이 있거든.
여: 그렇구나. 내 생각에는 우리가 퇴근 후에 조금 쉬어야 할 것 같아, 그러니까 7시부터 시작
하는 수업은 어때?
남: 좋아. 그렇다면 우리에게 두 가지 선택지가 남았어. 너는 어떤 쪽을 선호하니?
여: 사실, 나는 요즘 예산이 빠듯해서, 100달러 이상은 쓰고 싶지 않아.
남: 나도 그래. 더 저렴한 수업에 등록하자.

Rainbow Community Center 야간 수업

	수업	요일	시간(오후)	월 수업료
①	도자기	월	7:00 ~ 9:00	110달러
②	그림	화	6:30 ~ 8:00	80달러
③	프렌치 베이킹	수	6:30 ~ 8:00	90달러
④	요가	목	6:30 ~ 8:00	70달러
✔	사진	금	7:00 ~ 9:00	80달러

문제풀이

여자는 집에서 요가를 하기 때문에 시간표에서 Yoga(요가) 수업을 제외하고, 남자는 수요
일에 정기적인 모임이 있으니 수요일에 있는 French baking(프렌치 베이킹) 수업을 제외해
야 한다. 여자는 7시부터 시작하는 수업을 원하고 있어서 Pottery(도자기)와 Photography
(사진) 수업이 남는다. 그러나 100달러 이상은 쓰고 싶지 않다고 했으므로 정답은 ⑤
'Photography(사진)' 수업이 된다.

---

11 여자의 마지막 말에 대한 남자의 응답

고1 2018년 11월 1번 | 정답률 90% | ▶ 정답 ④

W: Hey, James, did you choose which club you're going to join?
선택하다   가입하다

M: Not yet. To be honest, I'd like to create a new academic club.
솔직히 말하면   새로운 학술 동아리

W: Great idea! What kind of club do you want to make?
만들고 싶다(want to V: ~하고 싶다)

M: (I'm thinking of making an English debate club.)
영어 토론 동아리

해석

여: 이봐, James, 어느 동아리에 가입할지 선택했니?
남: 아직 안 했어. 솔직히 말하면, 나는 새로운 학술 동아리를 만들고 싶어.
여: 좋은 생각이야! 어떤 종류의 동아리를 만들고 싶니?
남: (나는 영어 토론 동아리를 만들까 생각 중이야.)
① 너는 네 생각에 대해 정직해야 해.
② 나는 너에게 맞는 수업을 선택하도록 도울 수 있어.
③ 나는 이미 진로 상담 프로그램을 수강했어.
✔ 나는 영어 토론 동아리를 만들까 생각 중이야.
⑤ 너는 필요한 만큼 모든 학문적 조언을 얻을 거야.

---

12 남자의 마지막 말에 대한 여자의 응답

고1 2018년 11월 2번 | 정답률 85% | ▶ 정답 ③

M: What a nice hat, Kelly. It looks perfect on you.
~에 정말 잘 어울리다

W: Thanks. I got it from a local market. You can find many good
지역 시장
hand-made items there.
수제품들

M: Really? I'd love to go and look around the market.
가서 둘러보다

W: (Okay. Let's go there together next time.)

해석

남: 정말 멋진 모자구나, Kelly. 너에게 정말 잘 어울린다.
여: 고마워. 나는 그것을 지역 시장에서 샀어. 너는 그곳에서 좋은 수제품들을 많이 찾을 수
있어.
남: 정말? 나는 가서 시장을 둘러보고 싶어.
여: (좋아. 다음에 같이 그곳에 가자.)
① 물론이지. 나는 그것을 온라인에서 샀어.
② 천만에. 모자를 만드는 것은 재미있었어.
✔ 좋아. 다음에 같이 그곳에 가자.
④ 너였니? 나는 네가 그곳에 간 줄 몰랐어.
⑤ 정말이야. 나는 지역 시장에 가본 적이 없어.

---

13 여자의 마지막 말에 대한 남자의 응답

고1 2018년 11월 13번 | 정답률 85% | ▶ 정답 ①

W: That was a great documentary film, wasn't it, David?
다큐멘터리 영화

M: Yeah, I was really impressed by the Korean man, devoting his life to
~에게 정말 감동을 받았다   그의 삶을 돕는 데 바친
(be impressed by)   (devote A to B: A를 B에 바치다)
helping the poorest people of Africa.

W: Right, his life was so beautiful. Living one's life for others is truly
meaningful.
의미 있는

M: I think so, too. Evelyn, would you like to volunteer with me?
자원봉사를 하다

W: Great! What kind of volunteer work are you thinking about?

M: Actually, I've been working at the children's hospital as a volunteer
아동 병원   자원봉사 교사로
teacher.

W: Volunteer teacher?

M: Yeah, I teach children how to paint. The hospital is now looking for
그림을 그리는 법   지금 ~을 구하고 있다
more teachers.
(how to V: ~하는 법, paint: 그림을 그리다) (look for: 구하다, 찾다)

W: I'd like to, but can I be helpful?
도움이 되다

M: Sure, your major is art, so you might be a good fit.
전공   적임자이다

W: I've never taught anyone before, so I'm worried whether I can
teach them well.

M: (Come on. You'll do fine if you volunteer with a kind heart.)
친절한 마음으로

해석

여: 그것은 훌륭한 다큐멘터리 영화였어, 그렇지 않니, David?
남: 그래, 나는 그 한국 남자에게 정말 감동을 받았어, 그의 삶을 아프리카의 가장 가난한 사람
들을 돕는 데 바쳤잖아.
여: 맞아, 그의 삶은 매우 아름다웠어. 다른 사람들을 위한 삶을 사는 것은 정말 의미 있어.
남: 나도 그렇게 생각해. Evelyn, 나와 함께 자원봉사를 할래?
여: 좋아! 어떤 자원봉사 활동을 생각하고 있니?
남: 사실, 나는 아동 병원에서 자원봉사 교사로 일해 오고 있어.
여: 자원봉사 교사?
남: 응, 나는 아이들에게 그림을 그리는 법을 가르쳐. 병원에서 지금 더 많은 교사들을 구하
고 있어.
여: 나도 하고 싶은데, 내가 도움이 될 수 있을까?
남: 물론이지, 네 전공은 미술이니까, 네가 적임자일 수도 있어.
여: 나는 전에 아무도 가르쳐 본 적이 없어서, 내가 그들을 잘 가르칠 수 있을지 걱정이야.
남: (해 봐. 친절한 마음으로 자원봉사를 하면 너는 잘 할 거야.)
✔ 해 봐. 친절한 마음으로 자원봉사를 하면 너는 잘 할 거야.
② 좋아, 나를 위해 자원봉사 기회를 찾아 줄래?
③ 물론이지. 네가 다닐 수 있는 예술 학교 목록을 확인해 보자.
④ 그래, 너는 아프리카 여행을 미리 계획하는 게 좋을 거야.
⑤ 네 말이 맞아. 우리는 그 영화를 봤어야 했어.

문제풀이

남자의 자원봉사 제의에 여자는 누군가를 가르쳐 본 경험이 없어서 아이들을 잘 가르칠 수 있
는 교사가 될 수 있을까 걱정하고 있다. 이러한 상황에서 여자를 격려하는 말이 어울리므로 정
답은 ① 'Come on. You'll do fine if you volunteer with a kind heart.(해 봐. 친절한 마음으
로 자원봉사를 하면 너는 잘 할 거야.)'이다.

14 남자의 마지막 말에 대한 여자의 응답

▶ 정답 ④

M: You look so down these days. What's the matter, Alice?
매우 의기소침해 보이다

W: Do I look down? Actually, I am rather disappointed in myself, Dad.
~에 실망한

M: Oh, are you still discouraged about the school election results?
~에 대해 낙담한   학교 선거 결과

W: Yeah, I worked so hard to become the student president, but I
failed.
학생회장
실패했다

M: You weren't elected president, but challenging yourself was very
선출되지 않았다(be elected)   도전하는 것(challenge)
brave.

W: Everyone around me keeps telling me the same thing. But I can't
계속 말하다(keep V-ing: 계속 ~하다)
stop feeling like a failure.
느끼는 것을 멈출 수 없다   실패자
(stop V-ing: ~하는 것을 멈추다)

M: I understand it's hard to get over, but you proved yourself capable.
극복하다   너 자신이 유능하다는 것을 입증했다
(prove: 입증하다, capable: 유능한)

W: You really think so?

M: Sure, there were so many students who supported you.
지지했다

W: You're right. I hadn't thought about it that way.

M: Cheer up, Alice! This experience will help you become a better
경험
person in the end.
결국

W: (Thanks. I appreciate you for encouraging me to be positive.)
내가 긍정적으로 되도록 격려해 주는 것
(encourage A to V: A가 ~하도록 격려하다, positive: 긍정적인)

해석
남: 너 요즘 매우 의기소침해 보이는구나. 무슨 일이니, Alice?
여: 제가 의기소침해 보여요? 사실, 저는 제 자신에게 꽤 실망했어요, 아빠.
남: 오, 너 아직도 학교 선거 결과에 대해 낙담하고 있는 거니?
여: 네, 저는 학생회장이 되기 위해 정말 열심히 노력했지만, 실패했어요.
남: 너는 학생회장에 선출되지는 않았지만, 스스로에게 도전하는 것은 매우 용감했어.
여: 제 주위의 모든 사람들이 저에게 계속 같은 말을 해요. 그렇지만 저는 실패자처럼 느끼는 것을 멈출 수 없어요.
남: 극복하기 어렵다는 것은 이해하지만, 너는 너 자신이 유능하다는 것을 입증했어.
여: 정말 그렇게 생각하세요?
남: 물론이지, 너를 지지하는 정말 많은 학생들이 있었잖니.
여: 맞아요. 저는 그것에 대해 그렇게 생각하지 않았어요.
남: 기운 내렴, Alice! 이 경험은 결국 네가 더 나은 사람이 되도록 도움을 줄 거야.
여: (고맙습니다. 제가 긍정적으로 되도록 격려해 주셔서 감사해요.)
① 물론이죠. 아빠는 그 전략들로 당선될 수 있어요.
② 네, 저는 더 좋은 학교를 만들기 위한 아빠의 노력을 지지할 거예요.
③ 말도 안 돼요. 아빠 주변의 모든 사람들을 만족시키는 것은 불가능해요.
✓④ 고맙습니다. 제가 긍정적으로 되도록 격려해 주셔서 감사해요.
⑤ 맞아요. 우리는 서로 더 잘 이해하기 위해 더 많은 얘기를 해야 해요.

문제 풀이
학생회장으로 당선되지 못해 낙담하는 여자에게 남자는 그녀가 유능하며 그녀를 지지하던 많은 학생들을 생각하라는 말로 힘을 주고 있다. 이러한 상황에서는 그녀를 북돋아 주는 남자에게 고마움을 표현하는 말, 즉 ④ 'Thanks. I appreciate you for encouraging me to be positive.(고맙습니다. 제가 긍정적으로 되도록 격려해 주셔서 감사해요.)'가 답이다.

15 다음 상황에서 Sophia가 John에게 할 말

▶ 정답 ⑤

W: Sophia and John are classmates and they study math together in a
수학
study group. John spends lots of time studying math but his grades
스터디 그룹   공부하는 데 많은 시간을 보내다   성적
(spend time (on) V-ing: ~하는 데 시간을 보내다, study: 공부하다)
have not improved much. Sophia is good at math so John asks her
별로 향상되지 않았다   A에게 ~해달라고 부탁하다
(improve: 향상되다)   (ask A to V: A에게 ~해달라고 부탁하다)
to help him as a mentor. Sophia finds out that John always tries
조언자로서   풀려고 하다
(try to V: ~하려고 하다, solve: (문제) 풀다)
to solve difficult questions without practicing easier ones. Sophia
연습하지 않고
(without V-ing: ~하지 않고, practice: 연습하다)
thinks that in order to get a good grade, John has to go from easy
좋은 점수를 받기 위해
(in order to V: ~하기 위해, get a good grade: 좋은 점수를 받다)
questions to difficult ones step by step. So she wants to suggest to
쉬운 문제에서 어려운 문제로   단계적으로
(from A to B: A에서 B로)

John that he should solve easy math questions before going on to
어려운 문제로 넘어가기 전에
(go on to A: A로 넘어가다, challenging: 어려운)
challenging ones. In this situation, what would Sophia most likely
say to John?

Sophia: (Why don't you practice less challenging math questions
first?)

해석
여: Sophia와 John은 반 친구이고 스터디 그룹에서 수학을 함께 공부하고 있다. John은 수학을 공부하는 데 많은 시간을 보내지만 그의 성적은 별로 향상되지 않았다. Sophia는 수학을 잘해서 John은 그녀에게 조언자로서 그를 도와달라고 부탁한다. Sophia는 John이 항상 더 쉬운 문제를 연습하지 않고 어려운 문제를 풀려고 한다는 것을 알게 된다. Sophia는 좋은 점수를 받기 위해, John이 단계적으로 쉬운 문제에서 어려운 문제로 가야 한다고 생각한다. 그래서 그녀는 John에게 어려운 문제로 넘어가기 전에 쉬운 수학 문제를 풀어야 한다고 제안하고 싶다. 이러한 상황에서, Sophia는 John에게 뭐라고 말하겠는가?
Sophia: (덜 어려운 수학 문제를 먼저 연습하는 게 어떠니?)
① 우리가 다음 수업에서 배울 것을 예습하자.
② 실생활에 수학 이론을 적용하는 게 어떠니?
③ 수학 실력을 향상시키는 네 비결을 나에게 말해 줄래?
④ 너는 문제의 지시사항을 주의 깊게 읽어야 해.
✓⑤ 덜 어려운 수학 문제를 먼저 연습하는 게 어떠니?

문제 풀이
Sophia는 John이 수학 성적을 높이려면 단계적으로 쉬운 문제에서 어려운 문제로 나아가야 한다고 생각하고 있다. 따라서, 이러한 생각을 표현한 ⑤ 'Why don't you practice less challenging math questions first?(덜 어려운 수학 문제를 먼저 연습하는 게 어떠니?)'가 가장 적절하다.

16~17 1지문 2문항

M: Welcome to 'Smart Traveler.' I'm your host, Brian Lewis. While
현명한 여행자   진행자
traveling, shopping for souvenirs is one of the greatest pleasures,
기념품들을 사는 것
(shop for: ~을 사다, souvenir: 기념품)
and many people enjoy bringing small souvenirs back home. Today
가져오는 것을 즐기다
(enjoy V-ing: ~하는 것을 즐기다, bring: 가져오다)
I'll introduce some of the best souvenirs from around the world!
소개하다
First, when you travel to Beijing, jasmine tea is a great souvenir.
재스민 차
Scented tea in the morning will become a wonderful reminder of
향기로운   ~을 떠올리게 하는 멋진 추억물
all those memories there. Second, in Paris, Eiffel Tower keychains
에펠탑 열쇠고리들
are popular. With this little metal item hanging on your keys, you
인기가 있는   금속 제품   ~에 걸려 있는(hang on)
can remember the special moment of being at the top of the
특별한 순간
Eiffel Tower. Third, when visiting Hawaii, bring back a Hawaiian
춤추는 하와이안 인형
dancing doll. It'll remind you of the intense sun, crystal clear water,
생각나게 하다   강렬한   수정처럼 맑은 물
and amazing beaches. Last, in Venice, you can buy a traditional
놀라운   전통적인 베니스 가면
Venetian mask. Hanging the mask on the wall as a decoration, you
장식품으로
can feel the spirit of Venice at home long afterwards. I hope these
기분   한참 후에도
tips will help you in your souvenir shopping.

해석
남: 'Smart Traveler(현명한 여행자)'에 오신 것을 환영합니다. 저는 진행자인 Brian Lewis입니다. 여행을 하면서, 기념품들을 사는 것은 가장 큰 즐거움 중 하나이고, 많은 사람들이 집에 작은 기념품들을 가져오는 것을 즐깁니다. 오늘 저는 세계 최고의 기념품들 중 몇 가지를 소개할 것입니다. 첫째, 여러분이 베이징을 여행할 때, 재스민 차는 훌륭한 기념품입니다. 아침의 향기로운 차는 그곳의 모든 기억들을 떠올리게 하는 멋진 추억물이 될 것입니다. 둘째, 파리에서는, 에펠탑 열쇠고리가 인기가 있습니다. 이 작은 금속 제품이 여러분의 열쇠에 걸려 있으면, 여러분은 에펠탑의 꼭대기에 있었던 특별한 순간을 기억할 수 있습니다. 셋째, 하와이를 방문할 때, 춤추는 하와이안 인형을 가지고 오십시오. 그것은 여러분에게 강렬한 태양, 수정처럼 맑은 물, 그리고 놀라운 해변들을 생각나게 할 것입니다. 마지막으로, 베니스에서, 여러분은 전통적인 베니스 가면을 구입할 수 있습니다. 가면을 장식품으로 벽에 걸면, 여러분은 한참 후에도 집에서 베니스의 기분을 느낄 수 있습니다. 저는 이 조언이 여러분이 기념품을 살 때 도움이 되기를 바랍니다.

16 남자가 하는 말의 주제

고1 2018년 11월 16번 | 정답률 80%

▶ 정답 ①

☑ 여행에서 집으로 가져갈 수 있는 최고의 기념품들
② 자연을 촬영할 수 있는 세계의 인기 있는 장소들
③ 기념품 쇼핑에 돈을 절약하는 방법에 대한 조언들
④ 세계 문화 환경의 다양성
⑤ 명심해야 할 가장 중요한 여행 안전 규칙들

17 언급된 지역이 아닌 것

고1 2018년 11월 17번 | 정답률 90%

▶ 정답 ③

① 베이징　　　　② 파리　　　　☑ 시드니
④ 하와이　　　　⑤ 베니스

02 | 2019년 3월 학력평가

01	④	02	⑤	03	⑤	04	④	05	②
06	①	07	④	08	④	09	③	10	②
11	②	12	①	13	⑤	14	②	15	①
16	①	17	③							

01 남자가 하는 말의 목적

고1 2019년 3월 3번 | 정답률 85%

▶ 정답 ④

M: Hello, students. This is your vice principal Mike Westwood. I have
　　　　　　　　　　　　　　교감
an important announcement today. As the student lockers are
중요한　　　공지 사항　　　　　　　　　　　학생 사물함들
getting old, we've been receiving complaints from many of you. So
　　　　　　　　　　　　　　불평들
we've decided to replace the lockers over the weekend. We ask
　　　　교체하기로 결정한
(decide to V: ~하기로 결정하다, replace: 교체하다)
that you empty your lockers and leave them open by this Friday,
　　　　비우다　　　　　　　그것들을 열어 놓다
March 22nd. Make sure to take all the items from your lockers
　　　　　　반드시 ~하다　　　　　　　물건들
and leave nothing behind. Any items that are not removed will be
　　아무것도 남기지 않다
thrown away. Thank you for your cooperation.
버려지다　　　　　　　　　협조

해석
남: 안녕하세요, 학생 여러분. 저는 교감인 Mike Westwood입니다. 오늘 중요한 공지 사항이
있습니다. 학생 사물함이 점점 낡아감에 따라, 여러분 중 많은 분들에게서 불평을 받아왔
습니다. 그래서 주말에 사물함을 교체하기로 결정했습니다. 이번 주 금요일인 3월 22일까
지 여러분의 사물함을 비우고 그것들을 열어 놓으시길 부탁드립니다. 반드시 사물함에서
모든 물건들을 가져가고 아무것도 남기지 않도록 하십시오. 치우지 않은 물건들은 버려질
것입니다. 협조해 주셔서 감사합니다.
① 파손된 사물함 신고 절차를 안내하려고
② 사물함에 이름표를 부착할 것을 독려하려고
③ 사물함을 반드시 잠그고 다녀야 함을 강조하려고
☑ 사물함 교체를 위해 사물함을 비울 것을 당부하려고
⑤ 사물함 사용에 대한 학생 설문 조사 참여를 요청하려고

02 여자의 의견

고1 2019년 3월 4번 | 정답률 85%

▶ 정답 ⑤

W: Hey, Daniel. How are you getting ready for your trip to Seoul?
　　　　　　　　　　　　　~을 준비하는(get ready for)
M: Hi, Claire. Everything is going great, but I'm worried about food.
　　　　　　　　　　　　　　　　　　~에 대해 걱정하는
W: Why?
M: I heard that Korean food is very hot and spicy. I think I should bring
　　　　　　　　　　　　　　　맵고 자극적인
some food with me.
W: Oh, aren't you going to try any Korean food?
　　　　　　　　　　　먹어 보다

M: Well, I don't like trying new food. I feel comfortable with what I'm
　　　　먹어 보는 것을 좋아하다　　편안함을 느끼다　　　내가 익숙한 것
used to.
(like V-ing: ~하는 것을 좋아하다)　　　　　　(be used to A: A에 익숙하다)
W: But trying local food is the beauty of travel. It's the best way to get
　　　　　　현지 음식　　　　　　장점　　　여행
to the heart of the culture.
문화의 중심으로 가다
M: Maybe you're right. I'll give it a try during my travels.
　　　　　　　　　　　한번 시도해 보다
W: Good thinking. You can find some good Korean restaurants on the
web.
M: Okay. Thanks.

해석
여: 안녕, Daniel. 서울 여행은 어떻게 준비하고 있니?
남: 안녕, Claire. 모든 일이 잘 되고 있지만, 음식에 대해 걱정이 돼.
여: 왜?
남: 나는 한국 음식이 매우 맵고 자극적이라고 들었어. 음식을 좀 가져가야 할 것 같아.
여: 오, 너는 한국 음식을 안 먹어 볼 거야?
남: 글쎄, 나는 새로운 음식을 먹어 보는 것을 좋아하지 않아. 나는 내가 익숙한 것에 편안함
을 느끼거든.
여: 하지만 현지 음식을 먹어 보는 것은 여행의 장점이야. 그것은 문화의 중심으로 갈 수 있는
가장 좋은 방법이지.
남: 네 말이 맞을지도 몰라. 여행하는 동안 한번 시도해 볼게.
여: 잘 생각했어. 웹에서 좋은 한국 식당들을 찾을 수 있어.
남: 알겠어. 고마워.
① 무리한 여행 계획은 여행을 망칠 수 있다.
② 관광지에서 자연환경을 훼손하지 말아야 한다.
③ 여행할 지역의 문화를 미리 조사해 보는 것이 필요하다.
④ 남들이 추천하는 음식점에 꼭 가 볼 필요는 없다.
☑ 여행을 가면 현지 음식을 먹어 보는 것이 좋다.

03 두 사람의 관계

고1 2019년 3월 5번 | 정답률 80%

▶ 정답 ⑤

M: Hello, Ally! Long time no see.
W: Hi, Robert. It's been a long time since I came to your store.
M: You must have been busy.
　　　　바빴음에 틀림없다
(must have p.p.: ~했음에 틀림없다, busy: 바쁜)
W: Yeah. Did I tell you that I had to prepare for an exhibition?
　　　　　　　　　　　　　　　전시회를 준비하다
(prepare for: ~을 준비하다, exhibition: 전시회)
M: Oh, yeah. I remember. How did it go?
　　　　　　기억나다
W: It went well. It was finally over last week.
　　　　　　　마침내
M: Good. So what kind of hat are you looking for today?
　　　　　　　　　　　　　　~을 찾는(look for)
W: Actually I've changed my hair style, so I'm not sure which hat will
　　　　　　　　　　머리 모양
suit me.
어울리다
M: Oh, you cut your hair short! Why don't you try this hat? It goes well
당신의 머리카락을 짧게 자르다　　　　　　써 보다　　　~과 잘 어울리다
(cut one's hair short)
with short hair.
W: Let me try. [Pause] I love it!
M: It looks great on you.
　　　　　~에게 잘 어울리다
W: Thanks. I'll take it.

해석
남: 안녕하세요, Ally! 오랜만이에요.
여: 안녕하세요, Robert. 제가 당신 가게에 온 지 오래되었네요.
남: 당신은 바빴음에 틀림없군요.
여: 네. 제가 전시회를 준비해야 한다고 말씀드렸나요?
남: 오, 그래요. 기억나요. 그것은 어떻게 되었나요?
여: 잘 됐어요. 지난주에 마침내 끝났어요.
남: 좋네요. 그래서 오늘은 어떤 종류의 모자를 찾으시나요?
여: 사실 제가 머리 모양을 바꿔서, 어떤 모자가 저에게 어울릴지 모르겠어요.
남: 오, 머리카락을 짧게 자르셨군요! 이 모자를 써 보시는 건 어때요? 짧은 머리와 잘 어울
려요.
여: 써 볼게요. [잠시 후] 정말 마음에 들어요!
남: 당신에게 잘 어울리네요.
여: 감사해요. 그것을 살게요.
① 미용사 — 고객　　　　　　　② 화방 점원 — 화가

③ 미술관장 — 방문객　　　　　④ 패션 디자이너 — 모델
✔ 모자 가게 주인 — 손님

문제 풀이
여자가 가게에 온 지 오래되었다고 말했으므로 미술관장 — 방문객의 관계는 답과 거리가 멀어진다. 전시회에 대한 언급이 있었지만 오답을 선택하게 하려는 함정이니 주의해야 한다. 남자가 어떤 종류의 모자를 찾으시냐고 물었으므로 ⑤ '모자 가게 주인 — 손님'이 적절한 답이다.

04 그림에서 대화의 내용과 일치하지 않는 것
고1 2019년 3월 6번　정답률 85%　▶ 정답 ④

M: What are you looking at, Sumi?
W: Hi, David. I'm looking at the picture I took on my middle school
　　　　　　　　　　　　　　　　사진　　　　　　　　　　　중학교 졸업식 날
　graduation day.
M: Let me see it. [Pause] Wow! There are heart-shaped balloons
　　　　　　　　　　　　　　　　　　　하트 모양의 풍선들
　above the blackboard.
　　　　　칠판
W: Yeah. My friends and I put them there.
M: How nice! I also like the "Thank You" banner below the balloons.
　　　　　　　　　　　　　　　　　　　현수막
W: We really wanted to express our thanks to our homeroom teacher,
　　　　　　　　　　우리의 감사한 마음을 표현하다　　우리의 담임 선생님
　　　　　　　　　　　　(express one's thanks)
　Mr. Kim. I took this picture with him.
M: Oh, he's wearing a striped tie.
　　　　　　　　　줄무늬 넥타이
W: Right. He usually doesn't wear a tie, but it was a special day.
　　　　　　　보통
M: I see. What is it in your hand?
W: It's the school yearbook.
　　　　학교 졸업 앨범
M: And you're making a V-sign with your fingers.
　　　　　　　V 사인을 만드는
W: Yes. I was very happy and proud that day.
　　　　　　　　　　　　　자랑스러운

해석
남: 무엇을 보고 있니, Sumi?
여: 안녕, David. 나는 중학교 졸업식 날에 찍은 사진을 보고 있어.
남: 어디 보자. [잠시 후] 와! 칠판 위에 하트 모양의 풍선들이 있구나.
여: 그래. 내 친구들과 내가 그것들을 그곳에 놓았어.
남: 정말 멋지다! 나는 풍선들 아래에 있는 "Thank You" 현수막도 마음에 들어.
여: 우리는 정말 담임 선생님인 김 선생님께 감사한 마음을 표현하고 싶었어. 나는 그분과 함께 이 사진을 찍었어.
남: 오, 그분은 줄무늬 넥타이를 매고 계시는구나.
여: 맞아. 그분은 보통 넥타이를 매시지 않지만, 특별한 날이었거든.
남: 그렇구나. 네 손에 있는 것은 무엇이니?
여: 학교 졸업 앨범이야.
남: 그리고 너는 손가락으로 V 사인을 만들고 있구나.
여: 그래. 나는 그날 매우 행복하고 자랑스러웠어.

05 여자가 남자를 위해 할 일
고1 2019년 3월 7번　정답률 90%　▶ 정답 ②

W: Freddie, what are you doing on the computer?
M: I'm working on my music assignment, Mom.
　　　　　　　　　　　음악 과제
W: What is it about?
M: I have to write a song, but I can't think of a good melody.
　　　　　　작곡하다　　　　　　좋은 멜로디를 생각해 내다
W: When is the due date?
　　　　　　마감일
M: I only have a week to finish. I feel pressed for time.
　　　　　　　　　　　　　　　시간에 압박을 느끼다

W: Take it easy. Is there anything I can do for you?
M: I think I need to get some fresh air.
　　　　　　바람을 좀 쐬야 한다
　　(need to V: ~해야 하다, get some fresh air: 바람을 좀 쐬다)
W: Why don't you go to the beach? I can take you there.
　　　　　　　　　　해변에 가다
M: Great. It'll help me come up with some ideas. Thanks.
　　　　　　　　　　　~을 생각해 내다

해석
여: Freddie, 컴퓨터로 무엇을 하고 있니?
남: 음악 과제를 하고 있어요, 엄마.
여: 무엇에 관한 건데?
남: 작곡을 해야 하는데, 좋은 멜로디를 생각해 낼 수가 없어요.
여: 마감일이 언제니?
남: 끝내야 할 시간이 일주일 밖에 없어요. 저는 시간에 압박을 느끼고 있어요.
여: 진정하렴. 내가 너를 위해 할 수 있는 일이 있을까?
남: 저는 바람을 좀 쐬야 할 것 같아요.
여: 해변에 가는 게 어떠니? 내가 너를 그곳에 데려다 줄게.
남: 좋아요. 그것은 제가 아이디어를 생각해 내는 데 도움이 될 거예요. 감사해요.

① 악기 빌려다 주기
✔ 해변에 데려다 주기
③ 음악회에 함께 가기
④ 해양 스포츠 예약하기
⑤ 오디션 일정 확인해 주기

06 두 사람이 지불할 금액
고1 2019년 3월 9번　정답률 75%　▶ 정답 ①

M: Honey, I think Paul needs new shoes.
W: You're right. His shoes are getting too tight for his feet.
　　　　　　　　　　　　　　　　　　　~에 너무 꽉 끼는
M: Let's buy a pair online. I know a good store. [Clicking sound] Have
　　　　　　　한 켤레를 사다　　　　　　　　　　　가게
　a look.
W: Oh, how about these shoes? They're originally $100 a pair, but
　　　　~은 어때요?　　　　　　　　　　　원래
　they're 30% off now.
M: That's a good deal. Let's buy a pair.
W: Oh, there are shoe bags, too. Why don't we buy one?
　　　　　　　　　　　　　　　　　　우리 ~하는 게 어때요?
M: Okay. There are two kinds, a $10 bag and a $15 bag. Which one
　do you like?
W: The $10 one looks good enough.
　　　　　　충분히 좋아 보이다
M: Then let's take it. Is that all we need?
W: Yes. Oh, here it says that if you're a member of this online store,
　　　　　　　　　　　　　　　　　　　　　회원
　you'll get $5 off.
　　　5달러 할인을 받다
M: That's good. I'm a member. Let's buy them now.
W: Okay.

해석
남: 여보, Paul에게 새 신발이 필요한 것 같아요.
여: 당신 말이 맞아요. 그 애의 신발은 발에 점점 더 너무 꽉 끼고 있어요.
남: 온라인으로 한 켤레를 삽시다. 제가 좋은 가게를 알고 있어요. [클릭하는 소리] 봐요.
여: 오, 이 신발은 어때요? 원래 한 켤레에 100달러인데, 지금 30% 할인 중이에요.
남: 그거 괜찮은 거래네요. 한 켤레 삽시다.
여: 오, 신발 가방도 있어요. 우리 하나 사는 게 어때요?
남: 좋아요. 10달러짜리 가방과 15달러짜리 가방 두 종류가 있네요. 어떤 게 마음에 들어요?
여: 10달러짜리 가방도 충분히 좋아 보여요.
남: 그럼 그것을 삽시다. 우리 필요한 건 그게 다예요?
여: 네. 오, 여기 이 온라인 가게 회원이면, 5달러 할인을 받는다고 적혀 있어요.
남: 잘됐네요. 저는 회원이거든요. 지금 그것들을 삽시다.
여: 알겠어요.

✔ $75　　　　　　② $80　　　　　　③ $85
④ $105　　　　　⑤ $110

문제 풀이
신발의 원래 가격은 100달러인데 30% 할인 중이므로 70달러가 된다. 10달러짜리와 15달러짜리 신발 가방 중에 10달러짜리 가방을 사기로 했으므로 총 금액은 80달러가 된다. 그러나 남자가 온라인 가게 회원이라 5달러 할인을 받을 수 있으므로 최종 금액은 75달러가 된다. 따라서 정답은 ① '$75'이다.

07 남자가 발표 자료를 수정해야 하는 이유

고1 2019년 3월 8번 | 정답률 90% | ▶ 정답 ④

W: Tony, are you ready for your science presentation tomorrow?
~을 위한 준비가 된 / 과학 발표

M: Yes, Ms. Woods, thanks to your help. I've already printed out the
~ 덕분에 / 인쇄했다(print out)
presentation material.
발표 자료

W: Can I take a look at it? Hmm. I'm afraid you need to make some
~을 보다 / (유감스럽지만) ~인 것 같다 / 수정해야 하다
(need to V: ~해야 하다,
changes.
make a change: 수정하다)

M: Why? Are there any errors in the date or the names? I've checked
오류들
them twice.
두 번

W: No, they're correct.
정확한

M: Did I use old data?
오래된 자료

W: No, you used the latest data. But this picture of the planets is not
최신 자료 / 그림 / 행성들
clear.

M: Oh, my! I'll change it to a clearer picture.
그것을 더 선명한 그림으로 바꾸다
(change A to B: A를 B로 바꾸다)

W: Okay. I'm sure you'll do well tomorrow.

M: Thank you, Ms. Woods.

해석

여: Tony, 내일 과학 발표를 위한 준비는 되었니?
남: 네, Woods 선생님, 도와주신 덕분에요. 저는 이미 발표 자료를 인쇄했어요.
여: 내가 그것을 봐도 될까? 흠, 너는 좀 수정해야 할 것 같구나.
남: 왜요? 날짜나 명칭에 오류가 있나요? 두 번이나 확인했는데요.
여: 아니, 그것들은 정확해.
남: 제가 오래된 자료를 사용했나요?
여: 아니, 너는 최신 자료를 사용했구나. 그런데 행성들의 그림이 선명하지 않아.
남: 오, 이런! 그것을 더 선명한 그림으로 바꿀게요.
여: 좋아. 너는 내일 틀림없이 잘 할거야.
남: 감사합니다, Woods 선생님.

① 최신 자료가 아니어서
② 발표 일정이 바뀌어서
③ 명칭 표기에 오류가 있어서
✔ 그림 자료가 선명하지 않아서
⑤ 발표할 내용의 순서가 틀려서

08 Royal Botanic Garden에 관해 언급되지 않은 것

고1 2019년 3월 10번 | 정답률 85% | ▶ 정답 ④

W: Honey, it's spring. How about visiting the new botanic garden this
~하는 게 어때요? / 식물원
weekend?

M: Do you mean the Royal Botanic Garden located in Redwood Valley?
왕립 식물원 / ~에 위치한

W: Yes, it's not far from here. It's one of the biggest botanic gardens in
~에서 먼
the country.

M: That's right. I heard its size is about four times larger than a soccer
~보다 약 4배 더 큰 / 축구장
field.

W: Yeah. You know, they offer interesting programs such as tree
제공하다 / 나무 심기
planting and guided tours.
가이드 투어(가이드가 있는 투어)

M: Sounds great. Our kids will love planting trees.
나무를 심는 것을 좋아하다
(love V-ing: ~하는 것을 좋아하다)

W: Definitely. Let's go this Saturday. What time shall we leave?
출발하다

M: How about 9 in the morning? The botanic garden is open from 10
a.m. to 6 p.m.

W: Okay. It'll be fun.

해석

여: 여보, 봄이에요. 이번 주말에 새로 문을 연 식물원에 가보는 게 어때요?
남: Redwood Valley(레드우드 밸리)에 위치한 Royal Botanic Garden(왕립 식물원)을 말하는 거예요?
여: 네, 여기에서 멀지 않아요. 그것은 우리나라에서 가장 큰 식물원 중 하나잖아요.
남: 맞아요. 저는 그것의 크기가 축구장보다 약 4배 더 크다고 들었어요.
여: 네. 당신도 알다시피, 그곳에서는 나무 심기와 가이드 투어 같은 흥미로운 프로그램들을 제공해요.

남: 좋네요. 우리 아이들이 나무를 심는 것을 좋아할 거예요.
여: 당연하죠. 이번 주 토요일에 가요. 우리 몇 시에 출발할까요?
남: 아침 9시 어때요? 식물원은 오전 10시부터 오후 6시까지 문을 열어요.
여: 좋아요. 재미있을 거예요.

① 위치　　　　　② 크기　　　　　③ 프로그램
✔ 입장료　　　　⑤ 개관 시간

09 2019 Riverside High School Musical에 관한 내용과 일치하지 않는 것

고1 2019년 3월 11번 | 정답률 85% | ▶ 정답 ③

W: Hello, students. This is Janice Hawkins, your drama teacher. I'm
연극 교사
happy to invite you and your family to the 2019 Riverside High
초대하다 / 2019 리버사이드 고등학교 뮤지컬
School Musical. This year we're presenting Shrek, based on the
선보이는(present) / ~에 기반을 둔
famous animated film. It's full of singing, dancing, romance and
유명한 애니메이션 영화 / ~으로 가득 찬
lots of fun. The auditions for the show were in December last year.
오디션들
The cast and crew have been rehearsing for months to perfect
출연진과 제작진 / 리허설을 해 왔다(rehearse)
their performance. The musical will be held in the auditorium for
그들의 공연을 완벽하게 하다 / 열리다 / 강당
two days on March 15th and 16th. Tickets are $8 per person. You
1인당
can buy tickets in the drama club room. For more details, visit the
연극 동아리방
school website. Thank you.

해석

여: 안녕하세요, 학생 여러분. 저는 여러분의 연극 교사인 Janice Hawkins입니다. 여러분과 여러분의 가족을 2019 Riverside High School Musical(2019 리버사이드 고등학교 뮤지컬)에 초대하게 되어 기쁩니다. 올해 저희는 유명한 애니메이션 영화에 기반을 둔, 〈Shrek(슈렉)〉을 선보일 것입니다. 그것은 노래, 춤, 로맨스 그리고 많은 재미로 가득 차 있습니다. 공연의 오디션은 작년 12월에 있었습니다. 출연진과 제작진은 그들의 공연을 완벽하게 하기 위해 몇 달 동안 리허설을 해 왔습니다. 뮤지컬은 3월 15일과 16일 이틀 동안 강당에서 열릴 것입니다. 입장권은 1인당 8달러입니다. 연극 동아리방에서 입장권을 구입하실 수 있습니다. 더 자세한 정보를 원하시면, 학교 웹 사이트를 방문해 주십시오. 감사합니다.

① 공연작은 Shrek이다.
② 공연을 위한 오디션은 작년 12월에 있었다.
✔ 공연은 사흘간 진행된다.
④ 입장권은 1인당 8달러이다.
⑤ 입장권은 연극 동아리실에서 구입할 수 있다.

10 표에서 남자가 구입할 운동 매트

고1 2019년 3월 12번 | 정답률 80% | ▶ 정답 ②

W: Good morning. How may I help you?

M: I'm looking for an exercise mat for home training.
운동 매트 / 홈 트레이닝(집에서 간단한 기구를 사용하여 하는 운동)

W: Okay. Here are our best-selling models.
가장 잘 팔리는 모델들

M: They all look nice. Are thicker mats better?
더 두꺼운(thick: 두꺼운)

W: Not really. But I think it should be at least 5mm for home trainers.
적어도 5mm는 되다

M: I see. Then I have to choose from these four.
선택해야 하다
(have to V: ~해야 하다, choose: 선택하다)

W: How about this one? It's the most popular.
가장 인기가 있는

M: It's too expensive. I don't want to spend more than $40.
너무 비싼 / 쓰고 싶다
(want to V: ~하고 싶다, spend: (돈을) 쓰다)

W: Out of these two options left, I recommend this model with a
추천하다
non-slip surface. It keeps you from sliding around.
미끄럼 방지 표면이 있는 / 당신이 미끄러지는 것을 막다
(keep A from V-ing: A가 ~하는 것을 막다, slide around: 미끄러지다)

M: Okay. Safety is important. I'll take it.
안전

해석

여: 안녕하세요. 어떻게 도와드릴까요?
남: 저는 홈 트레이닝을 위한 운동 매트를 찾고 있어요.
여: 알겠습니다. 여기 저희의 가장 잘 팔리는 모델들이 있어요.
남: 모두 좋아 보이네요. 더 두꺼운 매트들이 더 좋을까요?
여: 꼭 그렇진 않아요. 하지만 제 생각에 홈 트레이너가 쓰려면 적어도 5mm는 되어야 할 것

같아요.

남: 그렇군요. 그럼 이 네 개 중에서 선택해야겠네요.

여: 이건 어떠세요? 가장 인기가 있는 것이에요.

남: 너무 비싸네요. 저는 40달러 이상은 쓰고 싶지 않아요.

여: 남은 두 개의 선택 중에서, 저는 미끄럼 방지 표면이 있는 이 모델을 추천해요. 그것은 당신이 미끄러지는 것을 막아주거든요.

남: 좋아요. 안전이 중요하죠. 그것을 살게요.

운동 매트

	모델	두께	가격	미끄럼 방지 표면
①	A	4mm	24달러	×
✓②	B	6mm	33달러	○
③	C	8mm	38달러	×
④	D	8mm	45달러	○
⑤	E	10mm	55달러	○

11 여자의 마지막 말에 대한 남자의 응답

고1 2019년 3월 1번 | 정답률 80% ▶ 정답 ②

W: Grandpa, is that a Spanish book you're reading?
스페인어 책

M: Yes, I just started to learn Spanish. You know learning a foreign
(start to V: ~하기 시작하다, learn: 배우다) 외국어
language is good for your brain.
~에 좋은   뇌

W: Sounds great. Are you learning it by yourself?
혼자서(by oneself)

M: (No, I'm taking a class in the community center.)
수업   지역 문화 센터

해석

여: 할아버지, 읽고 계신 것이 스페인어 책이에요?

남: 그래, 나는 막 스페인어를 배우기 시작했단다. 너도 외국어를 배우는 것이 뇌에 좋다는 것을 알고 있잖니.

여: 멋지네요. 그것을 혼자서 배우시는 거예요?

남: (아니, 나는 지역 문화 센터에서 수업을 받고 있어.)

① 미안하지만, 나 혼자 스페인에 가는 게 좋겠어.

✓② 아니, 나는 지역 문화 센터에서 수업을 받고 있어.

③ 그래, 너는 뇌를 위해 건강에 좋은 음식을 먹어야 해.

④ 그래, 너는 뇌에 대해 걱정할 필요가 없어.

⑤ 글쎄, 나는 스페인어를 배우는 데 관심이 없어.

12 남자의 마지막 말에 대한 여자의 응답

고1 2019년 3월 2번 | 정답률 75% ▶ 정답 ①

M: Sally, what are you looking for?
~을 찾고 있다(look for: ~을 찾다)

W: I can't find my jacket. I don't remember where I put it.
찾다   기억나다   두다

M: Why don't you check the gym? You were wearing it in P.E. class.
체육관을 확인하다   체육 수업 시간에

W: (That's right. I'll go there and see.)

해석

남: Sally, 무엇을 찾고 있니?

여: 내 재킷을 찾을 수가 없어. 그것을 어디에 두었는지 기억나지 않아.

남: 체육관을 확인해 보는 게 어떠니? 체육 수업 시간에 그것을 입고 있었잖아.

여: (맞아. 내가 그곳에 가서 볼게.)

✓① 맞아. 내가 그곳에 가서 볼게.

② 서두르자. 체육 수업이 곧 시작돼.

③ 좋은 생각이야. 체육관을 청소하는 것은 중요해.

④ 고마워. 내가 지금 분실물 보관소에 가 볼게.

⑤ 알았어. 내가 내일 그것을 돌려줄게.

13 여자의 마지막 말에 대한 남자의 응답

고1 2019년 3월 13번 | 정답률 85% ▶ 정답 ⑤

W: Hi, David. What are you looking at?

M: School club posters.
학교 동아리 포스터들

W: Is there any club you want to join?
가입하고 싶다
(want to V: ~하고 싶다, join: 가입하다)

M: I'm interested in drones, but there's no drone club.
~에 관심이 있는 (drone: 무선으로 조종하는 무인 비행기)

W: That's too bad. Why don't you make a new club yourself?
직접 새로운 동아리를 만들다(make A oneself: 직접 A를 만들다)

M: Oh, I haven't thought about it. What do I have to do first?
해야 하다(have to V: ~해야 하다)

W: You'll need at least five people to start a club.
최소한

M: Then I have to find people who are interested in drones.
찾다

W: How about using social media? It's an easy way to attract people.
소셜 미디어   쉬운 방법   끌어 모으다

M: (Right. I'll post an ad for a drone club I'm going to make.)
광고를 게시하다

해석

여: 안녕, David. 무엇을 보고 있니?

남: 학교 동아리 포스터들이야.

여: 가입하고 싶은 동아리가 있니?

남: 나는 드론에 관심이 있는데, 드론 동아리가 없어.

여: 안됐구나. 네가 직접 새로운 동아리를 만들어 보는 건 어떠니?

남: 오, 그건 생각하지 못했네. 내가 먼저 무엇을 해야 할까?

여: 동아리를 시작하기 위해서는 최소한 다섯 명이 필요할 거야.

남: 그럼 드론에 관심이 있는 사람들을 찾아야겠네.

여: 소셜 미디어를 사용하는 건 어떠니? 그것은 사람들을 끌어 모으는 쉬운 방법이잖아.

남: (맞아. 내가 만들 드론 동아리에 대한 광고를 게시할게.)

① 우리 동아리에는 새 회원을 위한 자리가 없어.

② 네가 동아리 면접에 통과하지 못했다니 유감이야.

③ 그건 사실이야. 우리가 그곳의 모든 정보를 신뢰할 수는 없어.

④ 고맙지만, 나는 드론 수업을 다시 듣고 싶지 않아.

✓⑤ 맞아. 내가 만들 드론 동아리에 대한 광고를 게시할게.

문제 풀이

드론 동아리를 만들어 보라는 여자의 제의에 남자가 수긍하며 자신처럼 드론에 관심 있는 사람들을 찾으려 하고 있다. 소셜 미디어를 사용해 사람들을 모아 보는 게 어떠냐는 여자의 제안에 남자가 긍정하고 있으므로 이어질 말은 ⑤ 'Right. I'll post an ad for a drone club I'm going to make.(맞아. 내가 만들 드론 동아리에 대한 광고를 게시할게.)'가 적절하다.

14 남자의 마지막 말에 대한 여자의 응답

고1 2019년 3월 14번 | 정답률 55% ▶ 정답 ②

M: What are you reading, Lily?

W: It's a book for my English class, Dad. We have to read a book and
영어 수업
write a review.
서평을 쓰다

M: Do you like the book?

W: Well, I'm not sure. Frankly it's too difficult for me.
솔직히

M: Why did you choose to read that book then?
읽기로 결정하다
(choose to V: ~하기로 결정하다, read: 읽다)

W: It was on the bestseller list and it looked interesting. It's very
베스트셀러 목록에   흥미로워 보였다(look interesting)
challenging, though.
어려운   하지만

M: Maybe you should try another book that suits your level.
시도하다   네 수준에 맞다

W: I know what you mean, but wouldn't I learn more from reading a
읽는 것으로부터 더 많은 것을 배우다
difficult book?
(learn A from B: B로부터 A를 배우다)

M: Well, what's the use of reading it if you can't understand it?
읽는 게 무슨 소용이 있니
(what's the use of V-ing: ~하는 게 무슨 소용이 있니)

W: (That makes sense. I'll switch to an easier book.)
~으로 바꾸다

해석

남: 무엇을 읽고 있니, Lily?

여: 제 영어 수업을 위한 책이에요, 아빠. 저희는 책을 읽고 서평을 써야 해요.

남: 그 책이 마음에 드니?

여: 음, 잘 모르겠어요. 솔직히 저에게는 너무 어려워요.

남: 그럼 너는 왜 그 책을 읽기로 결정했니?

여: 베스트셀러 목록에 있었고 흥미로워 보였거든요. 하지만 매우 어려워요.

남: 아마도 너는 네 수준에 맞는 다른 책을 시도해 봐야 할 것 같구나.

여: 무슨 말씀인지 알지만, 어려운 책을 읽는 것으로부터 더 많은 것을 배우지 않을까요?

남: 글쎄, 네가 이해하지 못한다면 그것을 읽는 게 무슨 소용이 있니.

여: (그거 일리가 있네요. 저는 더 쉬운 책으로 바꿀게요.)

① 맞아요. 그래서 제가 이 책을 선택한 거예요.

✓② 그거 일리가 있네요. 저는 더 쉬운 책으로 바꿀게요.

③ 알겠어요. 저는 다음에 베스트셀러 목록에서 하나를 고를 거예요.

④ 걱정하지 마세요. 그것은 제가 읽기에 그리 어렵지 않아요.
⑤ 네. 저는 더 많은 책을 읽기 위해 독서 동아리에 가입할 거예요.

문제 풀이

남자는 여자의 수준에 맞는 다른 책을 읽어보라며 이해하지 못하는 책을 읽을 필요가 없다는 입장을 보이고 있다. 따라서 남자의 주장을 수용하여 읽기에 좀 더 쉬운 책으로 바꿔보겠다는 ② 'That makes sense. I'll switch to an easier book.(그거 일리가 있네요. 저는 더 쉬운 책으로 바꿀게요.)'이 답으로 적절하다.

---

15 다음 상황에서 Becky가 Clara에게 할 말

M: Clara and Becky go to summer camp together every year. They are
planning to join one this year, too. Today Clara gets a flyer for an
interesting camp at the community center. She shows Becky the
flyer and asks her to sign up for the camp together. Checking the
dates, Becky finds out that she has a family vacation during that
period. When Becky tells Clara that she won't be able to join the
camp, Clara is very disappointed. So Becky wants to suggest to
Clara that they look for another camp. In this situation, what would
Becky most likely say to Clara?
Becky: (Why don't we find a camp on different dates?)

해석

남: Clara와 Becky는 매년 여름 캠프에 함께 간다. 그들은 올해에도 캠프에 참가할 계획이다. 오늘 Clara는 지역 문화 센터에서 흥미로운 캠프에 관한 전단지를 받는다. 그녀는 Becky에게 그 전단지를 보여주고 그녀에게 캠프에 함께 등록하자고 요청한다. 날짜를 확인하면서, Becky는 자신이 그 기간 동안 가족 휴가를 보낸다는 것을 알게 된다. Becky가 Clara에게 캠프에 참가할 수 없을 것이라고 말하자, Clara는 매우 실망한다. 그래서 Becky는 Clara에게 다른 캠프를 찾아보자고 제안하고 싶다. 이러한 상황에서, Becky는 Clara에게 뭐라고 말하겠는가?
Becky: (우리 다른 날짜의 캠프를 찾아보는 게 어때?)

✔️우리 다른 날짜의 캠프를 찾아보는 게 어때?
② 너는 이 전단지의 캠프 날짜를 먼저 확인해야 해.
③ 캠프에 참가하기 위해서 너는 부모님의 허락이 필요해.
④ 지금 당장 캠프에 등록하는 게 어때?
⑤ 올해는 캠프에 가지 말자.

16~17 1지문 2문항

W: Hello, class. You must have heard of the proverb, 'Birds of
a feather flock together.' We all know what this proverb means
because it's commonly used. Like this, there are many proverbs
in which animals appear. Let's talk about them today. First one
is, 'When the cat's away, the mice will play.' It is using the fun
relationship between the two animals. We can easily guess the
meaning of this proverb: the weaker do whatever they want
when the stronger are not around. The next one is, 'Don't count
your chickens before they're hatched.' It's using a chicken's life
cycle. From this proverb, we can learn the lesson that we should
not make hasty decisions. Now it's your turn to talk about a few
proverbs like these. You may have already thought about one with
dogs, like 'Every dog has its day.' Let's talk about some together.

해석

여: 안녕하세요, 여러분. 여러분은 '같은 깃털의 새들끼리 함께 모인다.'라는 속담을 들어봤음에 틀림없습니다. 이것은 흔히 쓰이기 때문에 우리 모두는 이 속담이 무엇을 의미하는지 알고 있습니다. 이처럼, 동물들이 등장하는 많은 속담들이 있습니다. 오늘은 그것들에 대해 이야기해 봅시다. 첫 번째 속담은, '고양이가 없으면, 쥐들이 설친다.'입니다. 그것은 두 동물들 사이의 재미있는 관계를 이용하고 있습니다. 우리는 이 속담의 의미를 쉽게 추측할 수 있습니다: 약자는 강자가 주위에 없을 때 그들이 원하는 게 무엇이든지 한다는 것입니다. 다음 속담은, '닭들이 부화하기도 전에 세지 마라.'입니다. 그것은 닭의 수명 주기를 이용하고 있습니다. 이 속담으로부터, 우리는 성급한 결정을 해서는 안 된다는 교훈을 배울 수 있습니다. 이제 여러분이 이와 같은 몇 가지 속담에 대해 이야기할 차례입니다. 여러분은 이미 '모든 개는 자기의 날을 가지고 있다.'와 같은, 개들이 나오는 속담에 대해 생각했을지도 모릅니다. 함께 이야기해 보겠습니다.

---

16 여자가 하는 말의 주제

✔️동물들이 나오는 속담들
② 다양한 문화권의 서로 다른 속담들
③ 속담이 이해하기 어려운 이유
④ 동물들의 행동을 연구하는 것의 중요성
⑤ 속담을 통해 가치를 가르치는 것의 이점

---

17 언급된 동물이 아닌 것

① 새들   ② 쥐들   ✔️소들
④ 닭들   ⑤ 개들

---

03 2019년 6월 학력평가

01	①	02	③	03	①	04	⑤	05	①
06	④	07	②	08	④	09	⑤	10	③
11	②	12	①	13	②	14	④	15	③
16	①	17	⑤						

---

01 여자가 하는 말의 목적

W: Good morning, everyone. This is Rachel Adams, your student
president. As you know, the student union is holding a charity
event from next Monday until Wednesday. Thank you to those who
have already donated a variety of useful items. We're selling all
of those items for five dollars or less, and all of the money will be
donated to a local charity. The event will be held in the school gym
from 3 p.m. to 5 p.m. I hope many students will participate in this
event for charity. Thank you for listening.

해석

여: 안녕하세요, 여러분. 저는 학생회장인 Rachel Adams입니다. 여러분도 알다시피, 학생회는 다음 주 월요일부터 수요일까지 자선 행사를 개최할 예정입니다. 이미 여러 가지 유용한 물건들을 기부하신 분들께 감사드립니다. 저희는 모든 물건들을 5달러 이하에 판매할 것이고, 모든 돈은 지역 자선 단체에 기부될 것입니다. 이 행사는 오후 3시부터 5시까지 학교 체육관에서 열릴 것입니다. 많은 학생들이 이 자선 행사에 참여하기를 바랍니다. 들어주셔서 감사합니다.

✔️자선 행사 개최를 공지하려고
② 경제 특강 참가자를 모집하려고
③ 물자 절약의 중요성을 강조하려고

④ 학생 회장 선거 후보자를 소개하려고
⑤ 학교 체육관 이용 방법을 안내하려고

02 남자의 의견

고1 2019년 6월 4번 | 정답률 85%
▶ 정답 ③

M: Brenda, my uncle bought a shrimp pizza. Help yourself.
새우 피자
W: Oh! But I don't like shrimp.
M: Really? Do you have an allergy to shrimp?
~에 알러지가 있다
W: No. I've heard shrimp is a little high in cholesterol. So, I think it isn't
콜레스테롤 함량이 조금 높다 (be high in A: A가 높다)
good for our health.
우리의 건강에 좋지 않다
(be good for: ~에 좋다, health: 건강)
M: Hmm, that's a misunderstanding about shrimp.
오해
W: You mean eating shrimp has a positive effect on health?
~에 긍정적인 영향을 미치다(have an effect on: ~에 영향을 미치다)
M: Of course. It can increase your level of good cholesterol.
증가시키다   너의 좋은 콜레스테롤 수치
W: Oh, I didn't know that.
M: Eating shrimp can give us vitamins and minerals. Plus, shrimp is
비타민들   미네랄들   게다가
low-calorie.
저칼로리의
W: Then it might be good to add shrimp to my diet.
새우를 내 식단에 추가하다
(add A to B: A를 B에 추가하다, diet: 식단)
M: Sure. It would be helpful to your health.
W: I guess I didn't know much about shrimp. I'll give it a try.
한번 시도해 보다

해석
남: Brenda, 우리 삼촌께서 새우 피자를 사주셨어. 많이 먹어.
여: 오! 하지만 나는 새우를 좋아하지 않아.
남: 정말? 너는 새우에 알레르기가 있니?
여: 아니. 나는 새우가 콜레스테롤 함량이 조금 높다고 들었어. 그래서, 나는 그것이 우리의 건강에 좋지 않다고 생각해.
남: 흠, 그것은 새우에 대한 오해야.
여: 새우를 먹는 것이 건강에 긍정적인 영향을 미친다는 말이니?
남: 물론이지. 그것은 너의 좋은 콜레스테롤 수치를 증가시킬 수 있어.
여: 오, 나는 그것을 몰랐어.
남: 새우를 먹는 것은 우리에게 비타민과 미네랄을 줄 수 있어. 게다가, 새우는 저칼로리야.
여: 그럼 새우를 내 식단에 추가하는 것이 좋을지도 모르겠네.
남: 물론이지. 그것은 네 건강에 도움이 될 거야.
여: 나는 새우에 대해 잘 몰랐던 것 같아. 한번 시도해 볼게.

① 다양한 영양소의 섭취는 성장에 필수적이다.
② 식품 구매 시 영양 성분의 확인이 필요하다.
✔ 새우를 섭취하는 것은 건강에 도움이 된다.
④ 체중 관리는 균형 잡힌 식단에서 비롯된다.
⑤ 음식을 조리할 때 위생 관리가 중요하다.

03 두 사람의 관계

고1 2019년 6월 5번 | 정답률 90%
▶ 정답 ①

W: Good afternoon. How may I help you?
M: I made a reservation online. It's under the name of Stennis.
예약했다(make a reservation)
W: Could you spell it, sir?
철자를 말하다
M: Sure. S-T-E-N-N-I-S.
W: All right. You've booked a double room with an ocean view for two
예약한(book)   바다가 보이는 전망이 있는
nights. Is that correct?
맞는
M: Yes. And I want to stay on a higher floor if possible.
더 높은 층에 머물다   가능하다면
W: Let me check. [Typing sound] We have rooms available on the 15th
이용 가능한
and 19th floors. Which one would you prefer?
선호하다
M: 19th is better.
W: Okay. You'll be staying in Room 1911. Here are your key and
breakfast coupons.
아침 식사 쿠폰들
M: Thanks. When does the morning buffet begin?
아침 뷔페
W: You can have breakfast from 7 to 9 a.m. at the restaurant on the
first floor. Have a nice stay.

해석
여: 안녕하세요. 어떻게 도와드릴까요?
남: 저는 온라인으로 예약했어요. Stennis라는 이름으로 되어 있어요.
여: 철자를 말씀해 주시겠어요, 손님?
남: 물론이죠. S-T-E-N-N-I-S.
여: 좋습니다. 바다가 보이는 전망이 있는 2인용 객실에 2박을 예약하셨네요. 맞습니까?
남: 네. 그리고 저는 가능하다면 더 높은 층에 머물고 싶어요.
여: 확인해 보겠습니다. [타자치는 소리] 15층과 19층에 이용 가능한 객실들이 있습니다. 어떤 것을 선호하시나요?
남: 19층이 더 좋아요.
여: 알겠습니다. 1911호에 머물게 되실 겁니다. 여기 열쇠와 아침 식사 쿠폰이 있습니다. 즐겁게 지내십시오.

✔ 호텔 직원 — 투숙객   ② 식당 지배인 — 요리사
③ 여행 가이드 — 여행객   ④ 열쇠 수리공 — 집주인
⑤ 부동산 중개인 — 세입자

04 그림에서 대화의 내용과 일치하지 않는 것

고1 2019년 6월 6번 | 정답률 80%
▶ 정답 ⑤

M: Mom, this is a picture from Science Day.
사진   과학의 날
W: Let me see. The woman wearing glasses must be your science
안경을 쓰고 있는(wear glasses)   과학 선생님
teacher.
M: Yes, she is. She helped me a lot. Do you see the rocket next to the
로켓
flower pot?
화분
W: Oh, it looks fantastic! Who made it?
M: I made it myself. I received a lot of good comments about it.
좋은 평을 많이 받았다 (receive: 받다, comment: (논)평)
W: Good job. What are the two pictures on the wall?
M: They are pictures of great scientists.
위대한 과학자들
W: I see. And there is a robot in front of the window.
로봇   ~ 앞에
M: Yeah, my class put all the parts of the robot together.
로봇의 모든 부품을 조립했다
(put A together: A를 조립하다, part: 부품)
W: Sounds great. I can see a star-shaped clock on the table, too.
별 모양의
M: My teacher showed us how to make it with a 3D-printer, and it was
만드는 법   3D 프린터
very exciting.
(how to V: ~하는 법)
W: You must've had a great time.
즐거운 시간을 보냈음에 틀림없다
(must have p.p.: ~했음에 틀림없다, have a great time: 즐거운 시간을 보내다)

해석
남: 엄마, 이것은 과학의 날 사진이에요.
여: 어디 보자. 안경을 쓰고 있는 여자분이 분명 네 과학 선생님이시겠구나.
남: 네, 맞아요. 그분께서 저를 많이 도와주셨어요. 화분 옆에 있는 로켓이 보이세요?
여: 오, 그것은 멋져 보이는구나! 누가 만들었니?
남: 제가 직접 만들었어요. 저는 그것에 대해 좋은 평을 많이 받았어요.
여: 잘했구나. 벽에 걸린 두 장의 사진은 무엇이니?
남: 그것들은 위대한 과학자들의 사진이에요.
여: 그렇구나. 그리고 창문 앞에 로봇이 있구나.
남: 네, 저희 반이 로봇의 모든 부품을 조립했어요.
여: 멋진데. 테이블 위에 별 모양의 시계도 보이는구나.
남: 선생님께서 3D 프린터로 그것을 만드는 법을 보여주셨는데, 매우 재미있었어요.
여: 너는 즐거운 시간을 보냈음에 틀림없구나.

05 남자가 할 일
고1 2019년 6월 7번   정답률 80%   ▶ 정답 ①

W: Brian, Mom and Dad are coming home within an hour.
　　　　　　　　　　　　　　　　　　　　한 시간 이내에
M: I hope they will like this surprise party for Parents' Day.
　　　　　　　　　　　　깜짝 파티　　　　　어버이날
W: Of course they will. [Pause] Good. We finished decorating the party
table.　　　　　　　　　　　　　　　　　장식하는 것을 끝냈다
　　　　　　　　(finish V-ing: ~하는 것을 끝내다, decorate: 장식하다)
M: I love the balloons on the wall. They're cute.
　　　　　　풍선들　　　　　　　　　　귀여운
W: I like them, too. And Dad will love this paper carnation. You did a
good job.　　　　　　　　　　　　　　종이 카네이션
잘했다(do a good job)
M: Thanks. Where is the cake for the party?
W: It's in the refrigerator. Let me take it out.
　　　　　냉장고　　　　　　그것을 꺼내다
M: What else do we need?
　　그 밖에
W: We have two more things to do, cooking pasta for dinner and
writing a thank-you letter.　　　　파스타를 요리하는 것
감사 편지를 쓰는 것
M: Mom does like your cooking, so you do the pasta. And I'll write the
letter.
W: Okay, I'll do that. Let's hurry.
　　　　　　　　　　　　서두르다

해석
여: Brian, 엄마와 아빠께서 한 시간 이내에 집에 오실 거야.
남: 부모님께서 어버이날을 위한 이 깜짝 파티를 마음에 들어 하셨으면 좋겠어.
여: 물론 그러실 거야. [잠시 후] 좋아. 우리는 파티 테이블을 장식하는 것을 끝냈어.
남: 나는 벽에 있는 풍선들이 정말 마음에 들어. 그것들은 귀여워.
여: 나도 마음에 들어. 그리고 아빠께서 이 종이 카네이션을 정말 좋아하실 거야. 잘했어.
남: 고마워. 파티를 위한 케이크는 어디에 있어?
여: 그것은 냉장고에 있어. 내가 그것을 꺼낼게.
남: 그 밖에 우리가 필요한 게 뭐가 있지?
여: 할 일이 두 가지가 더 있어, 저녁 식사로 파스타를 요리하는 것과 감사 편지를 쓰는 거야.
남: 엄마께서는 네 요리를 정말 좋아하시니까, 네가 파스타를 만들어. 그리고 나는 편지를 쓸게.
여: 알았어, 그렇게 하게. 서두르자.

✓ 감사 편지 쓰기　　　　　　　　② 풍선 장식하기
③ 파스타 요리하기　　　　　　　　④ 케이크 구매하기
⑤ 카네이션 만들기

문제 풀이
남자가 벽에 있는 풍선들이 마음에 든다고 했으므로 풍선 장식하기는 이미 한 일이다. 종이 카네이션을 잘 만들었다는 여자의 칭찬으로 보아 남자가 이미 카네이션을 만들었다는 것을 알 수 있다. 케이크는 냉장고에 있기 때문에 케이크 구매하기는 답과 멀다. 남자가 여자에게 파스타를 만들어 달라고 했고, 본인이 편지를 쓴다고 했으므로 답은 ① '감사 편지 쓰기'가 된다.

06 남자가 지불할 금액
고1 2019년 6월 9번   정답률 80%   ▶ 정답 ④

W: Hello. Can I help you?
M: Yes. I want to buy a baseball bat for my son. He is 11 years old.
　　　　　　　　　　야구 방망이
W: How about this baseball bat? It's the most popular. It's 30 dollars.
　　~은 어떠세요?　　　　　　　　　가장 인기 있는
M: Okay. I'll take one bat. Do you also have baseball gloves?
　　　　　　　　　　　　　　　　야구 글러브들
W: Sure. How about this glove? It's soft and comfortable.
　　　　　　　　　　　　　부드러운　　편안한
M: How much is it?
W: It's 15 dollars.
M: Hmm... That's reasonable. I'll buy two gloves.
　　　　　　　합리적인
W: Okay. Don't you need any safety balls for children? They are light
and soft.　　　　　필요하다　어린이용 안전공들　　　가벼운
M: I think I've got all I need. Can I use this coupon?
　　　　　　　　　　　　사용하다　쿠폰
W: Of course. Then you can get 10% off the total price.
　　　　　　　　　　　　총액에서 10% 할인을 받다
M: Great. I'll use the coupon and pay by credit card.
　　　　　　　　　　　　신용카드로 지불하다

해석
여: 안녕하세요. 도와드릴까요?
남: 네. 저는 제 아들을 위한 야구 방망이를 사고 싶어요. 그 애는 11살이에요.
여: 이 야구 방망이는 어떠세요? 가장 인기 있는 거예요. 30달러예요.
남: 좋네요. 야구 방망이 한 개를 살게요. 야구 글러브도 있나요?

여: 물론이죠. 이 글러브는 어떠세요? 부드럽고 편안해요.
남: 얼마죠?
여: 15달러예요.
남: 흠... 그것은 합리적이네요. 글러브 두 개를 살게요.
여: 알겠습니다. 어린이용 안전공은 필요하지 않으세요? 그것들은 가볍고 부드러워요.
남: 필요한 것은 모두 산 것 같아요. 이 쿠폰을 사용할 수 있나요?
여: 물론이죠. 그럼 총액에서 10% 할인을 받으실 수 있어요.
남: 잘됐네요. 쿠폰을 사용하고 신용카드로 지불할게요.

① $15　　　　　② $30　　　　　③ $48
✓ $54　　　　　⑤ $60

문제 풀이
남자가 30달러짜리 야구 방망이 한 개와 15달러짜리 야구 글러브 두 개를 사므로 총액은 60달러가 된다. 그러나 10퍼센트 할인 쿠폰을 사용하기 때문에 남자가 지불할 금액은 총액에서 6달러를 뺀 54달러이므로 정답은 ④ '$54'이다.

07 여자가 토론 대회에 참가할 수 없는 이유
고1 2019년 6월 8번   정답률 90%   ▶ 정답 ②

M: Linda, there'll be a team debate competition next week. The topic
is Social Network Services.　　팀 토론 대회　　　　　　　　주제
소셜 네트워크 서비스
W: Sounds interesting. Are you going to sign up?
　　　　　　　　　　　　　　　참가하다
M: Yes. I'm interested in debating. Do you want to be my teammate?
　　　~에 관심이 있는　　　　　　　　　　　　　팀 동료
W: I'd love to, but I can't.
M: Right. You said you're busy doing your writing assignment.
　　　　　　　　　네 글쓰기 과제를 하느라 바쁜
(busy V-ing: ~하느라 바쁜, writing assignment: 글쓰기 과제)
W: No, I've already finished it.
M: Well, do you find it hard to speak in front of others?
　　　　　　　~라고 생각하다　　　다른 사람들 앞에서 말하다
W: Not really. Actually, I'm preparing for a school musical performance.
It's next Thursday.　　　　　　~을 준비하는(prepare for)　학교 뮤지컬 공연
M: Oh, I see. You don't have enough time to join me this time.
　　　　　　　　　　　　충분한
W: Right. I hope you will find someone good to be your teammate.

해석
남: Linda, 다음 주에 팀 토론 대회가 있을 거야. 주제는 Social Network Services(소셜 네트워크 서비스)야.
여: 재미있겠다. 너는 참가할 거야?
남: 응. 나는 토론에 관심이 있거든. 너 내 팀 동료가 될래?
여: 그러고 싶지만, 안 되겠어.
남: 맞다. 너는 네 글쓰기 과제를 하느라 바쁘다고 했지.
여: 아니, 그것은 이미 끝났어.
남: 음, 다른 사람들 앞에서 말하는 게 힘들다고 생각하니?
여: 그렇진 않아. 사실, 나는 학교 뮤지컬 공연을 준비하고 있어. 다음 주 목요일이야.
남: 오, 그렇구나. 너는 이번에 나와 함께 할 충분한 시간이 없구나.
여: 맞아. 네가 팀 동료가 되기에 좋은 사람을 찾게 되길 바랄게.

① 남들 앞에서 말하는 것이 힘들어서
✓ 뮤지컬 공연 준비를 해야 해서
③ 수행평가 일정이 연기되어서
④ 글쓰기 과제를 해야 해서
⑤ 토론 주제가 어려워서

08 Career Vision Camp에 관해 언급되지 않은 것
고1 2019년 6월 10번   정답률 80%   ▶ 정답 ④

[Door knocks.]
M: Can I come in, Ms. Wilson?
W: Sure, come on in. [Pause] Oh, Peter. I was waiting for you to come.
How's your career search going?　　　　　　　　~을 기다리고 있는(wait for)
진로 탐색
M: I'm still trying to find some information about my future career.
　　　　　정보를 좀 찾으려고 노력하는　　　　　　　　　장래 직업
(try to V: ~하려고 노력하다, find information: 정보를 찾다)
W: Good. So I'd like to recommend the Career Vision Camp to you.
　　　　　　　　　　　　　추천하다　　　　직업 전망 캠프
M: Okay. I heard that the camp is only for high school students. Is that
right?　　　　　　　　　　　　　　　　　고등학생들
W: Yes. It'll be helpful. Plus, there's no registration fee.
　　　　　　도움이 되는　　　　　　　　등록비

M: Great. Hmm, can you tell me when the <u>application deadline</u> is?
지원 마감일

W: It's December 14th. You should <u>hurry</u> since it's <u>first come, first</u>
서두르다
<u>served</u>.
선착순

M: I see. I will <u>apply for</u> the camp <u>as soon as possible</u>.
~에 지원하다   가능한 한 빨리

W: It'll <u>be held</u> at the Lincoln Center near school. You can get there
열리다
easily.

M: Okay. Thank you.

해석

[문을 노크하는 소리.]

남: 들어가도 될까요, Wilson 선생님?

여: 물론이지, 어서 들어오너라. [잠시 후] 오, Peter. 나는 네가 오기를 기다리고 있었어. 진로 탐색은 어떻게 되어 가고 있니?

남: 저는 아직도 제 장래 직업에 대한 정보를 좀 찾으려고 노력하고 있어요.

여: 좋아. 그래서 나는 너에게 Career Vision Camp(직업 전망 캠프)를 추천하고 싶어.

남: 알겠어요. 저는 그 캠프가 고등학생들만을 위한 것이라고 들었어요. 맞나요?

여: 그래. 그것은 도움이 될 거야. 게다가, 등록비도 없단다.

남: 잘됐네요. 흠, 지원 마감일이 언제인지 말씀해 주실래요?

여: 12월 14일이야. 선착순이기 때문에 서둘러야 해.

남: 알겠어요. 가능한 한 빨리 캠프에 지원할게요.

여: 그것은 학교 근처의 Lincoln Center(링컨 센터)에서 열릴 거야. 너는 그곳에 쉽게 갈 수 있어.

남: 알겠어요. 감사해요.

① 참가 대상　　　　　② 등록 비용　　　　　③ 지원 마감일

✓④ 기념품　　　　　⑤ 행사 장소

09　Children's Book Fair에 관한 내용과 일치하지 않는 것　▶ 정답 ⑤

W: Good morning, residents. This is the <u>librarian</u> of the Jacksonville
사서   잭슨빌 지역 문화 센터
Community Center. We're holding the <u>Children's Book Fair</u> for
개최하는(hold)   아동 도서 박람회
three days, from June 21st to the 23rd. It will <u>offer</u> your children
제공하다
an <u>opportunity</u> to feel the joy of reading books. We'll <u>display a wide</u>
기회   전시하다 매우 다양한
<u>variety of</u> children's books <u>including</u> comic books, picture books,
~을 포함하여   만화책들   그림책들
and fairy tales. In addition, you will <u>be able to buy</u> all books <u>at 50%</u>
동화책들   게다가   구입할 수 있다
(be able to V: ~할 수 있다)
<u>off their original prices</u>. On the first day of the fair, you will be able
정가에서 50% 할인된 가격으로
to meet and talk with the <u>famous writer</u>, Andy Murphy. Also, every
유명한 작가
child visiting the fair will get a T-shirt <u>as a gift</u>. I hope you will enjoy
선물로
the fair. Thank you.

해석

여: 안녕하세요, 주민 여러분. 저는 Jacksonville Community Center(잭슨빌 지역 문화 센터)의 사서입니다. 저희는 6월 21일부터 23일까지, 3일 동안 Children's Book Fair(아동 도서 박람회)를 개최할 예정입니다. 그것은 여러분의 아이들에게 책을 읽는 기쁨을 느낄 수 있는 기회를 제공할 것입니다. 저희는 만화책, 그림책, 그리고 동화책을 포함한 매우 다양한 아동 도서들을 전시할 것입니다. 게다가, 여러분은 모든 책을 정가에서 50% 할인된 가격으로 구입하실 수 있을 것입니다. 박람회 첫날에, 여러분은 유명한 작가인 Andy Murphy(앤디 머피)와 만나 이야기를 나누실 수 있을 것입니다. 또한, 박람회를 방문하는 모든 어린이는 선물로 티셔츠를 받게 될 것입니다. 저는 여러분께서 박람회를 즐기시길 바랍니다. 감사합니다.

① 3일 동안 진행된다.

② 만화책을 포함한 아동용 도서를 전시한다.

③ 50% 할인된 가격으로 책을 살 수 있다.

④ 행사 첫 날에 유명 작가를 만날 수 있다.

✓⑤ 방문하는 모든 어린이는 책갈피를 선물로 받는다.

문제 풀이

박람회는 3일 동안 개최될 예정이고 거기서 만화책을 포함한 아동용 도서가 전시되며 정가에서 50퍼센트 할인된 가격으로 책을 구입할 수 있다. 또한 유명한 작가와 박람회 첫날에 만날 수도 있다. 박람회에 방문하는 모든 어린이는 티셔츠를 선물로 받게 될 것이므로 ⑤ '방문하는 모든 어린이는 책갈피를 선물로 받는다.'는 내용과 다르다.

10　표에서 여자가 구입할 전기면도기　▶ 정답 ③

M: Katie, what are you doing with your smartphone?

W: I'm searching for an <u>electric shaver</u> for my dad's birthday. Will you
전기면도기
help me find a good one?

M: Sure. Let me see... [Pause] How about this one?

W: Well, that's <u>too expensive</u>. I can't <u>spend</u> more than $100.
너무 비싼   (돈을) 쓰다

M: Okay. And I think a <u>20-minute battery life</u> is <u>too short to use</u>
20분의 배터리 수명   너무 짧아서 사용할 수 없는
conveniently.   (too A to V: 너무 A해서 ~할 수 없는)

W: I think so, too. It needs <u>frequent</u> <u>charging</u>.
빈번한   충전

M: You're right. Does it <u>need to</u> be <u>waterproof</u>?
~해야 하다   방수가 되다

W: Of course. He <u>shaves</u> in the shower every morning.
면도하다

M: Then we have only two <u>options</u> <u>left</u>. Which color do you think is
선택들 남은
better?

W: Dad likes black, so I'll buy the black one.

M: I think it's a nice choice.

해석

남: Katie, 스마트폰으로 무엇을 하고 있니?

여: 아빠 생신을 위한 전기면도기를 찾고 있어. 내가 좋은 것을 찾도록 네가 도와줄래?

남: 물론이지. 어디 보자... [잠시 후] 이것은 어때?

여: 글쎄, 그것은 너무 비싸. 나는 100달러 이상은 쓸 수 없어.

남: 알았어. 그리고 20분의 배터리 수명은 너무 짧아서 편리하게 사용할 수 없을 것 같아.

여: 나도 그렇게 생각해. 그것은 빈번한 충전이 필요하잖아.

남: 네 말이 맞아. 방수가 되어야 하니?

여: 물론이지. 아빠께서는 매일 아침 샤워하면서 면도를 하시거든.

남: 그럼 우리에게 두 가지 선택지만 남네. 너는 어떤 색이 더 좋다고 생각하니?

여: 아빠께서 검은색을 좋아하시니, 나는 검은색 면도기를 살 거야.

남: 좋은 선택인 것 같아.

전기면도기

	모델	가격	배터리 수명	방수 기능	색상
①	A	55달러	20분	×	검은색
②	B	70달러	40분	×	하얀색
✓③	C	85달러	60분	○	검은색
④	D	90달러	70분	○	하얀색
⑤	E	110달러	80분	○	검은색

문제 풀이

여자는 100달러 이상을 쓸 수 없다고 했으므로 모델 E는 답이 될 수 없다. 남자는 배터리 수명이 20분인 모델은 편리하게 사용할 수 없을 것 같다고 했으므로 모델 A도 제외가 된다. 방수가 되어야 하냐는 남자의 질문에 여자가 긍정했으므로 모델 B도 제외된다. 모델 C와 D중 여자가 검은색 면도기를 원하므로 답은 모델 C에 해당하는 ③번이다.

11　여자의 마지막 말에 대한 남자의 응답　▶ 정답 ②

W: Jason, I'm going to a <u>motor show</u> this Friday. Can you join me?
자동차 전시회   함께하다

M: I'd love to. But we have <u>classes</u> until 3 p.m. on that day.
수업들

W: <u>No worries</u>. The show is open until 8 p.m. Are you <u>free</u> <u>after school</u>?
걱정하지 마   한가한   방과 후에

M: (Sure. Let's go together.)

해석

여: Jason, 나는 이번 주 금요일에 자동차 전시회에 갈 거야. 나와 함께할 수 있어?

남: 나도 그러고 싶어. 하지만 우리는 그날 오후 3시까지 수업이 있잖아.

여: 걱정하지 마. 전시회는 오후 8시까지 열려. 너는 방과 후에 한가하니?

남: (물론이지. 함께 가자.)

① 그래. 내 차는 고장이 났어.

✓② 물론이지. 함께 가자.

③ 말도 안 돼. 그 전시회는 끝났어.

④ 그래. 나는 공부 모임에 가입할 거야.

⑤ 미안해. 나는 표를 찾을 수 없었어.

12 남자의 마지막 말에 대한 여자의 응답

▶ 정답 ①

M: Honey, look out the window. It's raining a lot.
　　　　　　창밖을 보다
W: Yeah, I think it might be dangerous to drive to work.
　　　　　　　　　　　　　위험한　　　　운전해서 출근하다
M: You're right. You'd better use public transportation today.
　　　　　　　　　　　　　　　　　　대중교통
W: (Okay. I'll take the subway then.)
　　　　　　　지하철을 타다

해석

남: 여보, 창밖을 봐요. 비가 많이 오네요.
여: 네, 제 생각에는 운전해서 출근하는 것은 위험할 것 같아요.
남: 당신 말이 맞아요. 당신 오늘은 대중교통을 이용하는 게 좋겠어요.
여: (알겠어요. 그럼 저는 지하철을 탈게요.)
✔ 알겠어요. 그럼 저는 지하철을 탈게요.
② 아니요. 저는 당신의 우산을 가져가지 않았어요.
③ 맞아요. 그것은 너무 힘든 일이었어요.
④ 네. 내일 비가 올 거예요.
⑤ 미안해요. 저는 차를 운전할 수 없어요.

13 남자의 마지막 말에 대한 여자의 응답

▶ 정답 ②

[Cellphone rings.]
W: Hello, this is Claire.
M: Hi, what's up?
W: I have something to tell you about the meeting for our economics
　　　　　　　　　　　　　　　　　　　　모임　　　　　　　　경제학 과제
assignment.
M: What happened? Is there a problem?
　　　　　　　　　　　　문제
W: Actually, my mom broke her ankle this morning. She can't walk
　　　　　그녀의 발목이 부러졌다(break one's ankle)
because of the pain.
　~ 때문에　　통증
M: I'm sorry to hear that. That must be hard for her.
　　　　　　　　　　　　　　　　　　~에게 힘들다
W: It is. So I will have to take care of her this weekend.
　　　　　　　　~을 돌봐야 하다
(have to V: ~해야 하다, take care of: ~을 돌보다)
M: Then we can't have our meeting this Saturday.
W: That's right. I'm terribly sorry, but I have to delay the meeting.
　　　　　　　　정말　　　　　　　　　　연기하다
M: Don't worry about that. So, when will you have time?
W: I guess any day next week is good for me.
　　　　　　　　　　　　~에게 좋은
M: Okay, then shall we make it next Monday?
W: (All right. Thank you for understanding.)

해석

[휴대전화가 울린다.]
여: 여보세요, 나 Claire야.
남: 안녕, 무슨 일이야?
여: 우리의 경제학 과제를 위한 모임에 대해 할 말이 있어.
남: 무슨 일인데? 문제가 있어?
여: 사실, 오늘 아침에 엄마께서 발목이 부러지셨어. 엄마께서는 통증 때문에 걸을 수 없으셔.
남: 정말 유감이다. 그것은 분명 그분에게 힘든 일일 거야.
여: 그렇지. 그래서 나는 이번 주말에 엄마를 돌봐야 할 것 같아.
남: 그럼 우리는 이번 주 토요일에 모임을 가질 수 없구나.
여: 맞아. 정말 미안하지만, 나는 모임을 연기해야 해.
남: 그것에 대해서는 걱정하지 마. 그럼, 너는 언제 시간이 될까?
여: 다음 주에는 어느 요일이건 나에게 좋을 것 같아.
남: 알겠어, 그럼 다음 주 월요일에 만날까?
여: (좋아. 이해해줘서 고마워.)
① 문제 없어. 나는 이미 그것을 제출했어.
✔ 좋아. 이해해줘서 고마워.
③ 물론이지. 나는 네가 곧 낫기를 바라.
④ 신경 쓰지 마. 내가 너를 병원에 데려다 줄게.
⑤ 미안해. 그 모임은 아직 취소되지 않았어.

문제 풀이

여자는 주말에 어머니를 돌봐야 하기 때문에 모임을 연기할 수밖에 없다고 남자에게 말했고, 남자는 흔쾌히 약속 날짜를 변경(다음 주 월요일)하자고 했으므로 이에 대해 여자가 고마움을 표현하는 것이 자연스럽다. 따라서 ② 'All right. Thank you for understanding.(좋아. 이해해줘서 고마워.)'이 답이다.

14 여자의 마지막 말에 대한 남자의 응답

▶ 정답 ④

M: Hi, Emily! How are your wedding preparations going?
　　　　　　　　　　　　　　결혼 준비는
W: They're going well so far. I reserved a wedding hall and ordered
　　　　　　　　　　　지금까지　　　　예식장을 예약했다
invitation cards.
초대장을 주문했다
M: Good. Everything's almost settled. It's on the first Saturday of July,
　　　　　　　　　　거의 결정된
right?
W: Yes. Can you come?
M: Of course. Is there anything that I can help you with?
W: Actually, I haven't decided who'll sing at the wedding. So, would
　　　　　결정하지 못했다(decide)　　결혼식에서 노래를 부르다
you sing for me?
M: I'd love to, but I've never done anything like that before.
W: I heard you singing at the college song festival, so I know you're a
　　　　　　　　　　　　　　대학가요제
good singer.
M: Thanks, but I'm afraid I may not sing well enough to do so at a
　　　　　　　(유감스럽지만)　　　　　　　그렇게 할 만큼 충분히 잘
wedding.　　~일 것 같다(be afraid)　　(A enough to V: ~할 만큼 충분히 A하게)
W: Oh, please! I'm sure it would be the best wedding gift. I'd look
　　　　　　　　　　　　　　　　　최고의 결혼 선물
forward to it.
~을 기대하다
M: (Okay, I'll sing for you. I hope you won't expect too much.)
　　　　　　　　　　　　　　　　　　기대하다

해석

남: 안녕, Emily! 결혼 준비는 어떻게 되어 가고 있니?
여: 지금까지는 잘 되어 가고 있어. 나는 예식장을 예약했고 초대장을 주문했어.
남: 잘됐구나. 모든 일이 거의 결정되었네. 7월 첫째 주 토요일이지, 그렇지?
여: 그래. 올 수 있겠어?
남: 물론이지. 내가 너를 도울 수 있는 일이 있을까?
여: 사실, 나는 결혼식에서 누가 노래를 부를지 결정하지 못했어. 그래서, 네가 나를 위해 노래를 불러 줄래?
남: 그러고 싶지만, 나는 전에 그런 것을 해 본 적이 없어.
여: 나는 네가 대학가요제에서 노래를 부르는 것을 들었어, 그래서 네가 노래를 잘한다는 것을 알지.
남: 고마워, 하지만 나는 결혼식에서 그렇게 할 만큼 충분히 노래를 잘 부르지는 못하는 것 같아.
여: 오, 제발! 나는 그것이 최고의 결혼 선물이 될 것이라고 확신해. 기대할게.
남: (알았어. 너를 위해 노래를 부를게. 나는 네가 너무 기대하지 않았으면 좋겠어.)
① 천만에. 나는 네가 선물을 정말 마음에 들어 해서 기뻐.
② 그것에 대해 걱정하지 마. 누구나 실수로부터 배울 수 있어.
③ 그래, 내가 그 노래를 불렀어. 나는 지금 화음을 넣어 노래하고 싶어.
✔ 알았어. 너를 위해 노래를 부를게. 나는 네가 너무 기대하지 않았으면 좋겠어.
⑤ 나는 그렇게 생각하지 않아. 결혼 반지를 고르는 것은 쉽지 않아.

문제 풀이

축가를 부를 만큼 노래를 잘 부르지는 못한다는 남자에게 여자가 격려의 말을 했으므로 용기를 내보겠다는 대답이 어울린다. 따라서 답은 ④ 'Okay, I'll sing for you. I hope you won't expect too much.(알았어. 너를 위해 노래를 부를게. 나는 네가 너무 기대하지 않았으면 좋겠어.)'가 된다.

15 다음 상황에서 Alex가 Olivia에게 할 말

▶ 정답 ③

W: Alex and Olivia have been close friends since they were children.
　　　　　　　　　　　　　　친한
They grew up in the same town, and they attend the same high
　　자랐다(grow up)　　　　　　　　　　　　　같은 고등학교에 다니다
school. One day, Alex tells Olivia that his father got a new job so
　　　　　　　　　　　　　　　　　　　새 직장을 구했다
　　　　　　　　　　　　　　　　　　(get a job: 직장을 구하다)
his family has to move to another city. That's why he's going to
　　　　　　다른 도시로 이사하다
transfer to a new school next week. Olivia feels sad because they
새 학교로 전학을 가다　　　　　　　　　　슬프다
have been friends for such a long time. Alex also hopes to keep
　　　　　　　　　　　매우 오랫동안
his friendship with her. So, Alex wants to suggest that they remain
그녀와의 우정을 유지하다
(keep one's friendship with: ~와의 우정을 유지하다)
in close touch even after he leaves the city. In this situation, what
친밀한 관계를 유지하다　　떠나다
would Alex most likely say to Olivia?
Alex: (Let's keep in touch even after we part.)
　　　　　　계속 연락하다　　　　　　헤어지다

해석

여: Alex와 Olivia는 어릴 때부터 친한 친구이다. 그들은 같은 마을에서 자랐고, 같은 고등학교에 다닌다. 어느 날, Alex는 Olivia에게 그의 아버지가 새 직장을 구해서 그의 가족이 다른 도시로 이사해야 한다고 말한다. 그런 이유로 그는 다음 주에 새 학교로 전학을 갈 예정이다. Olivia는 그들이 매우 오랫동안 친구였기 때문에 슬프다. Alex도 그녀와의 우정을 유지하기를 바란다. 그래서, Alex는 그가 도시를 떠난 후에도 그들이 친밀한 관계를 유지하자고 제안하고 싶다. 이러한 상황에서, Alex는 Olivia에게 뭐라고 말하겠는가?

Alex: (우리가 헤어진 후에도 계속 연락하자.)

① 새 직장을 구하다니 너는 정말 운이 좋구나.
② 네가 어디로 전학 가야 하는지 내가 알려 줄게.
✓③ 우리가 헤어진 후에도 계속 연락하자.
④ 나는 너의 친절한 말에 깊이 감동을 받았어.
⑤ 나는 네가 새 학교에 익숙해지기를 바라.

16~17 1지문 2문항

M: Hello, everyone. Last class we learned about the dangers of
climate change. Today, I'll tell you about some foods that might
disappear because of climate change. First of all, 70 percent
of the world's coffee could disappear by 2080 due to climate
change. In Africa, the amount of coffee produced has dropped
by more than 50 percent. Secondly, avocados are also in danger.
It usually takes 72 gallons of water to make just one pound of
avocados. Climate change in California has resulted in a lack of
water, so the avocado plants aren't producing enough fruit. Thirdly,
warmer temperatures affect apple trees, too. To grow properly,
apple trees need a certain period of cold weather. Lack of cold
weather time leads to lower apple production. Finally, the unstable
climatic conditions through crop season are causing a decrease in
strawberry production in Florida. Specifically, hotter-than-normal
weather has delayed the flowering and production of strawberries.
Now, let me show you some slides about this issue.

해석

남: 안녕하세요, 여러분. 지난 수업 시간에 우리는 기후 변화의 위험에 대해 배웠습니다. 오늘, 저는 기후 변화 때문에 사라질지도 모르는 몇몇 식품들에 대해 이야기할 것입니다. 첫 번째로, 기후 변화 때문에 2080년까지 세계 커피의 70퍼센트가 사라질 수도 있습니다. 아프리카에서는, 커피 생산량이 50퍼센트 이상 감소했습니다. 두 번째로, 아보카도도 위험에 처해 있습니다. 1파운드의 아보카도를 재배하는 데 보통 72갤런의 물을 필요로 합니다. 캘리포니아의 기후 변화는 물 부족을 초래해서, 아보카도 나무들이 충분한 열매를 맺지 않고 있습니다. 세 번째로, 더 따뜻해진 기온은 사과 나무에도 영향을 미칩니다. 제대로 자라기 위해서, 사과 나무들은 일정 기간의 추운 날씨를 필요로 합니다. 추운 날씨 기간의 부족은 더 낮은 사과 생산량으로 이어집니다. 마지막으로, 작물 기간 내내 불안정한 기후 상태는 플로리다의 딸기 생산량의 감소를 야기하고 있습니다. 구체적으로, 평소보다 더 더운 날씨는 딸기의 개화와 생산을 지연시켰습니다. 이제, 이 문제에 대한 몇 가지 슬라이드들을 보여드리겠습니다.

16 남자가 하는 말의 주제

고1 2019년 6월 16번 · 정답률 85% ▶ 정답 ①

✓① 기후 변화 때문에 위험에 처한 식품들
② 해수 온도가 상승하는 이유들
③ 수중 동물들과 식물들
④ 작물 재배의 요건들
⑤ 지구 온난화를 해결할 방법들

17 언급된 음식이 아닌 것

고1 2019년 6월 17번 · 정답률 85% ▶ 정답 ⑤

① 커피
② 아보카도
③ 사과
④ 딸기
✓⑤ 코코넛

04 2019년 9월 학력평가

01	①	02	③	03	②	04	④	05	⑤
06	④	07	②	08	④	09	⑤	10	⑤
11	⑤	12	①	13	②	14	①	15	③
16	①	17	③						

01 여자가 하는 말의 목적

고1 2019년 9월 3번 · 정답률 90% ▶ 정답 ①

W: Hello, students. Our annual school talent show is coming soon. I'm
glad that so many talented students signed up for the audition.
Now, I'd like to give you some tips on how to prepare for it. First,
practice your lines, your dance moves, or your songs over and over
until you memorize them perfectly. After that, rehearse with your
friends or in front of a mirror. Practicing again and again will help
you feel confident during the audition. Finally, wear clothes you'll
feel comfortable in. You can bring your own costumes if you want.
I wish all of you good luck and hope you shine on the stage. Thank
you.

해석

여: 안녕하세요, 학생 여러분. 우리의 연례 학교 장기 자랑이 곧 다가오고 있습니다. 저는 많은 재능 있는 학생들이 오디션에 지원해서 기쁩니다. 자, 저는 여러분에게 그것을 준비하는 방법에 관한 몇 가지 요령을 알려주고 싶습니다. 먼저, 여러분의 대사, 춤 동작, 또는 노래를 완벽하게 외울 때까지 반복해서 연습하세요. 그 후에, 여러분의 친구들과 함께 또는 거울 앞에서 예행 연습을 하세요. 반복해서 연습하는 것은 오디션 동안 여러분이 자신감을 갖는 데 도움을 줄 것입니다. 마지막으로, 여러분이 편안하게 느끼는 옷을 입으세요. 여러분이 원한다면 자신의 의상을 가져와도 됩니다. 여러분 모두에게 행운을 빌며 여러분이 무대에서 빛나기를 바랍니다. 감사합니다.

✓① 오디션 준비 요령을 알려주려고
② 학교 행사 아이디어를 공모하려고
③ 축제 홍보 활동 참여를 독려하려고
④ 공연 관람 규칙 준수를 당부하려고
⑤ 공연 리허설 장소 변경을 공지하려고

02 두 사람이 하는 말의 주제

고1 2019년 9월 4번 · 정답률 90% ▶ 정답 ③

M: Honey, where did you get all these potatoes?
W: My friend Jennifer runs a potato farm, so she gave me some.
M: This is a lot! Let's put them in the refrigerator.
W: Oh, no. Storing potatoes in a refrigerator gives them an unpleasant
taste.
M: Okay. Where should we keep them?
W: They should be stored in a cool and dark place.
M: Then the basement would be good.
W: That's perfect, but we also need to take the potatoes out of the

plastic bag. Potatoes <u>rot</u> easily in plastic bags.
썩다
M: I see. And I <u>remember reading</u> an <u>article</u> saying that storing
읽은 것을 기억하다   기사
potatoes with an apple <u>keeps them from sprouting</u>.
그것들이 싹이 나는 것을 막다(keep A from V-ing:
W: Really? That's good to know.   A가 ~하는 것을 막다, sprout: 싹이 나다)
M: I'll bring an apple, and we can keep them together.

해석
남: 여보, 이 감자들이 다 어디서 났어요?
여: 친구인 Jennifer가 감자 농장을 운영해서, 저에게 몇 개 줬어요.
남: 정말 많네요! 그것들을 냉장고에 넣읍시다.
여: 오, 안 돼요. 감자들을 냉장고에 보관하는 것은 그것들에게 불쾌한 맛을 줘요.
남: 알겠어요. 그것들을 어디에 보관해야 하죠?
여: 서늘하고 어두운 곳에 보관해야 해요.
남: 그럼 지하실이 좋겠네요.
여: 완벽하지만, 우리는 또한 감자들을 비닐봉지에서 꺼내야 해요. 감자들은 비닐봉지 안에
   서 쉽게 썩거든요.
남: 그렇군요. 그리고 저는 감자들을 사과와 함께 보관하면 그것들이 싹이 나는 것을 막을 수
   있다는 기사를 읽은 것을 기억해요.
여: 정말이에요? 알게 되어 다행이네요.
남: 제가 사과를 가져올게요, 그러면 우리는 그것들을 함께 보관할 수 있어요.

① 감자의 전파 과정
② 감자의 다양한 효능
✓③ 감자를 보관하는 방법
④ 감자를 이용한 요리법
⑤ 감자 재배 시 유의사항

03 두 사람의 관계
▶ 정답②

M: Hi, Kate. How do you feel today?
W: I feel better, but I still <u>have a sore throat</u>. How does my voice
목이 아프다
<u>sound</u>?
들리다
M: It sounds fine, so don't worry about it.
W: Thanks. Did you hear about one of the <u>audio books</u> we <u>recorded</u> in
오디오북   녹음했다
this studio last year?
M: You mean "The Dreaming Tree?" I heard it was the <u>best-selling</u>
가장 많이 팔리는
audio book of the year.
W: It was. The <u>sound effects</u> you <u>added</u> made the story <u>feel alive</u>.
음향 효과들   추가했다   살아있다고 느끼다
M: Thank you. <u>Most of all</u>, your <u>voice acting</u> was great in the <u>various</u>
무엇보다   목소리 연기   다양한
<u>roles</u>.
역할들
W: I'm flattered. Okay, I think I'm <u>ready</u> now. Is this the <u>script</u> for the
준비가 된   대본
radio drama we're working on today?
M: Yes. We can begin <u>once</u> you step into the <u>recording booth</u>. I'll
일단 ~하면   녹음실
<u>check</u> the <u>microphone</u>.
확인하다 마이크
W: All right. I'll start when you give me the <u>signal</u>.
신호

해석
남: 안녕하세요, Kate. 오늘은 기분이 어떠세요?
여: 괜찮아졌지만, 아직도 목이 아파요. 제 목소리는 어떻게 들려요?
남: 좋아요, 그러니까 그것에 대해서는 걱정하지 마세요.
여: 고마워요. 우리가 작년에 이 스튜디오에서 녹음한 오디오북 중 하나에 대해 들었어요?
남: 'The Dreaming Tree(꿈꾸는 나무)'를 말하는 거예요? 당해 가장 많이 팔린 오디오북이라
   고 들었어요.
여: 그렇죠. 당신이 추가한 음향 효과들이 그 이야기가 살아있다고 느끼게 만들었어요.
남: 고마워요. 무엇보다, 다양한 역할들 속에서 당신의 목소리 연기가 훌륭했어요.
여: 과찬이세요. 좋아요, 저는 이제 준비가 된 것 같아요. 이것이 오늘 우리가 작업을 하게 될
   라디오 드라마의 대본인가요?
남: 네. 일단 당신이 녹음실에 들어가면 우리는 시작할 수 있어요. 제가 마이크를 확인할게요.
여: 알겠어요. 당신이 제게 신호를 주면 시작할게요.

① 신문 기자 — 작가
✓② 녹음 기사 — 성우
③ 영화감독 — 배우
④ 매니저 — 가수
⑤ 의사 — 환자

04 그림에서 대화의 내용과 일치하지 않는 것
▶ 정답④

M: Ms. Morgan, how's the <u>preparation</u> for the <u>school talk show</u> going?
준비   학교 토크쇼
W: I've finished <u>setting up</u> the <u>stage</u>. How do you like it?
설치하는 것을 끝낸 무대
(finish V-ing: ~하는 것을 끝내다,
set up: 설치)
M: Great! I like the <u>banner</u> for the talk show at the top <u>between the</u>
현수막   커튼들 사이에
<u>curtains</u>.
W: Thanks. What do you think about the <u>picture</u> under the banner?
사진
M: I think the image of the <u>laptop computer</u> and the <u>lock</u> is <u>perfect for</u>
노트북 컴퓨터   자물쇠   ~에 완벽한
the talk show on "<u>Information Security</u>."
정보   보안
W: I think the picture shows the <u>topic clearly</u>.
주제 분명하게
M: It does. You put two <u>stereo speakers</u> below the picture.
스테레오 스피커들
W: Yes. They're the ones we bought <u>recently</u> for the show.
최근에
M: Okay. The students will sit and talk on those chairs on the <u>round</u>
<u>carpet</u>, right?   둥근 카펫
W: Exactly. I also put a white board next to the <u>standing microphone</u>.
Students <u>have asked me to set that up</u>.   스탠딩 마이크
나에게 그것을 설치해 달라고 부탁했다
(ask A to V: A에게 ~해 달라고 부탁하다)
M: Great! I'll <u>be looking forward to</u> the event.
~을 기대하고 있다

해석
남: Morgan 선생님, 학교 토크쇼 준비는 어떻게 되어가고 있나요?
여: 무대를 설치하는 것을 끝냈어요. 어떠세요?
남: 훌륭하네요! 커튼들 사이에 맨 위에 있는 토크쇼의 현수막이 마음에 들어요.
여: 감사해요. 현수막 아래에 있는 사진에 대해서는 어떻게 생각하세요?
남: 노트북 컴퓨터와 자물쇠의 이미지가 '정보 보안'에 관한 토크쇼에 완벽한 것 같아요.
여: 사진이 주제를 분명하게 보여주는 것 같아요.
남: 그렇네요. 사진 아래에 두 개의 스테레오 스피커를 놓았군요.
여: 네. 쇼를 위해 최근에 구매한 것들이에요.
남: 좋아요. 학생들은 둥근 카펫 위에 있는 의자들 위에 앉아서 이야기를 하겠군요, 그렇죠?
여: 맞아요. 저는 스탠딩 마이크 옆에 화이트 보드도 놓았어요. 학생들이 저에게 그것을 설치
   해 달라고 부탁했거든요.
남: 좋네요! 그 행사를 기대하고 있을게요.

05 남자가 할 일
▶ 정답⑤

M: Hey, Lucy! Where are you going?
W: Hi, Steve. I'm <u>on my way to</u> the bank to <u>exchange some money</u>.
~으로 가는 길에   환전을 좀 하다
M: Oh, is it for your trip to Europe? You must <u>be excited</u>. Did you buy
신나다
the big <u>backpack</u> you needed?
배낭
W: No, but I <u>borrowed</u> a nice one from my <u>cousin</u>. And I <u>ordered</u> the
빌렸다   사촌   주문했다
<u>guide book</u> you <u>recommended</u>.
안내 책자   추천했다
M: That's good. It'll be very <u>useful</u>. You seem to be all set for your trip.
유용한
W: Almost. I've <u>renewed</u> my <u>passport</u> and <u>booked the flight</u>. But I
갱신한(renew) 여권   예약한(book) 항공편
haven't <u>decided</u> on a hotel yet.
결정한(decide)
M: How come?
W: Because there are so many <u>different options</u>. It's difficult to find
다양한 선택들
the right <u>deal</u>.
상품

M: Why don't you use mobile applications to compare the hotel
　　　　　　　　　모바일 애플리케이션　　　비교하다
prices? It'll save you time and money.
　　　　　절약시키다
W: Mobile apps? Do you know of any good ones?
M: Yes, I know a few. I'll text you and let you know their names.
　　　　　　　　　　　　　　문자를 보내다
W: Thanks. I'll try them out.

해석

남: 이봐, Lucy! 어디 가니?
여: 안녕, Steve. 환전을 좀 하기 위해서 은행으로 가는 길이야.
남: 오, 네 유럽 여행을 위해서? 신나겠다. 네가 필요한 큰 배낭은 샀니?
여: 아니, 하지만 사촌에게 좋은 것을 빌렸어. 그리고 네가 추천한 안내 책자를 주문했어.
남: 잘했네. 그것은 매우 유용할 거야. 너는 여행 준비가 다 된 것 같아 보여.
여: 거의. 나는 여권을 갱신하고 항공편을 예약했어. 그런데 아직 호텔을 결정하지 못했어.
남: 어째서?
여: 너무 많은 다양한 선택들이 있기 때문이야. 제대로 된 상품을 찾는 게 어려워.
남: 호텔 가격을 비교하는 모바일 애플리케이션을 사용하는 건 어떠니? 그것은 너에게 시간과 돈을 절약시켜 줄 거야.
여: 모바일 앱? 너는 좋은 것을 알고 있니?
남: 응, 몇 개 알고 있어. 내가 너에게 문자를 보내서 이름을 알려 줄게.
여: 고마워. 그것들을 사용해 볼게.

① 배낭 빌려주기
② 항공권 예매하기
③ 은행에서 환전하기
④ 여행 안내 책자 주문하기
✔ 호텔 숙박비 비교 앱 알려 주기

06　남자가 지불할 금액

고1 2019년 9월 9번　정답률 70%　▶ 정답 ④

W: Hello, sir. How can I help you?
M: I'm looking for a teapot for my mother. She enjoys having tea with
　　　　　　　　찻주전자　　　　　　　　　차를 마시는 것을 즐기다
her friends.　　　　　　　　　　　　　　(enjoy V-ing: ~하는 것을 즐기다)
W: Okay. How about this teapot with a simple and classic design? It'll
　　　　　　　　　　　　　　　　단순한　　　고전적인
never go out of style.
유행에 뒤떨어지다
M: I think she'll like it. How much is it?
W: It's $20. But if you like this design, we also have this teapot set
that comes with the cups. It's only $30.
~이 딸려 있다
M: Great! I'll take the set. Can you recommend some tea as well?
　　　　　　　　　　　　　　　　추천하다
W: Sure. How about this lavender tea? It's definitely good for
　　　　　　　　　라벤더 차　　　　확실히
relaxation, and it's $10 a package.
휴식　　　　　　　　꾸러미
M: Sounds good. I'll take two packages. Can I use this discount
coupon?　　　　　　　　　　　　　　　　　할인 쿠폰
W: Absolutely. You'll get a 10% discount from the total price.
　　　　　　　　　　총액에서 10% 할인을 받다
M: Great. Here's my credit card.

해석

여: 안녕하세요, 손님. 어떻게 도와드릴까요?
남: 저는 어머니를 위한 찻주전자를 찾고 있어요. 그분은 친구들과 함께 차를 마시는 것을 즐기시거든요.
여: 알겠습니다. 단순하고 고전적인 디자인의 이 찻주전자는 어떠세요? 그것은 결코 유행에 뒤떨어지지 않을 거예요.
남: 어머니께서 좋아하실 것 같아요. 얼마죠?
여: 20달러예요. 하지만 이 디자인이 마음에 드신다면, 컵들이 딸려 있는 이 찻주전자 세트도 있어요. 그것은 고작 30달러예요.
남: 좋아요! 세트를 살게요. 차도 좀 추천해 주실래요?
여: 물론이죠. 이 라벤더 차는 어떠세요? 그것은 휴식에 확실히 좋고, 한 꾸러미에 10달러예요.
남: 좋을 것 같아요. 두 꾸러미를 살게요. 이 할인 쿠폰을 사용할 수 있나요?
여: 물론이죠. 총액에서 10% 할인을 받으실 거예요.
남: 좋네요. 여기 제 신용카드가 있어요.

① $27　　　　② $36　　　　③ $40
✔ $45　　　　⑤ $63

문제 풀이

남자는 처음에 20달러짜리 찻주전자를 소개받았지만 나중에 찻주전자에 컵들이 딸린 30달

러짜리 세트를 산다고 했다. 또한 한 꾸러미에 10달러짜리 라벤더 차를 두 꾸러미 산다고 했으므로 20달러가 더해진다. 총액 50달러에서 쿠폰을 사용해 10% 할인을 받으므로 45달러, 즉 ④ '$45'가 답이 된다.

07　여자가 El Bistro 레스토랑을 선택한 이유

고1 2019년 9월 8번　정답률 85%　▶ 정답 ②

M: Agnes, what are you doing?
W: I'm surfing the Internet to find a nice restaurant for my trip this
　　　　검색하는(surf)
weekend.
M: All the places on the website look nice.
　　　　　장소들
W: Yes, but I've finally decided where to go. It's this French restaurant
called El Bistro.　　　　　어디로 갈지
~이라는 이름의　　　　(where to V: 어디로 ~할지)
M: Oh, I've watched a travel TV show about that restaurant.
　　　　　　　　　　　여행 TV쇼
W: Have you?
M: Yes. It said it's so popular among the local people that they have to
　　　　　　　　　　　인기가 있는　　　지역의
wait in a long line to get in.
길게 줄을 서서 기다리다
W: I know. I don't like crowded places, but I think it'll be worth the wait
　　　　　　　　　(사람들로) 붐비는　　　　　기다릴 가치가 있다
because of its long tradition. The family's been running it since
1890.　　　　　　　전통　　　　　　　　운영하는(run)
M: Wow, that long?
W: Yes. I like old places that maintain their tradition. It's far from my
　　　　　　　　　　　　유지하다　　　　　　~에서 먼
hotel, but I'm willing to go anyway.
기꺼이 가는(willing to V: 기꺼이 ~하는)
M: I'm sure you'll enjoy the meal there.

해석

남: Agnes, 무엇을 하고 있니?
여: 이번 주말 여행을 위해 좋은 레스토랑을 찾으려고 인터넷을 검색하고 있어.
남: 웹 사이트에 있는 모든 장소들이 멋져 보여.
여: 그래, 하지만 나는 마침내 어디로 갈지 결정했어. El Bistro라는 이름의 프랑스 레스토랑이야.
남: 오, 나는 그 레스토랑에 관한 여행 TV쇼를 본 적이 있어.
여: 그래?
남: 응. 그곳은 지역 사람들 사이에서 매우 인기가 있어서 들어가려면 길게 줄을 서서 기다려야 한다고 했어.
여: 알아. 붐비는 장소들을 좋아하지는 않지만, 그곳의 오랜 전통 때문에 기다릴 가치가 있을 것 같아. 그 가족은 1890년부터 그곳을 운영해 오고 있거든.
남: 와, 그렇게 오래?
여: 응. 나는 그들의 전통을 유지하는 오래된 장소들을 좋아해. 그곳은 내 호텔에서 멀지만, 어쨌든 나는 기꺼이 갈 거야.
남: 나는 네가 그곳에서 식사를 즐길 거라고 확신해.

① 호텔에서 가까워서
✔ 오랜 전통이 있어서
③ 프랑스 요리로 유명해서
④ TV 프로그램에 소개되어서
⑤ 지역 주민에게 인기가 많아서

08　Stress Free Program에 관해 언급되지 않은 것

고1 2019년 9월 10번　정답률 90%　▶ 정답 ④

W: Hey, Ryan, did you hear about the Stress Free Program?
M: Stress Free Program? No, what is it? 스트레스 해방 프로그램
W: It's a new school program for students. You might want to join it.
You look really stressed out these days.　　참여하고 싶다
스트레스를 받다　　　　　　(want to V: ~하고 싶다, join: 참여하다)
M: Yeah, I really need to relax. What do I do there?
　　　　긴장을 풀어야 하다
(need to V: ~해야 하다, relax: 긴장을 풀다)
W: You can take part in various activities like coloring, e-sports, and
~에 참여하다　　　　다양한 활동들
board games.
M: Sounds interesting! How can I register for the program?
~에 등록하다
W: You can register in person or on the school website.
직접
M: Where's the program held?
열리는(hold)
W: It's held on the second floor of the Student Union building.
학생회관

04
19년 9월 학력평가

M: All right. Is the program available anytime?
　　　　　　　　　　　　　　　　이용 가능한

W: No, it runs from 3 to 7 p.m. There's a schedule for each activity.
　　　진행되다　　　　　　　　　　　　　　　　일정

M: Okay, I'll check the schedule first.
　　　　　확인하다

W: Great. I hope you can refresh your mind there.
　　　　　　　　　　　　네 마음을 맑게 하다

해석

여: 이봐, Ryan, Stress Free Program(스트레스 해방 프로그램)에 대해 들었니?

남: Stress Free Program? 아니, 그게 뭔데?

여: 학생들을 위한 새로운 학교 프로그램이야. 너는 그것에 참여하고 싶을지도 몰라. 너 요즘에 정말 스트레스를 받는 것처럼 보이거든.

남: 그래, 나는 정말 긴장을 풀어야 해. 그곳에서 내가 무엇을 하는 거야?

여: 색칠하기, e-스포츠, 그리고 보드게임 같은 다양한 활동들에 참여할 수 있어.

남: 재미있겠다! 어떻게 그 프로그램에 등록할 수 있어?

여: 직접 등록하거나 학교 웹 사이트에서 등록할 수 있어.

남: 어디에서 프로그램이 열리니?

여: 학생회관 2층에서 열려.

남: 알겠어. 그 프로그램은 언제나 이용 가능하니?

여: 아니, 그것은 오후 3시에서 7시까지 진행돼. 각 활동마다 일정이 있어.

남: 알았어, 내가 일정을 먼저 확인할게.

여: 좋아. 나는 네가 그곳에서 네 마음을 맑게 할 수 있었으면 좋겠어.

① 활동 종류　　　　　② 등록 방법　　　　　③ 운영 장소

☑ 참가비　　　　　⑤ 운영 시간

09

Show Me Your Dishes에 관한 내용과 일치하지 않는 것

▶ 정답 ⑤

M: Hello, listeners. I'm Nick Adams from Healthy Cooking. I'm pleased to make this announcement about the upcoming cooking contest,
　　　　　　　　　　　　　발표　　　　　　　　다가오는　　　요리 대회
Show Me Your Dishes. It's open to young adults aged 15 to 18 who
　　　　　　　　　　　　　　　　청소년들
want to become chefs. This contest is an annual event which has
　　　　　　　　요리사들　　　　　　　　연례 행사
been held every October since 2004. If you'd like to participate,
열려 왔다(be held)　　　　　　　　　　　　　　　참가하다
please upload your recipe to our contest website by September
　　　업로드하다　　　조리법
6th. The participants will have 90 minutes to cook up their best
　　　참가자들　　　　　　　　　　　　요리하다
dishes. Their dishes will be judged based on taste and nutritional
　　　　　　　　　　　　　~에 근거하여　맛　　　영양가
value by chefs from some of the most famous local restaurants.
　　　　　　　　　　　　가장 유명한 지역 레스토랑들
Don't miss this great opportunity to show off your cooking skills!
　　　놓치다　　　　기회　　　　자랑하다

해석

남: 안녕하세요, 청취자 여러분. 저는 Healthy Cooking(건강한 요리)의 Nick Adams입니다. 다가오는 요리 대회인 Show Me Your Dishes에 대해 이 발표를 하게 되어 기쁩니다. 그것은 요리사가 되고 싶어 하는 15세부터 18세의 청소년들에게 열려 있습니다. 이 대회는 2004년부터 매년 10월에 열려 온 연례 행사입니다. 참가하고 싶으시면, 9월 6일까지 저희의 대회 웹 사이트에 여러분의 조리법을 업로드해 주십시오. 참가자들은 자신들의 최고의 요리를 요리할 수 있는 90분을 가지게 될 것입니다. 그들의 요리는 몇몇 가장 유명한 지역 레스토랑들의 요리사들에 의해 맛과 영양가에 근거하여 심사될 것입니다. 여러분의 요리 솜씨를 자랑할 수 있는 이 좋은 기회를 놓치지 마십시오!

① 참가 대상은 15세부터 18세의 청소년이다.

② 2004년부터 매년 열리는 대회이다.

③ 참가하려면 조리법을 대회 웹 사이트에 업로드해야 한다.

④ 참가자에게 90분의 요리 시간이 주어진다.

☑ 심사의 기준은 맛과 창의성이다.

10

표에서 여자가 주문할 블루투스 키보드

▶ 정답 ②

M: Jessica, what are you doing on the computer?

W: I'm looking for a bluetooth keyboard that works with my
　　　　　　　　　　　블루투스 키보드　　　　　~에 작동하다
smartphone.

M: What do you need it for?

W: I need to type during meetings at work. Can you help me choose
　　타이핑을 해야 하다(need to V: ~해야 하다, type: 타이핑을 하다)
one?

M: Sure. How about this model? It looks great and is the cheapest.

W: I already have that model, but it's too heavy to carry around.
　　　　　　　　　　　너무 무거워서 가지고 다닐 수 없는
　　　　　　　　　　　(too A to V: 너무 A해서 ~할 수 없는)

M: Then, why don't you get something that weighs less than 300
　　　　　　　　　　　　　　　　　　　　　무게가 나가다
grams?

W: Yeah. That makes sense.

M: You can get this one. It also has a battery life of 100 hours.
　　　　　　　　　　　　　　　　배터리 수명

W: It's nice, but it's not foldable. I want to buy that one, instead.
　　　　　　　　　　접을 수 있는　　　　　　　　　　대신에

M: You mean this foldable keyboard?

W: Yeah, it'll take up much less space in my bag. I think I'll order it
　　　　　　공간을 훨씬 덜 차지하다　　　　　　　　주문하다
now.
(take up: 차지하다)

해석

남: Jessica, 컴퓨터로 무엇을 하고 있니?

여: 내 스마트폰에 작동하는 블루투스 키보드를 찾고 있어.

남: 왜 그것이 필요한데?

여: 직장에서 회의 동안에 타이핑을 해야 하거든. 내가 하나 고르는 것을 도와줄래?

남: 물론이지. 이 모델은 어떠니? 그것은 좋아 보이고 가장 싸잖아.

여: 나는 이미 그 모델을 가지고 있는데, 너무 무거워서 가지고 다닐 수가 없어.

남: 그럼, 무게가 300그램보다 덜 나가는 것을 사는 건 어떠니?

여: 그래. 일리 있는 말이야.

남: 이것을 살 수 있어. 배터리의 수명도 100시간이야.

여: 좋긴 한데, 접을 수 없잖아. 대신에, 나는 저것을 사고 싶어.

남: 이 접을 수 있는 키보드를 말하는 거야?

여: 그래, 그것은 내 가방에서 공간을 훨씬 덜 차지할 거야. 지금 그것을 주문해야겠다.

블루투스 키보드

모델	가격	무게	배터리 수명	접이식
① A	45달러	160g	100시간	×
☑ ② B	38달러	250g	82시간	○
③ C	30달러	280g	48시간	×
④ D	26달러	350g	10시간	○
⑤ E	15달러	420g	24시간	×

11

여자의 마지막 말에 대한 남자의 응답

▶ 정답 ⑤

W: Mike, I couldn't reach you on your cell phone yesterday.
　　　　　　　　연락하다　　　　　　　휴대전화

M: My cell phone wasn't working, so I took it to the repair shop.
　　　　　　　　작동하는(work)　　　　　　수리점

W: Really? We need to discuss our science project tonight. How can I
　　　　　　논의해야 하다　　과학 프로젝트
contact you? (need to V: ~해야 하다, discuss: 논의하다)
연락하다

M: (No worries. I'll get my phone back after school.)

해석

여: Mike, 나는 어제 네 휴대전화로 연락할 수가 없었어.

남: 내 휴대전화가 작동하지 않아서, 수리점에 가지고 갔어.

여: 정말? 우리는 오늘 밤에 과학 프로젝트에 대해 논의해야 해. 내가 어떻게 너에게 연락할 수 있어?

남: (걱정하지 마. 나는 방과 후에 휴대전화를 찾아올 거야.)

① 음, 그 프로젝트는 성공적이었어.

② 좋아! 너는 새 휴대전화를 살 수 있어.

③ 물론이지. 너는 내게 언제든지 연락할 수 있어.

④ 다행히도, 휴대전화를 수리하는 것은 비싸지 않았어.

☑ 걱정하지 마. 나는 방과 후에 휴대전화를 찾아올 거야.

12

남자의 마지막 말에 대한 여자의 응답

▶ 정답 ①

[Telephone rings.]

M: Hello. This is the Youth Volunteer Center. What can I do for you?
　　　　　　　　　　청소년 자원봉사 센터

W: I'm supposed to join the volunteer program tomorrow, but can I
　　　　참가하기로 되어 있다
(be supposed to V: ~하기로 되어 있다, join: 참가하다)
change my volunteering schedule?
변경하다　　　자원봉사 일정

M: Sure. You can choose from Thursday or Friday.
　　　　　　　선택하다

W: (All right. Either day is fine with me.)

해석

[전화벨이 울린다.]

남: 여보세요. Youth Volunteer Center(청소년 자원봉사 센터)입니다. 무엇을 도와드릴까요?

여: 제가 내일 자원봉사 프로그램에 참가하기로 되어 있는데요, 자원봉사 일정을 변경할 수 있을까요?

남: 물론이죠. 목요일이나 금요일 중에서 선택할 수 있습니다.

여: (알겠어요. 저는 어느 날이라도 좋아요.)

✓ 알겠어요. 저는 어느 날이라도 좋아요.
② 죄송해요. 당신은 날짜를 선택할 수 없어요.
③ 정말이에요? 저는 변경에 대해 몰랐어요.
④ 감사해요. 저는 자원봉사 프로그램을 즐겼어요.
⑤ 좋아요. 저는 이번 주말을 기대하고 있어요.

---

13 남자의 마지막 말에 대한 여자의 응답

고1 2019년 9월 13번 정답률 85% ▶ 정답 ②

M: Hi, Amy. What are you watching on your tablet?

W: Hi, Dan. It's a video clip on psychology. This lecture is really great!

M: I didn't know you were interested in psychology.

W: Actually, I'm thinking of becoming a counselor.

M: Great! I think it'll suit you. You're a good listener and you give good advice to others.

W: Thanks. I'd like to get some practical experience in counseling, but it's not easy to find opportunities.

M: How about checking the school's volunteer center? You might find something.

W: I've already checked it, but it didn't help much.

M: Oh, my uncle works at a local counseling center. Maybe he can help you.

W: (Really? Please ask him if I can visit him.)

해석

남: 안녕, Amy. 태블릿으로 무엇을 보고 있니?

여: 안녕, Dan. 심리학에 관한 동영상이야. 이 강의는 정말 훌륭해!

남: 나는 네가 심리학에 관심이 있는지 몰랐어.

여: 사실, 나는 상담사가 될까 생각 중이야.

남: 멋지다! 나는 그것이 너에게 어울릴 것 같아. 너는 말을 잘 들어주고 다른 사람들에게 좋은 조언을 해 주잖아.

여: 고마워. 나는 상담에 있어서 실질적인 경험을 좀 얻고 싶지만, 기회를 찾기가 쉽지 않아.

남: 학교 자원봉사 센터를 확인해 보는 건 어때? 무언가를 찾을 수 있을지도 몰라.

여: 나는 이미 그것을 확인했는데, 별로 도움이 안 됐어.

남: 오, 우리 삼촌께서 지역 상담 센터에서 일하고 계셔. 아마 그분이 너를 도와주실 거야.

여: (정말? 그분께 내가 방문해도 되는지 여쭤봐 줘.)

① 나도 알아. 심리학을 공부하는 것은 재미있어.
✓ 정말? 그분께 내가 방문해도 되는지 여쭤봐 줘.
③ 맞아. 직업을 결정하는 것은 쉽지 않아.
④ 음, 나는 상담 일이 너에게 맞는 것 같아.
⑤ 좋아. 내가 네 삼촌께 그 일에 지원하는 방법을 말해줄게.

문제풀이

상담사가 되고 싶은 여자는 상담 경험을 쌓고 싶지만 좀처럼 기회를 찾지 못하고 있다. 학교 자원봉사 센터도 별로 도움이 안 됐다는 여자의 말에 남자는 지역 상담 센터에서 일하고 계신 삼촌을 언급하며 그가 도와줄 수 있다는 말을 한다. 따라서 여자가 삼촌과 만날 수 있는 가능성을 비추고 있는 ② 'Really? Please ask him if I can visit him.(정말? 그분께 내가 방문해도 되는지 여쭤봐 줘.)'이 답이 된다.

---

14 여자의 마지막 말에 대한 남자의 응답

고1 2019년 9월 14번 정답률 75% ▶ 정답 ①

W: Chris, did you hear the weather forecast?

M: No, what did it say?

W: It said there would be heavy rain and strong winds this afternoon.

M: Oh, no! Our outdoor concert is supposed to start at 4 p.m. What should we do?

W: The teacher said we have to change the location of the concert to the school auditorium.

M: Okay. We still have several hours to set up the stage. But how can we inform people of the change?

W: I'll make a notice and put it up on the notice board at the outdoor concert hall.

M: Good. I'll go and ask the school broadcasting station to make an announcement about it.

W: Good idea. Is there any other way for us to spread the news to more people quickly?

M: (We can post the notice on social media.)

해석

여: Chris, 일기 예보 들었니?

남: 아니, 뭐라고 했는데?

여: 오늘 오후에 폭우가 내리고 강풍이 불 거라고 했어.

남: 오, 이런! 우리의 야외 콘서트가 오후 4시에 시작하기로 되어 있잖아. 어떻게 해야 하지?

여: 선생님께서 콘서트 장소를 학교 강당으로 바꿔야 한다고 말씀하셨어.

남: 알았어. 우리에게는 아직 무대를 설치할 몇 시간이 있어. 그런데 사람들에게 장소 변경을 어떻게 알릴까?

여: 내가 안내문을 만들어서 그것을 야외 콘서트장의 게시판에 붙일게.

남: 좋아. 나는 학교 방송국에 가서 그것에 대한 안내 방송을 해 달라고 부탁할게.

여: 좋은 생각이야. 우리가 더 많은 사람들에게 빠르게 소식을 퍼뜨릴 수 있는 다른 방법이 있을까?

남: (우리는 소셜 미디어에 안내문을 올릴 수 있어.)

✓ 우리는 소셜 미디어에 안내문을 올릴 수 있어.
② 그럼, 우리의 악기들을 실내로 옮기자.
③ 나는 이미 우리의 야외 콘서트를 취소했어.
④ 우리는 즉시 장소를 변경하는 게 좋겠어.
⑤ 우리는 앱을 이용해서 일기 예보를 확인할 수 있어.

문제풀이

좋지 않은 날씨 때문에 장소 변경을 알려야 하는 상황에서 여자는 콘서트장의 게시판에 안내문을 만들어 붙이고 남자는 학교 방송국에 안내 방송을 해 달라고 부탁하려 한다. 이 방법들보다 더 빠르게 소식을 퍼뜨릴 수 있는 다른 방법을 궁금해 하는 여자에게 방법을 제시하는 남자의 말, 즉 ① 'We can post the notice on social media.(우리는 소셜 미디어에 안내문을 올릴 수 있어.)'가 적절하다.

---

15 다음 상황에서 Jina가 어머니에게 할 말

고1 2019년 9월 15번 정답률 80% ▶ 정답 ③

M: Jina is a high school student. Her school is hosting a Market Day to raise money for the homeless in the neighborhood. Jina's teacher says that students who want to take part in the event should bring their own items to school. Jina wants to participate in the school market, so as soon as she gets home, she starts looking for items she can sell at the school Market Day. Finally, she finds her mother's old flower pot in the basement. Now, she wants to ask her mother for permission to take the flower pot to school. In this situation, what would Jina be most likely to say to her mother?

Jina: (Can I take this flower pot for a school event?)

해석

남: Jina는 고등학생이다. 그녀의 학교는 이웃의 노숙자들을 위한 돈을 모으기 위해 Market Day를 주최하고 있다. Jina의 선생님은 행사에 참가하고 싶은 학생들은 자신들의 물건들을 학교에 가져와야 한다고 말한다. Jina는 학교 시장에 참여하고 싶어서, 집에 오자마자, 학교 Market Day에 팔 수 있는 물건들을 찾기 시작한다. 마침내, 그녀는 지하실에서 어머

04 / 19년 9월 학력평가

니의 오래된 화분을 발견한다. 이제, 그녀는 어머니에게 학교에 화분을 가져갈 수 있도록 허락을 요청하고 싶다. 이러한 상황에서 Jina는 그녀의 어머니에게 뭐라고 말하겠는가?

Jina: (학교 행사를 위해 이 화분을 가져갈 수 있을까요?)

① 제가 좋은 화분을 고를 수 있도록 도와주세요.
② 저와 함께 Market Day에 가실래요?
✓③ 학교 행사를 위해 이 화분을 가져갈 수 있을까요?
④ 이 화분에 제 꽃을 심을 수 있을지 모르겠어요.
⑤ 우리 시장에서 팔 수 있는 물건을 찾아보는 게 어때요?

16~17 1지문 2문항

W: Hello, everyone! Today, I want you to consider this: do you have
(여러분이 생각하기를 바라다)
(want A to V: A가 ~하기를 바라다)
something you're not using in your home? Then, how about
sharing it with others? It enables products to be recycled and
그것을 다른 사람들과 나누는 것   물품들이 재활용되고 재사용될 수 있도록 하다
(share A with B: A를 B와 나누다)   (enable A to V: A가 ~할 수 있도록 하다,
                                          recycle: 재활용하다, reuse: 재사용하다)
reused, reducing the negative effects on the environment. For
                            부정적인 영향들
example, if you have a nice dress for a party, lend it to others who
                                              다른 사람들에게 그것을 빌려주다
                                              (lend A to B: B에게 A를 빌려주다)
need it. Then the materials used in making a new dress can be
                            재료들
saved. The same thing with toys. Every year, millions of toys that
절약되다   수백만 개의 장난감들
children no longer play with are thrown away. By sharing things
          더 이상 놀지 않다   버려지다(throw away)
with others, you can reduce waste. Also, you can benefit financially
                      쓰레기를 줄이다   이익을 얻다 경제적으로
by sharing your goods. If you have books you've finished reading,
register them on online sharing systems. Then, someone who
등록하다   온라인 공유 시스템
wants to read your books can rent them and you can make money
                                  빌리다   돈을 벌다
by sharing. Similarly, if you need a bicycle, you can find some
          마찬가지로
people who share theirs on bike-sharing systems and save money.
Why don't you awaken your "sleeping" goods?
              깨우다

해석

여: 안녕하세요, 여러분! 오늘, 저는 여러분께서 이것을 생각해 주시기를 바랍니다: 여러분의 집에 사용하지 않는 어떤 것이 있으신가요? 그렇다면, 그것을 다른 사람들과 나누는 것이 어떠십니까? 그것은 물품들이 재활용되고 재사용될 수 있도록 해서 환경에 대한 부정적인 영향들을 감소시킵니다. 예를 들면, 여러분께서 파티를 위한 멋진 옷을 가지고 계시다면, 그것을 필요로 하는 다른 사람들에게 그것을 빌려주십시오. 그러면 새 옷을 만드는 데 사용되는 재료들이 절약될 수 있습니다. 장난감들도 마찬가지입니다. 매년, 아이들이 더 이상 가지고 놀지 않는 수백만 개의 장난감들이 버려집니다. 다른 사람들과 물품들을 나눔으로써, 여러분은 쓰레기를 줄이실 수 있습니다. 또한, 여러분은 물품들을 나눔으로써 경제적으로 이익을 얻으실 수 있습니다. 여러분께서 다 읽으신 책들을 가지고 계신다면, 온라인 공유 시스템에 그것들을 등록하십시오. 그러면, 여러분의 책들을 읽고 싶어 하는 누군가가 그것들을 빌리고 여러분은 공유함으로써 돈을 버실 수 있습니다. 마찬가지로, 여러분께서 자전거가 필요하시다면, 여러분은 자전거 공유 시스템에서 자신들의 자전거를 공유하는 사람들을 찾으실 수 있고 돈을 절약하실 수 있습니다. 여러분의 '잠자고 있는' 물품들을 깨우시는 것은 어떠십니까?

16 여자가 하는 말의 주제
고1 2019년 9월 16번 | 정답률 85%
▶ 정답 ①

✓① 물품들을 공유하는 것의 이점들
② 중고 물품을 온라인에서 판매하는 방법들
③ 재활용 과정의 단계들
④ 정보를 공유하는 것의 필요성
⑤ 온라인 시장에 의해 야기된 문제들

17 언급된 물품이 아닌 것
고1 2019년 9월 17번 | 정답률 90%
▶ 정답 ③

① 옷   ② 장난감   ✓③ 자동차
④ 책   ⑤ 자전거

05 2019년 11월 학력평가

01	③	02	①	03	④	04	④	05	⑤
06	②	07	④	08	④	09	⑤	10	②
11	③	12	②	13	④	14	①	15	①
16	③	17	③						

01 남자가 하는 말의 목적
고1 2019년 11월 3번 | 정답률 90%
▶ 정답 ③

M: Hello, everyone. Welcome back to our show, 'Secrets to a Healthy
                                              건강한 삶의 비법들
Life.' I'm your host and health expert, Eric Bolton. You might have
          진행자   건강 전문가   들어봤을지도 모른다
                                                (might have p.p.: ~했을지도 모른다)
heard that many people suffer from dry skin as the weather gets
                      ~로 고생하다 건조한 피부 └~하면서
colder. Let me share some tips to keep your skin healthy in the
                            조언들
winter. When you take a bath, use water that is not very hot. A long
              목욕을 하다
hot bath in cold weather can make your skin dry and eventually
                                                          결국
cause skin trouble. And one more tip for your skin in the winter: Put
피부 트러블을 야기하다
lotion or oil on your skin as often as possible. I hope you can make
~에 로션이나 오일을 바르다 가능한 한 자주(as A as possible: 가능한 한 A한/A하게)
use of these tips to keep your skin healthy even in the winter.
~을 활용하다

해석

남: 안녕하세요, 여러분. 저희 쇼 'Secrets to a Healthy Life(건강한 삶의 비법들)'에 다시 오신 것을 환영합니다. 저는 진행자이자 건강 전문가인 Eric Bolton입니다. 여러분은 날씨가 더 추워지면서 많은 사람들이 건조한 피부로 고생한다는 것을 들어보셨을지도 모릅니다. 제가 겨울에 피부를 건강하게 유지하기 위한 몇 가지 조언들을 알려드리겠습니다. 목욕을 할 때, 너무 뜨겁지 않은 물을 사용하십시오. 추운 날씨에 오랫동안 뜨거운 물로 목욕을 하는 것은 피부를 건조하게 만들어서 결국 피부 트러블을 야기할 수 있습니다. 그리고 겨울철 피부를 위한 조언이 한 가지 더 있습니다: 가능한 한 자주 피부에 로션이나 오일을 바르십시오. 겨울에도 피부를 건강하게 유지하기 위해서 이러한 조언들을 활용하실 수 있기를 바랍니다.

① 유행성 독감 예방 접종을 권고하려고
② 열탕 목욕의 화상 위험성을 경고하려고
✓③ 겨울철 피부 건강 관리법을 소개하려고
④ 겨울철 체온 유지의 중요성을 강조하려고
⑤ 피부 트러블을 진정시키는 제품을 홍보하려고

02 여자의 의견
고1 2019년 11월 4번 | 정답률 95%
▶ 정답 ①

W: Hello, Jake. Is studying for the final exams going well?
                                  기말고사
M: Not really, Ms. Baker. I've been drinking energy drinks to stay
                                              에너지 음료들
awake.
자지 않고 깨어 있다
W: Well, I think you'd better not drink too many of them.
              너는 마시지 않는 게 좋겠다
        (had better not V: ~하지 않는 게 좋겠다)
M: Why? Do they have harmful effects?
                      해로운 영향들
W: Energy drinks have a lot of caffeine, so drinking them too much
                      많은 카페인
can disturb your sleep and make you feel dizzy.
    방해하다   현기증을 느끼다
M: That explains why I can't sleep well at night.
    설명하다
W: Right. Also, drinking them can make you nervous.
                                              과민한
M: Really? I thought it would relieve my stress instead.
                              내 스트레스를 완화하다 대신에
                              (relieve: 완화하다)
W: That's not true. And the more you drink energy drinks, the more
you become dependent on them.
      ~에 의존하게 되다
M: Do you mean I can become addicted to them?
                                  ~에 중독되다
W: That's right. So you should be careful not to drink too many of
                                주의하다
them.

M: Okay. I'll keep that in mind. Thanks, Ms. Baker.
　그것을 명심하다

해석　(keep A in mind: A를 명심하다)

여: 안녕, Jake. 기말고사 공부는 잘 되어가니?

남: 별로 그렇지 못해요, Baker 선생님. 저는 자지 않고 깨어 있기 위해서 에너지 음료를 마시고 있어요.

여: 음, 나는 네가 그것들을 너무 많이 마시지 않는 게 좋다고 생각해.

남: 왜요? 그것들이 해로운 영향을 미치나요?

여: 에너지 음료에는 많은 카페인이 들어 있어서, 그것들을 너무 많이 마시는 것은 너의 수면을 방해하고 네가 현기증을 느끼게 할 수도 있어.

남: 그것은 제가 왜 밤에 잠을 잘 못 자는지 설명해 주네요.

여: 그렇지. 또한, 그것들을 마시는 것은 너를 과민하게 만들 수 있어.

남: 정말이에요? 저는 그것이 대신에 제 스트레스를 완화할 것이라고 생각했어요.

여: 그렇지 않아. 그리고 네가 에너지 음료를 더 많이 마실수록, 너는 그것들에 더 많이 의존하게 돼.

남: 제가 그것들에 중독될 수도 있다는 말씀이세요?

여: 맞아. 그러니까 그것들을 너무 많이 마시지 않도록 주의해야 해.

남: 알겠어요. 그것을 명심할게요. 감사합니다, Baker 선생님.

☑① 에너지 음료의 과잉 섭취를 주의해야 한다.
② 적당량의 카페인은 긴장 완화에 효과적이다.
③ 어지럼증에는 충분한 수분을 공급하는 것이 좋다.
④ 명상은 일상의 불안감을 해소하는 데 도움이 된다.
⑤ 균형 잡힌 식단은 성적 향상에 긍정적인 영향을 준다.

03　두 사람의 관계　▶ 정답 ④

W: Hello. How can I help you?

M: Hi, I made an online reservation. Do I get the tickets here?
　　　　　　온라인 예약을 했다(make a reservation)

W: You don't have to get tickets if you have a reservation number. Just
　　표들을 받을 필요가 없다　　　　　　　　예약 번호
　(don't have to V: ~할 필요가 없다)

　show it at the entrance and you can enjoy the whole camping expo.
　　　　　입구에서　　　　　　　　　　　　　　캠핑 박람회

M: That's great. I heard there is a section for camping tables and
　　　　　　　　　　　　　　　　　구역　　　캠핑용 테이블들과 의자들

　chairs in the expo. Where can I find it?
　　　　　　　　　　찾다

W: When you go inside, you'll see it on your right. Look for camping
　　　　　안으로 들어가다　　　　　　　　　　　　　　　캠핑 제품들

　goods on display.
　캠핑 제품들　전시된

M: Thanks. Is there a cafeteria around here?
　　　　　　　　　식당

W: Yes, we have one on the second floor.
　　　　　　　　　　　2층에

M: Thank you so much for your help.

W: My pleasure. Enjoy your time in our camping expo.

해석

여: 안녕하세요. 어떻게 도와드릴까요?

남: 안녕하세요, 저는 온라인 예약을 했어요. 여기에서 표를 받는 건가요?

여: 예약 번호가 있으시면 표를 받으실 필요가 없어요. 그냥 입구에서 그것을 보여주시면 전체 캠핑 박람회를 즐기실 수 있어요.

남: 잘됐네요. 저는 박람회에 캠핑용 테이블과 의자에 관한 구역이 있다고 들었어요. 어디에서 그것을 찾을 수 있나요?

여: 안으로 들어가시면, 오른편에 있을 거예요. 전시된 캠핑 제품들을 찾아 보세요.

남: 감사합니다. 여기 근처에 식당이 있나요?

여: 네, 2층에 한 곳이 있어요.

남: 도와주셔서 정말 감사합니다.

여: 천만에요. 캠핑 박람회에서 즐거운 시간 보내세요.

① 호텔 직원 ― 투숙객　　　　② 식당 주인 ― 종업원
③ 가구 제작자 ― 의뢰인　　　☑④ 박람회장 안내원 ― 방문객
⑤ 전시 기획자 ― 실내 디자이너

문제 풀이

온라인 예약을 하고 캠핑 박람회장을 찾은 남자에게 여자는 예약 번호가 있으면 표를 받지 않아도 된다고 말하며, 캠핑용 테이블과 의자가 있는 구역과 식당의 위치 등에 대한 박람회장 정보를 안내하고 있다. 그러므로 ④ '박람회장 안내원 ― 방문객'이 적절한 답이다.

04　그림에서 대화의 내용과 일치하지 않는 것　▶ 정답 ④

M: What are you looking at, honey?
　　　　　　　　~을 보는(look at)

W: It's the picture Sally sent to me. She recommended that we go to
　　　　사진　　　　　　　　　　　　　　추천했다

　the new community park near her house.
　　　　지역 공원

M: Let me see it. [Pause] I like this big round table on the left. We can
　　　　　　　　　　　　　큰 원형 테이블

　have some sandwiches and talk there.

W: Sounds great. Look at the elephant face at the top of the slide. It
　　　　　　　　　　　코끼리 얼굴　　~의 맨 위에　　　미끄럼틀
　looks cute.

M: Yeah, there are also swings next to it. Our son would like this park,
　　　　　　　　　그네들　　~ 옆에
　too.

W: He sure would. Oh, there is a see-saw in front of the swings.
　　　　　　　　　　　　　　시소　　~ 앞에

M: Wow, this park has everything a child could want.

W: It's great to find a place where parents and children can have a
　　　　　　　　　찾다　　장소

　good time together.
　즐거운 시간을 보내다

M: It really is. Take a look at these flowers placed in the shape of a
　　　　　　　~을 보다　　　　　　　　놓여 있는(place: 놓다)　모양
　heart!

W: They're beautiful. How about going there this weekend?

M: Terrific! I can't wait to go there.
　　　　빨리 가고 싶다(can't wait to V: 빨리 ~하고 싶다)

해석

남: 무엇을 보고 있어요, 여보?

여: Sally가 제게 보낸 사진이에요. 그녀가 그녀의 집 근처에 새로 생긴 지역 공원에 가보라고 추천했어요.

남: 그것 좀 보여줘요. [잠시 후] 왼쪽에 있는 이 큰 원형 테이블이 마음에 드네요. 거기에서 샌드위치를 먹으며 얘기를 나눌 수 있겠네요.

여: 좋을 것 같아요. 미끄럼틀의 맨 위에 있는 코끼리 얼굴을 봐요. 귀여워 보이네요.

남: 그래요, 그것의 옆에 그네도 있어요. 우리 아들도 이 공원을 좋아할 거예요.

여: 그 애는 분명 그럴 거예요. 오, 그네 앞에 시소가 있어요.

남: 와, 이 공원에는 아이가 원하는 모든 것이 다 있네요.

여: 부모와 아이들이 함께 즐거운 시간을 보낼 수 있는 장소를 찾아서 좋네요.

남: 정말 그래요. 하트 모양 안에 놓여 있는 이 꽃들을 봐요!

여: 예쁘네요. 이번 주말에 그곳에 가는 게 어때요?

남: 좋아요! 그곳에 빨리 가고 싶네요.

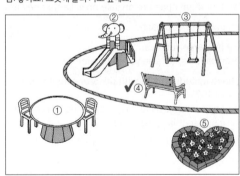

05　남자가 여자에게 부탁한 일　▶ 정답 ⑤

W: David, how are the preparations going for your meeting tomorrow?
　　　　　　　　　　준비들　　　　　　　　　회의

M: Hi, Jennifer. They're almost done. I'm about to check if everything
　　　　　　　　　　　　　　　　　　　　나는 막 확인하려는 참이다
　is ready.
　준비가 된　　　　　　　　　　　(be about to V: 막 ~하려는 참이다, check: 확인하다)

W: Sounds good. Since I finished my own work today, I can help you.
　　　　　　　　　~ 때문에　끝냈다

M: That's very kind of you. I confirmed the reservation for the meeting
　　　　　　　　　　　　　　확인했다　　　예약　　　　　　　회의실
　room and sent text messages informing the participants of
　　　　　　　　　　　　　　　　참석자들에게 내일 일정을 알리는
　tomorrow's schedule.
　　　　　　(inform A of B: A에게 B를 알리다, participant: 참석자, 참가자)

W: What about snacks for the meeting?
　　　　　　간식들

M: They're in my car. I'll get them tomorrow morning.

W: And, is there anything else left to do?
　　　　　　　　　　　　남은(leave)

M: Let me see... I need to make name tags to give to the participants.
　　　　　　　　　만들어야 하다　이름표들
　　　　　　　(need to V: ~해야 하다)

W: Do you want me to help you with that?
<u>내가 도와주기를 원하다</u>
(want A to V: A가 ~하기를 원하다)

M: No, thanks. I can <u>handle</u> it. Could you <u>print out</u> some <u>materials</u> for
<u>처리하다</u> <u>~을 출력하다</u> <u>자료들</u>
the meeting <u>instead</u>?
<u>대신에</u>

W: Sure. I'll do that for you.

M: I'll send you the <u>file</u> to print out right now. Thank you.
<u>파일</u>

해석

여: David, 내일 회의를 위한 준비는 어떻게 되어 가고 있어요?

남: 안녕하세요, Jennifer. 거의 다 되었어요. 저는 모든 것이 준비가 되었는지 막 확인하려는 참이에요.

여: 잘됐네요. 저는 오늘 제 일을 끝냈기 때문에, 당신을 도와줄 수 있어요.

남: 정말 친절하시네요. 저는 회의실 예약을 확인했고 참석자들에게 내일 일정을 알리는 문자 메시지를 보냈어요.

여: 회의를 위한 간식은 어때요?

남: 그것들은 제 차에 있어요. 제가 내일 아침에 가져올게요.

여: 그러면, 해야 할 남은 일이 있나요?

남: 어디 보자... 참석자들에게 줄 이름표를 만들어야 해요.

여: 제가 그것을 도와주기를 원하세요?

남: 아니요, 괜찮아요. 제가 처리할 수 있어요. 대신에 회의 자료를 좀 출력해 주실래요?

여: 물론이죠. 제가 할게요.

남: 지금 당장 출력할 파일을 보내드릴게요. 감사해요.

① 회의실 예약 확인하기 ② 일정 알림 문자 보내기
③ 차에서 간식 가져오기 ④ 참석자 이름표 만들기
✔ 회의 자료 출력하기

---

06 남자가 지불할 금액
▶ 정답 ②

W: Welcome to <u>Good Aroma Candle</u>. How may I help you?
<u>기분 좋은 향초</u>

M: Hi. I'm <u>looking for</u> scented candles for my parents. They like flower
<u>~을 찾는(look for)</u> <u>향초들</u> <u>꽃향기들</u>
scents.

W: Come over here and try this flower scent.
<u>(향기를) 맡아 보다</u>

M: Thanks. [Pause] I like this rose scented candle. How much is it?

W: Large candles and <u>medium</u> ones are <u>on sale</u> now. Large ones are
<u>중간의</u> <u>할인 판매 중인</u>
$20 and medium ones are $10 <u>each</u>.
<u>각각</u>

M: Well then, I'll take two large candles.

W: If you buy any three candles, we give you a <u>soap</u> for <u>free</u>.
<u>비누</u> <u>무료로</u>

M: Great. Then I'll have a medium one with the same scent <u>as well</u>.
<u>~도</u>
Did you say they're $10?

W: Exactly. You're getting two large candles and one medium candle.

M: That's right. Can I also use this <u>mobile coupon</u>?
<u>사용하다</u> <u>모바일 쿠폰</u>

W: Of course, you <u>get 10% off the total price</u> with that.
<u>총액에서 10% 할인을 받다</u>

M: Thank you. I'll <u>pay</u> by <u>credit card</u>.
<u>지불하다</u> <u>신용카드</u>

해석

여: Good Aroma Candle(기분 좋은 향초)에 오신 것을 환영합니다. 어떻게 도와드릴까요?

남: 안녕하세요. 제 부모님을 위한 향초를 찾고 있어요. 그분들은 꽃향기를 좋아하세요.

여: 이쪽으로 오셔서 이 꽃향기를 맡아 보세요.

남: 감사합니다. [잠시 후] 저는 이 장미 향초가 마음에 들어요. 얼마죠?

여: 큰 초와 중간 초는 지금 할인 판매 중이에요. 큰 초는 각각 20달러이고 중간 초는 각각 10달러예요.

남: 음 그럼, 큰 초 두 개를 살게요.

여: 어떤 초든 세 개를 사시면, 무료로 비누를 하나 드려요.

남: 좋네요. 그럼 같은 향으로 중간 초도 하나 살게요. 그것들은 10달러라고 하셨죠?

여: 맞아요. 손님은 큰 초 두 개와 중간 초 한 개를 사시게 되는군요.

남: 맞아요. 이 모바일 쿠폰도 사용할 수 있나요?

여: 물론이죠. 그것으로 총액에서 10% 할인을 받으시네요.

남: 감사합니다. 신용카드로 지불할게요.

① $40 ✔ $45 ③ $50
④ $54 ⑤ $60

문제 풀이

남자는 처음에 20달러짜리 큰 초 두 개만 사려고 했지만 어떤 초든 세 개를 사면 무료로 비누를 준다는 말에 10달러짜리 중간 초 한 개도 사기로 했다. 총 50달러이지만, 모바일 쿠폰을 사

용해서 총액에서 10% 할인을 받을 수 있으므로 최종 금액은 5달러를 뺀 45달러가 된다. 따라서 정답은 ② '$45'이다.

---

07 여자가 가족 여행을 갈 수 없는 이유
▶ 정답 ④

[Cell phone rings.]

M: Hello. Janis! What's up?

W: Hi, Chris. How are you <u>spending</u> your <u>vacation</u>?
<u>(시간을) 보내다(spend)</u> <u>방학</u>

M: I've been <u>doing a lot of cooking</u>. How about you? You said you're
<u>요리를 많이 하는(do cooking)</u>
<u>going on a family trip</u>.
<u>가족 여행을 가는(go on a trip)</u>

W: Yeah, I was supposed to, but I can't.

M: Really? Aren't there <u>flight tickets</u> <u>available</u>?
<u>항공권들</u> <u>이용 가능한</u>

W: Well, it's not about tickets.

M: Then why? Oh, is there still a <u>problem</u> with your <u>ankle</u>?
<u>아직도</u> <u>문제</u> <u>발목</u>

W: No, I'm okay now. Actually I <u>applied for an overseas volunteering</u>
<u>~에 지원했다(apply for)</u> <u>해외 자원봉사 프로그램</u>
program earlier and I was <u>accepted</u>.
<u>합격했다(be accepted)</u>

M: What a great <u>chance</u>! So you can't go on that family trip.
<u>기회</u>

W: You're right. I'll <u>be abroad</u> for a month. <u>I wanted to say goodbye to</u>
<u>해외에 있다</u> <u>너에게 작별 인사를 하고 싶었다</u>
<u>you</u> before I <u>leave</u>. (want to V: ~하고 싶다,
<u>떠나다</u> say goodbye to: ~에게 작별 인사를 하다)

M: Take good care of yourself. I'm sure you'll have a <u>meaningful</u>
<u>experience</u>. <u>의미 있는</u>
<u>경험</u>

W: Thank you for <u>supporting me</u>. Have a nice vacation!
<u>응원해주는 것(support: 응원하다)</u>

해석

[휴대전화가 울린다.]

남: 여보세요. Janis! 무슨 일이야?

여: 안녕, Chris. 방학을 어떻게 보내고 있니?

남: 나는 요리를 많이 하고 있어. 너는 어때? 너는 가족 여행을 갈 거라고 말했잖아.

여: 그래, 그렇게 하기로 되어 있었는데, 나는 갈 수가 없어.

남: 정말? 이용 가능한 항공권이 없니?

여: 음, 항공권에 대한 것이 아니야.

남: 그럼 왜? 오, 아직도 네 발목에 문제가 있는 거니?

여: 아니, 지금은 괜찮아. 사실 이전에 해외 자원봉사 프로그램에 지원했는데 합격했거든.

남: 정말 좋은 기회네! 그래서 네가 가족 여행을 갈 수 없구나.

여: 맞아. 나는 한 달 동안 해외에 있을 거야. 떠나기 전에 너에게 작별 인사를 하고 싶었어.

남: 몸 조심해. 나는 네가 의미 있는 경험을 할 것이라고 확신해.

여: 나를 응원해 줘서 고마워. 방학 잘 보내!

① 발목 상태가 좋지 않아서
② 항공권을 구입하지 못해서
③ 요리 대회에 참가해야 해서
✔ 해외 봉사 활동을 가야 해서
⑤ 부모님께 다른 일정이 생겨서

---

08 Junior Badminton Competition에 관해 언급되지 않은 것
▶ 정답 ④

M: Kelly, did you see this <u>Junior Badminton Competition</u> <u>leaflet</u>?
<u>청소년 배드민턴 대회</u> <u>전단</u>

W: No, not yet. Let me see. The competition is on November 21st, at
10 a.m.

M: It's after the <u>midterm exams</u>. Why don't we <u>sign up for the</u>
<u>중간고사</u> <u>~에 참가 신청을 하다</u>
competition <u>as a team</u>?
<u>한 팀으로</u>

W: Sounds exciting. It would be an <u>unforgettable</u> event <u>before</u>
<u>graduating</u>. <u>잊지 못할</u>
<u>졸업하기 전에(graduate: 졸업하다)</u>

M: Exactly. The <u>participation fee</u> is only $8.
<u>참가비</u>

W: That's <u>reasonable</u>. Oh, look at this. They <u>provide</u> lunch for <u>free</u>.
<u>합리적인</u> <u>제공하다</u> <u>무료로</u>

M: But here it says we <u>have to bring</u> our own rackets.
<u>가져와야 하다</u>
(have to V: ~해야 하다, bring: 가져오다)

W: Then, we should bring ours. How can we <u>apply for</u> the competition?
<u>~에 신청하다</u>

M: It says we can sign up online. Let's do it together now.

W: Okay. I'm really looking forward to it.
_{~을 기대하는(look forward to)}

해석

남: Kelly, 이 Junior Badminton Competition(청소년 배드민턴 대회) 전단 봤니?

여: 아니, 아직. 어디 보자. 그 대회는 11월 21일 오전 10시에 있구나.

남: 중간고사 이후야. 우리 한 팀으로 그 대회에 참가 신청을 하는 게 어때?

여: 재미있겠다. 그것은 졸업하기 전에 잊지 못할 일이 될 거야.

남: 맞아. 참가비는 겨우 8달러야.

여: 그거 합리적이네. 오, 이것을 봐. 그들은 무료로 점심 식사를 제공해.

남: 하지만 여기에 자신의 라켓을 가져와야 한다고 적혀 있어.

여: 그렇다면, 우리 것을 가져가야지. 어떻게 대회에 신청할 수 있어?

남: 온라인으로 신청할 수 있다고 적혀 있어. 지금 그것을 같이 하자.

여: 좋아. 나는 정말 기대돼.

① 대회 일시 ② 참가비 ③ 준비물

✔④ 우승 상품 ⑤ 신청 방법

---

09 Dream Children's Library에 관한 내용과 일치하지 않는 것
고1 2019년 11월 11번 | 정답률 65% | ▶ 정답 ⑤

W: Hello, listeners! I'm happy to introduce you to the first children's library in our town. It's the Dream Children's Library. Our library is for children in the sixth grade and younger. We have a variety of toys as well as books for different ages of children. There are special reading discussion programs for your children. Also, we offer movie showings for children every weekend. We're excited to tell you our library is now ready to open. Our opening day is November 24th. On opening day, we'll provide cartoon character bookmarks to all the visitors. Don't miss it! For more information, visit our website www.dreamchildrenslibrary.org.

해석

여: 안녕하세요, 청취자 여러분! 우리 마을 최초의 어린이 도서관을 여러분에게 소개하게 되어 기쁩니다. 그것은 Dream Children's Library입니다. 저희 도서관은 6학년까지의 어린이들을 대상으로 합니다. 저희는 다양한 연령층의 아이들을 위한 도서들뿐만 아니라 다양한 장난감들도 갖추고 있습니다. 여러분의 아이들을 위한 특별 독서 토론 프로그램들도 있습니다. 또한, 매주 주말에 아이들을 위한 영화 상영을 제공합니다. 저희 도서관이 이제 문을 열 준비가 되었다는 것을 여러분에게 전하게 되어 신이 납니다. 저희의 개관일은 11월 24일입니다. 개관일에, 저희는 모든 방문객들에게 만화 캐릭터 책갈피를 제공할 것입니다. 그것을 놓치지 마세요! 더 많은 정보를 원하시면, 저희 웹 사이트 www.dreamchildrenslibrary.org를 방문해 주세요.

① 6학년까지의 어린이를 대상으로 한다.

② 도서뿐 아니라 다양한 장난감이 있다.

③ 특별 독서 토론 프로그램을 운영한다.

④ 주말에 어린이들을 위해 영화를 상영한다.

✔⑤ 개관일에 만화 캐릭터 엽서를 제공한다.

문제 풀이

여자는 어린이 도서관의 개관일에 방문객들에게 만화 캐릭터 책갈피를 제공한다고 말하고 있다. 그러므로 여자의 말과 일치하지 않는 것은 ⑤ '개관일에 만화 캐릭터 엽서를 제공한다.'이다.

---

10 표에서 여자가 선택할 미술용품 세트
고1 2019년 11월 12번 | 정답률 85% | ▶ 정답 ②

M: Hey, Cathy! What are you looking at?
_{~을 보는(look at)}

W: Hi, Steve. I was searching for an art supplies set. I'm thinking about sending it as a Christmas gift to children in need.
_{~을 검색하는(search for) / 미술용품 세트 / 크리스마스 선물로 / 가난한 아이들(in need: 가난한)}

M: You're so kind. Do you need help choosing one?
_{필요하다}

W: Yeah, thank you. I want it to be under $20.
_{그것이 20달러 미만이기를 원하다(want A to V: A가 ~(이)기를 원하다)}

M: All right. Let me see. Which type of coloring tool would be good for them?
_{색칠 도구 / ~에게 좋다}

W: Hmm... I think watercolors are not very convenient. The kids would
_{수채 물감들 / 편리한}

---

need extra things like brushes.
_{추가적인 물건들 / 붓들}

M: I agree. The other tools would be better.

W: Right. How about the number of colors?
_{색깔 개수}

M: They'll need more than thirty colors to express what they want.
_{표현하다}

W: You're right. Then, there are two choices left.
_{선택지들 / 남은}

M: Yeah. Oh, there is a model which includes a sketchbook.
_{포함하다 / 스케치북}

W: Perfect! They might need it in their art classes. I'll choose that one.

해석

남: 이봐, Cathy! 무엇을 보고 있니?

여: 안녕, Steve. 나는 미술용품 세트를 검색하고 있었어. 가난한 아이들에게 크리스마스 선물로 그것을 보내줄까 생각 중이야.

남: 너는 참 착하구나. 고르는 데 도움이 필요하니?

여: 그래, 고마워. 나는 그것이 20달러 미만이기를 원해.

남: 좋아. 어디 보자. 어떤 종류의 색칠 도구가 그들에게 좋을까?

여: 흠... 수채 물감은 별로 편리하지 않은 것 같아. 아이들은 붓과 같은 추가적인 물건들이 필요하게 될 거야.

남: 나도 동의해. 다른 도구들이 더 낫겠어.

여: 맞아. 색깔 개수는 어때?

남: 그들이 원하는 것을 표현하기 위해서는 30색깔 이상이 필요할 거야.

여: 네 말이 맞아. 그럼, 두 가지 선택지가 남았어.

남: 그래. 오, 스케치북을 포함하는 모델이 있어.

여: 완벽해! 그들은 미술 수업에 그것이 필요할지도 몰라. 나는 그것을 선택할게.

아동용 미술용품 세트

	모델	가격	색칠 도구	색깔 개수	스케치북
①	A	12달러	크레용	24	X
✔②	B	16달러	크레용	32	O
③	C	17달러	수채 물감	28	O
④	D	18달러	마커	32	X
⑤	E	22달러	마커	36	O

---

11 남자의 마지막 말에 대한 여자의 응답
고1 2019년 11월 1번 | 정답률 90% | ▶ 정답 ③

M: Mom, look! It's raining outside. But we don't have umbrellas.
_{비가 오는(rain) / 밖에 / 우산들}

W: I think we need to buy one in this building.
_{사야 하다(need to V: ~해야 하다) / 건물}

M: Okay. Where can we buy one?

W: (We can buy one on the first floor.)
_{1층에서}

해석

남: 엄마, 보세요! 밖에 비가 오고 있어요. 그런데 우리는 우산이 없어요.

여: 이 건물에서 하나 사야 할 것 같구나.

남: 좋아요. 어디에서 살 수 있죠?

여: (우리는 1층에서 살 수 있어.)

① 그 건물은 여기에서 너무 멀어.

② 우리는 우산을 가져갈 필요가 없어.

✔③ 우리는 1층에서 살 수 있어.

④ 나는 너의 우산이 어디에 있는지 몰라.

⑤ 너는 일기 예보를 확인하는 게 좋겠어.

---

12 여자의 마지막 말에 대한 남자의 응답
고1 2019년 11월 2번 | 정답률 90% | ▶ 정답 ②

W: Mr. Smith, can you give me advice on how to edit my essay?
_{조언 / 편집하는 방법 / 에세이 / (how to V: ~하는 방법, edit: 편집하다)}

M: Sure. First, take a look at the hand-out I gave you last class. It has helpful examples.
_{~을 보다 / 유인물 / 유용한 / 예시들}

W: Really? Oh, I'm sorry. I'm afraid I lost it.
_{~인 것 같다 / 잃어버렸다(lose)}

M: (Don't worry. I can make a copy for you.)
_{복사하다}

해석

여: Smith 선생님, 제 에세이를 편집하는 방법에 대해 조언을 해 주시겠어요?

남: 물론이지. 먼저, 내가 지난 수업에서 너에게 준 유인물을 보렴. 그것에는 유용한 예시들

이 있단다.

여: 정말요? 오, 죄송해요. 저는 그것을 잃어버린 것 같아요.

남: (걱정하지 마. 내가 너에게 복사해 줄 수 있어.)

① 사실, 나는 네 에세이를 찾지 못했어.

✓② 걱정하지 마. 내가 너에게 복사해 줄 수 있어.

③ 유감이구나. 나는 마감 기한이 기억나지 않아.

④ 천만에. 나는 에세이를 쓰는 것을 시작하지 않았어.

⑤ 축하해! 나는 네가 해낼 줄 알았어.

---

13 여자의 마지막 말에 대한 남자의 응답

고1 2019년 11월 13번 정답률 80%

▶ 정답 ④

W: Brian, you look so tired today.

M: Yeah, even though I get enough rest, I feel exhausted these days.
피곤한 · 충분한 휴식을 취하다 · 기진맥진한

W: Hmm... maybe you need some exercise. You like swimming, don't you?
운동 · 수영하는 것을 좋아하다 (like V-ing: ~하는 것을 좋아하다)

M: I do, but I often feel lazy.
게으른

W: That's true for me, too. So, I made myself join a sports club at school.
학교 운동 동아리에 가입하다 (join: 가입하다)

M: What kind of sports club?

W: I exercise in a yoga club. I find it very helpful to work out with other people at a fixed time.
운동하다 · 요가 동아리 · 도움이 되는 · 운동하다 · 정해진 시간에

M: I guess exercising with others can help you keep motivated.
계속 동기부여가 되다(motivate: 동기를 부여하다)

W: Exactly. Why don't you join a sports club, too?
~하는 게 어때?

M: Actually, I'm interested in the swimming club, but as far as I know, the registration period ended.
~에 관심이 있는 · 내가 알기로는 · 등록 기간

W: It's too early to give up! I saw a notice that all the clubs extended their registration period to this Friday.
포기하다 · 공고 · 연장했다(extend)

M: (In that case, I'd better go and see if I can join the club.)
내가 가서 알아보는 게 좋겠다(had better V: ~하는 게 좋겠다)

해석

여: Brian, 너 오늘 매우 피곤해 보인다.

남: 응, 나는 충분한 휴식을 취하는데도, 요즘에 기진맥진해.

여: 흠... 아마도 너는 운동이 좀 필요할지도 몰라. 너 수영하는 것을 좋아하지, 그렇지 않니?

남: 그렇긴 하지만, 종종 게을러져.

여: 나도 그래. 그래서, 나는 학교 운동 동아리에 가입했어.

남: 어떤 종류의 운동 동아리?

여: 난 요가 동아리에서 운동하고 있어. 나는 정해진 시간에 다른 사람들과 운동하는 것이 매우 도움이 된다는 것을 알게 되었어.

남: 다른 사람들과 운동하는 것이 너에게 계속 동기부여가 되도록 도움을 주는 것 같아.

여: 맞아. 너도 운동 동아리에 가입하는 게 어때?

남: 사실, 나는 수영 동아리에 관심이 있는데, 내가 알기로는, 등록 기간이 끝났어.

여: 포기하기에는 너무 일러! 모든 동아리가 이번 주 금요일까지 등록 기간을 연장한다는 공고를 내가 봤어.

남: (그렇다면, 내가 그 동아리에 가입할 수 있는지 가서 알아보는 게 좋겠다.)

① 농담하지 마. 나는 요가 동아리에 관심이 없어.

② 너무 늦었어. 나는 너에게 내 등록증을 빌려줄 수 없어.

③ 너도 알다시피, 수영은 내가 가장 좋아하는 운동이 아니야.

✓④ 그렇다면, 내가 그 동아리에 가입할 수 있는지 가서 알아보는 게 좋겠다.

⑤ 나를 믿어. 나는 네가 훌륭한 운동 동아리 회장이 될 수 있다고 확신해.

문제 풀이

운동을 해야 하지만 게을러진다는 남자의 말에 여자는 학교 운동 동아리에 가입할 것을 제안한다. 남자는 관심이 있던 수영 동아리의 등록 기간이 끝난 것으로 알고 있었지만 등록 기간이 연장되었다는 말을 들었으므로 이어질 말은 ④ 'In that case, I'd better go and see if I can join the club.(그렇다면, 내가 그 동아리에 가입할 수 있는지 가서 알아보는 게 좋겠다.)'가 적절하다.

---

14 남자의 마지막 말에 대한 여자의 응답

고1 2019년 11월 14번 정답률 90%

▶ 정답 ①

M: Bonnie, what are you doing?

W: I'm checking my bank account. I'm running out of money again.
확인하는(check) · 은행 계좌 · 돈이 바닥나고 있는(run out of: ~이 바닥나다)

M: Haven't you gotten paid for your part-time job yet?
아르바이트

W: I have, but I already spent most of the money hanging out with my friends. At the end of month, I'll be broke.
내 친구들과 어울려 다니면서 그 돈의 대부분을 썼다 (spend A (on) V-ing: ~하면서 A를 쓰다, hang out with: ~와 어울려 다니다) · 빈털터리가 되다

M: Then, how about setting a weekly budget?
주간 예산을 짜는 것(set a budget: 예산을 짜다)

W: A weekly budget? What do you mean by that?

M: I usually set a budget for each week, and don't spend more than it allows. So I've cut down on everyday spending on chips and soda.
보통 · 매주 · 허용하다 · 매일의 지출을 줄인 (cut down on: ~을 줄이다, everyday spending: 매일의 지출)

W: Good for you. Can I save money if I make it a habit, too?
아끼다 · 그것을 습관으로 만들다

M: Of course, you can. If you consider your budget, you'll think twice before you spend money.
고려하다

W: That makes sense. Keeping a weekly budget seems advantageous.
일리가 있다 · 주간 예산의 범위를 지키는 것 · 도움이 되는 (keep a budget: 예산의 범위를 지키다)

M: Now that I keep a weekly budget, I spend money only where I need it. I bet it'll work for you, too.
~이니까 · 확신하다 · 효과가 있다

W: (Great. I should try to keep a weekly budget.)

해석

남: Bonnie, 무엇을 하고 있니?

여: 내 은행 계좌를 확인하고 있어. 나 또 돈이 바닥나고 있어.

남: 아직 아르바이트 급여를 받지 못했니?

여: 받았는데, 내 친구들과 어울려 다니면서 벌써 그 돈의 대부분을 썼어. 월말이면, 나는 빈털터리가 될 거야.

남: 그럼, 주간 예산을 짜는 게 어떠니?

여: 주간 예산? 그게 무슨 말이야?

남: 나는 보통 매주에 대한 예산을 짜고, 그것이 허용하는 것보다 더 많이 쓰지 않아. 그래서 과자와 음료에 대한 매일의 지출을 줄였어.

여: 잘했구나. 나도 그것을 습관으로 만들면 돈을 아낄 수 있을까?

남: 물론이지, 너도 할 수 있어. 네 예산을 고려한다면, 너는 돈을 쓰기 전에 두 번 생각하게 될 거야.

여: 그거 일리가 있네. 주간 예산의 범위를 지키는 것은 도움이 되는 것 같아.

남: 주간 예산의 범위를 지키니까, 나는 돈이 필요한 곳에만 돈을 써. 나는 그것이 너에게도 효과가 있을 것이라고 확신해.

여: (좋아. 나는 주간 예산의 범위를 지키려고 노력해야겠어.)

✓① 좋아. 나는 주간 예산의 범위를 지키려고 노력해야겠어.

② 행운을 빌어. 나는 네가 아르바이트를 구할 수 있기를 바라.

③ 어. 너는 내 식습관을 지도할 수 있어.

④ 말도 안 돼. 너는 쇼핑하는 데 그렇게 많은 돈을 쓸 수는 없어.

⑤ 나도 알아. 나는 친구들과 더 많은 시간을 보내야 해.

---

15 다음 상황에서 Ted가 Linda에게 할 말

고1 2019년 11월 15번 정답률 75%

▶ 정답 ①

M: Ted and Linda are classmates. Linda has some trouble with her friends because she often forgets her appointments with them.
그녀의 친구들과 약간의 문제가 있다 (have trouble with: ~와 문제가 있다) · 약속

In contrast, Ted is always on time and the other classmates think he's very responsible and reliable. Today, Linda even forgets to submit an important paper. She knows what she has to do, but it's not easy for her to remember everything. Disappointed in herself, she asks Ted for some help on how she can overcome her habit of forgetting. He thinks using a calendar app could help break her bad habit. So Ted wants to advise Linda to try using a calendar app to remind her of important things. In this situation, what would Ted most likely say to Linda?
그에 반해 · 시간을 지켜 · 책임감 있는 · 믿음직한 · 제출하는 것을 잊어버리다 (forget to V: ~하는 것을 잊어버리다, submit: 제출하다) · 알고 있는 · 기억하다 · ~에 실망한 · Ted에게 도움을 좀 요청하다 (ask A for help: A에게 도움을 요청하다) · 극복하다 · 일정표 앱 · 그녀의 나쁜 습관을 고치다 (break a habit: 습관을 고치다) · Linda에게 사용해보라고 조언하고 싶다 (advise A to V: A에게 ~하라고 조언하다, try V-ing: (시험 삼아) ~해보다) · 그녀에게 중요한 것들을 상기시키다(remind A of B: A에게 B를 상기시키다)

Ted: (Why don't you use a calendar app as a reminder?)
~하는 게 어때? · 기억 상기물로

해석

남: Ted와 Linda는 반 친구이다. Linda는 그녀의 친구들과 약간의 문제가 있는데 왜냐하면 그녀가 종종 그들과의 약속을 잊어버리기 때문이다. 그에 반해, Ted는 항상 시간을 지켜서 다른 반 친구들은 그가 매우 책임감 있고 믿음직하다고 생각한다. 오늘, Linda는 심지어 중요한 보고서를 제출하는 것조차 잊어버린다. 그녀는 자신이 무엇을 해야 하는지 알고 있지만, 그녀가 모든 것을 기억하는 것은 쉽지 않다. 자신에게 실망해서, 그녀는 그녀의 잊어버리는 습관을 어떻게 극복할 수 있는지에 대해 Ted에게 도움을 좀 요청한다. 그는 일정표 앱을 사용하는 것이 그녀의 나쁜 습관을 고치는 데 도움이 될 수 있을 거라고 생각한다. 그래서 Ted는 Linda에게 그녀에게 중요한 것들을 상기시키기 위해서 일정표 앱을 사용해 보라고 조언하고 싶다. 이러한 상황에서, Ted는 Linda에게 뭐라고 말하겠는가?

Ted: (기억 상기물로 일정표 앱을 사용하는 게 어때?)

✔① 기억 상기물로 일정표 앱을 사용하는 게 어때?
② 나는 네가 네 친구들에게 도움을 좀 요청하는 것을 추천해.
③ 너는 벽걸이용 달력이 더 좋니 아니면 탁상용 달력이 더 좋니?
④ 나는 네가 왜 제시간에 보고서를 제출하지 않았는지 궁금해.
⑤ 네가 어떻게 나쁜 습관을 극복했는지 나에게 말해 주겠니?

문제 풀이

Linda는 친구들과의 약속이나 보고서 제출과 같은 일들을 잊어버리는 나쁜 습관을 고치도록 Ted에게 도와달라고 요청한다. Linda와 달리, 시간을 잘 지키고 책임감이 있으며 믿음직한 Ted는 중요한 일들을 상기시키는 데 도움을 줄 수 있는 일정표 앱을 사용해보라고 권하고자 한다. 그러므로, Ted가 Linda에게 할 말로 가장 적절한 것은 ① 'Why don't you use a calendar app as a reminder?(기억 상기물로 일정표 앱을 사용하는 게 어때?)'이다.

16~17 1지문 2문항

W: Hello, students! Last class we learned about recycling. Today, I'll introduce you to something better than recycling. It's the process of turning waste into new items in a creative way. Let me show you some examples. First, one creative way is to make plastic bottles into vases for your home. Second, you can turn old cardboard boxes into fun chairs. All you need is just a little time and some paint. Third, an easy way to use empty cans creatively is turning them into fancy pencil holders for your desk. Lastly, when old newspapers pile up in your home, you can use them to wrap any present. It'll make your gift unique and memorable. In this way, you can create something new out of waste on your own. There are an endless number of ideas you can come up with if you use your imagination. Let's do something wonderful for our planet by this process, upcycling.

해석

여: 안녕하세요, 학생 여러분! 지난 수업 시간에 우리는 재활용에 대해서 배웠습니다. 오늘, 저는 여러분에게 재활용보다 더 좋은 것을 소개할 것입니다. 그것은 창의적인 방법으로 폐기물을 새로운 물건들로 바꾸는 과정입니다. 제가 여러분에게 몇 가지 예를 보여드리겠습니다. 첫째로, 한 가지 창의적인 방법은 플라스틱 병들을 여러분의 집을 위한 꽃병들로 만드는 것입니다. 둘째로, 여러분은 오래된 종이 상자들을 재미있는 의자들로 바꿀 수 있습니다. 여러분이 필요한 것은 단지 약간의 시간과 물감 조금입니다. 셋째로, 빈 깡통들을 창의적으로 사용하는 쉬운 방법은 그것들을 여러분의 책상을 위한 멋진 연필꽂이들로 바꾸는 것입니다. 마지막으로, 여러분의 집에 오래된 신문들이 쌓일 때, 여러분은 그것들을 선물을 포장하는 데 사용할 수 있습니다. 그것은 여러분의 선물을 독특하고 기억에 남게 만들 것입니다. 이러한 방식으로, 여러분은 스스로 폐기물로 새로운 것을 만들어 낼 수 있습니다. 여러분이 여러분의 상상력을 사용한다면 여러분이 생각해 낼 수 있는 끝없이 많은 아이디어들이 있습니다. 이러한 과정, 즉 업사이클링을 통해 우리의 행성(지구)을 위한 멋진 일을 해봅시다.

16 여자가 하는 말의 주제

고1 2019년 11월 16번 | 정답률 85%

▶ 정답 ③

① 에너지 절약 제품 생산의 한계들
② 십 대들에게 재활용을 가르치는 것의 중요성

③ 폐기물을 새로운 물건들로 바꾸는 창의적인 방법들
④ 가구를 쉽게 만드는 유용한 조언들
⑤ 친환경 소재를 사용하는 다양한 이유들

17 언급된 물건이 아닌 것

고1 2019년 11월 17번 | 정답률 90%

▶ 정답 ③

① 플라스틱 병 　　② 종이 상자 　　✔③ 유리잔
④ 깡통 　　⑤ 신문

---

06 2020년 3월 학력평가

01	①	02	⑤	03	③	04	④	05	⑤
06	②	07	⑤	08	②	09	③	10	②
11	②	12	①	13	①	14	③	15	⑤
16	⑤	17	④						

※2020년 4월 24일에 시행된 3월 전국연합 학력평가는 자율 원격 시험으로 시행되어 성적 발표를 하지 않았습니다. 이에 따라 교재에 기입된 정답률은 실제와 다를 수 있습니다.

01 남자가 하는 말의 목적

고1 2020년 3월 3번 | 정답률 90%

▶ 정답 ①

M: Hello, students. This is Mike Smith, your P.E. teacher. These days, the fine dust problem is getting serious. So, I'd like to explain what you should do when the fine dust level is high. First, close all the classroom windows to keep out the dust. Second, turn on the air purifier in the classroom. The air purifier will help keep the air clean. Third, drink water and wash your hands as often as possible. Last, it's important to wear a mask when you're outside. Thank you for listening.

해석

남: 안녕하세요, 학생 여러분. 저는 체육 교사인 Mike Smith입니다. 요즘 미세 먼지 문제가 심각해지고 있습니다. 그래서, 미세 먼지 수준이 높을 때 여러분이 무엇을 해야 하는지 설명하고자 합니다. 첫째, 먼지가 들어오지 못하게 하기 위해서 모든 교실 창문을 닫으십시오. 둘째, 교실에 있는 공기 청정기를 켜십시오. 공기 청정기는 공기를 깨끗하게 유지하는 데 도움을 줄 것입니다. 셋째, 가능한 한 자주 물을 마시고 손을 씻으십시오. 마지막으로, 밖에 있을 때는 마스크를 쓰는 것이 중요합니다. 들어주셔서 감사합니다.

✔① 미세 먼지 수치가 높을 때 대처 요령을 안내하려고
② 교실 내 공기 정화기 설치 일정을 알리려고
③ 체육 실기 시험 준비 방법을 설명하려고
④ 미세 먼지 방지용 마스크 배부 행사를 홍보하려고
⑤ 미세 먼지 감축을 위해 대중교통 이용을 독려하려고

02 여자의 의견

고1 2020년 3월 4번 | 정답률 90%

▶ 정답 ⑤

W: Look at all the shiny paper and ribbons! What are you doing, Tom?
M: I'm wrapping a birthday present for my friend Laura.
W: What are you going to give her?
M: A key chain. I hope she likes it.
W: That's a pretty big box for a key chain, isn't it?
M: Yes, I filled it with paper flowers. Now I'm going to wrap the box

with shiny paper and decorate it with ribbons.
그것을 리본으로 장식하다
(decorate A with B: A를 B로 장식하다)

W: I think it's a little too much. Most of the paper and ribbons will end
조금   대부분   결국 ~로 가게 되다
up in the trash can.
쓰레기통

M: Hmm.... You're right. My packaging will produce a lot of trash.
포장   만들다 많은

W: Yeah. We need to make gift packaging simple for the environment.
되게 해야 하다 선물   간소한   환경
(need to V: ~해야 하다, make: (상태가) 되게 하다)

M: I agree. I'll try to reduce the packaging then.
동의하다   줄이려고 노력하다
(try to V: ~하려고 노력하다, reduce: 줄이다)

W: Good thinking.

해석

여: 온통 반짝이는 종이와 리본들을 봐! 무엇을 하고 있는 거니, Tom?
남: 내 친구 Laura를 위한 생일 선물을 포장하고 있어.
여: 그녀에게 무엇을 줄 거야?
남: 열쇠고리. 그녀가 그것을 마음에 들어 했으면 좋겠어.
여: 그것은 열쇠고리에 비해 꽤 큰 상자야, 그렇지 않니?
남: 그래, 나는 그것을 종이꽃으로 채웠어. 이제 상자를 반짝이는 종이로 포장하고 그것을 리
   본들로 장식할 거야.
여: 그것은 조금 지나친 것 같아. 종이와 리본들의 대부분이 결국 쓰레기통으로 가게 될 거야.
남: 흠.... 네 말이 맞아. 내 포장은 많은 쓰레기를 만들 거야.
여: 그래. 우리는 환경을 위해 선물 포장을 간소하게 해야 해.
남: 동의해. 그럼 나는 포장을 줄이려고 노력해 볼게.
여: 좋은 생각이야.

① 받는 사람에게 필요한 것을 선물해야 한다.
② 정성 어린 선물 포장은 선물의 가치를 높인다.
③ 선물 포장을 위해 다양한 재료를 활용해야 한다.
④ 선물을 받으면 적절한 감사 인사를 하는 것이 좋다.
✅ 환경을 위해 선물 포장을 간소하게 할 필요가 있다.

---

03 두 사람의 관계

고1 2020년 3월 5번 | 정답률 80%
▶ 정답 ③

M: Come on in, Ms. Miller. It's been a while since your last visit.
                              ~ 이후로   마지막의   ↘방문
W: Good morning, Mr. Stevens. I've been in Europe for the last two
                                          유럽   지난 두 달 동안
   months.
M: Wow. Are you preparing for your second book?
            ~을 준비하는(prepare for)   책
W: Yes, I'm working on it.
         ~을 작업하는(work on)
M: I'm looking forward to it. So, what brings you here today?
   ~을 기대하는(look forward to+명사/V-ing) 오게 하다
W: I'd like to buy a wooden desk.
                   나무로 된 책상
M: I see. Do you have a particular design in mind?
                        특별한 디자인을 염두에 두다
(have A in mind: A를 염두에 두다, particular: 특별한, design: 디자인)
W: Just a plain rectangular one would be great.
        평범한 직사각형의
M: Okay. What color would you like?
              색상
W: I was thinking dark brown.
                 짙은 갈색
M: Great. We have a perfect one for you downstairs. Come this way.
                   꼭 알맞은   아래층에
W: All right.

해석

남: 들어오세요, Miller 씨. 마지막 방문 이후로 오랜만이네요.
여: 안녕하세요, Stevens 씨. 저는 지난 두 달 동안 유럽에 있었어요.
남: 와. 두 번째 책을 준비하고 계시는 거예요?
여: 네, 그것을 작업하고 있어요.
남: 저는 그것을 기대하고 있어요. 그럼, 오늘은 무슨 일로 오셨어요?
여: 나무로 된 책상을 사고 싶어요.
남: 그렇군요. 염두에 두신 특별한 디자인이 있나요?
여: 그냥 평범한 직사각형 책상이 좋을 것 같아요.
남: 알겠어요. 어떤 색상이 좋으세요?
여: 짙은 갈색을 생각하고 있었어요.
남: 좋아요. 아래층에 당신에게 꼭 알맞은 책상이 있어요. 이쪽으로 오세요.
여: 알겠어요.

① 정원사 — 집주인

---

② 출판사 직원 — 작가
✅ 가구 판매원 — 손님
④ 관광 가이드 — 관광객
⑤ 인테리어 디자이너 — 잡지 기자

---

04 그림에서 대화의 내용과 일치하지 않는 것

고1 2020년 3월 6번 | 정답률 85%
▶ 정답 ④

W: James, have you been to our new club room?
              너는 ~에 가본 적 있니?   동아리방
              (have been to: ~에 가본 적이 있다)
M: Unfortunately, I haven't.
   유감스럽게도
W: I have a picture of it. Do you want to take a look?
             사진   보고 싶다
                       (want to V: ~하고 싶다, take a look: 보다)
M: Sure. [Pause] Wow, I see lockers on the left side of the picture.
                           사물함들   왼쪽
W: Yes. We finally have our own lockers. Do you see the trophies on
        드디어   트로피들
   the lockers?
M: Yeah. There are two trophies. Are they the ones we won in the
                                                 수상했다(win)
   National School Band Contest?
   전국 학교 밴드 대회
W: Right. We won two years in a row. I'm so proud of our band.
                      연속으로   ~을 자랑스러워하는
M: Me, too. And the drums are under the clock.
                   드럼들   시계
W: Yes. And the right side of the picture is a round table with
              오른쪽   둥근   테이블
   chairs.
   의자들
M: Looks great. I also love the star-shaped rug in front of the drums.
                              별 모양의 깔개 ~ 앞에
W: I like it, too. We're really going to enjoy our new club room.
                                    누리다

해석

여: James, 우리의 새 동아리방에 가봤니?
남: 유감스럽게도, 못 가봤어.
여: 내가 그것의 사진을 가지고 있어. 보고 싶니?
남: 물론이지. [잠시 후] 와, 사진의 왼쪽에 사물함이 보이네.
여: 그래. 드디어 우리만의 사물함을 가지게 되었어. 사물함 위에 트로피들이 보이니?
남: 그래. 두 개의 트로피가 있어. National School Band Contest(전국 학교 밴드 대회)에서
   우리가 수상한 것이니?
여: 맞아. 우리는 2년 연속으로 수상했잖아. 나는 우리 밴드가 정말 자랑스러워.
남: 나도 그래. 그리고 시계 아래에 드럼이 있네.
여: 그래. 그리고 사진의 오른쪽에는 의자들이 함께 있는 둥근 테이블이 있어.
남: 멋져 보여. 나는 드럼 앞에 있는 별 모양의 깔개도 정말 마음에 들어.
여: 나도 마음에 들어. 우리는 정말 우리의 새 동아리방을 누리게 될 거야.

---

05 여자가 할 일

고1 2020년 3월 7번 | 정답률 90%
▶ 정답 ⑤

M: Ellie, the school orchestra's concert is just three days away. How's
            학교 오케스트라의 콘서트
   the preparation coming along?
   준비   되어 가는(come along)
W: Great, Mr. Brown. All of our orchestra members are very excited.
                                 단원들   흥분한
M: Good. Did everyone check their instruments?
                       점검하다   악기들
W: Of course. Everything sounded fine in practice today.
                          괜찮은   연습
M: I heard the posters were ready.
   들었다(hear) 포스터들 준비된

W: Yes. Here they are. One of the orchestra members designed them.
M: They look pretty nice. When are you going to put the posters up in the hallway?
W: I'm going to do that now.
M: You're doing a great job as the leader of the school orchestra. Have you arranged the chairs for the audience?
W: I already did it with some of the members.
M: Perfect.

해석
남: Ellie, 학교 오케스트라의 콘서트가 3일 앞으로 다가왔어. 준비는 어떻게 되어 가고 있니?
여: 잘 되고 있어요, Brown 선생님. 저희 오케스트라 단원들 모두가 매우 흥분해 있어요.
남: 좋아. 모두가 자신의 악기를 점검했니?
여: 물론이죠. 오늘 연습에서 모든 것이 괜찮게 들렸어요.
남: 나는 포스터가 준비되었다고 들었어.
여: 네. 여기 있어요. 오케스트라 단원들 중 한 명이 그것들을 디자인했어요.
남: 매우 멋져 보이는구나. 언제 복도에 포스터를 붙일 거니?
여: 이제 그것을 할 거예요.
남: 너는 학교 오케스트라의 단장으로서 아주 잘 하고 있구나. 관객을 위한 의자들은 배치했니?
여: 몇 명의 단원들과 이미 그것을 했어요.
남: 완벽하구나.

① 악기 점검하기
② 연습 시간 확인하기
③ 단원들에게 연락하기
④ 관객용 의자 배치하기
✓ 콘서트 포스터 붙이기

---

06 여자가 지불할 금액
고1 2020년 3월 9번 ┃ 정답률 90%
▶ 정답 ②

M: Good afternoon. How can I help you?
W: I'd like to buy some wireless earphones for my children. How much is this pair?
M: It's $60 for a pair. It's a very popular model.
W: Great. I'll take two pairs.
M: I see. Is there anything else you need?
W: Oh, I also need a portable speaker.
M: These two are the latest models.
W: How much are they?
M: This black one is $80 and the pink one is $100.
W: I'll take the black one.
M: Okay. Is that all you need?
W: Yes. Oh, I have this discount coupon. Can I use it?
M: Sure. You can get 10% off the total price with this coupon.
W: Great. Here's the coupon and here's my credit card.

해석
남: 안녕하세요. 어떻게 도와드릴까요?
여: 제 아이들을 위한 무선 이어폰을 사고 싶어요. 이 한 쌍은 얼마죠?
남: 한 쌍에 60달러예요. 그것은 매우 인기 있는 모델이에요.
여: 좋네요. 두 쌍을 살게요.
남: 알겠습니다. 다른 필요하신 건 없으세요?
여: 오, 휴대용 스피커도 필요해요.
남: 이 두 개가 최신 모델이에요.
여: 얼마죠?
남: 검은색은 80달러이고 분홍색은 100달러예요.
여: 검은색을 살게요.
남: 알겠습니다. 필요하신 건 그게 전부인가요?
여: 네. 오, 저는 이 할인 쿠폰을 가지고 있어요. 사용할 수 있나요?
남: 물론이죠. 이 쿠폰으로 총액에서 10% 할인을 받으실 수 있어요.
여: 잘됐네요. 쿠폰은 여기 있고 제 신용카드는 여기 있어요.

---

① $140　　　　✓ $180　　　　③ $200
④ $220　　　　⑤ $280

문제 풀이
여자는 60달러짜리 무선 이어폰 두 쌍과 80달러짜리 검은색 휴대용 스피커를 구매한다. 따라서 총 200달러를 지불해야 하지만 쿠폰을 사용해 10% 할인을 받으므로 180달러, 즉 ② '$180'가 정답이다.

---

07 남자가 이번 주말에 캠핑하러 갈 수 없는 이유
고1 2020년 3월 8번 ┃ 정답률 90%
▶ 정답 ⑤

W: Jason, you're going camping this weekend, right?
M: I reserved a campsite, but I'm afraid I can't go.
W: Why not? Is it going to rain?
M: No. It'll be sunny this weekend.
W: Then do you have to work this weekend? You said you're busy with your project.
M: No, I finished the project last week.
W: Then why can't you go camping?
M: My mother fell down the stairs and broke her arm.
W: Oh, no. Is she all right?
M: Well, she had surgery. So I have to take care of her in the hospital this weekend.
W: I see. I hope she'll get better soon.
M: Thanks.

해석
여: Jason, 너 이번 주말에 캠핑을 갈 거지, 그렇지?
남: 캠프장을 예약했는데, 못 갈 것 같아.
여: 왜 못 가? 비가 오는 거야?
남: 아니. 이번 주말에는 맑을 거야.
여: 그럼 이번 주말에 일해야 하는 거야? 프로젝트 때문에 바쁘다고 했잖아.
남: 아니, 지난주에 그 프로젝트를 끝냈어.
여: 그럼 왜 캠핑을 갈 수 없는 거야?
남: 어머니께서 계단에서 넘어지셔서 팔이 부러지셨어.
여: 오, 이런. 어머니께서는 괜찮으시니?
남: 음, 수술을 받으셨어. 그래서 내가 이번 주말에 병원에서 어머니를 돌봐드려야 해.
여: 그렇구나. 어머니께서 빨리 나으시길 바랄게.
남: 고마워.

① 계단을 수리해야 해서
② 캠프장을 예약할 수 없어서
③ 폭우로 인해 캠프장이 폐쇄되어서
④ 프로젝트를 마무리해야 해서
✓ 어머니를 돌봐야 해서

---

08 Pinewood Bake Sale에 관해 언급되지 않은 것
고1 2020년 3월 10번 ┃ 정답률 85%
▶ 정답 ②

W: Hi, Ross. What's on the flyer?
M: The Pinewood Bake Sale is this Friday. Would you like to go with me?
W: A bake sale? What's that?
M: In a bake sale, people raise money by selling bakery products. At the Pinewood Bake Sale, people will be selling doughnuts and cupcakes.
W: Sounds delicious. So all profits go to people in need, right?
M: That's right. The flyer says the profits will be donated to Pinewood Children's Hospital.
W: I'd like to join you. Where is it going to be held?

M: In the Pinewood High School gym.
　고등학교　체육관

W: Okay. Let's go together.

해석

여: 안녕, Ross. 그 전단지에 뭐가 있니?

남: Pinewood Bake Sale(Pinewood 빵 바자회)이 이번 주 금요일에 있대. 나와 같이 갈래?

여: 빵 바자회? 그게 뭔데?

남: 빵 바자회에서, 사람들은 빵 제품들을 판매함으로써 모금을 해. Pinewood Bake Sale에서는, 사람들이 도넛과 컵케이크를 판매할 거야.

여: 맛있겠다. 그럼 모든 수익금은 어려움에 처한 사람들에게 가는 거구나, 그렇지?

남: 맞아. 전단지에 따르면 수익금은 Pinewood 아동 병원에 기부될 거래.

여: 나도 너와 같이 가고 싶어. 어디에서 개최되니?

남: Pinewood 고등학교 체육관에서.

여: 좋아. 함께 가자.

① 개최 요일　　　　✓② 시작 시간　　　　③ 판매 제품
④ 수익금 기부처　　⑤ 개최 장소

09

2020 Global Village Festival에 관한 내용과 일치하지 않는 것　▶ **정답 ④**

W: Hello, Green City residents. This is Rachel White, the head of
　　　　　　　　　　주민들　　　　　　　　　　　　　　　부장
the Community Services Department. Are you ready to enjoy the
　　지역 사회 서비스부　　　　　　　　준비가 된 즐기다
2020 Global Village Festival? It'll be held on March 28th and
　　지구촌 축제　　　　　　　개최되다(hold: 개최하다)
29th at Green City Park. This two-day festival includes music
　　　　　　　　　　　　　　　　　　　　　포함하다　음악 공연들
performances and art exhibitions. Samples of food from around
　　　　　　　　미술 전시회들　　　샘플들　　　음식　　전 세계의
the world will be served. Prices of the food range from $2 to $5
　　　　　　제공되다　가격들　　　　　　　2달러에서 5달러까지이다
　　　(serve: 제공하다)　　(range from A to B: (범위가) A에서 B까지이다)
and you can pay by cash or credit card. The first 50 visitors will
　　　　　　　　　현금　　신용 카드　　　　　　방문객들
get special gifts. Parking will be available for $10 a car. For more
　　특별 선물들　주차　　　　이용 가능한　　　～당
information, visit the festival website. Thank you.
정보　　방문하다　　　웹사이트

해석

여: 안녕하세요, Green City 주민 여러분. 저는 지역 사회 서비스부의 부장인 Rachel White입니다. 2020 Global Village Festival(2020 지구촌 축제)을 즐길 준비가 되셨습니까? 그것은 Green City Park에서 3월 28일과 29일에 개최될 것입니다. 이 이틀간의 축제는 음악 공연과 미술 전시회를 포함합니다. 전 세계의 음식 샘플들이 제공될 것입니다. 음식의 가격은 2달러에서 5달러까지이며 현금이나 신용 카드로 지불하실 수 있습니다. 선착순 50명의 방문객들은 특별 선물을 받으실 것입니다. 주차는 차량당 10달러에 이용 가능할 것입니다. 더 많은 정보를 원하시면, 축제 웹사이트를 방문해 주십시오. 감사합니다.

① 이틀간 Green City Park에서 열린다.
② 음악 공연과 미술 전시회를 포함한다.
③ 현금이나 신용 카드로 음식을 구입할 수 있다.
✓④ 선착순 100명에게 특별 선물을 준다.
⑤ 차량당 주차비는 10달러이다.

문제 풀이

선착순 50명에게 특별 선물을 주므로 ④ '선착순 100명에게 특별 선물을 준다.'는 옳지 않다.

10

표에서 두 사람이 예약할 방　▶ **정답 ②**

M: Honey, what are you doing on your computer?

W: I'm trying to book a room at Wayne Island Hotel for our summer
　　　예약하려고 하는　　객실　　　　　호텔　　　여름 휴가
　(try to V: ~하려고 하다, book: 예약하다)
vacation.

M: Our summer vacation? Isn't it a bit early?
　　　　　　　　　　　　　조금 이른

W: We can get a room much cheaper if we book early.
　　　　　　　　　훨씬　더 싼　　　　　일찍

M: I see. Which room do you have in mind?
　　　어떤 객실을 염두에 두고 있어?
　　(have A in mind: A를 염두에 두다)

W: I was thinking a room with a city view. What do you think?
　생각하고 있었어(think)　　도심 전망

M: Well, a room with a mountain view or an ocean view would be
　　　　　　　산 전망　　　　　바다 전망
better.
더 나은

W: I agree. Shall we have breakfast in the hotel?
　동의하다　　　　　조식을 먹다

M: I don't think we need to. I heard there are some good restaurants
　　　　　　　　　　　　　들었다(hear)　　　　　　　식당들
near the hotel.
~근처에

W: Okay. Then we have two options left. I'd like to go with the cheaper
　　　　　　　　　　　선택들　남은　　　　　~을 선택하다
one.

M: Sounds good. Let's book this room then.

해석

남: 여보, 컴퓨터로 무엇을 하고 있어요?

여: 우리의 여름 휴가를 위해 Wayne Island 호텔에 객실을 예약하려고 해요.

남: 우리의 여름 휴가 말이에요? 조금 이르지 않아요?

여: 일찍 예약하면 객실을 훨씬 더 싸게 구할 수 있어요.

남: 그렇군요. 어떤 객실을 염두에 두고 있어요?

여: 도심 전망이 있는 객실을 생각하고 있었어요. 당신은 어떻게 생각해요?

남: 음, 산 전망이나 바다 전망이 있는 객실이 더 나을 거예요.

여: 동의해요. 호텔에서 조식을 먹을까요?

남: 그럴 필요는 없을 것 같아요. 호텔 근처에 좋은 식당들이 있다고 들었어요.

여: 알겠어요. 그럼 두 가지 선택지가 남았네요. 저는 더 싼 것을 선택하고 싶어요.

남: 좋아요. 그럼 이 객실을 예약해요.

Wayne Island 호텔 객실

	객실	전망	조식	요금
①	A	도심	X	70달러
✓②	B	산	X	80달러
③	C	산	○	95달러
④	D	바다	X	105달러
⑤	E	바다	○	120달러

11

남자의 마지막 말에 대한 여자의 응답　▶ **정답 ②**

M: This restaurant looks great. Have you been here before?
　　　식당　　　　~해 보이다

W: Yeah, it's one of my favorite restaurants. Let's see the menu.
　　　　　　　　가장 좋아하는　　　　　　　　　　메뉴

M: Everything looks so good. Can you recommend anything?
　　모든 것　　　　　　　　　　　　　　추천하다　무엇이든

W: (Sure. The onion soup is great here.)
　　　　　　양파 수프

해석

남: 이 식당은 근사해 보여. 전에 여기에 와본 적이 있어?

여: 응, 내가 가장 좋아하는 식당들 중 하나야. 메뉴를 보자.

남: 모든 것이 매우 좋아 보여. 무엇이든 추천해 줄 수 있어?

여: (물론이지. 여기 양파 수프가 정말 맛있어.)

① 괜찮아. 나는 이미 배불러.
✓② 물론이지. 여기 양파 수프가 정말 맛있어.
③ 모르겠어. 나는 전에 여기에 와본 적이 없어.
④ 그래. 나는 네가 제시간에 그곳에 가기를 추천해.
⑤ 동의해. 멕시코 식당에 가자.

12

여자의 마지막 말에 대한 남자의 응답　▶ **정답 ①**

W: Honey, don't forget to bring your umbrella to work today.
　　　　　　가져가는 것을 잊다　　　　　　우산　　일터, 직장
　(forget to V: ~하는 것을 잊다, bring: 가져가다)

M: Umbrella? The sky is clear now.
　　　　　　　하늘　　맑은

W: The weather forecast said it'd rain this afternoon.
　　　일기 예보　　　비오다

M: (I see. Thank you for letting me know.)

해석

여: 여보, 오늘 출근할 때 우산 가져가는 것을 잊지 마요.

남: 우산이요? 지금 하늘은 맑아요.

여: 일기 예보에서 오늘 오후에 비가 올 거라고 했어요.

남: (그렇군요. 알려줘서 고마워요.)

✓① 그렇군요. 알려줘서 고마워요.
② 불행히도, 저는 비를 맞았어요.
③ 음, 어제부터 비가 오고 있어요.

④ 맞아요. 오늘 오후에는 맑을 거예요.

⑤ 네. 이 우산들은 온라인에서 구할 수 있어요.

13 여자의 마지막 말에 대한 남자의 응답

고1 2020년 3월 13번 정답률 85% ▶ 정답 ①

W: Hey, Chris. What are you looking at on your cell phone?
~을 보는(look at)　휴대전화

M: I'm looking for an apartment to rent.
~을 찾는(look for)　아파트　임차하다

W: Aren't you sharing an apartment with William?
아파트를 William과 같이 쓰는
(share A with B: A를 B와 같이 쓰다)

M: Yeah, but I'm thinking about moving out.
이사 가는 것(move out)

W: Why? I thought you two get along well with each other.
~와 잘 지내다　서로

M: There have been a lot of problems between us. One thing
많은　문제들　~ 사이에
especially bothers me.
특히　신경 쓰이게 하다

W: Oh, what is it?

M: Actually, he never cleans up. The kitchen and the bathroom are
사실　청소하다　부엌　화장실
always messy.
지저분한

W: That's awful. Have you talked about this issue with him?
끔찍한　문제

M: (I have, but he didn't take it seriously.)
그것을 심각하게 받아들이다
(take A seriously: A를 심각하게 받아들이다)

해석

여: 이봐, Chris. 휴대전화로 무엇을 보고 있니?

남: 임차할 아파트를 찾고 있어.

여: 너는 아파트를 William과 같이 쓰고 있지 않니?

남: 그래, 하지만 나는 이사 가는 것에 대해 생각 중이야.

여: 왜? 나는 너희 둘이 서로 잘 지낸다고 생각했어.

남: 우리 사이에는 많은 문제가 있었어. 한 가지가 특히 나를 신경 쓰이게 해.

여: 오, 뭔데?

남: 사실, 그는 절대 청소를 하지 않아. 부엌과 화장실은 항상 지저분해.

여: 그거 끔찍하다. 이 문제에 대해 그와 이야기해 봤니?

남: (해 봤는데, 그는 그것을 심각하게 받아들이지 않았어.)

✔ 해 봤는데, 그는 그것을 심각하게 받아들이지 않았어.

② 걱정하지 마. 나는 그와 아무런 문제가 없어.

③ 음, 그는 항상 화장실을 깨끗하게 유지해.

④ 미안해. 나는 아파트에서 이사 가는 것을 연기했어.

⑤ 물론이지. 네가 새 아파트로 이사하는 것을 도와줄게.

문제 풀이

남자는 아파트를 같이 쓰는 William이 절대 청소를 하지 않아 이사 가는 것을 생각하고 있다. 여자가 청소 문제에 대해 William과 이야기해 보았냐고 물었으므로 제일 어울리는 답변은 ① 'I have, but he didn't take it seriously.(해 봤는데, 그는 그것을 심각하게 받아들이지 않았어.)'이다.

14 남자의 마지막 말에 대한 여자의 응답

고1 2020년 3월 14번 정답률 85% ▶ 정답 ③

M: Ms. Peterson! I heard you were looking for me.
들었다(hear)　~을 찾는(look for)

W: Yes, Louis. I need to tell you about the science competition
말해야 하다　과학 경연 대회
(need to V: ~해야 하다, tell: 말하다)
scheduled for next week.
~로 예정된

M: Okay. What's it about?

W: As you know, it'll be held in the school auditorium, but part of the
열리다(hold: 열다)　학교 강당　일부
floor needs repairing.
바닥　수리될 필요가 있다
(need V-ing: ~될 필요가 있다, repair: 수리하다)

M: Then is it going to be held somewhere else?
어딘가 다른 곳에서

W: No, but the competition will be delayed.
연기되다(delay: 연기하다)

M: Then when is it going to be held?

W: The date hasn't been decided yet, but it'll take at least two weeks
날짜 결정되지 않았다(decide: 결정하다)　최소한
to repair the floor. I'll text you the exact date later.
문자로 보내다　정확한　나중에

M: I see. I'll wait for your text message.
~을 기다리다　문자 메시지

W: (Okay. I'll let you know as soon as the date is set.)
~하는 대로　정해지다(set: 정하다)

해석

남: Peterson 선생님! 저를 찾으신다고 들었어요.

여: 그래, Louis. 다음 주로 예정된 과학 경연 대회에 관해서 너에게 말해야겠어.

남: 알겠어요. 뭔데요?

여: 너도 알다시피, 그것은 학교 강당에서 열릴 거야, 하지만 바닥의 일부가 수리될 필요가 있어.

남: 그럼 어딘가 다른 곳에서 열리는 건가요?

여: 아니, 하지만 경연 대회는 연기될 거야.

남: 그럼 언제 열리는데요?

여: 날짜는 아직 결정되지 않았지만, 바닥을 수리하는 데 최소한 2주가 걸릴 거야. 나중에 정확한 날짜를 너에게 문자로 보내줄게.

남: 알겠어요. 문자 메시지를 기다릴게요.

여: (좋아. 날짜가 정해지는 대로 너에게 알려줄게.)

① 바닥을 수리하는 데 얼마가 드는지 너에게 문자로 보내줄게.

② 맞아. 너는 경연 대회에 참가할 수 없을 것 같아.

✔ 좋아. 날짜가 정해지는 대로 너에게 알려줄게.

④ 하지만 강당은 지난주에 이미 수리되었어.

⑤ 경연 대회는 대신에 학교 체육관에서 열릴 거야.

15 다음 상황에서 Billy의 어머니가 Billy에게 할 말

고1 2020년 3월 15번 정답률 80% ▶ 정답 ⑤

M: Billy entered high school this year. In Billy's school, letters to
입학했다　고등학교　가정통신문
parents are given to the students. The letters include a lot of
포함하다　많은
information about school events such as parent-teacher meetings.
정보　행사들　~과 같은　학부모-교사　면담들
Students have to deliver them to their parents, but Billy often
그것들을 부모님들에게 전달하다
(deliver A to B: A를 B에게 전달하다)
forgets to bring them to his mother. Billy's mother is worried that
가져다주는 것을 잊다　걱정되는
(forget to V: ~하는 것을 잊다, bring: 가져다주다)
she may not get important information about school events. She
중요한
even missed some of them because she didn't get the letters.
심지어　놓쳤다
So she wants to tell Billy that he must give them to her. In this
말하고 싶다
(want to V: ~하고 싶다, tell: 말하다)
situation, what would Billy's mother most likely say to Billy?

Billy's mother: (Don't forget to bring me the letters.)

해석

남: Billy는 올해 고등학교에 입학했다. Billy의 학교에서는, 학생들에게 가정통신문이 주어진다. 가정통신문은 학부모-교사 면담과 같은 학교 행사들에 관한 많은 정보를 포함한다. 학생들은 그것들을 부모님들에게 전달해야 하지만, Billy는 그것들을 그의 어머니에게 가져다주는 것을 자주 잊는다. Billy의 어머니는 학교 행사들에 관한 중요한 정보를 얻지 못할까 봐 걱정이 된다. 그녀는 심지어 가정통신문을 받지 못해서 그것(행사)들 중 몇 개를 놓치기도 했다. 그래서 그녀는 Billy에게 그것들을 자신에게 주어야 한다고 말하고 싶다. 이러한 상황에서, Billy의 어머니는 Billy에게 뭐라고 말하겠는가?

Billy의 어머니: (나에게 가정통신문을 가져다주는 것을 잊지 말아라.)

① 반드시 편지에 답장을 해라.

② 학교 행사들에 자주 참가하려고 노력해라.

③ 나는 네가 좋은 친구를 사귈 수 있을 거라고 확신한다.

④ 너는 회의를 준비해야 한다.

✔ 나에게 가정통신문을 가져다주는 것을 잊지 말아라.

16~17 1지문 2문항

W: Good morning, class. What did you have for breakfast? I guess
아침 식사
some of you had your favorite cereal with milk. Have you ever
시리얼　우유
wondered where milk comes from? Most people would say it's
궁금해하는(wonder)　~에서 나오다　대부분의
from cows, and they're right. Around ninety percent of milk in
소들　옳은　대략
Canada and the U.S. comes from cows. But cows are not the only
유일한
source of milk. People around the world get milk from different
공급원　전 세계의　다양한

animals. <u>Water buffalos</u> are the main <u>source</u> of milk in <u>India</u>. They
　　　　　동물들　　　물소들　　　　주요한　　　　　　인도
<u>produce</u> half the milk <u>consumed</u> in the <u>country</u>. Some people in
생산하다 절반　　　소비되는(consume: 소비하다)　나라
the <u>northern</u> part of Finland drink <u>reindeer</u> milk because they are
　북부의　지역　핀란드　마시다　순록
the only <u>dairy animals</u> that can <u>survive</u> such a <u>cold</u> <u>environment</u>.
　　　착유 동물들　　　　　살아남다　　　추운　환경
People in <u>Romania</u> get milk from <u>sheep</u> and <u>use</u> it to make <u>cheese</u>.
　　　　루마니아　　　　　　양　　　사용하다　　　치즈
It has <u>twice</u> the <u>fat content</u> of cow milk. Now let's <u>watch</u> a <u>video</u>
　　두 배로　　　지방 함량　　　　　　　시청하다　영상
about these animals.

해석

여: 안녕하세요, 학생 여러분. 아침 식사로 무엇을 드셨나요? 여러분 중 일부는 우유와 함께 여러분이 가장 좋아하는 시리얼을 드셨을 거라 추측합니다. 여러분은 우유가 어디에서 나오는지 궁금해하신 적이 있나요? 대부분의 사람들은 그것이 소에서 나오는 것이라고 말할 것이며, 그들은 옳습니다. 캐나다와 미국의 우유 중 대략 90퍼센트는 소에서 나옵니다. 그러나 소가 우유의 유일한 공급원은 아닙니다. 전 세계의 사람들은 다양한 동물들로부터 우유를 얻습니다. 인도에서는 물소가 우유의 주요한 공급원입니다. 그것들은 그 나라에서 소비되는 우유의 절반을 생산합니다. 핀란드의 북부 지역에 사는 일부 사람들은 순록의 우유를 마시는데 그것들이 그토록 추운 환경에서 살아남을 수 있는 유일한 착유 동물이기 때문입니다. 루마니아 사람들은 양으로부터 우유를 얻어 치즈를 만드는 데 사용합니다. 그것은 소의 우유의 두 배의 지방 함량을 가지고 있습니다. 이제 이 동물들에 관한 영상을 시청하겠습니다.

---

16 여자가 하는 말의 주제

고1 2020년 3월 16번 | 정답률 85%
▶ 정답 ⑤

① 유제품의 주요 수출 국가들
② 우유를 주기적으로 마시는 것의 건강상 이점들
③ 전 세계의 독특한 음식 문화들
④ 착유 동물에 알맞은 환경들
✓ 여러 나라의 다양한 우유 공급원들

---

17 언급된 나라가 아닌 것

고1 2020년 3월 17번 | 정답률 85%
▶ 정답 ④

① 캐나다　　　② 인도　　　③ 핀란드
✓ 노르웨이　　⑤ 루마니아

---

07 2020년 6월 학력평가

01	②	02	②	03	②	04	④	05	③
06	③	07	⑤	08	④	09	⑤	10	②
11	②	12	⑤	13	①	14	③	15	①
16	②	17	④						

---

01 여자가 하는 말의 목적

고1 2020년 6월 3번 | 정답률 75%
▶ 정답 ②

W: Hello, students. This is <u>vice principal</u> Susan Lee. I know all of you
　　　　　　　　　　　　　　교감
are <u>busy preparing</u> for the <u>upcoming</u> school <u>festival</u>. There are
　　~을 준비하느라 바쁜　　　다가오는　　　　축제
(busy V-ing: ~하느라 바쁜, prepare for: ~을 준비하다)
<u>club activities</u> <u>going on</u> in every part of our school <u>building</u>. You
동아리　활동들　　진행되는(go on)　　　　　　건물
may <u>want to move</u> between <u>places</u> during activities. But I'd like to
　　이동하고 싶다　　　　장소들
(want to V: ~하고 싶다, move: 이동하다)
<u>ask</u> you <u>to work</u> in the <u>place</u> where you are <u>supposed to be</u>. Your
여러분에게 활동해 달라고 요청하다　　　　　　있어야 하다
(ask A to V: A에게 ~해 달라고 요청하다, work: 활동하다)　(be supposed to V: ~해야 하다)
teachers want to make your <u>safety</u> the <u>top priority</u>. <u>Once again</u>,
　　　　　　　　　　　　　안전　　　최우선 사항　다시 한번

---

make sure to prepare for the festival in your <u>prearranged</u> places.
반드시 준비하도록 하다　　　　　　　　　사전에 정해진
(make sure to V: 반드시 ~하도록 하다)
Thank you for your <u>cooperation</u>.
　　　　　　　　협조

해석

여: 안녕하세요, 학생 여러분. 저는 교감인 Susan Lee입니다. 여러분 모두 다가오는 학교 축제를 준비하느라 바쁘다는 것을 알고 있습니다. 우리 학교 건물 곳곳에서 진행되는 동아리 활동들이 있습니다. 여러분은 활동을 하는 동안에 장소들 사이를 이동하고 싶어 할지도 모릅니다. 그러나 저는 여러분에게 여러분이 있어야 하는 장소에서 활동해 달라고 요청하고 싶습니다. 선생님들은 여러분의 안전을 최우선 사항으로 삼고 싶어 합니다. 다시 한번, 반드시 여러분에게 사전에 정해진 장소에서 축제를 준비하도록 하십시오. 협조해 주셔서 감사합니다.

① 축제 관련자 안전 교육 참석을 공지하려고
✓ 정해진 장소에서 활동할 것을 요청하려고
③ 다양한 공연을 준비할 것을 독려하려고
④ 동아리 담당 교사 변경을 안내하려고
⑤ 적극적인 동아리 활동을 부탁하려고

문제 풀이

교감 선생님은 축제 준비를 위해 동아리 활동을 하는 학생들이 학교 건물 내의 여러 장소를 이동하는 상황을 우려하며 학생들의 안전을 위해 사전에 정해진 장소에서 동아리 활동을 할 것을 부탁하고 있으므로 답은 ② '정해진 장소에서 활동할 것을 요청하려고'이다.

---

02 남자의 의견

고1 2020년 6월 4번 | 정답률 90%
▶ 정답 ②

W: Hello, Chris. Why are you <u>sweating</u> like that?
　　　　　　　　　　　　땀을 흘리는(sweat)
M: Hi, Helen. I've just <u>jogged</u> <u>for an hour</u>.
　　　　　　　　　조깅한(jog)　한 시간 동안
W: For an hour? But, you don't look <u>tired</u> at all.
　　　　　　　　　　　~해 보이다　지친
M: That's because I had a <u>banana</u> before jogging.
　　　　　　　　　　　바나나
W: What do you mean?
M: If you eat something before running, you will <u>get more energy</u>.
섭취하다　　　　　　　　　　　　　더 많은 에너지를 얻다
W: Really? Does it <u>work</u>?
　　　　　　　효과가 있다
M: Yes! It gives your body more <u>power</u> for <u>exercise</u>.
　　　　　　　　　　　주다　힘　　　운동
W: That's why you look so <u>energetic</u> even after running <u>for a long time</u>.
　　　　　　　　　　　힘이 넘치는　　　　　　　　　　오랫동안
M: Yeah. <u>You should try it</u>.
　　　너도 한번 해 봐
W: Okay, I will.

해석

여: 안녕, Chris. 왜 그렇게 땀을 흘리고 있니?
남: 안녕, Helen. 방금 한 시간 동안 조깅을 했어.
여: 한 시간 동안? 그런데, 너는 전혀 지쳐 보이지 않는구나.
남: 그것은 내가 조깅하기 전에 바나나를 먹었기 때문이야.
여: 무슨 말이야?
남: 달리기를 하기 전에 무언가를 섭취하면, 더 많은 에너지를 얻을 거야.
여: 정말? 그것이 효과가 있어?
남: 그럼! 그것은 신체에 운동을 위한 더 많은 힘을 줘.
여: 그래서 네가 오랫동안 달리기를 한 후에도 그렇게 힘이 넘쳐 보이는구나.
남: 그래. 너도 한번 해 봐.
여: 알았어, 그럴게.

① 땀을 많이 흘린 후에는 수분 보충이 중요하다.
✓ 운동 전 음식 섭취가 운동을 위한 힘을 준다.
③ 운동은 땀을 흘릴 만큼 충분히 해야 한다.
④ 달리기 전 충분한 준비 운동을 해야 한다.
⑤ 꾸준한 운동이 건강한 신체를 만든다.

---

03 두 사람의 관계

고1 2020년 6월 5번 | 정답률 90%
▶ 정답 ②

[Telephone rings.]
M: Hello, this is Daniel Johnson.
W: Hello, Mr. Johnson. It's Elena Roberts. Have you thought about my <u>proposal</u>?
　　　　　　　　　　　　　　　　　　　　　　　　　　　　　　제안

M: Yes. You said you wanted to turn my novel into a movie, right?
내 소설을 영화로 바꾸다
(turn A into B: A를 B로 바꾸다, novel: 소설, movie: 영화)

W: That's right. I loved your novel, and it would make a great movie.

M: I'm glad to hear that. And if you directed the movie, it would be a
기쁜   감독하다(direct)
great honor for me.
~에게 큰 영광이다

W: Thank you for accepting my offer. I'd like us to speak about the
제안   ~에 대해 얘기 나누다
details of the story in person.
세부 사항들   이야기   직접

M: Then, shall I go to your office?
사무실

W: That would be great. Can you come tomorrow?

M: Sure. I'll be there by 10 a.m.

해석

[전화벨이 울린다.]

남: 여보세요, Daniel Johnson입니다.

여: 안녕하세요, Johnson 씨. Elena Roberts입니다. 제 제안에 대해 생각해 보셨나요?

남: 네. 제 소설을 영화로 바꾸고 싶다고 말씀하셨잖아요, 그렇죠?

여: 맞아요. 저는 당신의 소설을 정말 좋아했고, 그것은 멋진 영화가 될 거예요.

남: 그 말을 들으니 기쁘네요. 그리고 당신이 그 영화를 감독한다면, 저에게 큰 영광이 될 거예요.

여: 제 제안을 받아주셔서 감사해요. 저는 우리가 그 이야기의 세부 사항들에 대해 직접 얘기 나누었으면 좋겠어요.

남: 그럼, 제가 당신의 사무실로 갈까요?

여: 그래 주시면 좋을 것 같아요. 내일 오실 수 있나요?

남: 물론이죠. 오전 10시까지 갈게요.

① 구직자 — 채용 담당 직원
✓ 소설가 — 영화감독
③ 배우 — 방송 작가
④ 서점 직원 — 출판업자
⑤ 뮤지컬 배우 — 무대 감독

---

04 그림에서 대화의 내용과 일치하지 않는 것
고1 2020년 6월 6번 | 정답률 75%
▶ 정답 ④

W: Eugene, the stage is ready. Why don't you check it out?
무대   준비된   그것을 확인하다

M: Okay. Did you set up the TV I asked for?
~을 설치하다   ~을 부탁했다

W: Yeah, I put it on the wall above the sofa.
그것을 벽에 걸었다   소파

M: Great. I need to play video clips during the talk show.
재생해야 하다   동영상들   토크쇼
(need to V: ~해야 하다, play: 재생하다)

W: And I placed the floor lamp between the sofa and the flower pot.
놓았다   (바닥에 세우는) 전기 스탠드   화분
Do you like it?

M: Absolutely. It's simple but looks cool. Oh, I like the cushion with the
단순한   멋진   쿠션
striped pattern on the sofa.
줄무늬

W: So do I. How about the square table on the rug? Isn't it too big?
사각 테이블   깔개

M: It looks fine. But those two pictures below the clock don't seem to
fit well there.   그림들   잘 맞지 않는 것 같다
(seem to V: ~인 것 같다, fit well: 잘 맞다)

W: Then, I'll take them away.
그것들을 치우다

M: Thank you, Rebecca.

해석

여: Eugene, 무대가 준비됐어요. 그것을 확인해 보는 게 어때요?

남: 알았어요. 제가 부탁한 TV는 설치했나요?

여: 네, 그것을 소파 위의 벽에 걸었어요.

남: 좋아요. 토크쇼를 하는 동안 동영상들을 재생해야 해요.

여: 그리고 소파와 화분 사이에 전기 스탠드를 놓았어요. 마음에 드세요?

남: 당연하죠. 단순하지만 멋져 보여요. 오, 소파 위에 줄무늬가 있는 쿠션이 마음에 드네요.

여: 저도 그래요. 깔개 위의 사각 테이블은 어떠세요? 너무 크지 않나요?

남: 괜찮아 보여요. 그런데 시계 아래에 있는 저 두 개의 그림은 그곳에 잘 맞지 않는 것 같아요.

여: 그럼, 그것들을 치울게요.

남: 고마워요, Rebecca.

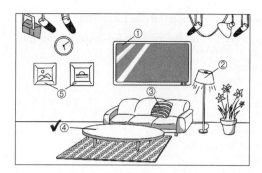

05 여자가 할 일
고1 2020년 6월 7번 | 정답률 85%
▶ 정답 ③

M: Honey, Nathan's birthday is tomorrow.

W: I can't believe he's almost ONE!
믿다   거의

M: Neither can I. He's already learning to walk.
벌써   걷는 법을 배우는
(learn to V: ~하는 법을 배우다, walk: 걷다)

W: I made a digital photo album for his birthday party.
디지털 사진 앨범   생일 파티

M: Wow! That's great! How do you plan to show it?
보여줄 계획이다(plan to V: ~할 계획이다, show: 보여주다)

W: How about showing the photos on the TV in the living room?
~하는 게 어때요?   거실

M: Sounds good. What else do we need?
필요하다

W: Every birthday party needs balloons and a cake.
풍선들   케이크

M: Okay. I'll decorate the living room with balloons.
거실을 풍선들로 장식하다(decorate A with B: A를 B로 장식하다)

W: Then, I'll bake the cake.
굽다

M: Great! He'll love it.

해석

남: 여보, Nathan의 생일이 내일이에요.

여: 그 애가 거의 한 살이 되었다는 게 믿어지지 않아요!

남: 저도 그래요. 벌써 걷는 법을 배우고 있잖아요.

여: 저는 그 애의 생일 파티를 위해 디지털 사진 앨범을 만들었어요.

남: 와! 그거 멋지네요! 어떻게 그것을 보여줄 계획이에요?

여: 거실에 있는 TV로 사진을 보여주는 게 어때요?

남: 좋을 것 같아요. 그 밖에 우리가 필요한 게 뭐죠?

여: 모든 생일 파티에는 풍선들과 케이크가 필요하잖아요.

남: 알겠어요. 제가 거실을 풍선들로 장식할게요.

여: 그럼, 저는 케이크를 구울게요.

남: 좋아요! 그 애가 그것을 정말 좋아할 거예요.

① 사진 앨범 만들기
② 파티 초대장 보내기
✓ 생일 케이크 만들기
④ 풍선으로 거실 장식하기
⑤ TV로 사진 영상 재생하기

---

06 여자가 지불할 금액
고1 2020년 6월 9번 | 정답률 85%
▶ 정답 ③

[Telephone rings.]

M: Good evening, John's Food Delivery. How may I help you?

W: Hi. I'd like to order some dinners.
주문하다   저녁 식사들

M: Okay. What would you like?

W: How much is a cheeseburger set?
치즈버거 세트

M: It's eight dollars. How many would you like?

W: I need two sets. Is there anything else you can recommend?
추천하다

M: Yes, our newest item, the avocado sandwich, is very delicious. It's
최신의   제품   아보카도 샌드위치   맛있는
seven dollars.

W: Good. Add two avocado sandwiches to my order, please.
내 주문에 아보카도 샌드위치 두 개를 추가하다
(add A to B: B에 A를 추가하다)

M: So two cheeseburger sets and two avocado sandwiches, right?

W: Yes. And I have a <u>discount coupon</u> for <u>new customers</u>.
　　　　　　　　　　　할인 쿠폰　　　　　신규 고객들
M: Okay, then you'll <u>get 10% off the total</u>. Where would you like your
　　　　　　　　　총액에서 10% 할인을 받다
　　food delivered?
W: 101 Fifth St., please.

해석

[전화벨이 울린다.]
남: 안녕하세요, John's Food Delivery입니다. 어떻게 도와드릴까요?
여: 안녕하세요. 저녁 식사들을 좀 주문하고 싶어요.
남: 알겠습니다. 무엇을 주문하시겠습니까?
여: 치즈버거 세트는 얼마죠?
남: 8달러입니다. 몇 개를 주문하시겠습니까?
여: 두 세트가 필요해요. 추천할 만한 다른 것이 있나요?
남: 네, 저희의 최신 제품인 아보카도 샌드위치가 아주 맛있어요. 그것은 7달러예요.
여: 좋네요. 제 주문에 아보카도 샌드위치 두 개를 추가해 주세요.
남: 그럼 치즈버거 세트 두 개와 아보카도 샌드위치 두 개네요, 맞습니까?
여: 네. 그리고 저는 신규 고객들을 위한 할인 쿠폰을 가지고 있어요.
남: 알겠습니다, 그럼 총액에서 10% 할인을 받으실 거예요. 음식을 어디로 배달해 드릴까요?
여: 5번가 101번지로 부탁드릴게요.

① $15　　　　　　　② $23　　　　　　　✓ $27
④ $30　　　　　　　⑤ $33

문제 풀이

여자는 8달러짜리 치즈버거 두 세트와 7달러짜리 아보카도 샌드위치 두 개를 주문했으므로 총액은 30달러인데, 신규 고객을 위한 할인 쿠폰을 사용해 10% 할인을 받을 수 있으므로 지불해야 할 금액은 27달러이다. 따라서 정답은 ③ '$27'이다.

07　남자가 수영장에 갈 수 없는 이유

고1 2020년 6월 8번 | 정답률 75%　▶ 정답 ⑤

W: Hey, Patrick. I have good news.
M: Hi, Jennifer. What is it?
W: The <u>outdoor swimming pool</u> at the <u>community center</u> opened last
　　　　　야외 수영장　　　　　　　지역 주민 센터
　　weekend.
M: I heard that. You know it is even open at night.
W: Cool! Let's <u>go swimming</u> tonight, then.
　　　　　　수영하러 가다
M: Well. I really want to, but I can't.
W: Do you have other <u>plans</u>?
　　　　　　　　　　계획들
M: Do you <u>remember</u> I had an <u>interview</u> for a <u>part-time job</u> yesterday?
　　　　　　기억하다　　　　　　면접　　　　　아르바이트
W: Sure, how did it go?
M: I got the job. So I have to <u>start working</u> this evening.
　　　　　　　　　　　일하기 시작하다(start V-ing: ~하기 시작하다, work: 일하다)
W: Oh well, we can go swimming <u>some other day</u>. Good luck!
　　　　　　　　　　　　　　　언젠가 다른 날

해석

여: 이봐, Patrick. 좋은 소식이 있어.
남: 안녕, Jennifer. 그게 뭔데?
여: 지역 주민 센터에 있는 야외 수영장이 지난 주말에 문을 열었어.
남: 들었어. 있잖아, 거기 밤에도 연대.
여: 멋지다! 그럼 오늘 밤에 수영하러 가자.
남: 음. 정말 그러고 싶지만, 갈 수 없어.
여: 다른 계획이 있는 거니?
남: 내가 어제 아르바이트 면접을 본 것을 기억하지?
여: 물론이지, 어떻게 됐어?
남: 나 일자리를 얻었어. 그래서 오늘 저녁에 일하기 시작해야 해.
여: 오 그래, 언젠가 다른 날에 수영하러 가면 되지. 행운을 빌어!

① 감기에 걸려서
② 취업 면접이 있어서
③ 친구와 약속이 있어서
④ 봉사 활동을 가야 해서
✓ 저녁에 일을 해야 해서

08　Rock Music Festival에 관해 언급되지 않은 것

고1 2020년 6월 10번 | 정답률 90%　▶ 정답 ④

W: Mike, did you see the <u>poster</u> for the <u>Rock Music Festival</u> in our
　　　　　　　　　　　　포스터　　　　　　록 음악 축제
　　town?

M: No, I didn't. Please give me some <u>details</u>. When will it be?
　　　　　　　　　　　　　　　　자세한 내용들
W: On June 13th at 8 p.m. Can you come with me?
M: Sure, I'd love to. How much are the <u>tickets</u> for the festival?
　　　　　　　　　　　　　　　　　입장권들
W: They're only ten dollars for <u>teens</u> like us.
　　　　　　　　　　　　　　십 대들
M: Wonderful! Where is the <u>event</u> <u>taking place</u>?
　　　　　　　　　　　　　행사　개최되는(take place)
W: It'll be <u>held</u> nearby, at <u>Central Stadium</u>.
　개최되다(hold: 개최하다)　　중앙 경기장
M: That's good. We can get there <u>on foot</u>. Who will be <u>playing</u>?
　　　　　　　　　　　　　걸어서　　　　　공연할 것이다(play)
W: <u>World famous</u> <u>musicians</u> Garcia and Martin will <u>perform</u>.
　세계적으로 유명한　음악가들　　　　　　　　공연하다
M: Wow! I <u>can't wait to see them</u>.
　　　　빨리 보고 싶다(can't wait to V: 빨리 ~하고 싶다)

해석

여: Mike, 우리 동네의 Rock Music Festival(록 음악 축제) 포스터를 봤니?
남: 아니, 못 봤어. 자세한 내용들 좀 알려줘. 그것은 언제 하니?
여: 6월 13일 오후 8시. 나와 같이 갈 수 있겠니?
남: 물론이지, 가고 싶어. 축제의 입장권은 얼마니?
여: 우리 같은 십 대들에겐 10달러밖에 안 해.
남: 멋진데! 그 행사는 어디에서 개최되니?
여: 근처의 Central Stadium(중앙 경기장)에서 개최될 거야.
남: 잘됐다. 우리는 그곳에 걸어서 갈 수 있잖아. 누가 공연을 하니?
여: 세계적으로 유명한 음악가들인 Garcia와 Martin이 공연할 거야.
남: 와! 빨리 그들을 보고 싶어.

① 개최 일시　　　　　② 입장료　　　　　③ 개최 장소
✓ 주차 요금　　　　　⑤ 참여 음악가

09　Westbank High School Science Fair에 관한 내용과 일치하지 않는 것　▶ 정답 ⑤

고1 2020년 6월 11번 | 정답률 70%

M: Hello, students. This is Kyle Evans, your <u>physics teacher</u>. I'm very
　　　　　　　　　　　　　　　　　　　　물리 교사
　　glad to tell you about the Westbank <u>High School</u> <u>Science Fair</u>.
　　　　　　　　　　　　　　　　　　　　고등학교　　　과학 박람회
　　It'll <u>be held</u> on July 21st in the school <u>auditorium</u>. You'll <u>present</u>
　　　　열리다(hold: 열다)　　　　　　　　　　강당　　　　　발표하다
　　your <u>projects</u> in front of <u>judges</u> and <u>visitors</u>. The judges will be
　　　　　과제들　　　　　　　평가자들　　방문객들
　　<u>professors</u> and teachers from other schools. They'll all <u>provide</u>
　　　교수님들　　　　　　　　　　　　　　　　　　　　주다
　　<u>feedback</u> and <u>comments</u> to each team. <u>Awards</u> will be given in
　　　피드백　　　　　의견들　　　　　　　　상들
　　three areas: <u>Physics</u>, <u>Chemistry</u>, and <u>Biology</u>. Also, the first 100
　　　　　　　　분야들　물리　　　화학　　　　생물
　　visitors will get T-shirts <u>for free</u>. <u>Spread the word</u> and please <u>invite</u>
　　　　　　　　　　　　무료로　　소문을 내다
　　<u>your friends and parents to come</u>. I hope you enjoy the fair.
　　여러분의 친구들과 부모님들께 와 달라고 부탁하다(invite A to V: A에게 ~해 달라고 부탁하다)

해석

남: 안녕하세요, 학생 여러분. 저는 물리 교사인 Kyle Evans입니다. 여러분에게 Westbank 고등학교 과학 박람회에 대해 알려드리게 되어 매우 기쁩니다. 그것은 7월 21일에 학교 강당에서 열릴 것입니다. 여러분은 평가자들과 방문객들 앞에서 과제를 발표할 것입니다. 평가자들은 다른 학교의 교수님들과 선생님들이 될 것입니다. 그분들께서는 모두 각 팀에게 피드백과 의견을 주실 것입니다. 상은 물리, 화학, 그리고 생물의 세 분야에 주어질 것입니다. 또한, 선착순 100명의 방문객들께 무료로 티셔츠를 드릴 것입니다. 소문을 내 주시고 여러분의 친구들과 부모님들께 와 달라고 부탁해 주십시오. 여러분이 박람회를 즐기시길 바랍니다.

① 7월 21일에 열린다.
② 평가자와 방문객 앞에서 과제 발표가 이루어진다.
③ 각 팀에게 피드백이 주어진다.
④ 세 분야에 상이 주어진다.
✓ 모든 방문객에게 무료로 티셔츠를 준다.

문제 풀이

남자의 말에 따르면 Westbank 고등학교 과학 박람회의 방문객들 중 선착순 100명에게 무료로 티셔츠를 준다고 했으므로 ⑤ '모든 방문객에게 무료로 티셔츠를 준다.'는 본문의 내용과 일치하지 않는다.

10　표에서 여자가 수강할 수업

고1 2020년 6월 12번 | 정답률 85%　▶ 정답 ②

M: Linda, what are you <u>looking at</u>?
　　　　　　　　　　　~을 보는(look at)

W: Hi, James. I'm thinking of taking one of the summer programs on
　　　　　　　　　　　　　　　　　　　　　　　　　　　　　 여름 프로그램들
this time table.
시간표
M: Let me see. What program would you like to take?
W: Well, I took English Conversation last year. This time I want to take
　　　　　　　　 영어 회화　　　　　　　　　　　　　　　 수강하고 싶다
something different.　　　　　　　　　　　　　　　 (want to V: ~하고 싶다)
　　　　　　 다른
M: If I were you, I would take this class.
　　　　　　　　　　　　　　　　 수업
W: I'd love to, but I plan to volunteer on Fridays this summer.
　　　　　　　　　　 자원봉사를 할 계획이다
　　　　　　　　　 (plan to V: ~할 계획이다, volunteer: 자원봉사를 하다)
M: I see. Then, how about this one?
　　　　　　　　 ~은 어때?
W: Sounds good, but I have to be home by six for dinner with my family.
　　　　　　　　　　　　　　　　　　　　　　　　 저녁 식사
M: Then, you're left with two options. Which one do you prefer?
　　　　　　~이 남은　　　　 선택들　　　　　　　 ~을 더 좋아하다
W: Well, considering my budget, I'll take the cheaper one.
　　　~을 고려하면　　 예산

해석
남: Linda, 무엇을 보고 있니?
여: 안녕, James. 나는 이 시간표에서 여름 프로그램들 중 하나를 수강할까 생각 중이야.
남: 어디 보자. 어떤 프로그램을 수강하고 싶니?
여: 음, 나는 작년에 영어 회화를 수강했어. 이번에는 다른 것을 수강하고 싶어.
남: 내가 너라면, 난 이 수업을 수강할 거야.
여: 나도 그러고 싶지만, 이번 여름에는 금요일마다 자원봉사를 할 계획이야.
남: 그렇구나. 그럼, 이것은 어때?
여: 좋긴 한데, 가족과의 저녁 식사를 위해 6시까지 집에 가야 해.
남: 그럼, 너에게는 두 가지 선택지가 남았어. 어떤 것이 더 좋니?
여: 음, 내 예산을 고려하면, 더 저렴한 것을 선택할게.

여름 프로그램 시간표

	수업	요일	시간	월 수강료
①	영어 회화	월요일	오전 9시	50달러
✓	만화 창작	화요일	오전 10시	60달러
③	수중 에어로빅	수요일	오전 10시	75달러
④	축구	목요일	오후 6시	80달러
⑤	소묘	금요일	오후 3시	75달러

---

11 여자의 마지막 말에 대한 남자의 응답

고1 2020년 6월 1번 ｜ 정답률 85%
▶ 정답 ①

W: Jimmy, what are you looking for?
　　　　　　　　　 ~을 찾는(look for)
M: My cellphone. I forgot where I left it.
　　 휴대전화　　└ 잊어버렸다(forget) └ 두었다(leave)
W: Why don't you look for it in your room first?
　 ~하는 게 어때?
M: (I already did, but I couldn't find it.)
　　 이미　　　　　　　　　 찾다

해석
여: Jimmy, 무엇을 찾고 있니?
남: 내 휴대전화. 그것을 어디에 두었는지 잊어버렸어.
여: 네 방에서 먼저 그것을 찾아보는 게 어때?
남: (나는 이미 그랬는데, 그것을 찾을 수 없었어.)
✓ 나는 이미 그랬는데, 그것을 찾을 수 없었어.
② 알았어, 나는 거실에서 기다릴게.
③ 너는 휴대전화를 수리해야 해.
④ 나는 분실물 보관소에 전화했어.
⑤ 여기에서는 와이파이를 이용할 수 없어.

---

12 남자의 마지막 말에 대한 여자의 응답

고1 2020년 6월 2번 ｜ 정답률 85%
▶ 정답 ⑤

M: Excuse me. I'd like to buy some flowers for my wife.
　　　　　　　　　　　　 사다　　 꽃들　　　　 아내
W: Do you have any kind in mind?
　　　　 어떤 종류를 염두에 두다
　　　 (have A in mind: A를 염두에 두다, kind: 종류)
M: Not really. What do you recommend?
　　　　　　　　　　　 추천하다
W: (White roses are nice at this time of year.)
　　　 장미들　　　　　　 매년 이맘때에

해석
남: 실례합니다. 저는 아내를 위해 꽃들을 좀 사고 싶어요.

여: 염두에 둔 어떤 종류가 있으신가요?
남: 그렇진 않아요. 어떤 것을 추천해 주시겠어요?
여: (매년 이맘때에는 하얀 장미가 좋아요.)
① 해바라기 축제를 방문하는 것이 좋을 거예요.
② 당신은 그녀에게 생일 카드를 보낼 수 없어요.
③ 당신의 친절은 항상 보답을 받아요.
④ 제가 꽃들을 무료로 포장해 드릴게요.
✓ 매년 이맘때에는 하얀 장미가 좋아요.

---

13 여자의 마지막 말에 대한 남자의 응답

고1 2020년 6월 13번 ｜ 정답률 70%
▶ 정답 ①

W: Hi, Thomas. Are you okay? You look worried.
　　　　　　　　　　　　　　　　　　　　 걱정스러운
M: Cindy, may I ask you a favor?
　　 너에게 부탁을 하다(ask A a favor: A에게 부탁을 하다)
W: Sure! Just tell me what you need.
M: As you know, I'm going on a family trip for three weeks.
　　 알다시피　　　　 가족 여행을 가는(go on a trip: 여행을 가다)
W: To Europe this Sunday, right?
M: Yes. Can you look after my plants while I'm away?
　　　　　　　 ~을 돌보다　　 식물들　 내가 없는 동안
W: I'd love to, but I don't know how to take care of them.
　　　　　　　　　　　　　 ~을 돌보는 방법(how to V: ~하는 방법, take care of: ~을 돌보다)
M: No worries. It's really easy. You just need to remember one thing:
　　　　　　　　　　　　　　　　　　　　 기억해야 하다
Water them regularly.　　　　　 (need to V: ~해야 하다, remember: 기억하다)
물을 주다　 규칙적으로
W: I can do that. Do I have to water them every day?
M: (No. Just once a week.)
　　　　 일주일에 한 번

해석
여: 안녕, Thomas. 너 괜찮니? 걱정스러워 보여.
남: Cindy, 내가 너에게 부탁을 하나 해도 될까?
여: 물론이지! 무엇이 필요한지 말해봐.
남: 알다시피, 나는 3주 동안 가족 여행을 갈 거야.
여: 이번 주 일요일에 유럽으로 가잖아, 맞지?
남: 그래. 내가 없는 동안 내 식물들을 돌봐 주겠니?
여: 그러고 싶지만, 나는 그것들을 돌보는 방법을 몰라.
남: 걱정하지 마. 그것은 정말 쉬워. 한 가지만 기억하면 되는데, 그것들에게 규칙적으로 물을 주는 거야.
여: 그것은 할 수 있어. 매일 물을 줘야 하는 거야?
남: (아니. 일주일에 한 번만.)
✓ 아니. 일주일에 한 번만.
② 물론이지. 매일 그것을 마셔.
③ 미안해. 나는 할 수 없을 것 같아.
④ 그래. 여기에서 멀지 않아.
⑤ 바로 그거야. 너도 같이 여행을 갈 거야.

---

14 남자의 마지막 말에 대한 여자의 응답

고1 2020년 6월 14번 ｜ 정답률 65%
▶ 정답 ③

M: Ms. White, you look so busy tonight.
　　　　　　　　　　　　 바쁜
W: I am. I have to check my students' homework.
　　　　　　　 확인하다　　　　 숙제
M: Wow, I can't believe students made these.
　　　　　　 믿다
W: Yeah, I was surprised how creative they were when making their
　　　　　　　 놀란　　　 창의적인
videos.
동영상들
M: By making videos, students could learn several aspects of Korean
　 만듦으로써(by V-ing: ~함으로써)　　　　　　　 측면들
culture and share them in a fun way.
문화　　　 공유하다　　 재미있는 방법으로
W: You're right. That's why I assigned them this homework.
　　　　　　　　　　　　 (숙제를) 냈다
M: I see. Which is your favorite one?
　　　　　　　　 가장 좋아하는
W: I think this one is the best, because it shows 'Ganggangsullae'
　　　　　　　　　　　　　　　　　　　 보여주다
performed by many students in harmony.
공연된(perform: 공연하다)　　　 조화롭게
M: It would be excellent if it were shared on the Internet.
　　　　　　 멋진
W: (Good idea. It will introduce Korean culture to the world.)
　　　　　　　　　 알리다

해석
남: White 선생님, 오늘 밤에 매우 바빠 보이시네요.

여: 네. 제 학생들의 숙제를 확인해야 하거든요.
남: 와, 학생들이 이것들을 만들었다니 믿을 수가 없네요.
여: 그래요, 저는 그들이 동영상을 만들 때 얼마나 창의적인지에 놀랐어요.
남: 동영상을 만듦으로써, 학생들은 한국 문화의 몇 가지 측면들을 배울 수 있고 재미있는 방법으로 그것들을 공유할 수 있죠.
여: 맞아요. 그래서 제가 그들에게 이 숙제를 낸 거예요.
남: 그렇군요. 선생님께서 가장 좋아하시는 것은 어떤 거예요?
여: 저는 이것이 가장 좋은 것 같아요, 왜냐하면 그것은 많은 학생들에 의해 조화롭게 공연된 '강강술래'를 보여주기 때문이에요.
남: 그것이 인터넷에서 공유된다면 멋질 거예요.
여: (좋은 생각이에요. 그것은 한국 문화를 세계에 알릴 거예요.)

① 물론이죠. 숙제는 제시간에 제출해야 해요.
② 맞아요. 학생들은 적절한 인터넷 예절을 갖춰야 해요.
✔좋은 생각이에요. 그것은 한국 문화를 세계에 알릴 거예요.
④ 고마워요. 저희를 한국에 초대해 주셔서 정말 감사해요.
⑤ 좋아요. 제가 가서 그들을 위해 표를 사 올게요.

문제 풀이

한국 문화에 대해 배우는 학생들이 만든 동영상 중에서 '강강술래'를 하는 동영상이 가장 좋다는 여자의 말에 남자는 그것을 인터넷에 올려 여러 사람들이 볼 수 있도록 공유하면 멋질 것이라고 말한다. 따라서 이에 대한 여자의 응답으로 적절한 것은 ③ 'Good idea. It will introduce Korean culture to the world.(좋은 생각이에요. 그것은 한국 문화를 세계에 알릴 거예요.)'이다.

---

15 다음 상황에서 Olivia가 온라인 쇼핑몰 고객센터 직원에게 할 말

고1 2020년 6월 15번 | 정답률 75% | ▶ 정답 ①

W: Olivia likes to shop online. She ordered a pair of blue pants from a famous online shopping mall a few days ago. When they are delivered, she finds out that the pants are not blue, but black. So she calls the customer service center. When she explains her situation, the employee who answers her call apologizes for their mistake and tells her that the blue pants are sold out. So, Olivia wants to return the black pants and get her money back. In this situation what would Olivia most likely say to the customer service employee?
Olivia: (I'd like to send the pants back and get a refund.)

(deliver: 배송하다)
(want to V: ~하고 싶다, return: 반품하다)

해석

여: Olivia는 온라인으로 쇼핑하는 것을 좋아한다. 그녀는 며칠 전에 유명한 온라인 쇼핑몰에서 파란색 바지 한 벌을 주문했다. 그것이 배송되었을 때, 그녀는 바지가 파란색이 아니라 검은색인 것을 알게 된다. 그래서 그녀는 고객 서비스 센터에 전화를 한다. 그녀가 그녀의 상황을 설명할 때, 그녀의 전화를 받은 직원은 자신들의 실수에 대해 사과하고 그녀에게 파란색 바지는 품절되었다고 말한다. 그래서, Olivia는 검은색 바지를 반품하고 그녀의 돈을 돌려받고 싶다. 이러한 상황에서 Olivia는 고객 서비스 센터 직원에게 뭐라고 말하겠는가?
Olivia: (저는 바지를 반품하고 환불을 받고 싶어요.)

✔저는 바지를 반품하고 환불을 받고 싶어요.
② 바지를 내일까지 배송해 주실 수 있을까요?
③ 파란색 바지가 입고되면 알려주세요.
④ 그것을 파란색 바지로 교환할 수 있을까요?
⑤ 저는 배송 상태를 확인하고 싶어요.

문제 풀이

파란색 바지가 품절되어서 Olivia는 원하던 바지를 얻을 수 없게 되었다. 그래서 검은색 바지를 반품하고 그녀의 돈을 돌려받고 싶어하는 상황이므로 ① 'I'd like to send the pants back and get a refund.(저는 바지를 반품하고 환불을 받고 싶어요.)'가 답이 된다.

16~17 1지문 2문항

M: Good morning, listeners. This is Dr. Cooper of Daily HealthLine Radio. These days, you can see many people around you who suffer from back pain. Any incorrect positioning of your body or lifting of heavy objects may cause it. So, today, I'll share some useful types of exercise to help reduce your own back pain. First, biking can decrease back pain by building your core muscles.

(by V-ing: ~함으로써, build: 형성하다)

Second, swimming is good because you can do it without much stress on your back muscles. Also, yoga is a helpful way to stretch safely and strengthen your back as well. Finally, walking is the easiest exercise to keep your spine in a natural position to avoid back pain. I hope this will be helpful information for you and allow you to be fit again.

(allow A to V: A가 ~할 수 있게 해주다, fit: 건강한)

해석

남: 안녕하세요, 청취자 여러분. 저는 Daily HealthLine Radio의 Cooper 박사입니다. 요즈음에, 여러분은 주변에서 요통으로 고생하는 사람들을 많이 볼 수 있습니다. 어떠한 신체의 옳지 못한 자세 잡기나 무거운 물건 들어 올리기라도 그것을 유발할 수 있습니다. 그래서, 오늘, 저는 여러분 자신의 요통을 감소시키는 데 도움을 줄 수 있는 몇 가지 유용한 종류의 운동을 공유할 것입니다. 첫째, 자전거 타기는 중심 근육들을 형성함으로써 요통을 줄일 수 있습니다. 둘째, 수영은 허리 근육들에 많은 압박을 가하지 않고 그것을 할 수 있기 때문에 좋습니다. 또한, 요가는 안전하게 몸을 뻗고 허리를 강화할 수 있는 유용한 방법입니다. 마지막으로, 걷기는 척추를 자연스러운 자세로 유지해 요통을 피하게 해주는 가장 쉬운 운동입니다. 이것이 여러분에게 유용한 정보가 되고 여러분이 다시 건강할 수 있게 해주기를 바랍니다.

---

16 남자가 하는 말의 주제

고1 2020년 6월 16번 | 정답률 85% | ▶ 정답 ②

① 체중 감량을 위한 다양한 유산소 운동들
✔요통 감소를 위한 효과적인 운동들
③ 당신의 신체를 유연하게 만드는 활동들
④ 올바른 자세를 취하는 것의 중요성
⑤ 근육통의 흔한 증상들

---

17 언급된 운동이 아닌 것

고1 2020년 6월 17번 | 정답률 90% | ▶ 정답 ④

① 자전거 타기　　② 수영　　③ 요가
✔등산　　⑤ 걷기

---

08 2020년 9월 학력평가

01	⑤	02	①	03	①	04	④	05	①
06	⑤	07	⑤	08	③	09	⑤	10	③
11	⑤	12	①	13	④	14	②	15	⑤
16	①	17	②						

---

01 여자가 하는 말의 목적

고1 2020년 9월 3번 | 정답률 90% | ▶ 정답 ⑤

W: Hello, everyone. Thank you for visiting Dream Amusement Park. To celebrate our 20th anniversary, we have a special musical performance for children, *The Winter Princess*, all through this week. It was awarded the Best Children's Musical last year and features many famous musical artists that you love. Today, the performance will start at 4 p.m. at the Rainbow Theater. If you'd

like to join the show, you need to <u>make a reservation</u> at any
예약하다
<u>information center</u> nearby. We hope you all have a wonderful time
안내소
with us. Thank you.

해석

여: 안녕하세요, 여러분. Dream Amusement Park(Dream 놀이공원)를 방문해 주셔서 감사
합니다. 20주년을 기념하기 위해서, 저희는 이번 주 내내 어린이들을 위한 특별한 뮤지컬
공연, 'The Winter Princess(겨울 공주)'를 합니다. 그것은 작년에 최우수 어린이 뮤지컬상
을 수상했으며 여러분이 정말 좋아하는 많은 유명한 뮤지컬 배우들이 출연합니다. 오늘,
공연은 Rainbow Theater(Rainbow 극장)에서 오후 4시에 시작될 것입니다. 공연을 함께
하고 싶으시면, 가까운 안내소에서 예약을 하셔야 합니다. 여러분 모두 저희와 함께 즐거
운 시간을 보내시길 바랍니다. 감사합니다.

① 놀이공원의 개장을 홍보하려고
② 어린이 뮤지컬 배우를 모집하려고
③ 뮤지컬 시상식 일정을 공지하려고
④ 어린이 안전사고 예방을 당부하려고
✓ 어린이 뮤지컬 특별 공연을 안내하려고

---

02 두 사람이 하는 말의 주제

고1 2020년 9월 4번 | 정답률 85% | ▶ 정답 ①

M: Hey, Sarah. What are you going to <u>choose</u> for your <u>after-school</u>
선택하다   방과 후 활동
<u>activity</u>?
W: I'm not sure, Dad.
M: What about taking a <u>coding course</u>?
~하는 게 어때?   코딩 수업
W: A coding course? Why should I do that?
M: I think learning to code can give you <u>important</u> <u>skills</u> for the <u>future</u>.
중요한 기술들 미래
W: Oh, I <u>remember</u> my teacher saying that coding is a skill that can
기억나다
<u>increase</u> the <u>chances</u> of getting a job. But it sounds <u>difficult</u>.
높이다   가능성들   어려운
M: It might be, but it can help you learn <u>how to plan and organize</u> your
계획하고 정리하는 방법
thoughts.   (how to V: ~하는 방법, plan: 계획하다, organize: 정리하다)
W: Good to know. And I heard coding helps with <u>math</u>. Right?
수학
M: Definitely. <u>Plus</u>, it <u>improves</u> your <u>problem-solving skills</u>.
게다가 향상시키다   문제 해결 능력들
W: Cool! I think I'm going to take the course.

해석

남: 얘, Sarah야. 방과 후 활동으로 무엇을 선택할 거니?
여: 잘 모르겠어요, 아빠.
남: 코딩 수업을 듣는 게 어떠니?
여: 코딩 수업이요? 제가 왜 그것을 해야 하죠?
남: 코딩 학습은 너에게 미래를 위한 중요한 기술들을 알려줄 수 있다고 생각해.
여: 오, 저희 선생님께서 코딩이 취업의 가능성들을 높일 수 있는 기술이라고 말씀하신 게 기
억나요. 하지만 그것은 어렵게 들려요.
남: 그럴지도 모르지만, 그것은 네가 계획하고 생각들을 정리하는 방법을 배우는 데 도움을
줄 수 있어.
여: 좋은 정보네요. 그리고 저는 코딩이 수학에 도움이 된다고 들었어요. 맞아요?
남: 물론이지. 게다가, 그것은 너의 문제 해결 능력들을 향상시킨단다.
여: 멋지네요! 그 수업을 들어야겠어요.

✓ 코딩 학습의 이점
② 코딩 시 주의할 점
③ 코딩 기술이 필요한 직업
④ 조기 코딩 교육의 문제점
⑤ 코딩 초보자를 위한 학습법

---

03 두 사람의 관계

고1 2020년 9월 5번 | 정답률 85% | ▶ 정답 ①

W: Hello, Mr. Williams.
M: Please come on in, Ms. Jackson. How are you doing?
W: I'm good. <u>Recently</u> our company <u>published</u> <u>several</u> books, so I've
최근에   출판했다   여러 권의
been really <u>busy</u>.
바쁜
M: Oh, I hope you get some time off soon.
W: I hope so, too. Well, I've read your <u>work</u>, *The Great Man*. I think you
작품

---

nicely <u>expressed</u> the feeling of the <u>original book</u>.
잘 표현했다(express)   원작
M: Thank you. Which book will I <u>translate</u> this time?
번역하다
W: It is a <u>novel</u> written by a Spanish <u>writer</u>, Isabel Martinez.
소설   작가
M: Sounds good. I'm so happy to translate the book.
W: My <u>boss</u> said that the book <u>needs to be released</u> by December. So,
상사   발간되어야 하다
(need to V: ~해야 하다, release: 발간하다)
is it <u>possible</u> to get the <u>first draft</u> by the end of October?
가능한   초안
M: No problem.

해석

여: 안녕하세요, Williams 씨.
남: 들어오세요, Jackson 씨. 어떻게 지내세요?
여: 잘 지내요. 최근에 저희 회사에서 여러 권의 책들을 출판해서, 정말 바빴어요.
남: 오, 당신이 빨리 쉬는 시간을 좀 가졌으면 좋겠네요.
여: 저도 그랬으면 좋겠어요. 음, 'The Great Man(위대한 사람)'이라는 당신의 작품을 읽었어
요. 원작의 느낌을 잘 표현하신 것 같아요.
남: 감사해요. 이번에는 어떤 책을 번역할까요?
여: 스페인 작가인 Isabel Martinez가 쓴 소설이에요.
남: 좋을 것 같아요. 그 책을 번역하게 되어 정말 기뻐요.
여: 제 상사께서 그 책이 12월까지는 발간되어야 한다고 말씀하셨어요. 그래서, 10월 말까지
초안을 받는 것이 가능할까요?
남: 문제 없어요.

✓ 출판사 직원 — 번역가
② 여행 가이드 — 관광객
③ 도서관 사서 — 학생
④ 서점 직원 — 고객
⑤ 잡지 기자 — 배우

---

04 그림에서 대화의 내용과 일치하지 않는 것

고1 2020년 9월 6번 | 정답률 85% | ▶ 정답 ④

M: Lisa, how's the <u>poster</u> for our <u>magic show</u> going?
포스터   마술 쇼
W: I have <u>changed</u> a few things. <u>Take a look</u>.
바꿨다(change)   보다
M: Oh, I like the two birds at the top.
W: And I <u>wrote</u> the <u>date</u> and the time under the <u>title</u>, Magic Show.
썼다(write) 날짜   제목
M: Nice choice. It's more <u>eye-catching</u>.
선택   더 눈길을 끄는
W: What do you think of the rabbit in the hat?
M: I really like it. It's so cute. And you put the <u>round table</u> <u>instead of</u>
원형 테이블   ~ 대신에
the <u>square</u> one.
사각 테이블
W: Yes, but I'm <u>still</u> not sure about the <u>shape</u> of the table.
아직도   모양
M: I think the round one looks much better.
W: Okay. And as you <u>suggested</u>, I drew a <u>magician holding</u> a magic
제안했다(suggest)   마술사   들고 있는(hold)
stick.
M: Nice. I think it's <u>perfect</u> now.
완벽한
W: Yeah, finally. Thanks for your help.

해석

남: Lisa, 우리의 마술 쇼 포스터는 어떻게 되어 가니?
여: 내가 몇 가지를 바꿨어. 봐봐.
남: 오, 나는 맨 위에 있는 새 두 마리가 마음에 들어.
여: 그리고 나는 Magic Show라는 제목 아래에 날짜와 시간을 썼어.
남: 좋은 선택이야. 그것이 더 눈길을 끄는구나.
여: 모자 속에 있는 토끼는 어때?
남: 정말 마음에 들어. 아주 귀여워. 그리고 사각 테이블 대신에 원형 테이블을 넣었구나.
여: 그래, 하지만 테이블의 모양에 대해서는 아직도 잘 모르겠어.
남: 나는 원형 테이블이 훨씬 더 좋은 것 같아.
여: 알았어. 그리고 네가 제안한 대로, 마술봉을 들고 있는 마술사를 그렸어.
남: 좋아. 이제 완벽한 것 같아.
여: 좋았어, 드디어 다 됐어. 도와줘서 고마워.

Magic Show
October 15th, 3:00 p.m.

05 여자가 할 일

고1 2020년 9월 7번 | 정답률 85% | ▶ 정답 ①

W: Chris, what are you doing?
M: I'm writing interview questions for the feature story of our next
　　　　　　　　인터뷰 질문들　　　　　　　특집 기사
　school magazine.
　학교 잡지
W: Who are you interviewing?
M: The new English teacher. I'm going to interview him tomorrow.
W: Do you need any help with the interview questions?
　　　　필요하다　　도움
M: No, I'm almost done. But I'm still looking for someone to take
　　　　　거의　　　　　　　　아직도　　~을 찾고 있는(look for)
　photos during the interview.
　사진들을 찍다(take a photo)
W: Why don't you ask Cindy? She's good at taking photos.
　　~하는 게 어때?　　　　　　　　　~을 잘한다(be good at)
M: I already asked her, but she said she has an important presentation
　　　　　　　　　　　　　　　　　　　　　중요한　　　발표
　tomorrow.
W: Well, how about Tom? He's a member of the photo club.
　　　　~은 어때?　　　　　　　회원　　　사진 동아리
M: You mean the one in our chemistry class?
　　　　　　　　　　　　　화학
W: Yes. I think he's the right person. Do you want me to call him to see
　　　　　　　　　　적임자
　if he's available tomorrow?
　　　시간이 있는
M: That would be great. Thanks.

해석
여: Chris, 무엇을 하고 있니?
남: 우리의 다음 호 학교 잡지의 특집 기사를 위해 인터뷰 질문들을 작성하고 있어.
여: 누구를 인터뷰하는 거야?
남: 새로 오신 영어 선생님이야. 내일 그분을 인터뷰할 거야.
여: 인터뷰 질문들을 작성하는 데 도움이 필요하니?
남: 아니, 거의 다 했어. 그런데 아직도 인터뷰하는 동안 사진들을 찍을 사람을 찾고 있어.
여: Cindy에게 부탁하는 게 어떠니? 그녀는 사진들을 잘 찍잖아.
남: 이미 부탁했는데, 그녀는 내일 중요한 발표가 있어.
여: 음, Tom은 어때? 그는 사진 동아리의 회원이야.
남: 우리 화학 수업에 있는 그 애 말이니?
여: 그래. 나는 그가 적임자인 것 같아. 내가 전화해서 그가 내일 시간이 있는지 알아봐 줄까?
남: 그러면 좋겠어. 고마워.

✔①Tom에게 전화하기
②화학 과제 제출하기
③인터뷰 사진 촬영하기
④Cindy와 발표 준비하기
⑤인터뷰 질문지 작성하기

문제 풀이
내일 영어 선생님을 인터뷰하는 동안 사진을 촬영할 사람을 찾고 있는 남자에게 여자는 화학 수업을 같이 듣는 Tom을 추천하고, 그에게 전화를 걸어 내일 시간이 있는지 알아봐 주겠다고 말하고 있다. 따라서 여자가 할 일은 ① 'Tom에게 전화하기'이다.

06 여자가 지불할 금액

고1 2020년 9월 9번 | 정답률 65% | ▶ 정답 ⑤

M: Hello, ma'am. Welcome to the Aerospace Exhibition.
　　　　　　　　　　　　　　　　항공 우주 전시회
W: Hi, I'd like to get tickets for the exhibition.
M: Sure. We have two options, a full-day ticket and a half-day ticket.
　　　　　　　　　　선택권들　　　전일 입장권　　　　　반일 입장권
W: I'll take the half-day ticket. How much is it?

M: It's $30 for adults and $20 for children. How many tickets do you
　need?
　필요하다
W: One adult and two children's tickets, please. I have a membership
　　　　　　　　　　　　　　　　　　　　　　　　　　　　회원 카드
　card. Do you offer a discount?
　　　　제공하다　　할인
M: Yes. Gold membership holders get 20% off the total, and silver
　　　　　　　　　　보유자들　　총액에서 20% 할인을 받다
　membership holders get 10% off the total.
W: Great. I have a silver membership.
M: Okay. May I have your membership card?
W: Here it is. And I'll be paying with cash.
　　　　　　　　　　　　　　　　현금

해석
남: 안녕하세요, 손님. 항공 우주 전시회에 오신 것을 환영합니다.
여: 안녕하세요, 전시회 입장권들을 사고 싶어요.
남: 알겠습니다. 두 가지 선택권이 있는데, 전일 입장권과 반일 입장권입니다.
여: 반일 입장권을 살게요. 얼마죠?
남: 어른은 30달러이고 어린이는 20달러입니다. 몇 장의 입장권이 필요하십니까?
여: 어른 한 장과 어린이 두 장 주세요. 저는 회원 카드를 가지고 있어요. 할인을 제공하시나요?
남: 네, 골드 회원등급 보유자들은 총액에서 20% 할인을 받고, 실버 회원등급 보유자들은 총액에서 10% 할인을 받으십니다.
여: 잘됐네요. 저는 실버 회원등급을 가지고 있어요.
남: 알겠습니다. 회원 카드를 주시겠습니까?
여: 여기 있어요. 그리고 현금으로 지불할게요.

① $40　　　　　② $45　　　　　③ $50
④ $56　　　　✔⑤ $63

문제 풀이
30달러인 어른 반일 입장권 한 장, 20달러인 어린이 반일 입장권 두 장을 사면 총액은 70달러가 된다. 실버 회원등급 보유자는 총액에서 10% 할인을 받을 수 있으므로 정답은 ⑤ '$63'가 된다.

07 남자가 Winter Sports Camp에 참가할 수 없는 이유

고1 2020년 9월 8번 | 정답률 80% | ▶ 정답 ⑤

W: James, check out the poster. It's about this year's Winter Sports
　　　　　~을 보다　　포스터　　　　　　　　　　　동계 스포츠 캠프
　Camp.
M: I remember we had a great time at last year's camp.
　　　기억나다
W: Yes, we did. Let's go to the camp together again.
M: I'm afraid I can't.
W: Why not? Do you still have ankle pain?
　　　　　　　　아직도　　발목　통증
M: I'm still taking my pills, but don't worry. I'm fine.
　　　　(약을) 먹는(take)　약들　　걱정하다
W: Ah, you must have another family trip scheduled.
　　　　　　　　　　　　가족 여행　　예정된
M: No, not this time. Actually, it's because of my science project.
　　　　　　　　　　　　　　　~ 때문에　　　과학 프로젝트
W: Haven't you finished it yet?
M: I've already handed in the final report for the project, but Mr. Miller
　　　　　　~을 제출한(hand in)　최종 보고서
　said that I have to participate in the National Science Contest with
　　　　　　　　　~에 참가하다　　　　　전국 과학 경시대회
　it.
W: That's great. You should definitely spend your whole winter
　　　　　　　　　　　　　　　　　　~을 준비하면서 네 겨울방학 전부를 보내다
　vacation preparing for it, then.
　　　　　　　　　(spend A (on) V-ing: ~하면서 A를 보내다,
M: I'm going to do my best. Have fun for me.　prepare for: ~을 준비하다)
　　　　　　최선을 다하다(do one's best)

해석
여: James, 포스터를 봐. 올해 Winter Sports Camp(동계 스포츠 캠프)에 관한 거야.
남: 우리가 작년 캠프에서 즐거운 시간을 보냈던 것이 기억난다.
여: 응, 그랬지. 다시 함께 캠프에 가자.
남: 유감스럽지만 안 될 것 같아.
여: 왜 안 돼? 아직도 발목 통증이 있니?
남: 아직도 약들을 먹고 있지만, 걱정하지마. 난 괜찮아.
여: 아, 예정된 다른 가족 여행이 있구나.
남: 아니, 이번에는 아니야. 사실, 과학 프로젝트 때문이야.
여: 아직 그것을 끝내지 못했니?
남: 프로젝트에 대한 최종 보고서는 이미 제출했는데, Miller 선생님께서 내가 그것을 가지고 전국 과학 경시대회에 참가해야 한다고 말씀하셨어.
여: 잘됐네. 그럼, 넌 분명 그것을 준비하면서 네 겨울방학 전부를 보내야겠구나.
남: 나는 최선을 다할 거야. 나 대신 즐겁게 보내.

①다른 캠프 일정과 겹쳐서

② 발목 통증이 낫지 않아서
③ 가족 여행이 예정되어 있어서
④ 과학 보고서를 제출하지 못해서
✓전국 과학 대회 참가를 준비해야 해서

08 Mind-Up Program에 관해 언급되지 않은 것
고1 2020년 9월 10번 | 정답률 85% ▶ 정답 ③

W: Hey, Sam. Have you heard about the Mind-Up Program?
M: No, I haven't. What is it?
W: It's a program for high school students. Its purpose is to encourage
us to build a positive mindset. You should come.
(encourage A to V: A가 ~하도록 장려하다)
M: It sounds interesting. Please tell me more about it.
W: There will be a lot of activities to help relieve stress. Also, we'll get
to listen to special lectures from successful young CEOs.
M: Awesome! I should sign up. When is it?
W: This Friday. It starts at 6 p.m.
M: Cool. How much is the admission fee?
W: It's free for all students. You can apply for the program on our
school website.
M: Great. I'll do it now.

해석
여: 이봐, Sam. Mind-Up Program에 대해 들어본 적이 있니?
남: 아니, 들어본 적 없어. 그것이 뭐니?
여: 고등학생들을 위한 프로그램이야. 그것의 목적은 우리가 긍정적인 사고방식을 형성하도록 장려하는 것이야. 너는 와야 해.
남: 흥미롭게 들린다. 그것에 대해 좀 더 말해줘.
여: 스트레스를 완화하는 데 도움이 되는 많은 활동들이 있을 거야. 또한, 우리는 성공한 젊은 CEO들의 특별 강연을 듣게 될 거야.
남: 멋지다! 신청해야겠어. 언제야?
여: 이번 주 금요일이야. 오후 6시에 시작해.
남: 좋아. 입장료는 얼마니?
여: 모든 학생들에게 무료야. 우리 학교 웹사이트에서 그 프로그램에 지원할 수 있어.
남: 좋아. 지금 할게.

① 목적　　　　② 특별 강연　　　✓개최 장소
④ 시작 시간　　⑤ 입장료

09 Plata Tea Festival에 관한 내용과 일치하지 않는 것
고1 2020년 9월 11번 | 정답률 85% ▶ 정답 ⑤

M: Hello, listeners. I'm Ted Potter, the manager of the Plata Community
Center. I'd like to tell you about the upcoming Plata Tea Festival.
It's an annual tea festival held at City Hall. This year it'll take
place on September 5th and 6th. More than 20 tea companies
will participate in this festival. During the festival, you can enjoy
blind tea tasting and food pairing events. Also, you can learn tea
etiquette from experts. The admission fee is $10 and children
under 5 enter for free. Reservations are not necessary. Come to
this festival and share a cup of tea with your friends and family.

해석
남: 안녕하세요, 청취자 여러분. 저는 Plata Community Center(Plata 주민 센터)의 관리자인 Ted Potter입니다. 여러분께 다가오는 Plata Tea Festival(Plata 차 축제)에 대해 알려드리고 싶습니다. 그것은 매년 시청에서 개최되는 차 축제입니다. 올해는 9월 5일과 6일에 열릴 것입니다. 20개가 넘는 차 회사들이 이 축제에 참여할 것입니다. 축제 기간 동안에, 블라인드 차 시음회와 푸드 페어링 행사들을 즐기실 수 있습니다. 또한, 여러분은 전문들로부터 차 예절도 배우실 수 있습니다. 입장료는 10달러이며 5세 미만 어린이들은 무료로 입장할 수 있습니다. 예약은 필요하지 않습니다. 친구들과 가족과 함께 이 축제에 오셔서 한 잔의 차를 나누세요.

① 시청에서 개최되는 행사이다.
② 20개가 넘는 차 회사가 참여할 것이다.
③ 전문가로부터 차 예절을 배울 수 있다.
④ 5세 미만 어린이의 입장료는 무료이다.
✓예약을 해야만 참가할 수 있다.

10 표에서 여자가 구입할 휴대용 선풍기
고1 2020년 9월 12번 | 정답률 90% ▶ 정답 ③

M: Julie, what are you looking at?
W: I'm thinking of buying a new handheld fan. Can you help me pick
one?
M: Sure. Hmm, how about this one?
W: It looks good, but I don't want to spend more than $30.
M: Okay. And I think you should get one with a battery that lasts more
than 8 hours.
W: I think so, too. I usually spend more than 8 hours outside.
M: What about the fan speed levels? Do you need a fan with 4 levels?
W: No. Three levels will be enough for me.
M: Then you have two models left. I recommend the foldable one.
W: What's special about it?
M: If you fold the handle, it'll easily fit into your handbag. It can also
stand up on your desk.
W: That sounds convenient. I'll buy that one.

해석
남: Julie, 무엇을 보고 있니?
여: 나는 새 휴대용 선풍기를 살까 생각 중이야. 하나 고르는 것을 도와줄래?
남: 물론이지. 흠, 이것은 어때?
여: 좋아 보이지만, 나는 30달러 이상을 쓰고 싶지 않아.
남: 알았어. 그리고 너는 8시간 이상 지속되는 배터리가 있는 것을 사야 할 것 같아.
여: 나도 그렇게 생각해. 나는 보통 밖에서 8시간 이상을 보내거든.
남: 선풍기 속도 단계는 어때? 4단계가 있는 선풍기가 필요하니?
여: 아니. 내게 3단계면 충분할 거야.
남: 그럼 두 개의 모델이 남았어. 나는 접이식 모델을 추천해.
여: 그것은 무엇이 특별한데?
남: 손잡이를 접으면, 네 핸드백에 쉽게 들어갈 거야. 그것은 또한 책상 위에 세워져 있을 수도 있어.
여: 그거 편리할 것 같아. 그것을 살게.

휴대용 선풍기

	모델	가격	배터리 지속 시간	선풍기 속도 단계	접이식
①	A	20달러	6시간	2	X
②	B	23달러	9시간	3	X
✓③	C	25달러	9시간	3	O
④	D	28달러	12시간	4	O
⑤	E	33달러	12시간	4	O

11 여자의 마지막 말에 대한 남자의 응답
고1 2020년 9월 1번 | 정답률 80% ▶ 정답 ⑤

W: Did you hear that Golden Bookstore will hold a book signing event
for Lora Johnson?
M: Oh, she is one of my favorite writers. I've read all of her novels.
When is it?
W: This Sunday afternoon. Do you want to come with me?
M: (Yes. I can't believe I'm going to see her in person.)

해석
여: Golden Bookstore(Golden 서점)에서 Lora Johnson의 책 사인회를 개최할 것이라는 소식을 들었니?
남: 오, 그녀는 내가 가장 좋아하는 작가들 중 한 명이야. 나는 그녀의 소설들을 모두 읽었어. 그것은 언제니?
여: 이번 주 일요일 오후야. 나와 함께 갈래?

남: (응. 그녀를 직접 만나게 될 거라는 게 믿어지지가 않아.)

① 정말? 나는 그녀를 만나야 했어.

② 말도 안 돼. 나는 네가 많이 그리울 거야.

③ 아니. 나는 그날 서점에 가지 않았어.

④ 미안해. 나는 그녀의 글에 관심이 없어.

✓응. 그녀를 직접 만나게 될 거라는 게 믿어지지가 않아.

---

12 남자의 마지막 말에 대한 여자의 응답

▶ 정답 ①

M: Jane, are you almost done setting up your drone?
거의   설치하는 것(set up)   드론

W: Not yet. I'm having a hard time understanding the instructions.
이해하는 데 어려움을 겪는   사용 설명서
(have a hard time V-ing: ~하는 데 어려움을 겪다)

M: Watching some video clips might be helpful. I'm sure you'll find
동영상들   도움이 되는
some showing you how to do it.
하는 방법(how to V: ~하는 방법)

W: (Good idea! I'll look for some videos online.)
~을 찾다

해석

남: Jane, 드론을 설치하는 것을 거의 다 했니?

여: 아직이야. 나는 사용 설명서를 이해하는 데 어려움을 겪고 있어.

남: 동영상들을 좀 보는 것이 도움이 될지도 몰라. 나는 네가 그것을 하는 방법을 보여주는 것들을 찾을 수 있을 거라고 확신해.

여: (좋은 생각이야! 온라인으로 동영상들을 좀 찾아볼게.)

✓①좋은 생각이야! 온라인으로 동영상들을 좀 찾아볼게.

②잘됐다! 나에게 동영상 만드는 방법을 가르쳐줘.

③와! 너는 드론을 잘 조종하는구나.

④좋아. 함께 새 드론을 사러 가자.

⑤맞아. 나는 사용 설명서를 읽어야 해.

---

13 여자의 마지막 말에 대한 남자의 응답

▶ 정답 ④

W: Hi, Andrew. I heard that your tennis club is competing in the City
참가할 것이다(compete)
Tennis Tournament.
시 테니스 대회

M: Yes. We've been practicing a lot these days.
연습하는(practice)   요즘에

W: I'm sure you'll do well.

M: Thanks. But our school tennis court is going to be under construction
테니스장   공사 중이다
starting next week, so we won't have a place to practice.
장소

W: What about the community center? It has several tennis courts.
주민 센터   여러 개의

M: We already checked. But all the courts are fully booked.
이미   확인했다   예약된(book: 예약하다)

W: That's too bad. Oh, wait! My sister told me her school tennis courts
would be open to the public starting this Saturday.
일반인에게 개방되다

M: Really? That's great news. Do I need a reservation?
예약

W: Yes. I remember she said that reservations would start at 9 a.m.
기억나다
tomorrow.

M: (I hope I can reserve a court to continue practicing.)
예약하다   (continue V-ing: 계속해서 ~하다)

해석

여: 안녕, Andrew. 네 테니스 클럽이 시 테니스 대회에 참가할 것이라고 들었어.

남: 맞아. 우리는 요즘에 연습을 많이 하고 있어.

여: 나는 네가 잘할 거라고 확신해.

남: 고마워. 하지만 다음 주부터 우리 학교 테니스장이 공사 중일 예정이라서, 우리는 연습할 장소가 없을 거야.

여: 주민 센터는 어때니? 그곳엔 여러 개의 테니스장이 있잖아.

남: 이미 확인했어. 그런데 모든 경기장이 예약이 꽉 찼어.

여: 그거 안됐다. 오, 잠깐! 내 여동생이 이번 주 토요일부터 그녀의 학교 테니스장이 일반인에게 개방될 것이라고 말했어.

남: 정말? 그거 좋은 소식이다. 예약이 필요하니?

여: 응. 내 여동생이 예약은 내일 오전 9시에 시작할 것이라고 말했던 기억이 나.

남: (내가 계속해서 연습할 수 있도록 경기장을 예약할 수 있으면 좋겠어.)

①네 여동생은 그것들을 예약하는 데 어려움을 겪었어.

②공사가 곧 끝날 것이라고 확신해.

③주민 센터는 내일 이용할 수 있을 거야.

✓④내가 계속해서 연습할 수 있도록 경기장을 예약할 수 있으면 좋겠어.

⑤그들은 우리가 체육관에서 연습하는 것을 허락하지 않을 것 같아.

---

14 남자의 마지막 말에 대한 여자의 응답

▶ 정답 ②

W: Hey, Minho. What are you doing?

M: Hi, Mrs. Sharon. I'm writing an application letter for college.
지원서

W: Can I take a look at it?
~을 보다

M: Of course. Please give me some advice after you're finished
조언
reading it.

W: Hmm.... You only listed the activities you've done without being
열거했다(list)   활동들   구체적으로 밝히지 않고
specific.
(without V-ing: ~하지 않고, specific: 구체적인)

M: Yeah. Isn't it good to include as many activities as possible?
포함하다   가능한 한 많은 활동들
(as A as possible: 가능한 한 A한/하게)

W: No. If you do that, your application letter won't be memorable.
기억에 남는

M: But I thought if I wrote down a lot of activities, I would stand out.
~을 적었다(write down)   돋보이다

W: It's actually the opposite. You should focus on a few things and
사실   반대   ~에 집중하다
write about them in detail.
상세하게

M: I never thought about that. Do you really think it'll work?
효과가 있다

W: (Of course. The more specific, the better.)

해석

여: 안녕, Minho. 무엇을 하고 있니?

남: 안녕하세요, Sharon 선생님. 대학 지원서를 쓰고 있어요.

여: 내가 봐도 될까?

남: 물론이죠. 그것을 다 읽으신 후에 저에게 조언을 좀 해 주세요.

여: 흠.... 너는 구체적으로 밝히지 않고 네가 한 활동들을 열거하기만 했구나.

남: 네. 가능한 한 많은 활동들을 포함하는 것이 좋지 않나요?

여: 아니. 그렇게 하면, 네 지원서는 기억에 남지 않을 거야.

남: 하지만 저는 많은 활동들을 적으면, 제가 돋보일 것이라고 생각했어요.

여: 사실 그 반대야. 몇 가지 일들에 집중해서 그것들에 대해 상세하게 써야 해.

남: 저는 그것에 대해 생각하지 못했어요. 정말 그것이 효과가 있을 것이라고 생각하세요?

여: (당연하지. 더 구체적일수록, 더 좋단다.)

①물론이지. 가능한 한 많은 활동들을 쓰렴.

✓②당연하지. 더 구체적일수록, 더 좋단다.

③고맙구나. 하지만 이번에는 내 방식대로 할 거란다.

④잘됐다. 네가 드디어 대학에 합격했구나.

⑤맞아. 선착순이란다.

문제 풀이

대학 지원서에 많은 활동 내역을 단순히 열거하는 대신 몇 가지에 집중해서 상세하게 적으라고 조언하는 여자의 말에 남자는 그것이 효과가 있을지 묻고 있다. 따라서 여자의 답변으로는 ② 'Of course. The more specific, the better.(당연하지. 더 구체적일수록, 더 좋단다.)'가 가장 적절하다.

---

15 다음 상황에서 Cathy가 Brian에게 할 말

▶ 정답 ⑤

M: Cathy and Brian are members of the same orchestra. They are
단원들   오케스트라
practicing together for the upcoming concert. Lately, Brian doesn't
연습하고 있다(practice)   다가오는   최근에
look so good and seems to be unable to concentrate during
~해 보이다   집중하지 못하다
(be unable to V: ~하지 못하다, concentrate: 집중하다)
practice. When Cathy asks why, he tells her that it's because of
~ 때문에
his back pain. He sits for long periods of time preparing for the
요통   오랫동안   ~을 준비하면서(prepare for)
concert, so his back hurts. Cathy understands his pain because
아프다   통증
she had the same problem last year. However, after she started
문제
yoga, her back pain disappeared. She wants to suggest to Brian
요가   사라졌다(disappear)
that he start yoga. In this situation, what would Cathy most likely
say to Brian?

Cathy: (Why don't you try yoga for your back pain?)
~하는 게 어때?

해석

남: Cathy와 Brian은 같은 오케스트라의 단원들이다. 그들은 다가오는 연주회를 위해 함께 연습하고 있다. 최근에, Brian은 안색이 좋아 보이지 않고 연습 동안에 집중하지 못하는 것처럼 보인다. Cathy가 이유를 묻자, 그는 그녀에게 그것은 그의 요통 때문이라고 말한다. 그는 연주회를 준비하면서 오랫동안 앉아 있기 때문에, 허리가 아프다. Cathy는 작년에 같은 문제를 겪었기 때문에 그의 통증을 이해한다. 하지만, 그녀가 요가를 시작한 후에, 그녀의 요통이 사라졌다. 그녀는 Brian에게 요가를 시작하라고 제안하고 싶다. 이러한 상황에서, Cathy는 Brian에게 뭐라고 말하겠는가?

Cathy: (네 요통을 위해 요가를 해 보는 게 어때?)

① 내가 너에게 연주를 더 잘하는 방법을 알려줄게.
② 너는 방과 후에 연습을 더 해야 해.
③ 나와 함께 연주회에 갈래?
④ 너는 의사의 지시를 따라야 해.
☑ 네 요통을 위해 요가를 해 보는 게 어때?

16~17 1지문 2문항

W: Hello, class! Last time we learned about LED technology. I hope all
of you have a clear idea of what an LED is now. Today, I'll talk about
how LEDs make our lives better. First, one of the advantages of
LEDs is the long lifespan. LED bulbs are used in lamps and last for
over 17 years before you need to change them. Second, LEDs use
very low amounts of power. For example, a television using LEDs
in its backlight saves a lot of energy. Next, LEDs are brighter than
traditional bulbs. So, they make traffic lights more visible in foggy
conditions. Finally, thanks to their small size, LEDs can be used in
various small devices. Any light you see on a computer keyboard is
an LED light. Now, let's think about other products that use LEDs.

해석

여: 안녕하세요, 학생 여러분! 지난 시간에 우리는 LED(Light-Emitting Diode, 발광 다이오드) 기술에 대해 배웠습니다. 저는 이제 여러분 모두가 LED가 무엇인지 확실히 알고 있기를 바랍니다. 오늘은, LED가 어떻게 우리의 삶을 더 좋게 만드는지에 대해 얘기하겠습니다. 첫째, LED의 장점 중 하나는 긴 수명입니다. LED 전구들은 전등들에 사용되며 그것들을 교체해야 하기 전까지 17년 이상 동안 지속됩니다. 둘째, LED는 매우 적은 양의 전력을 사용합니다. 예를 들어, 배면광에 LED를 사용하는 텔레비전은 많은 에너지를 절약합니다. 다음으로, LED는 전통적인 전구들보다 더 밝습니다. 그래서, 그것들은 안개가 낀 기상 상태에서 신호등이 눈에 더 잘 띄게 합니다. 마지막으로, 그것들의 작은 크기 덕분에, LED는 다양한 작은 장치들에 사용될 수 있습니다. 여러분이 컴퓨터 키보드에서 보는 모든 불빛은 LED 불빛입니다. 이제, LED를 사용하는 다른 제품들에 대해 생각해봅시다.

16 여자가 하는 말의 주제
고1 2020년 9월 16번 | 정답률 80% | ▶ 정답 ①

☑ LED 사용의 장점들
② LED가 발명된 방식
③ LED에 대한 오해들
④ LED 시장에서의 경쟁
⑤ LED 기술을 발전시키는 방법들

17 언급된 물건이 아닌 것
고1 2020년 9월 17번 | 정답률 90% | ▶ 정답 ②

① 전등   ☑ 시계   ③ 텔레비전
④ 신호등   ⑤ 컴퓨터 키보드

09 2020년 11월 학력평가

01	②	02	①	03	②	04	③	05	③
06	③	07	②	08	⑤	09	②	10	④
11	⑤	12	④	13	①	14	⑤	15	③
16	④	17	④								

01 남자가 하는 말의 목적
정답률 90% | ▶ 정답 ②

M: Hello, welcome to Fun Bike Touring. I'm Harry Wilson, your tour
guide. Before starting the tour, let me tell you the safety rules.
First, always keep your helmet on. Wearing a helmet protects you
from serious injuries in case of an accident. Second, you should
use bicycle-only lanes. If you ride out of the lane, there is a chance
that you could be hit by a car. Lastly, don't use your cell phone
while riding. Taking pictures or talking on the phone while riding
can be really dangerous to you and others. Now, are you ready to
start? Let's go!

해석

남: 안녕하세요, Fun Bike Touring에 오신 것을 환영합니다. 저는 여러분의 투어 가이드인 Harry Wilson입니다. 투어를 시작하기 전에, 안전 규칙들을 알려드리겠습니다. 첫째, 항상 헬멧을 착용하고 있으십시오. 헬멧을 착용하는 것은 사고가 발생할 시에 심각한 부상들로부터 여러분을 보호해 줍니다. 둘째, 여러분은 자전거 전용 도로를 이용해야 합니다. 도로를 벗어나서 자전거를 타면, 차에 치일 가능성이 있습니다. 마지막으로, 자전거를 타면서 휴대전화를 사용하지 마십시오. 자전거를 타면서 사진을 찍거나 전화 통화를 하는 것은 여러분과 다른 사람들에게 정말 위험할 수 있습니다. 이제, 출발할 준비가 되셨나요? 가시죠!

① 교통사고 발생 시 대처 요령을 안내하려고
☑ 자전거 투어 시 안전 규칙을 설명하려고
③ 자전거 전용 도로 확충을 요청하려고
④ 단체 관광 일정 변경을 공지하려고
⑤ 자전거 대회 참가를 독려하려고

02 여자의 의견
정답률 90% | ▶ 정답 ①

M: Good morning, Rosa.
W: Hi, Tony. You look tired. Are you all right?
M: Yeah, I'm okay. I'm just having a hard time falling asleep these
days.
W: Why? Are you worried about something?
M: No. Since I started exercising late at night, it's been hard to fall
asleep.
W: What time do you exercise?
M: I usually go to the gym around 10 p.m. When I come back, it's
almost midnight.
W: Hmm, I think that's why you can't sleep well.
M: Really?
W: As far as I know, when you exercise, your heart rate and temperature
go up, which makes you stay awake. These can disturb your sleep.
M: Oh, that makes sense.
W: So, it's not a good idea to exercise right before going to bed.
M: I'll keep that in mind. Thanks for your advice.

해석
남: 안녕, Rosa.
여: 안녕, Tony. 너 피곤해 보인다. 괜찮니?
남: 그래, 괜찮아. 단지 요즘에 잠드는 데 힘든 시간을 보내고 있어.
여: 왜? 무슨 걱정이라도 있니?
남: 아니. 밤늦게 운동하기 시작한 이후로, 잠들기가 힘들어.
여: 몇 시에 운동하니?
남: 보통 밤 10시쯤에 체육관에 가. 돌아오면, 거의 자정이지.
여: 흠, 그것이 네가 잠을 잘 못 자는 이유인 것 같아.
남: 정말?
여: 내가 알기로는, 운동할 때, 심박수와 체온이 올라가는데, 그것이 너를 깨어 있게 만드는 거야. 이것들은 너의 수면을 방해할 수 있어.
남: 오, 그거 일리가 있네.
여: 그래서, 잠들기 직전에 운동하는 것은 좋은 생각이 아니야.
남: 그것을 명심할게. 조언해 줘서 고마워.
☑잠들기 직전의 운동은 수면을 방해할 수 있다.
②운동은 규칙적으로 하는 것이 효과적이다.
③과격한 운동은 심장에 무리를 줄 수 있다.
④충분한 수면은 건강 관리에 도움이 된다.
⑤지나친 스트레스는 건강을 해친다.

문제 풀이
여자는 운동할 때 상승하는 심박수와 체온이 신체를 깨어 있게 만들어 수면을 방해할 수 있음을 알려주면서 밤늦게 운동을 하는 남자에게 잠들기 직전에 하는 운동은 좋지 않다고 말하고 있다. 따라서 여자의 의견으로 적절한 것은 ① '잠들기 직전의 운동은 수면을 방해할 수 있다'이다.

03 두 사람의 관계

정답률 90%
▶ 정답 ②

[Door knocks.]
W: Hello, Mr. Cooper. Come on in. Have a seat, please.
M: Thank you.
W: You came here last week <u>because of</u> a <u>sunburn</u>. How are the
   <u>symptoms</u> now?
M: Much better.
W: Great. Let me <u>look at</u> the sunburn. [Pause] The <u>redness</u> is <u>almost</u>
   gone.
M: Yeah. The cream you <u>prescribed</u> was really <u>helpful</u>.
W: Good. Do you <u>still</u> have any <u>pain</u>?
M: Not anymore.
W: I'm glad to hear that. If you <u>put the cream on</u> for a few days more,
   your <u>skin</u> will <u>completely recover</u>.
M: Okay. But I don't have any more cream. Could you write me
   another <u>prescription</u>?
W: Sure. [Typing sound] If you have any <u>problems</u>, please come back.
M: Thank you.

해석
[문을 노크하는 소리]
여: 안녕하세요, Cooper 씨. 어서 들어오세요. 앉으세요.
남: 감사합니다.
여: 지난주에 일광화상 때문에 여기에 오셨죠. 지금 증상들은 어떤가요?
남: 훨씬 나아졌어요.
여: 잘됐네요. 제가 일광화상을 볼게요. [잠시 후] 홍조는 거의 없어졌네요.
남: 네. 처방해 주신 크림이 정말 도움이 되었어요.
여: 다행이네요. 아직도 통증이 있나요?
남: 이제 없어요.
여: 그 말을 들으니 기쁘네요. 며칠 더 크림을 바르면, 피부가 완전히 회복될 거예요.
남: 좋아요. 하지만 크림이 더는 없어요. 처방전을 한 장 더 써 주시겠어요?
여: 물론이죠. [타자치는 소리] 문제가 있으면, 다시 오세요.
남: 감사합니다.
①구급 대원 ― 간호사
☑피부과 의사 ― 환자
③화장품 판매원 ― 손님
④제약 회사 직원 ― 약사

⑤물리 치료사 ― 운동선수

04 그림에서 대화의 내용과 일치하지 않는 것

정답률 80%
▶ 정답 ③

M: Hi, Claire. What did you do yesterday?
W: Hi, Henry. I <u>set up</u> an <u>exercise room</u> in my house. Look at this
   <u>picture</u>.
M: Cool! The <u>indoor bike</u> under the clock looks nice.
W: Thanks. I bought the bike <u>a few days ago</u>.
M: Good. Is that a <u>hula-hoop</u> under the <u>calendar</u>?
W: Yes. I <u>exercise</u> with it for 30 minutes every day. What do you think
   of the <u>mat</u> with the <u>flower pattern</u> on the floor?
M: I love it. <u>By the way</u>, what's the big ball next to the door?
W: It's a <u>gym ball</u>. I use it for <u>back stretches</u>.
M: Good. Oh, I know that T-shirt on the wall.
W: Yeah. It's from the <u>marathon</u> we <u>ran</u> together.
M: Great. It <u>matches well</u> with your room.
W: Thanks. Next time, come over and we'll exercise together.

해석
남: 안녕, Claire. 어제 무엇을 했니?
여: 안녕, Henry. 나는 집에 운동실을 마련했어. 이 사진을 봐.
남: 멋진데! 시계 아래의 실내 자전거가 좋아 보인다.
여: 고마워. 나는 며칠 전에 그 자전거를 샀어.
남: 잘했어. 달력 아래에 있는 것은 훌라후프니?
여: 응. 나는 매일 30분 동안 그것으로 운동해. 바닥에 있는 꽃무늬가 있는 매트에 대해 어떻게 생각하니?
남: 정말 마음에 들어. 그런데, 문 옆에 있는 큰 공은 뭐야?
여: 그것은 짐볼이야. 나는 그것을 허리 스트레칭을 위해 사용해.
남: 좋아. 오, 나는 벽에 걸린 저 티셔츠를 알아.
여: 그래. 우리가 함께 달렸던 마라톤에서 받은 거야.
남: 멋지다. 네 방과 잘 어울려.
여: 고마워. 다음에는, 와서 같이 운동하자.

05 여자가 할 일

정답률 85%
▶ 정답 ③

W: Simon, I think we're <u>ready for</u> the <u>fundraising event</u>.
M: Right. Let's <u>do one last check</u>.
W: Okay. We're going to <u>play a short video clip</u> for the event. Is the
   screen <u>working</u>?
M: Yes. I checked the screen and there's no <u>problem</u> at all.
W: Great. <u>What about</u> the <u>speakers</u>?
M: I already <u>tried using</u> them, and they worked fine. Did you bring the
   <u>donation box</u>?
W: Yes. Look. I made it <u>by myself</u>.
M: Wow! It looks nice.
W: Thanks. All the <u>items</u> we're going to sell are nicely <u>set up</u> on the
   table.

M: Okay. The only thing left is to put the price tags on. I'll do that later
남은(leave)　　　　　　　　가격표들을 붙이다　　　　　　　　나중에
(put A on: A를 붙이다, price tag: 가격표)
because I have to go to my part-time job now.
아르바이트

W: Oh, don't worry. I'll put the price tags on.

M: Really? Thanks.

해석

여: Simon, 우리는 모금 행사를 위한 준비가 된 것 같아.

남: 그래. 마지막으로 한 번 더 확인해 보자.

여: 좋아. 우리는 행사를 위해 짧은 동영상을 보여줄 거야. 화면이 작동하고 있니?

남: 응. 화면을 확인했는데 전혀 문제가 없어.

여: 좋아. 스피커는 어때?

남: 내가 이미 사용해 봤는데, 잘 작동했어. 너는 모금함을 가져왔니?

여: 그래. 봐. 내가 그것을 혼자 힘으로 만들었어.

남: 와! 멋져 보여.

여: 고마워. 우리가 판매할 모든 물품들은 테이블 위에 잘 배치되어 있어.

남: 좋아. 남은 유일한 일은 가격표를 붙이는 거야. 나는 지금 아르바이트를 가야 하기 때문에
나중에 그것을 할게.

여: 오, 걱정하지 마. 내가 가격표를 붙일게.

남: 정말? 고마워.

① 모금함 만들기
② 물품 배치하기
✓ 가격표 붙이기
④ 스피커 점검하기
⑤ 동영상 제작하기

06 남자가 지불할 금액 　　　정답률 80%　　▶ 정답 ③

M: Good afternoon.

W: Hello. Welcome to Happy Pet World. How can I help you?

M: I'm looking for a cushion for my dog.
　　~을 찾는(look for)　　쿠션

W: Okay, how about these? These are the most popular models.
　　~은 어떠세요?　　　　　　　　　　　　인기 있는

M: The pink one looks cute. How much is it?

W: Originally, it was $40. But due to a special promotion, you can get
원래　　　　　　　　　　~때문에　　특별 판촉 활동
a 10 percent discount on cushions.
10% 할인을 받다

M: Great. I'll buy one cushion, then.

W: Sure. Anything else?

M: Do you have dog biscuits?
개 먹이용 비스킷들

W: Of course. They're right over here. Each box of biscuits is $5.

M: I'll buy two boxes of biscuits. Do I get a discount on the biscuits,
too?

W: I'm sorry. We don't offer a discount on biscuits.
제공하다

M: Okay, then. Here's my credit card.
신용카드

해석

남: 안녕하세요.

여: 안녕하세요. Happy Pet World에 오신 것을 환영합니다. 어떻게 도와드릴까요?

남: 저는 제 강아지를 위한 쿠션을 찾고 있어요.

여: 알겠습니다, 이것들은 어떠세요? 가장 인기 있는 모델들이에요.

남: 분홍색이 귀여워 보이네요. 얼마죠?

여: 원래, 40달러였어요. 그런데 특별 판촉 활동 때문에, 쿠션에 10% 할인을 받으실 수 있
어요.

남: 잘됐네요. 그럼 쿠션 한 개를 살게요.

여: 알겠습니다. 그밖에 다른 필요한 것이 있으세요?

남: 개 먹이용 비스킷이 있나요?

여: 물론이죠. 바로 이쪽에 있습니다. 비스킷 한 상자당 5달러예요.

남: 비스킷 두 상자를 살게요. 비스킷도 할인을 받나요?

여: 죄송합니다. 비스킷에는 할인을 제공하지 않아요.

남: 알겠어요, 그럼. 여기 제 신용카드가 있어요.

① $41　　　　　② $45　　　　　✓ $46
④ $50　　　　　⑤ $54

문제 풀이

원래 가격이 40달러인 쿠션은 10% 할인을 받을 수 있으므로 36달러이다. 한 상자에 5달러
인 비스킷은 할인이 되지 않는다. 따라서 쿠션 한 개와 비스킷 두 상자를 사면 총액은 46달러

이므로 답은 ③ '$46'이다.

07 남자가 학생 패션쇼에 갈 수 없는 이유 　　정답률 90%　　▶ 정답 ②

[Cell phone rings.]

W: Hello.

M: Hi, Linda. Did you call me earlier? I was in my book club meeting.
　　　　　　　　　전화하다　　　　　　　　　독서 동아리 모임
What's up?

W: I called you to make sure you can come to the student fashion
　　　　　　　　　확인하다　　　　　　　　　　　학생 패션쇼
show. The schedule has changed.
일정

M: Really? When is the show now?

W: It has changed to 6 p.m. next Friday. The place we were going to
　　　　　　　　　　　　　　　　　　　　　장소
use is being repaired this week.
수리될 예정이다(repair: 수리하다)

M: I see. I'm afraid I can't go then.
그때

W: Oh, didn't you say you're going to a concert next Friday?
콘서트

M: No, that's next Saturday.

W: Then, why can't you come?

M: It's my mom's birthday. So, I'm going to have dinner with my family.
~와 저녁 식사를 하다

W: Oh, I understand. Have a good time.

M: Thanks.

해석

[휴대전화가 울린다.]

여: 여보세요.

남: 안녕, Linda. 아까 전화했니? 나는 독서 동아리 모임에 있었어. 무슨 일이야?

여: 네가 학생 패션쇼에 올 수 있는지 확인하려고 전화했어. 일정이 변경되었거든.

남: 정말? 그럼 쇼는 언제야?

여: 다음 주 금요일 오후 6시로 바뀌었어. 우리가 사용하려던 장소가 이번 주에 수리될 예정
이거든.

남: 그렇구나. 나는 그때 못 갈 것 같아.

여: 오, 너는 다음 주 금요일에 콘서트에 갈 거라고 말하지 않았니?

남: 아니, 그것은 다음 주 토요일이야.

여: 그럼, 왜 못 오니?

남: 엄마 생신이야. 그래서, 가족들과 저녁 식사를 할 거야.

여: 오, 알겠어. 즐거운 시간 보내.

남: 고마워.

① 친구 생일 선물을 사야 해서
✓ 가족과 식사를 하기로 해서
③ 집수리를 도와줘야 해서
④ 회의에 참석해야 해서
⑤ 콘서트에 가기로 해서

08 World Dinosaur Exhibition에 관해 언급되지 않은 것 　정답률 90%　▶ 정답 ⑤

M: Honey, what are you reading?

W: Look at this article. There will be a World Dinosaur Exhibition this
기사　　　　　　　　　　　　세계 공룡 전시회
Saturday. Why don't we bring the kids?
우리 ~하는 게 어때요?

M: That sounds great! Where's the exhibition held?

W: At the Redstone Science Museum.　　　열린(hold: 열다)
과학 박물관

M: Good. I know where that is.

W: There are fun programs for children like making dinosaur toys and
재미있는　　　　　　　　　　　　　　　　　　　　장난감들
watching a 3D dinosaur movie.
영화

M: Our kids will love them. What time shall we go?

W: Since the exhibition runs from 10 a.m. to 5 p.m., how about going
운영되다　　　　　　　　　　　　　~하는 게 어때요?
there in the afternoon?

M: Okay. How much is the admission fee?
입장료

W: It's $10 for an adult and $5 for a child and if we register online, we
등록하다
can get a discount.
할인을 받다

M: Really? Let's register now.

W: Okay.

해석

남: 여보, 무엇을 읽고 있어요?

여: 이 기사를 봐요. 이번 주 토요일에 World Dinosaur Exhibition(세계 공룡 전시회)이 열릴 거예요. 우리 아이들을 데려가는 게 어때요?

남: 좋을 것 같아요! 전시회가 어디에서 열려요?

여: Redstone Science Museum(Redstone 과학 박물관)이요.

남: 좋아요. 저는 그곳이 어디에 있는지 알아요.

여: 공룡 장난감 만들기와 3D 공룡 영화 관람하기와 같은 아이들을 위한 재미있는 프로그램들이 있네요.

남: 우리 아이들은 그것들을 정말 좋아할 거예요. 몇 시에 갈까요?

여: 전시회가 오전 10시부터 오후 5시까지 운영되니까, 오후에 가는 게 어때요?

남: 좋아요. 입장료는 얼마죠?

여: 어른은 10달러이고 어린이는 5달러인데 온라인으로 등록하면 할인을 받을 수 있어요.

남: 정말이에요? 지금 등록합시다.

여: 좋아요.

① 장소　　　　② 프로그램　　　　③ 운영 시간

④ 입장료　　　✓교통편

---

09 Greenville Animation Film Festival에 관한 내용과 일치하지 않는 것 ▶ 정답 ⑤

정답률 85%

W: Hello, listeners! Are you excited for the Greenville Animation Film
애니메이션 영화 축제
Festival? This festival, one of Greenville's largest events, began
행사들　　시작되었다(begin)
in 1995. This year, it'll start on December 5th and continue for
계속되다
one week. The theme for this year is friendship. Throughout the
주제　　　　　우정
festival, visitors can watch different animation movies related to
방문객들　　다양한　　　　　　　　　　　　과 관련한
the theme every night. The movie schedule will be posted on our
일정　　　게시되다(post: 게시하다)
website. Remember, there's no parking lot nearby. So, please use
기억하다　　　　주차장　　근처에
public transportation. For more information, visit www.GAFF.com.
대중교통　　　　　　정보
Thank you.

해석

여: 안녕하세요, 청취자 여러분! Greenville Animation Film Festival(Greenville 애니메이션 영화 축제)에 들떠 있으신가요? Greenville의 가장 큰 행사들 중 하나인 이 축제는 1995년에 시작되었습니다. 올해는, 12월 5일에 시작해서 일주일 동안 계속될 것입니다. 올해의 주제는 우정입니다. 축제 기간 내내, 방문객들은 매일 밤 주제와 관련된 다양한 애니메이션 영화들을 볼 수 있습니다. 영화 일정은 저희 웹사이트에 게시될 것입니다. 기억하세요, 근처에 주차장이 없습니다. 그러므로, 대중교통을 이용해 주세요. 더 많은 정보를 원하시면, www.GAFF.com을 방문해 주세요. 감사합니다.

① 1995년에 시작된 행사이다.

② 일주일 동안 열린다.

③ 올해의 주제는 우정이다.

④ 영화 스케줄은 웹사이트에 게시될 것이다.

✓근처에 주차장이 있다.

---

10 표에서 여자가 등록할 그리기 강좌 ▶ 정답 ④

정답률 70%

M: Jane, what are you doing?

W: Dad, I'm searching for a one-day drawing lesson, but it's not easy
일일 그리기 강좌　　　　　　　쉬운
to choose one. Can you help me?
선택하다

M: Sure. Is there any particular drawing material you want to use?
특별한　　　　　재료

W: I've done pastel drawing before. So, this time I want to try a new
파스텔화　　　　　　　　　　　사용해 보다
material, not pastel.

M: Okay. Do you want to have a private lesson?
개인의

W: No, I want to learn in a group.
배우다　　그룹으로

M: Okay. You have piano lessons Monday mornings, right?

W: Yes. So I should choose a lesson on Wednesday or Friday.

M: That leaves you two choices.
남기다　　　선택들

W: Let me think. [Pause] I'd rather take a lesson in the morning.

M: There's only one left then.

W: Yes. I'll register for that lesson. Thank you, Dad.
등록하다

해석

남: Jane, 무엇을 하고 있니?

여: 아빠, 저는 일일 그리기 강좌를 찾고 있는데, 선택하기가 쉽지 않아요. 저를 도와주실래요?

남: 물론이지. 사용하고 싶은 어떤 특별한 그리기 재료가 있니?

여: 저는 전에 파스텔화를 그려본 적이 있어요. 그래서, 이번에는 파스텔이 아닌 새로운 재료를 사용해 보고 싶어요.

남: 알겠어. 개인 강좌를 듣고 싶니?

여: 아니요, 그룹으로 배우고 싶어요.

남: 알겠어. 너는 월요일 오전에 피아노 강좌가 있지, 그렇지?

여: 네. 그래서 수요일이나 금요일에 있는 강좌를 선택해야 해요.

남: 두 가지 선택지가 남았구나.

여: 생각해 볼게요. [잠시 후] 저는 오전에 강좌를 듣고 싶어요.

남: 그럼 한 가지만 남았어.

여: 네. 저는 그 강좌에 등록할 거예요. 고마워요, 아빠.

일일 그리기 강좌

	수업	재료	강좌 유형	요일	시간
①	A	유화 물감	그룹	월요일	오전 11시
②	B	아크릴 물감	개인	수요일	오전 11시
③	C	크레용	그룹	수요일	오후 6시
✓ D	D	색연필	그룹	금요일	오전 11시
⑤	E	파스텔	개인	금요일	오후 6시

---

11 남자의 마지막 말에 대한 여자의 응답 ▶ 정답 ⑤

정답률 90%

M: Emma, it smells good in here. What's that you're cooking?
좋은 냄새가 나다　　　　　　　　　　요리하는(cook)

W: I cooked some *Bulgogi*. Try some.
먹어 보다

M: Okay. Wow, it's really delicious. Where did you get the recipe?
맛있는　　　　　　　조리법

W: (I got the recipe from the Internet.)

해석

남: Emma, 여기에서 좋은 냄새가 나. 무엇을 요리하고 있니?

여: '불고기'를 요리했어. 좀 먹어 봐.

남: 알겠어. 와, 정말 맛있다. 조리법은 어디에서 구했어?

여: (나는 인터넷에서 조리법을 구했어.)

① '불고기'는 이미 품절되었어.

② 너는 무엇을 먹을지 선택할 수 있어.

③ 우리는 식당에서 만날 거야.

④ 나는 내일 먹을 음식을 주문할 거야.

✓나는 인터넷에서 조리법을 구했어.

---

12 여자의 마지막 말에 대한 남자의 응답 ▶ 정답 ④

정답률 65%

W: Honey, where are the speakers we used when we went camping?
스피커들　　　　　　　　　　　　캠핑을 갔다(go camping)

M: Oh, I just left them in my car.
놓고 왔다(leave)

W: Really? I need to use them tomorrow.
사용해야 하다(need to V: ~해야 하다)

M: (Okay. I'll bring you the speakers now.)

해석

여: 여보, 우리가 캠핑을 갔을 때 사용했던 스피커는 어디에 있어요?

남: 오, 그냥 제 차에 놓고 왔어요.

여: 정말이에요? 저는 내일 그것들을 사용해야 해요.

남: (알겠어요. 제가 지금 스피커를 가져다 줄게요.)

① 문제없어요. 당신의 차는 수리되었어요.

② 미안해요. 저는 당신과 함께 캠핑을 갈 수 없어요.

③ 물론이죠. 당신은 제 텐트를 빌릴 수 있어요.

✓알겠어요. 제가 지금 스피커를 가져다 줄게요.

⑤ 걱정하지 마세요. 제가 이미 그것들을 껐어요.

---

13 남자의 마지막 말에 대한 여자의 응답

정답률 70% ▶ 정답 ①

M: Kelly, what are you doing?
W: Hey, Paul. I'm trying to sell my old sweater using the Local Market app.
M: Local Market app? What's that?
W: It's a kind of online marketplace for used items. I can buy or sell items with this app.
M: Interesting! How do you use it?
W: If I upload pictures of my sweater, somebody who needs a sweater will see and buy it.
M: That's great. Have you ever bought anything using the app?
W: Sure. Look at this bag. I bought it for only $5.
M: Wow, that's a good deal! I also have a lot of things to sell.
W: (Then, you should sell the items using this app.)

해석
남: Kelly, 무엇을 하고 있니?
여: 안녕, Paul. 나는 Local Market(로컬 마켓) 앱을 이용해서 내 오래된 스웨터를 팔려고 해.
남: Local Market 앱? 그게 뭐니?
여: 중고품을 위한 일종의 온라인 시장이야. 나는 이 앱으로 물건들을 사고 팔 수 있어.
남: 흥미로운데! 그것을 어떻게 이용하니?
여: 내가 스웨터 사진들을 업로드하면, 스웨터를 필요로 하는 사람이 그것을 보고 살 거야.
남: 멋지다. 너는 그 앱을 이용해서 어떤 것을 산 적이 있니?
여: 물론이지. 이 가방을 봐. 나는 그것을 겨우 5달러에 샀어.
남: 와, 그거 괜찮은 거래네! 나도 팔 물건들을 많이 가지고 있어.
여: (그럼, 너는 이 앱을 이용해서 물건들을 팔아야 해.)
✔ 그럼, 너는 이 앱을 이용해서 물건들을 팔아야 해.
② 좋아. 시장에서 스웨터를 사자.
③ 알겠어. 이 가방은 온라인으로 주문하기 쉬워.
④ 걱정하지 마. 내가 너에게 돈을 좀 빌려줄게.
⑤ 음, 너는 새 옷을 사는 게 좋겠어.

문제 풀이
앱을 이용해 중고품을 거래한다는 여자의 말을 듣고 여자가 실제로 구매한 가방을 본 남자는 긍정적으로 반응하며 자신도 팔 물건들이 많다고 말하고 있다. 이에 대해 앱 이용을 권하는 여자의 응답이 적절하므로 답은 ① 'Then, you should sell the items using this app.(그럼, 너는 이 앱을 이용해서 물건들을 팔아야 해.)'이다.

14 여자의 마지막 말에 대한 남자의 응답

정답률 85% ▶ 정답 ⑤

W: Honey, look at this bill. Have you been using a movie streaming service?
M: No. But a few months ago, I used a one-month free trial.
W: Look. A $15 membership fee has been charged for three months.
M: Oh, no! There must be something wrong.
W: Did you get any notice about that?
M: Well, I did, but I didn't pay much attention to it when I signed up for it.
W: Let's check it now.
M: Wait. [Clicking sound] Hmm, it says the membership fee will be charged if I don't cancel it after the free trial.
W: Well, one of my friends was in the same situation and she tried to get a refund but she couldn't.
M: Then, what should I do?
W: Hmm, the only thing you can do is to end the membership.
M: (Okay. I'll call customer service to cancel the membership.)

해석
여: 여보, 이 고지서 좀 봐요. 당신이 영화 스트리밍 서비스를 이용해 왔어요?
남: 아니요. 하지만 몇 달 전에, 1개월 무료 체험 서비스를 이용했어요.
여: 봐요. 3개월 동안 15달러의 회비가 부과되어 왔어요.

남: 오, 이런! 뭔가 잘못된 게 틀림없어요.
여: 그것에 대해 어떤 통지를 받았어요?
남: 음, 그랬죠. 하지만 그것을 신청할 때 별로 주의를 기울이지 않았어요.
여: 지금 확인해 봐요.
남: 잠시만요. [클릭하는 소리] 흠, 무료 체험 서비스 이후에 그것을 취소하지 않으면 회비가 부과된다고 쓰여 있네요.
여: 음, 제 친구들 중 한 명이 같은 상황에 있었는데 그녀는 환불을 받으려고 했지만 받지 못했어요.
남: 그럼, 어떻게 해야 하죠?
여: 흠, 당신이 할 수 있는 유일한 일은 멤버십을 종료하는 거예요.
남: (알겠어요. 제가 고객 서비스 센터에 전화해서 멤버십을 취소할게요.)

① 걱정하지 마요. 제가 당신에게 이메일로 통지서를 보낼게요.
② 좋아요. 당신의 서비스를 이용하는 방법을 알려주세요.
③ 저는 동의하지 않아요. 당신은 영수증 없이 환불을 받을 수 있어요.
④ 좋아요. 저는 오늘 밤에 영화를 보는 것을 기대하고 있어요.
✔ 알겠어요. 제가 고객 서비스 센터에 전화해서 멤버십을 취소할게요.

15 다음 상황에서 Ms. Brown이 Chris에게 할 말

정답률 80% ▶ 정답 ③

M: Ms. Brown teaches English in high school. Chris is one of the students who takes her class. Since he wants to major in English Literature at university, he thinks English writing skills are important. To get advice, Chris visits Ms. Brown and asks how to improve his English writing skills. Ms. Brown thinks that writing in English regularly is important. So she wants to suggest that Chris keep a diary for his English writing skills. In this situation, what would Ms. Brown most likely say to Chris?
Ms. Brown: (Why don't you start writing a diary in English?)

해석
남: Brown 선생님은 고등학교에서 영어를 가르친다. Chris는 그녀의 수업을 듣는 학생들 중 한 명이다. 그는 대학에서 영문학을 전공하고 싶기 때문에, 영어 작문 실력이 중요하다고 생각한다. 조언을 얻기 위해, Chris는 Brown 선생님을 찾아가서 그의 영어 작문 실력을 향상시키는 방법을 묻는다. Brown 선생님은 규칙적으로 영어로 글을 쓰는 것이 중요하다고 생각한다. 그래서 그녀는 Chris가 그의 영어 작문 실력을 위해 일기를 쓸 것을 제안하고 싶다. 이러한 상황에서 Brown 선생님은 Chris에게 뭐라고 말하겠는가?
Ms. Brown: (영어로 일기를 쓰는 것을 시작하는 게 어떠니?)
① 네 전공에 대해 걱정하는 것을 그만둬야 해.
② 너는 매일 영어책을 읽는 게 좋겠어.
✔ 영어로 일기를 쓰는 것을 시작하는 게 어떠니?
④ 너는 영어 단어를 많이 배워야 할 것 같아.
⑤ 외국인들과 대화를 하는 게 어떠니?

16~17 1지문 2문항

W: Hello, everyone. I'm Monica Dale from Blue River Animal Center. Today, let's talk about the different ways animals communicate. First, smell is probably the most basic type of animal communication. For example, dogs mark their areas with their smell to send a clear message to others to stay away. Second, when animals make sounds, those usually convey certain messages. For instance, dolphins get the attention of others in the area by using various sounds. Sometimes, they sing to their mates. Third, visual signals are widely used by many animals. Gorillas stick out their tongues to show anger. Lastly, many animals make use of touch to communicate their feelings to others. Giraffes

press their necks together when they're attracted to each other.
누르다   ~에게 매력을 느끼는
Now, let's take a look at a video clip that contains interesting
~을 보다   담고 있다
animal communication.

해석

여: 안녕하세요, 여러분. 저는 Blue River 동물 센터의 Monica Dale입니다. 오늘은, 동물들이 의사소통을 하는 다양한 방법들에 대해 이야기해 봅시다. 첫째, 냄새는 아마도 동물 의사소통의 가장 기본적인 형태일 것입니다. 예를 들어, 개들은 다른 개들에게 떨어져 있으라는 분명한 메시지를 보내기 위해 자신들의 냄새로 영역을 표시합니다. 둘째, 동물들이 소리를 낼 때, 그것들은 보통 특정한 메시지를 전달합니다. 예를 들어, 돌고래들은 다양한 소리를 사용함으로써 영역에서 다른 돌고래들의 주의를 끕니다. 때때로, 그들은 자신들의 짝에게 노래를 불러줍니다. 셋째, 시각 신호는 많은 동물들에 의해 널리 사용됩니다. 고릴라들은 분노를 나타내기 위해 혀를 내밉니다. 마지막으로, 많은 동물들이 자신들의 감정을 다른 동물들에게 전달하기 위해 촉각을 사용합니다. 기린들은 서로에게 매력을 느낄 때 목을 함께 누릅니다. 이제, 흥미로운 동물 의사소통을 담고 있는 동영상을 봅시다.

16 여자가 하는 말의 주제

정답률 90%
▶ 정답 ④

① 동물들을 기르는 것의 긍정적인 효과들
② 동물 행동 기록을 위한 유용한 조언들
③ 바다 동물들이 가진 공통 특성들
☑ 동물들이 의사소통하기 위해 사용하는 다양한 방법들
⑤ 멸종 위기에 처한 종을 보호하는 것의 중요성

17 언급된 동물이 아닌 것

정답률 80%
▶ 정답 ④

① 개   ② 돌고래   ③ 고릴라
☑ 코끼리   ⑤ 기린

---

10 2021년 3월 학력평가

01	④	02	④	03	①	04	③	05	④
06	③	07	①	08	②	09	⑤	10	②
11	①	12	①	13	②	14	③	15	④
16	②	17	④								

01 남자가 하는 말의 목적

정답률 90%
▶ 정답 ④

M: Good morning, students. This is Mr. Lewis from the school
administration office. Last night there was a heavy rainstorm. The
학교 행정실   심한   폭풍우
pouring rain left some of the school's hallways wet and slippery.
호우   남겼다(leave)   복도들   젖은   미끄러운
The first floor hallway and the central stairway are especially
중앙 계단   특히
dangerous to walk on. Please be extra careful when you walk
위험한   각별히 조심하다
through these areas. You could get seriously hurt if you slip on the
구역들   심각하게 다치다   미끄러지다
(get hurt: 다치다, seriously: 심각하게)
wet floor. We're doing our best to take care of the situation. Thank
최선을 다하는   ~을 처리하다   상황
you.   (do one's best)

해석

남: 안녕하세요, 학생 여러분. 저는 학교 행정실의 Lewis 선생님입니다. 지난밤에 심한 폭풍우가 있었습니다. 호우가 학교의 복도 일부를 젖고 미끄러운 상태로 남겨 놓았습니다. 1층 복도와 중앙 계단이 걷기에 특히 위험합니다. 이 구역들을 통과해서 걸을 때 각별히 조심하십시오. 젖은 바닥에서 미끄러지면 심각하게 다칠 수 있습니다. 저희는 상황을 처리하기 위해 최선을 다하고 있습니다. 감사합니다.

① 교내 청소 일정을 공지하려고

② 학교 시설 공사의 지연에 대해 사과하려고
③ 하교 시 교실 창문을 닫을 것을 요청하려고
☑ 교내의 젖은 바닥을 걸을 때 조심하도록 당부하려고
⑤ 깨끗한 교실 환경 조성을 위한 아이디어를 공모하려고

02 여자의 의견

정답률 85%
▶ 정답 ④

W: Mike, you look very tired today.
피곤한
M: I am. I'm having trouble sleeping at night these days.
잠을 자는 데 어려움을 겪는
(have trouble V-ing: ~하는 데 어려움을 겪다)
W: What's the matter?
M: I don't know. I just can't fall asleep until late at night.
잠들다   밤늦게까지
W: I feel bad for you.
M: I need to find a way to sleep better.
찾아야 하다 방법
(need to V: ~해야 하다, find: 찾다)
W: Can I share how I handled my sleeping problem?
처리했다   수면 문제
M: Sure.
W: After I changed my pillow, I was able to sleep much better.
베개   잠을 잘 수 있었다
(be able to V: ~할 수 있다)
Changing your pillow can help you with your sleeping problem.
M: Thanks for the tip. I hope that works for me, too.
조언   효과가 있다

해석

여: Mike, 너 오늘 매우 피곤해 보여.
남: 피곤해. 나는 요즘 밤에 잠을 자는 데 어려움을 겪고 있어.
여: 문제가 뭐야?
남: 모르겠어. 그냥 밤늦게까지 잠들 수가 없어.
여: 안됐구나.
남: 잠을 더 잘 잘 수 있는 방법을 찾아야 해.
여: 내가 내 수면 문제를 어떻게 처리했는지 말해도 될까?
남: 물론이지.
여: 베개를 바꾼 후에, 나는 잠을 훨씬 더 잘 잘 수 있었어. 베개를 바꾸는 것은 네 수면 문제에 도움을 줄 수 있어.
남: 조언해 줘서 고마워. 그것이 내게도 효과가 있었으면 좋겠어.

① 짧은 낮잠은 업무 효율을 높인다.
② 야식은 숙면에 방해가 될 수 있다.
③ 사람마다 최적의 수면 시간이 다르다.
☑ 베개를 바꾸면 숙면에 도움이 될 수 있다.
⑤ 숙면을 위해 침실을 서늘하게 하는 것이 좋다.

03 두 사람의 관계

정답률 90%
▶ 정답 ①

M: Hi, I'm Daniel Jones. I'm glad to finally meet you.
드디어
W: Welcome. Mr. Harvey told me you're coming.
M: He told me nice things about you.
W: Thanks. I hear that you're holding a party at your house in two
주최하는(hold)   2주 후에
weeks.
M: That's right. I'm hoping you could take charge of the food for my
~을 맡다
party.
W: Sure. You can always depend on a chef like me.
~에 의지하다   요리사
M: Great. Is there anything I need to prepare for you?
준비해야 하다
(need to V: ~해야 하다, prepare: 준비하다)
W: No need. I'll be taking care of the party food from start to finish.
~을 관리하고 있다(take care of)   처음부터 끝까지
M: Sounds fantastic.   (from A to B: A부터 B까지)
환상적인
W: Now let's talk about the menu.
메뉴

해석

남: 안녕하세요, 저는 Daniel Jones입니다. 드디어 당신을 만나게 되어 기쁘네요.
여: 어서 오세요. Harvey 씨가 당신이 올 거라고 했어요.
남: 그가 당신에 대해 좋은 얘기를 해 줬어요.
여: 감사해요. 당신이 2주 후에 당신의 집에서 파티를 주최한다고 들었어요.
남: 맞아요. 당신이 제 파티를 위한 음식을 맡아주셨으면 좋겠어요.

여: 물론이죠. 당신은 언제나 저와 같은 요리사에게 의지할 수 있어요.
남: 좋아요. 당신을 위해 제가 준비해야 하는 것이 있나요?
여: 그러실 필요 없어요. 제가 파티 음식을 처음부터 끝까지 관리할 거예요.
남: 환상적으로 들리네요.
여: 이제 메뉴에 대해 얘기해 봐요.
☑️ 파티 주최자 — 요리사
② 슈퍼마켓 점원 — 손님
③ 배달 기사 — 음식점 주인
④ 영양학자 — 식품 제조업자
⑤ 인테리어 디자이너 — 의뢰인

04 그림에서 대화의 내용과 일치하지 않는 것

정답률 75% ▶ 정답 ③

W: Is that the photo of our school's new studio?
    사진
M: Yes. We can shoot online lectures here.
         촬영하다   온라인 강의들
W: Can I have a look?
         보다
M: Sure. Do you see that camera facing the chair? It's the latest
                        향하는(face)   최신의
    model.
W: I see. What is that ring on the stand next to the camera?
              고리 모양의 것   스탠드
M: That's the lighting. It's to brighten the teacher's face.
         조명   밝게 하다
W: Hmm.... The round clock on the wall looks simple and modern.
              원형 시계   단순한   현대적인
M: Teachers can check the time on the clock while shooting.
              확인하다
W: The microphone on the table looks very professional.
         마이크   전문적인
M: It really does. Also, I like the tree in the corner. It goes well with the
                                        구석   ~과 잘 어울리다
    studio.

해석
여: 그것이 우리 학교의 새로운 스튜디오 사진이니?
남: 그래. 우리는 여기에서 온라인 강의를 촬영할 수 있어.
여: 내가 좀 볼 수 있을까?
남: 물론이지. 의자를 향하고 있는 저 카메라가 보이니? 그것은 최신 모델이야.
여: 그렇구나. 카메라 옆의 스탠드 위에 있는 고리 모양의 것은 뭐니?
남: 그건 조명이야. 선생님의 얼굴을 밝게 하기 위한 것이야.
여: 흠.... 벽에 걸린 원형 시계는 단순하고 현대적으로 보여.
남: 촬영하는 동안 선생님들이 시계의 시간을 확인할 수 있어.
여: 테이블 위에 있는 마이크는 매우 전문적으로 보여.
남: 정말 그렇지. 또한, 나는 구석에 있는 나무도 마음에 들어. 그것은 스튜디오와 잘 어울리거든.

05 남자가 할 일

정답률 85% ▶ 정답 ④

M: Hi, Jamie. You remember we're going to the movies later today,
              기억하다   영화를 보러 가는(go to the movies)
    right?
W: Of course. I'll see you after class.
M: Didn't you say there's a student discount on the movie ticket?
                        학생 할인   영화 티켓
W: Yes, I did. Don't forget to bring your student ID card.
              가져오는 것을 잊다   학생증
         (forget to V: ~하는 것을 잊다, bring: 가져오다)
M: But I've lost my ID. Is there any other way to get the discount?
         잃어버린(lose)
W: Probably not. Why don't you go get a new ID card from the school
                  ~하는 게 어때?   학교 사무실
    office?

M: Do you know where the office is?
W: Yes. It's on the first floor.
M: Okay. I'll go there right away.
                        당장

해석
남: 안녕, Jamie. 우리가 오늘 늦게 영화를 보러 가는 거 기억하지, 그렇지?
여: 물론이지. 수업 끝나고 보자.
남: 네가 영화 티켓에 학생 할인이 있다고 말하지 않니?
여: 응, 그랬지. 네 학생증을 가져오는 것을 잊지마.
남: 하지만 나는 학생증을 잃어버렸어. 할인을 받을 수 있는 다른 방법이 있니?
여: 아마도 없을 거야. 학교 사무실에 가서 새 학생증을 발급받는 게 어때?
남: 사무실이 어디에 있는지 아니?
여: 응. 1층에 있어.
남: 알겠어. 당장 갈게.
① 영화 예매하기
② 지갑 가져오기
③ 시간표 출력하기
☑️ 학생증 재발급받기
⑤ 영화 감상문 제출하기

06 여자가 지불할 금액

정답률 75% ▶ 정답 ③

W: Hi, I'm looking for camping chairs. Can you recommend one?
                        캠핑용 의자들   추천하다
M: Good morning. This is our bestselling chair. They're $20 each.
                              가장 잘 팔리는
W: That sounds good. I'll take it.
M: How many do you need?
              필요하다
W: I need four chairs.
M: Okay. Is there anything else you need?
W: I also need a camping knife.
              캠핑용 칼
M: How about this one? It's $20.
    ~은 어떠세요?
W: That looks convenient. I'll buy one. Do you offer any discounts?
              편리한   할인을 제공하다
M: Yes. Since your total purchase is over $80, we'll give you a 10%
    ~ 하기 때문에   총 구매액
    discount on the total amount.
                  총액
W: That sounds nice. I'll pay with my credit card.
                        지불하다   신용카드

해석
여: 안녕하세요, 저는 캠핑용 의자를 찾고 있어요. 하나 추천해 주시겠어요?
남: 안녕하세요. 이것이 가장 잘 팔리는 의자예요. 개당 20달러예요.
여: 좋은 것 같네요. 그것을 살게요.
남: 몇 개가 필요하신가요?
여: 의자 4개가 필요해요.
남: 알겠습니다. 그밖에 더 필요하신 게 있으신가요?
여: 캠핑용 칼도 필요해요.
남: 이것은 어떠세요? 20달러예요.
여: 편리해 보이네요. 하나 살게요. 할인을 제공하시나요?
남: 네. 손님의 총 구매액이 80달러를 넘기 때문에, 총액에서 10% 할인을 해 드릴게요.
여: 좋아요. 신용카드로 지불할게요.

① $72   ② $80   ☑️ $90
④ $100   ⑤ $110

문제풀이
20달러짜리 캠핑용 의자 4개와 20달러짜리 캠핑용 칼 1개를 사면 총액은 100달러이다. 총 구매액이 80달러를 넘으면 10% 할인을 받을 수 있다고 했으므로 여자가 지불할 금액은 90달러이다. 따라서 답은 ③ '$90'이다.

07 남자가 보고서를 완성하지 못한 이유

정답률 70% ▶ 정답 ①

M: Hi, Rebecca. What's up?
W: Hey, Tom. Can I borrow your laptop today?
                        빌리다   노트북 컴퓨터
M: Yes, but I have to finish my science report first.
                  끝내다   과학 보고서
W: Really? Wasn't the science report due last week?
                              ~하기로 되어 있는
M: Yes, it was. But I couldn't finish it.

W: What happened? I thought your experiment went well.
　　　　　　　　　　　　　　　　　실험
M: Actually, it didn't. I made a mistake in the experimental process.
　　　　　　　　　　　　실수를 했다　　　　　　실험 과정
W: Oh, no. Did you have to do the experiment all over again?
　　　　　　　　　　　　　　　　　　　　　　　처음부터 다시
M: Yes, it took a lot of time. So I haven't finished my report yet.
　　　　　　　　　많은
W: I see. Let me know when you're done.

해석
남: 안녕, Rebecca. 무슨 일이야?
여: 안녕, Tom. 오늘 네 노트북 컴퓨터를 빌릴 수 있을까?
남: 그래, 하지만 나는 과학 보고서를 먼저 끝내야 해.
여: 정말? 과학 보고서는 지난주에 제출하기로 되어 있지 않니?
남: 응, 그랬지. 하지만 나는 그것을 끝내지 못했어.
여: 무슨 일이 있었니? 나는 네 실험이 잘 되었다고 생각했는데.
남: 사실, 그렇지 않았어. 나는 실험 과정에서 실수를 했어.
여: 오, 저런. 실험을 처음부터 다시 해야 했니?
남: 그래, 많은 시간이 걸렸어. 그래서 아직 보고서를 끝내지 못했지.
여: 그렇구나. 다 하면 나에게 알려줘.

✅ ① 실험을 다시 해서
② 제출일을 착각해서
③ 주제가 변경되어서
④ 컴퓨터가 고장 나서
⑤ 심한 감기에 걸려서

문제 풀이
과학 보고서 작성을 위한 실험 과정에서 실수를 했다는 말을 듣고 여자가 실험을 처음부터 다시 해야 했냐고 묻자 남자는 그렇다고 대답한다. 따라서 남자가 과학 보고서를 기한 내에 완성하지 못한 이유는 ① '실험을 다시 해서'이다.

08 Spring Virtual Run에 관해 언급되지 않은 것

정답률 85%
▶ 정답 ②

W: Hi, Asher. What are you doing on the computer?
M: I'm signing up for an event called the Spring Virtual Run.
　　~에 등록하는(sign up for)　　　　　　　봄 가상 달리기
W: The Spring Virtual... Run?
M: It's a race. Participants upload their record after running either a
　　　　경주　　　참가자들　업로드하다　　　기록
three-mile race or a ten-mile race.
　　3마일 경주 또는 10마일 경주
　　(either A or B: A 또는 B)
W: Can you run at any location?
　　　　　　　　　　지역
M: Yes. I can choose any place in the city.
　　　　　선택하다　　　장소
W: That sounds interesting. I want to participate, too.
　　　　　　　　　　　　　　　참가하다
M: Then you should sign up online and pay the registration fee. It's
　　　　　　　　　　　　　　　　지불하다　　등록비
twenty dollars.
W: Twenty dollars? That's pretty expensive.
　　　　　　　　　　　　꽤　　비싼
M: But souvenirs are included in the fee. All participants will get a
　　　　기념품들　포함되다(include: 포함하다)
T-shirt and a water bottle.
　　　　　　　물병
W: That's reasonable. I'll sign up.
　　　　합리적인

해석
여: 안녕, Asher. 컴퓨터로 무엇을 하고 있니?
남: Spring Virtual Run(봄 가상 달리기)이라고 불리는 행사에 등록하고 있어.
여: Spring Virtual... Run?
남: 그것은 경주야. 참가자들은 3마일 경주 또는 10마일 경주를 한 후에 자신들의 기록을 업로드해.
여: 어느 지역에서나 달릴 수 있는 거야?
남: 그래. 시내의 어느 장소든 선택할 수 있어.
여: 재미있겠다. 나도 참가하고 싶어.
남: 그럼 온라인으로 등록하고 등록비를 지불해야 해. 20달러야.
여: 20달러? 꽤 비싸구나.
남: 하지만 기념품이 등록비에 포함되어 있어. 모든 참가자들은 티셔츠와 물병을 받을 거야.
여: 합리적이네. 나도 등록할게.

① 달리는 거리　　　✅ ② 참가 인원　　　③ 달리는 장소
④ 참가비　　　⑤ 기념품

09 Family Night at the Museum에 관한 내용과 일치하지 않는 것

정답률 75%
▶ 정답 ⑤

W: Do your children love adventures? Here's a great adventure for
　　　　　　　　　　　　모험들
you and your children. The Museum of Natural History is starting a
　　　　　　　　　　　　　　자연사 박물관
special program — Family Night at the Museum. When the regular
특별한　　　　　　　가족의 밤
museum hours are over, you and your children get to walk around
박물관 정규 운영 시간　　　　　　　　　　　　　　~를 돌아다니게 되다
the museum with a flashlight. After your adventure is complete,
　　　　　　　　손전등　　　　　　　　　　　　　완료된
you will sleep under the amazing models of planets and stars.
　　　　　　　　　　　놀라운　모형들　　행성들
Sleeping bags, snacks, and water will be provided. This program is
침낭들　　간식들　　　　　　제공되다
for children ages 6 to 13. All those who want to join must register
　　　　　　　　　　　　　　　　　　　　　　　　　　등록하다
in advance. On-site registration is not accepted. Why not call today
사전에　　　현장 등록
and sign up?
신청하다

해석
여: 여러분의 자녀들이 모험을 정말 좋아하나요? 여기 여러분과 여러분의 자녀들을 위한 멋진 모험이 있습니다. 자연사 박물관은 Family Night at the Museum(박물관에서의 가족의 밤)이라는 특별한 프로그램을 시작할 것입니다. 박물관 정규 운영 시간이 끝나면, 여러분과 여러분의 자녀들은 손전등을 들고 박물관을 돌아다니게 됩니다. 모험이 완료된 후에, 여러분은 놀라운 행성과 별 모형 아래에서 잠을 잘 것입니다. 침낭, 간식, 그리고 물이 제공될 것입니다. 이 프로그램은 6세부터 13세까지의 아이들을 위한 것입니다. 참가하기를 원하는 모든 사람들은 사전에 등록해야 합니다. 현장 등록은 허용되지 않습니다. 오늘 전화해서 신청하시는 것은 어떠십니까?

① 박물관 정규 운영 시간 종료 후에 열린다.
② 행성과 별 모형 아래에서 잠을 잔다.
③ 참가자들에게 침낭이 제공된다.
④ 6세부터 13세까지를 위한 프로그램이다.
✅ ⑤ 사전 등록 없이 현장에서 참가할 수 있다.

10 표에서 여자가 구매할 스마트 워치

정답률 80%
▶ 정답 ②

M: Hi, how can I help you today?
W: Hi, I'm looking for a smart watch.
　　　　　　　　　　　　스마트 워치
M: Sure. We have these five models.
W: Hmm.... I want to wear it when I swim.
　　　　　　착용하고 싶다　　　　수영하다
　　(want to V: ~하고 싶다, wear: 착용하다)
M: Then you're looking for one that's waterproof.
　　　　　　　　　　　　　　　　방수의
W: That's right. Do you think a one-year warranty is too short?
　　　　　　　　　　　　　　　1년의 보증 기간
M: Yes. I recommend one that has a warranty longer than one year.
　　　　추천하다
W: Okay. I'll take your advice.
　　　　　　　　조언
M: That leaves you with these two options. I'd get the cheaper one
　　남기다　　　　　　　　　　선택들　　　　　　　더 싼
because it's as good as the other one.
　　　　~만큼 좋은
W: I see. Then I'll go with the cheaper one.
M: Good choice.
　　　선택

해석
남: 안녕하세요, 오늘 어떻게 도와드릴까요?
여: 안녕하세요, 저는 스마트 워치를 찾고 있어요.
남: 그렇군요. 저희는 이 다섯 가지 모델을 가지고 있어요.
여: 흠.... 저는 수영할 때 그것을 착용하고 싶거든요.
남: 그럼 방수가 되는 제품을 찾고 계시는군요.
여: 맞아요. 1년의 보증 기간은 너무 짧다고 생각하시나요?
남: 네. 저는 1년보다 더 긴 보증 기간을 가진 제품을 추천해요.
여: 알겠어요. 당신의 조언을 따를게요.
남: 그럼 이 두 가지 선택지가 남아요. 저라면 더 싼 제품을 살 텐데 왜냐하면 그것이 다른 제품만큼 좋기 때문이죠.
여: 그렇군요. 그럼 더 싼 제품을 살게요.
남: 훌륭한 선택이에요.

스마트 워치

모델	방수	보증 기간	가격
① A	X	2년	90달러
✓ B	O	3년	110달러
③ C	O	1년	115달러
④ D	X	2년	120달러
⑤ E	O	4년	125달러

11 여자의 마지막 말에 대한 남자의 응답
정답률 80% ▶ 정답 ①

W: Liam, how did your shopping go?
M: It was good, Mom. I got this shirt at a good price.
　　　　　　　　　　　　　　　　셔츠　　　좋은 가격에
W: It looks nice. Wait! It's missing a button.
　　　　　　　　　　　　　없는(miss)　단추
M: (Oh, I should get it exchanged.)
　　　　　　　그것을 교환하다(exchange: 교환하다)

해석
여: Liam, 쇼핑은 어땠니?
남: 좋았어요, 엄마. 저는 이 셔츠를 좋은 가격에 샀어요.
여: 멋져 보이네. 잠깐! 단추가 없구나.
남: (오, 저는 그것을 교환해야겠어요.)
✓오, 저는 그것을 교환해야겠어요.
② 물론이죠. 제가 당신을 위해 셔츠를 주문할게요.
③ 음, 그것은 저에게 너무 비싸요.
④ 아니요. 더 작은 사이즈로 찾아주세요.
⑤ 죄송하지만, 이 셔츠는 할인 판매하지 않아요.

12 남자의 마지막 말에 대한 여자의 응답
정답률 75% ▶ 정답 ①

M: Alicia, these donuts are delicious. Can you tell me where you
　　　　　　　　도넛들　　맛있는
bought them?
샀다(buy)
W: They're from a new donut shop. I can take you there if you want.
　　　　　　　　　　　　　　　　　데려다 주다
M: That'd be nice. How's today after work?
　　　　　　　　　　　　　　퇴근 후에
W: (Good. Let's meet around six.)
　　　　　　　　만나다

해석
남: Alicia, 이 도넛들은 맛있구나. 그것들을 어디에서 샀는지 알려 주겠니?
여: 새로 생긴 도넛 가게에서 산 거야. 네가 원한다면 내가 데려다 줄 수 있어.
남: 그게 좋겠어. 오늘 퇴근 후에 어때?
여: (좋아. 6시쯤에 만나자.)
✓좋아. 6시쯤에 만나자.
② 괜찮아. 나는 도넛을 좋아하지 않아.
③ 나는 내 도넛 가게를 열고 싶어.
④ 걱정하지 마. 나는 그것을 혼자 할 수 있어.
⑤ 네 도넛 조리법을 공유해 줘서 고마워.

13 여자의 마지막 말에 대한 남자의 응답
정답률 75% ▶ 정답 ②

W: Brandon, I'm sorry I'm late.
　　　　　　　　　　늦은
M: That's okay. Let's order our drinks. I'll get my coffee in my personal
　　　　　　　　　주문하다　　　　　　　　　　　　　　　개인의
cup.
W: Oh, you brought your own cup?
M: Yes, it is a reusable cup. I'm trying to reduce my plastic footprint.
　　　　　　재사용할 수 있는　　줄이려고 노력하는　　플라스틱 발자국
　　　　　　　　　　　(try to V: ~하려고 노력하다, reduce: 줄이다)
W: What is plastic footprint?
M: It is the total amount of plastic a person uses and throws away.
　　　　　　총량　　　　　　　　　사용하다　　　버리다
W: You care a lot about the environment.
　　~에 신경을 많이 쓰다　　　　환경
M: I do. Plastic waste is a huge environmental problem.
　　　　　　　　　　　　거대한　　환경 문제
W: I should use a reusable cup, too. What else can I do to reduce my
plastic footprint?

M: (You can stop using plastic straws.)
　　　　　사용하는 것을 중단하다
　　　　　(stop V-ing: ~하는 것을 중단하다)

해석
여: Brandon, 늦어서 미안해.
남: 괜찮아. 음료를 주문하자. 나는 내 개인 컵에 커피를 받을게.
여: 오, 너 자신의 컵을 가져왔어?
남: 그래, 그것은 재사용할 수 있는 컵이야. 나는 내 플라스틱 발자국을 줄이려고 노력하고 있어.
여: 플라스틱 발자국이 뭐야?
남: 그것은 한 사람이 사용하고 버리는 플라스틱의 총량이야.
여: 너는 환경에 신경을 많이 쓰는구나.
남: 그래. 플라스틱 쓰레기는 거대한 환경 문제야.
여: 나도 재사용할 수 있는 컵을 써야겠어. 내 플라스틱 발자국을 줄이기 위해 그밖에 또 무엇을 할 수 있을까?
남: (너는 플라스틱 빨대를 사용하는 것을 중단할 수 있어.)
① 이 커피 전문점은 매우 인기가 있어.
✓너는 플라스틱 빨대를 사용하는 것을 중단할 수 있어.
③ 네가 준비가 되면 내가 음료를 주문할게.
④ 네 음료는 곧 준비가 될 거야.
⑤ 컵은 다양한 색상과 모양으로 나와.

문제 풀이
플라스틱 발자국을 줄이기 위해 재사용 가능한 컵을 쓰는 남자를 보고 여자는 자신도 그렇게 하겠다고 말하며 플라스틱 발자국을 줄일 수 있는 또 다른 방법에 대해 묻고 있다. 이에 대해 구체적인 방법을 제시하는 응답이 적절하므로 답은 ② 'You can stop using plastic straws. (너는 플라스틱 빨대를 사용하는 것을 중단할 수 있어.)'이다.

14 남자의 마지막 말에 대한 여자의 응답
정답률 85% ▶ 정답 ③

M: Good morning, Kathy. That's a cool helmet.
　　　　　　　　　　　　　　　　　　헬멧
W: Hi, Alex. It's for biking. I rode my bike to school.
　　　　　　　　　　　　　탔다(ride)
M: How often do you ride your bike to school?
　　얼마나 자주
W: I try to do it every day. It's very refreshing.
　　하려고 하다　　　　　　　　　　상쾌한
　(try to V: ~하려고 하다)
M: Sounds nice. I'm thinking of riding to school, too.
W: Good! We should ride together.
　　　　　　　　　　　함께
M: Let's do that, but I'm not very good at biking.
　　　　　　　　　　　~을 잘하지 못하는
W: It's okay. We can go slowly. Also, remember to wear your helmet.
　　　　　　　　　　천천히　　　　착용하는 것을 기억하다
　　　　　　　　　　　　(remember to V: ~하는 것을 기억하다, wear: 착용하다)
M: But I don't have a helmet yet.
W: (You really need one for your own safety.)
　　　　　　　　　　　　　　　　안전

해석
남: 안녕, Kathy. 멋진 헬멧이구나.
여: 안녕, Alex. 그것은 자전거용이야. 나는 자전거를 타고 등교했어.
남: 얼마나 자주 자전거를 타고 등교하니?
여: 나는 매일 그렇게 하려고 해. 매우 상쾌하거든.
남: 좋은 것 같아. 나도 자전거를 타고 등교할까 생각 중이야.
여: 좋아! 우리 함께 타야겠다.
남: 그렇게 하자, 그런데 난 자전거를 잘 타지 못해.
여: 괜찮아. 우리는 천천히 가면 돼. 또한, 헬멧을 착용하는 것을 기억해.
남: 하지만 나는 아직 헬멧이 없어.
여: (너는 정말로 너 자신의 안전을 위해 헬멧이 필요해.)
① 다행히도, 나는 사고에서 다치지 않았어.
② 나는 새 자전거를 사기에 충분한 돈을 가지고 있어.
✓너는 정말로 너 자신의 안전을 위해 헬멧이 필요해.
④ 자전거를 타고 등교한 후에는 졸릴지도 몰라.
⑤ 우리는 학교 주차장에 자전거를 둘 수 있어.

15 다음 상황에서 Jasper가 Mary에게 할 말
정답률 80% ▶ 정답 ④

W: Jasper and Mary are trying to form a rock band for the school band
　　　　　　　　　　　결성하려고 하고 있다　　　　　록 밴드
　　　　　　　　　　(try to V: ~하려고 하다, form: 결성하다)

10
21년 3월 학력평가

competition. Mary plays the guitar, and Jasper is the <u>drummer</u>.
　　　　　대회　　　　　　　　　　　　　　　　　　　　　드럼 연주자
They <u>pick</u> a <u>keyboard player</u> through an <u>audition</u>. Now, they need
　　　뽑다　건반 연주자　　　　　　오디션
a <u>lead singer</u>. Although the band is not <u>completely</u> formed, they
　리드 싱어　비록 ~이지만　　　　　　　완전히
begin their first <u>practice</u> today. <u>Since</u> they don't have a lead singer
　　　　　　연습　　　　　~ 때문에
yet, Mary sings while playing the guitar. Hearing her sing, the other
members are <u>amazed</u>. Mary has the <u>perfect voice</u> for rock music!
　　　　　　놀란　　　　　　　완벽한　목소리
So Jasper wants to tell Mary to be the lead singer for their band. In
this situation, what would Jasper most likely say to Mary?
Jasper: (I think you should be our lead singer.)

해석

여: Jasper와 Mary는 학교 밴드 대회를 위해 록 밴드를 결성하려고 하고 있다. Mary는 기타를 연주하고, Jasper는 드럼 연주자이다. 그들은 오디션을 통해 건반 연주자를 뽑는다. 이제, 그들은 리드 싱어가 필요하다. 비록 밴드가 완전히 결성되지는 않았지만, 그들은 오늘 첫 연습을 시작한다. 그들은 아직 리드 싱어가 없기 때문에, Mary가 기타를 연주하면서 노래를 부른다. 그녀가 노래를 부르는 것을 듣고, 다른 멤버들은 놀란다. Mary가 록 음악에 완벽한 목소리를 가지고 있는 것이다! 그래서 Jasper는 Mary에게 밴드의 리드 싱어가 되어 달라고 말하고 싶다. 이러한 상황에서, Jasper는 Mary에게 뭐라고 말하겠는가?

Jasper: (네가 우리의 리드 싱어가 되어야 할 것 같아.)

① 오디션은 어디에서 열리니?
② 네가 직접 곡을 쓰는 게 어때?
③ 이번에는 다른 노래를 연주하자.
✔④ 네가 우리의 리드 싱어가 되어야 할 것 같아.
⑤ 우리는 연습이 더 필요하다고 생각하지 않니?

16~17 1지문 2문항

M: Good afternoon, everybody. Today, we'll talk about what our
<u>animal companions</u> love: Toys. How do toys help our pets? First,
　반려동물들
toys <u>play a very important role in keeping</u> your pet happy. A toy like
　　~하게 하는 데 매우 중요한 역할을 하다
(play an important role in V-ing: ~하는 데 중요한 역할을 하다)
a <u>scratcher</u> helps to <u>reduce</u> your cat's stress. Second, toys are a
　　스크래처　　　　　　줄이다
great <u>tool</u> for a pet to <u>get exercise</u>. For example, a <u>hamster</u> loves to
　　　도구　　　　　　운동하다　　　　　　　햄스터
<u>run on a wheel toy</u>. Third, toys <u>build a bond</u> between you and your
　바퀴 장난감 위를 달리다　　　　유대감을 형성하다
pet. Playing with a small soft ball will give you and your dog a <u>joyful</u>
<u>experience</u>. Lastly, toys help keep your pet <u>entertained</u>. A small
　경험　　마지막으로　　　　　　　　　　재미있어하는(entertain)
hiding tent will make your <u>parrot</u> feel <u>less bored</u> when you are not
　　　　　　　　　　　　　앵무새　　　덜 지루한
around. Now let's watch a video of pets playing with their toys.

해석

남: 안녕하세요, 여러분. 오늘, 우리는 우리의 반려동물들이 정말 좋아하는 것, 즉 장난감들에 대해 이야기할 것입니다. 장난감들은 우리의 애완동물들에게 어떤 도움을 줄까요? 첫째, 장난감들은 여러분의 애완동물을 행복하게 하는 데 매우 중요한 역할을 합니다. 스크래처와 같은 장난감은 고양이의 스트레스를 줄이는 데 도움을 줍니다. 둘째, 장난감들은 애완동물이 운동을 할 수 있는 훌륭한 도구입니다. 예를 들어, 햄스터는 바퀴 장난감 위를 달리는 것을 매우 좋아합니다. 셋째, 장난감들은 여러분과 애완동물 사이에 유대감을 형성합니다. 작고 부드러운 공으로 노는 것은 여러분과 여러분의 개에게 즐거운 경험을 줄 것입니다. 마지막으로, 장난감들은 여러분의 애완동물을 재미있게 하는 데 도움을 줍니다. 작은 숨는 텐트는 여러분이 주위에 없을 때 여러분의 앵무새가 덜 지루하게 느끼도록 할 것입니다. 이제 장난감들을 가지고 노는 애완동물들의 영상을 봅시다.

16 남자가 하는 말의 주제
〔정답률 80%〕　▶ 정답 ②

① 애완동물을 위한 친환경 장난감
✔② 애완동물의 행복에 있어 장난감의 역할
③ 애완동물의 특이한 행동 유형
④ 애완동물에게 위험한 음식
⑤ 아이들을 애완동물과 함께 기를 때의 어려움

17 언급된 동물이 아닌 것
〔정답률 85%〕　▶ 정답 ④

① 고양이　　　　② 햄스터　　　　③ 개
✔④ 거북이　　　　⑤ 앵무새

11 | 2021년 6월 학력평가

01	②	02	②	03	②	04	④	05	④
06	①	07	③	08	③	09	④	10	③
11	②	12	⑤	13	①	14	⑤	15	③
16	③	17	④						

01 남자가 하는 말의 목적
〔정답률 85%〕　▶ 정답 ②

M: Hello, students. This is Allan, your <u>school nurse</u>. Many students
　　　　　　　　　　　　　　　　　보건 교사
get sick with <u>seasonal influenza</u>. Some cases can lead to serious
　　　　　　계절성 독감
<u>pain</u> or even <u>hospitalization</u>. I would <u>recommend</u> you to <u>get a flu</u>
　통증　　　입원　　　　　　　권장하다　　　독감 백신을 맞다
<u>vaccine</u>. A flu shot can keep you from getting sick. Also, since flu
　독감 예방 주사
viruses <u>keep changing</u>, flu vaccines <u>are updated</u> to <u>protect</u> against
　　　계속 변하다　　　　　　업데이트되다　보호하다
(keep V-ing: 계속 ~하다)　(update: 업데이트하다)
such viruses. Please get a flu shot offered in <u>doctors' offices</u> or
　　　　　　　　　　　　　　　　　　　　　병원들
<u>health departments</u> by the end of this month. Thank you.
　보건소들

해석

남: 안녕하세요, 학생 여러분. 저는 보건 교사인 Allan입니다. 많은 학생들이 계절성 독감에 걸립니다. 어떤 경우는 심각한 통증이나 심지어 입원까지 초래할 수 있습니다. 저는 여러분에게 독감 백신을 맞을 것을 권장합니다. 독감 예방 주사는 여러분이 병에 걸리는 것을 막아줄 수 있습니다. 또한, 독감 바이러스는 계속 변하기 때문에, 독감 백신은 그러한 바이러스로부터 보호하기 위해 업데이트됩니다. 이번 달 말까지 병원이나 보건소에서 제공되는 백신 예방 주사를 맞으십시오. 감사합니다.

① 건강 검진 일정을 공지하려고
✔② 독감 예방 접종을 권장하려고
③ 개인 위생 관리를 당부하려고
④ 보건소 운영 기간을 안내하려고
⑤ 독감 예방 접종 부작용을 경고하려고

02 여자의 의견
〔정답률 85%〕　▶ 정답 ②

M: Irene, where are you heading?
W: Hello, Mason. I'm going to the <u>bookstore</u> to buy some books.
　　　　　　　　　　　　　　　서점
M: The bookstore? Isn't it <u>more convenient</u> to <u>order</u> books online?
　　　　　　　　　　　　　　더 편리한　　주문하다
W: Yes, but I like to <u>flip through the pages</u> at bookstores.
　　　　　　　책장을 넘기며 훑어보다
M: Yeah, but buying books online is cheaper.
W: Right. But we can help bookstore <u>owners</u> when we buy books from
　　　　　　　　　　　　　　　　주인들
them.
M: I guess you're right. The bookstore near my house <u>shut down</u> last
　　　　　　　　　　　　　　　　　　　　　　　문을 닫았다
month.
W: It's a pity to see <u>local</u> bookstores <u>going out of business</u> nowadays.
　　　　　　　　지역의　　　　　폐업하는(go out of business)
M: I agree. Next time I need a book, I'll <u>try to go</u> to a local bookstore.
　　　　　　　　　　　　　　　　　　　가려고 노력하다
　　　　　　　　　　　　　　　　(try to V: 하려고 노력하다)

해석

남: Irene, 어디로 가는 거야?
여: 안녕, Mason. 책을 좀 사러 서점에 가는 중이야.
남: 서점? 온라인으로 책을 주문하는 것이 더 편리하지 않니?
여: 응, 그런데 나는 서점에서 책장을 넘기며 훑어보고 싶어.
남: 그래, 하지만 온라인으로 책을 사는 것이 더 저렴하잖아.

여: 맞아. 하지만 우리는 서점 주인들에게 책을 살 때 그들을 도울 수 있어.
남: 네 말이 맞는 것 같아. 우리 집 근처의 서점은 지난달에 문을 닫았어.
여: 요즘에 지역 서점들이 폐업하는 것을 보면 안타까워.
남: 동의해. 다음에 책이 필요할 때는, 지역 서점에 가려고 노력할게.

① 독서 습관을 기르자.
✓② 지역 서점을 이용하자.
③ 지역 특산품을 애용하자.
④ 중고 서점을 활성화시키자.
⑤ 온라인을 통한 도서 구입을 늘리자.

---

03 두 사람의 관계

정답률 85%

▶ 정답 ②

[Telephone rings.]
M: Hello. This is G-Solution. How may I help you?
W: Hello. I'm locked out of my home. The keypad on my door isn't
　밖에 있는 채로 ~의 문이 잠겼는데 열 수 없는　　키패드
responding.
반응하지 않고 있다(respond)
M: It might be an electric problem. It's probably a simple fix and it
　　　　　　　전기적인　　　　　　　　간단히 고칠 수 있는 것
won't cost much.
비용이 들다
W: How much is it?
M: It's 30 dollars including the service charge. But you'll have to pay
　　　　　　　~을 포함해서　　서비스 요금　　　추가 요금을 지불하다
extra if there're any additional problems.
　　　　　　　　추가적인
W: I got it. Can you come over right away?
　　　　　　　　　　　　곧바로
M: I'm afraid not. I'm doing a job at the Capital Bank.
W: How long will it take you to finish?
M: Just one hour. I'll call you as soon as I'm done. Address, please?
　　　　　　　　　　　　~하자마자　　　　　주소
W: 705 Cozy Street near Lee's Dental Clinic.
　　　　　　　　　　　　　　치과
M: Okay. See you soon.

해석
[전화벨이 울린다.]
남: 안녕하세요. G-Solution입니다. 어떻게 도와드릴까요?
여: 안녕하세요. 제가 밖에 있는 채로 집 문이 잠겼는데 열 수가 없어요. 문의 키패드가 반응하지 않고 있어요.
남: 전기적인 문제일 수도 있어요. 그것은 아마도 간단히 고칠 수 있고 비용이 많이 들지 않을 거예요.
여: 얼마인데요?
남: 서비스 요금을 포함해서 30달러입니다. 하지만 추가적인 문제가 있다면 추가 요금을 지불하셔야 할 거예요.
여: 알겠어요. 곧바로 오실 수 있나요?
남: 안 될 것 같아요. 저는 Capital Bank에서 작업 중이거든요.
여: 끝내시는 데 얼마나 걸릴까요?
남: 한 시간이면 됩니다. 제가 끝나자마자 전화를 드릴게요. 주소를 알려주시겠어요?
여: Lee 치과 근처의 Cozy Street 705번지예요.
남: 알겠습니다. 곧 뵐게요.

① 호텔 직원 — 투숙객
✓② 열쇠 수리공 — 집주인
③ 경비원 — 입주민
④ 은행원 — 고객
⑤ 치과의사 — 환자

---

04 그림에서 대화의 내용과 일치하지 않는 것

정답률 60%

▶ 정답 ④

M: Grace, let me show you my newly designed room.
　　　　　　　　　　　　　　새롭게 디자인된
W: Wow, Jake! It's so cool.
M: Look at the monitor between the speakers. I changed my old
　　　　　　모니터　　　　　　스피커들
monitor for this new one.
W: Looks nice. But isn't your desk too crowded to put your electric
　　　　　　　　　　　　　　너무 가득 차서 놓을 수 없는　　전기 키보드
keyboard on it?
　　　　　　(too A to V: 너무 A해서 ~할 수 없는)
M: It's fine with me. I find it convenient there.
W: Is that a microphone in the corner? Do you sing?
　　　　　　　마이크　　　　　구석

M: Yes. Singing is my all-time favorite hobby.
　　　　　　　　언제나 가장 좋아하는
W: What's that star-shaped medal on the wall? Where did you get it?
　　　　　　　별 모양의
M: I won that medal at a guitar contest with my dad.
　　　　　　　　　　　기타 대회
W: Incredible! Do you often practice the guitar with your dad?
　　　　　　　　　　　　연습하다
M: Sure. That's why there're two guitars in the room.

해석
남: Grace, 새롭게 디자인된 내 방을 보여줄게.
여: 와, Jake! 정말 멋지다.
남: 스피커들 사이에 있는 모니터를 봐. 내 오래된 모니터를 이 새 모니터로 바꿨어.
여: 좋아 보인다. 하지만 네 책상은 너무 가득 차서 그 위에 전기 키보드를 놓을 수 없지 않니?
남: 괜찮아. 나는 그것이 그곳에 있는 게 편하다고 생각하거든.
여: 구석에 있는 것은 마이크니? 너 노래를 해?
남: 응. 노래하는 것은 내가 언제나 가장 좋아하는 취미야.
여: 벽에 걸린 저 별 모양의 메달은 뭐니? 어디에서 받았어?
남: 아빠와 함께 나간 기타 대회에서 저 메달을 땄어.
여: 놀라운데! 아빠와 함께 자주 기타를 연습하니?
남: 물론이지. 그래서 방에 두 개의 기타가 있는 거야.

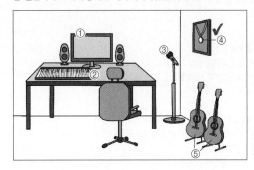

---

05 남자가 여자를 위해 할 일

정답률 75%

▶ 정답 ④

W: Smells nice, Daniel. What did you make for lunch?
M: Creamy pasta. I found the recipe online.
　　　　　　　　　　요리법
W: Fantastic. But don't you think the kitchen is a little bit messy?
　　　　　　　　　　　　　　　　　　　　조금　　지저분한
M: Sorry. I'll clean it up later.
　　　　　그것을 청소하다
W: You promise?
M: Yes. Let's have lunch. [Pause] By the way, do you remember you
have to pick up our daughter from the library this afternoon?
　　　　데려오다　　　　　　　　　　도서관
W: Oh, my! I totally forgot. What should I do? My friend Amy is coming
　　　　　　완전히
in an hour.
M: Don't worry. I planned to go camera shopping, but I'll pick up Betty,
　　　　　　　갈 계획이었다
instead.　　(plan to V: ~할 계획이다)
대신
W: Thanks. How sweet of you! Then I'll clean the kitchen.

해석
여: 냄새가 좋네요, Daniel. 점심으로 무엇을 만들었어요?
남: 크림 파스타예요. 온라인에서 요리법을 찾았어요.
여: 환상적이네요. 그런데 부엌이 조금 지저분하다고 생각하지 않아요?
남: 미안해요. 내가 나중에 그것을 청소할게요.
여: 약속해요?
남: 네. 점심을 먹읍시다. [잠시 후] 그런데, 당신 오늘 오후에 우리 딸을 도서관에서 데려와야 하는 것을 기억하죠?
여: 오, 이런! 완전히 잊고 있었어요. 어떻게 해야 하죠? 제 친구인 Amy가 한 시간 후에 올 거예요.
남: 걱정하지 마요. 카메라 쇼핑을 갈 계획이었는데, 제가 대신 Betty를 데려올게요.
여: 고마워요. 당신은 정말 친절해요! 그럼 제가 부엌을 청소할게요.

① 부엌 청소하기
② 점심 준비하기
③ 카메라 구매하기
✓④ 딸 데리러 가기
⑤ 요리법 검색하기

06 여자가 지불할 금액

정답률 80% ▶ 정답 ①

M: Good afternoon. May I help you?
W: Yes, please. I want to buy a bag for my laptop. Can you recommend one?
　　　　　　　　　　　노트북 컴퓨터　　　　　　　추천하다
M: How about this one? It's only 30 dollars on sale. The original price was 65 dollars.
　　　　　　　　　　　　　　　　　　　　　　　　　　　원래의
W: Wow, more than 50% off?
M: It's a very good deal.
　　　　　　　　거래
W: I like the design and color, but it's not big enough.
　　　　　　　　　　　　　　　　　　　　　　충분히
M: If you want something bigger, how about this one? It has a USB charging port, too.
충전 포트
W: I like it, but it looks expensive.
　　　　　　　　　　　비싼
M: It's 70 dollars. But I can give you a 10% discount.
　　　　　　　　　　　　　　10% 할인해 주다
W: Well... It's still beyond my budget. Let me look at the first one again.
　　　　　　　　　　　예산
M: Here it is. 30 dollars is a bargain.
　　　　　　　　　　　　　　싸게 사는 물건
W: Okay. I'll take it.

해석
남: 안녕하세요. 도와드릴까요?
여: 네, 부탁해요. 제 노트북 컴퓨터를 넣을 가방을 사고 싶어요. 하나 추천해 주시겠어요?
남: 이것은 어떠세요? 할인해서 겨우 30달러예요. 원래 가격은 65달러였어요.
여: 와, 50% 이상 할인하시는 거예요?
남: 아주 좋은 거래죠.
여: 디자인과 색상이 마음에 들지만, 충분히 크지 않네요.
남: 더 큰 것을 원하시면, 이것은 어떠세요? USB 충전 포트도 있어요.
여: 마음에 들지만, 비싸 보이네요.
남: 70달러예요. 하지만 10% 할인해 드릴 수 있어요.
여: 음... 그것은 여전히 제 예산을 초과하네요. 첫 번째 것을 다시 볼게요.
남: 여기 있어요. 30달러면 싸게 사는 물건이에요.
여: 좋아요. 그것을 살게요.

✓$30　　②$50　　③$63
④$65　　⑤$70

문제 풀이
남자가 여자에게 보여준 첫 번째 가방은 할인해서 30달러이고 두 번째 가방은 70달러이다. 여자는 자신의 예산을 초과하는 가격 때문에 첫 번째 가방을 다시 보여달라고 했고 싼 가격에 구매를 결정했다. 따라서 여자가 지불할 금액은 30달러이므로, 답은 ① '$30'이다.

07 남자가 공연장에 갈 수 없는 이유

정답률 75% ▶ 정답 ③

W: Hi, Chris. How was your business trip?
　　　　　　　　　　　　　　출장
M: It went fine. By the way, I heard Emma is moving out this Saturday.
W: You're right. She's very busy preparing to move. So she gave me
　　　　　　　　　준비를 하느라 매우 바쁘다
　　　　　(be busy V-ing: ~하느라 바쁘다, prepare: 준비를 하다)
two tickets for a musical because she can't go.
M: Good for you. What's the name of the musical?
W: It's "Heroes."
M: Really? I heard it's popular. Who are you going with?
　　　　　　　　　　　인기 있는
W: No one, yet. My sister turned me down because she has to finish her homework.
　　　　　　　　　　나를 거절했다
　　　　숙제
M: Well, can I go with you instead?
W: Sure. Why not? The show is at 8 p.m. this Friday.
M: Friday? Oh, no! I promised to take care of my niece at that time.
　　　　　　　　　　~를 돌보기로 약속했다　　　　조카
　　　(promise to V: ~하기로 약속하다, take care of: ~를 돌보다)
W: No problem. I'll ask Susan to go with me then.

해석
여: 안녕, Chris. 출장은 어땠니?
남: 잘 됐어. 그런데, Emma가 이번 주 토요일에 이사를 간다고 들었어.
여: 네 말이 맞아. 그녀는 이사 준비를 하느라 매우 바빠. 그래서 그녀는 갈 수 없기 때문에 나에게 뮤지컬 티켓 두 장을 줬어.
남: 잘 됐네. 뮤지컬의 이름이 뭐니?

여: 'Heroes(영웅들)'야.
남: 정말? 나는 그것이 인기 있다고 들었어. 누구랑 갈 거야?
여: 아직 아무도 없어. 내 여동생은 숙제를 끝내야 하기 때문에 나를 거절했어.
남: 음, 대신에 내가 너와 함께 가도 될까?
여: 물론이지. 왜 안 돼? 쇼는 이번 주 금요일 저녁 8시야.
남: 금요일? 오, 이런! 나는 그때 조카를 돌보기로 약속했어.
여: 괜찮아. 그럼 Susan에게 같이 가자고 부탁할게.

① 출장을 가야 해서
② 숙제를 끝내야 해서
✓ 조카를 돌봐야 해서
④ 이사 준비를 해야 해서
⑤ 친구와 만날 약속을 해서

08 강아지 키우기에 관해 언급되지 않은 것

정답률 70% ▶ 정답 ③

W: Dad, I want to have a puppy just like my friend, Julie.
M: Why not? But do you know how hard it is to raise a dog?
　　　　　　　　　　　　　　　　　　힘든　　　　기르다
W: Yes, but I'm ready. I think I will name my puppy Toby.
　　　　　　준비된
M: Okay. But will you walk Toby every day?
　　　　　　　　산책시키다
W: That'll be easy.
M: Also, you'll have to feed Toby three times a day.
　　　　　　　　　　먹이를 주다
W: No big deal. Anything else?
M: You'll have to toilet train Toby, too.
W: Really?　　배변 훈련을 시키다
M: Of course. Plus, you'll need to clean up the dog's pee pads.
　게다가　　　　　　　　　　　　　　　　　　소변 패드들
W: Hmm... Dad, you'll help me, right?
M: Sometimes. But remember having a dog takes responsibility.
　　　　　　　　　　　　　　　　　　　책임을 지다

해석
여: 아빠, 저는 제 친구인 Julie처럼 강아지를 키우고 싶어요.
남: 왜 안 되겠어? 그런데 개를 기르는 것이 얼마나 힘든지 알고 있니?
여: 네, 하지만 저는 준비됐어요. 제 강아지 이름을 Toby라고 지을 것 같아요.
남: 좋아. 그런데 매일 Toby를 산책시킬 거니?
여: 그것은 쉬울 거예요.
남: 또한, 하루에 세 번 Toby에게 먹이를 줘야 할 거야.
여: 별일 아니에요. 또 다른 건 없나요?
남: Toby에게 배변 훈련도 시켜야 할 거야.
여: 정말이에요?
남: 물론이지. 게다가, 개의 소변 패드들 치워야 할 거야.
여: 흠... 아빠, 저를 도와주실 거죠, 그렇죠?
남: 가끔. 하지만 개를 키우는 것은 책임을 지는 것이라는 것을 기억하렴.

① 산책시키기
② 먹이 주기
✓ 목욕시키기
④ 배변 훈련시키기
⑤ 소변 패드 치우기

09 Sharing Friday Movement에 관한 내용과 일치하지 않는 것

정답률 85% ▶ 정답 ④

W: Good afternoon, listeners. Why don't you join the Sharing Friday
　　　　　　　　　　　　　　　　　　　　　　　　　금요일 공유 운동
Movement and donate two dollars to our fund every Friday? This
　　　　　　　　기부하다　　　　　　　　기금
movement started in 2001 in Finland as an idea to encourage
　　　　　　　　　　　　　　　　　　　　아이디어로
people to do good. Since then, this idea has grown into a global
사람들이 선행을 하도록 장려하다　　　　　　　　　　　　세계적인
(encourage A to V: A가 ~하도록 장려하다, do good: 선행을 하다)
movement. Most of the donations go to poor areas across the
　　　　　　　　기부금들　　　　　가난한 지역들
world and help people get clean water. This year, scholarships
　　　　　　　　　　　　　　　　　　　　　　　　　장학금들
were given to 100 students in these areas to celebrate our 20th
　　　　　　　　　　　　　　　　　　　우리의 20주년을 기념하다
anniversary. Please join us, and help make a difference. If you
　　　　　　　　　　　　　　　　　　　변화를 가져오다
want to get more information, visit our homepage.

해석

여: 안녕하세요, 청취자 여러분. Sharing Friday Movement(금요일 공유 운동)에 참여하고 매주 금요일에 저희 기금에 2달러씩 기부해 보시는 건 어떠세요? 이 운동은 사람들이 선행을 하도록 장려하기 위한 아이디어로 2001년 핀란드에서 시작되었습니다. 그 이후로, 이 아이디어는 세계적인 운동으로 성장해 왔습니다. 기부금의 대부분은 전 세계의 가난한 지역으로 가서 사람들이 깨끗한 물을 얻는 데 도움을 줍니다. 올해, 저희의 20주년을 기념하기 위해 이 지역의 100명의 학생들에게 장학금이 지급되었습니다. 저희와 함께 해 주시고 변화를 가져오는 데 도움을 주십시오. 더 많은 정보를 원하시면, 저희 홈페이지를 방문해 주십시오.

① 매주 금요일에 2달러씩 기부하는 운동이다.
② 2001년 핀란드에서 시작되었다.
③ 기부금은 가난한 지역에 깨끗한 물을 공급하는 데 쓰인다.
☑④ 올해 20명의 학생에게 장학금을 지급했다.
⑤ 추가 정보는 홈페이지를 통해 얻을 수 있다.

문제 풀이

Sharing Friday Movement의 20주년을 기념하는 의미로 전 세계의 가난한 지역에 사는 100명의 학생들에게 장학금을 지급했다고 했으므로 ④ '올해 20명의 학생에게 장학금을 지급했다.'는 내용과 일치하지 않는다.

10 표에서 여자가 구입할 모델
정답률 85% ▶ 정답 ③

W: Kevin, I'm looking for a selfie stick. Can you help me?
M: Sure, Mom. You can buy one on your smart phone. *[Pause]* What kind of selfie stick do you want?
W: I'd prefer a light one.
M: Then I don't recommend a selfie stick over 200 grams. How about the length?
W: I have no idea. What's your opinion?
M: Hmm... It should extend up to 80cm at least.
W: Okay. I also want a bluetooth remote control. I heard they're convenient to use.
M: Then you have two options left. Which one do you want?
W: I'll buy this cheaper one.
M: Great choice.

해석

여: Kevin, 나는 셀카봉을 찾고 있단다. 도와주겠니?
남: 물론이죠, 엄마. 스마트폰으로 하나 살 수 있어요. *[잠시 후]* 어떤 종류의 셀카봉을 원하세요?
여: 나는 가벼운 것이 좋아.
남: 그럼 200그램 이상인 셀카봉은 추천하지 않아요. 길이는 어떠세요?
여: 모르겠어. 네 의견은 어떠니?
남: 흠... 최소한 80cm까지는 늘어나야 해요.
여: 알았어. 나는 블루투스 리모컨도 원해. 사용하기에 편리하다고 들었거든.
남: 그럼 두 가지 선택지가 남았어요. 어떤 것을 원하세요?
여: 더 싼 이것을 살게.
남: 좋은 선택이에요.

셀카봉

	모델	무게	최대 길이	블루투스 리모컨	가격
①	A	150g	60cm	X	10달러
②	B	150g	80cm	O	30달러
☑③	C	180g	80cm	O	20달러
④	D	180g	100cm	X	15달러
⑤	E	230g	100cm	O	25달러

11 남자의 마지막 말에 대한 여자의 응답
정답률 80% ▶ 정답 ②

M: Have you finished packing your bags for your trip to Mount Jiri?
W: I think so. Look! What else do I need?
M: You'd better prepare for the cold weather at night.
W: (You're right. I'll take a warm jacket.)

해석

남: 지리산 여행을 위해 가방을 싸는 것을 끝냈니?
여: 그런 것 같아. 봐! 그밖에 또 뭐가 필요할까?
남: 너는 밤에 추운 날씨에 대비하는 게 좋겠어.
여: (네 말이 맞아. 따뜻한 재킷을 가져갈게.)
① 또? 너는 가방을 두 번이나 잃어버렸어.
☑② 네 말이 맞아. 따뜻한 재킷을 가져갈게.
③ 왜? 나는 네가 추운 날씨를 더 좋아한다고 알고 있어.
④ 뭐? 나는 너를 위한 선물을 포장하는 것을 끝냈어.
⑤ 미안해. 하지만 너는 이 시점에 여행에 동참할 수 없어.

12 여자의 마지막 말에 대한 남자의 응답
정답률 70% ▶ 정답 ⑤

W: Honey, we can't eat out tomorrow evening.
M: Why not? I've already booked a table at the restaurant.
W: I'm sorry. I have an important business meeting at that time.
M: (Sorry to hear that. I'll cancel the reservation now.)

해석

여: 여보, 우리 내일 저녁에 외식할 수 없어요.
남: 왜 안 돼요? 이미 식당에 자리를 예약했어요.
여: 미안해요. 그때 중요한 업무 회의가 있어요.
남: (그 말을 들으니 유감이네요. 지금 예약을 취소할게요.)
① 고맙지만 괜찮아요. 충분히 먹었어요.
② 좋아요. 6시에 5명 예약할게요.
③ 좋은 선택이에요. 음식이 훌륭해요.
④ 알았어요. 회의 장소와 시간을 정할게요.
☑⑤ 그 말을 들으니 유감이네요. 지금 예약을 취소할게요.

13 남자의 마지막 말에 대한 여자의 응답
정답률 80% ▶ 정답 ①

M: Why do you look so busy?
W: I'm working on a team project.
M: What's it about?
W: It's about 'Climate Change.'
M: Sounds interesting. Who's on your team?
W: You know Chris? He's the leader.
M: I know him very well. He's responsible and smart.
W: Jenny is doing the research and Alex is making the slides.
M: What a nice team! Then what's your role?
W: (I'm in charge of giving the presentation.)

해석

남: 너 왜 그렇게 바빠 보이니?
여: 조별 과제를 하고 있어.
남: 무엇에 관한 거야?
여: '기후 변화'에 관한 거야.
남: 재미있겠다. 네 조에는 누가 있니?
여: Chris 알지? 그가 조장이야.
남: 나는 그를 매우 잘 알아. 그는 책임감이 있고 똑똑해.
여: Jenny는 조사를 하고 있고 Alex는 슬라이드를 만들고 있어.
남: 정말 좋은 조구나! 그럼 네 역할은 뭐니?
여: (나는 발표를 하는 일을 맡았어.)
☑① 나는 발표를 하는 일을 맡았어.
② 나는 네가 그 역할에 적임자라고 생각해.
③ 네 조를 신중하게 선택하는 것이 중요해.
④ 과제는 모레까지 마감 기한이야.
⑤ 우리가 그 과제를 끝내기 위해 늦게까지 깨어 있지 않았으면 좋겠어.

문제 풀이

여자와 조별 과제를 함께 하는 조원들이 각자 담당하고 있는 일에 대해 들은 남자가 여자의 역할은 무엇인지 물었으므로 이에 대한 응답으로는 ① 'I'm in charge of giving the presentation.(나는 발표를 하는 일을 맡았어.)'가 가장 적절하다.

14 여자의 마지막 말에 대한 남자의 응답
정답률 75%
▶ 정답 ⑤

M: Hi, Diana. You look down. What's the problem?
우울해 보이다

W: Hi, Peter. I missed the deadline for the speech contest. It was
놓쳤다   마감일   말하기 대회
yesterday.

M: No way. You'd been waiting for it for a long time.
오랫동안

W: Yeah. It totally slipped my mind. I'm so forgetful.
잊어버렸다(slip one's mind)   건망증이 있는

M: Why don't you write notes to remember things?
메모를 하다

W: I've tried, but it doesn't work. I even forget where I put the notes.
효과가 있다

M: How about using a time management application like me?
시간 관리 앱

W: Well... What's good about your app?

M: (It helps me keep deadlines to complete specific tasks.)
완료하다   특정한

해석
남: 안녕, Diana. 너 우울해 보여. 문제가 뭐니?
여: 안녕, Peter. 말하기 대회의 마감일을 놓쳤어. 어제였거든.
남: 말도 안 돼. 너는 오랫동안 그것을 기다려 왔잖아.
여: 그래. 완전히 잊어버렸어. 나는 건망증이 심해.
남: 일들을 기억하기 위해서 메모를 하는 게 어때?
여: 시도해 봤는데, 효과가 없어. 나는 심지어 내가 어디에 메모를 두었는지도 잊어버려.
남: 나처럼 시간 관리 앱을 사용하는 게 어때?
여: 음... 네 앱은 어떤 점이 좋니?
남: (그것은 내가 특정 작업을 완료하기 위한 마감일을 지키는 데 도움을 줘.)

① 나는 사람들 앞에서 말하는 것을 잘해.
② 과제를 잊어버려서 미안해.
③ 불행히도, 내 자명종은 나를 깨우지 않아.
④ 말하기 대회가 얼마 남지 않았어.
✔ 그것은 내가 특정 작업을 완료하기 위한 마감일을 지키는 데 도움을 줘.

15 다음 상황에서 Harold가 Kate에게 할 말
정답률 65%
▶ 정답 ③

M: Harold is a tennis coach. He's been teaching Kate, a talented and
재능 있는
passionate player, for years. While practicing for an upcoming
열정적인   연습하는 동안에
(while: ~하는 동안에, practice: 연습하다)
match, Kate injured her elbow badly. Her doctor strongly
경기   다치게 했다
recommends she stop playing tennis for a month. However, Kate
치는 것을 중단하다
(stop V-ing: ~하는 것을 중단하다)
insists on playing the match. Harold knows how heart-broken she
할 것을 고집하다   마음이 아픈
(insist on V-ing: ~할 것을 고집하다)
would be to miss the match. But he's concerned about her tennis
career if her elbow doesn't recover. So he wants to persuade her to
경력   회복되다   설득하다
calm down and focus on her recovery. In this situation, what would
진정하다   ~에 집중하다   회복
Harold most likely say to Kate?

Harold: (Take it easy. Take good care of yourself first.)

해석
남: Harold는 테니스 코치이다. 그는 수년 동안 재능 있고 열정적인 선수인 Kate를 가르쳐 오
고 있다. 다가오는 경기를 위해 연습하는 동안에, Kate는 팔꿈치를 심하게 다쳤다. 그녀의
주치의는 한 달 동안 테니스를 치는 것을 중단하라고 강력히 권고한다. 하지만, Kate는 그
경기를 할 것을 고집한다. Harold는 그녀가 그 경기를 놓치면 얼마나 마음이 아플지 알고
있다. 그러나 그는 그녀의 팔꿈치가 회복되지 않을 경우 그녀의 테니스 경력에 대해 걱정
하고 있다. 그래서 그는 그녀가 진정하고 그녀의 회복에 집중하도록 설득하고 싶다. 이러
한 상황에서, Harold는 Kate에게 뭐라고 말하겠는가?
Harold: (진정해. 먼저 너 자신을 잘 돌보도록 해.)
① 알았어. 너는 그 경기에 최선의 노력을 다하는 게 좋을 거야.
② 그렇구나. 너는 그녀 대신에 그 경기를 해야 해.
✔ 진정해. 먼저 너 자신을 잘 돌보도록 해.
④ 너는 그럴 만한 자격이 있어. 연습이 완벽을 만들어.
⑤ 걱정하지 마. 너는 이번 경기를 이길 거야.

16~17 1지문 2문항

W: This is Linda from "Life and Science." Did you know light pollution
빛 공해
from bright lights at night can drive wildlife to death? For example,
야생동물을 죽음으로 몰고 가다
(drive A to B: A를 B로 몰고 가다)
sea turtles lay eggs on beaches and their babies find their way to
바다거북들   알을 낳다
the sea with the help of moonlight. But artificial lights can confuse
달빛   인공적인   혼란스럽게 하다
them and cause them not to reach the sea and die. Fireflies have
그들이 도달하지 못하게 하다   반딧불이들
(cause A to V: A가 ~하게 하다, reach: 도달하다)
been disappearing across the globe. Male fireflies get disturbed
사라지고 있다(disappear)   방해를 받다
by artificial lights when they try to attract mates. This means less
유혹하려고 하다
(try to V: ~하려고 하다, attract: 유혹하다)
fireflies are born. Also, salmon migrate randomly when exposed
연어   이동하다   ~에 노출되었을 때
(expose: 노출하다)
to artificial lights at night. This threatens their chances of survival.
위협하다   생존 가능성
Lastly, light pollution interrupts the mating calls of tree frogs at
방해하다   짝짓기 울음소리   청개구리들
night. As male frogs reduce the number of their mating calls, the
줄이다
females don't reproduce. So light pollution can be a matter of life
번식하다   문제
and death for some animals.

해석
여: 저는 '삶과 과학'의 Linda입니다. 여러분은 밤에 밝은 빛으로 인한 빛 공해가 야생동물을
죽음으로 몰고 갈 수 있다는 것을 알고 있었나요? 예를 들어, 바다거북은 해변에 알을 낳
고 그들의 새끼들은 달빛의 도움으로 바다로 가는 길을 찾습니다. 하지만 인공적인 빛은
그들을 혼란스럽게 하고 그들이 바다에 도달하지 못하고 죽게 할 수 있습니다. 반딧불이
는 전 세계적으로 사라지고 있습니다. 수컷 반딧불이는 짝을 유혹하려고 할 때 인공적인
빛에 의해 방해를 받습니다. 이것은 더 적은 수의 반딧불이가 태어난다는 것을 의미합니
다. 또한, 연어는 밤에 인공적인 빛에 노출되었을 때 무작위로 이동합니다. 이것은 그들
의 생존 가능성을 위협합니다. 마지막으로, 빛 공해는 밤에 청개구리의 짝짓기 울음소리
를 방해합니다. 수컷 개구리가 짝짓기 울음소리의 수를 줄이기 때문에, 암컷 개구리는 번
식하지 않습니다. 그래서 빛 공해는 몇몇 동물들에게 삶과 죽음의 문제가 될 수 있습니다.

16 여자가 하는 말의 주제
정답률 75%
▶ 정답 ③

① 불법 사냥과 관련된 문제들
② 이동하는 동물의 특성들
✔ 빛 공해가 야생동물에게 미치는 영향들
④ 멸종 위기의 동물을 구하기 위한 다양한 방법들
⑤ 수질 오염으로 인한 동물 서식지 변화

17 언급된 동물이 아닌 것
정답률 85%
▶ 정답 ④

① 바다거북
② 반딧불이
③ 연어
✔ 꿀벌
⑤ 청개구리

12 2021년 9월 학력평가

01	④	02	②	03	③	04	③	05	⑤
06	③	07	③	08	③	09	④	10	②
11	①	12	①	13	③	14	①	15	④
16	②	17	③							

01 남자가 하는 말의 목적

정답률 80%
▶ 정답 ④

M: Hello, citizens of Portland. This is Jerry Wilson, your Mayor. As you know, Port Elementary School has opened, and it is so nice to hear the kids playing. To ensure the safety of the students at the school, we've been communicating with the New Jersey State Police and requested that they enforce speed limits in the area around the school. This is in response to the many complaints City Hall has received regarding excessive speeding, especially in front of the school. Please obey speed limits for the safety of the kids and your fellow citizens. Thank you for your cooperation. Stay safe and healthy.

해석
남: 안녕하십니까, Portland 시민 여러분. 저는 시장인 Jerry Wilson입니다. 여러분도 아시다시피, Port 초등학교가 문을 열었고, 아이들이 노는 소리를 듣는 것은 매우 즐겁습니다. 학교 학생들의 안전을 확보하기 위해, 저희는 New Jersey 주 경찰과 소통해왔으며 학교 주변 지역에 속도 제한을 시행해 줄 것을 요청했습니다. 이것은 특히 학교 앞에서의 과속에 관해 시청이 받아온 많은 불만들에 대응한 것입니다. 아이들과 시민 여러분의 안전을 위해 속도 제한을 준수해주십시오. 협조해주셔서 감사합니다. 안전하고 건강하게 지내십시오.

① 시민 자율 방범 단원을 모집하려고
② 어린이 안전 교육 장소를 안내하려고
③ 초등학교 개교 기념행사를 홍보하려고
✔ 학교 주변 제한 속도 준수를 독려하려고
⑤ 시청에서 열리는 공청회 일정을 공지하려고

02 남자의 의견

정답률 85%
▶ 정답 ②

M: Lily, what's wrong? Are you all right?
W: Oh, it's nothing.
M: Are you sure? You look pretty worried.
W: Actually, I said something mean to my sister and I feel really bad about it.
M: What did you say to her?
W: I said she's the worst sister because she wore my favorite jacket again!
M: Jeez! She must have been really hurt by that.
W: Yeah, but I told her not to wear my jacket a million times. She never listens.
M: Still, you should be more careful when you talk to someone close to you.
W: I know, but I was so angry.
M: People get hurt more easily when someone close to them says mean things.
W: Yeah, you're right. I'll apologize to her when I get home.

해석
남: Lily, 무슨 일이니? 괜찮아?

여: 오, 아무것도 아니야.
남: 확실해? 매우 걱정스러워 보여.
여: 사실, 내가 언니에게 심술궂은 말을 했는데 그것 때문에 정말 기분이 안 좋아.
남: 무슨 말을 했는데?
여: 그녀가 내가 제일 좋아하는 재킷을 또 입어서 최악의 언니라고 했어.
남: 저런! 그녀는 그것에 정말 상처를 받았음에 틀림없어.
여: 그래, 하지만 나는 그녀에게 내 재킷을 입지 말라고 수도 없이 말했어. 그녀는 절대 듣지 않아.
남: 그래도, 가까운 사람과 이야기할 때는 더 조심해야 해.
여: 알아, 하지만 나는 너무 화가 났어.
남: 사람들은 가까운 사람이 심술궂은 말을 할 때 더 쉽게 상처를 받아.
여: 그래, 네 말이 맞아. 집에 가면 그녀에게 사과할게.

① 고민이 있을 때는 가족이나 친구와 대화해야 한다.
✔ 가까운 사람일수록 말을 신중하게 하는 것이 좋다.
③ 사과를 받아들일 수 있는 넓은 마음이 필요하다.
④ 일어나지 않은 일을 미리 걱정할 필요는 없다.
⑤ 가족이라도 개인 공간을 존중해야 한다.

03 두 사람의 관계

정답률 90%
▶ 정답 ③

W: Hi, listeners! Now we have one person on the line. He has something special to share with us. Hello, you're on the air!
M: Hello. Wow! I'm surprised that I got through to you. Thank you for taking my call.
W: Sure. Please introduce yourself.
M: I'm Jin, a high school student. I'm a big fan of the show.
W: Thank you, Jin. By the way, you left a message on our website, didn't you?
M: Yes. Today is my parents' 20th wedding anniversary. I wanted to honor them on the show.
W: I see. Are your parents listening now?
M: Yes, they listen to your show every day.
W: That's great. What is your message to your parents?
M: Hmm... Mom and Dad, you're amazing parents. Happy Anniversary to you both!
W: What a lovely message! Thank you for calling us today, Jin.
M: Thanks again for taking my call.

해석
여: 안녕하세요, 청취자 여러분! 지금 한 분이 연결되어 있습니다. 그는 우리와 나눌 특별한 일이 있습니다. 안녕하세요, 방송 중이에요!
남: 안녕하세요. 와! 당신과 전화 연결이 됐다니 놀랍네요. 제 전화를 받아주셔서 감사해요.
여: 네. 자기 소개를 해 주세요.
남: 저는 고등학생인 Jin입니다. 쇼의 열혈 팬이에요.
여: 고마워요, Jin. 그런데, 저희 웹 사이트에 메시지를 남겼죠, 그렇지 않나요?
남: 네. 오늘이 제 부모님의 20주년 결혼 기념일이에요. 저는 쇼에서 그분들께 경의를 표하고 싶었어요.
여: 그렇군요. 부모님께서 지금 듣고 계신가요?
남: 네, 부모님은 매일 당신의 쇼를 들으세요.
여: 잘됐네요. 부모님께 전하는 메시지는 무엇인가요?
남: 흠... 엄마와 아빠, 두 분은 멋진 부모님이에요. 두 분 모두 행복한 기념일 되세요!
여: 정말 사랑스러운 메시지네요! 오늘 전화 주셔서 고마워요, Jin.
남: 제 전화를 받아주셔서 다시 한 번 감사드려요.

① 교사 — 학생
② 방송 작가 — 배우
✔ 라디오 진행자 — 청취자
④ 이벤트 업체 직원 — 고객
⑤ 설문 조사원 — 설문 응답자

04 그림에서 대화의 내용과 일치하지 않는 것

정답률 65%
▶ 정답 ③

W: Hi, Tim. How's everything going with the festival?
M: Hey, Julie! It's going great. This is a picture of what our booth will

look like.

W: What will people do at your booth?

M: They'll be asked to answer questions and be given snacks if they
<u>질문들</u> <u>과자들</u>
answer correctly.
<u>정확하게</u>

W: Okay, that sounds good. I like the banner that says 'Guessing Time'
<u>현수막</u> <u>알아맞히기 시간</u>
in the center.

M: Thanks. What do you think about the photos that are under the
clock?

W: Great idea! What are you using the round table for?
<u>원형 테이블</u>

M: We're going to put the snacks on it.

W: That makes sense. Then, what about the globe on the floor?
<u>일리가 있다</u> <u>지구본</u> <u>바닥</u>

M: It's for choosing countries. We're going to ask people geography
<u>나라들</u> <u>지리</u>
questions.

W: That should be interesting. What's that crown on the left side?
<u>왕관</u>

M: That's a photo zone for all participants.
<u>포토존</u> <u>참가자들</u>

W: Cool. I can't wait for this year's festival!

해석

여: 안녕, Tim. 축제는 어떻게 되어가고 있니?

남: 안녕, Julie! 잘 되어가고 있어. 이것은 우리 부스가 어떻게 보일지 나타내는 그림이야.

여: 부스에서 사람들이 무엇을 하게 되는 거야?

남: 그들은 질문에 대답하도록 요청을 받고 정확하게 대답을 하면 과자를 받게 될 거야.

여: 알았어, 좋은 것 같네. 나는 중앙에 있는 'Guessing Time(알아맞히기 시간)'이라고 적힌 현수막이 마음에 들어.

남: 고마워. 시계 아래에 있는 사진들은 어때?

여: 좋은 생각이야! 원형 테이블은 무슨 용도로 사용할 거야?

남: 그 위에 과자를 올려놓을 거야.

여: 그거 일리가 있네. 그럼, 바닥에 있는 지구본은 뭐야?

남: 그것은 나라를 선택하기 위한 거야. 우리는 사람들에게 지리 질문을 할 거야.

여: 그거 재미있을 것 같아. 왼쪽에 있는 왕관은 뭐야?

남: 모든 참가자들을 위한 포토존이야.

여: 멋지다. 나는 올해 축제가 무척 기다려져.

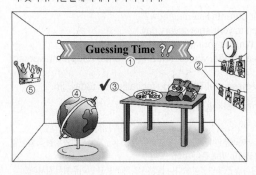

05 남자가 할 일

▶ 정답 ⑤

M: Kasey, how's everything coming along for grandma's birthday this
<u>되어 가고 있는</u>
Sunday?
(come along: (원하는 대로) 되어가다; 도착하다; 함께 가다[오다])

W: Hey, Dad. I wrote a card for her and got some decorations yesterday.
<u>썼다(write)</u> <u>장식품들</u>

M: That's good!

W: Have you gotten anything for her yet?

M: I already bought a sweater. Can I help with decorating the living
<u>샀다(buy)</u> <u>스웨터</u> <u>장식하는 것(decorate)</u>
room for the party?

W: Clara will take care of that. Also, she's picking up a birthday cake.
<u>~을 맡다</u> <u>찾아올 것이다(pick up)</u>

M: Awesome! Your grandma will be so happy because you guys are
going to make her birthday so special.

W: I hope so. What about food? What can we make for her?

M: How about grilled salmon sandwiches? She loves those!
<u>구운 연어 샌드위치들</u>

W: Good idea, but I won't have time to handle that on my own.
<u>처리하다</u> <u>나 혼자서(on one's own)</u>

M: Then, I'll order salmon and vegetables online today.
<u>주문하다</u>

W: Thanks, Dad! That's a big help.

해석

남: Kasey, 이번 주 일요일 할머니 생신을 위한 준비는 어떻게 되어가고 있니?

여: 네, 아빠. 어제 할머니를 위한 카드를 쓰고 장식품들을 좀 샀어요.

남: 잘했구나!

여: 할머니를 위한 무언가를 벌써 마련하셨어요?

남: 나는 이미 스웨터를 샀단다. 파티를 위해 거실을 장식하는 것을 도와줄까?

여: Clara가 그 일을 맡아 줄 거예요. 또한, 그녀는 생일 케이크도 찾아올 거예요.

남: 멋지구나! 너희들이 생신을 매우 특별하게 만들어 드리니까 할머니께서 굉장히 행복해 하실 거야.

여: 그랬으면 좋겠어요. 음식은요? 할머니를 위해 무엇을 만들 수 있을까요?

남: 구운 연어 샌드위치는 어떠니? 할머니께서 그것을 정말 좋아하시잖아!

여: 좋은 생각이지만, 저 혼자서 그 일을 처리할 시간은 없을 거예요.

남: 그럼, 내가 오늘 온라인으로 연어와 채소를 주문할게.

여: 감사해요, 아빠! 큰 도움이 되네요.

① 생일 카드 쓰기
② 스웨터 구매하기
③ 거실 장식하기
④ 케이크 찾아오기
☑ 샌드위치 재료 주문하기

문제 풀이

할머니의 생신을 위해 구운 연어 샌드위치를 준비하고 싶지만 시간이 없다는 여자의 말에 남자는 자신이 온라인으로 샌드위치의 재료인 연어와 채소를 주문해 주겠다고 말한다. 따라서 정답은 ⑤ '샌드위치 재료 주문하기'이다.

06 여자가 지불할 금액

▶ 정답 ③

M: Hello. How can I help you?

W: Hi, how much is the ice cream?

M: It depends on the size. The small cup is $5, the medium is $10,
<u>~에 따라 다르다</u>
and the large is $15. What size would you like?

W: I'll take two smalls and one medium.

M: Okay. What flavor would you like?
<u>맛</u>

W: I'll take chocolate for all three cups.

M: Sounds good. Do you want any toppings on your ice cream? We
<u>토핑들</u>
have chocolate chips and crunchy nuts. Toppings cost $1 each.
<u>초콜릿 칩들</u> <u>바삭바삭한 견과류</u> <u>(값·비용이) ~이다</u>

W: Oh, yes. I'll have crunchy nuts only on the medium and nothing on
the small cups.

M: Good choice. Do you need anything else?

W: No, that's it.

M: How would you like to pay? Cash or credit?
<u>지불하다</u>

W: I'll pay with my credit card.

해석

남: 안녕하세요. 어떻게 도와드릴까요?

여: 안녕하세요, 아이스크림은 얼마인가요?

남: 크기에 따라 달라요. 작은 컵은 5달러, 중간 컵은 10달러, 큰 컵은 15달러예요. 어떤 크기로 드릴까요?

여: 작은 컵 두 개와 중간 컵 한 개를 살게요.

남: 알겠습니다. 어떤 맛으로 드릴까요?

여: 세 컵 모두 초콜릿으로 살게요.

남: 좋습니다. 아이스크림 위에 토핑을 올려드릴까요? 초콜릿 칩과 바삭바삭한 견과류가 있어요. 토핑은 각각 1달러예요.

여: 오, 네. 중간 컵에만 바삭바삭한 견과류를 주시고 작은 컵에는 아무것도 주지 마세요.

남: 훌륭한 선택이네요. 그 밖에 또 필요한 것이 있으신가요?

여: 아니요, 그게 다예요.

남: 지불은 어떻게 하시겠어요? 현금으로 하시겠습니까, 아니면 신용카드로 하시겠습니까?

여: 신용카드로 지불할게요.

① $16 ② $20 ☑ $21
④ $23 ⑤ $26

문제 풀이

아이스크림을 사는 여자는 5달러인 작은 컵 2개와 10달러인 중간 컵 1개를 선택하고 1달러인 견과류 토핑을 중간 컵에만 올려달라고 주문했으므로 여자가 지불할 총 금액은 21달러이다. 따라서 정답은 ③ '$21'이다.

07 남자가 헬스장 회원권을 연장하지 않은 이유

정답률 90% ▶ 정답 ③

M: Mom, I'm home.
W: Hi. Did you go to the gym?
M: Yes. My <u>membership</u> ended today, but I didn't <u>renew</u> it.
　　　　　　　회원권　　　　　　　　　　　　　갱신하다
　　체육관
W: Why? Does your shoulder still <u>hurt</u>?
　　　　　　　　　　　　　　　아프다
M: No, my shoulder feels <u>completely</u> fine.
　　　　　　　　　　　　完전히
W: So, what's the problem? I thought you were <u>enjoying exercising</u>.
　　　　　　　　　　　　　　　　운동하는 것을 즐기고 있었다
M: I was. It's actually been <u>fun</u>. (enjoy V-ing: ~하는 것을 즐기다, exercise: 운동하다)
　　　　　　　　　　재미있는
W: Then why didn't you renew your membership?
M: Well, the <u>shower facilities</u> at the gym are too old, and there's not
　　　　　　샤워 시설
<u>enough</u> <u>space</u> in the <u>shower stalls</u>.
충분한　공간　　　　　샤워실
W: I see. Why don't you <u>check out</u> the new health club <u>nearby</u>? It may
　　　　　　　　　　　확인하다　　　　　　　　　　　　근처에
be <u>more expensive</u>, but the facilities are probably <u>a lot</u> better.
　　더 비싼　　　　　　　　　　　　　　　　　　　　훨씬
M: Okay. Maybe I should visit there tomorrow <u>on my way home</u> after
school.　　　　　　　　　　　　　　　　　집에 오는 길에
W: That sounds like a good plan!

해석
남: 엄마, 저 왔어요.
여: 그래. 체육관에 갔었니?
남: 네. 제 회원권이 오늘 끝났는데, 갱신하지 않았어요.
여: 왜? 어깨가 아직도 아프니?
남: 아니요, 어깨는 완전히 좋아졌어요.
여: 그럼, 문제가 뭐니? 나는 네가 운동하는 것을 즐기고 있다고 생각했어.
남: 그랬죠. 사실 재미있었어요.
여: 그럼 왜 회원권을 갱신하지 않았어?
남: 음, 체육관에 있는 샤워 시설이 너무 낡았고, 샤워실에 충분한 공간이 없어요.
여: 그렇구나. 근처에 새로 생긴 헬스클럽을 확인해 보는 건 어떠니? 더 비쌀지도 모르지만,
아마도 시설이 훨씬 좋을 거야.
남: 네. 내일 방과 후에 집에 오는 길에 방문해 봐야겠어요.
여: 좋은 계획인 것 같구나!

① 어깨 부상이 회복되지 않아서
② 운동에 흥미를 잃어서
✓ 샤워 시설이 낡고 좁아서
④ 가격이 인상되어서
⑤ 방과후 수업에 참여해야 해서

08 Tour of Liberty University에 관해 언급되지 않은 것

정답률 90% ▶ 정답 ③

W: Hey, Bruce! I'm going to <u>take a tour of</u> Liberty University. Do you
want to come?　　　　　　　　　　~을 탐방하다
M: Absolutely! That's one of the schools that I'm <u>interested in</u>. When
is the tour?　　　　　　　　　　　　　　　　~에 관심이 있는
W: There's one on October 3rd and another one on October 10th.
They're both Saturdays. Which <u>date</u> is better for you?
　　　　　　　　　　　　　　　날짜
M: October 10th is better for me. What will we do during the tour?
W: We'll get to see the <u>campus</u> in the morning and then we'll meet
　　　　　　　　　　　캠퍼스
with an <u>admissions counselor</u> in the afternoon. You can ask them
　　　　입학 상담사
questions about the <u>admissions process</u> when we see them.
　　　　　　　　　　입학 절차
M: Okay, then I should <u>make a list of questions</u>. I have <u>a lot</u> of things
to ask them.　　　　　　질문 목록을 만들다　　　　　　　많은
W: That's a good idea. Also, everyone who goes on the tour will get a
<u>free</u> Liberty University T-shirt as <u>a souvenir</u>.
무료의　　　　　　　　　　　　　　기념품으로 (souvenir: 기념품)
M: Really? That's cool. So how do I <u>sign up for</u> the tour?
　　　　　　　　　　　　　　　　~을 신청하다
W: You can sign up on their website.
M: Okay, I will do that. Thank you so much for telling me about it.

해석
여: 안녕, Bruce! 나는 Liberty 대학교를 탐방할 예정이야. 너도 가고 싶니?
남: 당연하지! 그것은 내가 관심이 있는 학교들 중 하나야. 탐방이 언제니?

여: 하나는 10월 3일이고 다른 하나는 10월 10일에 있어. 둘 다 토요일이야. 어떤 날짜가 더
좋니?
남: 나는 10월 10일이 더 좋아. 탐방하는 동안 우리는 무엇을 하는 거야?
여: 오전에는 캠퍼스를 구경하고 그런 다음 오후에는 입학 상담사를 만날 거야. 그들을 만나
면 입학 절차에 대한 질문을 할 수 있어.
남: 좋아, 그럼 질문 목록을 만들어야겠다. 나는 그들에게 물어볼 게 많거든.
여: 좋은 생각이야. 또한, 탐방에 참가하는 모든 사람은 기념품으로 Liberty 대학교 티셔츠를
무료로 받을 거야.
남: 정말이야? 그거 멋진데. 그럼 어떻게 탐방을 신청하는 거니?
여: 대학교 웹 사이트에서 신청할 수 있어.
남: 좋아, 그렇게 할게. 그것에 대해 말해줘서 정말 고마워.

① 날짜　　　　② 활동 내용　　　✓ 참가 가능 인원수
④ 기념품　　　⑤ 신청 방법

09 Green Action Photo Contest에 관한 내용과 일치하지 않는 것

정답률 70% ▶ 정답 ④

W: Are you taking <u>actions</u> to help the <u>environment</u>? Then, why don't
　　　　　　행동을 취하고 있는(take action)　　환경
you join our <u>Green Action Photo Contest</u>? <u>As long as</u> you are a
　　　　　　　녹색 행동 사진 대회　　　　　　　~이라면
<u>resident</u> of our town, you can be the winner! From September
주민
1st until September 30th, 2021, you can <u>upload</u> photos of you
　　　　　　　　　　　　　　　　　　　　업로드 하다
<u>participating in</u> <u>eco-friendly activities</u> on social media. By <u>tagging</u>
참여하는 (participate in)　친환경 활동들　　　　　(by V-ing: ~함으로써, tag: 태그를 붙이다)
your photos with the hash tag #GreenAction, you can <u>automatically</u>
　　　　　　　　　　해시태그　　　　　　　　　　　　자동으로
participate in our contest. The maximum number of photos you
can post is five. The winner will be <u>announced</u> on October 4th. The
　　게시하다　　　　　　　　　　　발표되다(announce: 발표하다)
<u>prize</u> for the winner will be <u>delivered</u> by October 11th. The winning
상품　　　　　　　　　　배송되다(deliver: 배송하다)
photos will be posted on the town's website until the end of this
year. Show us your green actions. No action is too small!

해석
여: 여러분은 환경을 돕기 위한 행동들을 취하고 있나요? 그렇다면, Green Action Photo
Contest(녹색 행동 사진 대회)에 참가하시는 건 어떠세요? 여러분이 우리 마을의 주
민이라면 우승자가 될 수 있습니다! 2021년 9월 1일부터 9월 30일까지, 소셜 미디어
에 친환경 활동에 참여하는 여러분의 사진을 업로드 할 수 있습니다. 여러분의 사진에
#GreenAction이라는 해시태그를 붙임으로써 자동으로 대회에 참가할 수 있습니다. 게
시할 수 있는 최대 사진 수는 5장입니다. 우승자는 10월 4일에 발표될 것입니다. 우승 상
품은 10월 11일까지 배송될 것입니다. 우승 사진은 올해 말까지 마을 웹 사이트에 게시될
것입니다. 여러분의 녹색 행동을 보여주세요. 그 어떤 행동도 너무 작은 것은 없습니다!

① 9월 한 달간 사진을 업로드 할 수 있다.
② 정해진 해시태그를 붙이면 자동으로 참가하게 된다.
③ 사진은 5장까지 올릴 수 있다.
✓ 우승 상품은 10월 11일까지 직접 찾아가야 한다.
⑤ 우승 사진은 연말까지 마을 웹 사이트에 게시된다.

10 표에서 여자가 주문할 Rolling Cart

정답률 85% ▶ 정답 ②

M: Hey, Jessica. What are you <u>working on</u>?
　　　　　　　　　　　　　　하고 있는
　　　　　　　　　　(work on: ~을 (공들여) 하다, 착수하다)
W: Hey! I'm <u>trying to</u> order a new <u>rolling cart</u> for our <u>school's library</u>. Do
　　　　주문하려고 하고 있다　이동식 카트　　　학교 도서관
(try to V: ~하려고 하다, order: 주문하다)
you want to help me?
M: Sure. Let's see. Hmm... How about this plastic one? It looks like it's
<u>easy</u> to use.
쉬운
W: Well, the cart we have now is plastic and it's not <u>strong enough</u>, so,
　　　　　　　　　　　　　　　　　　　　　　　　튼튼한　충분히
I'd prefer to buy one that's made of metal or wood.
M: That makes sense. Then, let's get one that's made of metal or
wood. What about the number of <u>shelves</u>?
　　　　　　　　　　　　　　　　선반들
W: I think it would be nice to have a cart that has <u>at least</u> three shelves.
　　　　　　　　　　　　　　　　　　　　　　최소한
M: That's a good idea. I would also <u>recommend</u> one that has <u>lockable</u>
　　　　　　　　　　　　　　　　추천하다　　　　　잠금식 바퀴
<u>wheels</u> because that makes it easier to <u>control</u>.
　　　　　　　　　　　　　　　　　　　　제어하다

W: You're right! The one we have now doesn't have lockable wheels, so it's really hard to control.
M: I understand. That leaves us with these two options.
W: Well, we don't have much left in our budget. I can't spend more than $100.
M: All right. Then, this one would be the best choice.
W: Okay, then I'll order this one. Thanks for your help.

해석

남: 안녕, Jessica. 너는 무엇을 하고 있니?
여: 안녕! 학교 도서관에서 쓸 새 이동식 카트를 주문하려고 하고 있어. 나 좀 도와줄래?
남: 그래. 어디 보자. 흠… 이 플라스틱 카트는 어때? 사용하기에 쉬워 보이는데.
여: 음, 우리가 지금 가지고 있는 카트가 플라스틱인데 그것이 충분히 튼튼하지 않아서, 금속이나 나무로 만들어진 것을 사고 싶어.
남: 그거 일리가 있네. 그럼, 금속이나 나무로 만들어진 것을 사자. 선반의 수는 어때?
여: 최소한 3개의 선반이 있는 카트를 사는 것이 좋을 것 같아.
남: 좋은 생각이야. 나는 또한 제어하기 더 쉽기 때문에 잠금식 바퀴가 있는 것을 추천하고 싶어.
여: 네 말이 맞아! 우리가 지금 가지고 있는 것은 잠금식 바퀴가 없어서, 제어하기가 정말 힘들어.
남: 이해해. 그러면 우리에게 이 두 가지 선택지가 남아.
여: 음, 우리는 예산이 얼마 남지 않았어. 100달러 이상은 쓸 수 없어.
남: 알았어. 그럼, 이것이 제일 좋은 선택일 것 같아.
여: 좋아, 그럼 이것을 주문할게. 도와줘서 고마워.

이동식 카트

	모델	재질	선반 수	잠금식 바퀴	가격
①	A	금속	2	O	80달러
✔	B	금속	3	O	95달러
③	C	나무	3	O	105달러
④	D	나무	4	X	110달러
⑤	E	플라스틱	4	X	75달러

11 여자의 마지막 말에 대한 남자의 응답
정답률 75% ▶ 정답 ①

W: Hey, Sean! Is this your dog? He's adorable!
M: He's actually not my dog. I think he's lost, but I don't know what to do.
W: Oh, really? [Pause] Look at the couple over there! It seems like they're looking for something.
M: (Okay. Then let's ask them if they lost their dog.)

해석

여: 안녕, Sean! 이 개가 네 개니? 귀엽다!
남: 사실 내 개가 아니야. 길을 잃은 것 같은데, 내가 무엇을 해야 할지 모르겠어.
여: 오, 그래? [잠시 후] 저기 커플 좀 봐! 그들은 뭔가를 찾고 있는 것 같아.
남: (좋아. 그럼 그들에게 개를 잃어버렸는지 물어보자.)
✔ 좋아. 그럼 그들에게 개를 잃어버렸는지 물어보자.
② 진정해. 이 개는 전혀 위험하지 않아.
③ 미안해. 최선을 다했는데, 그것을 찾을 수 없었어.
④ 정말 다행이다! 나는 내 개를 영원히 잃어버린 줄 알았어.
⑤ 맞아! 개 주인들은 하루에 두 번 애완견을 산책시켜야 해.

12 남자의 마지막 말에 대한 여자의 응답
정답률 90% ▶ 정답 ①

M: Hi, we just wanted to see if we could still sit and order dinner.
W: Umm… I'm sorry but the kitchen closes in five minutes, so we won't be able to serve you.
M: That's disappointing. What time do you open tomorrow?
W: (We're open from 11 o'clock in the morning.)

해석

남: 안녕하세요, 아직 앉아서 저녁 식사를 주문할 수 있는지 알고 싶어요.
여: 음… 죄송하지만 주방이 5분 후에 문을 닫아서, 손님께 (음식을) 제공할 수 없습니다.
남: 실망스럽네요. 내일은 몇 시에 문을 여시나요?
여: (저희는 오전 11시부터 문을 엽니다.)

✔ 저희는 오전 11시부터 문을 엽니다.
② 최송하지만, 지금 모든 테이블이 꽉 찼습니다.
③ 오늘의 특선 요리는 바비큐 치킨입니다.
④ 저희 식당을 방문해 주셔서 감사합니다.
⑤ 저는 요리할 충분한 시간이 없어요.

13 여자의 마지막 말에 대한 남자의 응답
정답률 65% ▶ 정답 ③

M: Good morning, ma'am. May I help you?
W: Yes, please. I just heard that my flight will be delayed for six hours.
M: Oh, I'm sorry to hear that. Is there anything I can do for you?
W: Well, I know I have to check out of my room by 11, but that means I would be waiting at the airport for almost eight hours.
M: I understand. That's a long time to sit around and wait.
W: Is it possible for me to stay in my room for a couple more hours until I leave this afternoon?
M: Let me check to see if the room is available. [Pause] Luckily, ma'am, the room hasn't been booked for today.
W: Okay, then if I stay for a couple more hours, do I have to pay an additional charge?
M: (Yes. But you don't have to pay for a full day.)

해석

남: 안녕하세요, 고객님. 도와드릴까요?
여: 네. 방금 제 항공편이 6시간 지연될 것이라고 들었어요.
남: 오, 그렇다니 유감이네요. 제가 도와드릴 일이 있을까요?
여: 음, 11시까지 제 방에서 체크아웃해야 하는 것을 알지만, 그것은 제가 공항에서 거의 8시간 동안 기다릴 것이라는 뜻이에요.
남: 이해합니다. 앉아서 기다리기에 긴 시간이죠.
여: 오늘 오후에 떠날 때까지 제 방에서 몇 시간 더 머무르는 게 가능할까요?
남: 그 방이 이용 가능한지 확인해 보겠습니다. [잠시 후] 다행히도, 고객님, 그 방은 오늘 예약되지 않았습니다.
여: 좋아요, 그럼 몇 시간 더 머무르면 추가 요금을 지불해야 하나요?
남: (네. 하지만 하루치 요금을 지불할 필요는 없습니다.)
① 걱정하지 마세요. 다른 호텔을 예약하셔도 됩니다.
② 맞아요. 이미 요금을 지불하셨습니다.
✔ 네. 하지만 하루치 요금을 지불할 필요는 없습니다.
④ 죄송해요. 예약을 취소하셨어야 합니다.
⑤ 물론이죠. 오후까지 로비에 계셔도 됩니다.

14 남자의 마지막 말에 대한 여자의 응답
정답률 65% ▶ 정답 ①

W: Hi, James. Is everything okay? I heard there was a huge storm in your area last night.
M: Yeah, we had some really intense thunderstorms throughout the night. There was some damage.
W: Did anyone get hurt?
M: Thankfully, no, but there were a lot of fallen trees, and the roads were blocked.
W: Oh my! That must have been scary!
M: Yeah, it was. Then the electricity went out while the roads were being cleared.
W: So you didn't have any power last night?

M: No, I couldn't turn on any lights or use any electronic devices, but
　　　　　　 켜다　　　　　　　　　　　　　　　 전자 기기들
　　it's okay now.

W: That must have been so frustrating. Is there anything you need
　　　　　　　　　　　　답답하게 하는
　　help with?

M: Well, my basement is a mess. The water is up to my knees and all
　　　　　지하실　　 엉망진창　　　　　　　 ~까지
　　of my stuff down there is wet.
　　　 물건들

W: (Oh, no! I can come over today to help you clear it out.)

해석

여: 안녕, James. 모두 괜찮아? 어젯밤에 너희 지역에 큰 폭풍이 불었다고 들었어.
남: 그래, 밤새도록 정말 강한 뇌우가 있었어. 피해도 좀 있었지.
여: 다친 사람이 있니?
남: 다행스럽게도 없어, 하지만 쓰러진 나무들이 많이 있고 도로들이 막혔어.
여: 맙소사! 무서웠겠다!
남: 응, 그랬지. 그리고 나서 도로들이 치워지는 동안 전기가 나갔어.
여: 그래서 어젯밤에 전력이 없었어?
남: 응, 불을 켜거나 전자 기기들을 사용할 수 없었는데 지금은 괜찮아.
여: 정말 답답했겠다. 도움이 필요한 일이 있어?
남: 음, 내 지하실이 엉망진창이야. 물이 무릎까지 차 있고 저 아래에 있는 내 물건들이 다 젖었어.
여: (오, 저런! 내가 오늘 들러서 네가 그것을 청소하는 것을 도와줄 수 있어.)
✓오, 저런! 내가 오늘 들러서 네가 그것을 청소하는 것을 도와줄 수 있어.
② 신경 쓰지 마. 모두가 결정을 내릴 시간이 필요해.
③ 좋아. 우리는 위험에 처하면 지하실로 갈 수 있어.
④ 그래. 나무에 물을 더 자주 주는 게 어때?
⑤ 미안해. 나는 전구를 가는 방법을 몰라.

문제 풀이

여자는 폭풍 때문에 피해를 입은 남자에게 도움이 필요한지 물었고 남자는 지하실에 물이 차서 물건들이 다 젖었다고 말했다. 엉망이 된 지하실을 청소해야 하므로, 정답은 ① 'Oh, no! I can come over today to help you clear it out.(오, 저런! 내가 오늘 들러서 네가 그것을 청소하는 것을 도와줄 수 있어.)'이 가장 적절하다.

15 다음 상황에서 Emily가 Chris에게 할 말

정답률 60%
▶ 정답 ④

M: Emily and Chris are classmates. Emily is making cookies when she
　　gets a call from Chris. He says he is going to see a movie with his
　　　　 전화를 받다
　　friends and asks if she can join them. She says that she would love
　　to, but she can't go because her parents aren't home and she has
　　to watch her younger brother. Chris suggests that Emily bring her
　　　　　　　　　　　　　　　　　　　　제안하다　　　　　 데리고 가다
　　brother with her to the movie. Emily explains to Chris that her little
　　　　　　　　　　　　　　　　　　　　설명하다
　　brother has homework to finish, so he can't go either. She wants
　　　　　　　　 숙제　　 끝내다
　　to tell Chris that she has to look after her brother. In this situation,
　　　　　　　　　　　　　　　　　 ~을 돌보다
　　what would Emily most likely say to Chris?

Emily: (I'm sorry, but I need to take care of my brother.)
　　　　　　　　　　　　 ~을 돌봐야 하다
　　(need to V: ~해야 하다, take care of: ~을 돌보다)

해석

남: Emily와 Chris는 반 친구이다. Emily는 Chris에게 전화를 받을 때 쿠키를 만들고 있다. 그는 친구들과 영화를 보러 갈 예정이라고 말하며 그녀가 그들과 함께 갈 수 있는지 물어본다. 그녀는 가고 싶지만 그녀의 부모님께서 집에 안 계셔서 남동생을 봐야 하기 때문에 갈 수 없다고 말한다. Chris는 Emily에게 그녀의 남동생을 데리고 영화를 보러 가자고 제안한다. Emily는 Chris에게 남동생이 끝내야 할 숙제가 있어서 그도 갈 수 없다고 설명한다. 그녀는 Chris에게 그녀의 남동생을 돌봐야 한다고 말하고 싶다. 이러한 상황에서, Emily는 Chris에게 뭐라고 말하겠는가?

Emily: (미안하지만, 나는 내 남동생을 돌봐야 해.)
① 다행히도, 나는 숙제를 끝냈어.
② 내 남동생과 함께 영화를 봐도 될까?
③ 고마워, 그리고 네 쿠키 잘 먹을게.
✓미안하지만, 나는 내 남동생을 돌봐야 해.
⑤ 잠깐만 내 남동생 좀 봐줄래?

16~17 1지문 2문항

W: Everyone loves a good night's sleep, but for wild animals, finding
　　　　　　　　　　　　　 숙면
　　the right time and place can be difficult. Whether it's staying safe,
　　　　　　　　　　　　　　　　　　　　　　　　　　　　 안전한
　　keeping warm, or remembering to breathe, animals have a lot to
　　　　　　　　　 호흡하는 것을 기억하는 것
　　　　　　 (remember to V: ~하는 것을 기억하다, breathe: 호흡하다)
　　consider before they go to bed. As a result, they've come up with
　　고려하다　　　　　　　　　　　　　　　 그 결과　　 ~을 생각해냈다(come up with)
　　some clever and interesting solutions. To start with, bats sleep
　　　　　　　　　　　　　　 해결책들　　　　　 우선　　　　　 박쥐들
　　in caves while hanging upside down. Doing that not only keeps
　　　　 동굴들　　 매달리는(hang)　 거꾸로
　　them away from enemies but also means they are in the perfect
　　~으로부터 그들을 멀리 떨어지게 하다 ●적들
　　position to fly away if necessary. Meanwhile, ducks sleep side by
　　　 위치　　　　　　　 필요할 경우　　　　　　 오리들　　　　 나란히
　　side in rows. The ducks on the outside of the rows sleep with one
　　　　 줄지어　　　　　　　　　　　　　　　　　　 한쪽 눈을 뜬 채
　　eye open to watch for danger, while the ducks on the inside sleep
　　　　　　　　 위험을 살피다
　　with both eyes closed. Giraffes require little rest, sleeping for only
　　　　 양쪽 눈을 감은 채　　 기린들　　　　 휴식
　　five minutes at a time or as little as 30 minutes a day. They sleep
　　　　　　　　　 한 번에　　　　　　 고작 30분　　　　 하루에
　　in short intervals, sometimes sitting down or even standing up,
　　　 짧은 간격으로　　　　　　 때때로
　　so that they're ready to run. Finally, dolphins have to consciously
　　　　 달릴 준비가 되다　　　　 돌고래들　　　　　 의식적으로
　　　 (be ready to V: ~할 준비가 되다)
　　think in order to breathe, even when they're sleeping. They only let
　　　　 호흡하기 위해서
　　　 (in order to V: ~하기 위해서)
　　part of their brain relax and keep one eye open as they sleep.
　　　 일부　　　　　　　　　 쉬다

해석

여: 모두가 숙면을 좋아하지만, 야생동물의 경우, 적당한 시간과 장소를 찾는 것이 어려울 수 있다. 그것이 안전하게 머무는 것이든, 따뜻하게 지내는 것이든, 아니면 호흡하는 것을 기억하는 것이든, 동물들은 잠자리에 들기 전에 고려해야 할 것이 많다. 그 결과, 그들은 영리하고 흥미로운 몇 가지 해결책을 생각해냈다. 우선, 박쥐는 동굴에서 거꾸로 매달려서 잠을 잔다. 그렇게 하는 것은 그들을 적들로부터 멀리 떨어지게 할 뿐만 아니라 필요할 경우 그들이 날아갈 수 있는 완벽한 위치에 있다는 것을 의미한다. 한편, 오리는 나란히 줄지어 잠을 잔다. 줄의 바깥쪽에 있는 오리는 위험을 살피기 위해 한쪽 눈을 뜬 채 잠을 자고, 반면에 안쪽에 있는 오리는 양쪽 눈을 감은 채 잠을 잔다. 기린은 휴식을 거의 필요로 하지 않는데, 한 번에 겨우 5분 또는 하루에 고작 30분 동안 잠을 잔다. 그들은 달릴 준비가 되어 있도록 때때로 앉거나 심지어 서서 짧은 간격으로 잠을 잔다. 마지막으로, 돌고래는 잠을 자고 있을 때조차도 호흡하기 위해서 의식적으로 생각해야 한다. 그들은 잠을 잘 때 뇌의 일부만 쉬게 하고 한쪽 눈을 뜨고 있다.

16 여자가 하는 말의 주제

정답률 90%
▶ 정답 ②

① 다양한 문화권에서 인기 있는 여러 동물들
✓동물들이 생존을 위해 사용하는 독특한 수면 습관들
③ 멸종 위기종이 되고 있는 야생동물들
④ 동물들이 먹는 방식을 바꾼 방법
⑤ 사람들에게 행운을 가져다 주는 동물들

17 언급된 동물이 아닌 것

정답률 90%
▶ 정답 ③

① 박쥐　　　　　　② 오리　　　　　　✓침팬지
④ 기린　　　　　　⑤ 돌고래

13 2021년 11월 학력평가

01	②	02	③	03	①	04	⑤	05	②
06	③	07	①	08	④	09	④	10	③
11	①	12	①	13	⑤	14	②	15	③
16	④	17	⑤

01 남자가 하는 말의 목적

정답률 60% ▶ 정답 ②

[Chime bell rings.]

M: Hello, passengers. I'm James Walker from the Greenville Subway
System. As you know, the international film festival will be held in
our city next month. Throughout the festival, some movies will run
till late at night. So, for our citizens' convenience, the Greenville
City Council has decided to provide longer subway service hours
during the festival. All Greenville subway lines will run extra hours
while the festival is going on. You can easily check the extended
service schedules using the Greenville Subway App. I hope you can
make the most of the festival experience with our services. Thank
you.

해석

[차임벨이 울린다.]
남: 안녕하세요, 승객 여러분. 저는 Greenville Subway System(Greenville 지하철 시스템)의
James Walker입니다. 아시다시피, 다음 달에 우리 시에서 국제 영화제가 열릴 것입니다.
축제 기간 내내, 일부 영화들은 밤늦게까지 상영될 것입니다. 그래서, 우리 시민들의 편의
를 위해, Greenville 시의회는 축제 기간 동안 더 긴 지하철 운행 시간을 제공하기로 결정
했습니다. 축제가 진행되는 동안 모든 Greenville 지하철 노선은 추가 시간 운행될 것입니
다. Greenville 지하철 앱을 이용하면 연장 운행 일정을 쉽게 확인하실 수 있습니다. 저희
의 서비스로 축제 경험을 최대한 활용하시기 바랍니다. 감사합니다.

① 지하철 앱 출시를 홍보하려고
☑ 지하철 연장 운행을 안내하려고
③ 지하철 운행 지연에 대해 사과하려고
④ 지하철 시설 보수 공사 일정을 공지하려고
⑤ 지하철 내 영화 촬영에 대한 양해를 구하려고

02 여자의 의견

정답률 95% ▶ 정답 ③

W: Good morning, Jason. It's sports day today. Do you have everything
you need?
M: Yes, Mom. I put a water bottle, some snacks, and a towel in my
bag. Is there anything I forgot?
W: What about sunblock? Did you put it on?
M: Sunblock? It's not sunny outside.
W: Jason, you should wear sunblock even on a cloudy day.
M: But I don't feel the sun in weather like this.
W: Even if you don't feel the sun on your skin, the harmful light from
the sun can damage your skin because the clouds don't block it.
M: Really? You mean I can still get a sunburn even on a cloudy day?
W: Yes. That's why you shouldn't forget to wear sunblock even if it's
not sunny outside.
M: I didn't know that. I'll put it on now.

해석

여: 좋은 아침이야, Jason. 오늘은 운동회 날이구나. 필요한 모든 것을 가지고 있니?

남: 네, 엄마. 제 가방에 물병, 과자, 그리고 수건을 넣었어요. 제가 잊어버린 게 있나요?
여: 자외선 차단제는 어때? 그것을 발랐니?
남: 자외선 차단제요? 밖은 화창하지 않아요.
여: Jason, 흐린 날에도 자외선 차단제를 발라야 해.
남: 하지만 이런 날에는 햇빛이 느껴지지 않아요.
여: 피부로 햇빛을 느끼지 못한다 하더라도, 구름이 그것을 막는 것은 아니기 때문에 태양으
로부터 나오는 해로운 빛이 피부를 손상시킬 수 있어.
남: 정말이에요? 흐린 날에도 여전히 햇빛에 심하게 탈 수 있다는 말씀이세요?
여: 그래. 그런 이유로 밖이 화창하지 않다 하더라도 자외선 차단제를 바르는 것을 잊어버리
면 안 되는 거란다.
남: 저는 그것을 몰랐어요. 지금 바를게요.

① 날씨가 더울수록 수분 보충이 중요하다.
② 적당한 준비 운동이 부상 위험을 줄인다.
☑ 흐린 날에도 자외선 차단제를 발라야 한다.
④ 햇빛이 강한 날에는 야외 활동을 자제해야 한다.
⑤ 화상을 입었을 때 신속하게 응급 처치를 해야 한다.

03 두 사람의 관계

정답률 85% ▶ 정답 ①

M: Hello, Ms. Green. You came just on time.
W: Really? I thought I was early.
M: No. Your car is over there. Follow me, please.
W: Wow. All the dirt is gone. It looks like a new car.
M: Yeah. But some stains were difficult to remove. It's better to have
your car washed right after it gets dirty.
W: I went on a business trip for a month, so I didn't have time. I'll keep
that in mind.
M: Anyway, while cleaning the inside, we found this earring under the
driver's seat.
W: Really? I thought I had lost that. Thank you.
M: You're welcome. Would you like to pay by credit card or in cash?
W: I'll pay in cash. Here you are.
M: Okay. [Pause] Here is your receipt. And this is a discount coupon
for our car wash center. You can use it on your next visit.
W: That's nice. Thank you.

해석

남: 안녕하세요, Green 씨. 제시간에 오셨네요.
여: 그래요? 저는 일찍 왔다고 생각했어요.
남: 아니에요. 당신의 차는 저쪽에 있어요. 저를 따라오세요.
여: 와. 먼지가 다 없어졌네요. 새 차처럼 보여요.
남: 네. 그런데 몇몇 얼룩들은 제거하기 어려웠어요. 더러워진 후에 바로 당신의 차를 세차하
는 것이 더 좋아요.
여: 제가 한 달 동안 출장을 다녀와서, 시간이 없었어요. 그것을 명심할게요.
남: 어쨌든, 내부를 청소하다가, 저희가 운전석 밑에서 이 귀걸이를 찾았어요.
여: 정말이에요? 저는 그것을 잃어버린 줄 알았어요. 감사해요.
남: 천만에요. 신용카드로 지불하시겠어요 아니면 현금으로 지불하시겠어요?
여: 현금으로 지불할게요. 여기 있어요.
남: 알겠습니다. [잠시 후] 영수증 여기 있어요. 그리고 이것은 저희 세차장 할인 쿠폰이에요.
다음에 방문하실 때 그것을 사용하실 수 있어요.
여: 잘됐네요. 감사해요.

☑ 세차장 직원 ― 고객
② 청소 업체 직원 ― 집주인
③ 중고차 판매원 ― 구매자
④ 분실물 센터 직원 ― 방문자
⑤ 액세서리 디자이너 ― 의뢰인

04 그림에서 대화의 내용과 일치하지 않는 것

정답률 80% ▶ 정답 ⑤

W: Hi, Harry. Congratulations on your wedding. Did you finish
decorating the new house?

M: I just finished the living room. Look at this picture, Linda.

W: Wow. I love the striped curtains on the window.
<u>줄무늬 커튼들</u>

M: Thanks. Do you see those two cushions on the sofa? My sister
<u>쿠션들</u>
made them as wedding gifts.
<u>결혼 선물</u>

W: That's lovely. Oh, you put a round table on the rug.
<u>원형 테이블</u>

M: Yeah. We spend time reading books around the table. What do you
<u>책을 읽으면서 시간을 보내다(spend time V-ing: ~하면서 시간을 보내다)</u>
think of the clock on the bookshelf?
<u>시계</u> <u>책꽂이</u>

W: It looks good in that room. By the way, is that a plant under the
<u>식물</u>
calendar?
<u>달력</u>

M: Yes. I placed it there because the plant helps to clean the air.
<u>놓았다(place)</u> <u>공기를 깨끗하게 하다</u>

W: You decorated your house really well.

M: Thanks. I'll invite you over when we have the housewarming party.
<u>집들이</u>

해석

여: 안녕, Harry. 결혼을 축하해. 새 집을 꾸미는 것을 끝냈니?

남: 방금 거실을 끝냈어. 이 사진 좀 봐, Linda.

여: 와. 나는 창문에 있는 줄무늬 커튼이 정말 마음에 들어.

남: 고마워. 소파 위에 있는 저 쿠션 두 개 보이니? 내 여동생이 결혼 선물로 그것들을 만들었어.

여: 멋지다. 오, 깔개 위에 원형 테이블을 놓았구나.

남: 그래. 우리는 테이블 주변에서 책을 읽으면서 시간을 보내거든. 책꽂이 위에 있는 시계는 어떠니?

여: 그 방에 잘 어울려. 그런데, 달력 아래에 있는 것은 식물이니?

남: 그래. 식물이 공기를 깨끗하게 하는 데 도움을 주기 때문에 거기에 놓았어.

여: 너는 집을 정말 잘 꾸몄구나.

남: 고마워. 우리가 집들이를 할 때 너를 초대할게.

05 남자가 할 일

정답률 85%

▶ 정답 ②

M: Jane, the Stop Using Plastic campaign starts tomorrow. Let's do a
<u>플라스틱 사용 중지 캠페인</u>
final check.
<u>최종 점검을 하다</u>

W: Okay, Robin. I just finished editing a video clip about plastic waste.
<u>동영상 편집을 끝냈다(edit: 편집하다, video clip: 동영상)</u>

M: Then, I'm going to check the screen that we'll use for the video.

W: No worries. I've already done it, and it works well.
<u>이미</u> <u>잘 작동하다</u>

M: That's nice. I uploaded a campaign poster on our organization's
<u>업로드했다</u> <u>포스터</u> <u>단체의 웹사이트</u>
website.

W: Yeah. Some of my friends saw it and texted me they're coming.
<u>문자를 보냈다</u>

M: My friends, too. They showed a huge interest in the reusable bag
<u>~에 큰 관심을 보였다</u> <u>재사용 가능한</u>
decorating activity. The bags are ready in that box.
<u>활동</u>

W: Good. By the way, where are the badges you ordered for visitors?
<u>배지들</u>

M: Oh, I left the badges in my car. I'll bring them right away.
<u>두고 왔다(leave)</u>

W: Great. It seems that everything is prepared.
<u>준비되다(prepare: 준비하다)</u>

해석

남: Jane, 플라스틱 사용 중지 캠페인이 내일 시작돼. 최종 점검을 해 보자.

여: 알겠어, Robin. 나는 방금 플라스틱 쓰레기에 대한 동영상 편집을 끝냈어.

남: 그럼, 나는 우리가 영상을 위해 사용할 스크린을 점검할게.

여: 걱정하지 마. 내가 이미 점검했는데, 그것은 잘 작동해.

남: 잘됐다. 내가 우리 단체의 웹사이트에 캠페인 포스터를 업로드했어.

여: 그래. 내 친구들 중 몇 명이 그것을 보고 오겠다고 나에게 문자를 보냈어.

남: 내 친구들도 그랬어. 그들은 재사용 가능한 가방 꾸미기 활동에 큰 관심을 보였어. 가방들은 저 상자 안에 준비되어 있어.

여: 좋아. 그런데, 방문객을 위해 네가 주문한 배지들은 어디에 있니?

남: 오, 내 차에 배지들을 두고 왔어. 지금 바로 그것들을 가져올게.

여: 좋아. 모든 것이 준비된 것 같아.

① 가방 준비하기
✔② 배지 가져오기
③ 스크린 점검하기
④ 동영상 편집하기
⑤ 포스터 업로드하기

문제 풀이

여자가 방문객에게 주기 위해 주문한 배지가 어디에 있는지 묻자 남자는 자신의 차에 두고 온 배지를 가져오겠다고 대답하고 있다. 따라서 남자가 할 일은 ②'배지 가져오기'이다.

06 여자가 지불할 금액

정답률 80%

▶ 정답 ③

M: Welcome to Kids Clothing Club. How may I help you?

W: I'm looking for a muffler for my son. He's 5 years old.
<u>~을 찾고 있다(look for)</u> <u>목도리</u>

M: Okay. Follow me. [Pause] This red muffler is one of the best sellers
<u>가장 잘 팔리는 제품들</u>
in our shop.

W: I love the color. How much is it?

M: It's $50. This one is popular because of the cartoon character
<u>인기가 있는</u> <u>만화 캐릭터</u>
here.

W: Oh, that's my son's favorite character. I'll buy one red muffler, then.

M: Great. Anything else?

W: How much are these winter socks?
<u>겨울 양말</u>

M: A pair of socks is $5.

W: All right. I'll buy two pairs.

M: So, one red muffler and two pairs of winter socks, right?

W: Yes. Can I use this discount coupon?

M: Of course. With that coupon, you can get 10% off the total price.
<u>총액에서 10% 할인을 받다</u>

W: Good. Here's my credit card.

해석

남: Kids Clothing Club에 오신 것을 환영합니다. 어떻게 도와드릴까요?

여: 제 아들에게 줄 목도리를 찾고 있어요. 그 애는 5살이에요.

남: 알겠습니다. 저를 따라오세요. [잠시 후] 이 빨간 목도리는 저희 가게에서 가장 잘 팔리는 제품 중 하나예요.

여: 색상이 정말 마음에 드네요. 얼마죠?

남: 50달러예요. 이 제품은 여기에 있는 만화 캐릭터 때문에 인기가 있어요.

여: 오, 그것은 제 아들이 가장 좋아하는 캐릭터예요. 그럼 빨간 목도리를 하나 살게요.

남: 알겠습니다. 또 다른 필요한 건 없으세요?

여: 이 겨울 양말은 얼마인가요?

남: 양말 한 켤레는 5달러예요.

여: 알겠어요. 두 켤레 살게요.

남: 그럼, 빨간 목도리 하나와 겨울 양말 두 켤레네요, 맞죠?

여: 네. 이 할인 쿠폰을 사용할 수 있나요?

남: 물론이죠. 그 쿠폰으로 총액에서 10% 할인을 받으실 수 있어요.

여: 좋아요. 여기 제 신용카드가 있어요.

① $45 ② $50 ✔③ $54
④ $55 ⑤ $60

문제 풀이

가격이 50달러인 목도리 한 개와 한 켤레에 5달러인 양말 두 켤레를 사면 총액은 60달러이다. 여기에 쿠폰을 사용해 10% 할인을 받을 수 있다고 했으므로 여자가 지불할 금액은 54달러이다. 따라서 답은 ③'$54'이다.

07 남자가 London Walking Tour에 참여하지 못한 이유

정답률 85%

▶ 정답 ①

W: Hi, Jeremy. How was your trip to London?

M: It was fantastic, Julia. I watched the musical you recommended.
<u>추천했다</u>

W: Good. What about the London Walking Tour? Did you enjoy it?
<u>런던 도보 투어</u>

M: Unfortunately, I couldn't join the tour.
<u>안타깝게도</u> <u>참여하다</u>

W: Why? Didn't you say you booked it?
예약했다
M: Yes. I made a reservation for the tour in advance.
예약을 했다(make a reservation)   미리
W: Oh, was the tour canceled because of the weather?
취소된(cancel: 취소하다)
M: No. The weather was no problem at all.
W: Then, why couldn't you join the tour?
M: Actually, I fell down the day before the tour, so I had some pain in
넘어졌다(fall down)   통증
my ankle. That's why I couldn't make it.
발목   (모임 등에) 가다
W: I'm sorry to hear that. Is it okay, now?
M: Yes. It's completely fine now. Oh, I forgot to bring the souvenir I
완전히   기념품
bought for you. I'll bring it tomorrow.
W: That's so sweet. Thanks.

해석
여: 안녕, Jeremy. 런던 여행은 어땠니?
남: 환상적이었어, Julia. 나는 네가 추천한 뮤지컬을 관람했어.
여: 잘했어. London Walking Tour(런던 도보 투어)는 어땠어? 즐거웠니?
남: 안타깝게도, 나는 그 투어에 참여할 수 없었어.
여: 왜? 너는 그것을 예약했다고 하지 않았어?
남: 그래. 미리 투어 예약을 했지.
여: 오, 날씨 때문에 투어가 취소됐니?
남: 아니. 날씨는 전혀 문제가 없었어.
여: 그럼, 왜 투어에 참여하지 못했어?
남: 사실, 투어 전날에 넘어져서, 발목에 통증이 있었어. 그래서 가지 못했어.
여: 정말 안됐다. 지금은 괜찮니?
남: 응. 이제 완전히 괜찮아. 오, 너를 위해 산 기념품을 가져오는 것을 잊었어. 내일 가져올게.
여: 정말 친절하구나. 고마워.

✔ 발목에 통증이 있어서
② 뮤지컬을 관람해야 해서
③ 투어 예약을 하지 못해서
④ 기념품을 사러 가야 해서
⑤ 날씨로 인해 투어가 취소되어서

08 Winter Lake Festival에 관해 언급되지 않은 것
정답률 90%   ▶ 정답 ④

M: What are you doing, Laura?
W: Hi, Tim. I'm looking for winter festivals to visit during vacation.
방학 동안에
M: Is there anything good?
W: Yes, look at this. There is a new local event called the Winter Lake
지역의   겨울 호수 축제
Festival.
M: Awesome. When does it start?
W: December 18th and it'll be held for two weeks.
M: Cool. Oh, it'll take place in Stevenson Park.
개최되다
W: Great. It's near our school. If you don't have any plans during
vacation, let's go together.
M: Of course. Is there an entrance fee?
입장료
W: Yes. Here, it says $3. It's not expensive.
비싼
M: Good. Look! There are so many kinds of activities to enjoy.
활동
W: Yeah, there is ice skating, ice fishing, and a snowball fight.
빙상 스케이팅   얼음 낚시   눈싸움
M: They all sound exciting. Let's have fun there.

해석
남: 무엇을 하고 있니, Laura?
여: 안녕, Tim. 방학 동안에 방문할 겨울 축제를 찾고 있어.
남: 뭐 좋은 게 있니?
여: 응, 이것 좀 봐. Winter Lake Festival(겨울 호수 축제)이라고 하는 새로운 지역 행사가 있어.
남: 멋지다. 언제 시작하니?
여: 12월 18일이고 2주 동안 열릴 거야.
남: 좋네. 오, Stevenson 공원에서 개최되는 구나.
여: 잘됐다. 그것은 우리 학교 근처에 있잖아. 네가 방학 동안에 아무 계획이 없으면, 같이 가자.
남: 물론이지. 입장료가 있니?
여: 응. 여기, 3달러라고 쓰여 있어. 비싸지 않아.

남: 좋아. 봐! 즐길 수 있는 많은 종류의 활동들이 있어.
여: 그래, 빙상 스케이팅, 얼음 낚시, 그리고 눈싸움이 있네.
남: 모두 흥미롭게 들려. 거기서 재미있게 놀자.
① 기간   ② 장소   ③ 입장료
✔ 기념품   ⑤ 활동 종류

09 Mascot Design Contest에 관한 내용과 일치하지 않는 것
정답률 85%   ▶ 정답 ④

W: Hello, supporters! I'm Christine Miller, manager of Western
서포터들
Football Club. This year, we're holding a Mascot Design Contest
마스코트 디자인 대회
to celebrate our team's 1st championship. Anyone who loves our
기념하다   첫 우승
team can participate in this contest. The mascot design should be
~에 참여하다
related to our team's slogan "One team, one spirit." The winning
~과 관련되다   정신
design will be chosen through a fan vote. And the winner will
팬 투표를 통해
receive a team uniform as a prize. People who want to participate
팀 유니폼   상으로
should send their design by email by December 5th. Show your
이메일로 ~까지
creativity and love for our team through active participation. For
창의력   적극적인   참여
more information, please visit our website. Thank you.

해석
여: 안녕하세요, 서포터 여러분! 저는 Western Football Club의 매니저인 Christine Miller입니다. 올해, 저희는 저희 팀의 첫 우승을 기념하기 위해 Mascot Design Contest(마스코트 디자인 대회)를 개최합니다. 저희 팀을 사랑하는 누구든 이 대회에 참여할 수 있습니다. 마스코트 디자인은 저희 팀의 슬로건인 '하나의 팀, 하나의 정신'과 관련되어야 합니다. 수상 디자인은 팬 투표를 통해 선정될 것입니다. 그리고 수상자는 상으로 팀 유니폼을 받게 될 것입니다. 참여를 원하시는 분들은 12월 5일까지 디자인을 이메일로 보내야 합니다. 적극적인 참여를 통해 저희 팀에 대한 여러분의 창의력과 사랑을 보여주세요. 더 많은 정보를 원하시면, 저희 웹사이트를 방문해 주세요. 감사합니다.
① 팀을 사랑하는 누구든 참여할 수 있다.
② 디자인은 팀 슬로건과 관련되어야 한다.
③ 수상작은 팬 투표로 선정될 것이다.
✔ 수상자는 상으로 시즌 티켓을 받게 될 것이다.
⑤ 참가 희망자는 디자인을 이메일로 보내야 한다.

10 표에서 두 사람이 예약할 캠핑장
정답률 85%   ▶ 정답 ③

W: Honey, what are you looking at?
M: This is a list of the best campsites in 2021. How about going to one
목록   가장 좋은 캠핑장들
of them next month?
W: Sounds great. Let me see. [Pause] There are five different
campsites.
M: Yeah. Since we went to Seaside campsite last time, let's choose
among the other four.
W: Good. Hmm, I don't want to spend more than $100 per night. It's
(돈을) 쓰다   1박에
too expensive.
M: I agree with that. What do you think of staying in a camping car?
~에 동의하다   머무는 것(stay) 캠핑카
W: Oh, I want to try it. It'll be a special experience.
특별한
M: Then, we can choose between these two.
W: What about going to this campsite? Since this has a kids'
playground, our children can have more fun.
어린이 놀이터
M: Cool! I'll make a reservation for this campsite.
예약하다(reservation: 예약)

해석
여: 여보, 무엇을 보고 있어요?
남: 이것은 2021년의 가장 좋은 캠핑장들 목록이에요. 다음 달에 그곳들 중 한 곳에 가는 게 어때요?
여: 좋아요. 어디 보자. [잠시 후] 다섯 곳의 다른 캠핑장이 있네요.
남: 네. 우리는 지난번에 Seaside 캠핑장에 갔으니까, 다른 네 곳 중에서 골라봐요.
여: 알겠어요. 흠, 저는 1박에 100달러 이상을 쓰고 싶지는 않아요. 그건 너무 비싸요.
남: 저도 동의해요. 캠핑카에 머무는 것에 대해 어떻게 생각해요?
여: 오, 저는 그것을 해보고 싶어요. 그것은 특별한 경험이 될 거예요.

남: 그럼, 우리는 이 두 곳 중에서 선택할 수 있어요.
여: 이 캠핑장에 가는 게 어때요? 이곳은 어린이 놀이터가 있기 때문에, 우리 아이들이 더 재미있게 놀 수 있잖아요.
남: 멋지네요! 이 캠핑장을 예약할게요.

2021 가장 좋은 캠핑장

	캠핑장	위치	가격(1박)	종류	어린이 놀이터
①	A	Seaside	65달러	텐트	X
②	B	Jungle Hut	70달러	텐트	O
✔	C	Rose Valley	85달러	캠핑카	O
④	D	Blue Forest	90달러	캠핑카	X
⑤	E	Pine Island	110달러	캠핑카	O

11 남자의 마지막 말에 대한 여자의 응답
정답률 85% ▶ 정답 ①

M: Kate, I heard your company moved to a new office. How is it?
W: It's all good except one thing. It's far from my house.
M: Oh, really? How long does it take to get there?
W: (It takes an hour by bus.)

해석
남: Kate, 당신의 회사가 새 사무실로 이전했다고 들었어요. 어때요?
여: 한 가지를 제외하고는 다 좋아요. 그곳은 제 집에서 멀어요.
남: 오, 정말이에요? 거기에 가려면 얼마나 걸리나요?
여: (버스로 한 시간 걸려요.)
✔ 버스로 한 시간 걸려요.
② 그것은 당신의 사무실보다 더 커요.
③ 당신은 집에서 더 일찍 나왔어야 했어요.
④ 그 회사는 지난달에 이전했어요.
⑤ 저는 그 일자리를 구하느라 힘들었어요.

12 여자의 마지막 말에 대한 남자의 응답
정답률 90% ▶ 정답 ①

W: Honey, you know my nephew is coming over this evening. How about ordering pizza for dinner?
M: Sure. Which topping does he prefer, grilled beef or shrimp?
W: Oh, he doesn't like beef. He loves seafood.
M: (Okay. I'll order a shrimp pizza.)

해석
여: 여보, 제 조카가 오늘 저녁에 올 예정인 거 알잖아요. 저녁으로 피자를 주문하는 게 어때요?
남: 좋아요. 그는 구운 소고기와 새우 중 어떤 토핑을 선호하죠?
여: 오, 그는 소고기를 좋아하지 않아요. 해산물을 정말 좋아해요.
남: (알겠어요. 제가 새우 피자를 주문할게요.)
✔ 알겠어요. 제가 새우 피자를 주문할게요.
② 고마워요. 당신은 요리를 잘하네요.
③ 아니요. 피자가 아직 배달되지 않았어요.
④ 물론이죠. 언제든지 오세요.
⑤ 네. 식사를 거르는 것은 당신의 건강에 해로워요.

13 남자의 마지막 말에 대한 여자의 응답
정답률 80% ▶ 정답 ⑤

M: Honey, did you read this leaflet on the table?
W: Not yet. What's it about?
M: It says the local children's library is going to hold some events to celebrate their reopening.
W: Is there anything good?
M: Let me see. [Pause] There will be a Meet-the-Author event. Rebecca Moore is coming.
W: Oh, she's one of our son's favorite writers.

M: Yes. He'll be excited if he can meet her in person.
W: Let's take him to that event. When is it?
M: It's next Saturday, 1 p.m.
W: But we have a lunch reservation at the French restaurant at that time.
M: Oh, I forgot. Then how about rescheduling lunch? It's a rare chance to meet the author.
W: (You're right. I'll change the reservation now.)

해석
남: 여보, 테이블 위에 있는 이 전단을 읽어 봤어요?
여: 아직이요. 무엇에 관한 거예요?
남: 지역 어린이 도서관이 재개관을 축하하기 위해 몇 가지 행사를 개최할 예정이라고 하네요.
여: 뭐 좋은 거 있어요?
남: 어디 보자. [잠시 휴] 작가와의 만남 행사가 있을 거예요. Rebecca Moore가 오네요.
여: 오, 그녀는 우리 아들이 가장 좋아하는 작가 중 한 명이잖아요.
남: 그래요. 아이가 그녀를 직접 만날 수 있다면 기뻐할 거예요.
여: 아이를 그 행사에 데려가요. 언제죠?
남: 다음 주 토요일, 오후 1시네요.
여: 하지만 우리는 그 시간에 프랑스 식당에 점심 예약이 되어 있잖아요.
남: 오, 잊어버렸어요. 그럼 점심 식사 일정을 다시 잡는 게 어때요? 그 작가를 만나는 것은 드문 기회잖아요.
여: (당신 말이 맞아요. 제가 지금 예약을 변경할게요.)
① 너무 늦었어요. 회의는 이미 끝났어요.
② 물론이죠. 프랑스 요리책이 많이 있어요.
③ 동의해요. 당신은 독서에 너무 많은 시간을 보내요.
④ 아니요. 우리는 도서관에서 음식을 먹을 수 없어요.
✔ 당신 말이 맞아요. 제가 지금 예약을 변경할게요.

14 여자의 마지막 말에 대한 남자의 응답
정답률 80% ▶ 정답 ②

[Cell phone rings.]
W: This is Fairview Laptop Repair. How may I help you?
M: Hello, this is David Brown. I missed your call this morning.
W: Oh, Mr. Brown. You requested the screen repair yesterday, right?
M: Yes. Is there any problem?
W: The screen is all repaired. But we found another problem with your laptop. You need to replace the battery.
M: Oh, I didn't know that. How bad is it?
W: Even when the battery is fully charged, it won't last longer than an hour.
M: Really? How much does it cost to change the battery?
W: It's $70. It's on sale now.
M: That sounds great. But, I'm worried it'll delay the laptop pick-up time, 5 p.m. today.
W: Don't worry. You can still pick it up at that time.
M: (Then, I'd like to replace the battery.)

해석
[휴대전화가 울린다.]
여: Fairview Laptop Repair입니다. 어떻게 도와드릴까요?
남: 안녕하세요, 저는 David Brown입니다. 제가 오늘 오전에 전화를 못 받았어요.
여: 오, Brown 씨. 어제 화면 수리를 요청하셨네요, 그렇죠?
남: 네. 무슨 문제라도 있나요?
여: 화면은 모두 수리되었어요. 그런데 저희가 고객님의 노트북에서 다른 문제를 발견했어요. 배터리를 교체하셔야 해요.
남: 오, 저는 그것을 몰랐어요. 얼마나 안 좋은가요?
여: 배터리가 완전히 충전되어도, 한 시간 이상 지속되지 않을 거예요.
남: 정말이에요? 배터리를 바꾸는데 얼마나 드나요?
여: 70달러예요. 지금 세일 중이에요.
남: 그거 잘됐네요. 그런데, 저는 그것 때문에 오늘 오후 5시인 노트북 픽업 시간이 지연될까 봐 걱정이네요.

여: 걱정하지 마세요. 여전히 그 시간에 그것을 찾으러 오실 수 있어요.
남: (그럼, 저는 배터리를 교체하고 싶어요.)
① 죄송해요. 제 노트북을 가져오는 것을 잊었어요.
✓② 그럼, 저는 배터리를 교체하고 싶어요.
③ 음, 화면이 여전히 잘 안 나와요.
④ 좋아요. 어제 새로운 수리점이 문을 열었어요.
⑤ 사실, 저는 환불을 위한 영수증이 없어요.

문제 풀이
노트북 수리를 맡겼던 남자는 배터리도 교체해야 한다는 여자의 말에 오늘 오후 5시로 예정된 픽업 시간이 지연될 것을 걱정하고 있다. 그러나 여자가 같은 시간에 노트북을 가져갈 수 있다고 했으므로 이에 대한 남자의 응답은 ② 'Then, I'd like to replace the battery. (그럼, 저는 배터리를 교체하고 싶어요.)'가 적절하다.

15 다음 상황에서 Amy가 Terry에게 할 말 ▶ 정답 ③
정답률 85%

M: Amy is the leader of a high school band and Terry is one of the
  band members. The band is going to hold a mini concert in the
  school festival, and Terry is in charge of making a concert poster.
  When he completes the poster, he shows it to the band members.
  Even though the poster has all the necessary information, it's hard
  to read it because the size of the letters is too small. Amy thinks
  if Terry changes the font size to a larger one, it could be easier to
  notice. So, Amy wants to suggest that Terry increase the size of the
  letters on the poster. In this situation, what would Amy most likely
  say to Terry?
Amy: (Can you make the letter size bigger on the poster?)

해석
남: Amy는 고등학교 밴드의 리더이고 Terry는 밴드 멤버 중 한 명이다. 그 밴드는 학교 축제에서 미니 콘서트를 개최할 예정이며, Terry는 콘서트 포스터 제작을 담당하고 있다. 포스터를 완성하자, 그는 그것을 밴드 멤버들에게 보여준다. 포스터는 필요한 모든 정보를 담고 있음에도 불구하고, 글자의 크기가 너무 작아서 읽기가 힘들다. Amy는 Terry가 글자 크기를 더 큰 것으로 바꾸면 더 쉽게 알아차릴 수 있을 것이라고 생각한다. 그래서, Amy는 Terry가 포스터에 있는 글자의 크기를 늘릴 것을 제안하고 싶다. 이러한 상황에서, Amy는 Terry에게 뭐라고 말하겠는가?
Amy: (포스터의 글자 크기를 더 크게 해줄 수 있겠니?)
① 포스터에 다채로운 글씨체를 사용하는 건 어떠니?
② 너는 네 친구들에게 콘서트에 대해 알리는 게 좋겠다.
✓③ 포스터의 글자 크기를 더 크게 해줄 수 있겠니?
④ 우리 학교 축제에서 콘서트를 여는 게 어떠니?
⑤ 너는 포스터에 중요한 정보를 넣어야 해.

16~17 1지문 2문항

W: Hello, students. Previously, we discussed why gardening is a great
  hobby. But not everyone has a sunny front yard. So, today we'll
  learn about plants that grow even in shade. First, lemon balm
  survives in full shade. So if your place is sunless, it's the plant
  you should choose. Next, ivy is the ultimate shade-loving plant.
  Its ability to grow in shade makes it survive under trees where
  most plants can't. Also, there's mint. It lives well under low-light
  conditions, so you can grow it in a small pot indoors. Lastly,
  camellia grows better in partial shade. Especially when it's a young
  plant, it needs protection from the sun. Many plants like these can
  live even in the shade. Isn't it fascinating? Now, let's watch a video
  clip about how to grow these plants.

해석
여: 안녕하세요, 학생 여러분. 이전에, 우리는 정원 가꾸기가 왜 훌륭한 취미인지에 대해서 논의했습니다. 하지만 모든 사람들이 햇빛이 잘 드는 앞마당을 가지고 있는 것은 아닙니다. 그래서, 오늘 우리는 그늘에서도 자라는 식물들에 대해 배울 것입니다. 우선, 레몬밤은 완전한 그늘에서 생존합니다. 그래서 여러분의 장소가 햇빛이 들지 않는다면, 그것은 여러분이 선택해야 할 식물입니다. 다음으로, 담쟁이덩굴은 그늘을 사랑하는 최고의 식물입니다. 그늘에서 자라는 그것의 능력은 대부분의 식물들이 살 수 없는 나무 아래에서 생존하도록 만듭니다. 또한, 박하가 있습니다. 그것은 조도가 낮은 환경에서 잘 살기 때문에, 여러분은 실내에서 작은 화분에 그것을 키울 수 있습니다. 마지막으로, 동백나무는 부분적인 그늘에서 더 잘 자랍니다. 특히 그것이 어린 식물일 때는, 햇빛으로부터 보호가 필요합니다. 이와 같은 많은 식물이 심지어 그늘에서 살 수 있습니다. 대단히 흥미롭지 않나요? 이제, 이 식물들을 기르는 방법에 대한 동영상을 시청합시다.

16 여자가 하는 말의 주제 ▶ 정답 ④
정답률 80%

① 식물 질병을 예방하는 방법들
② 식물 성장에 영향을 미치는 요인들
③ 집에서 식물을 재배하는 것의 이점들
✓④ 그늘진 곳에서 자랄 수 있는 식물들
⑤ 식물이 그늘에서 자라는 데 도움을 주는 재료들

17 언급된 식물이 아닌 것 ▶ 정답 ⑤
정답률 85%

① 레몬밤
② 담쟁이덩굴
③ 박하
④ 동백나무
✓⑤ 라벤더

14 2022년 3월 학력평가

01	①	02	③	03	②	04	④	05	④
06	③	07	①	08	③	09	⑤	10	③
11	①	12	⑤	13	②	14	②	15	①
16	④	17	④						

01 남자가 하는 말의 목적 ▶ 정답 ①
정답률 80%

M: Good afternoon, everybody. This is Student President Sam Wilson.
  As you know, the lunch basketball league will begin soon. Many
  students are interested in joining the league and waiting for the
  sign-up sheet to be handed out at the gym. For easier access,
  we've decided to change the registration method. Instead of going
  to the gym to register, simply log into the school website and fill out
  the registration form online. Thank you for listening and let's have
  a good league.

해석
남: 안녕하세요, 여러분. 저는 학생회장인 Sam Wilson입니다. 아시다시피, 점심 농구 리그가 곧 시작될 것입니다. 많은 학생들이 리그에 참가하는 데 관심을 가지고 있고 체육관에서 참가 신청서가 배부되기를 기다리고 있습니다. 더 쉽게 접근할 수 있도록, 저희는 등록 방법을 변경하기로 결정했습니다. 등록하기 위해 체육관에 가는 대신, 간단히 학교 웹사이트에 로그인해서 온라인으로 등록 양식을 작성해 주십시오. 들어주셔서 감사하며 좋은 리그를 만들어 봅시다.
✓① 농구 리그 참가 등록 방법의 변경을 알리려고
② 확정된 농구 리그 시합 일정을 발표하려고
③ 농구 리그의 심판을 추가 모집하려고

④ 농구 리그 경기 관람을 권장하려고
⑤ 농구 리그 우승 상품을 안내하려고

02 여자의 의견

▶ 정답 ③

W: Daniel, what are you doing in front of the mirror?
M: I have skin problems these days. I'm trying to pop these pimples
　　　　　　피부 문제들　　　　　　　터뜨리려고 하는　　　여드름들
on my face.
　(try to V: ~하려고 하다, pop: 터뜨리다)
W: Pimples are really annoying, but I wouldn't do that.
　　　　　　　　　　짜증나는
M: Why not?
W: When you pop them with your hands, you're touching your face.
　　　　　　　　　　　　　　　　　　　　　만지는(touch)
M: Are you saying that I shouldn't touch my face?
W: Exactly. You know our hands are covered with bacteria, right?
　　　　　　　　　　　　　　　박테리아로 덮여 있다
M: So?　　　　　　(be covered with: ~으로 덮여 있다, bacteria: 박테리아)
W: You'll be spreading bacteria all over your face with your hands. It
　　퍼뜨릴 것이다(spread)　　　　전체에
could worsen your skin problems.
　　악화시키다
M: Oh, I didn't know that.
W: Touching your face with your hands is bad for your skin.
　　　　　　　　　　　　　　　　　　　　　~에 해롭다(be bad for)
M: Okay, I got it.

해석
여: Daniel, 거울 앞에서 무엇을 하고 있니?
남: 나는 요즘에 피부 문제가 있어. 얼굴에 난 이 여드름을 터뜨리려고 하는 중이야.
여: 여드름은 정말 짜증나지만, 나라면 그렇게 하지 않을 거야.
남: 왜?
여: 네가 그것들을 손으로 터뜨릴 때, 얼굴을 만지고 있잖아.
남: 얼굴을 만지면 안 된다는 말이야?
여: 바로 그거야. 너는 우리의 손이 박테리아로 덮여 있는 것을 알고 있잖아, 그렇지?
남: 그래서?
여: 너는 손으로 얼굴 전체에 박테리아를 퍼뜨리게 될 거야. 그것은 네 피부 문제를 악화시킬 수 있어.
남: 오, 나는 그것을 몰랐어.
여: 얼굴을 손으로 만지는 것은 네 피부에 해로워.
남: 그래, 알겠어.
① 평소에 피부 상태를 잘 관찰할 필요가 있다.
② 여드름을 치료하려면 피부과 병원에 가야 한다.
✔ 얼굴을 손으로 만지는 것은 얼굴 피부에 해롭다.
④ 지성 피부를 가진 사람은 자주 세수를 해야 한다.
⑤ 손을 자주 씻는 것은 감염병 예방에 도움이 된다.

03 두 사람의 관계

▶ 정답 ②

M: Excuse me. You're Chloe Jones, aren't you?
W: Yes, I am. Have we met before?
M: No, but I'm a big fan of yours. I've watched your speeches on
　　　　　　　열혈 팬　　　　　　　　　　　　　　연설들
climate change, and they're very inspiring.
　기후 변화　　　　　　　　　　영감을 주는
W: Thank you. I'm so glad to hear that.
M: And, I also think your campaign about plastic pollution has been
　　　　　　　　　　　　　　　　　　　　플라스틱 오염
very successful.
　　성공적인
W: As an environmental activist, that means a lot to me.
　　　　환경 운동가
M: May I make a suggestion? I thought it'd be nice if more children
　　　　　제안을 하다
could hear your ideas.
W: That's what I was thinking. Do you have any good ideas?
M: Actually, I'm a cartoonist. Perhaps I can make comic books based
　　　　　　　　만화가　　　　　　　　　　　　만화책들　　　~을 바탕으로
on your work.
W: That is a wonderful idea. Can I contact you later to discuss it more?
　　　　　　　　　　　　　　　　연락하다　　　　　　상의하다
M: Sure. By the way, my name is Jack Perse. Here's my business card.
　　　　　　　　　　　　　　　　　　　　　　　　　명함

해석
남: 실례합니다. 당신은 Chloe Jones죠, 그렇지 않나요?
여: 네, 맞아요. 우리가 전에 만난 적이 있나요?
남: 아니요, 하지만 저는 당신의 열혈 팬이에요. 기후 변화에 관한 당신의 연설들을 봤는데, 그

것들은 매우 영감을 줬어요.
여: 감사해요. 그 말을 들으니 정말 기쁘네요.
남: 그리고, 저는 또한 플라스틱 오염에 대한 당신의 캠페인이 매우 성공적이었다고 생각해요.
여: 환경 운동가로서, 그것은 저에게 많은 의미가 있어요.
남: 제가 제안을 해도 될까요? 저는 더 많은 아이들이 당신의 생각을 들을 수 있으면 좋겠다고 생각했어요.
여: 저도 그렇게 생각하고 있었어요. 좋은 아이디어가 있나요?
남: 사실, 저는 만화가예요. 아마도 당신의 활동을 바탕으로 만화책을 만들 수 있을 것 같아요.
여: 그거 멋진 생각이네요. 그것에 대해 좀 더 상의하기 위해 나중에 연락해도 될까요?
남: 물론이죠. 그나저나, 제 이름은 Jack Perse예요. 여기 제 명함이 있어요.
① 방송 작가 ― 연출자
✔ 만화가 ― 환경 운동가
③ 촬영 감독 ― 동화 작가
④ 토크쇼 진행자 ― 기후학자
⑤ 제품 디자이너 ― 영업 사원

04 그림에서 대화의 내용과 일치하지 않는 것

▶ 정답 ④

W: Yesterday, I decorated my fish tank like a beach.
　　　　　　　꾸몄다　　　　　어항　　　　해변
M: I'd like to see it. Do you have a picture?
W: Sure. Here. [Pause] Do you recognize the boat in the bottom left
　　　　　　　　　　　　　　　　알아보다　　　　　　　왼쪽 아래 구석에
corner?
M: Yes. It's the one I gave you, isn't it?
W: Right. It looks good in the fish tank, doesn't it?
M: It does. I love the beach chair in the center.
　　　　　　　　　　　　　　　　　　가운데에
M: I see a starfish next to the chair.
　　　　　불가사리
W: Isn't it cute? And do you see these two surf boards on the right
　　　　　　　　　　　　　　　　　　　서핑 보드들　　　~의 오른쪽에
side of the picture?
M: Yeah. I like how you put both of them side by side.
　　　　　　　　　　　　　　　　　나란히
M: Your fish in the top left corner looks happy with its new home.
W: I hope so.　　왼쪽 위 구석에

해석
여: 어제, 내 어항을 해변처럼 꾸몄어.
남: 그것을 보고 싶어. 사진이 있니?
여: 물론이지. 여기. [잠시 후] 왼쪽 아래 구석에 있는 배를 알아보겠니?
남: 그래. 내가 너에게 준 것이구나, 그렇지 않니?
여: 맞아. 어항에 잘 어울리지, 그렇지 않니?
남: 그래. 나는 가운데에 있는 해변 의자가 마음에 들어.
여: 그래. 나도 마음에 들어.
남: 의자 옆에 불가사리가 보이네.
여: 귀엽지 않니? 그리고 사진의 오른쪽에 이 두 개의 서핑 보드가 보여?
남: 그래. 두 개를 나란히 놓은 게 마음에 들어.
여: 그게 멋져 보일 것이라고 생각했어.
남: 왼쪽 위 구석에 있는 물고기는 새 집에 만족하는 것처럼 보여.
여: 그랬으면 좋겠어.

05 여자가 남자에게 부탁한 일

▶ 정답 ④

[Cell phone rings.]
M: Hello, honey. I'm on the way home. How's setting up Mike's
　　　　　　　　　　　　　　　　　　　　　　　　준비하는 것(set up)
birthday party going?

W: Good, but I still have stuff to do. Mike and his friends will get here soon.
　　　　　　　　　　　　일

M: Should I pick up the birthday cake?
　　　　　　가지러 가다

W: No, that's okay. I already did that.
　　　　　　　　　　이미

M: Then, do you want me to put up the balloons around the doorway when I get there?
　　　　　　　　　　　　　　풍선들을 달다　　　　　　　　　현관

W: I'll take care of it. Can you take the table out to the front yard?
　　　~을 처리하다　　　　　　　탁자를 ~로 옮기다　　　앞마당

M: Sure. Are we having the party outside?

W: Yes. The weather is beautiful so I made a last minute change.
　　　　　날씨　　　　　　　　　마지막 순간에 바꿨다(make a change: 바꾸다)

M: Great. The kids can play with water guns in the front yard.
　　　　　　　　　　~을 가지고 놀다

W: Good idea. I'll go to the garage and grab the water guns.
　　　　　　　　　　　　차고　　　　가져오다

해석

[휴대전화가 울린다.]

남: 여보세요, 여보. 저는 집에 가는 길이에요. Mike의 생일 파티를 준비하는 것은 어떻게 되어 가요?

여: 좋아요, 그런데 아직도 할 일이 있어요. Mike와 그의 친구들이 곧 여기에 도착할 거예요.

남: 제가 생일 케이크를 가지러 갈까요?

여: 아니요, 괜찮아요. 제가 이미 했어요.

남: 그럼, 도착하면 현관 주위에 풍선을 달아줄까요?

여: 그 일은 제가 처리할게요. 당신은 탁자를 앞마당으로 옮겨줄래요?

남: 물론이죠. 우리 밖에서 파티를 하는 거예요?

여: 네. 날씨가 좋아서 마지막 순간에 바꿨어요.

남: 좋네요. 아이들이 앞마당에서 물총을 가지고 놀 수 있잖아요.

여: 좋은 생각이에요. 제가 차고로 가서 물총을 가져올게요.

① 장난감 사 오기
② 풍선 달기
③ 케이크 가져오기
✔ 탁자 옮기기
⑤ 아이들 데려오기

06 남자가 지불할 금액
정답률 80% ▶ 정답 ③

W: Welcome to Green Eco Shop. How can I help you?

M: Hi, do you sell eco-friendly toothbrushes?
　　　　　　　　친환경적인　　칫솔들

W: Yes, we have a few types over here. Which do you like?
　　　　　　　몇 가지 종류들

M: Hmm.... How much are these?

W: They're $2 each. They are made from bamboo.
　　　　　　　　　　대나무로 만들어졌다
　　　　　　　　　(be made from: ~으로 만들어지다, bamboo: 대나무)

M: All right. I'll take four of them.

W: Excellent choice. Anything else?

M: I also need bath sponges.
　　　　　　　목욕용 스펀지들

W: They're right behind you. They're plastic-free and only $3 each.
　　　　　　　　　　　　　　　플라스틱이 없는

M: Okay. I'll also take four of them. That'll be all.

W: If you have a store membership, you can get a 10% discount off the total price.
　　　　　　매장 회원권　　　　　　　　총액에서 10% 할인을 받다

M: Great. I'm a member. Here are my credit and membership cards.

해석

여: Green Eco Shop에 오신 것을 환영합니다. 어떻게 도와드릴까요?

남: 안녕하세요, 친환경 칫솔을 판매하시나요?

여: 네, 여기 몇 가지 종류가 있어요. 어떤 게 좋으세요?

남: 흠.... 이것들은 얼마죠?

여: 한 개에 2달러예요. 그것들은 대나무로 만들어졌어요.

남: 그렇군요. 네 개를 살게요.

여: 훌륭한 선택이에요. 또 다른 건 없으신가요?

남: 목욕용 스펀지도 필요해요.

여: 그것들은 바로 뒤에 있어요. 플라스틱이 없고 한 개에 3달러밖에 안 해요.

남: 알겠어요. 그것도 네 개를 살게요. 그게 다예요.

여: 매장 회원권을 가지고 계시면, 총액에서 10% 할인을 받으실 수 있어요.

남: 잘됐네요. 저는 회원이에요. 여기 제 신용카드와 회원카드가 있어요.

① $14　　② $16　　✔ $18　　④ $20　　⑤ $22

문제 풀이

한 개에 2달러인 친환경 칫솔과 한 개에 3달러인 목욕용 스펀지를 각각 네 개씩 사면 총액은 20달러이다. 매장 회원권을 가지고 있는 남자는 10% 할인을 받을 수 있으므로 지불할 금액은 2달러가 할인된 18달러이다. 따라서 답은 ③ '$18'이다.

07 두 사람이 오늘 실험을 할 수 없는 이유
정답률 85% ▶ 정답 ①

[Cell phone rings.]

M: Hey, Suji. Where are you?

W: I'm in the library checking out books. I'll be heading out to the science lab for our experiment in a couple of minutes.
　　　~로 갈 것이다(head out to)
　　과학실　　　　　실험

M: I guess you haven't checked my message yet. We can't do the experiment today.

W: Really? Isn't the lab available today?
　　　　　　　　　이용할 수 있는

M: Yes, it is, but I canceled our reservation.
　　　　　　　　취소했다　　　예약

W: Why? Are you still suffering from your cold?
　　　　　　　　감기를 앓고 있는(suffer from: ~을 앓다, cold: 감기)

M: No, I'm fine now.

W: That's good. Then why aren't we doing the experiment today? We need to hand in the science report by next Monday.
　　　　　　제출하다　　과학 보고서

M: Unfortunately, the experiment kit hasn't been delivered yet. It'll arrive tomorrow.
　　　　　　　　　　　　　　　배달되지 않았다(deliver: 배달하다)
　　도착하다

W: Oh, well. The experiment has to wait one more day, then.

해석

[휴대전화가 울린다.]

남: 이봐, Suji. 어디에 있니?

여: 도서관에서 책을 빌리고 있어. 몇 분 후에 우리의 실험을 위해 과학실로 갈 거야.

남: 네가 아직 내 메시지를 확인하지 않은 것 같구나. 우리는 오늘 실험을 할 수 없어.

여: 정말? 오늘 과학실을 이용할 수 없는 거야?

남: 아니, 이용할 수 있지만, 내가 예약을 취소했어.

여: 왜? 아직도 감기를 앓고 있니?

남: 아니, 지금은 괜찮아.

여: 잘됐다. 그럼 우리 오늘 왜 실험을 안 하는 거야? 우리는 다음 주 월요일까지 과학 보고서를 제출해야 해.

남: 안타깝게도, 실험용 키트가 아직 배달되지 않았어. 그것은 내일 도착할 거야.

여: 오, 그렇구나. 그럼, 실험은 하루 더 기다려야겠네.

✔ 실험용 키트가 배달되지 않아서
② 실험 주제를 변경해야 해서
③ 과학실을 예약하지 못해서
④ 보고서를 작성해야 해서
⑤ 남자가 감기에 걸려서

08 Stanville Free-cycle에 관해 언급되지 않은 것
정답률 85% ▶ 정답 ③

W: Honey, did you see the poster about the Stanville Free-cycle?
　　　　　　　　　　　　　　　　　　　　　　　　무료 순환

M: Free-cycle? What is that?

W: It's another way of recycling. You give away items you don't need and anybody can take them for free.
　　　　　　　　　재활용　　　　나눠주다　물건들
　　　　　　　　　　　　　　무료로

M: Oh, it's like one man's garbage is another man's treasure. Who can participate?
　　　　　　　　　　　　쓰레기　　　　　　　　보물
　　참가하다

W: It's open to everyone living in Stanville.

M: Great. Where is it taking place?
　　　　　　　　　　열리는(take place)

W: At Rose Park on Second Street.

M: When does the event start?
　　　　　　　행사

W: It starts on April 12th and runs for a week.
　　　　　　　　　　　　　계속되다

M: Let's see what we can free-cycle, starting from the cupboard.
　　　　　　　　　　　　　　　　　　　　　　찬장

W: Okay. But breakable items like glass dishes or cups won't be accepted.
　　　　　깨지기 쉬운　　　　　　　　　　받아들여지지 않을 것이다
　　　　　　　　　　　　　　　　　　　　(accept: 받아들이다)

M: I see. I'll keep that in mind.
　　　　　　그것을 명심하다

M: The one with a washable filter would be a better choice.
  세척 가능한
W: I got it. Then I'll order this one.

해석

여: Ben, 시간 좀 있니?
남: 물론이지. 무슨 일이야?
여: 이 다섯 가지 모델 중에서 소형 진공청소기를 사려고 해. 하나 고르는 것을 도와줄래?
남: 좋아. 너는 얼마를 쓸 의향이 있니?
여: 130달러 이하야.
남: 그럼 우리는 이것을 제외할 수 있어. 작동 시간은 어때?
여: 10분보다 더 길어야 할 것 같아.
남: 그럼 이 세 가지로 범위를 좁히겠네.
여: 더 가벼운 것 중 하나를 골라야 할까?
남: 그래. 청소할 때 더 가벼운 것이 다루기에 더 편해.
여: 알겠어. 필터는 어때?
남: 세척 가능한 필터가 있는 것이 더 나은 선택이 될 거야.
여: 알겠어. 그럼 이것을 주문할게.

소형 진공청소기

	모델	가격	작동 시간	무게	세척 가능 필터
①	A	50달러	8분	2.5kg	X
②	B	80달러	12분	2.0kg	O
✓③	C	100달러	15분	1.8kg	O
④	D	120달러	20분	1.8kg	X
⑤	E	150달러	25분	1.6kg	O

---

09 River Valley Music Camp에 관한 내용과 일치하지 않는 것

정답률 85% ▶ 정답 ⑤

M: Hello, River Valley High School students. This is your music teacher, Mr. Stailor. Starting on April 11th, we are going to have the River Valley Music Camp for five days. You don't need to be a
  음악 캠프   (don't need to V: ~할 필요는 없다)
member of the school orchestra to join the camp. You may bring
  학교 오케스트라
your own instrument or you can borrow one from the school. On
  자신의   악기   빌리다
the last day of camp, we are going to film our performance and
                              촬영하다   공연
play it on screen at the school summer festival. Please keep in
  그것을 스크린에 상영하다   축제
mind the camp is limited to 50 students. Sign-ups start this Friday,
  제한되다(limit: 제한하다)   등록
on a first-come-first-served basis. Come and make music together!
  선착순으로

해석

남: 안녕하세요, River Valley 고등학교 학생 여러분. 저는 음악 교사인 Stailor 선생님입니다. 4월 11일부터, 우리는 5일 동안 River Valley Music Camp(River Valley 음악 캠프)를 개최할 예정입니다. 캠프에 참가하기 위해서 학교 오케스트라의 단원일 필요는 없습니다. 여러분은 자신의 악기를 가져오거나 학교에서 빌릴 수 있습니다. 캠프의 마지막 날에, 공연을 촬영하고 학교 여름 축제에서 그것을 스크린에 상영할 것입니다. 캠프는 50명으로 인원이 제한되어 있다는 것을 명심하세요. 등록은 이번 주 금요일에 선착순으로 시작됩니다. 오셔서 함께 음악을 만들어 보세요!

① 4월 11일부터 5일 동안 진행된다.
② 학교 오케스트라 단원이 아니어도 참가할 수 있다.
③ 자신의 악기를 가져오거나 학교에서 빌릴 수 있다.
④ 마지막 날에 공연을 촬영한다.
✓⑤ 참가 인원에는 제한이 없다.

문제 풀이

음악 캠프에 참가할 수 있는 인원은 50명으로 제한되어 있다고 했으므로 ⑤ '참가 인원에는 제한이 없다.'는 일치하지 않는 내용이다.

---

11 남자의 마지막 말에 대한 여자의 응답

정답률 75% ▶ 정답 ①

M: My eyes are sore today.
             아픈
W: Too bad. Maybe some dust got in your eyes.
                        먼지
M: You're probably right. What should I do?
        아마도
W: (Why don't you rinse your eyes with clean water?)
                  씻다

해석

남: 오늘 눈이 아파.
여: 저런. 눈에 먼지가 좀 들어갔나 봐.
남: 아마도 네 말이 맞을 거야. 어떻게 해야 하지?
여: (깨끗한 물로 눈을 씻는 게 어때?)

✓① 깨끗한 물로 눈을 씻는 게 어때?
② 대기 오염에 대해 더 설명해 줄 수 있겠니?
③ 나는 새 안경을 사야 해.
④ 나는 미세먼지가 심각한 문제라는 것에 동의해.
⑤ 우리는 밖에 나가서 산책해야 해.

---

10 표에서 여자가 주문할 소형 진공청소기

정답률 80% ▶ 정답 ③

W: Ben, do you have a minute?
M: Sure. What is it?
W: I'm trying to buy a handheld vacuum cleaner among these five
                      소형 진공청소기
   models. Could you help me choose one?
M: Okay. How much are you willing to spend?
                          쓸 의향이 있는
                          (willing to V: ~할 의향이 있는, spend: (돈을) 쓰다)
W: No more than $130.
M: Then we can cross this one out. What about the working time?
              이것을 제외하다(cross out: 제외하다)   작동 시간
W: I think it should be longer than 10 minutes.
M: Then that narrows it down to these three.
            범위를 ~으로 좁히다
W: Should I go with one of the lighter ones?
                            더 가벼운
M: Yes. Lighter ones are easier to handle while cleaning.
                                  다루다
W: All right. What about the filter?
                            필터

---

12 여자의 마지막 말에 대한 남자의 응답

정답률 75% ▶ 정답 ⑤

W: Excuse me. Would you mind if I sit here?
                              앉다
M: I'm sorry, but it's my friend's seat. He'll be back in a minute.
                              자리   돌아오다   곧
W: Oh, I didn't know that. Sorry for bothering you.
                                  귀찮게 해서 미안하다
                      (sorry for V-ing: ~해서 미안하다, bother: 귀찮게 하다)
M: (That's okay. I think the seat next to it is available.)

해석

여: 실례해요. 여기에 앉아도 될까요?
남: 죄송한데, 제 친구 자리예요. 그는 곧 돌아올 거예요.
여: 오, 저는 몰랐어요. 귀찮게 해서 미안해요.
남: (괜찮아요. 그 옆의 자리는 비어 있는 것 같아요.)

① 그건 공평하지 않아요. 제가 이 자리를 먼저 예약했어요.
② 고마워요. 제 친구가 그것을 알면 기뻐할 거예요.
③ 천만에요. 뭐든지 물어보세요.
④ 별 말씀을. 저는 당신과 자리를 바꿔도 상관없어요.
✓⑤ 괜찮아요. 그 옆의 자리는 비어 있는 것 같아요.

13 남자의 마지막 말에 대한 여자의 응답

정답률 85%

▶ 정답 ②

M: Hey, Jasmine.
W: Hi, Kurt. Are you going to be at home tomorrow afternoon?
M: Yeah, I'm going to watch the <u>baseball game</u> with my friends at home.
　　　　　　　　　　　　　　　　야구 경기
W: Good. Can I <u>drop by</u> your house and give you back the <u>hammer</u> I borrowed?
　　　　　　　잠깐 들르다　　　　　　　　　　　　　　　　　　　망치
　　빌렸다
M: Sure. Come over any time. By the way, why don't you join us and watch the game?
W: I'd love to. Which teams are playing?
M: Green Thunders and Black Dragons.
W: That'll be <u>exciting</u>. What time should I come?
　　　　　　흥미진진한
M: Come at five. We'll <u>have pizza</u> before the game.
　　　　　　　　　피자를 먹다
W: Perfect. Do you want me to bring anything?
M: Maybe some <u>snacks</u> to eat while watching the game.
　　　　　　　간식들
W: (Great. I'll bring chips and popcorn.)

해석
남: 안녕, Jasmine.
여: 안녕, Kurt. 내일 오후에 집에 있을 거니?
남: 그래, 집에서 친구들과 야구 경기를 시청할 거야.
여: 잘 됐다. 내가 네 집에 잠깐 들러서 빌린 망치를 돌려줘도 될까?
남: 물론이지. 언제든지 와. 그런데, 우리와 함께 경기를 보는 게 어때?
여: 그러고 싶어. 어느 팀이 경기를 하니?
남: Green Thunders와 Black Dragons야.
여: 흥미진진하겠다. 몇 시에 가면 될까?
남: 5시에 와. 우리는 경기 전에 피자를 먹을 거야.
여: 완벽해. 내가 뭐 좀 가져갈까?
남: 경기를 보는 동안 먹을 간식이 좀 있으면 좋을 것 같아.
여: (알겠어. 내가 감자칩과 팝콘을 가져갈게.)
① 냄새가 좋다. 피자를 먹어봐도 될까?
✔ 알겠어. 내가 감자칩과 팝콘을 가져갈게.
③ 문제 없어. 내가 표를 취소할게.
④ 미안해. 나는 야구를 보는 것을 좋아하지 않아.
⑤ 물론이야. 여기 내가 빌린 망치가 있어.

14 여자의 마지막 말에 대한 남자의 응답

정답률 85%

▶ 정답 ②

W: Hi, Tom.
M: Hi, Jane. What are you reading?
W: It's a <u>novel</u> by Charles Dickens. I'm going to talk about it with my
　　　　소설
<u>book club members</u> this weekend.
　독서 동아리 회원들
M: Oh, you're in a book club?
W: Yes. I <u>joined</u> it a few months ago. And now I read much more than
　　　　가입했다
before.
M: Really? Actually one of my <u>new year's resolutions</u> is to read more
　　　　　　　　　　　　　　　　새해 목표들
books.
W: Then, joining a book club will <u>surely</u> help.
　　　　　　　　　　　　　　분명히
M: Hmm.... What other <u>benefits</u> can I get if I join one?
　　　　　　　　　혜택들
W: You can also <u>share your reading experiences with others</u>.
　　　　　　　　네 독서 경험을 다른 사람들과 공유하다
M: That'd be nice.　(share A with B: A를 B와 공유하다, experience: 경험)
W: Yeah, it really <u>broadens</u> your mind. I really <u>recommend you to join</u>
　　　　　　　　넓히다　　　　　　　　　　　네가 가입하기를 추천하다
a book club.
　　　　　　　　(recommend A to V: A가 ~하기를 추천하다)
M: (Sounds cool. I'll join a book club, too.)

해석
여: 안녕, Tom.
남: 안녕, Jane. 무엇을 읽고 있니?
여: Charles Dickens의 소설이야. 나는 이번 주말에 독서 동아리 회원들과 그것에 대해 이야기할 거야.
남: 오, 너 독서 동아리에서 활동하니?
여: 응. 몇 달 전에 가입했어. 그리고 지금은 전보다 훨씬 더 많은 책을 읽어.

남: 정말? 사실 나의 새해 목표 중 하나가 더 많은 책을 읽는 거야.
여: 그렇다면, 독서 동아리에 가입하는 것이 분명히 도움이 될 거야.
남: 흠.... 가입하면 또 어떤 혜택을 얻을 수 있니?
여: 네 독서 경험을 다른 사람들과 공유할 수도 있어.
남: 그거 좋을 것 같아.
여: 그래, 그것은 정말 네 사고방식을 넓혀줘. 나는 네가 독서 동아리에 가입하기를 정말 추천해.
남: (멋질 것 같아. 나도 독서 동아리에 가입할게.)
① 맞아. 이것은 베스트셀러 소설이야.
✔ 멋질 것 같아. 나도 독서 동아리에 가입할게.
③ 그렇진 않아. 책은 좋은 선물이 돼.
④ 새해 목표는 지키기 어려워.
⑤ 네 독서 동아리를 위해 책을 좀 사자.

문제 풀이
새해 목표가 많은 책을 읽는 것이라고 말하는 남자에게 여자는 독서 동아리 활동을 통해 얻을 수 있는 여러 가지 혜택들에 대해 설명하며 가입할 것을 추천하고 있다. 이에 대한 남자의 응답으로는 ② 'Sounds cool. I'll join a book club, too.(멋질 것 같아. 나도 독서 동아리에 가입할게.)'가 적절하다.

15 다음 상황에서 Brian이 Sally에게 할 말

정답률 85%

▶ 정답 ①

M: Brian and Sally are walking down the street together. A <u>blind man</u>
　　　　　　　　　　　　　　　　　　　　　　　　　　　　시각 장애인
and his <u>guide dog</u> are walking towards them. Sally likes dogs
　　　　안내견
very much, so she <u>reaches out</u> to touch the guide dog. Brian
　　　　　　　　　손을 뻗다
doesn't think that Sally should do that. The guide dog needs to
<u>concentrate on guiding</u> the blind person. If someone touches the
안내하는 데 집중하다
(concentrate on V-ing: ~하는 데 집중하다, guide: 안내하다)
dog, the dog can <u>lose its focus</u>. So Brian wants to tell Sally not to
　　　　　　　　집중력을 잃다(lose one's focus)
touch the guide dog <u>without the permission of</u> the dog <u>owner</u>. In
　　　　　　　　　　　~의 허락 없이　　　　　　　주인
this situation, what would Brian most likely say to Sally?
Brian: (You shouldn't touch a guide dog without permission.)

해석
남: Brian과 Sally는 함께 거리를 걷고 있다. 한 시각 장애인과 그의 안내견이 그들을 향해 걸어 오고 있다. Sally는 개를 매우 좋아해서, 안내견을 만지기 위해 손을 뻗는다. Brian은 Sally가 그렇게 하면 안 된다고 생각한다. 안내견은 시각 장애인을 안내하는 데 집중해야 한다. 누군가가 안내견을 만진다면, 안내견은 집중력을 잃을 수 있다. 그래서 Brian은 Sally에게 안내견 주인의 허락 없이 안내견을 만지지 말라고 말하고 싶다. 이러한 상황에서 Brian은 Sally에게 뭐라고 말하겠는가?
Brian: (너는 허락 없이 안내견을 만지면 안 돼.)
✔ 너는 허락 없이 안내견을 만지면 안 돼.
② 우리가 음식을 좀 주면 그 개는 좋아할 거야.
③ 나는 그것이 안내견이 될 만큼 충분히 똑똑하다고 확신해.
④ 나는 네가 매일 개를 산책시킬 것을 제안해.
⑤ 유감스럽지만 이곳에는 개가 들어올 수 없어.

16~17 1지문 2문항

W: Hello, everybody. Welcome to the health workshop. I'm Alanna
Reyes, the <u>head trainer</u> from Eastwood Fitness Center. As you
　　　　　수석 트레이너
know, <u>joints</u> are body parts that <u>link</u> bones together. And doing
　　　관절들　　　　　　　　　　　　　　연결하다
certain <u>physical activities</u> <u>puts stress on</u> the joints. But the good
　　　　신체 활동들　　　　　~에 부담을 주다
news is that people with bad joints can still do certain <u>exercises</u>.
　　　　　　　　　　　　　　　　　　　　　　　　　　　　　운동들
They have <u>relatively low impact on</u> the joints. Here are some
~에 비교적 적은 충격을 주다
(relatively: 비교적, impact: 충격, 영향)
examples. The first is <u>swimming</u>. While swimming, the water
　　　　　　　　　　수영
<u>supports</u> your <u>body weight</u>. The second is <u>cycling</u>. You put almost
지탱하다　　　체중　　　　　　　　　　　자전거 타기　　　거의
no stress on the knee joints when you <u>pedal smoothly</u>. Horseback
　　　　　　　　　　　　　　　　　　　　페달을 밟다 부드럽게　　승마

riding is another exercise that puts very little stress on your knees. Lastly, walking is great because it's low-impact, unlike running. If you have bad joints, don't give up exercising. Instead, stay active and stay healthy!

걷기 / 운동하는 것을 포기하다 / 대신 / 활동적인

(give up V-ing: ~하는 것을 포기하다, exercise: 운동하다)

해석

여: 안녕하세요, 여러분. 건강 워크숍에 오신 것을 환영합니다. 저는 Eastwood 피트니스 센터의 수석 트레이너인 Alanna Reyes입니다. 아시다시피, 관절은 뼈를 서로 연결하는 신체 부위입니다. 그리고 특정한 신체 활동들을 하는 것은 관절에 부담을 줍니다. 하지만 좋은 소식은 관절이 좋지 않은 사람들이 여전히 특정한 운동들을 할 수 있다는 것입니다. 그것들은 관절에 비교적 적은 충격을 줍니다. 여기 몇 가지 예가 있습니다. 첫 번째는 수영입니다. 수영하는 동안, 물은 체중을 지탱합니다. 두 번째는 자전거 타기입니다. 부드럽게 페달을 밟을 때 무릎 관절에 거의 부담을 주지 않습니다. 승마는 무릎에 매우 적은 부담을 주는 또 다른 운동입니다. 마지막으로, 걷기는 달리기와 달리 충격이 적기 때문에 매우 좋습니다. 관절이 좋지 않다 하더라도, 운동하는 것을 포기하지 마세요. 대신, 활동적으로 지내며 건강을 유지하세요!

16 여자가 하는 말의 주제
정답률 70% ▶ 정답 ④

① 근육을 형성하는 데 도움을 주는 활동들
② 일상생활에서 스트레스를 조절하는 방법들
③ 노인들의 관절 문제 유형들
✔ 관절이 좋지 않은 사람들을 위한 충격이 적은 운동들
⑤ 체중 조절을 위해 매일 하는 운동의 중요성

17 언급된 운동이 아닌 것
정답률 85% ▶ 정답 ④

① 수영 ② 자전거 타기 ③ 승마
✔ 볼링 ⑤ 걷기

15 | 2022년 6월 학력평가

01	②	02	①	03	⑤	04	⑤	05	①
06	③	07	①	08	⑤	09	⑤	10	④
11	①	12	③	13	③	14	④	15	④
16	②	17	③						

01 남자가 하는 말의 목적
정답률 90% ▶ 정답 ②

M: Good afternoon, this is the building manager, Richard Carson. We are planning to have the walls painted on our building next week. The working hours will be from 9 a.m. to 6 p.m. Don't be surprised to see workers outside your windows. Please keep your windows closed while they are painting. There might be some smell from the paint. But don't worry. It is totally safe and eco-friendly. Sorry for any inconvenience and thank you for your cooperation.

건물 관리자 / 벽에 페인트를 칠하다 / 작업 시간 / 놀라다 / 작업자들 / 창문을 닫아 두다 / 안전한 / 친환경적인 / 불편 / 협조

해석

남: 안녕하세요, 저는 건물 관리자인 Richard Carson입니다. 다음 주에 건물 벽에 페인트를 칠할 계획입니다. 작업 시간은 오전 9시부터 오후 6시까지일 것입니다. 창문 밖의 작업자들을 보고 놀라지 마십시오. 그들이 페인트를 칠하는 동안에 창문을 닫아 두십시오. 페인트에서 약간의 냄새가 날 수도 있습니다. 하지만 걱정하지 마십시오. 그것은 완전히 안전하고 친환경적입니다. 불편을 드려 죄송하며 협조해 주셔서 감사합니다.

① 사생활 보호의 중요성을 강조하려고
✔ 건물 벽 페인트 작업을 공지하려고

③ 회사 근무시간 변경을 안내하려고
④ 새로운 직원 채용을 공고하려고
⑤ 친환경 제품 출시를 홍보하려고

02 여자의 의견
정답률 90% ▶ 정답 ①

M: Hello, Veronica.
W: Hi, Jason. I heard that you are trying to get a driver's license these days. How is it going?

운전면허증을 따려고 하고 있다

(try to V: ~하려고 하다, get a driver's license: 운전면허증을 따다)

M: You know what? I already got it. Look!
W: Oh, good for you! How was the driving test?

운전면허 시험

M: Well, while taking the driving test, I was very nervous because some people were driving so fast.

긴장한

W: But there are speed limit signs everywhere.

제한 속도 표지판들

M: Right, there are. But so many drivers ignore speed limits these days.

운전자들 / 무시하다

W: That's terrible. Those drivers could cause serious car accidents.

일으키다 / 교통사고들

M: That's true. Driving too fast can be dangerous for everybody.

위험한

W: Exactly. In my opinion, all drivers should follow the speed limits.

내 생각에는

M: I totally agree with you.

전적으로

해석

남: 안녕, Veronica.
여: 안녕, Jason. 나는 네가 요즘 운전면허증을 따려고 하고 있다고 들었어. 어떻게 되어 가니?
남: 그거 알아? 나는 이미 그것을 땄어. 봐!
여: 오, 잘됐다! 운전면허 시험은 어땠니?
남: 음, 운전면허 시험을 보는 동안, 몇몇 사람들이 너무 빨리 운전을 하고 있어서 매우 긴장됐어.
여: 하지만 어디에나 제한 속도 표지판들이 있잖아.
남: 그래, 있어. 그런데 요즘 너무 많은 운전자들이 제한 속도를 무시해.
여: 그거 끔찍하다. 그 운전자들은 심각한 교통사고를 일으킬 수 있어.
남: 맞아. 너무 빨리 운전하는 것은 모두에게 위험할 수 있어.
여: 그래. 내 생각에는, 모든 운전자들은 제한 속도를 지켜야 해.
남: 네 말에 전적으로 동의해.

✔ 운전자는 제한 속도를 지켜야 한다.
② 교통경찰을 더 많이 배치해야 한다.
③ 보행자의 부주의가 교통사고를 유발한다.
④ 교통사고를 목격하면 즉시 신고해야 한다.
⑤ 대중교통을 이용하면 이동시간을 줄일 수 있다.

03 두 사람의 관계
정답률 90% ▶ 정답 ⑤

W: Excuse me. Can you help me find some books for my homework?

숙제

M: Sure. What is your homework about?
W: It's for my history class. The topic is the relationship between France and Germany.

역사 수업 / 주제 / 관계

M: What about this world history book?
W: It looks good. Do you have any other books?
M: I can also recommend this European history book.

추천하다

W: Great. How many books can I borrow at a time?

빌리다 / 한 번에

M: You can borrow up to four books for three weeks each.

~까지

W: Okay. I'll take these two books, then.
M: All right. [Beep sound] Don't forget to return them on time.

반납하는 것을 잊지 않다 / 제때에

(forget to V: ~하는 것을 잊다, return: 반납하다)

해석

여: 실례합니다. 제 숙제를 위한 책을 찾도록 도와주시겠어요?
남: 물론이죠. 숙제는 무엇에 관한 건가요?
여: 역사 수업을 위한 건데요. 주제는 프랑스와 독일 사이의 관계예요.
남: 이 세계사 책은 어떠세요?
여: 좋아 보여요. 다른 책들도 있나요?
남: 저는 이 유럽 역사 책도 추천해 줄 수 있어요.

여: 좋네요. 한 번에 몇 권의 책을 빌릴 수 있나요?
남: 각 3주 동안 4권까지 빌릴 수 있어요.
여: 알겠습니다. 그럼, 이 두 권의 책을 빌릴게요.
남: 알겠습니다. [삐 소리] 그것들을 제때에 반납하는 것을 잊지 마세요.

① 작가 — 출판사 직원
② 관람객 — 박물관 해설사
③ 손님 — 주방장
④ 탑승객 — 항공 승무원
✔ 학생 — 사서

04 그림에서 대화의 내용과 일치하지 않는 것

정답률 80% ▶ 정답 ⑤

M: Honey, come to Lucy's room. Look at what I did for her.
W: It looks great. Is that a toy bear on the bed?
  곰 인형
M: Yes. That's right. She can sleep with the toy bear.
W: It's cute. Oh, and I like the round clock on the wall.
  둥근 시계
M: The round clock goes well with the room, doesn't it? How do you
  ~과 잘 어울리다
  like the family picture next to the window?
  가족 사진
W: That's so sweet. I also love the striped curtains on the window.
  줄무늬의
M: I'm happy you like them. What do you think of the star-shaped rug
  on the floor?   별 모양의   깔개
  바닥
W: It is lovely. Lucy will feel safe and warm on the rug.
M: Looks like everything's prepared.
  준비되다(prepare: 준비하다)
W: Thanks, honey. You've done a great job.

해석

남: 여보, Lucy의 방으로 와요. 내가 그 애를 위해 한 일을 봐요.
여: 멋져 보이네요. 침대 위에 있는 것은 곰 인형이에요?
남: 네. 맞아요. 그 애는 곰 인형과 함께 잘 수 있어요.
여: 귀엽네요. 오, 그리고 저는 벽에 걸린 둥근 시계가 마음에 들어요.
남: 둥근 시계가 방과 잘 어울리죠, 그렇지 않나요? 창문 옆에 있는 가족 사진은 어때요?
여: 정말 좋아요. 창문에 있는 줄무늬 커튼도 마음에 들어요.
남: 당신이 마음에 든다니 기쁘네요. 바닥에 있는 별 모양의 깔개에 대해 어떻게 생각해요?
여: 사랑스러워요. Lucy가 깔개 위에서 안전하고 따뜻하게 느낄 거예요.
남: 모든 것이 준비된 것 같아요.
여: 고마워요, 여보. 수고 많았어요.

05 남자가 할 일

정답률 90% ▶ 정답 ①

W: David, did you fix your bicycle yesterday?
  수리하다
M: Yes. Luckily, I was able to fix it by myself. How was your soccer
  수리할 수 있었다 혼자서(by oneself)   축구 연습
  practice, Christine?
  (be able to V: ~할 수 있다)
W: A new coach came to our soccer club and we practiced very hard.
  감독   열심히
M: You must be so tired. Do you still want to see a movie this
  afternoon?   피곤한
W: Of course, I booked the tickets two weeks ago.
  예매했다
M: All right. Let's get going.

W: Wait, did you email your science report to Mr. Smith? It's due today.
  이메일로 보내다   과학 보고서
M: [Pause] Oh, no! I finished it but forgot to send it. What should I do?
  끝냈다   보내는 것을 잊어버렸다
  (send: 보내다)
W: Why don't you send it before meeting me at the movie theater?
  영화관
M: Good idea. I'll go home quickly and send the report, but can you
  buy some popcorn for me before I get there?
W: No problem. See you there.

해석

여: David, 어제 네 자전거를 수리했니?
남: 응. 다행히도, 혼자서 수리할 수 있었어. 네 축구 연습은 어땠니, Christine?
여: 새 감독님이 우리 축구 클럽에 오셔서 우리는 매우 열심히 연습했어.
남: 매우 피곤하겠구나. 너는 아직도 오늘 오후에 영화를 보고 싶니?
여: 물론이지, 2주 전에 티켓을 예매했어.
남: 알았어. 가자.
여: 잠깐, 너 Smith 선생님에게 과학 보고서를 이메일로 보냈니? 오늘까지 제출해야 해.
남: [잠시 후] 오, 이런! 나는 그것을 끝냈는데 보내는 것을 잊어버렸어. 어떻게 해야 하지?
여: 영화관에서 나를 만나기 전에 그것을 보내는 게 어떠니?
남: 좋은 생각이야. 빨리 집에 가서 보고서를 보낼게, 그런데 내가 그곳에 도착하기 전에 팝콘 좀 사다 줄 수 있어?
여: 문제 없어. 거기서 보자.

✔ 보고서 제출하기
② 티켓 예매하기
③ 자전거 수리하기
④ 축구 연습하기
⑤ 팝콘 구입하기

문제 풀이

기한이 오늘까지인 과학 보고서를 제출하지 않은 남자에게 여자는 영화관에서 만나기 전에 보고서를 보낼 것을 제안한다. 이 말에 남자는 집에 가서 보고서를 보내겠다고 답하고 있으므로 남자가 할 일은 ① '보고서 제출하기'이다.

06 여자가 지불할 금액

정답률 80% ▶ 정답 ③

M: Good morning. Welcome to Happy Land.
W: Hello. I'd like to buy some tickets. How much are they?
M: $20 for the amusement park and $10 for the water park. How
  놀이공원   수상공원
  many tickets do you need?
W: We're five people in total, and we only want to go to the
  amusement park.   모두 합해서
M: Okay. Do you have any discount coupons?
  할인 쿠폰들
W: I printed out a birthday coupon from your website. It's my birthday
  출력했다   today.
M: It's your birthday? Just let me check your ID, please.
W: Here you are.   신분증
M: Oh, happy birthday! With your birthday coupon, your ticket is free.
  무료의
W: That's great. Please give me five tickets including my ticket.
  ~을 포함해서
M: Let me see. That'll be four people at the original price, and one
  person with a birthday coupon.   원래 가격
W: Right. Here is my credit card.

해석

남: 안녕하세요. Happy Land에 오신 것을 환영합니다.
여: 안녕하세요. 티켓을 좀 사고 싶은데요. 얼마죠?
남: 놀이공원은 20달러이고 수상공원은 10달러예요. 몇 장의 티켓이 필요하신가요?
여: 저희는 모두 합해서 5명이고, 놀이공원에만 가고 싶어요.
남: 알겠습니다. 할인 쿠폰을 가지고 계신가요?
여: 웹사이트에서 생일 쿠폰을 출력했어요. 오늘이 제 생일이거든요.
남: 생일이신가요? 신분증을 좀 확인할게요.
여: 여기 있어요.
남: 오, 생일 축하드려요! 생일 쿠폰으로, 고객님의 티켓은 무료예요.
여: 잘됐네요. 제 티켓 포함해서 5장의 티켓을 주세요.
남: 어디 보자. 원래 가격으로 4명이고, 생일 쿠폰이 있는 1명이시네요.
여: 맞아요. 여기 제 신용카드가 있어요.

① $40   ② $60   ✓③ $80
④ $100   ⑤ $120

문제풀이
여자의 일행은 총 5명이므로, 1장에 20달러인 놀이공원 티켓 5장을 구입하면 총액은 100달러이다. 생일 쿠폰을 사용하는 여자의 티켓은 무료라고 했으므로 나머지 4장에 대한 금액인 80달러만 지불하면 된다. 따라서 답은 ③ '$80'이다.

---

07 남자가 음식 부스에 갈 수 없는 이유
정답률 90%   ▶ 정답 ①

W: Hi, Alex. How is it going?
M: I'm good. Thanks. I've just finished my English project. How about you, Tracy?
　　　　　　　　　　　　　　　영어 프로젝트
W: I'm a little busy preparing for my food booth.
　　~을 준비하느라 좀 바쁜　　　　음식 부스
　(busy V-ing: ~하느라 바쁜, prepare for: ~을 준비하다)
M: A food booth? What for?
W: My school festival is next Tuesday. I'm running a food booth that day.
　　　　　　　　　　　　　　　　　운영하는(run)
M: That is so cool. What is on the menu?
　　　　　　　　　　　　　　메뉴
W: We're making sandwiches. You should come.
M: I'd love to, but I can't.
W: You can't? I was really looking forward to seeing you at my school.
　　　　　　　보기를 정말 기대하고 있었다
　　　　(look forward to V-ing: ~하기를 기대하다)
M: I'm terribly sorry. I have to practice for a band audition.
　　　　　　　　　　　　　　　　　　밴드 오디션
W: Oh, I see. Well, good luck with your audition.
　　　　　　　　　　~에 행운을 빌다
M: Thank you.

해석
여: 안녕, Alex. 어떻게 지내니?
남: 좋아. 고마워. 나는 방금 영어 프로젝트를 끝냈어. 너는 어때, Tracy?
여: 나는 음식 부스를 준비하느라 좀 바빠.
남: 음식 부스? 무엇 때문에?
여: 우리 학교 축제가 다음 주 화요일이야. 나는 그날 음식 부스를 운영할 거야.
남: 그거 정말 멋지다. 메뉴에 무엇이 있니?
여: 우리는 샌드위치를 만들 거야. 너도 꼭 와.
남: 그러고 싶지만, 안 되겠어.
여: 안 돼? 나는 우리 학교에서 너를 보기를 정말 기대하고 있었어.
남: 정말 미안해. 나는 밴드 오디션을 위해 연습을 해야 해.
여: 오, 그렇구나. 음, 오디션에 행운을 빌게.
남: 고마워.

✓① 밴드 오디션 연습을 해야 해서
② 보드게임 부스를 설치해야 해서
③ 영어 프로젝트를 끝내야 해서
④ 샌드위치를 준비해야 해서
⑤ 친구를 만나러 가야 해서

---

08 Spanish culture class에 관해 언급되지 않은 것
정답률 90%   ▶ 정답 ⑤

[Telephone rings.]
W: Hello, this is the World Culture Center. How can I help you?
　　　　　　　　　　세계 문화 센터
M: Hi, I'm calling about a Spanish culture class for my teenage son.
　　　　　　　　　　　　스페인 문화 수업
W: Okay. We have an interesting class for teenagers.
　　　　　　　　　　흥미로운
M: Great. Who teaches it?
　　　　　　　가르치다
W: A Korean teacher and a native speaker teach it together.
　　　　　　　　　　　　원어민
M: What kind of activities are there in the class?
　　　　　　　　활동들
W: Students can cook traditional foods, learn new words, and try on
　　　　　　　　요리하다　전통의　　　　　　　　　　　　　~을 입어 보다
　traditional clothing.
M: On what day is the class?
W: It's on Wednesday and Friday afternoons.
M: I see. Is there anything my son should prepare before the class?
W: He just needs to bring a pen and a notebook. The center provides
　　　　　　　　가져오다

---

all the other class materials.
　　　　　　　자료들
M: Perfect. Thanks for the information.

해석
[전화벨이 울린다.]
여: 여보세요, 세계 문화 센터입니다. 어떻게 도와드릴까요?
남: 안녕하세요, 저는 십 대 아들을 위한 스페인 문화 수업 때문에 전화를 드렸어요.
여: 네. 십 대들을 위한 흥미로운 수업이 있어요.
남: 잘됐네요. 누가 그것을 가르치나요?
여: 한국인 선생님과 원어민이 함께 가르쳐요.
남: 수업에는 어떤 종류의 활동들이 있나요?
여: 학생들은 전통 음식을 요리하고, 새로운 단어를 배우고, 전통 의상을 입어 볼 수 있어요.
남: 수업이 무슨 요일에 있나요?
여: 수요일과 금요일 오후예요.
남: 그렇군요. 제 아들이 수업 전에 준비해야 할 것이 있나요?
여: 펜과 공책만 가져오면 됩니다. 센터에서 다른 모든 수업 자료를 제공해요.
남: 완벽하네요. 알려주셔서 감사합니다.

① 강사   ② 활동 종류   ③ 수업 요일
④ 준비물   ✓⑤ 수강료

---

09 Summer Flea Market에 관한 내용과 일치하지 않는 것
정답률 85%   ▶ 정답 ⑤

W: Good afternoon, residents. This is the head of the Pineville
　　　　　　　　　　주민들　　　　　　　　대표
　Community Center. We're holding the Summer Flea Market for one
　　주민 센터　　　　　　　　　　　여름 벼룩시장
　week. It'll be held in the parking lot of Pineville Middle School. You
　　　　　　　　　　　　주차장
　can get many different kinds of items such as toys and candles at
　　　　　　　　　　　　物品들　　　　　　　　　　　양초들
　reasonable prices. You can also sell any of your own used items if
　합리적인　　　　　　판매하다　　　　　　　　　중고의
　they are in good condition. On the first day, every resident visiting
　　　　　상태가 좋은
　the market will get a shopping bag as a gift. For more information,
　　　　　　　　　　장바구니　　선물로
　please check out the community center's website.

해석
여: 안녕하세요, 주민 여러분. 저는 Pineville 주민 센터의 대표입니다. 저희는 일주일 동안 Summer Flea Market(여름 벼룩시장)을 개최할 예정입니다. 그것은 Pineville 중학교 주차장에서 열릴 것입니다. 여러분은 합리적인 가격에 장난감과 양초와 같은 매우 다양한 종류의 물품들을 살 수 있습니다. 또한 여러분 소유의 중고 물품이 상태가 좋다면 판매할 수도 있습니다. 첫날에, 시장을 방문하는 모든 주민은 장바구니를 선물로 받을 것입니다. 더 많은 정보를 원하시면, 주민 센터의 웹사이트를 확인하시기 바랍니다.

① 일주일 동안 진행된다.
② 학교 주차장에서 열린다.
③ 장난감, 양초와 같은 물품을 살 수 있다.
④ 상태가 좋은 중고 물품을 판매할 수 있다.
✓⑤ 첫날 방문하면 할인 쿠폰을 선물로 받는다.

---

10 표에서 여자가 구입할 운동화
정답률 80%   ▶ 정답 ④

W: Kyle, I'm looking for some sneakers. Can you help me find some
　　　　　　　　　　　　운동화들
　good ones?
M: Of course. Let me see... [Pause] Look. These are the five best-selling
　　　　　　　　　　　　　　　　　　　　　　　　　　가장 많이 팔리는
　ones.
W: Wow, they all look so cool. It's hard to choose among them.
　　　　　　　　　　　　　　어려운
M: Well, what's your budget?
　　　　　　　　예산
W: I don't want to spend more than 80 dollars.
　　　　　　　(돈을) 쓰다
M: All right. Which style do you want, active or casual?
　　　　　　　　　　　　　　　　活動적인　　편안한
W: I prefer casual ones. I think they match my clothes better.
　　　　　　　　　　　　　　　　　어울리다
M: Good. And I'd like to recommend waterproof shoes for rainy days.
　　　　　　　　　　　　추천하다　　방수의
W: Okay, I will take your advice.
　　　　　　　　조언
M: So you have two options left. Which color do you prefer?
W: Most of my shoes are black, so I'll buy white ones this time.
M: You made a good choice.

해석
여: Kyle, 나는 운동화를 찾고 있어. 좋은 것을 찾도록 도와줄 수 있겠니?
남: 물론이지. 어디 보자... [잠시 후]봐. 이것들이 가장 많이 팔리는 다섯 가지야.
여: 와, 모두 너무 멋져 보여. 그 중에서 고르는 것은 어려워.
남: 음, 예산은 얼마니?
여: 80달러 이상은 쓰고 싶지 않아.
남: 알았어. 활동적인 것과 편안한 것 중 어떤 스타일을 원하니?
여: 편안한 것이 더 좋아. 그것들이 내 옷과 더 잘 어울리는 것 같아.
남: 좋아. 그리고 나는 비 오는 날을 위해 방수 신발을 추천하고 싶어.
여: 알았어, 네 조언을 들을게.
남: 그럼 두 가지 선택지가 남았어. 어떤 색상이 더 좋니?
여: 내 신발은 대부분 검은색이라서, 이번에는 흰색을 살 거야.
남: 잘 선택했어.

운동화

	모델	가격	스타일	방수	색상
①	A	50달러	편안한	X	검은색
②	B	60달러	활동적인	X	흰색
③	C	65달러	편안한	O	검은색
✔ D	D	70달러	편안한	O	흰색
⑤	E	85달러	활동적인	O	흰색

11 여자의 마지막 말에 대한 남자의 응답

정답률 55%
▶ 정답 ①

W: Justin, what are you reading?
M: An advertisement. There's a special event at Will's Bookstore downtown.
　　　광고　　　　　　　특별 행사　　　　　서점
W: What kind of event is it?
M: (All children's books are 20% off.)
　　아동 도서들

해석
여: Justin, 무엇을 읽고 있니?
남: 광고야. 시내에 있는 Will's Bookstore(Will의 서점)에서 특별 행사가 있어.
여: 어떤 종류의 행사니?
남: (모든 아동 도서가 20% 할인돼.)
✔ ① 모든 아동 도서가 20% 할인돼.
② 좋은 기사를 쓰는 데는 시간이 걸려.
③ 나는 액션 모험 도서를 읽는 것을 좋아해.
④ TV에는 광고가 너무 많아.
⑤ 그 가게는 지난달부터 문을 닫았어.

12 남자의 마지막 말에 대한 여자의 응답

정답률 80%
▶ 정답 ③

M: You look so worried. What's wrong, Liz?
　　　　　　　　걱정스러운
W: I didn't do well on my presentation yesterday.
　　~을 잘하지 못했다　　　　발표
M: Sorry about that. To help take your mind off of it, how about having a nice meal?
　　　　　　　　　　~을 잊어버리다(take one's mind off of)
W: (Okay. Good food always makes me feel better.)
　　　　　　　　　　　　　　기분이 나아지다

해석
남: 너 아주 걱정스러워 보여. 무슨 일이니, Liz?
여: 어제 발표를 잘하지 못했어.
남: 유감이구나. 그것을 잊어버리는 데 도움을 주도록, 맛있는 식사를 하는 게 어떠니?
여: (좋아. 좋은 음식은 항상 내 기분이 나아지게 해주거든.)
① 천만에. 나는 너를 도울 수 있어서 기뻐.
② 그건 사실이 아니야. 나는 네 도움으로 그것을 만들었어.
✔ ③ 좋아. 좋은 음식은 항상 내 기분이 나아지게 해주거든.
④ 정말? 너는 나중에 꼭 극장에 방문해야 해.
⑤ 신경 쓰지 마. 너는 다음 발표를 더 잘할 거야.

13 여자의 마지막 말에 대한 남자의 응답

정답률 80%
▶ 정답 ③

M: Jenny, what class do you want to take this summer vacation?
　　　　　　　　　　　　　　　　　　여름 방학
W: Well, [Pause] I'm thinking of the guitar class.
M: Cool! I'm interested in playing the guitar, too.
　　　　　~에 관심이 있는
W: Really? It would be exciting if we took the class together.
M: I know, but I am thinking of taking a math class instead. I didn't do well on the final exam.
　　　　　　　　　　　　　　　　　　대신에
　　　　　기말고사
W: Oh, there is a math class? I didn't know that.
M: Yes. Mrs. Kim said she is offering a math class for first graders.
　　　　　　　　개설할 예정이다(offer)　　　1학년
W: That might be a good chance to improve my skills, too. Where can I check the schedule for the math class?
　　　　　　　　기회　　향상시키다
　　　　　시간표
M: (You can find it on the school website.)

해석
남: Jenny, 이번 여름 방학에 무슨 수업을 듣고 싶어?
여: 음, [잠시 후] 나는 기타 수업을 생각하고 있어.
남: 멋지다! 나도 기타를 치는 것에 관심이 있어.
여: 정말? 우리가 그 수업을 함께 들으면 재미있을 거야.
남: 알아, 하지만 나는 대신에 수학 수업을 들을 생각이야. 기말고사를 잘 못 봤거든.
여: 오, 수학 수업이 있니? 나는 몰랐어.
남: 그래. Kim 선생님께서 1학년들을 위해 수학 수업을 개설할 예정이라고 말씀하셨어.
여: 그것은 내 실력을 향상시킬 수 있는 좋은 기회일 수도 있겠어. 어디에서 수학 수업 시간표를 확인할 수 있니?
남: (학교 웹 사이트에서 그것을 찾을 수 있어.)
① 나는 새 기타를 사게 되어 신나.
② 여름 방학은 금요일에 시작해.
✔ ③ 학교 웹 사이트에서 그것을 찾을 수 있어.
④ 학교 축제에 함께 가자.
⑤ 너는 방학 동안 휴식을 취할 수 있어.

문제 풀이
여름 방학 기간에 Kim 선생님이 수학 수업을 할 것이라는 남자의 말을 듣고 여자는 자신의 수학 실력을 향상시킬 수 있는 기회라고 말하며 수업 시간표를 확인할 수 있는 곳에 대해 묻고 있다. 이에 대한 남자의 응답으로는 ③ 'You can find it on the school website.(학교 웹 사이트에서 그것을 찾을 수 있어.)'가 적절하다.

14 남자의 마지막 말에 대한 여자의 응답

정답률 85%
▶ 정답 ④

M: Hi, Claire! How are you doing?
W: I'm good. You're looking great!
M: Thanks. I've been working out these days.
　　　　　　　　운동을 하다(work out)
W: I need to start working out, too. What kind of exercise do you do?
　　　　　　　　　　　　　　　　　　　운동
M: I do yoga and some stretching at home.
　　　요가　　　　스트레칭　　집에서
W: At home? Do you exercise alone?
　　　　　　　　　　혼자
M: Yes and no. I exercise online with other people.
W: Exercising online with others? What do you mean by that?
M: I'm taking an online fitness course. We work out together on the Internet every evening at 7.
　　　　　　　피트니스 강좌
W: (That sounds great. Can I join the course, too?)

해석
남: 안녕, Claire! 어떻게 지내니?
여: 잘 지내. 너는 멋져 보이는구나!
남: 고마워. 나는 요즘 운동을 하고 있어.
여: 나도 운동을 시작해야겠어. 너는 어떤 종류의 운동을 하니?
남: 나는 집에서 요가와 스트레칭을 좀 해.
여: 집에서? 혼자 운동을 하는 거야?
남: 그렇기도 하고 그렇지 않기도 해. 다른 사람들과 온라인으로 운동을 하거든.
여: 다른 사람들과 온라인으로 운동을 한다고? 그게 무슨 말이니?
남: 나는 온라인 피트니스 강좌를 수강하고 있어. 우리는 매일 저녁 7시에 인터넷으로 함께 운동을 해.
여: (그거 좋겠다. 나도 그 강좌에 참여할 수 있을까?)
① 동의해. 체육관에서 운동하는 것에는 많은 이점이 있어.

② 네 말이 맞아. 모든 운동이 뇌에 도움이 되는 것은 아니야.

③ 걱정하지 마. 내가 운동을 하는 것은 그렇게 힘들지 않아.

☑ 그거 좋겠다. 나도 그 강좌에 참여할 수 있을까?

⑤ 정말 안됐다. 빨리 낫기를 바랄게.

15 다음 상황에서 Ted가 Monica에게 할 말   ▶ 정답 ④
정답률 80%

M: Ted is a high school student. He is planning to run for school president this year. He really wants to win the election. He thinks using posters is an effective way to make a strong impression on his schoolmates. But he is not good at drawing. His friend, Monica, is a member of a drawing club and she is good at drawing. So, he wants to ask her to help him draw posters. In this situation, what would Ted most likely say to Monica?

Ted: (Can you help me make posters for the election?)

해석

남: Ted는 고등학생이다. 그는 올해 학생회장에 출마할 계획이다. 그는 정말 선거에서 이기고 싶어 한다. 그는 포스터를 이용하는 것이 학교 친구들에게 강한 인상을 남길 수 있는 효과적인 방법이라고 생각한다. 하지만 그는 그림을 잘 그리지 못한다. 그의 친구인 Monica는 미술 동아리의 회원이고 그림을 잘 그린다. 그래서, 그는 그녀에게 포스터를 그리는 것을 도와달라고 부탁하고 싶다. 이러한 상황에서, Ted는 Monica에게 뭐라고 말하겠는가?

Ted: (선거를 위한 포스터를 만드는 것을 도와주겠니?)

① 포스터에 네 동아리 회원들을 그려도 될까?

② 내 미술 동아리에 가입하는 데 관심이 있니?

③ 선거에서 투표하는 방법에 대해 알려주겠니?

☑ 선거를 위한 포스터를 만드는 것을 도와주겠니?

⑤ 너는 다음 학생회장 선거에 출마할 거야?

16~17 1지문 2문항

W: Good morning, listeners. This is your host Rachel at the Morning Radio Show. What do you eat for breakfast? Today I will introduce a healthy breakfast food list. Eggs are an excellent choice because they are high in protein. High-protein foods such as eggs provide energy for the brain. Cheese is another good option. It reduces hunger so it supports weight loss. Yogurt is also great to eat in the morning. It contains probiotics that can improve digestion. Eating berries such as blueberries or strawberries is another perfect way to start the morning. They are lower in sugar than most other fruits, but higher in fiber. Add them to yogurt for a tasty breakfast. Start every day with a healthy meal. Thank you.

해석

여: 안녕하세요, 청취자 여러분. 저는 Morning Radio Show의 진행자인 Rachel입니다. 여러분께서는 아침 식사로 무엇을 드시나요? 오늘, 저는 건강에 좋은 아침 식사 음식 목록을 소개하겠습니다. 달걀은 단백질의 함유량이 높기 때문에 훌륭한 선택입니다. 달걀과 같은 고단백 음식은 에너지를 뇌에 제공합니다. 치즈는 또 다른 좋은 선택입니다. 그것은 배고픔을 줄여주어서 체중 감량을 도와줍니다. 요거트도 아침에 먹기에 좋습니다. 그것은 소화력을 향상시킬 수 있는 활생균을 함유하고 있습니다. 블루베리나 딸기와 같은 베리류를 먹는 것은 아침을 시작하는 또 다른 완벽한 방법입니다. 그것들은 대부분의 다른 과일들보다 당분의 함유량이 더 낮지만, 섬유소의 함유량은 더 높습니다. 맛있는 아침 식사를 위해 그것들을 요거트에 첨가하세요. 건강에 좋은 식사로 매일 시작하세요. 감사합니다.

16 여자가 하는 말의 주제   ▶ 정답 ②
정답률 90%

① 기름진 음식의 단점들

☑ 건강에 좋은 아침 식사 음식들

③ 간식 섭취를 피하는 방법들

④ 5분 안에 요리하기 쉬운 음식들

⑤ 균형 잡힌 식사의 중요성

17 언급된 음식이 아닌 것   ▶ 정답 ③
정답률 90%

① 달걀　　② 치즈　　☑ 감자

④ 요거트　　⑤ 베리류

16 2022년 9월 학력평가

01	③	02	⑤	03	②	04	④	05	④
06	③	07	②	08	②	09	⑤	10	③
11	③	12	①	13	①	14	③	15	④
16	①	17	④						

01 여자가 하는 말의 목적   ▶ 정답 ③
정답률 85%

W: Good evening, Vermont citizens. I'm Elizabeth Bowen, the Director of the Vermont City Library. I'd like to tell you about our online 15-Minute Book Reading program. This program is designed to help your children form good reading habits at home. Every day, individual tutoring is provided for 15 minutes. It's completely personalized to your child's reading level! Don't hesitate to sign up your children for this amazing opportunity to build their reading habits! For more information, please visit the Vermont City Library. Thank you.

해석

여: 안녕하세요, Vermont 시민 여러분. 저는 Vermont 시립 도서관장인 Elizabeth Bowen입니다. 저희의 온라인 15분 독서 프로그램에 대해 알려드리고 싶습니다. 이 프로그램은 여러분의 자녀들이 집에서 좋은 독서 습관을 형성하도록 도움을 주기 위해 고안되었습니다. 매일, 15분 동안 개별 지도가 제공됩니다. 그것은 여러분의 자녀의 독서 수준에 완전히 맞춰져 있습니다! 그들의 독서 습관을 기를 수 있는 이 놀라운 기회를 위해 주저하지 말고 여러분의 자녀들을 등록하세요! 더 많은 정보를 원하시면, Vermont 시립 도서관을 방문하세요. 감사합니다.

① 도서관 확장 이전을 공지하려고

② 도서관 이용 안내 영상을 소개하려고

☑ 독서 습관 형성 프로그램을 홍보하려고

④ 독해력 향상 방안에 대한 의견을 구하려고

⑤ 독서 프로그램 만족도 조사 참여를 요청하려고

02 남자의 의견   ▶ 정답 ⑤
정답률 85%

M: Clara, why the long face?

W: Aw, Dad, I bought this hair dryer, but the cool air mode doesn't work.

M: Where did you get it?

W: I bought it second-hand online.

M: Did you check the condition before you ordered it?

W: I did, but I missed the seller's note that said the cool air mode doesn't work.

M: Oh dear. It's important to check all the details when you buy second-hand items.

W: You're right. I was just so excited because it was much cheaper than other hair dryers.

M: Some second-hand items are almost like new, but others are not. So, you should read every detail of the item carefully.

W: Thanks, Dad. I'll keep that in mind.

(keep A in mind: A를 명심하다)

해석

남: Clara, 왜 우울한 얼굴이니?

여: 아, 아빠, 제가 이 헤어 드라이어를 샀는데, 냉풍 모드가 작동하지 않아요.

남: 그것을 어디에서 샀니?

여: 온라인에서 중고로 샀어요.

남: 주문하기 전에 상태를 확인했니?

여: 했는데, 냉풍 모드가 작동하지 않는다는 판매자의 메모를 못 봤어요.

남: 오, 이런. 중고품을 살 때는 모든 세부 사항을 확인하는 것이 중요해.

여: 맞아요. 저는 그저 그것이 다른 헤어 드라이어보다 훨씬 싸서 너무 신이 났었어요.

남: 어떤 중고품들은 거의 새것과 같지만, 다른 것들은 그렇지 않아. 그래서, 물품의 모든 세부 사항을 주의 깊게 읽어야 한단다.

여: 고마워요, 아빠. 그것을 명심할게요.

① 중고품은 직접 만나서 거래해야 한다.

② 물품 구매 시 여러 제품을 비교해야 한다.

③ 계획적으로 예산을 세워 물품을 구매해야 한다.

④ 온라인 거래 시 개인 정보 유출에 유의해야 한다.

✔ 중고품 구매 시 세부 사항을 꼼꼼히 확인해야 한다.

03 두 사람의 관계

정답률 90% ▶ 정답 ②

M: Hello, Ms. Adams! It's been a while since you were here.

W: Last time I came, you told me I should get a checkup every year.

M: That's right. When did you last visit us?

W: I guess I came here last October.

M: Okay. Then, let me check your vision. Please sit here. *[Pause]* Hmm... your eyesight got a little worse.

W: Yeah, maybe it's because I've been working on a computer for too long.

M: Actually, the blue light from computers and smartphones makes your eyes tired.

W: Really? Is there a lens that blocks the light?

M: Sure. You can wear these blue light blocking lenses.

W: That sounds perfect. But I'd like to use this frame again.

M: No problem, you can just change the lenses. You can come pick them up in a week.

W: Okay, thank you so much. See you then.

해석

남: 안녕하세요, Adams 씨! 여기에 오신 지 꽤 됐네요.

여: 지난번에 왔을 때, 제게 매년 검진을 받아야 한다고 말씀하셨잖아요.

남: 맞아요. 마지막으로 방문하신 게 언제죠?

여: 작년 10월에 왔던 것 같아요.

남: 알겠어요. 그럼, 시력을 확인해 볼게요. 여기에 앉으세요. *[잠시 후]* 흠... 시력이 조금 더 나빠졌네요.

여: 네, 아마 너무 오랫동안 컴퓨터 작업을 해오고 있어서 그럴 거예요.

남: 사실, 컴퓨터와 스마트폰에서 나오는 청색광은 눈을 피로하게 만들어요.

여: 정말이에요? 청색광을 차단하는 렌즈가 있나요?

남: 물론이죠. 이 청색광 차단 렌즈를 착용하실 수 있어요.

여: 완벽할 것 같네요. 그런데 저는 이 안경테를 다시 사용하고 싶어요.

남: 문제 없어요, 그냥 렌즈만 바꿀 수 있거든요. 일주일 후에 찾으러 오시면 돼요.

여: 알겠어요, 정말 감사해요. 그때 뵐게요.

① 의사 — 간호사

✔ 안경사 — 고객

③ 보건 교사 — 학부모

④ 사진사 — 모델

⑤ 앱 개발자 — 의뢰인

04 그림에서 대화의 내용과 일치하지 않는 것

정답률 90% ▶ 정답 ④

W: Carl, what are you looking at?

M: Oh, hi, Amy. Come take a look. It's a picture of my grandparents' house. I was there last weekend.

W: What a beautiful house! There's even a pond under the tree!

M: Yes, my grandfather dug it himself. And how about that flower-patterned tablecloth?

W: I love it. It makes the table look cozy.

M: Did you see the painting of a bear on the door?

W: Oh! Did you paint that?

M: Yeah, I did it when I was 8 years old.

W: It's cute. And there are two windows on the roof.

M: Right, we get a lot of sunlight through the windows.

W: I like that! And can you still ride the swings next to the house?

M: Of course. That's the best spot to see the sunset.

W: Wow, your grandparents' house looks like a nice place!

해석

여: Carl, 무엇을 보고 있니?

남: 오, 안녕, Amy. 와서 좀 봐. 이건 내 조부모님 집의 사진이야. 나는 지난 주말에 거기에 있었어.

여: 정말 아름다운 집이구나! 나무 아래에 연못도 있어!

남: 응, 할아버지께서 그것을 직접 파셨어. 그리고 저 꽃무늬 테이블보는 어때?

여: 마음에 들어. 그것은 테이블을 아늑하게 보이게 해.

남: 문에 있는 곰 그림을 봤니?

여: 오! 네가 그렸어?

남: 그래, 내가 8살 때 그렸어.

여: 귀엽다. 그리고 지붕에는 2개의 창문이 있네.

남: 맞아, 그 창문을 통해서 햇빛이 많이 들어와.

여: 마음에 들어! 그리고 아직도 집 옆에 있는 그네를 탈 수 있니?

남: 물론이지. 그곳은 일몰을 보기에 가장 좋은 장소야.

여: 와, 너희 조부모님 집은 좋은 곳처럼 보여!

05 여자가 할 일

정답률 70% ▶ 정답 ④

M: Honey, there's a box in the doorway. What is it?

W: I ordered some groceries online. Would you bring it in?

M: Sure. Is this for the house-warming party today?

W: Yeah. Since I had to have my car repaired, I couldn't go shopping yesterday.

M: Sorry, I should've taken you to the market.

(should have p.p.: ~했어야 했다)

W: That's okay. You worked late to meet the deadline for your report.
Would you open the box for me?

M: Sure. *[Pause]* Oh no, some eggs are broken! Have a look.

W: Ah... that's never happened before.

M: Why don't we call the customer center about it?

W: Okay. I'll do it right now.

M: While you do that, I'll put the other food in the fridge.

W: Thanks.

해석

남: 여보, 현관에 상자가 있네요. 뭐예요?

여: 온라인으로 식료품을 좀 주문했어요. 가지고 들어와 줄래요?

남: 물론이죠. 이것은 오늘 집들이를 위한 거예요?

여: 네. 제 차의 수리를 맡겨야 해서, 어제 장을 보러 갈 수 없었어요.

남: 미안해요, 내가 당신을 시장에 데려다 주었어야 했는데요.

여: 괜찮아요. 당신은 보고서의 마감 기한을 맞추기 위해 늦게까지 일했잖아요. 저 대신 상자를 열어줄래요?

남: 물론이죠. *[잠시 후]* 오 이런, 계란 몇 개가 깨졌네요! 봐요.

여: 아... 전에는 그런 일이 한 번도 없었는데요.

남: 우리 그것에 대해 고객 센터에 전화하는 게 어때요?

여: 알겠어요. 지금 바로 할게요.

남: 당신이 그것을 하는 동안, 제가 다른 식품을 냉장고에 넣을게요.

여: 고마워요.

① 식료품 주문하기
② 자동차 수리 맡기기
③ 보고서 제출하기
✓ 고객 센터에 전화하기
⑤ 냉장고에 식료품 넣기

---

06 남자가 지불할 금액   ▶ 정답 ③

정답률 80%

W: Hello, welcome to Kelly's Bake Shop. How can I help you?

M: Hi, I'd like to order a carrot cake.

W: Okay, we have two sizes. A small one is $25 and a large one is $35. Which one would you like?

M: Well, we're four people, so a large one would be good.

W: Great. Do you need candles?

M: No thanks, but can you write on the cake?

W: We can. It costs $5. What would you like the message to say?

M: Please write "Thank You Mom" on it.

W: Sure. It takes about half an hour. Is that okay?

M: No problem. Can I use this 10% off coupon?

W: Certainly. You get 10% off the total.

M: Thanks. Here's my credit card.

해석

여: 안녕하세요, Kelly's Bake Shop에 오신 것을 환영합니다. 어떻게 도와드릴까요?

남: 안녕하세요, 당근 케이크를 주문하고 싶어요.

여: 네, 두 가지 사이즈가 있어요. 작은 것은 25달러이고 큰 것은 35달러예요. 어떤 것으로 하시겠어요?

남: 음, 저희는 4명이니까 큰 것이 좋겠네요.

여: 알겠습니다. 초가 필요하신가요?

남: 아니요, 그런데 케이크 위에 글씨를 써 주실 수 있나요?

여: 네. 그것은 5달러예요. 어떤 내용의 메시지를 원하시나요?

남: '엄마 감사해요'라고 써주세요.

여: 알겠습니다. 30분 정도 걸려요. 괜찮으신가요?

남: 문제 없어요. 이 10% 할인 쿠폰을 사용할 수 있나요?

여: 물론이죠. 총액에서 10% 할인을 받게 돼요.

남: 고마워요. 여기 제 신용카드가 있어요.

① $27   ② $30   ✓ $36
④ $40   ⑤ $45

문제 풀이

큰 사이즈의 당근 케이크는 35달러이고, 케이크 위에 글씨를 쓰는 데 드는 비용은 5달러이므로 총액은 40달러이다. 10% 할인 쿠폰을 사용할 수 있으므로 남자가 지불할 금액은 4달러가 할인된 36달러이다. 따라서 답은 ③ '$36'이다.

---

07 여자가 가방을 구입한 이유   ▶ 정답 ②

정답률 90%

M: Anna, I haven't seen you use this bag before. Did you buy a new one?

W: Hi, Jason. Yeah, I bought it online last week.

M: I saw some celebrities posting about it on their social media.

W: Really? I didn't know that, but this bag seems to be popular.

M: It does, but its design isn't that unique. It's too plain.

W: Yeah, and it's a little expensive compared to other bags.

M: Well, then why did you buy it?

W: I bought it because it's made from recycled materials.

M: Oh, you're a responsible consumer.

W: Exactly. So, I'm recommending it to all my friends.

M: Good idea. I'll check the website for more information.

해석

남: Anna, 나는 네가 이 가방을 사용하는 것을 전에 본 적이 없어. 새 가방을 샀니?

여: 안녕, Jason. 그래, 지난주에 온라인에서 샀어.

남: 몇몇 유명 연예인들이 그들의 소셜 미디어에 그것에 대해 게시하는 것을 봤어.

여: 정말? 그건 몰랐는데, 이 가방이 인기가 있는 것 같아.

남: 그렇긴 하지만, 디자인이 그렇게 독특하지는 않아. 너무 평범해.

여: 그래, 그리고 다른 가방들에 비해서 조금 비싸.

남: 음, 그럼 왜 그것을 샀니?

여: 재활용 소재로 만들어졌기 때문에 샀어.

남: 오, 너는 책임감 있는 소비자구나.

여: 맞아. 그래서 나는 그것을 모든 친구들에게 추천하고 있어.

남: 좋은 생각이야. 나도 더 많은 정보를 위해 웹사이트를 확인해 볼게.

① 유명 연예인들이 착용해서
✓ 재활용 소재를 사용해서
③ 많은 친구들이 추천해서
④ 디자인이 독특해서
⑤ 가격이 저렴해서

---

08 Youth Street Dance Contest에 관해 언급되지 않은 것   ▶ 정답 ②

정답률 85%

W: Jimmy, what are you doing with your smartphone?

M: I'm looking at a poster about the Youth Street Dance Contest.

W: Oh, isn't it a street dance contest for high school students?

M: Yeah. Why don't you enter? I know you're good at dancing.

W: Hmm... when is it?

M: The competition is October 22nd, but the deadline for entry is September 30th.

W: Okay, good. I have a few months to practice.

M: And look! The winner gets $2,000!

W: That's amazing! What types of dancing are there?

M: It says participants should choose one of these three types: hip-hop, locking, and breakdancing.

W: I'm really into breakdancing lately, so I'll enter with that. How do I apply?

M: You just download the application form from the website and submit it by email.

W: Okay! It'll be a great experience for me to try out.

해석

여: Jimmy, 스마트폰으로 무엇을 하고 있니?

남: Youth Street Dance Contest(청소년 길거리 댄스 대회)에 대한 포스터를 보고 있어.

여: 오, 그것은 고등학생들을 위한 길거리 댄스 대회 아니야?

남: 그래. 참가하는 게 어때? 나는 네가 춤을 잘 추는 것을 알아.

여: 흠... 언제야?

남: 대회는 10월 22일인데, 신청 마감일은 9월 30일이야.

여: 그래, 좋아. 연습할 시간이 몇 달 있네.

남: 그리고 봐! 우승자는 2,000달러를 받게 돼!

여: 그거 놀라운데! 어떤 종류의 댄스가 있어?

남: 참가자는 힙합, 락킹, 그리고 브레이크댄스의 세 종류 중 하나를 선택해야 한다고 되어 있어.

여: 나는 최근에 브레이크댄스에 푹 빠져 있어서, 그것으로 참가할 거야. 어떻게 신청하면 되니?

남: 웹사이트에서 신청서를 다운로드해서 이메일로 제출하기만 하면 돼.

여: 알겠어! 그것은 내가 시도해 볼 좋은 경험이 될 거야.

① 신청 마감일　　　②심사 기준 ✔　　　③우승 상금액
④ 참가 부문　　　⑤신청 방법

09 Lakewoods Plogging에 관한 내용과 일치하지 않는 것

정답률 60%　▶ 정답 ⑤

M: Hello, Lakewoods High School students! I'm Lawrence Cho, president of the student council. I'm happy to announce a special new event to reduce waste around our school: Lakewoods Plogging! Since plogging is the activity of picking up trash while running, all participants should wear workout clothes and sneakers. We provide eco-friendly bags for the trash, so you don't need to bring any. The event will be held on October 1st from 7 a.m. to 9 a.m. You can sign up for the event on the school website starting tomorrow. The first 30 participants will get a pair of sports socks. For more information, please visit our school website. Don't miss this fun opportunity!

해석

남: 안녕하세요, Lakewoods 고등학교 학생 여러분! 저는 학생회 회장인 Lawrence Cho 입니다. 우리 학교 주변의 쓰레기를 줄이기 위한 특별하고 새로운 행사인 Lakewoods Plogging(Lakewoods 플로깅)에 대해 알려드리게 되어 기쁩니다. 플로깅은 달리면서 쓰레기를 줍는 활동이기 때문에, 모든 참가자들은 운동복과 운동화를 착용해야 합니다. 쓰레기를 담을 친환경 봉투를 제공하므로, 어떤 것도 가져오실 필요가 없습니다. 행사는 10월 1일 오전 7시부터 9시까지 열릴 것입니다. 내일부터 학교 웹사이트에서 행사에 참가 신청을 할 수 있습니다. 선착순 30명의 참가자들은 스포츠 양말 한 켤레를 받을 것입니다. 더 많은 정보를 원하시면, 우리 학교 웹사이트를 방문해 주세요. 이 재미있는 기회를 놓치지 마세요!

① 참가자는 운동복과 운동화를 착용해야 한다.
② 쓰레기를 담을 봉투가 배부된다.
③ 10월 1일 오전 7시부터 진행될 것이다.
④ 학교 웹사이트에서 신청할 수 있다.
✔ 참가자 모두 스포츠 양말을 받을 것이다.

문제 풀이

플로깅 행사의 참가 신청은 학교 웹사이트에서 할 수 있는데 참가자 중에서 선착순 30명에게만 스포츠 양말 한 켤레를 줄 것이라고 했으므로 ⑤ '참가자 모두 스포츠 양말을 받을 것이다.'는 내용과 일치하지 않는다.

10 표에서 두 사람이 주문할 휴대용 캠핑 히터

정답률 85%　▶ 정답 ③

M: Honey, what are you doing?

W: I'm looking at a website to order a portable heater for winter camping. Would you like to choose one together?

M: Sure, let me see.

W: We should be able to carry it easily, so its weight is important. I think we should get one of these under 4kg.

M: Good point. Oh, this one is pretty expensive.

W: I know. Let's choose one of these for less than $100.

M: Okay. And I think an electric heater would be good. What do you think?

W: I agree. It's safer to use.

M: Now we have these two models left.

W: I'd like the one with a five-star customer rating.

M: All right. Let's order this one.

해석

남: 여보, 무엇을 하고 있어요?

여: 겨울 캠핑을 위한 휴대용 히터를 주문하기 위해서 웹 사이트를 보고 있어요. 같이 하나 고를래요?

남: 물론이죠, 어디 봐요.

여: 쉽게 운반할 수 있어야 하니까, 무게가 중요해요. 이 4kg 이하의 제품들 중에서 하나를 사야 할 것 같아요.

남: 좋은 지적이에요. 오, 이 제품은 꽤 비싸네요.

여: 그러게요. 100달러 이하로 이것들 중에서 하나를 골라요.

남: 좋아요. 그리고 전기 히터가 좋을 것 같아요. 어떻게 생각해요?

여: 동의해요. 사용하기에 더 안전하잖아요.

남: 이제 이 두 가지 모델들이 남았네요.

여: 저는 소비자 평가가 별 다섯 개인 제품이 마음에 들어요.

남: 알겠어요. 이 제품을 주문합시다.

휴대용 캠핑 히터

모델	무게(kg)	가격	에너지원	소비자 평가
① A	4.2	85달러	기름	★★★
② B	3.6	90달러	기름	★★★★
✔ ③ C	3.4	92달러	전기	★★★★★
④ D	3.2	95달러	전기	★★★★
⑤ E	2.8	115달러	전기	★★★★★

11 여자의 마지막 말에 대한 남자의 응답

정답률 60%　▶ 정답 ③

W: Kevin, is this bike yours?

M: Yes, I bought it for my bike tour.

W: Really? Where are you planning to go?

M: (I haven't decided the place, yet.)

해석

여: Kevin, 이 자전거 네 거야?

남: 응, 자전거 여행을 위해 그것을 샀어.

여: 정말? 어디로 갈 계획이니?

남: (아직 장소는 결정하지 않았어.)

① 너도 여행에 참여할 수 있어.
② 그 자전거는 그렇게 비싸지 않았어.
✔ 아직 장소는 결정하지 않았어.
④ 나는 공원에서 자전거를 빌릴 거야.
⑤ 가을은 여행하기에 가장 좋은 계절이야.

12 남자의 마지막 말에 대한 여자의 응답

정답률 85%　▶ 정답 ①

[Telephone rings.]

M: Hello, this is Ashley's Dental Clinic. How may I help you?

W: Hello, this is Emily Gibson. Can I see the dentist today? I have a terrible toothache.

M: Just a second. Let me check. [Pause] He's available at 4:30 this afternoon.

W: (Great. I'll be there at that time.)

해석

[전화벨이 울린다.]

남: 안녕하세요, Ashley's Dental Clinic(Ashley's 치과)입니다. 어떻게 도와드릴까요?

여: 안녕하세요, 저는 Emily Gibson이에요. 오늘 치과 진료를 받을 수 있을까요? 치통이 심해서요.

남: 잠시만요. 확인해 볼게요. [잠시 후] 선생님께서 오늘 오후 4시 30분에 시간이 되시네요.

여: (잘됐네요. 그 시간에 갈게요.)

✔ 잘됐네요. 그 시간에 갈게요.
② 알겠어요. 칫솔을 바꿀게요.
③ 안타깝네요. 당신이 빨리 낫기를 바랄게요.
④ 걱정하지 마세요. 진통제가 효과가 좋네요.
⑤ 물론이죠. 그가 언제 시간이 되는지 알려주세요.

13 여자의 마지막 말에 대한 남자의 응답
정답률 75%　▶ 정답 ①

W: Hey, Justin. Do you know where those students are going?
M: They're <u>probably</u> going to the <u>gym</u> to <u>practice</u> badminton.
　　　　　아마　　　　　체육관　　연습하다
W: Why are so many students practicing badminton?
M: Haven't you heard about the School Badminton <u>Tournament</u>? Many of the students <u>have already signed up for it.</u>
　　　　　　　　　　　　　대회
　　　~에 이미 등록했다
　　(already: 이미, sign up for: ~에 등록하다)
W: Really? Why is it so <u>popular</u>?
　　　　　　　　인기가 있는
M: The winners will get a big <u>scholarship</u> and there are lots of other prizes as well.
　　　장학금
　　상들
W: That's nice! Why don't you sign up for it, too?
M: I'd like to, but only <u>doubles</u> can <u>participate</u>. And I haven't found a partner, yet.
　　　　　　복식　　　참가하다
W: Actually, I used to be a badminton player in my <u>elementary school</u>.
　　　　　(과거에) ~이었다　　　　　　　　　초등학교
M: Wow! I have a top <u>expert</u> right here! How about we <u>partner up</u>?
　　　　　　　전문가　　　　　　　　　파트너가 되다
W: Sure. Not an expert, but I can try.
M: (Fantastic! We'll be a really good team.)

해석
여: 안녕, Justin. 저 학생들이 어디로 가고 있는지 아니?
남: 아마 배드민턴을 연습하러 체육관에 가고 있을 거야.
여: 왜 그렇게 많은 학생들이 배드민턴을 연습하고 있는 거야?
남: 너는 학교 배드민턴 대회에 대해 들어본 적 없니? 많은 학생들이 그것에 이미 등록했어.
여: 정말? 왜 그렇게 인기가 있는 거야?
남: 우승자는 많은 장학금을 받게 되고 다른 상들도 많이 있거든.
여: 그거 좋은데! 너도 등록하는 게 어때?
남: 그러고 싶지만, 복식만 참가할 수 있어. 그런데 나는 아직 파트너를 찾지 못했어.
여: 사실, 나는 초등학교 때 배드민턴 선수였어.
남: 와! 바로 여기에 최고 전문가가 있네! 우리 파트너가 되는 게 어떠니?
여: 그래. 전문가는 아니지만, 해 볼게.
남: (좋아! 우리는 정말 좋은 팀이 될 거야.)
✔ 좋아! 우리는 정말 좋은 팀이 될 거야.
② 미안해. 나는 네가 왜 그것을 좋아하는지 이해가 안 돼.
③ 좋은 생각이야! 내가 너를 위해 다른 파트너를 찾아줄게.
④ 문제없어. 나는 내 라켓을 사용해서 연습할 수 있어.
⑤ 알아. 모든 사람은 스포츠 경기를 보는 것을 좋아해.

문제 풀이
파트너가 없어서 복식만 참가할 수 있는 학교 배드민턴 대회에 등록하지 못한 남자는 초등학교 때 선수였다는 여자의 말에 파트너가 될 것을 제안하고 여자는 이에 동의한다. 따라서 여자의 말에 대한 남자의 응답으로는 ① 'Fantastic! We'll be a really good team.(좋아! 우리는 정말 좋은 팀이 될 거야.)'가 적절하다.

14 남자의 마지막 말에 대한 여자의 응답
정답률 80%　▶ 정답 ③

M: Hey, Natalie. What are you doing on your computer?
W: Hi, Dave. I'm working on my <u>presentation</u> for <u>social studies class.</u> It's about <u>traditional games</u> in Asia.
　　　　　　　　　발표　　　　사회 수업
　　　전통 놀이들
M: Sounds interesting. Can I see it?
W: Sure. I'll <u>introduce</u> some games with these pictures.
　　　　　소개하다
M: That's a great idea, but I think you have too many words on the slides.
W: You're right. I'm worried it might be <u>boring</u>.
　　　　　　　　　　　　　지루한
M: Then, how about <u>shortening</u> your <u>explanation</u> and using some
　　　　　　짧게 하는 것(shorten)　　설명
questions? It would make your presentation more interesting.
W: Great idea! What do you think about <u>True-or-False questions</u>?
　　　　　　　　　　　　　　　　　　OX 질문들
M: That's good. Your <u>audience</u> will be able to <u>focus on</u> your
　　　　　　　　청중　　　　　　　　~에 집중하다
presentation while thinking about the answers.
W: But... what if they don't know the answers?
M: It doesn't <u>matter</u>. They'll have fun just doing it.
　　　　　　중요하다

W: (Okay. I'll make some questions right away.)

해석
남: 안녕, Natalie. 컴퓨터로 무엇을 하고 있니?
여: 안녕, Dave. 나는 사회 수업을 위한 발표를 준비하고 있어. 그것은 아시아의 전통 놀이에 관한 거야.
남: 재미있겠다. 내가 봐도 될까?
여: 물론이지. 이 사진들로 몇 가지 놀이를 소개할 거야.
남: 좋은 생각이지만, 슬라이드에 너무 많은 단어가 있는 것 같아.
여: 네 말이 맞아. 나는 그것이 지루할까 봐 걱정이야.
남: 그럼, 설명을 짧게 하고 몇 가지 질문을 사용하는 게 어때? 그것이 네 발표를 더 흥미롭게 만들어 줄 거야.
여: 좋은 생각이야! OX 질문에 대해 어떻게 생각해?
남: 좋은데. 청중은 답에 대해 생각하는 동안 네 발표에 집중할 수 있을 거야.
여: 그런데... 그들이 답을 모르면 어떻게 하지?
남: 그것은 중요하지 않아. 그들은 그것을 하는 것만으로도 즐거워할 거야.
여: (알겠어. 지금 바로 몇 가지 질문을 만들게.)
① 좋아! 나는 네가 무엇을 물어볼지 궁금해.
② 물론이지. 너는 퀴즈를 위해 열심히 공부해야 해.
✔ 알겠어. 지금 바로 몇 가지 질문을 만들게.
④ 좋아. 사진을 더 추가할 수 있는지 알아볼게.
⑤ 걱정하지 마. 대답하는 데 너무 오래 걸리지 않을 거야.

15 다음 상황에서 Ms. Olson이 Steven에게 할 말
정답률 70%　▶ 정답 ④

W: Steven is a high school student and Ms. Olson is a <u>career counselor</u> at his school. Steven <u>has much interest in</u> the video
　　직업 상담사　　　　　　　　　　　　　~에 많은 관심을 가지다
game <u>industry</u>. A few days ago, Ms. Olson <u>recommended</u> a book
　　　산업　　　　　　　　　　　　　　추천했다
written by a CEO who <u>runs</u> a famous gaming company. After
　　　　　　　　　　운영하다
reading the book, Steven told her that the CEO is his <u>role model</u>.
　　　　　　　　　　　　　　　　　　　　역할 모델
This morning, Ms. Olson hears the news that the CEO is going to
have a <u>book-signing</u> at a <u>bookstore</u> nearby. She thinks Steven
　　　책 사인회　　　서점
would love to meet his role model <u>in person</u>. So, Ms. Olson wants
　　　　　　　　　　　　　직접
to tell Steven that he should go see the CEO at the event. In this
situation, what would Ms. Olson most likely say to Steven?
Ms. Olson: (How about going to your role model's book-signing?)

해석
여: Steven은 고등학생이고 Olson 선생님은 그의 학교의 직업 상담사이다. Steven은 비디오 게임 산업에 많은 관심을 가지고 있다. 며칠 전, Olson 선생님은 유명한 게임 회사를 운영하는 CEO가 쓴 책을 추천했다. 그 책을 읽은 후에, Steven은 그녀에게 그 CEO가 그의 역할 모델이라고 말했다. 오늘 아침에, Olson 선생님은 그 CEO가 근처 서점에서 책 사인회를 가질 것이라는 소식을 듣는다. 그녀는 Steven이 그의 역할 모델을 직접 만나고 싶어 할 것이라고 생각한다. 그래서, Olson 선생님은 Steven에게 그 행사에 가서 그 CEO를 만나 보라고 말하고 싶다. 이러한 상황에서, Olson 선생님은 Steven에게 뭐라고 말하겠는가?
Ms. Olson: (네 역할 모델의 책 사인회에 가는 게 어떠니?)
① 네가 원할 때 언제든지 나를 보러 와도 돼.
② 네가 그 CEO를 만났다는 말을 들으니 기쁘구나.
③ 너는 왜 게임 회사를 운영하고 싶어 하니?
✔ 네 역할 모델의 책 사인회에 가는 게 어떠니?
⑤ 너는 네 역할 모델이 쓴 책을 더 사야 해.

16~17 1지문 2문항

M: Hello, students. Last class, we took a brief look at <u>how to tune</u> your
　　　　　　　　　　　　　　　　　　　　　　　　조율하는 방법
　　　　　　　　　　　　　　　　　(how to V: ~하는 방법, tune: 조율하다)
<u>musical instruments</u>. Today, we're going to talk a bit about how to
　　악기들
<u>take care of</u> and <u>maintain</u> your instruments. First, let's take <u>flutes</u>.
　~을 관리하다　　유지하다　　　　　　　　　　　　　플루트들
They may have <u>moisture</u> from the air <u>blown</u> through them, so you
　　　　　　습기　　　　　　　　불어넣어진(blow: 불다)
should clean and <u>wipe</u> the <u>mouth piece</u> before and after playing.
　　　　　　　닦다　　　마우스피스

Next are trumpets. They can be taken apart, so you should air dry
<u>트럼펫들</u>   <u>분해되다</u>   <u>자연 건조하다</u>
(take apart: 분해하다)
the parts in a cool dry place, away from <u>direct sunlight</u>. And as for
<u>직사광선</u>
pianos, they don't need everyday care, but it's <u>essential</u> to protect
<u>피아노들</u>   <u>관리</u>   <u>필수적인</u>
the keys by covering them with a <u>protective pad</u> when not in use.
<u>건반들</u>   <u>보호 패드</u>   <u>사용하고 있는</u>
The last ones are string instruments like <u>guitars</u>. Their <u>strings</u>
<u>기타들</u>   <u>줄들</u>
need <u>replacement</u>. When you <u>replace</u> the strings, it's good to do
<u>교체</u>   <u>교체하다</u>
it <u>gradually</u>, <u>one at a time</u>. Proper care can <u>lengthen</u> the <u>lifespan</u>
<u>점차적으로</u> <u>한 번에</u>   <u>연장하다</u>   <u>수명</u>
of your musical instruments. I hope this lesson helps you to keep
your musical instruments safe from <u>damage</u>.
<u>손상</u>

해석
남: 안녕하세요, 학생 여러분. 지난 수업 시간에, 우리는 악기를 조율하는 방법에 대해 간략하게 살펴보았습니다. 오늘, 우리는 악기를 관리하고 유지하는 방법에 대해 이야기를 좀 할 것입니다. 먼저, 플루트를 살펴보겠습니다. 플루트는 그것들을 통해 불어넣어진 공기로 인해 습기를 지닐 수 있기 때문에, 연주하기 전과 후에 마우스피스를 청소하고 닦아야 합니다. 다음은 트럼펫입니다. 그것들은 분해될 수 있기 때문에, 직사광선을 피해 서늘하고 건조한 곳에서 부품을 자연 건조해야 합니다. 그리고 피아노에 대해 말하자면, 그것들은 일상적인 관리를 필요로 하지 않지만 사용하고 있지 않을 때는 보호 패드로 건반을 덮어서 보호하는 것이 필수적입니다. 마지막은 기타와 같은 현악기입니다. 그것들의 줄은 교체되어야 합니다. 줄을 교체할 때는, 한 번에 하나씩 점차적으로 하는 것이 좋습니다. 적절한 관리는 악기의 수명을 연장할 수 있습니다. 이 수업이 여러분의 악기를 손상으로부터 안전하게 지키는 데 도움이 되기를 바랍니다.

16 남자가 하는 말의 주제
정답률 80%
▶ 정답 ①

☑ 악기 관리에 대한 조언들
② 좋은 악기를 고르는 방법들
③ 날씨가 악기에 미치는 영향들
④ 어릴 때 악기를 배우는 것의 이점들
⑤ 자신만의 악기를 만드는 것의 어려움들

17 언급된 악기가 아닌 것
정답률 90%
▶ 정답 ④

① 플루트   ② 트럼펫   ③ 피아노
☑ 드럼   ⑤ 기타

---

17 2022년 11월 학력평가

01	①	02	①	03	②	04	④	05	⑤
06	④	07	①	08	③	09	④	10	②
11	①	12	②	13	③	14	①	15	②
16	②	17	④						

01 남자가 하는 말의 목적
정답률 85%
▶ 정답 ①

[Chime bell rings.]
M: Good morning. This is Ethan Cooper from the Reindeer Mountain
maintenance office. Last night, we had 20cm of <u>heavy snow</u>. Most
<u>관리 사무소</u>   <u>폭설</u>
of the snow <u>melted away</u> with the sun out in the morning, but some
<u>녹아 없어졌다</u>(melt away)
of it <u>froze</u> in the <u>shade</u>. For hikers' <u>safety</u>, we've closed some of the
<u>얼었다</u>(freeze) <u>그늘</u>   <u>안전</u>
<u>trails</u> <u>covered with</u> ice. At this moment, Sunrise Trail and Lakeview
<u>등산로들</u> <u>~으로 덮인</u>
Trail are <u>unavailable</u> for hikers. I'll <u>make an announcement</u> later
<u>이용할 수 없는</u>   <u>안내 방송을 하다</u>

when the trails are ready to be <u>reopened</u>. Until then, <u>keep in mind</u>
<u>재개통되다</u>   <u>~을 명심하다</u>
that Sunrise Trail and Lakeview Trail are closed. Thank you.

해석
[차임벨이 울린다.]
남: 좋은 아침입니다. 저는 Reindeer Mountain 관리 사무소의 Ethan Cooper입니다. 지난 밤에, 20cm의 폭설이 내렸습니다. 아침에 해가 뜨면서 대부분의 눈은 녹아 없어졌지만, 일부는 그늘에서 얼었습니다. 등산객들의 안전을 위해서, 저희는 얼음으로 덮인 일부 등산로를 폐쇄했습니다. 현재, Sunrise Trail과 Lakeview Trail은 등산객들이 이용할 수 없습니다. 등산로가 재개통될 준비가 되면 추후에 안내 방송을 하겠습니다. 그때까지, Sunrise Trail과 Lakeview Trail은 폐쇄된다는 것을 명심하십시오. 감사합니다.

☑ 얼음으로 덮인 일부 등산로 폐쇄를 공지하려고
② 등산객에게 야간 산행의 위험성을 경고하려고
③ 겨울 산행을 위한 안전 장비를 안내하려고
④ 긴급 제설에 필요한 작업자를 모집하려고
⑤ 일출 명소인 전망대를 소개하려고

02 남자의 의견
정답률 90%
▶ 정답 ①

M: Honey, what are you doing?
W: I'm looking for the <u>measuring spoons</u>. Do you know where they
<u>계량 스푼들</u>
are?
M: They're in the first <u>drawer</u>. Why do you need them?
<u>서랍</u>
W: The <u>recipe</u> says four teaspoons of sugar.
<u>조리법</u>
M: Dear, you <u>don't have to</u> follow the recipe <u>as it is</u>.
<u>따를 필요는 없다</u>   <u>있는 그대로</u>
(don't have to V: ~할 필요는 없다, follow: 따르다)
W: What do you mean?
M: A recipe is just an <u>example</u>. You don't need to <u>add</u> the same
<u>예시</u>   <u>첨가하다</u>
amount of <u>ingredients</u> as <u>stated</u> in the recipe.
<u>양</u>   <u>재료들</u>   <u>명시된</u>
(state: 명시하다)
W: Hmm. Right. <u>Sometimes</u> the food is too sweet when I cook <u>based</u>
<u>가끔</u>   <u>~을 바탕으로</u>
<u>on</u> the recipe <u>instructions</u>.
<u>지시 사항들</u>
M: See? You don't need to <u>stick to</u> the recipe.
<u>~을 고수하다</u>
W: Okay. I'll remember that.

해석
남: 여보, 무엇을 하고 있어요?
여: 계량 스푼을 찾고 있어요. 어디에 있는지 알아요?
남: 첫 번째 서랍에 있어요. 그것들이 왜 필요해요?
여: 조리법에 설탕 4 티스푼이라고 쓰여 있거든요.
남: 여보, 조리법을 있는 그대로 따를 필요는 없어요.
여: 무슨 말이에요?
남: 조리법은 단지 예시일 뿐이에요. 조리법에 명시된 것과 똑같은 양의 재료를 첨가할 필요는 없어요.
여: 흠. 맞아요. 가끔 조리법 지시 사항을 바탕으로 요리를 하면 음식이 너무 달아요.
남: 그렇죠? 조리법을 고수할 필요는 없어요.
여: 알겠어요. 그것을 기억할게요.

☑ 조리법을 있는 그대로 따를 필요는 없다.
② 요리 도구를 정기적으로 소독해야 한다.
③ 설탕 섭취는 단기 기억력을 향상시킨다.
④ 열량이 높은 음식은 건강에 좋지 않다.
⑤ 신선한 재료는 요리의 풍미를 높인다.

03 두 사람의 관계
정답률 85%
▶ 정답 ②

[Door knocks.]
W: Can I come in?
M: Yes. Oh, Ms. Smith. Did you read the email I sent?
W: I did. I liked your game scenario. The <u>characters exploring</u> space
<u>등장인물들</u> <u>탐험하는</u>(explore)
were very <u>mysterious</u>. How did you create the characters?
<u>신비로운</u>

M: Actually, old science fiction movies inspired me to design those
                                         내가 디자인하도록 영감을 주다
    characters.   (inspire A to V: A가 ~하도록 영감을 주다)

W: Interesting. Now, could you describe the main character more
                                 설명하다   더 구체적으로
    specifically? It'll be helpful when I compose the theme song for the
                                  작곡하다   주제가
    character.

M: Well, he's a thrill seeker. So, a strong, bold, and rhythmic sound
               스릴을 추구하는 사람   대담한
    would suit him.
         어울리다

W: Okay. Do you need anything else?

M: I also want you to make some background music.
                               배경 음악

W: Of course. When do you need them?

M: By December 21st. I'd like to start putting the music into the game
                            음악을 게임에 넣기 시작하다
    by then.   (start V-ing: ~하기 시작하다, put A into B: A를 B에 넣다)

W: All right. Then I'll talk to you later.

해석

[문을 노크하는 소리.]
여: 들어가도 될까요?
남: 네. 오, Smith 씨. 제가 보낸 이메일을 읽어보셨어요?
여: 읽어봤어요. 저는 당신의 게임 시나리오가 마음에 들었어요. 우주를 탐험하는 등장인물들
    이 매우 신비로웠어요. 어떻게 그 등장인물들을 만들었나요?
남: 사실, 오래된 공상 과학 영화들이 제가 그 등장인물들을 디자인하도록 영감을 주었어요.
여: 흥미롭네요. 자, 주인공에 대해 더 구체적으로 설명해 주시겠어요? 제가 그 등장인물을 위
    한 주제가를 작곡할 때 도움이 될 거예요.
남: 음, 그는 스릴을 추구하는 사람이에요. 그래서 강하고, 대담하고, 율동적인 소리가 그에
    게 어울릴 거예요.
여: 알겠어요. 그 밖에 또 필요한 것이 있나요?
남: 저는 당신이 배경 음악도 좀 만들어 줬으면 해요.
여: 좋아요. 언제 필요하세요?
남: 12월 21일까지요. 그때쯤에는 음악을 게임에 넣기 시작하고 싶어요.
여: 알겠어요. 그럼 나중에 얘기할게요.

① 음악 평론가 — 방송 연출가
✓ 작곡가 — 게임 제작자
③ 독자 — 웹툰 작가
④ 삽화가 — 소설가
⑤ 영화감독 — 배우

04   그림에서 대화의 내용과 일치하지 않는 것

정답률 80%   ▶ 정답 ④

M: Hi, Chelsea. Did you finish your art assignment?
                                      미술 과제

W: Oh, my dream room drawing? Yes. Here's the picture.

M: Wow, it's so creative. There is a staircase next to the door.
               창의적인   계단

W: Yes. I've always dreamed of a room with two floors. Look at the
                                    2층짜리 방
    three light bulbs above the staircase.
           전구들

M: They look very stylish. And I like the flower picture above the sofa.
                   멋진
    It'll bring warmth to your room.
               따뜻함

W: Thanks. Check out the square-shaped rug on the floor.
                        사각형 모양의   깔개   바닥

M: It goes well with this place. Oh, there is a bookshelf by the sofa.
        ~과 잘 어울리다   책꽂이

W: You're right. I want to keep my favorite books nearby.
                             가까운 곳에

M: That's a good idea.

해석

남: 안녕, Chelsea. 미술 과제는 다 했니?
여: 오, 내 꿈의 방 그리기? 응. 여기 그 그림이 있어.
남: 와, 정말 창의적이다. 문 옆에 계단이 있구나.
여: 응. 나는 항상 2층짜리 방을 꿈꿔왔거든. 계단 위에 있는 3개의 전구를 봐.
남: 그것들은 매우 멋져 보여. 그리고 나는 소파 위쪽에 있는 꽃 그림이 마음에 들어. 그것은 네
    방에 따뜻함을 가져다 줄 거야.
여: 고마워. 바닥에 있는 사각형 모양의 깔개를 봐.
남: 그것은 이 장소와 잘 어울려. 오, 소파 옆에 책꽂이가 있구나.
여: 맞아. 나는 좋아하는 책들을 가까운 곳에 두고 싶어.
남: 그거 좋은 생각이야.

05   남자가 할 일

정답률 90%   ▶ 정답 ⑤

W: Jamie, is the cartoon artist on her way?
               만화가

M: Yes. She'll arrive at our studio in an hour.
          도착하다

W: Perfect. Let's check if we have everything ready for our talk show.
                                         토크쇼

M: Okay. I set up a chair for our guest yesterday.
         설치했다(set up)   손님

W: Great. And I bought a drink and put it on the table.
                   음료

M: Good. Did you prepare a pencil? The artist said she'll draw
              준비하다   그리다
    caricatures of us during the live show.
       캐리커처들

W: Oh, she told me that she'll bring her own pencil.

M: She did? Then we don't need it.

W: Yeah. By the way, where's the sketchbook?
           그런데   스케치북

M: Oops. I left it in my car. I'll go get it right now.
        두고 왔다(leave)

W: Fine. Then I'll check the microphones.
                     마이크들

M: Thanks.

해석

여: Jamie, 만화가는 오는 중이에요?
남: 네. 그녀는 한 시간 내에 우리 스튜디오에 도착할 거예요.
여: 완벽해요. 우리 토크쇼를 위한 준비가 다 되었는지 확인해 봅시다.
남: 알겠어요. 제가 어제 손님을 위한 의자를 설치했어요.
여: 잘했어요. 그리고 저는 음료를 사서 테이블 위에 놓아두었어요.
남: 좋아요. 연필은 준비했나요? 그 만화가가 라이브쇼 동안에 우리의 캐리커처를 그려줄 것
    이라고 했어요.
여: 오, 그녀가 자신의 연필을 가져올 거라고 했어요.
남: 그랬어요? 그럼 그것은 필요하지 않겠네요.
여: 네. 그런데, 스케치북은 어디에 있어요?
남: 이런. 제 차에 두고 왔어요. 지금 당장 가서 가져올게요.
여: 좋아요. 그럼 저는 마이크를 점검할게요.
남: 고마워요.

① 음료 구매하기
② 연필 준비하기
③ 의자 설치하기
④ 마이크 점검하기
✓ 스케치북 가져오기

06   여자가 지불할 금액

정답률 65%   ▶ 정답 ④

M: Welcome to Crispy Fried Chicken. What would you like to order?
                                                주문하다

W: What kind of chicken do you have?

M: We only have two kinds. Fried chicken is $15 and barbecue
    chicken is $20.

W: I'll have one fried and one barbecue chicken.

M: Okay. Would you like some potato chips with your order? They're
                              감자칩
    our most popular side dish.
       가장 인기 있는   곁들임 요리

W: How much are they?

M: One basket of potato chips is $2.
        바구니

17

22
년
11
월
학
력
평
가

W: Then I'll get one basket.
M: Will that be all?
W: Yes. And can I use this coupon for a free soda?
M: Of course. You can grab any soda from the fridge.
               가져가다   냉장고
W: Great. Here's my credit card.

해석
남: Crispy Fried Chicken에 오신 것을 환영합니다. 무엇을 주문하시겠어요?
여: 어떤 종류의 치킨이 있나요?
남: 두 종류만 있습니다. 프라이드 치킨은 15달러이고 바비큐 치킨은 20달러입니다.
여: 프라이드 치킨 하나와 바비큐 치킨 하나를 살게요.
남: 알겠습니다. 감자칩을 함께 주문하시겠어요? 그것들은 가장 인기 있는 곁들임 요리입니다.
여: 얼마인가요?
남: 감자칩 한 바구니에 2달러입니다.
여: 그럼 한 바구니를 살게요.
남: 그게 전부인가요?
여: 네. 그리고 무료 탄산음료에 이 쿠폰을 사용할 수 있나요?
남: 물론입니다. 냉장고에서 아무 탄산음료나 가져가시면 됩니다.
여: 좋아요. 여기 제 신용카드가 있어요.

① $17   ② $22
③ $35   ✔④ $37
⑤ $39

문제 풀이
15달러인 프라이드 치킨 하나, 20달러인 바비큐 치킨 하나, 2달러인 감자칩 한 바구니를 사면 총액은 37달러이다. 쿠폰을 사용해 구매한 탄산음료는 무료이므로 여자가 지불할 금액은 37달러이다. 따라서 답은 ④ '$37'이다.

---

07   남자가 얼음낚시를 갈 수 없는 이유   정답률 85%   ▶ 정답 ①

[Cell phone rings.]
W: Leo, I'm sorry I missed your call. What's up?
M: Well, I just called to tell you that I can't go ice fishing with you this
      weekend.   얼음낚시를 하러 가다
W: Oh, no. I heard the weather will be perfect this weekend.
                     날씨
M: I'm sorry. I really wish I could go.
W: Didn't you say you're off from work this weekend?
M: I am. It's not because of work. Actually, I hurt my wrist.
             ~ 때문에   다쳤다(hurt) 손목
W: That's terrible. Are you okay?
M: Don't worry. I'll be fine.
W: How did you get injured?
             부상을 당하다
M: I was playing basketball with a friend and sprained my wrist.
                              삐었다
W: Did you go to the hospital?
          병원에 가다
M: I did. The doctor told me that it'll be better in a month.
W: That's good. I hope you feel better soon.

해석
[휴대전화가 울린다.]
여: Leo, 네 전화를 못 받아서 미안해. 무슨 일이야?
남: 음, 이번 주말에 너와 얼음낚시를 하러 갈 수 없다고 말하려고 전화했어.
여: 오, 이런. 나는 이번 주말에 날씨가 완벽할 거라고 들었어.
남: 미안해. 나도 정말 갈 수 있으면 좋겠어.
여: 이번 주말에 일을 쉰다고 말하지 않았어?
남: 그래. 일 때문은 아니야. 사실, 손목을 다쳤어.
여: 그거 큰일이구나. 괜찮아?
남: 걱정하지 마. 괜찮을 거야.
여: 어쩌다 부상을 당한 거니?
남: 친구와 농구를 하다가 손목을 삐었어.
여: 병원에 갔어?
남: 갔어. 의사가 한 달 후면 나을 거라고 했어.
여: 잘됐네. 빨리 회복되기를 바랄게.

✔① 손목을 다쳐서
② 병원에 입원해야 해서
③ 직장에 출근해야 해서

---

④ 기상 여건이 나빠져서
⑤ 친구와 농구를 해야 해서

08   Kids' Pottery Class에 관해 언급되지 않은 것   정답률 85%   ▶ 정답 ③

M: Honey, look at this flyer about Kids' Pottery Class.
                 전단   어린이 도자기 수업
W: Okay. Let's take a look.
M: I think our little Austin would love to make his own cereal bowl.
                                      시리얼 그릇
W: I think so, too. It says that the class is held on October 8th. We can
    take him there on that day.   열리다(hold: 열다, 개최하다)
M: Great. And it's held in Pottery Village. It's a 10-minute drive from
    our home.   ~에서 차로 10분 걸리는 거리
W: That's so close. And check out the price. The class costs only $15.
                               비용이 들다
M: That's reasonable. We should sign up. How can we register for the
    class?   합리적인   신청하다   등록하다
W: It says you can simply scan the QR code to register online.
                    스캔하다
M: Okay. Let's do it right away.

해석
남: 여보, Kids' Pottery Class(어린이 도자기 수업)에 관한 이 전단 좀 봐요.
여: 알겠어요. 어디 한번 봐요.
남: 우리 어린 Austin은 자신의 시리얼 그릇을 만들고 싶어 할 것 같아요.
여: 저도 그렇게 생각해요. 수업은 10월 8일에 열린다고 되어 있어요. 우리는 그날 그 애를 그곳에 데려갈 수 있어요.
남: 잘됐네요. 그리고 그것은 Pottery Village(도자기 마을)에서 열려요. 집에서 차로 10분 걸리는 거리예요.
여: 매우 가깝네요. 그리고 가격을 확인해 봐요. 그 수업은 비용이 15달러밖에 들지 않아요.
남: 합리적이네요. 신청해야겠어요. 어떻게 수업에 등록할 수 있어요?
여: 그냥 QR 코드를 스캔해서 온라인으로 등록할 수 있다고 되어 있어요.
남: 알겠어요. 지금 바로 합시다.

① 날짜   ② 장소
✔③ 수강 인원   ④ 수강료
⑤ 등록 방법

---

09   2022 Online Whistling Championship에 관한 내용과 일치하지 않는 것   ▶ 정답 ④   정답률 80%

W: Hello, listeners. The most interesting music competition is back!
                                      경연 대회
    You can now sign up for the 2022 Online Whistling Championship.
          ~에 참가 신청을 하다   온라인 휘파람 불기 대회
    You can select any song that you like, but note that the length
              선택하다   주의하다   길이
    of your whistling video is limited to three minutes. To enter the
                       ~으로 제한되다(be limited to)
    competition, you must upload your video on our website by
                     업로드하다
    December 4th. When recording your whistling, be sure to turn off
                                    반드시 끄다
                  (be sure to V: 반드시 ~하다, turn off: 끄다)
    the echo effect on the microphone. Winners will be decided by
          에코 효과   수상자들
    public online voting. The result will be announced on our website.
         공개 온라인 투표   발표되다(announce: 발표하다)
    We look forward to your enthusiastic participation.
      ~을 기대하다   열정적인   참여

해석
여: 안녕하세요, 청취자 여러분. 가장 흥미로운 음악 경연 대회가 돌아왔습니다! 지금 2022 Online Whistling Championship(2022 온라인 휘파람 불기 대회)에 참가 신청을 할 수 있습니다. 여러분은 좋아하는 어떤 노래든 선택할 수 있지만, 휘파람 동영상의 길이는 3분으로 제한된다는 점을 주의하십시오. 경연 대회에 참가하기 위해서는, 12월 4일까지 저희 웹사이트에 동영상을 업로드해야 합니다. 휘파람을 녹음할 때는, 마이크의 에코 효과를 반드시 꺼야 합니다. 수상자는 공개 온라인 투표에 의해 결정될 것입니다. 결과는 저희 웹사이트에 발표될 것입니다. 여러분의 열정적인 참여를 기대합니다.

① 좋아하는 어떤 노래든 선택할 수 있다.
② 12월 4일까지 동영상을 업로드해야 한다.
③ 녹음 시 마이크의 에코 효과를 반드시 꺼야 한다.
✔④ 운영진의 심사에 의해 수상자들이 결정될 것이다.
⑤ 결과는 웹사이트에 발표될 것이다.

문제 풀이
온라인 휘파람 불기 대회의 수상자는 공개 온라인 투표를 통해서 결정된다고 했기 때문에 ④ '운영진의 심사에 의해 수상자들이 결정될 것이다.'는 내용과 일치하지 않는다.

③ 당신은 올바른 줄에 서 있어요.
④ 저는 당신을 기다릴 충분한 시간이 있어요.
⑤ 당신은 1년 안에 공사를 끝낼 수도 있어요.

10 표에서 두 사람이 선택할 커튼
정답률 65%
▶ 정답 ②

M: Honey, I'm looking at a shopping site to choose curtains for our bedroom. But there are too many options to consider.
W: Okay. Let's pick one together.
M: I don't think we should spend more than $100.
W: I agree. Let's drop this one. And some of them are machine washable at home.
M: Fantastic. We won't have to pay for dry cleaning all the time.
W: Good for us. Let's cross out this one then. What about a blackout option?
M: We definitely need it. It'll completely block sunlight, so we won't be disturbed. And which color do you like?
W: I don't mind any color except for gray.
M: Okay. Then we narrowed it down to one.
W: Well then, let's choose this one.

해석
남: 여보, 저는 우리 침실에 쓸 커튼을 고르려고 쇼핑 사이트를 보고 있어요. 그런데 고려할 선택 사항들이 너무 많네요.
여: 알겠어요. 같이 하나 골라봐요.
남: 저는 우리가 100달러 이상을 써야 한다고 생각하지 않아요.
여: 동의해요. 이것은 탈락시킵시다. 그리고 그것들 중 일부는 집에서 세탁기 세탁이 가능해요.
남: 환상적이네요. 우리는 번번이 드라이클리닝 비용을 지불하지 않아도 될 거예요.
여: 잘됐네요. 그럼 이것을 제외해요. 암막 선택 사항은 어때요?
남: 꼭 필요해요. 그것이 햇빛을 완전히 차단해서, 우리는 방해를 받지 않을 거예요. 그리고 당신은 어떤 색상이 좋아요?
여: 회색을 제외하고는 어떤 색상도 상관없어요.
남: 알겠어요. 그럼 하나로 좁혔네요.
여: 그렇다면, 이것을 선택해요.

커튼

	제품	가격	관리 지침	암막	색상
①	A	70달러	세탁기 세탁 가능	×	남색
②	B	80달러	세탁기 세탁 가능	○	갈색
③	C	90달러	드라이클리닝 전용	○	상아색
④	D	95달러	세탁기 세탁 가능	○	회색
⑤	E	110달러	드라이클리닝 전용	×	흰색

11 남자의 마지막 말에 대한 여자의 응답
정답률 85%
▶ 정답 ①

M: Excuse me. Is this really the line for the rollercoaster?
W: Yes. This is the line for the ride.
M: Oh, no. I can't believe it. There are so many people standing in line. How long have you been waiting here?
W: (I've been waiting for 30 minutes.)

해석
남: 실례합니다. 이게 정말 롤러코스터를 위한 줄인가요?
여: 네. 그 놀이 기구를 위한 줄이에요.
남: 오, 이런. 믿을 수가 없네요. 줄을 서 있는 사람들이 정말 많군요. 얼마나 오래 여기서 기다리고 있었죠?
여: (저는 30분 동안 기다리고 있어요.)
① 저는 30분 동안 기다리고 있어요.
② 저는 이 놀이 기구를 아주 재미있게 탔어요.

12 여자의 마지막 말에 대한 남자의 응답
정답률 80%
▶ 정답 ②

W: Chris, what are you looking at?
M: A little boy is crying and wandering around the park. He's all by himself.
W: Oh, I see him, too. We should ask him if he's lost.
M: (Okay. Let's see if he needs our help.)

해석
여: Chris, 무엇을 보고 있어?
남: 어떤 어린 남자 아이가 울면서 공원을 돌아다니고 있어. 그는 혼자야.
여: 오, 나도 보여. 우리는 그에게 길을 잃었는지 물어봐야 해.
남: (알겠어. 그가 우리의 도움이 필요한지 알아보자.)
① 말도 안 돼. 나는 누가 길을 잃었는지 몰라.
② 알겠어. 그가 우리의 도움이 필요한지 알아보자.
③ 맞아. 어린애처럼 울지 좀 마.
④ 물론이지. 그는 공원을 돌아다니는 것을 좋아해.
⑤ 고마워. 우리는 아들에 대해 걱정했어.

13 남자의 마지막 말에 대한 여자의 응답
정답률 85%
▶ 정답 ③

M: Hi, Ava.
W: Hi, Samuel. Are you all set for the job interview?
M: I'm still working on it. I've come up with a list of questions the interviewer might ask.
W: Good job. Preparing answers to those questions will help you for the interview.
M: But I think I'm not ready.
W: Hmm. Have you thought about how you'll make a good first impression?
M: Could you be more specific?
W: You know a smile makes you look confident. Also, people usually dress up to give a favorable impression.
M: That's a good point.
W: I believe you'll get a good interview result with a proper presentation of yourself.
M: Okay. Then I'm going to practice smiling and look for my best suit.
W: (Good. Your effort will give a good impression on the interviewer.)

해석
남: 안녕, Ava.
여: 안녕, Samuel. 취업 면접을 위한 준비는 다 됐니?
남: 아직 하고 있어. 나는 면접관이 물어볼 수 있는 질문들의 목록을 마련했어.
여: 잘했어. 그 질문들에 대한 답을 준비하는 것은 면접에 도움이 될 거야.
남: 그런데 나는 준비가 안 된 것 같아.
여: 흠. 어떻게 좋은 첫인상을 남길지에 대해 생각해 봤니?
남: 더 구체적으로 말해 줄 수 있어?
여: 너는 미소가 자신감 있게 보이도록 해주는 것을 알잖아. 또한, 사람들은 보통 좋은 인상을 주기 위해서 옷을 갖춰 입어.
남: 좋은 지적이야.
여: 나는 적절한 너의 모습을 보여주면 네가 좋은 면접 결과를 얻을 것이라고 믿어.
남: 알았어. 그럼 미소를 짓는 연습을 하고 가장 좋은 정장을 찾아봐야겠다.
여: (좋아. 네 노력은 면접관에게 좋은 인상을 줄 거야.)
① 잘됐네. 나는 이전의 내 제안이 네 회사에 유익할 것이라고 믿어.
② 미안해. 네 면접은 다음 주 수요일로 연기되었어.
③ 좋아. 네 노력은 면접관에게 좋은 인상을 줄 거야.
④ 훌륭해. 두 번째 후보자의 경력이 내 눈길을 끌었어.
⑤ 걱정하지 마. 너는 다가오는 파티를 위해 멋진 옷을 살 수 있어.

문제 풀이

여자로부터 취업 면접관에게 좋은 첫인상을 남길 수 있는 방법에 대해 조언을 들은 남자는 자신감 있어 보이도록 미소를 짓는 연습을 하고 옷을 갖춰 입기 위해 정장을 찾아보겠다고 말한다. 이에 대한 여자의 응답으로 가장 적절한 것은 ③ 'Good. Your effort will give a good impression on the interviewer.(좋아. 네 노력은 면접관에게 좋은 인상을 줄 거야.)'이다.

14 여자의 마지막 말에 대한 남자의 응답

정답률 85% ▶ 정답 ①

W: Excuse me.
M: Yes, ma'am. How can I help you?
W: How much are those shoes?
M: They're $60. But today only, we're offering a 30% discount.
　　　　　　　　　　　　　　　　　　　　　　　　　　할인
W: That's a good price. Do you have a size six?
M: Sure. Here they are. Take a seat here and try them on.
　　　　　　　　　　　　　　　　　　　　그것들을 신어 보다
W: Thank you. [Pause] Well, these shoes are a little tight for me. Can I
get a size six and a half?　　　　　　　　　　　　　　　　꽉 끼는
M: I'm sorry. That size in this color is sold out.
　　　　　　　　　　　　　　　품절되다(be sold out)
W: Do you have these shoes in a different color?
M: Let me check. [Typing sounds] We have red and green in storage.
　　　　　　　　　　　　　　　　　　　　　　　　　　　입고되어 있는
W: A green pair sounds good. I want to try them on.
M: (Please wait. I'll be back with the shoes in a minute.)
　　　　　　　　　　　돌아오다　　　　　　　　금방

해석

여: 실례합니다.
남: 네, 손님. 어떻게 도와드릴까요?
여: 저 신발은 얼마인가요?
남: 60달러예요. 하지만 오늘만 30% 할인해 드려요.
여: 좋은 가격이네요. 6 사이즈 있나요?
남: 물론이죠. 여기 있어요. 여기에 앉아서 그것들을 신어 보세요.
여: 감사해요. [잠시 후] 음, 이 신발은 제게 좀 꽉 끼네요. 6.5 사이즈를 볼 수 있을까요?
남: 죄송합니다. 이 색상의 그 사이즈는 품절되었어요.
여: 이 신발로 다른 색상은 있나요?
남: 확인해 볼게요. [타자 치는 소리] 빨간색과 초록색이 입고되어 있네요.
여: 초록색 신발이 좋을 것 같아요. 그것들을 신어 보고 싶어요.
남: (기다려 주세요. 금방 그 신발을 가지고 돌아올게요.)
✔ 기다려 주세요. 금방 그 신발을 가지고 돌아올게요.
② 서두르세요. 당신은 이것을 하기에 충분한 시간이 없어요.
③ 물론이죠. 당신은 이 신발에 대해 환불을 받을 수 있어요.
④ 걱정하지 마세요. 저에게 색상은 중요하지 않아요.
⑤ 죄송해요. 빨간색 신발은 이미 품절되었어요.

15 다음 상황에서 Amelia가 Jacob 교수에게 할 말

정답률 70% ▶ 정답 ②

M: Amelia is a high school student. She is working on a psychology
　　　　　　　　　　　　　　　　　　　　　　　　　　　심리학 과제
project. She thinks that an interview with an expert in the field
　　　　　　　　　　　　　　　　　　　　　　전문가　　　　분야
will make her project even better. She emails Professor Jacob,
　　　　　　　　　　　　훨씬
who is a renowned psychology professor. Even though he's busy,
　　　　　　유명한
she manages to set up an interview with him. Unfortunately, on
　　　가까스로 인터뷰 약속을 잡다　　　　　　　　유감스럽게도
(manage to V: 가까스로 ~하다, set up an interview: 인터뷰 약속을 잡다)
that morning, she eats a sandwich and feels sick. She knows this
　　　　　　　　　　　　　　　　　　　속이 안 좋다
interview is important, and difficult to set up again. But she can't
go meet him because of a severe stomachache. So she wants to
　　　　　　　　　　　　　심한　　복통
ask him if he can reschedule their meeting. In this situation, what
　　　　　　　　　　　일정을 변경하다
would Amelia most likely say to Professor Jacob?
Amelia: (Would it be possible to change our appointment?)
　　　　　　　　　　　　　　　　　　　약속

해석

남: Amelia는 고등학생이다. 그녀는 심리학 과제를 수행하고 있다. 그녀는 그 분야의 전문가와의 인터뷰가 자신의 과제를 훨씬 더 좋게 만들 것이라고 생각한다. 그녀는 Jacob 교수에게 이메일을 보내는데, 그는 유명한 심리학 교수이다. 그는 바쁘지만, 그녀는 가까스로 그와의 인터뷰 약속을 잡는다. 유감스럽게도, 그날 오전에, 그녀는 샌드위치를 먹고 속이 안 좋다. 그녀는 이 인터뷰가 중요하고 다시 약속을 잡기 어렵다는 것을 알고 있다. 하

지만 그녀는 심한 복통 때문에 그를 만나러 갈 수가 없다. 그래서 그녀는 그에게 만남의 일정을 변경할 수 있는지 묻고 싶다. 이러한 상황에서, Amelia는 Jacob 교수에게 뭐라고 말하겠는가?
Amelia: (우리의 약속을 변경하는 것이 가능할까요?)

① 과제의 마감 기한을 연장해 주실 수 있나요?
✔ 우리의 약속을 변경하는 것이 가능할까요?
③ 제 최종 심리학 과제에 참여하는 게 어때요?
④ 안내 센터에서 만나기를 원하시나요?
⑤ 진찰을 받으러 병원에 가는 게 어때요?

16~17 1지문 2문항

W: Good morning, students. These days we can easily send
messages to each other using phones or computers. However,
communication has not always been as simple as it is today.
통신
Here are a few ways people in the past used to carry their
　　　　　　　　　　　　　　　　　　　　　　전달하다
messages. First, some tribes used a special drum. They were
　　　　　　　　　부족들　　　　　　북
able to send warnings or important information by varying the
　　　　　　　경보　　　　　　　　　　　　　변화를 줌으로써
　　　　　　　　　　　　　　　　　　(by V-ing: ~함으로써, vary: 변화를 주다)
pitch or beat. Next, other people used smoke to send messages
음의 높이　박자　　　　　　　　　　　　연기
over long distances. For example, our ancestors used smoke
장거리에 걸쳐　　　　　　　　　조상들
to signal attacks from enemies. Third, a pigeon was a reliable
(신호로) 알리다　　적들　　　　　비둘기　　　믿을 수 있는
means of communication. It always found its way home with
수단
messages attached to its legs. Finally, a horse was one of the most
　　　　~에 부착된　　　　　　　　　말
efficient ways to communicate. The horse with a messenger on
효율적인　　　통신을 하다　　　　　　　배달원
its back delivered mail more quickly than runners. Now you may
　　　전달했다　　　　　　　　　　파발꾼들
understand the ways of sending messages back in the old days.
Then let's take a look in detail at each communication method.
　　　　　　　　　　자세히　　　　　　　　　방법

해석

여: 좋은 아침입니다, 학생 여러분. 요즘 우리는 전화나 컴퓨터를 사용하여 서로에게 쉽게 메시지를 보낼 수 있습니다. 하지만, 통신이 오늘날처럼 항상 간단했던 것은 아닙니다. 여기 과거의 사람들이 메시지를 전달하기 위해 사용했던 몇 가지 방법들이 있습니다. 먼저, 몇몇 부족들은 특별한 북을 사용했습니다. 그들은 음의 높이나 박자에 변화를 줌으로써 경보나 중요한 정보를 보낼 수 있었습니다. 다음으로, 다른 사람들은 장거리에 걸쳐 메시지를 보내기 위해 연기를 사용했습니다. 예를 들어, 우리 조상은 적들의 공격을 알리기 위해 연기를 사용했습니다. 셋째, 비둘기는 믿을 수 있는 통신 수단이었습니다. 그것은 항상 자신의 다리에 메시지를 부착한 채 집으로 가는 길을 찾았습니다. 마지막으로, 말은 통신을 하기 위한 가장 효율적인 방법 중 하나였습니다. 배달원을 등에 태운 말은 파발꾼보다 더 빨리 우편물을 전달했습니다. 이제 여러분은 옛날에 메시지를 보냈던 방법을 이해할 수 있을 것입니다. 그럼 각각의 통신 방법을 자세히 살펴봅시다.

16 여자가 하는 말의 주제

정답률 85% ▶ 정답 ②

① 거짓된 정보의 확산을 막는 방법
✔ 과거의 메시지 전달 방법
③ 현대의 통신 방식
④ 목적에 따른 연설의 형식
⑤ 선사 시대의 생존 수단

17 언급된 수단이 아닌 것

정답률 85% ▶ 정답 ④

① 북　　　　　　　　　　② 연기
③ 비둘기　　　　　　　　✔ 깃발
⑤ 말

18 | 2023년 3월 학력평가

01	⑤	02	⑤	03	③	04	⑤	05	②
06	②	07	①	08	③	09	④	10	②
11	②	12	①	13	③	14	①	15	③
16	③	17	④						

01 남자가 하는 말의 목적

정답률 80%   ▶ 정답 ⑤

M: Hello, Villeford High School students. This is principal Aaron Clark. As a big fan of the Villeford ice hockey team, I'm very excited about the upcoming National High School Ice Hockey League. As you all know, the first game will be held in the Central Rink at 6 p.m. this Saturday. I want as many of you as possible to come and cheer our team to victory. I've seen them put in an incredible amount of effort to win the league. It will help them play better just to see you there cheering for them. I really hope to see you at the rink. Thank you.

해석

남: 안녕하세요, Villeford 고등학교 학생 여러분. 저는 교장인 Aaron Clark입니다. Villeford 아이스하키 팀의 열렬한 팬으로서, 저는 다가오는 '전국 고등학교 아이스하키 리그'에 매우 흥분하고 있습니다. 모두 아시다시피, 이번 주 토요일 오후 6시에 Central Rink에서 첫 경기가 열릴 것입니다. 가능한 한 많은 분들께서 오셔서 우리 팀이 승리하도록 응원해 주시기 바랍니다. 저는 그들이 리그에서 우승하기 위해 엄청난 양의 노력을 기울이는 것을 보았습니다. 여러분이 그곳에서 그들을 응원하는 것을 보는 것만으로도 그들이 경기를 더 잘 하는 데 도움을 줄 것입니다. 링크에서 여러분을 뵙기를 진심으로 바랍니다. 감사합니다.

① 아이스하키부의 우승을 알리려고
② 아이스하키부 훈련 일정을 공지하려고
③ 아이스하키부 신임 감독을 소개하려고
④ 아이스하키부 선수 모집을 안내하려고
✓ 아이스하키부 경기의 관람을 독려하려고

02 여자의 의견

정답률 85%   ▶ 정답 ⑤

W: Honey, are you okay?
M: I'm afraid I've caught a cold. I've got a sore throat.
W: Why don't you go see a doctor?
M: Well, I don't think it's necessary. I've found some medicine in the cabinet. I'll take it.
W: You shouldn't take that medicine. That's what I got prescribed last week.
M: My symptoms are similar to yours.
W: Honey, you shouldn't take medicine prescribed for others.
M: It's just a cold. I'll get better if I take your medicine.
W: It could be dangerous to take someone else's prescription.
M: Okay. Then I'll go see a doctor this afternoon.

해석

여: 여보, 괜찮아요?
남: 감기에 걸린 것 같아요. 목이 아프네요.
여: 병원에 가는 게 어때요?
남: 음, 그럴 필요는 없을 것 같아요. 수납장에서 약을 찾았거든요. 그것을 먹을게요.
여: 그 약은 먹으면 안 돼요. 제가 지난주에 처방받은 것이에요.
남: 제 증상은 당신의 것과 비슷해요.
여: 여보, 다른 사람들에게 처방된 약을 먹으면 안 돼요.

남: 그냥 감기잖아요. 당신의 약을 먹으면 나을 거예요.
여: 다른 사람의 처방된 약을 먹는 것은 위험할 수 있어요.
남: 알겠어요. 그럼 오늘 오후에 병원에 갈게요.

① 과다한 항생제 복용을 자제해야 한다.
② 오래된 약을 함부로 폐기해서는 안 된다.
③ 약을 복용할 때는 정해진 시간을 지켜야 한다.
④ 진료 전에 자신의 증상을 정확히 확인해야 한다.
✓ 다른 사람에게 처방된 약을 복용해서는 안 된다.

03 두 사람의 관계

정답률 80%   ▶ 정답 ③

W: Hi, Mr. Thomson. How are your preparations going?
M: You arrived at the right time. I have something to tell you.
W: Okay. What is it?
M: Well, I'm afraid that we have to change the exhibition room for your paintings.
W: May I ask why?
M: Sure. We have some electrical problems there.
W: I see. Then where are you going to exhibit my works?
M: Our gallery is going to exhibit your paintings in the main hall.
W: Okay. Can I see the hall now?
M: Sure. Come with me.

해석

여: 안녕하세요, Thomson 씨. 준비는 어떻게 되어 가나요?
남: 제 때에 도착하셨네요. 드릴 말씀이 있어요.
여: 좋아요. 무엇인가요?
남: 음, 당신 그림의 전시실을 바꿔야 할 것 같아요.
여: 이유를 여쭤봐도 될까요?
남: 물론이죠. 그곳에 전기적인 문제가 좀 있어요.
여: 그렇군요. 그럼 제 작품을 어디에 전시하실 건가요?
남: 저희 미술관은 당신의 그림을 본관에 전시할 예정이에요.
여: 알겠어요. 지금 본관을 볼 수 있을까요?
남: 물론이에요. 저와 함께 가시죠.

① 관람객 — 박물관 관장
② 세입자 — 건물 관리인
✓ 화가 — 미술관 직원
④ 고객 — 전기 기사
⑤ 의뢰인 — 건축사

04 그림에서 대화의 내용과 일치하지 않는 것

정답률 85%   ▶ 정답 ⑤

M: Hi, Grace. What are you looking at on your phone?
W: Hi, James. It's a photo I took when I did some volunteer work. We painted pictures on a street wall.
M: Let me see. Wow, I like the whale with the flower pattern.
W: I like it, too. How do you like the house under the whale?
M: It's beautiful. What are these two chairs for?
W: You can take a picture sitting there. The painting becomes the background.
M: Oh, I see. Look at this tree! It has heart-shaped leaves.
W: That's right. We named it the Love Tree.
M: The butterfly on the tree branch is lovely, too.
W: I hope a lot of people enjoy the painting.

해석

남: 안녕, Grace. 휴대전화로 무엇을 보고 있니?
여: 안녕, James. 내가 자원봉사를 할 때 찍은 사진이야. 우리는 거리의 벽에 그림을 그렸어.
남: 어디 보자. 와, 나는 꽃무늬가 있는 고래가 마음에 들어.
여: 나도 그래. 고래 아래에 있는 집은 어떠니?

남: 아름다워. 이 두 개의 의자는 무슨 용도야?
여: 거기에 앉아서 사진을 찍을 수 있어. 그 그림이 배경이 되는 거야.
남: 오, 그렇구나. 이 나무를 봐! 하트 모양의 나뭇잎을 가지고 있어.
여: 맞아. 우리는 그것에 '사랑의 나무'라는 이름을 붙였어.
남: 나뭇가지에 있는 나비도 사랑스러워.
여: 나는 많은 사람들이 그림을 즐겼으면 좋겠어.

05 남자가 할 일
정답률 85%
▶ 정답 ②

M: Hi, Stella. How are you doing these days?
W: Hi, Ryan. I've been busy helping my granddad with his concert. He
   돕느라 바빴다(be busy V-ing: ~하느라 바쁘다)
   made a rock band with his friends.
         록 밴드
M: There must be a lot of things to do.
W: Yeah. I reserved a place for the concert yesterday.
           예약했다   장소
M: What about posters and tickets?
           포스터들   티켓들
W: Well, I've just finished designing a poster.
M: Then I think I can help you.
W: Really? How?
M: Actually, I have a music blog. I think I can upload the poster there.
                   음악 블로그   업로드하다
W: That's great!
M: Just send the poster to me, and I'll post it online.
        보내다   게시하다
W: Thanks a lot.

해석
남: 안녕, Stella. 요즘 어떻게 지내니?
여: 안녕, Ryan. 나는 할아버지의 콘서트를 돕느라 바빴어. 할아버지께서 친구들과 록 밴드
   를 만드셨거든.
남: 할 일이 많겠구나.
여: 그래. 어제는 콘서트를 위한 장소를 예약했어.
남: 포스터와 티켓은?
여: 음, 방금 포스터 디자인을 끝냈어.
남: 그럼 내가 도와줄 수 있을 것 같아.
여: 정말? 어떻게?
남: 사실, 내가 음악 블로그를 가지고 있어. 거기에 포스터를 업로드할 수 있을 것 같아.
여: 잘됐다!
남: 나한테 포스터를 보내주면, 그것을 온라인에 게시할게.
여: 정말 고마워.
① 티켓 디자인하기
✔② 포스터 게시하기
③ 블로그 개설하기
④ 밴드부원 모집하기
⑤ 콘서트 장소 대여하기

06 여자가 지불할 금액
정답률 75%
▶ 정답 ②

M: Good morning. How may I help you?
W: Hi. I want to buy a coffee pot.
                    커피포트
M: Okay. You can choose from these coffee pots.
W: I like this one. How much is it?

M: It was originally $60, but it's now on sale for $50.
          원래   할인 판매 중인
W: Okay, I'll buy it. I'd also like to buy this red tumbler.
                                                 텀블러
M: Actually, it comes in two sizes. This smaller one is $20 and a
   bigger one is $30.
W: The smaller one would be easier to carry around. I'll buy two
                          더 쉬운   휴대하다
   smaller ones.
M: All right. Is there anything else you need?
W: No, that's all. Thank you.
M: Okay. How would you like to pay?
W: I'll pay by credit card. Here you are.

해석
남: 좋은 아침입니다. 어떻게 도와드릴까요?
여: 안녕하세요. 커피포트를 사고 싶은데요.
남: 알겠습니다. 이 커피포트들 중에서 고르시면 됩니다.
여: 이것이 마음에 드네요. 얼마인가요?
남: 원래 60달러인데, 지금 50달러로 할인 판매 중입니다.
여: 좋네요, 그것을 살게요. 이 빨간색 텀블러도 사고 싶어요.
남: 사실, 그것은 두 가지 사이즈로 나옵니다. 이 작은 것은 20달러이고 큰 것은 30달러입
   니다.
여: 작은 것이 휴대하기 더 쉬울 거예요. 작은 것 두 개를 살게요.
남: 알겠습니다. 그 밖에 더 필요하신 게 있나요?
여: 아니요, 그게 다예요. 감사해요.
남: 알겠습니다. 계산은 어떻게 하시겠어요?
여: 신용카드로 계산할게요. 여기 있어요.

① $70   ✔② $90
③ $100   ④ $110
⑤ $120

문제 풀이
여자는 커피포트 한 개와 작은 텀블러 두 개를 사겠다고 했다. 원래 가격이 60달러인 커피포
트는 50달러에 할인 판매하고 있고, 작은 텀블러는 20달러이므로 여자가 지불할 총 금액은
90달러이다. 따라서 답은 ② '$90'이다.

07 남자가 지갑을 구매하지 못한 이유
정답률 85%
▶ 정답 ①

[Cell phone rings.]
W: Hi, Brian.
M: Hi, Mom. I'm in line to get on the plane.
                              비행기에 타다
W: Okay. By the way, did you drop by the duty free shop in the airport?
                           ~에 들르다   면세점
M: Yes, but I couldn't buy the wallet you asked me to buy.
                              지갑
W: Did you forget the brand name?
                    브랜드명
M: No. I remembered that. I took a memo.
                                  메모
W: Then did you arrive late at the airport?
                       늦게
M: No, I had enough time to shop.
           충분한   쇼핑을 하다
W: Then why couldn't you buy the wallet?
M: Actually, because they were all sold out.
                         다 팔렸다(be all sold out)
W: Oh, really?
M: Yeah. The wallet must be very popular.
                            인기 있는
W: Okay. Thanks for checking anyway.

해석
[휴대전화가 울린다.]
여: 안녕, Brian.
남: 네, 엄마. 저는 비행기에 타려고 줄을 서 있어요.
여: 알겠어. 그런데, 공항 면세점에 들렀니?
남: 네, 하지만 사다라고 부탁하신 지갑을 못 샀어요.
여: 브랜드명을 잊어버렸니?
남: 아니요. 기억하고 있어요. 메모를 했거든요.
여: 그럼 공항에 늦게 도착했니?
남: 아니요, 쇼핑을 할 충분한 시간이 있었어요.
여: 그럼 왜 지갑을 사지 못했니?
남: 사실, 그것들이 다 팔렸기 때문이에요.
여: 오, 정말이니?

남: 네. 그 지갑이 분명 매우 인기 있는 것 같아요.
여: 알겠어. 어쨌든 알아봐줘서 고마워.

✔①해당 상품이 다 팔려서
②브랜드명을 잊어버려서
③계산대의 줄이 길어서
④공항에 늦게 도착해서
⑤면세점이 문을 닫아서

---

08 Youth Choir Audition에 관해 언급되지 않은 것

정답률 80% ▶ 정답 ③

M: Lucy, look at this.
W: Wow. It's about the Youth Choir Audition.
　　　　　　　　　　　　청소년 합창단 오디션
M: Yes. It's open to anyone aged 13 to 18.
W: I'm interested in joining the choir. When is it?
　　　~에 관심이 있는
M: April 2nd, from 9 a.m. to 5 p.m.
W: The place for the audition is the Youth Training Center. It's really far
　　　　　　　　　　　　　　　　　청소년 수련원
　　from here.
M: I think you should leave early in the morning.
　　　　　　　　　　　출발하다
W: That's no problem. Is there an entry fee?
　　　　　　　　　　　　　　　참가비
M: No, it's free.
　　　　　무료의
W: Good. I'll apply for the audition.
　　　　　~에 지원하다
M: Then you should fill out an application form on this website.
　　　　　　　　　　　작성하다　　　　신청서
W: All right. Thanks.

해석
남: Lucy, 이것 좀 봐.
여: 와. Youth Choir Audition(청소년 합창단 오디션)에 관한 거구나.
남: 응. 그것은 13세에서 18세까지 누구에게나 열려 있어.
여: 나는 합창단에 가입하는 데 관심이 있어. 언제야?
남: 4월 2일 오전 9시부터 오후 5시까지야.
여: 오디션 장소는 Youth Training Center(청소년 수련원)야. 여기에서 정말 멀어.
남: 너는 아침 일찍 출발해야 할 것 같아.
여: 그건 문제 없어. 참가비가 있니?
남: 아니, 무료야.
여: 잘됐다. 나는 오디션에 지원할 거야.
남: 그럼 이 웹사이트에서 신청서를 작성해야 해.
여: 알겠어. 고마워.
①지원 가능 연령　　　　　　　②날짜
✔③심사 기준　　　　　　　　　④참가비
⑤지원 방법

---

09 2023 Career Week에 관한 내용과 일치하지 않는 것

정답률 85% ▶ 정답 ④

W: Hello, Rosehill High School students! I'm your school counselor,
　　　　　　　　　　　　　　　　　　　　　　　　　학교 상담사
　　Ms. Lee. I'm so happy to announce a special event, the 2023
　　　　　　　　　　　　　　알리다　　　　행사
　　Career Week. It'll be held from May 22nd for five days. There will
　　직업 체험 주간
　　be many programs to help you explore various future jobs. Please
　　　　　　　　　　　　　　　　　탐색하다　　　　미래 직업들
　　kindly note that the number of participants for each program is
　　　주의하다　　　　　　　　　　　참가자들
　　limited to 20. A special lecture on future career choices will be
　　~으로 제한되다(be limited to)　　　　강연
　　presented on the first day. Registration begins on May 10th. For
　　　　　　　　　　　　　　　　　　등록
　　more information, please visit our school website. I hope you can
　　come and enjoy the 2023 Career Week!

해석
여: 안녕하세요, Rosehill 고등학교 학생 여러분! 저는 학교 상담사인 Lee 선생님입니다. 저는 특별 행사인 2023 Career Week(2023 직업 체험 주간)에 대해 알려드리게 되어 매우 기쁩니다. 그것은 5월 22일부터 5일 동안 열릴 것입니다. 여러분이 다양한 미래 직업을 탐색할 수 있도록 도움을 주는 많은 프로그램이 있을 것입니다. 각 프로그램에 대한 참가자의 수는 20명으로 제한된다는 점을 주의해 주십시오. 미래 직업 선택에 관한 특별 강연이 첫날에 있을 것입니다. 등록은 5월 10일에 시작됩니다. 더 많은 정보를 원하시면, 우리 학교 웹사이트를 방문해 주십시오. 오셔서 2023 Career Week를 즐기길 바랍니다!

---

①5일 동안 열릴 것이다.
②미래 직업 탐색을 돕는 프로그램이 있을 것이다.
③프로그램 참가 인원에 제한이 있다.
✔④특별 강연이 마지막 날에 있을 것이다.
⑤등록은 5월 10일에 시작된다.

문제 풀이
5월 22일부터 5일 동안 진행되는 행사 기간 중에서 미래 직업 선택에 관한 특별 강연은 행사 첫날에 있을 것이라고 했으므로 ④ '특별 강연이 마지막 날에 있을 것이다.'는 내용과 일치하지 않는다.

---

10 표에서 여자가 구입할 프라이팬

정답률 85% ▶ 정답 ②

M: Jessica, what are you doing?
W: I'm trying to buy one of these five frying pans.
　　　　　　　　　　　　　　　　프라이팬들
M: Let me see. This frying pan seems pretty expensive.
　　　　　　　　　　　　　　　　　　팩　　비싼
W: Yeah. I don't want to spend more than $50.
M: Okay. And I think 9 to 12-inch frying pans will work for most of your
　　　　　　　　　　　　　　　　　　　　　　　　　유용하다　대부분
　　cooking.
　　요리
W: I think so, too. An 8-inch frying pan seems too small for me.
M: What about the material? Stainless steel pans are good for fast
　　　　　　　　　　　재질　　　스테인리스 스틸 팬들
　　cooking.
W: I know, but they are heavier. I'll buy an aluminum pan.
　　　　　　　　　　더 무거운　　　　　알루미늄 팬
M: Then you have two options left. Do you need a lid?
　　　　　　　　　　　　　　　　　　　　　　뚜껑
W: Of course. A lid keeps the oil from splashing. I'll buy this one.
　　　　　　　　　기름이 튀는 것을 막다
M: Good choice.　기름이 튀는 것을 막다
　　　　　　　(keep A from V-ing: A가 ~하는 것을 막다, oil: 기름, splash: 튀다)

해석
남: Jessica, 무엇을 하고 있니?
여: 이 다섯 가지 프라이팬 중에 하나를 사려고 하고 있어.
남: 어디 보자. 이 프라이팬은 꽤 비싼 것 같아.
여: 그래. 나는 50달러 이상은 쓰고 싶지 않아.
남: 알겠어. 그리고 9에서 12인치의 프라이팬이 대부분의 요리에 유용할 것 같아.
여: 나도 그렇게 생각해. 8인치 프라이팬은 나한테 너무 작은 것 같아.
남: 재질은 어때? 스테인리스 스틸 팬은 빠른 요리에 좋아.
여: 알지만, 그것들은 더 무거워. 나는 알루미늄 팬을 살 거야.
남: 그럼 두 가지 선택지가 남았어. 뚜껑이 필요하니?
여: 물론이지. 뚜껑은 기름이 튀는 것을 막아줘. 이것을 살게.
남: 좋은 선택이야.

프라이팬

	모델	가격	크기(인치)	재질	뚜껑
①	A	30달러	8	알루미늄	○
✔②	B	32달러	9.5	알루미늄	○
③	C	35달러	10	스테인리스 스틸	×
④	D	40달러	11	알루미늄	×
⑤	E	70달러	12.5	스테인리스 스틸	○

---

11 남자의 마지막 말에 대한 여자의 응답

정답률 80% ▶ 정답 ②

M: Have you finished your team's short-movie project?
　　　　　　　　　　　　　　　단편 영화 과제
W: Not yet. I'm still editing the video clip.
　　　　　　　　　　편집하는(edit)　동영상
M: Oh, you edit? How did you learn to do that?
W: (I learned it by myself through books.)
　　　　　　　혼자(by oneself)

해석
남: 너희 팀의 단편 영화 과제는 끝냈니?
여: 아직이야. 나는 여전히 동영상을 편집하고 있어.
남: 오, 너 편집하니? 어떻게 그것을 하는 법을 배웠어?
여: (나는 책을 통해서 그것을 혼자 공부했어.)
①그때까지 그것을 편집하는 것을 끝낼 수 없을 것 같아.
✔②나는 책을 통해서 그것을 혼자 공부했어.
③이 단편 영화는 매우 흥미로워.
④너는 다른 동영상을 만들어야 해.

18
23년 3월 학력평가

⑤ 나는 팀 과제에서 A⁺를 받았어.

12 여자의 마지막 말에 대한 남자의 응답
정답률 80%
▶ 정답 ①

[Cell phone rings.]
W: Daddy, are you still working now?
M: No, Emma. I'm about to get in my car and drive home.
막 타려고 하다
(be about to V: 막 ~하려고 하다, get in: (차 등을) 타다)
W: Great. Can you give me a ride? I'm at the City Library near your
나를 태워 주다   시립 도서관
office.
사무실   (give A a ride: A를 태워주다)
M: (All right. I'll come pick you up now.)

해석
[휴대전화가 울린다.]
여: 아빠, 지금도 여전히 일하고 계세요?
남: 아니, Emma. 막 차를 타고 운전해서 집에 가려고 했어.
여: 잘됐네요. 저를 태워 주실 수 있어요? 저는 아빠 사무실 근처에 있는 시립 도서관에 있
  어요.
남: (알겠어. 지금 너를 데리러 갈게.)

✔️① 알겠어. 지금 너를 데리러 갈게.
② 미안해. 도서관은 오늘 문을 닫았어.
③ 문제없어. 너는 내 책을 빌릴 수 있어.
④ 정말 고마워. 지금 너를 내려줄게.
⑤ 맞아. 나는 사무실의 인테리어를 바꿨어.

13 남자의 마지막 말에 대한 여자의 응답
정답률 80%
▶ 정답 ③

M: Claire, how's your farm doing?
농장
W: Great! I harvested some cherry tomatoes and cucumbers last
수확했다   방울토마토들   오이들
weekend. Do you want some?
M: Of course. I'd like some very much.
W: Okay. I'll bring you some tomorrow.
M: Thanks. Are you going to the farm this weekend too?
W: Yes. The peppers are almost ready to be picked.
고추들   거의   따지다(pick: 따다)
M: Can I go with you? I'd like to look around your farm and help you
둘러보다
pick the peppers.
W: Sure. It would be fun to work on the farm together.
재미있는
M: Sounds nice. Is there anything I need to prepare?
준비해야 하다
(need to V: ~해야 하다, prepare: 준비하다)
W: (Just wear comfortable clothes and shoes.)
편한

해석
남: Claire, 네 농장은 어때?
여: 좋아! 지난 주말에 방울토마토와 오이를 수확했어. 좀 줄까?
남: 물론이지. 정말 먹고 싶어.
여: 알겠어. 내일 가져다 줄게.
남: 고마워. 이번 주말에도 농장에 갈 거니?
여: 응. 고추를 딸 때가 거의 되었거든.
남: 같이 가도 될까? 네 농장을 둘러보고 네가 고추를 따는 것을 도와주고 싶어.
여: 물론이지. 농장에서 함께 일하면 재미있을 거야.
남: 좋아. 내가 준비해야 할 것이 있어?
여: (그냥 편한 옷과 신발을 착용하면 돼.)

① 이 토마토와 오이를 먹어봐.
② 나는 고추가 피부에 좋은 줄 몰랐어.
✔️③ 그냥 편한 옷과 신발을 착용하면 돼.
④ 토마토가 빨간색일 때 딸 수 있어.
⑤ 네가 농장에서 채소를 재배하는 것을 도와줄게.

14 여자의 마지막 말에 대한 남자의 응답
정답률 85%
▶ 정답 ①

W: Daniel, what's wrong?
M: Hi, Leila. I had an argument with Olivia.
~와 말다툼을 했다(have an argument with)

W: Was it serious?
심각한
M: I'm not sure, but I think I made a mistake.
실수를 했다(make a mistake)
W: So that's why you have a long face.
시무룩한 얼굴
M: Yeah. I want to get along with her, but she's still angry at me.
~와 잘 지내다   화가 난
W: Did you say you're sorry to her?
M: Well, I texted her saying that I'm sorry.
문자 메시지를 보냈다
W: I don't think it's a good idea to express your apology through a text
표현하다   사과
message.
M: Do you think so? Now I know why I haven't received any response
답장
from her yet.
W: I think it'd be best to go and talk to her in person.
직접
M: (You're right. I'll meet her and apologize.)
사과하다

해석
여: Daniel, 무슨 일 있어?
남: 안녕, Leila. Olivia와 말다툼을 했어.
여: 심각했어?
남: 확실하지는 않지만, 내가 실수를 한 것 같아.
여: 그래서 시무룩한 얼굴을 하고 있는 거구나.
남: 그래. 나는 그녀와 잘 지내고 싶지만, 그녀는 여전히 내게 화가 나 있어.
여: 그녀에게 미안하다고 말했니?
남: 음, 미안하다고 문자 메시지를 보냈어.
여: 문자 메시지를 통해서 사과를 표현하는 것은 좋은 생각이 아닌 것 같아.
남: 그렇게 생각해? 왜 아직도 그녀에게 아무런 답장을 받지 못했는지 이제야 알겠어.
여: 가서 그녀에게 직접 이야기하는 것이 가장 좋을 것 같아.
남: (네 말이 맞아. 그녀를 만나서 사과할게.)

✔️① 네 말이 맞아. 그녀를 만나서 사과할게.
② 네 의견에 동의해. 그래서 내가 그것을 한 거야.
③ 고마워. 사과해 줘서 고마워.
④ 걱정하지 마. 그것은 네 잘못이 아닌 것 같아.
⑤ 유감이야. 나는 너희 둘이 잘 지냈으면 좋겠어.

문제 풀이
여자는 남자에게 말다툼을 한 친구에게 문자 메시지로 사과를 하는 것은 좋은 방법이 아니
므로 찾아가서 직접 말하라고 조언하고 있다. 이에 대한 남자의 응답으로 가장 적절한 것은
① 'You're right. I'll meet her and apologize.(네 말이 맞아. 그녀를 만나서 사과할게.)'이다.

15 다음 상황에서 John이 Ted에게 할 말
정답률 75%
▶ 정답 ③

M: Ted and John are college freshmen. They are climbing Green
대학 신입생들   오르고 있다(climb)
Diamond Mountain together. Now they have reached the campsite
캠프장
near the mountain top. After climbing the mountain all day, they
정상
have a relaxing time at the campsite. While drinking coffee, Ted
편안한
suggests to John that they watch the sunrise at the mountain top
제안하다   일출
the next morning. John thinks it's a good idea. So, now John wants
to ask Ted how early they should wake up to see the sunrise. In this
일찍   일어나다
situation, what would John most likely say to Ted?
John: (What time should we get up tomorrow morning?)

해석
남: Ted와 John은 대학 신입생들이다. 그들은 함께 Green Diamond Mountain을 오르고 있
  다. 이제 그들은 산 정상 근처의 캠프장에 도착했다. 하루 종일 산을 오른 후에, 그들은 캠
  프장에서 편안한 시간을 보낸다. 커피를 마시면서, Ted는 John에게 다음날 아침에 산 정상
  에서 일출을 볼 것을 제안한다. John은 그것이 좋은 아이디어라고 생각한다. 그래서, 이제
  John은 Ted에게 일출을 보기 위해 얼마나 일찍 일어나야 하는지 묻고 싶다. 이러한 상황
  에서, John은 Ted에게 뭐라고 말하겠는가?
John: (우리 내일 아침에 몇 시에 일어나야 하지?)

① 우리 어떻게 가장 좋은 일출 명소를 찾을 수 있을까?
② 왜 너는 그렇게 자주 등산을 하러 가는 거니?
✔️③ 우리 내일 아침에 몇 시에 일어나야 하지?
④ 우리 언제 산 정상에서 내려와야 하지?
⑤ 우리 밤에 산에서는 어디에서 머물러야 하지?

16~17 1지문 2문항

W: Good morning, everyone. Do you spend a lot of time with your family? One of the best ways to spend time with your family is to enjoy sports together. Today, I will share some of the best sports that families can play together. The first one is badminton. The whole family can enjoy the sport with minimal equipment. The second one is basketball. You can easily find a basketball court near your house. The third one is table tennis. It can be played indoors anytime. The last one is bowling. Many families have a great time playing it together. When you go home today, how about playing one of these sports with your family?

해석

여: 좋은 아침입니다, 여러분. 여러분은 가족과 많은 시간을 보내나요? 가족과 시간을 보내는 가장 좋은 방법 중 하나는 함께 스포츠를 즐기는 것입니다. 오늘, 저는 가족들이 함께 할 수 있는 최고의 스포츠 몇 가지를 이야기하겠습니다. 첫 번째는 배드민턴입니다. 모든 가족이 최소한의 장비로 그 스포츠를 즐길 수 있습니다. 두 번째는 농구입니다. 여러분은 집 근처에서 농구장을 쉽게 찾을 수 있습니다. 세 번째는 탁구입니다. 그것은 실내에서 언제든지 할 수 있습니다. 마지막은 볼링입니다. 많은 가족들이 그것을 함께 하면서 즐거운 시간을 보냅니다. 오늘 집에 가면, 여러분의 가족과 이 스포츠들 중 하나를 해 보는 것은 어떠세요?

16 여자가 하는 말의 주제 ▶ 정답 ③ 정답률 90%

① 노인들에게 좋은 실내 스포츠
② 스포츠에서 규칙을 배우는 것의 중요성
✓ 가족들이 함께 즐길 수 있는 최고의 스포츠
④ 스포츠 경기에서 승리하기 위한 유용한 조언들
⑤ 전통적인 가족 스포츠의 역사

17 언급된 스포츠가 아닌 것 ▶ 정답 ④ 정답률 90%

① 배드민턴 ② 농구
③ 탁구 ✓ 축구
⑤ 볼링

19 2023년 6월 학력평가

01	②	02	①	03	①	04	④	05	⑤
06	③	07	④	08	③	09	⑤	10	④
11	①	12	③	13	②	14	⑤	15	⑤
16	③	17	④						

01 여자가 하는 말의 목적 ▶ 정답 ② 정답률 85%

W: Good afternoon, everybody. This is your student council president, Monica Brown. Our school's annual e-sports competition will be held on the last day of the semester. For the competition, we need some volunteers to help set up computers. If you're interested in helping us make the competition successful, please fill out the volunteer application form and email it to me. For more information, please visit our school website. I hope many of you will join us. Thank you for listening.

해석

여: 안녕하세요, 여러분. 저는 학생 회장인 Monica Brown입니다. 우리 학교의 연례 e스포츠 대회가 학기의 마지막 날에 개최될 것입니다. 대회를 위해, 컴퓨터를 설치하는 데 도움을 줄 자원봉사자들이 필요합니다. 대회를 성공시키는 데 도움을 줄 의향이 있으시면, 자원봉사 신청서를 작성하여 이메일로 저에게 보내주시기 바랍니다. 더 많은 정보를 원하시면, 우리 학교 웹사이트를 방문해 주십시오. 많은 분들께서 저희와 함께 해주시기를 바랍니다. 들어주셔서 감사합니다.

① 체육대회 종목을 소개하려고
✓ 대회 자원봉사자를 모집하려고
③ 학생 회장 선거 일정을 공지하려고
④ 경기 관람 규칙 준수를 당부하려고
⑤ 학교 홈페이지 주소 변경을 안내하려고

02 남자의 의견 ▶ 정답 ① 정답률 85%

M: Hannah, how's your design project going?
W: Hey, Aiden. I'm still working on it, but I'm not making much progress.
M: Can you tell me what the problem is?
W: Hmm... [Pause] It's hard to think of creative ideas. I feel like I'm wasting my time.
M: I understand. Why don't you take a walk?
W: How can that help me to improve my creativity?
M: It will actually make your brain more active. Then you'll see things differently.
W: But I don't have time for that.
M: You don't need a lot of time. Even a short walk will help you to come up with creative ideas.
W: Then I'll try it. Thanks for the tip.

해석

남: Hannah, 디자인 과제는 어떻게 되어 가고 있니?
여: 안녕, Aiden. 나는 아직도 작업을 하고 있는데, 많은 진전을 이루지 못하고 있어.
남: 무엇이 문제인지 말해줄 수 있어?
여: 흠... [잠시 휴] 창의적인 아이디어를 생각해 내는 것이 어려워. 나는 시간을 낭비하는 것 같아.
남: 이해해. 산책을 하는 게 어떠니?
여: 그것이 내가 창의력을 향상시키는 데 어떻게 도움을 줄 수 있니?
남: 그것은 실제로 뇌를 더 활동적으로 만들어 줄 거야. 그러면 너는 상황을 다르게 보게 될 거야.
여: 하지만 나는 그것을 위한 시간이 없어.
남: 많은 시간이 필요하지는 않아. 짧은 산책도 네가 창의적인 아이디어를 생각해 내는 데 도움을 줄 거야.
여: 그럼 한번 해 볼게. 알려줘서 고마워.

✓ 산책은 창의적인 생각을 할 수 있게 돕는다.
② 식사 후 과격한 운동은 소화를 방해한다.
③ 지나친 스트레스는 집중력을 감소시킨다.
④ 독서를 통해 창의력을 증진할 수 있다.
⑤ 꾸준한 운동은 기초체력을 향상시킨다.

03 두 사람의 관계 ▶ 정답 ① 정답률 85%

W: Excuse me. Could you please tell me where I can put this box?
M: Right here on this counter. How can I help you today?
W: I'd like to send this to Jeju Island.
M: Sure. Are there any breakable items in the box?
W: No, there are only clothes in it.
M: Then, there should be no problem.
W: I see. What's the fastest way to send it?

M: You can send the package by express mail, but there's an extra
　　　　　　　　　소포　　　　　속달 우편　　　　　　　추가 요금
　charge.
W: That's okay. I want it to be delivered as soon as possible. When will
　　　　　　　　　　　　배달되다(deliver: 배달하다)　가능한 한 빨리
　it arrive in Jeju if it goes out today?
　　도착하다
M: If you send it today, it will be there by this Friday.
W: Oh, Friday will be great. I'll do the express mail.

해석
여: 실례합니다. 이 상자를 어디에 놓으면 되는지 말씀해 주시겠어요?
남: 바로 여기 이 접수대 위에 놓으시면 됩니다. 오늘 어떻게 도와드릴까요?
여: 이것을 제주도에 보내고 싶어요.
남: 네. 상자 안에 깨지기 쉬운 물품이 있나요?
여: 아니요, 그 안에는 옷만 있어요.
남: 그렇다면, 문제가 없을 거예요.
여: 그렇군요. 그것을 보내는 가장 빠른 방법은 무엇인가요?
남: 그 소포는 속달 우편으로 보낼 수 있지만, 추가 요금이 있어요.
여: 괜찮아요. 저는 그것이 가능한 한 빨리 배달되기를 원해요. 오늘 발송하면 언제 제주에 도
　착할까요?
남: 오늘 보내면, 이번 주 금요일까지 도착할 거예요.
여: 오, 금요일이면 좋겠네요. 속달 우편으로 할게요.

☑ 고객 — 우체국 직원
② 투숙객 — 호텔 지배인
③ 여행객 — 여행 가이드
④ 아파트 주민 — 경비원
⑤ 손님 — 옷가게 주인

04　그림에서 대화의 내용과 일치하지 않는 것
정답률 85%　▶ 정답 ④

M: Kayla, I heard you went busking on the street last weekend.
　　　　　　　　　　　　　　　버스킹(길거리 공연)
W: It was amazing! I've got a picture here. Look!
　　　　　굉장한
M: Oh, you're wearing the hat I gave you.
　　　　　　　　　　　모자
W: Yeah, I really like it.
M: Looks great. This boy playing the guitar next to you must be your
　　　　　　　　　　　　　　　　기타
　brother Kevin.
W: You're right. He played while I sang.
　　　　　　　　　　　　　　노래를 했다(sing)
M: Cool. Why did you leave the guitar case open?
　　　　　　　　　　　기타 케이스를 열어 놓다(leave A open: A를 열어 놓다)
W: That's for the audience. If they like our performance, they give us
　　　　　　　　관객　　　　　　　　　　　　　공연
　some money.
M: Oh, and you set up two speakers!
　　　　　　　　　　　스피커들
W: I did. I recently bought them.
　　　　　　최근에
M: I see. And did you design that poster on the wall?
　　　　　　　　　　　　　　포스터
W: Yeah. My brother and I worked on it together.
M: It sounds like you really had a lot of fun!

해석
남: Kayla, 네가 지난 주말에 거리에서 버스킹을 했다고 들었어.
여: 그것은 굉장했어! 여기 사진이 있어. 봐!
남: 오, 너는 내가 준 모자를 쓰고 있구나.
여: 그래, 나는 그것이 정말 마음에 들어.
남: 좋아 보여. 네 옆에서 기타를 연주하는 이 소년은 분명 네 남동생인 Kevin이구나.
여: 맞아. 내가 노래를 하는 동안 그는 연주를 했어.
남: 멋지다. 왜 기타 케이스를 열어 놓았니?
여: 그것은 관객을 위한 거야. 우리의 공연을 좋아하면, 그들은 우리에게 약간의 돈을 줘.
남: 오, 그리고 너는 두 개의 스피커를 설치했구나!
여: 그랬지. 최근에 그것들을 샀어.
남: 그렇구나. 그리고 벽에 있는 저 포스터는 네가 디자인했니?
여: 그래. 남동생과 내가 함께 그것을 작업했어.
남: 너는 정말 재미있는 시간을 보낸 것 같아!

05　남자가 할 일
정답률 85%　▶ 정답 ⑤

W: Honey, are we ready for Jake's birthday party tomorrow?
M: I sent the invitation cards last week. What about other things?
　　　　　　　　초대장들
W: I'm not sure. Let's check.
M: We are expecting a lot of guests. How about the dinner menu?
　　　　　　　　　　　　　손님들
W: I haven't decided yet.
　　　결정하지 못했다(decide)
M: We won't have much time to cook, so let's just order pizza.
　　　　　　　　　　　　　　　　요리하다　　　　　주문하다
W: Okay. I'll do it tomorrow. What about the present?
　　　　　　　　　　　　　　　　　선물
M: Oh, you mean the smartphone? I forgot to get it!
　　　　　　　　　　　　　　　　사는 것을 잊어버렸어
　　　　　　　　　　　(forget to V: ~하는 것을 잊어버리다)
W: That's alright. Can you go to the electronics store and buy it now?
　　　　　　　　　　　　　　　　　전자 제품 매장
M: No problem. I'll do it right away.
W: Good. Then, I'll clean up the living room while you're out.
　　　　　　　　　청소하다

해석
여: 여보, 내일 Jake의 생일 파티를 위한 준비는 다 됐어요?
남: 제가 지난주에 초대장을 보냈어요. 다른 것들은 어때요?
여: 잘 모르겠어요. 확인해 봐요.
남: 우리는 많은 손님들이 올 것으로 예상하고 있어요. 저녁 메뉴는 어때요?
여: 아직 결정하지 못했어요.
남: 요리할 시간이 많지 않을 테니, 그냥 피자를 주문해요.
여: 알겠어요. 제가 내일 할게요. 선물은 어때요?
남: 오, 스마트폰을 말하는 거예요? 사는 것을 잊어버렸어요!
여: 괜찮아요. 지금 전자 제품 매장에 가서 살 수 있겠어요?
남: 문제 없어요. 즉시 할게요.
여: 좋아요. 그럼, 당신이 외출한 동안 제가 거실을 청소할게요.

① 초대장 보내기
② 피자 주문하기
③ 거실 청소하기
④ 꽃다발 준비하기
☑ 스마트폰 사러 가기

문제 풀이
Jake의 생일 선물인 스마트폰을 사지 않았다는 남자의 말에 여자는 지금 전자제품 매장으로
가서 살 수 있을지를 물었다. 남자는 그러겠다고 대답했으므로 남자가 할 일은 ⑤ '스마트폰
사러 가기'이다.

06　여자가 지불할 금액
정답률 75%　▶ 정답 ③

M: Good morning! How can I help you?
W: Hi. I'm looking for a blanket and some cushions for my sofa.
　　　　　　　　　　　　담요　　　　　　　쿠션들
M: Okay. We've got some on sale. Would you like to have a look?
　　　　　　　　　　　할인 판매 중인　　　　　　　　　　　보다
W: Yes. How much is this green blanket?
M: That's $40.
W: Oh, I love the color green. Can you also show me some cushions
　that go well with this blanket?
　　~과 잘 어울리다
M: Sure! How about these?

W: They look good. I need two of them. How much are they?

M: The cushions are $20 each.

W: Okay. I'll take one green blanket and two cushions. Can I use this coupon?

M: Sure. It will give you 10% off the total.
__총액에서 10%를 할인해 주다__

W: Thanks! Here's my credit card.

해석

남: 안녕하세요! 어떻게 도와드릴까요?

여: 안녕하세요. 저는 소파에 놓을 담요와 쿠션을 좀 찾고 있어요.

남: 알겠습니다. 할인 판매 중인 것이 몇 개 있습니다. 보시겠습니까?

여: 네. 이 초록색 담요는 얼마인가요?

남: 그것은 40달러입니다.

여: 오, 초록색이 정말 마음에 드네요. 이 담요와 잘 어울리는 쿠션도 좀 보여주실래요?

남: 물론입니다! 이것들은 어떠십니까?

여: 좋아 보이네요. 저는 두 개가 필요해요. 얼마인가요?

남: 쿠션은 각각 20달러입니다.

여: 알겠어요. 초록색 담요 한 개와 쿠션 두 개를 살게요. 이 쿠폰을 사용할 수 있나요?

남: 그럼요. 그것은 총액에서 10%를 할인해 줄 것입니다.

여: 감사해요! 여기 제 신용카드가 있어요.

① $54   ② $60

☑ $72   ④ $76

⑤ $80

문제 풀이

가격이 40달러인 초록색 담요 한 개와 개당 20달러인 쿠션 두 개를 사면 총액이 80달러이다. 쿠폰을 사용하면 10% 할인을 받을 수 있다고 했으므로 여자가 지불할 금액은 8달러가 할인된 72달러이다. 따라서 답은 ③ '$72'이다.

07 남자가 록 콘서트에 갈 수 없는 이유 ▶ 정답 ④

정답률 85%

W: Hello, Justin. What are you doing?

M: Hi, Ellie. I'm doing my project for art class.
__미술 수업__

W: Can you go to a rock concert with me this Saturday? My sister gave
__록 콘서트__
me two tickets!

M: I'd love to! [Pause] But I'm afraid I can't.

W: Do you have to work that day?
__(have to V: ~해야 하다, work: 일을 하다)__

M: No, I don't work on Saturdays.

W: Then, why not? I thought you really like rock music.
__록 음악__

M: Of course I do. But I have to take care of my friend's dog this
__~을 돌보다__
Saturday.

W: Oh, really? Is your friend going somewhere?

M: He's visiting his grandmother that day.

W: Okay, no problem. I'm sure I can find someone else to go with me.
__다른 사람__

해석

여: 안녕, Justin. 무엇을 하고 있니?

남: 안녕, Ellie. 나는 미술 수업을 위한 과제를 하고 있어.

여: 이번 주 토요일에 나와 함께 록 콘서트에 갈 수 있니? 내 언니가 티켓 두 장을 줬거든!

남: 가고 싶어! [잠시 후] 하지만 갈 수 없을 것 같아.

여: 그날 일을 해야 하니?

남: 아니, 토요일에는 일을 하지 않아.

여: 그럼, 왜 안 돼? 나는 네가 록 음악을 정말 좋아한다고 생각했어.

남: 물론 그렇지. 그런데 이번 주 토요일에 친구의 개를 돌봐야 해.

여: 오, 정말이야? 네 친구가 어디에 가는 거니?

남: 그는 그날 자신의 할머니를 방문할 거야.

여: 알겠어, 괜찮아. 분명 나와 함께 갈 다른 사람을 찾을 수 있을 거야.

① 일을 하러 가야 해서

② 피아노 연습을 해야 해서

③ 할머니를 뵈러 가야 해서

☑ 친구의 개를 돌봐야 해서

⑤ 과제를 아직 끝내지 못해서

08 Eco Day에 관해 언급되지 않은 것 ▶ 정답 ③

정답률 85%

W: Scott, did you see this Eco Day poster?

M: No, not yet. Let me see. [Pause] It's an event for picking up trash
__행사__ __쓰레기__
while walking around a park.
__공원__

W: Why don't we do it together? It's next Sunday from 10 a.m. to 5 p.m.

M: Sounds good. I've been thinking a lot about the environment lately.
__환경__ __최근에__

W: Me, too. Also, the event will be held in Eastside Park. You know, we
__열리다(hold: 열다, 개최하다)__
often used to go there.
__가곤 했다__
__(used to V: ~하곤 했다)__

M: That's great. Oh, look at this. We have to bring our own gloves and
__장갑들__
small bags for the trash.
__봉투들__

W: No problem. I have extra. I can bring some for you as well.
__여분(의 물건)__

M: Okay, thanks. Do we have to sign up for the event?
__~에 등록하다__

W: Yes. The poster says we can do it online.

M: Let's do it right now. I'm looking forward to it.
__~을 기대하고 있다(look forward to)__

해석

여: Scott, 이 Eco Day 포스터 봤니?

남: 아니, 아직이야. 어디 보자. [잠시 후] 그것은 공원을 돌아다니면서 쓰레기를 줍는 행사구나.

여: 우리 그것을 함께 하는 게 어떠니? 다음 주 일요일 오전 10시부터 오후 5시까지야.

남: 좋을 것 같아. 나는 최근에 환경에 대해 많은 생각을 해 왔어.

여: 나도 그래. 또한, 그 행사는 Eastside Park에서 열릴 거야. 알잖아, 우리는 종종 그곳에 가곤 했어.

남: 잘됐다. 오, 이것을 봐. 우리는 자신만의 장갑과 작은 쓰레기 봉투를 가져가야 해.

여: 문제 없어. 나는 여분을 가지고 있어. 내가 너를 위해 몇 개 가져갈 수도 있어.

남: 알겠어, 고마워. 행사에 등록해야 하니?

여: 응. 포스터에 온라인으로 할 수 있다고 쓰여 있어.

남: 지금 당장 하자. 나는 그것을 기대하고 있어.

① 행사 시간   ② 행사 장소

☑ 참가비   ④ 준비물

⑤ 등록 방법

09 Eastville Dance Contest에 관한 내용과 일치하지 않는 것 ▶ 정답 ⑤

정답률 75%

M: Hello, Eastville High School students. This is your P.E. teacher, Mr.
__체육 교사__
Wilson. I'm pleased to let you know that we're hosting the first
__개최하는(host)__
Eastville Dance Contest. Any Eastville students who love dancing
__춤 경연 대회__
can participate in the contest as a team. All kinds of dance are
__~에 참가하다__
allowed. If you'd like to participate, please upload your team's
__허용되다(allow: 허용하다)__ __업로드하다__
dance video to our school website by August 15th. Students
__춤 영상__
can vote for their favorite video from August 16th to 20th. The
__~에 투표하다__
winning team will receive a trophy as a prize. Don't miss this great
__우승팀__ __트로피__ __상__
opportunity to show off your talents!
__자랑하다__ __재능들__

해석

남: 안녕하세요, Eastville 고등학교 학생 여러분. 저는 체육 교사인 Wilson 선생님입니다. 저희가 Eastville Dance Contest(Eastville 춤 경연 대회)를 처음으로 개최할 예정이라는 것을 알려드리게 되어 기쁩니다. 춤을 사랑하는 Eastville 학생들은 누구나 팀으로 경연 대회에 참가할 수 있습니다. 모든 종류의 춤이 허용됩니다. 참가하고 싶다면, 팀의 춤 영상을 8월 15일까지 우리 학교 웹사이트에 업로드하기 바랍니다. 학생들은 8월 16일부터 20일까지 자신들이 가장 좋아하는 영상에 투표할 수 있습니다. 우승팀은 상으로 트로피를 받게 될 것입니다. 여러분의 재능을 자랑할 수 있는 이 좋은 기회를 놓치지 마세요!

① 처음으로 개최되는 경연이다.

② 모든 종류의 춤이 허용된다.

③ 춤 영상을 8월 15일까지 업로드해야 한다.

④ 학생들은 가장 좋아하는 영상에 투표할 수 있다.

☑ 우승팀은 상으로 상품권을 받게 될 것이다.

10 표에서 두 사람이 구입할 정수기

정답률 85% ▶ 정답 ④

M: Honey, we need a water purifier for our new house.
정수기
W: You're right. Let's order one online.
M: Good idea. [Clicking Sound] Look! These are the five bestsellers.
잘 나가는 상품들
W: I see. What's our budget?
예산
M: Well, I don't want to spend more than 800 dollars.
W: Okay, how about the water tank capacity?
수조 용량
M: I think the five-liter tank would be perfect for us.
5리터   ~에 꼭 알맞은
W: I think so, too. And I like the ones with a power-saving mode.
절전 모드
M: Okay, then we can save electricity. Now, there are just two options
전기
left.
W: Let's look at the warranties. The longer, the better.
품질 보증 기간들
M: I agree. We should order this model.

해석
남: 여보, 우리의 새 집을 위해 정수기가 필요해요.
여: 당신 말이 맞아요. 온라인으로 하나 주문해요.
남: 좋은 생각이에요. [클릭하는 소리]봐요! 이것들이 다섯 가지 잘 나가는 상품들이에요.
여: 그렇군요. 우리의 예산은 얼마죠?
남: 음, 저는 800달러 이상을 쓰고 싶지는 않아요.
여: 알겠어요, 수조 용량은 어때요?
남: 5리터 수조가 우리에게 꼭 알맞을 것 같아요.
여: 저도 그렇게 생각해요. 그리고 저는 절전 모드가 있는 것이 마음에 들어요.
남: 알겠어요, 그럼 우리는 전기를 절약할 수 있죠. 이제, 두 가지 선택지만 남았네요.
여: 품질 보증 기간을 봐요. 더 길수록, 더 좋아요.
남: 동의해요. 우리는 이 모델을 주문해야겠네요.

정수기

	모델	가격	수조 용량(리터)	절전 모드	품질 보증 기간
①	A	570달러	4	×	1년
②	B	650달러	5	○	1년
③	C	680달러	5	×	3년
✓	D	740달러	5	○	3년
⑤	E	830달러	6	○	3년

11 남자의 마지막 말에 대한 여자의 응답

정답률 70% ▶ 정답 ①

M: Let's get inside. I'm so excited to see this auto show.
안으로 들어가다   자동차 전시회
W: Look over there. So many people are already standing in line to
이미 줄을 서고 있다(stand in line: 줄을 서다)
buy tickets.
M: Fortunately, I bought our tickets in advance.
다행스럽게도   미리
W: (Great. We don't have to wait in line.)

해석
남: 안으로 들어가자. 나는 이 자동차 전시회를 보게 되어 매우 신나.
여: 저기 좀 봐. 정말 많은 사람들이 표를 사기 위해서 이미 줄을 서고 있어.
남: 다행스럽게도, 나는 우리의 표를 미리 샀어.
여: (잘됐다. 우리는 줄을 서서 기다릴 필요가 없어.)
✓잘됐다. 우리는 줄을 서서 기다릴 필요가 없어.
② 괜찮아. 우리는 나중에 다시 올 수 있어.
③ 잘했어. 표를 사자.
④ 걱정하지 마. 내가 줄을 설게.
⑤ 안타까워. 나는 그 차를 살 수 없어.

12 여자의 마지막 말에 대한 남자의 응답

정답률 70% ▶ 정답 ③

W: Hi, Chris. Did you check your grade for the history test we took last
성적   역사 시험
week?
M: Yes. But I think there's something wrong with my grade.
잘못된

W: Don't you think you should go ask Mr. Morgan about it?
M: (Right. I should go to his office now.)
사무실

해석
여: 안녕, Chris. 지난주에 본 역사 시험의 성적을 확인했니?
남: 응. 그런데 내 성적에 잘못된 게 있는 것 같아.
여: Morgan 선생님에게 가서 그것에 대해 물어봐야 할 것 같지 않니?
남: (맞아. 나는 지금 그의 사무실로 가야겠어.)
① 그래. 너는 온라인으로 등록할 수 있어.
② 미안해. 나는 다음 주에 너를 볼 수 없어.
✓맞아. 나는 지금 그의 사무실로 가야겠어.
④ 환상적이야! 나는 내일 시험을 볼 거야.
⑤ 물론이지. 그가 내 도움을 필요로 하면 나는 그를 도울 수 있어.

13 여자의 마지막 말에 대한 남자의 응답

정답률 75% ▶ 정답 ②

M: Mom, did you write this note?
쪽지
W: What's that?
M: I found this in the book you gave me.
W: Oh, the one I bought for you at the secondhand bookstore last
중고 서점
week?
M: Yes. At first I thought it was a bookmark, but it wasn't. It's a note
처음에는   책갈피
with a message!
W: What does it say?
M: It says, "I hope you enjoy this book."
W: How sweet! That really brings a smile to my face.
~에 미소를 가져다주다
M: Yeah, mom. I love this message so much.
W: Well, then, why don't we leave a note if we resell this book later?
남기다   되팔다
M: (Great idea! Our message would make others smile.)

해석
남: 엄마, 이 쪽지를 쓰셨어요?
여: 그게 뭐니?
남: 저에게 주신 책에서 이것을 찾았어요.
여: 오, 내가 지난주에 중고 서점에서 너에게 사준 책이니?
남: 네. 처음에는 책갈피라고 생각했는데, 아니었어요. 메시지가 담긴 쪽지예요!
여: 뭐라고 쓰여 있니?
남: "이 책을 재미있게 읽기 바랍니다."라고 쓰여 있어요.
여: 정말 자상하다! 그것은 진정으로 내 얼굴에 미소를 가져다주는구나.
남: 네, 엄마. 저는 이 메시지가 아주 마음에 들어요.
여: 음, 그럼, 우리가 나중에 이 책을 되팔게 되면 쪽지를 남기는 게 어떠니?
남: (좋은 생각이에요! 우리의 메시지는 다른 사람들을 미소 짓게 만들 거예요.)
① 동의해요. 중고품으로 사면 많이 절약할 수 있어요.
✓좋은 생각이에요! 우리의 메시지는 다른 사람들을 미소 짓게 만들 거예요.
③ 죄송해요. 저는 책에 메시지를 쓰는 것을 잊어버렸어요.
④ 맞아요. 수업 중에 필기를 하는 것은 중요해요.
⑤ 알겠어요. 우리는 지금 떠나면 제시간에 도착할 수 있어요.

문제 풀이
중고 서점에서 구입한 책에 들어 있던 쪽지의 메시지를 마음에 들어 하는 남자에게 여자는 그 책을 다시 팔게 될 경우에 똑같이 쪽지를 남기자고 제안한다. 이에 대한 남자의 응답으로 가장 적절한 것은 ② 'Great idea! Our message would make others smile.(좋은 생각이에요! 우리의 메시지는 다른 사람들을 미소 짓게 만들 거예요.)'이다.

14 남자의 마지막 말에 대한 여자의 응답

정답률 85% ▶ 정답 ⑤

M: Do you have any plans for this weekend, Sandy?
W: Hey, Evan. I'm planning to go camping with my family.
캠핑을 가다
M: I've never gone before. Do you go camping often?
W: Yes. Two or three times a month at least.
적어도
M: That's cool. Why do you like it so much?
W: I like spending time in nature with my family. It makes me feel
자연
closer to them.
~와 더 가깝다고 느끼다
M: I understand. It's like a family hobby, right?
취미

W: Yes, you're right. Camping helps me relieve all my stress, too.
　　　　　　　　　　　　　　　　　나의 모든 스트레스를 풀다
M: Sounds interesting. I'd love to try it.
W: If you go camping with your family, you'll see what I mean.
M: I wish I could, but I don't have any equipment for it.
　　　　　　　　　　　　　　　　　　　장비
W: (No problem. You can use my equipment.)

해석
남: 이번 주말에 무슨 계획이 있니, Sandy?
여: 안녕, Evan. 나는 가족과 함께 캠핑을 갈 계획이야.
남: 나는 전에 캠핑을 가본 적이 없어. 너는 자주 캠핑을 가니?
여: 응. 적어도 한 달에 두세 번은 가.
남: 멋지다. 왜 그렇게 그것을 좋아하는 거니?
여: 나는 가족과 함께 자연에서 시간을 보내는 것을 좋아해. 그것은 내가 그들과 더 가깝다고 느끼게 만들어 주거든.
남: 이해해. 가족 취미와 같은 거구나, 그렇지?
여: 응, 네 말이 맞아. 캠핑은 나의 모든 스트레스를 푸는 데도 도움을 줘.
남: 흥미롭게 들린다. 나도 그것을 한번 해 보고 싶어.
여: 가족과 함께 캠핑을 가면, 내 말이 무슨 뜻인지 알게 될 거야.
남: 나도 갈 수 있으면 좋겠지만, 그것을 위한 장비가 없어.
여: (문제없어. 너는 내 장비를 사용해도 돼.)
① 왜 안 돼? 우리가 캠핑을 갈 때 나는 음식을 좀 가져갈 수 있어.
② 미안해. 그 낚시 장비는 판매용이 아니야.
③ 나는 그렇게 생각하지 않아. 가격이 가장 중요해.
④ 정말? 나는 네 가족을 만나고 싶어.
✓ 문제없어. 너는 내 장비를 사용해도 돼.

15 다음 상황에서 Violet이 Peter에게 할 말

정답률 85%　▶ 정답 ⑤

W: Violet and Peter are classmates. They're doing their science group
　　　　　　　　　　　　　　　　　　　　　　　　　　과학 조별 과제
assignment together. On Saturday morning, they meet at the
public library. They decide to find the books they need in different
공공 도서관　　　　찾기로 결정하다
　　　　　　　(decide to V: ~하기로 결정하다)
sections of the library. Violet finds two useful books and tries to
구역들　　　　　　　　　　　　　　　　　　그것들을 대출받으려고 하다
　　　　　　　　　　　　　　　　　　(try to V: ~하려고 하다, check out: 대출받다)
check them out. Unfortunately, she suddenly realizes that she
　　　　　　　안타깝게도　　　　　　　　깨닫다
didn't bring her library card. At that moment, Peter walks up to
　　　　　　　　　　　　　　　　　　　　　　~에게 다가가다
Violet. So, Violet wants to ask Peter to check out the books for her
because she knows he has his library card. In this situation, what
would Violet most likely say to Peter?
Violet: (Can you borrow the books for me with your card?)
　　　　　　　　　　빌리다

해석
여: Violet과 Peter는 반 친구이다. 그들은 과학 조별 과제를 함께 하고 있다. 토요일 아침에, 그들은 공공 도서관에서 만난다. 그들은 도서관의 다른 구역에서 필요한 책을 찾기로 결정한다. Violet은 두 권의 유용한 책을 찾아서 그것들을 대출받으려고 한다. 안타깝게도, 그녀는 문득 도서관 카드를 가져오지 않았다는 것을 깨닫는다. 그 순간, Peter가 Violet에게 다가간다. 그래서, Violet은 Peter가 도서관 카드를 가지고 있다는 것을 알기 때문에 그에게 그녀를 위해 책을 대출받아달라고 부탁하고 싶다. 이러한 상황에서, Violet은 Peter에게 뭐라고 말하겠는가?
Violet: (네 카드로 나를 위해 책을 빌려줄 수 있겠니?)
① 과학 동아리에 함께 가입하겠니?
② 음료를 결제하기 위해 카드를 사용해도 괜찮니?
③ 도서관에 우리의 책을 기부하는 게 어떠니?
④ 점심을 먹으러 구내식당에 가는 게 어떠니?
✓ 네 카드로 나를 위해 책을 빌려줄 수 있겠니?

16~17 1지문 2문항

M: Hello, everyone. I'm Shawn Collins, a doctor at Collins Sleep Clinic.
　　　　　　　　　　　　　　　　　　　　　　　　　　　수면 클리닉
Sleep is one of the most essential parts of our daily lives. So today,
　　　　　　　　　　　　　중요한　　부분들
I'm going to introduce the best foods for helping you sleep better.
　　　　　　소개하다

First, kiwi fruits contain a high level of hormones that help you
　　　　　　　　함유하다　　　　　　　　호르몬들
fall asleep more quickly, sleep longer, and wake up less during
잠들다　　　　　　　　　　　　　　　　　　깨다
the night. Second, milk is rich in vitamin D and it calms the mind
　　　　　　　　　　　　~이 풍부한　　　　　　　　진정시키다
and nerves. If you drink a cup of milk before you go to bed, it will
　　　신경
definitely help you get a good night's sleep. Third, nuts can help
　　　　　　　　　　충분히 숙면을 취하다
to produce the hormone that controls your internal body clock
생산하다　　　　　　　　　　　　조절하다　　　체내 시계
and sends signals for the body to sleep at the right time. The last
　　　　　신호들
one is honey. Honey helps you sleep well because it reduces the
　　　　　　　　　　　　　　　　　　　　　　　감소시키다
hormone that keeps the brain awake! Now, I'll show you some
　　　　　　　　　뇌를 깨어있게 하다
　　　　　　　　　(keep A awake: A를 깨어있게 하다)
delicious diet plans using these foods.
　　　　　　　식단들

해석
남: 안녕하세요, 여러분. 저는 Collins Sleep Clinic(Collins 수면 클리닉)의 의사인 Shawn Collins입니다. 수면은 우리의 일상 생활에서 가장 중요한 부분들 중 하나입니다. 그래서 오늘, 저는 여러분이 수면을 더 잘 취하도록 돕는 최고의 음식들을 소개하려고 합니다. 첫째, 키위는 여러분이 더 빨리 잠들고, 더 오래 자고, 밤에 덜 깨는 데 도움을 주는 높은 수준의 호르몬을 함유하고 있습니다. 둘째, 우유는 비타민 D가 풍부하고 마음과 신경을 진정시킵니다. 잠자리에 들기 전에 우유 한 컵을 마시면, 그것은 분명히 여러분이 충분히 숙면을 취하는 데 도움을 줄 것입니다. 셋째, 견과류는 체내 시계를 조절하고 신체가 적절한 시간에 수면을 취하도록 신호를 보내는 호르몬을 생산하는 데 도움을 줄 수 있습니다. 마지막은 꿀입니다. 꿀은 뇌를 깨어있게 하는 호르몬을 감소시키기 때문에 여러분이 수면을 잘 취하도록 도와줍니다! 이제, 이 음식들을 이용한 맛있는 식단들을 몇 가지 보여드리겠습니다.

16 남자가 하는 말의 주제

정답률 90%　▶ 정답 ③

① 수면 장애의 여러 가지 원인들
② 음식을 신선하게 유지하는 다양한 방법들
✓ 수면의 질을 향상시키는 음식들
④ 유기농 식품의 인기에 대한 이유들
⑤ 세계적으로 인기 있는 음식의 기원들

17 언급된 음식이 아닌 것

정답률 85%　▶ 정답 ④

① 키위　　　　　　　　　　② 우유
③ 견과류　　　　　　　　　✓ 토마토
⑤ 꿀

20 2023년 9월 학력평가

01	⑤	02	①	03	③	04	⑤	05	①
06	③	07	④	08	③	09	④	10	④
11	①	12	④	13	①	14	③	15	⑤
16	③	17	③						

01 남자가 하는 말의 목적

정답률 90%　▶ 정답 ⑤

M: Attention, Fargo High School students. This is your music teacher,
Mr. Nelson. Our school rock band was supposed to hold its concert
　　　　　　　　　　　　　　　　　　개최하기로 되어 있었다
　　　　　　　　　　　　　　(be supposed to V: ~하기로 되어 있다, hold: 개최하다)
in the auditorium today. I'm sure you've been looking forward to
　　　　　강당
the concert. Unfortunately, the rain yesterday caused a leak in
　　　　　　　　안타깝게도　　　　　　　　　　　누수를 야기했다

the ceiling of the auditorium. The ceiling needs to be fixed, so we
<u>천장</u> <u>수리되다</u>(fix: 수리하다)
decided to change the location of the concert. The rock band will
<u>변경하기로 결정했다</u> <u>장소</u>
(decide to V: ~하기로 결정하다)
now perform in the school theater. The time for the concert hasn't
<u>공연하다</u> <u>학교 극장</u>
changed. I hope you'll enjoy the performance.
<u>공연</u>

해석
남: 주목하세요, Fargo 고등학교 학생 여러분. 저는 음악 교사인 Nelson 선생님입니다. 오늘 우리 학교 록 밴드가 강당에서 공연을 개최하기로 되어 있었습니다. 여러분은 분명 공연을 기대해 왔을 것입니다. 안타깝게도, 어제 내린 비가 강당 천장에 누수를 야기했습니다. 천장을 수리해야 해서, 공연 장소를 변경하기로 결정했습니다. 록 밴드는 이제 학교 극장에서 공연할 것입니다. 공연 시간은 바뀌지 않았습니다. 공연을 즐기시기를 바랍니다.

① 강당의 천장 수리 기간을 공지하려고
② 콘서트 관람 규칙 준수를 요청하려고
③ 학교 축제에서 공연할 동아리를 모집하려고
④ 폭우에 대비한 교실 시설 관리를 당부하려고
☑ 학교 록 밴드 공연의 장소 변경을 안내하려고

02 여자의 의견
정답률 95% ▶ 정답 ①

W: Simon, are you doing anything after school?
<u>방과 후에</u>
M: Nothing special. What about you?
<u>특별한</u>
W: I'm planning to go for a run in the park. It's a five-kilometer route.
<u>달리기를 하러 가다</u> <u>구간</u>
M: The weather is perfect for running. Can I go with you?
<u>날씨</u>
W: Why not? [Pause] Wait! You're wearing slippers. Those aren't good
for running.
M: It's okay. I can run in slippers.
W: No way. Slippers aren't designed for running. You can get hurt if
<u>고안되지 않다</u>(design: 고안하다) <u>다치다</u>
you run in them.
M: You mean I need to put on running shoes?
<u>운동화를 신다</u>
W: You got it. You need to wear the right shoes for running.
<u>알맞은</u>
M: All right. I'll go home and change.

해석
여: Simon, 방과 후에 할 일이 있니?
남: 특별한 것은 없어. 너는 어때?
여: 나는 공원에서 달리기를 하러 갈 계획이야. 그것은 5km 구간이야.
남: 날씨가 달리기에 딱 좋네. 내가 너와 같이 가도 될까?
여: 왜 안 되겠어? [잠시 후]잠깐만! 너 슬리퍼를 신고 있구나. 그것들은 달리기에 좋지 않아.
남: 괜찮아. 나는 슬리퍼를 신고 달릴 수 있어.
여: 절대 안 돼. 슬리퍼는 달리기를 위해 고안된 것이 아니야. 그것들을 신고 달리면 다칠 수도 있어.
남: 운동화를 신어야 한다는 말이지?
여: 그래. 달리기에 알맞은 신발을 신어야 해.
남: 알겠어. 집에 가서 갈아 신을게.

☑ 달리기를 할 때 적합한 신발을 신어야 한다.
② 운동을 한 후에 충분한 물을 섭취해야 한다.
③ 야외 활동 전에 일기예보를 확인하는 것이 좋다.
④ 달리기 전 스트레칭은 통증과 부상을 예방해 준다.
⑤ 초보자의 경우 달리는 거리를 점진적으로 늘려야 한다.

03 두 사람의 관계
정답률 85% ▶ 정답 ③

M: Good morning, Ms. Clapton. It's nice to meet you.
W: Nice to meet you, too. I'm a fan of your articles.
<u>기사들</u>
M: You won many awards at the film festival this year. Congratulations!
<u>많은 상을 받았다</u> <u>영화제</u>
(win an award: 상을 받다)
W: Thank you. I was lucky to work with a great director and talented
<u>감독</u>
actors.
<u>배우들</u>
M: The clothes and accessories in the movie are impressive. How do
<u>인상적인</u>

you start your costume designs?
<u>의상 디자인</u>
W: I read the script to fully understand the characters. Then I research
<u>대본</u> <u>등장인물들</u> <u>연구하다</u>
the characters' backgrounds.
<u>배경들</u>
M: That sounds like a lot of work. Which of the costumes from this
film is your favorite?
W: It's hard to pick just one because I love all of my designs.
<u>어려운</u> <u>고르다</u>
M: I totally understand. Thank you for sharing your story with the
readers of our magazine.
<u>독자들</u> <u>잡지</u>
W: It was my pleasure.

해석
남: 안녕하세요, Clapton 씨. 만나서 반갑습니다.
여: 저도 만나서 반갑습니다. 저는 당신의 기사를 아주 좋아해요.
남: 올해 영화제에서 많은 상을 받았네요. 축하합니다!
여: 감사합니다. 운 좋게도 훌륭한 감독님과 재능 있는 배우들과 함께 작업했어요.
남: 영화 속의 의상과 장신구들이 인상적입니다. 의상 디자인은 어떻게 시작하시나요?
여: 등장인물들을 충분히 이해하기 위해서 대본을 읽어요. 그런 다음 등장인물들의 배경을 연구해요.
남: 일이 많을 것 같네요. 이번 영화의 의상들 중 어떤 것을 가장 좋아하시나요?
여: 제 디자인을 다 좋아해서 하나만 고르기는 어렵네요.
남: 충분히 이해합니다. 저희 잡지의 독자들과 본인의 이야기를 공유해 주셔서 감사합니다.
여: 저도 즐거웠어요.

① 관객 — 영화감독
② 연극 배우 — 시나리오 작가
☑ 잡지 기자 — 의상 디자이너
④ 토크쇼 진행자 — 영화 평론가
⑤ 배우 지망생 — 연기 학원 강사

04 그림에서 대화의 내용과 일치하지 않는 것
정답률 80% ▶ 정답 ⑤

W: Come look at the new reading room in the library.
<u>열람실</u>
M: Wow! It's much better than I thought.
W: Same here. I like the rug in the center of the room.
<u>깔개</u> <u>중앙</u>
M: The striped pattern of the rug makes the room feel warm.
<u>줄무늬</u> <u>따뜻한 느낌이 들다</u>
W: I agree. I think putting the sofa between two plants was a good
<u>두 개의 식물 사이에</u>
idea.
M: Right. We can sit there and read for hours.
<u>몇 시간 동안</u>
W: There's a round clock on the wall.
<u>원형 시계</u>
M: I have the same clock at home. Oh, the bookshelf under the clock
<u>책장</u>
is full of books.
<u>~으로 가득 차다</u>
W: We can read the books at the long table.
M: Yeah, it looks like a good place to read. The two lamps on the table
<u>전등들</u>
will make it easy to focus.
<u>집중하다</u>
W: Good lighting is important for reading.
<u>조명</u>
M: I can't wait to start using the reading room.
<u>빨리 시작하고 싶다</u>
(can't wait to V: 빨리 ~하고 싶다)

해석
여: 와서 도서관에 새로 생긴 열람실을 좀 봐.
남: 나도 내가 생각했던 것보다 훨씬 더 좋아.
여: 나도 그래. 나는 열람실의 중앙에 있는 깔개가 마음에 들어.
남: 깔개의 줄무늬가 열람실이 따뜻한 느낌이 들게 만드는구나.
여: 동의해. 두 개의 식물 사이에 소파를 놓은 것은 좋은 생각이었던 같아.
남: 맞아. 거기에 앉아서 몇 시간이고 책을 읽을 수 있어.
여: 벽에 원형 시계가 걸려 있어.
남: 나도 집에 똑같은 시계가 있어. 오, 시계 아래에 있는 책장이 책으로 가득 차 있어.
여: 긴 테이블에서 책을 읽을 수 있어.
남: 그래, 책을 읽기에 좋은 장소인 것 같아. 테이블 위에 있는 두 개의 전등이 집중하기 쉽게 만들어 줄 거야.
여: 좋은 조명은 독서에 있어서 중요해.
남: 나는 빨리 열람실을 사용하고 싶어.

05 여자가 할 일

정답률 85%

▶ 정답 ①

M: Kelly, the school musical is tomorrow. Shall we go over the final checklist together?
학교 뮤지컬 / 검토하다 / 최종 점검표
W: Let's do it. What's first? [Pause] Oh, the posters. We put them up around school last week.
그것들을 붙였다 (put A up: A를 붙이다)
M: Right. Do we have extra batteries for the wireless microphones?
여분의 / 무선 마이크들
W: Yeah. I bought them yesterday. We should check that the microphones work well with the sound system.
작동하다 / 음향 기기
M: I did that this morning. They sound terrific.
W: How about the stage lights?
무대 조명들
M: They work perfectly. I think everyone will love the lighting design you made.
완벽하게
W: Really? Thanks. It looks like we've finished everything.
M: No, wait. The chairs for the audience haven't been arranged yet.
관객 / 배치되지 않았다(arrange: 배치하다)
W: You're right! I'll go take care of that now.
~을 처리하다
M: The musical is going to be fantastic.

해석
남: Kelly, 학교 뮤지컬이 내일이야. 최종 점검표를 함께 검토해볼까?
여: 하자. 뭐가 먼저야? [잠시 후]오, 포스터야. 우리는 지난주에 학교 근처에 그것들을 붙였어.
남: 맞아. 우리에게 무선 마이크에 쓸 여분의 배터리가 있니?
여: 응. 내가 어제 그것들을 구매했어. 우리는 마이크가 음향 기기와 함께 잘 작동하는지 점검해야 해.
남: 내가 오늘 아침에 했어. 소리가 잘 들려.
여: 무대 조명은 어때?
남: 완벽하게 작동해. 모든 사람이 네가 만든 조명 디자인을 좋아할 것 같아.
여: 정말? 고마워. 우리 다 끝낸 것 같아.
남: 아니야, 잠시만. 관객용 의자가 아직 배치되지 않았어.
여: 네 말이 맞아! 내가 지금 가서 그것을 처리할게.
남: 뮤지컬은 환상적일 거야.
① 관객용 의자 배치하기 ② 마이크 음향 점검하기
③ 공연 포스터 붙이기 ④ 무대 조명 설치하기
⑤ 배터리 구매하기

문제 풀이
관객용 의자가 아직 배치되지 않았다는 남자의 말에 여자는 자신이 그 일을 처리하겠다고 대답한다. 따라서 여자가 할 일은 ① '관객용 의자 배치하기'이다.

06 남자가 지불할 금액

정답률 80%

▶ 정답 ③

W: Welcome to Libby's Flowers. How can I help you?
M: I'd like to order a rose basket for my parents' wedding anniversary.
장미 바구니 / 결혼 기념일
W: All right. Our rose baskets come in two sizes.
M: What are the options?
W: The regular size is 30 dollars, and the large size is 50 dollars.
표준의
M: Hmm.... I think the bigger one is better.

W: Good choice. So, you'll get one rose basket in the large size. By the way, we're giving a 10-percent discount on all purchases this week.
그런데 / 모든 구매품을 10% 할인해 주고 있다 (give a discount: 할인하다, purchase: 구매품)
M: Excellent! When will my order be ready?
준비되다
W: It'll be ready around 11 a.m. If you can't pick it up, we offer a delivery service. It's 10 dollars.
그것을 찾으러 오다 (pick A up: A를 찾으러 오다) / 배달 서비스
M: Oh, great. I'd like it to be delivered. Here's my credit card.

해석
여: Libby's Flowers에 오신 것을 환영합니다. 어떻게 도와드릴까요?
남: 부모님의 결혼 기념일을 위해 장미 바구니를 주문하고 싶어요.
여: 알겠습니다. 저희 장미 바구니는 두 가지 사이즈로 나옵니다.
남: 어떤 선택사항이 있나요?
여: 표준 사이즈는 30달러이고, 큰 사이즈는 50달러입니다.
남: 흠.... 더 큰 것이 더 좋은 것 같네요.
여: 좋은 선택입니다. 그럼, 장미 바구니 한 개를 큰 사이즈로 구매하시네요. 그런데, 저희가 이번 주에 모든 구매품을 10% 할인해 드리고 있습니다.
남: 좋네요! 주문한 상품은 언제 준비될까요?
여: 오전 11시쯤에 준비될 거예요. 그것을 찾으러 오실 수 없으면, 저희가 배달 서비스를 제공합니다. 그것은 10달러입니다.
남: 오, 잘됐네요. 배달해 주셨으면 좋겠어요. 여기 제 신용카드가 있어요.
① $37 ② $45 ✔ $55
④ $60 ⑤ $80

문제 풀이
50달러인 큰 사이즈의 장미 바구니에 대해 10% 할인을 받을 수 있다고 했으므로 장미 바구니의 가격은 5달러가 할인된 45달러이다. 여기에 비용이 10달러인 배달 서비스를 신청했으므로 남자가 지불할 총 금액은 55달러이다. 따라서 답은 ③ '$55'이다.

07 여자가 스키 여행을 갈 수 없는 이유

정답률 90%

▶ 정답 ④

M: You seem busy this morning, Olivia.
W: I am. I had to see Professor Martin about my history test.
역사 시험
M: Oh, I see. Do you remember that our club's ski trip is this weekend?
기억하다 / 스키 여행
W: Yeah. I heard that a nice ski resort has been booked for the trip.
스키장 / 예약되었다(book: 예약하다)
M: I didn't know that. I'm so excited to go skiing at a nice resort.
스키를 타러 가다(go V-ing: ~하러 가다)
W: I bet it'll be great, but I don't think I can go this time.
M: Why? You don't work at the cafe on the weekends, do you?
W: No, I don't. But I need to take care of my cat. She's recovering from surgery.
~을 돌보다 / 수술
M: Isn't there anyone else who can look after your cat?
~을 보살피다
W: No one but me. My parents are visiting relatives in Canada. They won't be back for two weeks.
친척들 / 돌아오다
M: I'm sorry that you can't join us.
W: Me, too. Have fun this weekend.

해석
남: 오늘 오전에 바쁜 것 같아, Olivia.
여: 맞아. 역사 시험 때문에 Martin 교수님을 뵈어야 했어.
남: 오, 그렇구나. 우리 동아리의 스키 여행이 이번 주말인 것을 기억하니?
여: 응. 여행을 위해 좋은 스키장을 예약했다는 것을 들었어.
남: 난 몰랐어. 좋은 스키장에 스키를 타러 가게 되어 매우 신나.
여: 틀림없이 멋질 것 같은데, 나는 이번에 못 갈 것 같아.
남: 왜? 너는 주말에 카페에서 일하지 않잖아, 그렇지?
여: 그래, 일하지 않아. 하지만 내 고양이를 돌봐야 해. 수술에서 회복하고 있거든.
남: 고양이를 보살펴 줄 수 있는 다른 사람은 없는 거야?
여: 나 말고는 없어. 부모님께서는 캐나다에 사는 친척들을 방문하실 거야. 2주 동안 돌아오지 않으실 거야.
남: 네가 우리와 함께 할 수 없다니 유감이야.
여: 나도 그래. 이번 주말에 재미있게 보내.
① 카페에서 일해야 해서
② 숙소를 예약하지 못해서
③ 역사 시험 공부를 해야 해서

20
23년 9월 학력평가

✅수술받은 고양이를 돌봐야 해서
⑤ 캐나다에 사는 친척을 방문해야 해서

③ 초콜릿 5개를 만든다.
✅사전 등록 없이 참가할 수 있다.
⑤ 등록비에 재료비가 포함된다.

08 Street Photography Contest에 관해 언급되지 않은 것

정답률 85% ▶ 정답 ③

W: What are you doing, Tim?
M: I'm looking at the Street Photography Contest website.
   거리 사진 공모전
W: I've heard about that. It's a contest for college students, right?
   대학생들
M: Actually, it's open to high school students, too. Why don't you try it?
W: Really? Maybe I will. Does the contest have a theme?
   주제
M: Sure. This year's theme is Daily Life.
   일상 생활
W: That sounds interesting. When is the deadline?
   마감일
M: You have to submit your photographs by September 15th.
   제출하다
W: That's sooner than I expected.
   예상했던(expect)
M: You should hurry and choose your photos. The winner will receive a
   서두르다   우승자
   laptop as a prize.
   상품으로
W: Okay! Wish me luck.

해석

여: 무엇을 하고 있니, Tim?
남: Street Photography Contest(거리 사진 공모전) 웹 사이트를 보고 있어.
여: 나는 그것에 대해 들었어. 대학생들을 위한 공모전이지, 그렇지?
남: 사실, 고등학생들에게도 열려 있어. 한번 해 보는 게 어떠니?
여: 정말? 그래야겠어. 공모전의 주제가 있니?
남: 물론이야. 올해의 주제는 Daily Life(일상 생활)야.
여: 흥미롭게 들리네. 마감일이 언제니?
남: 9월 15일까지 사진을 제출해야 해.
여: 내가 예상했던 것보다 더 빠르구나.
남: 서둘러서 사진을 골라야 해. 우승자는 상품으로 노트북 컴퓨터를 받을 거야.
여: 알겠어! 행운을 빌어줘.

① 참가 대상   ② 주제   ✅심사 기준
④ 제출 마감일   ⑤ 우승 상품

09 Twin Stars Chocolate Day에 관한 내용과 일치하지 않는 것

정답률 90% ▶ 정답 ④

M: Hello, listeners. I'm Charlie Anderson from the Twin Stars Chocolate Museum. I'm happy to introduce the Twin Stars
                   초콜릿 박물관
Chocolate Day, a special opportunity to create your own delicious
초콜릿의 날   기회
chocolates. It'll be held on November 12th from 1 p.m. to 4 p.m. First,
         열리다(hold: 열다, 개최하다)
you'll listen to a lecture about the history of chocolate. Then you'll
                   강의
have a chance to taste our most popular flavors. At the end of the
         기회   맛보다   맛들
event, you'll make five chocolates yourself. If you want to take part in
                                           ~에 참가하다
the event, you must register in advance. You can sign up on our
                   등록하다 사전에   등록하다
website until November 1st. The registration fee is 20 dollars,
                            등록비
which includes the cost of ingredients. Don't miss this sweet
      포함하다   재료비   놓치다
opportunity!

해석

남: 안녕하세요, 청취자 여러분. 저는 Twin Stars Chocolate Museum(쌍둥이 별 초콜릿 박물관)의 Charlie Anderson입니다. 여러분 자신만의 맛있는 초콜릿을 만들 수 있는 특별한 기회인 Twin Stars Chocolate Day(쌍둥이 별 초콜릿의 날)를 소개하게 되어 기쁩니다. 그것은 11월 12일 오후 1시부터 4시까지 열릴 것입니다. 먼저, 여러분은 초콜릿의 역사에 관한 강의를 들을 것입니다. 그리고 나서 저희의 가장 인기 있는 맛들을 맛볼 수 있는 기회를 가질 것입니다. 행사가 끝날 무렵에, 여러분은 5개의 초콜릿을 직접 만들 것입니다. 행사에 참가하고 싶다면, 사전에 등록해야 합니다. 11월 1일까지 저희 웹 사이트에서 등록할 수 있습니다. 등록비는 20달러이며, 재료비가 포함되어 있습니다. 이 달콤한 기회를 놓치지 마세요!

① 11월 12일 오후에 열린다.
② 초콜릿의 역사에 관한 강의가 진행된다.

10 표에서 두 사람이 주문할 실내 사이클링 자전거

정답률 85% ▶ 정답 ④

M: Honey, what are you looking at?
W: I'm looking at indoor cycling bikes. Would you like to choose one
              실내 사이클링 자전거들
   together?
M: Sure, let me see. [Pause] The price differs by model.
                                  다르다
W: I don't want to pay more than 300 dollars. That's too expensive.
                                                   비싼
M: I agree. Which color do you like?
W: I prefer a dark color because it goes well with our living room.
                              ~과 잘 어울리다
M: Okay. Then we shouldn't get a white one. What do you think about
   the foldable one?
       접이식의
W: We definitely need that. It'll take up less storage space.
                              차지하다   저장 공간
M: We have just two options left. Which one should we get?
W: I think we should go with the one with a higher customer rating.
                                              고객 평점
   The reviews are based on actual customers' experiences.
          ~을 바탕으로 하다   실제의
M: Sounds good. Let's order this one.

해석

남: 여보, 무엇을 보고 있어요?
여: 실내 사이클링 자전거를 보고 있어요. 같이 하나 고르겠어요?
남: 물론이죠, 어디 보자. [잠시 후]모델에 따라 가격이 다르네요.
여: 저는 300달러 이상을 지불하고 싶지는 않아요. 그것은 너무 비싸요.
남: 동의해요. 어떤 색상이 좋아요?
여: 우리 거실과 잘 어울리기 때문에 어두운 색상이 더 좋아요.
남: 알겠어요. 그럼 흰색 모델은 사지 않아야겠어요. 접이식 모델에 대해 어떻게 생각해요?
여: 꼭 필요해요. 그것은 더 적은 저장 공간을 차지할 거예요.
남: 이제 두 개의 선택지만 남았어요. 어떤 것을 살까요?
여: 고객 평점이 더 높은 모델을 선택해야 할 것 같아요. 그 후기들은 실제 고객의 경험을 바탕으로 한 거예요.
남: 좋아요. 이것을 주문합시다.

실내 사이클링 자전거

	모델	가격	색상	접이식	고객 평점
①	A	100달러	흰색	×	★★★★
②	B	150달러	검은색	×	★★★
③	C	190달러	검은색	○	★★★★
✅	D	250달러	검은색	○	★★★★★
⑤	E	320달러	흰색	×	★★★★★

11 여자의 마지막 말에 대한 남자의 응답

정답률 85% ▶ 정답 ①

W: Jason, is that a new sweater? It looks good on you.
                        스웨터   ~에게 잘 어울리다
M: Thanks. I bought it online. It was on sale.
                              할인 판매 중인
W: I'd love to buy the same one for my brother. Can you tell me where
   you got it?
M: (Sure. I'll send you a link to the website.)

해석

여: Jason, 그거 새 스웨터니? 너에게 잘 어울려.
남: 고마워. 온라인으로 샀어. 할인 판매 중이었거든.
여: 내 남동생에게 같은 것을 사주고 싶어. 어디에서 샀는지 말해줄 수 있어?
남: (물론이지. 웹 사이트 링크를 보내줄게.)

✅물론이지. 웹 사이트 링크를 보내줄게.
② 다른 색상이 더 잘 어울릴 것 같아.
③ 미안해. 네 스웨터를 가져오는 것을 잊어버렸어.
④ 그것을 반품하려면 영수증이 필요해.
⑤ 내 남동생도 할인 판매할 때 그것을 샀어.

12 남자의 마지막 말에 대한 여자의 응답

정답률 75% ▶ 정답 ④

M: Becky, did you order our food for dinner?
W: Yes. I ordered pizza about an hour ago.
약 한 시간 전에
M: An hour ago? Delivery usually takes less than 40 minutes.
배달   보통
W: (I'll call the restaurant and check our order.)

해석
남: Becky, 저녁 식사 음식을 주문했니?
여: 그래. 약 한 시간 전에 피자를 주문했어.
남: 한 시간 전에? 배달은 보통 40분도 안 걸려.
여: (내가 식당에 전화해서 주문을 확인해 볼게.)

① 남은 음식을 집으로 가져가자.
② 나는 피자보다 프라이드 치킨을 더 좋아해.
③ 나는 오늘 점심 먹으러 나가고 싶지 않아.
☑ 내가 식당에 전화해서 주문을 확인해 볼게.
⑤ 편지가 잘못된 주소로 배달되었어.

13 여자의 마지막 말에 대한 남자의 응답

정답률 80% ▶ 정답 ①

W: I haven't seen you in the cafeteria this week. Where have you
구내식당
been?
M: I've been in the library working on my science project.
도서관   과학 과제
W: Does that mean you've been skipping lunch?
걸러 왔다(skip)
M: Yeah. This project is really important for my grade.
성적
W: You shouldn't do that. It's not good for your health.
건강
M: Don't worry. I always have a big dinner when I get home.
저녁을 많이 먹다
W: That's the problem. Skipping meals makes you overeat later.
식사들   과식하다
M: I hadn't thought of that. Then what should I do?
W: It's simple. You should eat regularly to stay healthy.
규칙적으로   건강을 유지하다
M: (You're right. I won't skip meals anymore.)

해석
여: 이번 주에 구내식당에서 너를 못 봤어. 어디에 있었니?
남: 도서관에서 과학 과제를 하고 있었어.
여: 점심을 걸러 왔다는 말이니?
남: 그래. 이번 과제는 내 성적에 정말 중요해.
여: 그러면 안 돼. 그것은 네 건강에 좋지 않아.
남: 걱정하지 마. 집에 가면 항상 저녁을 많이 먹어.
여: 그게 문제야. 식사를 거르는 것은 나중에 과식하게 만들어.
남: 나는 그런 생각을 하지 못했어. 그럼 어떻게 해야 하지?
여: 간단해. 건강을 유지하기 위해 규칙적으로 먹어야 해.
남: (네 말이 맞아. 더 이상 식사를 거르지 않을게.)

☑ 네 말이 맞아. 더 이상 식사를 거르지 않을게.
② 나를 위해 네가 준비해준 점심 잘 먹었어.
③ 너는 구내식당이 언제 문을 여는지 확인해야 해.
④ 나를 믿어. 내가 너에게 좋은 식사 예절을 가르쳐 줄 수 있어.
⑤ 문제없어. 우리는 과학 과제를 제시간에 끝낼 거야.

14 남자의 마지막 말에 대한 여자의 응답

정답률 70% ▶ 정답 ③

M: Excuse me, Ms. Lopez. Can I ask you something?
W: Sure, Tony. What can I do for you?
M: I want to do better in Spanish, but I don't know how to improve.
향상시키는 방법
(how to V: ~하는 방법, improve: 향상시키다)
W: You seem to do well during class. Do you study when you're at
home?
M: I do all my homework and try to learn 20 new words every day.
암기하려고 노력하다   단어들
(try to V: ~하려고 노력하다, learn: 암기하다)
W: That's a good start. Do you also practice saying those words
말하는 것을 연습하다
repeatedly?
반복해서
(practice V-ing: ~하는 것을 연습하다)

M: Do I need to do that? That sounds like it'll take a lot of time.
많은 시간이 걸리다
W: It does. But since you're still a beginner, you have to put in more
초보자   더 많은 노력을 기울이다
effort to get used to new words.
~에 익숙해지다
M: I see. So are you suggesting that I practice them over and over?
반복해서
W: (Exactly. Learning a language starts with repetition.)

해석
남: 실례합니다, Lopez 선생님. 뭐 좀 여쭤봐도 될까요?
여: 물론이지, Tony. 무엇을 도와줄까?
남: 스페인어를 더 잘하고 싶은데, 향상시키는 방법을 모르겠어요.
여: 너는 수업 시간에 잘하는 것 같아. 집에 있을 때 공부를 하니?
남: 숙제를 다 하고 매일 20개의 새로운 단어를 암기하려고 노력해요.
여: 좋은 출발이구나. 그 단어를 말하는 것을 반복해서 연습하기도 하니?
남: 그것을 해야 하나요? 많은 시간이 걸릴 것 같아요.
여: 그렇지. 하지만 너는 아직 초보자이기 때문에, 새로운 단어에 익숙해지기 위해 더 많은 노력을 기울여야 해.
남: 그렇군요. 그럼 그것들을 반복해서 연습하라는 말씀이신가요?
여: (맞아. 언어를 배우는 것은 반복에서 시작된단다.)

① 아니. 나는 스페인어를 배우는 것이 어렵지 않아.
② 네가 드디어 어휘 시험에 통과했다니 기쁘구나.
☑ 맞아. 언어를 배우는 것은 반복에서 시작된단다.
④ 글쓰기를 하면서 사전을 사용하는 것은 매우 유용해.
⑤ 너는 오늘 오후까지 숙제를 제출해야 해.

문제풀이
스페인어 실력을 향상시키는 방법을 묻는 남자에게 여자는 많은 시간과 노력이 들더라도 새롭게 익히는 단어에 익숙해지도록 말하는 연습을 여러 번 반복해서 해야 한다고 조언하고 있다. 따라서 남자의 마지막 말에 대한 여자의 응답으로 적절한 것은 ③ 'Exactly. Learning a language starts with repetition.(맞아. 언어를 배우는 것은 반복에서 시작된단다.)'이다.

15 다음 상황에서 Brian이 Melissa에게 할 말

정답률 80% ▶ 정답 ⑤

W: Brian is a class leader. He is passionate about environmental
반장   열정적인   환경 문제들
issues and saving energy. Recently, he's noticed that his
최근에
classmates don't turn the lights off when they leave the classroom.
불을 끄다(turn A off: A를 끄다)
Brian thinks this is very careless. He wants to make stickers that
부주의한
remind his classmates to save energy by turning off the lights. He
상기시키다
tells this idea to his classmate Melissa, and she agrees it's a good
동의하다
idea. Brian knows Melissa is a great artist, so he wants to ask her
to design stickers that encourage their classmates to save energy.
그들의 반 친구들이 절약하도록 장려하다
(encourage A to V: A가 ~하도록 장려하다)
In this situation, what would Brian most likely say to Melissa?
Brian: (Will you design stickers that encourage energy saving?)

해석
여: Brian은 반장이다. 그는 환경 문제와 에너지 절약에 열정적이다. 최근에, 그는 반 친구들이 교실을 나갈 때 불을 끄지 않는다는 것을 알게 되었다. Brian은 이것이 매우 부주의하다고 생각한다. 그는 반 친구들에게 불을 꺼서 에너지를 절약하도록 상기시키는 스티커를 만들고 싶어 한다. 그는 이 생각을 반 친구인 Melissa에게 말하고, 그녀는 그것이 좋은 생각이라는 것에 동의한다. Brian은 Melissa가 그림을 매우 잘 그리는 것을 알고 있어서, 그녀에게 그들의 반 친구들이 에너지를 절약하도록 장려하는 스티커를 디자인해 달라고 부탁하고 싶다. 이러한 상황에서, Brian은 Melissa에게 뭐라고 말하겠는가?
Brian: (에너지 절약을 장려하는 스티커를 디자인해 주겠니?)

① 미술 수업 후에 교실을 청소하자.
② 게시판에서 스티커를 제거했니?
③ 방에서 나갈 때 히터를 꺼 줘.
④ 디자인 수업 수강을 신청하는 최종 날짜가 언제니?
☑ 에너지 절약을 장려하는 스티커를 디자인해 주겠니?

16~17 1지문 2문항

M: Good afternoon, everyone. Last time, we learned that overtourism
과잉 관광
happens when there are too many visitors to a particular
특정한
destination. Today, we'll learn how cities deal with the problems
목적지   ~을 처리하다
caused by overtourism. First, some cities limit the number of
제한하다
hotels so there are fewer places for visitors to stay. In Barcelona,
머무르다
building new hotels is not allowed in the city center. Second,
짓는 것(build: 짓다)   도시 중심부
other cities promote areas away from popular sites. For instance,
홍보하다
Amsterdam encourages tourists to visit less-crowded areas. Third,
덜 붐비는
many cities have tried to limit access. For example, Venice has
접근
tried to reduce tourism overall by stopping large cruise ships from
감소시키다   대형 유람선이 정박하는 것을 막음으로써
(by V-ing: ~함으로써, stop A from V-ing: A가 ~하는 것을 막다, dock: 정박하다)
docking on the island. Similarly, Paris has focused on reducing
(focus on)
tourism to certain parts of the city by having car-restricted areas.
자동차 제한 구역들
Now, let's watch some video clips.

해석
남: 안녕하세요, 여러분. 지난 시간에, 우리는 특정한 목적지에 방문객이 너무 많을 때 과잉 관광이 발생한다는 것을 배웠습니다. 오늘, 우리는 도시들이 과잉 관광으로 인한 문제들을 어떻게 처리하는지 배울 것입니다. 첫 번째로, 일부 도시들은 호텔의 수를 제한해서 방문객이 머무를 수 있는 장소가 더 적어지게 합니다. 바르셀로나에서는, 도시 중심부에 새로운 호텔을 짓는 것이 허용되지 않습니다. 두 번째로, 다른 도시들은 인기 있는 장소로부터 떨어진 지역을 홍보합니다. 예를 들어, 암스테르담은 관광객들이 덜 붐비는 지역을 방문하도록 장려합니다. 세 번째로, 많은 도시들이 접근을 제한하려고 노력해 왔습니다. 예를 들어, 베니스는 대형 유람선들이 섬에 정박하는 것을 막음으로써 전반적으로 관광을 감소시키려고 노력해 왔습니다. 마찬가지로, 파리는 자동차 제한 구역을 지정함으로써 그 도시의 특정한 지역에 대한 관광을 감소시키는 데 집중해 왔습니다. 이제, 몇 개의 동영상을 시청하겠습니다

16 남자가 하는 말의 주제
정답률 75%
▶ 정답 ③

① 도시에서 주택을 임대하는 것의 장점들
② 관광객들이 오래된 도시 방문을 선호하는 이유들
✔ 도시들이 과잉 관광 문제들을 처리하는 방법들
④ 도시의 규모와 과잉 관광 사이의 상관관계
⑤ 도시들이 노후화된 교통 체계를 직면하는 방법

17 언급된 도시가 아닌 것
정답률 85%
▶ 정답 ③

① 바르셀로나   ② 암스테르담   ✔ 런던
④ 베니스   ⑤ 파리

21 2023년 11월 학력평가

01	②	02	①	03	⑤	04	④	05	①
06	⑤	07	⑤	08	④	09	③	10	③
11	①	12	②	13	④	14	③	15	⑤
16	①	17	⑤						

01 남자가 하는 말의 목적
정답률 90%
▶ 정답 ②

[Chime bell rings.]
M: Hello, visitors. This is Scott Wolfman from the Edison Convention

Center management office. We're doing our best to make sure
관리사무소   최선을 다하고 있다(do one's best)
that visitors have a wonderful experience in our convention center.
경험
As part of our effort, our center provides a robot guide service. The
~의 일환으로   로봇 안내 서비스
robot offers guided-tours of our exhibitions. Foreign languages,
전시회들   외국어
such as Chinese and Spanish, are available. And if you lose your
이용 가능한
way, the robot will accompany you to where you want to go. So,
길을 잃다(lose one's way)   동행하다
please feel free to ask our friendly robot guide, and it'll kindly help
편하게 문의하다   상냥한
(feel free to V: 편하게 ~하다)
you. I hope this service makes your experience even better. Thank
you.

해석
[차임벨이 울린다.]
남: 안녕하세요, 관람객 여러분. 저는 Edison 컨벤션 센터 관리사무소의 Scott Wolfman입니다. 저희는 관람객 여러분이 저희 컨벤션 센터에서 멋진 경험을 하도록 최선을 다하고 있습니다. 노력의 일환으로, 저희 센터는 로봇 안내 서비스를 제공합니다. 로봇은 전시회의 안내가 있는 관람을 제공합니다. 중국어와 스페인어 같은 외국어도 이용 가능합니다. 그리고 길을 잃으면, 로봇은 여러분이 가고 싶어 하는 곳까지 동행할 것입니다. 그러니, 저희의 상냥한 로봇 안내원에게 편하게 문의해 주세요, 그러면 친절하게 도와드릴 것입니다. 이 서비스가 여러분의 경험을 훨씬 더 좋게 만들기를 바랍니다. 감사합니다.

① 로봇 프로그램 만족도 조사 참여를 독려하려고
✔ 관람객을 위한 안내 로봇 서비스를 소개하려고
③ 전시 작품 해설 서비스 중단을 안내하려고
④ 오디오 가이드 대여 장소를 공지하려고
⑤ 전시관 온라인 예약 방법을 설명하려고

02 여자의 의견
정답률 90%
▶ 정답 ①

W: Kevin, what are you doing?
M: Mom, I'm writing a letter to my sponsored child in Congo.
편지   후원 아동
W: That's why you're writing in French. Your French has gotten better
and better.   점점 더 좋은
M: Actually, I got help from a translation program.
번역 프로그램
W: I see. [Pause] Did you check the translated text before copying it?
글   옮겨 적기 전에
(copy: 옮겨 적다)
M: No, I didn't. Do you think I have to?
W: Yes. You'd better check the translation.
M: Well, I think the translation program does a better job than I can.
W: Not exactly. The translation could have meanings different from
what you intended.   의미들   ~과 다른
의도했다
M: Hmm, you may be right. The translated text often loses the
meaning of my original writing.
원래 글
W: See? When translating a text with a translation program, you need
to check the results.
결과
M: Okay. Thanks for your advice.

해석
여: Kevin, 무엇을 하고 있니?
남: 엄마, 저는 콩고에 있는 제 후원 아동에게 편지를 쓰고 있어요.
여: 그래서 프랑스어로 쓰고 있구나. 네 프랑스어 실력이 점점 더 좋아지고 있네.
남: 사실, 번역 프로그램의 도움을 받았어요.
여: 그렇구나. [잠시 휴]번역된 글을 옮겨 적기 전에 확인했니?
남: 아니요, 안 했어요. 해야 한다고 생각하세요?
여: 응. 번역문을 검토하는 것이 좋단다.
남: 음, 저는 번역 프로그램이 제가 할 수 있는 것보다 더 잘한다고 생각해요.
여: 꼭 그렇지는 않아. 번역문이 네가 의도했던 것과 다른 의미를 가질 수도 있어.
남: 흠, 그럴 수도 있겠네요. 번역된 글은 종종 제 원래 글의 의미를 놓쳐버리기도 해요.
여: 그렇지? 번역 프로그램으로 글을 번역할 때, 너는 결과를 확인해야 해.
남: 알겠어요. 조언해 주셔서 감사해요.

✔ 번역 프로그램으로 번역한 글은 검토가 필요하다.
② 읽기 학습을 통해 쓰기 능력을 향상시킬 수 있다.
③ 글을 인용할 때는 출처를 명확히 밝혀야 한다.
④ 예상 독자를 고려하여 글을 작성해야 한다.
⑤ 번역기 사용은 외국어 학습에 효과적이다.

문제풀이

번역 프로그램을 이용할 때 번역문을 그대로 옮겨 적는다고 말하는 남자에게 여자는 글의 의미가 의도와 다르게 번역되는 경우도 있으므로 검토할 필요가 있다고 조언한다. 따라서 답은 ①'번역 프로그램으로 번역한 글은 검토가 필요하다.'이다.

03 두 사람의 관계

정답률 80%   ▶ 정답 ⑤

[Cell phone rings.]

M: Hello. This is Johnny. We've been messaging each other on the online marketplace.
온라인 시장

W: Oh, hi. You have more questions about the air conditioner, right?
에어컨

M: Yes. Could you tell me how long you've been using it?

W: I bought it a year ago. It works well and is like new as you can see
잘 작동하다
from the photo.

M: Then why do you want to sell it?
팔다

W: Because I don't need it anymore. I'm moving to a place with a
~로 이사 갈 예정이다
built-in air conditioner.
붙박이의   (be V-ing: ~할 예정이다, move to: ~로 이사 가다)

M: I see. I'd like to buy it, then. It's $400, correct?

W: That's right. When can you pick it up?
그것을 가지러 오다

M: Maybe tomorrow. I need to find a truck to load it on first.
그것을 싣다

W: Okay. Let me know when you're ready.
준비가 된

M: Thanks. I'll call you again.

해석

[휴대전화가 울린다.]

남: 안녕하세요. 저는 Johnny예요. 우리 온라인 시장에서 서로 메시지를 보내고 있었죠.

여: 오, 안녕하세요. 에어컨에 대해 더 궁금하신 점이 있군요, 그렇죠?

남: 네. 얼마나 오래 그것을 사용하셨는지 말씀해 주시겠어요?

여: 1년 전에 샀어요. 잘 작동하고 사진에서 볼 수 있듯이 새것 같아요.

남: 그럼 왜 팔려고 하시는 거예요?

여: 더 이상 필요하지 않기 때문이에요. 붙박이 에어컨이 있는 곳으로 이사를 갈 예정이거든요.

남: 그렇군요. 그럼 구매하고 싶은데요. 400달러죠, 맞나요?

여: 맞아요. 언제 그것을 가지러 오실 수 있나요?

남: 아마 내일 가능할 것 같아요. 우선 그것을 실을 트럭을 찾아야 해요.

여: 알겠어요. 준비가 되면 알려주세요.

남: 감사해요. 다시 연락드릴게요.

① 광고 제작자 — 사진작가
② 이사업체 직원 — 의뢰인
③ 고객 — 에어컨 설치 기사
④ 트럭 운전사 — 물류 창고 직원
✓⑤ 구매자 — 중고 물품 개인 판매자

04 그림에서 대화의 내용과 일치하지 않는 것

정답률 85%   ▶ 정답 ④

W: Hi, Benjamin. Did you finish your work for the student lounge
학생 휴게실
design contest?
디자인 대회

M: Yes. I'm confident that I'm going to win. Here's my design for it.
자신 있는   우승하다

W: Awesome. Is that a hanging plant in front of the window?
공중 식물

M: Yes. The plant will give a fresh feel to the lounge. What do you think
신선한 느낌을 주다
about the banner on the wall?
현수막

W: I love it. The slogan "TO THE WORLD" goes well with the world map.
구호   ~와 잘 어울리다

M: I hope this place helps students dream big.
꿈을 크게 가지다

W: That's cool. And the two cushions on the sofa make the
atmosphere cozier.
분위기   더 아늑한(cozy)

M: You're right. Check out the square-shaped table as well.
사각형 모양의

W: Good. It can be useful. Most of all, students will love the vending
유용한   무엇보다도   자판기
machine under the clock.

M: You bet!

해석

여: 안녕, Benjamin. 학생 휴게실 디자인 대회를 위한 작업은 끝냈니?

남: 응. 나는 우승할 자신 있어. 여기 내 디자인이야.

여: 대단한데. 창문 앞에 있는 저것은 공중 식물이니?

남: 그래. 식물이 휴게실에 신선한 느낌을 줄 거야. 벽에 걸린 현수막에 대해서는 어떻게 생각해?

여: 정말 마음에 들어. "TO THE WORLD"라는 구호가 세계 지도와 잘 어울려.

남: 이 장소가 학생들이 꿈을 크게 가지는 데 도움이 되었으면 좋겠어.

여: 멋지다. 그리고 소파 위에 있는 두 개의 쿠션이 분위기를 더 아늑하게 만들어 줘.

남: 네 말이 맞아. 사각형 모양의 테이블도 봐.

여: 좋네. 그것은 유용할 수 있어. 무엇보다도, 학생들은 시계 아래에 있는 자판기를 정말 좋아할 거야.

남: 당연하지!

05 남자가 할 일

정답률 90%   ▶ 정답 ①

M: Ms. Kim, Empty Your Plate Day is coming. How's the preparation
식판 비우는 날   준비
going?

W: I've finally decided on the lunch menu for that day.
점심 메뉴

M: You did! How did you do that?

W: I did a survey of students' favorite foods.
설문 조사

M: Good idea! Can I help you with anything?

W: Actually, Mr. Han, I'm not sure how to motivate students to
학생들이 참여하도록 동기를 부여하다
participate.   (motivate A to V: A가 ~하도록 동기를 부여하다, participate: 참여하다)

M: How about an award for the class with the fewest leftovers?
상   남은 음식

W: Sounds great. But how will we find that class?

M: You could give a sticker to the students who leave nothing on their
스티커   남기다
plates. And then, you can find the class with the most stickers.

W: Excellent. Could you prepare some stickers for me?
준비하다

M: Sure. I'll do that for you.

W: Thanks. Then I'll put a notice on the bulletin board.
안내문을 붙이다   게시판

해석

남: Kim 선생님, Empty Your Plate Day(식판 비우는 날)가 다가오고 있어요. 준비는 어떻게 되어 가나요?

여: 드디어 그날 점심 메뉴를 정했어요.

남: 그랬군요! 어떻게 하신 거예요?

여: 학생들이 가장 좋아하는 음식에 대한 설문 조사를 했어요.

남: 좋은 생각이네요! 제가 도와드릴 일이 있나요?

여: 사실, 한 선생님, 저는 학생들이 참여하도록 동기를 부여하는 방법을 잘 모르겠어요.

남: 남은 음식이 가장 적은 학급에 상을 주는 건 어때요?

여: 좋을 것 같네요. 그런데 그 학급을 어떻게 찾을까요?

남: 식판에 아무것도 남기지 않은 학생들에게 스티커를 줄 수 있어요. 그런 다음, 스티커가 가장 많은 학급을 찾으면 돼요.

여: 훌륭하네요. 저를 위해 스티커를 좀 준비해 주시겠어요?

남: 물론이죠. 제가 선생님을 위해 그 일을 할게요.

여: 감사해요. 그럼 저는 게시판에 안내문을 붙일게요.

✓① 스티커 준비하기
② 안내문 게시하기
③ 급식 메뉴 선정하기
④ 설문 조사 실시하기
⑤ 우수 학급 시상하기

06 남자가 매달 지불할 금액
▶ 정답 ⑤

W: Welcome to Boom Telecom. How can I help you?
M: Hi. I'm thinking of changing my internet provider. What service
plans do you have?
인터넷 공급 업체 / 서비스 요금제들
W: Okay. We have the Economic plan that's $20 per month. And the
매달
Supreme plan, which is faster, is $30 per month.
M: I prefer the faster one.
W: Alright. We also have an OTT service for an extra $10 per month.
추가의
What do you think?
M: Awesome. I'd like that as well.
W: Excellent choice. Then you'll have the Supreme plan with the OTT
service, right?
M: Correct. Can I get a discount?
할인을 받다
W: I'm afraid that the 10% discount promotion is over.
판촉 행사
M: That's a shame. But I'll take it anyway.
W: Thank you. Please fill in this paper with your payment information.
기입하다 / 결제 정보
M: Okay. [Writing sound] Here you are.

해석

여: Boom Telecom에 오신 것을 환영합니다. 어떻게 도와드릴까요?
남: 안녕하세요. 저는 인터넷 공급 업체를 바꾸려고 생각 중이에요. 어떤 서비스 요금제가 있
나요?
여: 알겠습니다. 저희에게 매달 20달러의 이코노믹 요금제가 있습니다. 그리고 속도가 더 빠
른 슈프림 요금제가 있는데, 매달 30달러입니다.
남: 저는 더 빠른 것이 좋아요.
여: 알겠습니다. 매달 추가 10달러에 OTT 서비스도 제공하고 있습니다. 어떻게 생각하시나요?
남: 멋지네요. 그것도 하고 싶어요.
여: 훌륭한 선택입니다. 그럼 OTT 서비스를 포함하는 슈프림 요금제로 하시는 거네요, 그렇죠?
남: 맞아요. 할인을 받을 수 있나요?
여: 유감스럽게도 10% 할인 판촉 행사는 끝났어요.
남: 아쉽네요. 하지만 어쨌든 그것으로 할게요.
여: 감사합니다. 이 서류에 결제 정보를 기입해 주세요.
남: 네. [글씨를 쓰는 소리] 여기 있어요.

① $20   ② $27
③ $30   ④ $36
☑ $40

문제 풀이

남자는 월 사용료가 30달러인 슈프림 요금제와 추가로 10달러를 내면 이용할 수 있는 OTT
서비스를 선택했다. 여자가 10% 할인을 제공하는 판촉 행사는 이미 끝났다고 했으므로 남자
가 매달 지불해야 하는 금액은 총 40달러이다. 따라서 답은 ⑤ '$40'이다.

07 여자가 토크 쇼를 방청하러 갈 수 없는 이유
▶ 정답 ⑤

[Cell phone rings.]
M: Hi, Isabella.
W: Hi, Lorenzo. Did you finish your part-time job?
아르바이트
M: Yes. I'm on my way to a meeting for a chemistry project. What's up?
~에 가는 길인(on one's way to) / 화학 프로젝트
W: Your favorite talk show is The Alice Mitchell Show, right?
토크 쇼
M: Yeah, I'm a big fan of hers. I even went to her book signing event.
열렬한 팬 / 책 사인회
W: I knew it! I got two tickets for her talk show. It's next Saturday
evening.
M: Whoa! Can you please take me with you?
W: Actually, I'm not available that day. The tickets are all yours.
시간이 있는
M: Wait, why can't you go? Is it because of the family gathering you
가족 모임
mentioned before?
말했다(mention)
W: No, that's in two weeks. Next Saturday I have to attend my friend's
2주 후에 / 참석하다
wedding.
결혼식
M: Oh, I see. Then I'll take the tickets with pleasure. Thank you so
기쁜 마음으로
much.

해석

[휴대전화가 울린다.]
남: 안녕, Isabella.
여: 안녕, Lorenzo. 아르바이트는 다 끝났니?
남: 응. 나는 화학 프로젝트를 위한 모임에 가는 길이야. 무슨 일이니?
여: 네가 가장 좋아하는 토크 쇼가 'Alice Mitchell Show'잖아, 맞지?
남: 그래, 나는 그녀의 쇼의 열렬한 팬이야. 심지어 그녀의 책 사인회에도 갔어.
여: 그럴 줄 알았어! 내게 그녀의 토크 쇼 티켓 2장이 있어. 다음 주 토요일 저녁이야.
남: 우와! 나도 데려가 줄 수 있어?
여: 사실, 나는 그날 시간이 없어. 티켓은 모두 네 거야.
남: 잠깐, 왜 못 가는 거야? 전에 말한 가족 모임 때문에 그러는 거니?
여: 아니, 그것은 2주 후야. 다음 주 토요일에는 친구의 결혼식에 참석해야 해.
남: 오, 그렇구나. 그럼 기쁜 마음으로 티켓을 받을게. 정말 고마워.

① 가족 모임에 가야 해서
② 아르바이트를 해야 해서
③ 책 사인회를 준비해야 해서
④ 화학 프로젝트를 해야 해서
☑ 친구 결혼식에 참석해야 해서

08 Polar Bear Swim에 관해 언급되지 않은 것
▶ 정답 ④

W: Michael, look at this poster. The Polar Bear Swim will be held soon.
북극곰 수영 대회 / 개최되다(hold: 개최하다)
M: I know! I've been really looking forward to it. [Pause] It's on
~을 정말 기대하고 있었다
December 23rd.
(look forward to: ~을 기대하다)
W: Yeah. We can enjoy winter sea-swimming.
M: How nice! To join this event, we must hand in a medical check-up
제출하다 / 건강진단서
paper.
W: I think it's a good policy for everyone's health since the water is icy
정책 / ~하기 때문에 / 얼음처럼
cold.
차가운
M: I agree. By the way, it says that there's a limit of 100 people.
제한
W: Oh, we must hurry. Look! Registration starts this Saturday.
서두르다 / 등록
M: I'll set a reminder on my phone.
알림을 설정하다
W: Great idea. And the entry fee is just $15.
참가비
M: Yes. And all entry fees will be donated to charity.
~에 기부되다 / 자선 단체
(donate A to B: A를 B에 기부하다)
W: Cool. Let's have some icy fun while doing a good deed.
선행

해석

여: Michael, 이 포스터를 봐. 북극곰 수영 대회가 곧 개최될 거야.
남: 알고 있어! 나는 그것을 정말 기대하고 있었어. [잠시 후] 12월 23일이구나.
여: 그래. 우리는 겨울 바다 수영을 즐길 수 있어.
남: 정말 좋아! 이 행사에 참가하려면, 우리는 건강진단서를 제출해야 해.
여: 물이 얼음처럼 차갑기 때문에 그것은 모두의 건강을 위한 좋은 정책인 것 같아.
남: 동의해. 그런데 인원을 100명으로 제한한다고 적혀 있어.
여: 오, 우리 서둘러겠다. 봐! 등록이 이번 주 토요일부터 시작돼.
남: 내 휴대폰에 알림을 설정할게.
여: 좋은 생각이야. 그리고 참가비가 15달러밖에 안 해.
남: 그래. 그리고 모든 참가비는 자선 단체에 기부될 거야.
여: 멋지다. 선행을 하면서 추위를 즐겨보자.

① 행사 날짜   ② 제출 서류
③ 최대 참가 인원   ☑ 기념품
⑤ 참가비

09 Walk in the Snow에 관한 내용과 일치하지 않는 것
▶ 정답 ③

W: Hello, listeners! Are you a winter person? Then, Walk in the Snow
겨울을 좋아하는 사람 / 눈밭 걷기
might just be the adventure for you. It's a one-day tour program at
모험 / 1일 투어 프로그램
Great White Mountain. Regardless of hiking experience, anyone
~에 상관없이
who is interested in hiking can participate in the tour. Participants
~에 관심이 있는 / ~에 참여하다 / 참여자들

are required to bring their own snowshoes and poles. But
가져오도록 요구되다
(require A to V: A가 ~하도록 요구하다)
equipment is also available to rent for a small fee. The registration
장비   적은 요금으로   등록비
fee is $10, and we offer discounts to students. Don't forget that
                            할인을 제공하다
you must register in advance to participate. For more information,
                            사전에
please visit our website, www.walkinthesnow.com. Thank you.

해석

여: 안녕하세요, 청취자 여러분! 여러분은 겨울을 좋아하는 사람인가요? 그렇다면, Walk in the Snow(눈밭 걷기)가 여러분에게 딱 맞는 모험이 될 수도 있습니다. 그것은 Great White Mountain에서의 1일 투어 프로그램입니다. 하이킹 경험에 상관없이, 하이킹에 관심이 있는 누구나 투어에 참여할 수 있습니다. 참여자들은 자신의 설상화와 등산스틱을 가져와야 합니다. 하지만 장비는 적은 요금으로 대여할 수도 있습니다. 등록비는 10달러이며, 학생에게 할인을 제공합니다. 참여하기 위해서는 사전에 등록해야 한다는 것을 잊지 마세요. 더 많은 정보를 원하시면, 저희 웹 사이트 www.walkinthesnow.com을 방문해 주세요. 감사합니다.

① 1일 투어 프로그램이다.
② 하이킹에 관심이 있는 누구든 참여할 수 있다.
✔ 장비를 무료로 대여할 수 있다.
④ 학생에게 등록비 할인을 해 준다.
⑤ 참여하려면 사전에 등록해야 한다.

---

10 표에서 두 사람이 선택할 달력   정답률 75%   ▶ 정답 ③

M: Honey, what are you looking at?
W: It's a brochure for a new calendar. Why don't we choose one
        안내 책자   달력
    together?
M: Great. How much do you want to spend?
W: I think more than $20 is not reasonable.
                                    합리적인
M: Agreed. How about trying a new format instead of a wall calendar?
                                    형태   ~ 대신에
    We've only used wall calendars so far.
                                    지금까지
W: Good idea. Let's pick the standing desk format, then.
M: Okay. And I prefer one that's made of recyclable paper.
                                                재활용 가능 종이
W: Me, too. It's more eco-friendly than those that cannot be recycled.
                            친환경적인
M: Then, let's cross this out. Now, we have two options left. Which one
            이것을 제외하다   남은
    do you prefer?
W: I think the classic art theme doesn't match our interior design.
            고전 미술   테마, 주제   어울리다
M: Good point. Then, let's choose this one.

해석

남: 여보, 무엇을 보고 있어요?
여: 새로운 달력을 위한 안내 책자예요. 같이 하나 고르는 게 어때요?
남: 좋아요. 얼마를 쓰고 싶어요?
여: 20달러 이상은 합리적이지 않은 것 같아요.
남: 동의해요. 벽걸이용 달력 대신에 새로운 형태를 시도해 보는 건 어때요? 우리는 지금까지 벽걸이용 달력만 사용했잖아요.
여: 좋은 생각이에요. 그럼 탁상용 형태를 선택해요.
남: 알겠어요. 그리고 저는 재활용 가능 종이로 만들어진 것이 더 좋아요.
여: 저도 그래요. 재활용할 수 없는 것보다 더 친환경적이잖아요.
남: 그럼, 이것을 제외합시다. 이제, 두 가지 선택지가 남았어요. 어떤 것이 더 좋아요?
여: 고전 미술 테마는 우리의 인테리어 디자인과 어울리지 않는 것 같아요.
남: 좋은 지적이에요. 그럼, 이것을 선택합시다.

달력

	제품	가격	형태	재활용 가능 종이	테마
①	A	8달러	탁상용	×	현대 미술
②	B	10달러	탁상용	○	고전 미술
✔	C	12달러	탁상용	○	영화
④	D	16달러	벽걸이용	○	자연
⑤	E	22달러	벽걸이용	×	동물

---

11 여자의 마지막 말에 대한 남자의 응답   정답률 50%   ▶ 정답 ①

W: Congratulations, Lucas! I heard you were invited to speak at the
                                                        연설하다
    National Assembly.
        국회
M: Thanks. It's a real honor. I think the article I wrote in the newspaper
                    영광   기사
    made a strong impression.
        강한 인상을 남겼다
W: I'm so proud of you. What did you mostly write about?
            자랑스러운   주로
M: (I covered the worrying state of marine life.)
    다뤘다   상태   해양의

해석

여: 축하해요, Lucas! 국회에서 연설해 달라는 초청을 받았다고 들었어요.
남: 감사해요. 정말 영광이에요. 제가 신문에 쓴 기사가 강한 인상을 남긴 것 같아요.
여: 당신이 정말 자랑스러워요. 주로 무엇에 대해 썼나요?
남: (저는 해양 생물의 걱정스러운 상태를 다뤘어요.)

✔ 저는 해양 생물의 걱정스러운 상태를 다뤘어요.
② 저는 생물학과에 기사를 보냈어요.
③ 당신이 무엇을 했든, 그것에 대해 말하지 맙시다.
④ 저는 그 연설을 준비하는 데 많은 시간을 보냈어요.
⑤ 기사는 주로 학생들이 읽었어요.

---

12 남자의 마지막 말에 대한 여자의 응답   정답률 70%   ▶ 정답 ②

M: Claire, why are you sweating? It's pretty cold outside.
                            땀을 흘리는(sweat)   추운
W: Hey, Jamie. I ran to be in time for class. It's too far to walk from the
                            수업 시간에 맞추다
    subway station to our college, don't you think?
        지하철역   대학교
M: Yes, but the shuttle bus began running last week. You can take it
                            운행하기 시작했다
    instead.   (begin V-ing: ~하기 시작하다, run: 운행하다)
    대신
W: (Good news. Thanks for letting me know.)

해석

남: Claire, 왜 땀을 흘리니? 밖은 꽤 춥잖아.
여: 안녕, Jamie. 수업 시간에 맞추기 위해서 뛰어왔어. 지하철역에서 우리 대학교까지 걷기에는 너무 멀어, 그렇게 생각하지 않니?
남: 그래, 그런데 지난주부터 셔틀버스가 운행하기 시작했어. 너는 대신 그것을 탈 수 있어.
여: (좋은 소식이구나. 알려줘서 고마워.)

① 몸조심해. 날씨가 너무 추워.
✔ 좋은 소식이구나. 알려줘서 고마워.
③ 서둘러. 버스가 곧 출발할 거야.
④ 진짜? 그럼 걸어보는 게 좋겠어.
⑤ 정말? 나도 셔틀버스에 타고 있었어.

---

13 여자의 마지막 말에 대한 남자의 응답   정답률 80%   ▶ 정답 ④

W: Good morning, Pablo.
M: Hi, Eva. Look at my new tablet PC.
W: Wow. How do you like it?
M: It's opened a brand new world to me. But I have a small problem.
                    완전히 새로운
W: What is it? Maybe I can be of help.
                            도움이 되다
M: This file works well on my laptop, but it won't open on my tablet.
                잘 작동하다
W: Did you install a file-reading app? You need one to open the file on
            설치하다   파일 읽기 앱
    a tablet.
M: I already did that a week ago.
        이미
W: Then, I'll check a few things. [Tapping sound] I got it. The free trial
    period of this app is over.   무료 체험 기간
M: Oh, that's why it doesn't work. Do you think I should pay for this
    app?
W: Well, it depends on you. You can consider it if you need this app.
            ~에게 달려 있다   고려하다
M: (I see. I'll give it some thought before buying this app.)

해석

여: 좋은 아침이야, Pablo.

남: 안녕, Eva. 나의 새 태블릿 PC를 좀 봐.

여: 와. 그것은 어때?

남: 그것은 내게 완전히 새로운 세상을 열어주었어. 그런데 작은 문제가 있어.

여: 뭔데? 내가 도움이 될 수도 몰라.

남: 이 파일이 내 노트북 컴퓨터에서는 잘 작동하는데, 태블릿에서는 열리지 않아.

여: 파일 읽기 앱을 설치했니? 태블릿에서 파일을 열려면 파일 읽기 앱이 필요해.

남: 일주일 전에 이미 했어.

여: 그럼, 내가 몇 가지 확인해 볼게. [가볍게 치는 소리] 알았어. 이 앱의 무료 체험 기간이 끝났어.

남: 오, 그래서 작동이 안 되는구나. 이 앱에 돈을 지불해야 한다고 생각해?

여: 음, 그것은 네게 달려 있어. 이 앱이 필요하면 그것을 고려해 볼 수 있지.

남: (그렇구나. 이 앱을 구매하기 전에 생각을 좀 해볼게.)

① 물론이지. 그래서 앱에 대해 환불을 받은 거야.

② 미안해. 내 태블릿 PC를 더 일찍 수리했어야 했어.

③ 맞아. 문서들은 알파벳순으로 정리되어 있었어.

☑④ 그렇구나. 이 앱을 구매하기 전에 생각을 좀 해볼게.

⑤ 걱정하지 마. 아직 무료 체험 기간이 며칠 더 남았어.

문제 풀이

파일 읽기 앱의 무료 체험 기간이 끝나서 사용할 수 없다는 말을 들은 남자는 여자에게 앱에 돈을 지불해야 할지를 묻는다. 여자는 앱의 필요 여부에 따라 결정해야 한다고 조언한다. 따라서, 이에 대한 남자의 응답은 ④ 'I see. I'll give it some thought before buying this app.(그렇구나. 이 앱을 구매하기 전에 생각을 좀 해볼게.)'가 가장 적절하다.

14   남자의 마지막 말에 대한 여자의 응답

정답률 85%
▶ 정답 ③

M: Hi, Naomi. What are you up to?

W: Hi. I'm looking for volunteer work. Didn't you say you're volunteering?
   자원봉사 활동

M: Yes. I'm working as a note-taker.
   노트 필기자

W: You mean helping students with hearing difficulties?
   청각 장애

M: Right. It helps deaf students understand the class better.
   청각 장애가 있는

W: Interesting. Could you tell me more?

M: I type everything during class, even jokes. The more detailed, the
   타자로 치다   상세한
   more understandable.
   이해하기 쉬운

W: It sounds like a unique and valuable experience.
   특별한   소중한

M: Yeah. Are you thinking about joining?

W: Absolutely. But can I join in the middle of the semester?
   학기

M: It could be possible. I heard one member quit a few days ago.
   그만두었다(quit)

W: Lucky me. Is the position still available?
   자리

M: Hmm, I'm not sure, but if you ask the student volunteer center,
   you'll get an answer immediately.
   답변을 받다   바로

W: (Okay. Wish me luck in getting this volunteer work.)

해석

남: 안녕, Naomi. 무엇을 하고 있니?

여: 안녕. 나는 자원봉사 활동을 찾고 있어. 너는 자원봉사를 하고 있다고 하지 않았니?

남: 그래. 나는 노트 필기자로 일하고 있어.

여: 청각 장애가 있는 학생들을 돕는다는 말이니?

남: 맞아. 청각 장애가 있는 학생들이 수업을 더 잘 이해할 수 있도록 도와주는 거야.

여: 흥미롭네. 좀 더 말해 주겠니?

남: 나는 수업 시간에 모든 것을 타자로 쳐, 심지어 농담도 말이야. 더 상세할수록, 더 이해하기 쉽거든.

여: 그것은 특별하고 소중한 경험인 것 같아.

남: 그래. 참여할 생각이니?

여: 당연하지. 그런데 학기 중간에 참여할 수 있을까?

남: 가능할 수도 있어. 며칠 전에 회원 한 명이 그만두었다고 들었거든.

여: 운이 좋네. 아직 그 자리가 비어 있니?

남: 흠, 잘 모르겠지만 학생 자원봉사 센터에 문의하면 바로 답변을 받을 수 있을 거야.

여: (알겠어. 내가 이 자원봉사 활동을 할 수 있도록 행운을 빌어줘.)

① 좋은 생각이야. 수화를 읽는 법을 배우자.

② 네 말이 맞아. 내가 그를 돕고 싶었기 때문이야.

☑③ 알겠어. 내가 이 자원봉사 활동을 할 수 있도록 행운을 빌어줘.

④ 나를 믿어. 분명 너는 노트 필기자로 선정될 거야.

⑤ 멋지다. 수업 중에 나를 위해 필기를 해 줘서 고마워.

15   다음 상황에서 Tony가 Kate에게 할 말

정답률 70%
▶ 정답 ⑤

M: Tony and Kate are members of the bread lovers club. They plan
   to go on a bakery tour every month. To make a list of places to
       빵집 투어를 가다   ~의 목록을 만든다
   visit, they're sharing their ideas about must-visit bakeries. Kate
                                       꼭 방문해야 하는
   proposes a bakery whose bread she thinks is super delicious.
   제안하다   매우 맛있는
   However, Tony finds out that the baker there quit and since then
                                제빵사
   there have been lots of reviews complaining about the bread
                          후기들   불평하는(complain)
   quality getting worse. So, he wants to suggest that they choose a
   품질
   better bakery for their where-to-go list. In this situation, what would
                           방문 목록
   Tony most likely say to Kate?

Tony: (How about finding a different bakery for the list?)

해석

남: Tony와 Kate는 빵 애호가 동아리의 회원이다. 그들은 매달 빵집 투어를 갈 계획이다. 방문할 장소의 목록을 만들기 위해, 그들은 꼭 방문해야 하는 빵집에 대한 자신들의 생각을 공유하고 있다. Kate는 빵이 매우 맛있다고 생각하는 빵집을 하나 제안한다. 하지만 Tony는 그곳의 제빵사가 그만두었고, 그 이후로 빵의 품질이 더 나빠진 것에 대해 불평하는 후기가 많아졌다는 것을 알게 된다. 그래서 그는 자신들의 방문 목록을 위해 더 나은 빵집을 선택해야 한다고 제안하고 싶다. 이러한 상황에서, Tony는 Kate에게 뭐라고 말하겠는가?

Tony: (목록에 들어갈 다른 빵집을 찾아보는 게 어떠니?)

① 우리 이 빵집에 대한 후기를 올리는 게 어떨까?

② 그녀에게 이달의 제빵사 상을 주자.

③ 우리가 대기 명단에 있는지 확인하는 게 좋겠어.

④ 우리는 나중에 수리가 끝나면 와야겠어.

☑⑤ 목록에 들어갈 다른 빵집을 찾아보는 게 어떠니?

16~17   1지문 2문항

W: Hello, students. Last time, we learned why it's good for us to eat
   fruits and veggies. But what's good for us isn't always good for
   과일들   채소들
   animals. Today, let's find out what fruits to avoid when feeding
                          알아보다   피하다
   dogs. First, grapes are known to be highly toxic to dogs. You should
              포도들   ~에게 매우 유독하다
                                   (highly: 매우, toxic: 유독한)
   be careful because even a single grape can cause severe health
                                              유발하다   심각한
   damage. Now, let's take a look at cherries. If a dog swallows their
                                       체리들   삼키다
   seeds, the dog is likely to have difficulties breathing. Next, if your
   씨앗들   숨을 쉬는 데 어려움을 겪다
                      (have difficulty V-ing: ~하는 데 어려움을 겪다, breathe: 숨을 쉬다)
   dog doesn't eat avocados, it would be for the best. That's because
                   아보카도들
   eating large amounts of avocados can make your dog sick. Finally,
          많은 양의
   don't let your dog snack on grapefruits. The fruit contains so much
                      ~을 간식으로 먹다 자몽들   함유하다
   acid that some dogs can develop stomach problems. Now, you
   산(酸)   배탈이 나다
   may understand why some fruits are said to be harmful to dogs.
                                                  해로운
   I hope this information will help you and your dog in living a happy
   life.

해석

여: 안녕하세요, 학생 여러분. 지난 시간에, 우리는 과일과 채소를 먹는 것이 왜 좋은지에 대해 배웠습니다. 하지만 우리에게 좋은 것이 동물에게 항상 좋은 것은 아닙니다. 오늘은 개에게 먹이를 줄 때 피해야 할 과일은 무엇인지 알아보겠습니다. 첫 번째로, 포도는 개에게 매우 유독한 것으로 알려져 있습니다. 포도 한 알도 심각한 건강 손상을 유발할 수 있기 때문에 조심해야 합니다. 이제, 체리를 살펴봅시다. 만약 개가 그 씨앗을 삼킨다면, 숨을 쉬는 데 어려움을 겪을 가능성이 있습니다. 다음으로, 여러분의 개가 아보카도를 먹지 않는다면, 그것이 최선일 것입니다. 많은 양의 아보카도를 먹는 것은 개를 아프게 할 수 있기 때문

입니다. 마지막으로, 여러분의 개가 자몽을 간식으로 먹지 못하게 하세요. 이 과일은 너무 많은 산(酸)을 함유하고 있어서 일부 개들은 배탈이 날 수 있습니다. 이제, 여러분은 왜 몇 몇 과일이 개에게 해롭다고 하는지 이해할 수 있을 것입니다. 이 정보가 여러분과 여러분의 개가 행복한 삶을 사는 데 도움이 되기를 바랍니다.

16 여자가 하는 말의 주제

정답률 85% ▶ 정답 ①

☑ ① 개의 건강에 위험을 초래할 수 있는 과일들
② 개가 과일의 맛을 즐기도록 돕는 방법들
③ 동물로부터 정원의 과일을 보호하기 위한 조언들
④ 개의 식단에 과일이 포함되어야 하는 이유들
⑤ 과일과 채소를 캐릭터로 사용한 이야기들

17 언급된 과일이 아닌 것

정답률 90% ▶ 정답 ⑤

① 포도
② 체리
③ 아보카도
④ 자몽
☑ ⑤ 크랜베리

---

22 2024년 3월 학력평가

01	⑤	02	②	03	⑤	04	⑤	05	②
06	③	07	⑤	08	④	09	④	10	③
11	③	12	⑤	13	②	14	①	15	①
16	①	17	④								

01 남자가 하는 말의 목적

정답률 90% ▶ 정답 ⑤

M: Good afternoon, students! This is your vice principal, Jack Eliot. Due to the heavy rain last night, there's some damage on the road and the road condition is not good. So we decided to make some rearrangements to the school shuttle bus schedule. From tomorrow, keep in mind that the bus schedule will be delayed by 15 minutes. We want to make sure all of you are safe. This bus schedule change will continue for one week. We appreciate your understanding and cooperation. Thank you for your attention!

해석
남: 안녕하세요, 학생 여러분! 저는 교감인 Jack Eliot입니다. 어젯밤 폭우 때문에, 도로에 약간의 손상이 있고 도로 상태가 좋지 않습니다. 그래서 저희는 학교 셔틀버스 일정을 약간 재조정하기로 결정했습니다. 내일부터, 버스 일정이 15분 정도 지연될 것이라는 점을 명심하십시오. 저희는 여러분 모두의 안전을 확실하게 하고 싶습니다. 이번 버스 일정 변경은 일주일 동안 계속될 것입니다. 여러분의 이해와 협조에 대해 감사드립니다. 들어주셔서 감사합니다!

① 학교 체육관 공사 일정을 알리려고
② 학교 수업 시간표 조정을 안내하려고
③ 학교 통학 시 대중교통 이용을 권장하려고
④ 학교 방과 후 수업 신청 방식을 설명하려고
☑ ⑤ 학교 셔틀버스 운행 시간 변경을 공지하려고

02 여자의 의견

정답률 85% ▶ 정답 ②

W: Brian, I heard that you are thinking of buying an electric bicycle.
M: Yes, that's right.
W: That's good. But be careful when you ride it.
M: Yeah, I know what you mean. On my way here I saw a man riding an electric bicycle without wearing a helmet.
W: Some riders don't even follow basic traffic rules.
M: What do you mean by that?
W: These days many people ride electric bicycles on sidewalks.
M: Yes, it's so dangerous.
W: Right. There should be stricter rules about riding electric bicycles.
M: I totally agree with you.

해석
여: Brian, 네가 전기 자전거를 사는 것을 생각 중이라고 들었어.
남: 응, 맞아.
여: 잘됐네. 하지만 그것을 탈 때 조심해.
남: 그래, 무슨 말인지 알겠어. 여기 오는 길에 헬멧을 쓰지 않고 전기 자전거를 타는 남자를 봤어.
여: 일부 탑승자들은 기본적인 교통 규정을 따르지도 않아.
남: 그게 무슨 말이야?
여: 요즘 많은 사람들이 보도에서 전기 자전거를 타잖아.
남: 그래, 그것은 너무 위험해.
여: 맞아. 전기 자전거를 타는 것에 관한 더 엄격한 규정이 있어야 해.
남: 전적으로 네 말에 동의해.

① 전기 자전거 이용 전에 배터리 상태를 점검하여야 한다.
☑ ② 전기 자전거 운행에 관한 규정이 더 엄격해야 한다.
③ 전기 자전거의 속도 규정에 대한 논의가 필요하다.
④ 전기 자전거 구입 시 가격을 고려해야 한다.
⑤ 전기 자전거 이용 시 헬멧을 착용해야 한다.

03 여자가 하는 말의 요지

정답률 85% ▶ 정답 ⑤

W: Hello, this is your student counselor, Susan Smith. You might be worried about your new school life as a freshman. You have a lot of things to do in the beginning of the year. Today, I'm going to give you a tip about time management. Make a to-do list! Write down the tasks you have to do on a list and check off what you finish, one by one. By doing this, you won't miss the things you need to do. Using a to-do list will help you manage your time efficiently. Good luck to you and don't forget to start today.

해석
여: 안녕하세요, 저는 학생 상담사인 Susan Smith입니다. 여러분은 신입생으로서 새로운 학교 생활에 대해 걱정할지도 모릅니다. 여러분은 연초에 해야 할 일이 많습니다. 오늘, 저는 여러분에게 시간 관리에 대한 조언을 해 드릴 것입니다. 할 일 목록을 만드세요! 여러분이 해야 할 일을 목록에 적고 끝마친 일에 하나씩 확인 표시를 하세요. 이렇게 함으로써, 여러분은 해야 할 일들을 놓치지 않을 것입니다. 할 일 목록을 사용하는 것은 여러분이 시간을 효율적으로 관리하는 데 도움을 줄 것입니다. 행운을 빌며 오늘부터 시작하는 것을 잊지 마세요.

① 학업 목표를 분명히 설정하는 것이 필요하다.
② 친구와의 협력은 학교생활의 중요한 덕목이다.
③ 과제 제출 마감 기한을 확인하고 준수해야 한다.
④ 적절한 휴식은 성공적인 과업 수행의 핵심 요소이다.
☑ ⑤ 할 일의 목록을 활용하는 것이 시간 관리에 유용하다.

문제 풀이
학생 상담사로서 신입생의 학교 생활에 대해 조언하는 여자는 해야 할 일들을 놓치지 않기 위해 할 일 목록을 만들면 해야 할 일들을 놓치지 않고 시간을 효율적으로 관리할 수 있다고 말한다. 따라서 답은 ⑤ '할 일의 목록을 활용하는 것이 시간 관리에 유용하다.'이다.

04 그림에서 대화의 내용과 일치하지 않는 것
정답률 85% ▶ 정답 ⑤

M: Hi, Amy. I heard that you've joined the English Newspaper Club.
영자 신문 동아리

W: Yes, Tom. I went to the club room yesterday and took a picture of
~의 사진을 찍었다(take a picture of)
it. Look.

M: Wow, the place looks nice. I like the lockers on the left.
사물함들   왼쪽에

W: Yes, they're good. We also have a star-shaped mirror on the wall.
별 모양의   거울

M: It looks cool. What's that on the bookshelf?
책장

W: Oh, that's the trophy my club won for 'Club of the Year'.
트로피   수상했다(win)

M: You must be very proud of it. There's also a computer on the right
~을 매우 자랑스러워하다   ~의 오른쪽에
side of the room.

W: Yeah, we use the computer when we need it.

M: Great. I can see a newspaper on the table.

W: Yes, it was published last December.
발행되었다(publish: 발행하다)

해석
남: 안녕, Amy. 네가 영자 신문 동아리에 가입했다고 들었어.
여: 응, Tom. 나는 어제 동아리방에 가서 그것의 사진을 찍었어. 봐.
남: 와, 장소가 좋아 보이네. 나는 왼쪽에 있는 사물함이 마음에 들어.
여: 맞아, 그것들은 괜찮아. 벽에는 별 모양의 거울도 있어.
남: 멋져 보이네. 책장 위에 있는 저것은 뭐니?
여: 오, 우리 동아리가 '올해의 동아리'로 수상한 트로피야.
남: 너는 그것을 매우 자랑스러워하겠구나. 방의 오른쪽에 컴퓨터도 있어.
여: 그래, 우리는 필요할 때 그 컴퓨터를 사용해.
남: 좋네. 테이블 위에 신문이 보여.
여: 응, 그것은 작년 12월에 발행되었어.

05 남자가 할 일
정답률 90% ▶ 정답 ②

W: Mike, I think we've got most of the camping supplies ready now.
캠핑 용품들

M: Yeah, the tent, sleeping bags, and cooking tools are all set.
침낭들   조리 도구들   모두 준비된

W: Perfect. I bought some easy-to-cook meals and snacks for us.
간편식들   간식들

M: Great. What about some warm clothes? It might get cold at night.
따뜻한 옷   추워지다

W: I've packed some warm jackets for us, too. Anything else we need
챙겼다(pack)
to consider?
고려하다

M: We need something fun for the camping night. I already packed
재미있는
some books to read.

W: How about playing board games?
보드 게임을

M: Nice. I have a chess set at home.
체스 세트

W: Cool, can you bring it?
가져오다

M: Of course! I'll take it with me.
가져가다

해석
여: Mike, 이제 캠핑 용품 대부분이 준비가 된 것 같아.
남: 그래, 텐트, 침낭, 그리고 조리 도구가 모두 준비되어 있어.
여: 완벽해. 나는 우리를 위한 간편식과 간식을 좀 샀어.
남: 좋아. 따뜻한 옷은 어떠니? 밤에 추워질 수도 있어.
여: 내가 우리를 위한 따뜻한 재킷도 챙겼어. 우리가 또 고려해야 할 것이 있니?

남: 우리는 캠핑하는 밤을 위한 재미있는 무언가가 필요해. 나는 이미 읽을 책을 챙겼어.
여: 보드 게임을 하는 건 어때?
남: 좋아. 집에 체스 세트가 있어.
여: 잘됐네, 그것을 가져올 수 있어?
남: 물론이지! 내가 가져갈게.

① 따뜻한 옷 챙기기
✓ 체스 세트 가져가기
③ 읽을 책 고르기
④ 간편식 구매하기
⑤ 침낭 준비하기

06 여자가 지불할 금액
정답률 85% ▶ 정답 ③

M: Hello, what can I help you with today?

W: Hi! I want to buy some fruit and vegetables. What's fresh today?
신선한

M: We just got some apples in.
사과들

W: How much are they?

M: They are ten dollars for one bag.
한 봉지

W: Fantastic! I'll take two bags of apples.

M: Okay, what else do you need?

W: I'd like to buy some carrots, too.
당근들

M: The carrots are five dollars for one bag. How many do you need?

W: I need two bags of carrots.

M: Okay, you need two bags of apples and two bags of carrots.

W: Right. And I have a coupon. I can get a discount with this, right?
쿠폰   할인을 받다

M: Yes. You can get a ten percent discount off the total price.
총액에서

W: Good. Here's the coupon and my credit card.

해석
남: 안녕하세요, 오늘은 무엇을 도와드릴까요?
여: 안녕하세요! 과일과 채소를 좀 사고 싶은데요. 오늘은 어떤 게 신선한가요?
남: 방금 사과가 들어왔어요.
여: 얼마죠?
남: 한 봉지에 10달러예요.
여: 환상적이네요! 사과 두 봉지를 살게요.
남: 네, 그 밖에 무엇이 더 필요하신가요?
여: 당근도 좀 사고 싶어요.
남: 당근은 한 봉지에 5달러예요. 얼마나 필요하신가요?
여: 당근 두 봉지가 필요해요.
남: 네, 사과 두 봉지와 당근 두 봉지가 필요하시군요.
여: 맞아요. 그리고 저는 쿠폰이 있어요. 이것으로 할인을 받을 수 있어요, 그렇죠?
남: 네. 총액에서 10퍼센트 할인을 받으실 수 있어요.
여: 좋네요. 여기 쿠폰과 제 신용카드를 드릴게요.

① $15   ② $20
✓ $27   ④ $30
⑤ $33

문제 풀이
한 봉지에 10달러인 사과 두 봉지와 5달러인 당근 두 봉지를 사면 총액은 30달러이다. 쿠폰을 사용하면 10퍼센트 할인을 받을 수 있다고 했으므로, 여자가 지불할 금액은 30달러에서 3달러가 할인된 27달러이다. 따라서 답은 ③ '$27'이다.

07 남자가 체육 대회 연습을 할 수 없는 이유
정답률 90% ▶ 정답 ⑤

W: Hey, Jake! How was your math test yesterday?
수학 시험

M: Better than I expected.
예상했다(expect)

W: That's great. Let's go and practice for Sports Day.
연습하다   체육 대회

M: I'm so sorry but I can't make it.
(모임 등에) 가다

W: Come on, Jake! Sports Day is just around the corner.
얼마 남지 않은

M: I know. That's why I brought my soccer shoes.
축구화

W: Then, why can't you practice today? Do you have a club interview?
M: No, I already had the interview last week.
W: Then, does your leg still hurt?
M: Not really, it's okay, now. Actually, I have to attend a family dinner gathering tonight for my mother's birthday.
W: Oh, that's important! Family always comes first. Are you available tomorrow, then?
M: Sure. Let's make up for the missed practice.

해석

여: 안녕, Jake! 어제 수학 시험은 어땠니?
남: 예상했던 것보다 더 좋았어.
여: 잘됐네. 가서 체육 대회를 위한 연습을 하자.
남: 정말 미안한데 나는 갈 수 없어.
여: 제발, Jake! 체육 대회가 얼마 남지 않았어.
남: 알아. 그래서 축구화를 가져온 거야.
여: 그럼, 오늘 왜 연습을 할 수 없는 거야? 동아리 면접이니?
남: 아니, 이미 지난주에 면접을 봤어.
여: 그럼, 다리가 아직도 아픈 거야?
남: 별로 그렇진 않아, 지금은 괜찮아. 사실, 오늘 밤에 어머니 생신을 위한 가족 저녁 식사 모임에 참석해야 해.
여: 오, 그건 중요하지! 가족이 항상 최우선이야. 그럼 내일은 시간이 있니?
남: 물론이야. 놓친 연습을 보충하자.

① 시험공부를 해야 해서
② 동아리 면접이 있어서
③ 축구화를 가져오지 않아서
④ 다리가 완전히 회복되지 않아서
☑ 가족 식사 모임에 참석해야 해서

08 Science Open Lab Program에 관해 언급되지 않은 것
정답률 85% ▶ 정답 ④

W: Hey, Chris. Have you heard about the Science Open Lab Program?
M: Yes, I heard about it. But I don't know what it is exactly.
W: In that program, we can design any science experiment we want.
M: That sounds pretty cool. Do you want to join the program?
W: Sure, it's only for freshmen like us. Let's join it together.
M: Great! Do we need to buy some materials for experiments?
W: No, they'll prepare everything for us. We just need to send the application form online.
M: When is the deadline for applying?
W: It's tomorrow. We need to hurry.
M: Oh, I see. Is there any special prize?
W: Yes. I heard they're giving out prizes for the most creative projects.
M: Perfect! I'm so excited.

해석

여: 안녕, Chris. Science Open Lab Program(과학 연구실 체험 프로그램)에 대해 들어 본 적이 있니?
남: 응, 들어 봤어. 하지만 정확히 무엇인지는 모르겠어.
여: 그 프로그램에서, 우리는 우리가 원하는 어떤 과학 실험이든 설계할 수 있어.
남: 아주 멋진 것 같아. 그 프로그램에 참가하고 싶니?
여: 물론이지, 그것은 우리 같은 신입생만을 위한 거야. 같이 참가하자.
남: 좋아! 우리가 실험 재료를 사야 하니?
여: 아니, 우리를 위해 다 준비해 줄 거야. 우리는 지원서를 온라인으로 보내기만 하면 돼.
남: 지원 마감일은 언제야?
여: 내일이야. 우리 서둘러야 해.
남: 오, 그렇구나. 특별상은 있어?
여: 응. 가장 창의적인 프로젝트에 상을 준다고 들었어.
남: 완벽해! 정말 기대된다.

① 지원 가능 학년　　　　② 실험 재료 구입 필요성
③ 지원서 제출 기한　　　☑ 참가 인원수
⑤ 시상 여부

09 Triwood High School Volunteer Program에 관한 내용과 일치하지 않는 것
정답률 90% ▶ 정답 ④

W: Hello, students! Are you looking for a chance to help others? Then, I recommend you to join Triwood High School Volunteer Program to help senior citizens. You're supposed to help the senior citizens face-to-face. You teach them how to use their smartphones for things such as sending text messages or taking pictures. You will also teach seniors how to use various apps. The program will require volunteers to participate for two hours every Saturday. If you are interested in joining our program, please send us an application form through email.

해석

여: 안녕하세요, 학생 여러분! 여러분은 다른 사람들을 도울 기회를 찾고 있나요? 그렇다면, 저는 여러분에게 노인들을 도와주는 Triwood High School Volunteer Program(Triwood 고등학교 자원봉사 프로그램)에 참가하는 것을 추천합니다. 여러분은 대면으로 노인들을 도울 예정입니다. 여러분은 그들에게 문자 메시지를 보내거나 사진을 찍는 것과 같은 일들을 위해 스마트폰을 사용하는 방법을 가르칩니다. 또한 노인들에게 다양한 앱을 사용하는 방법도 가르칠 것입니다. 그 프로그램은 자원봉사자들이 매주 토요일에 두 시간 동안 참여하도록 요구할 것입니다. 저희 프로그램에 참가하는 것에 관심이 있다면, 우리에게 이메일로 신청서를 보내주세요.

① 노인을 도와주는 봉사 활동이다.
② 봉사자는 대면으로 활동한다.
③ 스마트폰 사용 방법 교육을 한다.
☑ 봉사자는 매주 토요일에 세 시간씩 참여한다.
⑤ 지원자는 이메일로 참가 신청서를 보내야 한다.

10 표에서 여자가 주문할 휴대용 선풍기
정답률 85% ▶ 정답 ③

M: Sophie, what are you looking for?
W: I'm trying to choose one of these portable fans as a gift for my friend Cathy.
M: Oh, let me help you. How many speed options do you think she would want?
W: She would like it if the fan has more than two options.
M: Okay, then, what color do you have in mind?
W: Cathy's old one was white. I want to choose a different color.
M: Good idea. Do you want an LED display to show the remaining battery power?
W: Hmm, I don't think she will need it.
M: You're left with two options. Which one do you prefer?
W: Well, I'll take the cheaper one.

해석

남: Sophie, 무엇을 찾고 있니?
여: 내 친구 Cathy를 위한 선물로 이 휴대용 선풍기들 중 하나를 고르려고 해.
남: 오, 내가 도와줄게. 그녀가 몇 개의 속도 옵션을 원할 것 같니?
여: 선풍기에 두 개 이상의 옵션이 있으면 그녀가 좋아할 거야.
남: 알겠어, 그럼, 너는 어떤 색상을 생각해 두었니?
여: Cathy의 예전 것은 흰색이었어. 나는 다른 색상을 선택하고 싶어.
남: 좋은 생각이야. 배터리 잔량을 보여주는 LED 표시등을 원하니?
여: 흠, 그녀는 그것을 필요로 하지 않을 것 같아.
남: 두 가지 선택지가 남았어. 너는 어떤 것을 선호하니?
여: 음, 더 저렴한 것을 살게.

휴대용 선풍기

	모델	속도 옵션 개수	색상	LED 표시등	가격
①	A	1개	파란색	×	15달러
②	B	3개	흰색	○	26달러
☑	C	3개	노란색	×	31달러
④	D	4개	분홍색	×	37달러
⑤	E	5개	초록색	○	42달러

11 남자의 마지막 말에 대한 여자의 응답

정답률 80% ▶ 정답 ③

M: What's wrong, Jane? You look so upset.
속상한
W: I lost my purse! I have been searching for it for an hour, but I can't
잃어버렸다(lose) ~을 찾고 있었다(search for)
find it.
M: When did you last have it?
마지막으로
W: (I had it before biology class.)
생물학 수업

해석
남: 무슨 일이야, Jane? 매우 속상해 보여.
여: 내 지갑을 잃어버렸어! 한 시간 동안 찾고 있었는데, 찾을 수가 없어.
남: 언제 마지막으로 그것을 가지고 있었니?
여: (나는 생물학 수업 전에 그것을 가지고 있었어.)
① 나는 네가 그것을 찾도록 도울 수 있어.
② 나는 이미 새것을 샀어.
✓나는 생물학 수업 전에 그것을 가지고 있었어.
④ 너는 경찰에 신고해야 해.
⑤ 그것은 아빠가 주신 생일 선물이었어.

12 여자의 마지막 말에 대한 남자의 응답

정답률 75% ▶ 정답 ⑤

W: Honey, what do you have in mind for lunch this Saturday?
염두에 두다
M: I was thinking we should try the new Italian restaurant.
이탈리아 식당
W: Hmm... I heard that it's hard to make a reservation there these
힘든 예약하다
days.
M: (That's too bad. Why don't we try another restaurant?)

해석
여: 여보, 이번 주 토요일 점심으로 무엇을 염두에 두고 있어요?
남: 새로 생긴 이탈리아 식당에 가봐야겠다고 생각 중이었어요.
여: 흠... 요즘 그곳을 예약하는 게 힘들다고 들었어요.
남: (안타깝네요. 우리 다른 식당에 가보는 게 어때요?)
① 고마워요. 모든 것이 맛있어 보여요.
② 네. 저는 이번 주 토요일에 약속이 있어요.
③ 천만에요. 저는 그것을 아빠의 조리법으로 만들었어요.
④ 좋네요. 몇 시에 예약했어요?
✓안타깝네요. 우리 다른 식당에 가보는 게 어때요?

13 남자의 마지막 말에 대한 여자의 응답

정답률 85% ▶ 정답 ②

M: Mom! I've started to record audiobooks for kids.
녹음하다 오디오북들
W: That's great! How did you get involved in that?
~에 참여하게 되다(involve: 참여시키다)
M: My teacher told me that a local organization is looking for students
지역 단체
to record audiobooks.
W: Fantastic! Are you having fun with it?
M: Well, actually, I'm struggling with my voice acting.
고군분투하는(struggle) 목소리 연기
W: Oh? Is that so?
M: Yes, it's a bit challenging to get the right tone for kids.
어려운 ~에게 맞는 어조로 말하다
W: I'm sure you'll get better with practice soon.
좋아지다 연습
M: Thanks. I'm trying my best.
W: That's wonderful. Anything I can help you with?
M: Can you recommend a good book for my audiobook recording?
추천하다
W: (Sure. Let's choose one from your old children's books.)

해석
남: 엄마! 저는 아이들을 위한 오디오북을 녹음하기 시작했어요.
여: 잘됐네! 어떻게 그 일에 참여하게 되었니?
남: 선생님께서 한 지역 단체에서 오디오북을 녹음할 학생들을 찾고 있다고 말씀하셨어요.
여: 멋지다! 그 일은 재미있니?
남: 음, 사실, 목소리 연기 때문에 고군투 중이에요.
여: 오? 그러니?

남: 네, 아이들에게 맞는 어조로 말하는 것이 조금 어려워요.
여: 연습하면 곧 좋아질 것이라고 확신해.
남: 감사해요. 저는 최선을 다하고 있어요.
여: 대단하구나. 내가 도와줄 일이 있을까?
남: 오디오북 녹음에 좋은 책을 추천해 주시겠어요?
여: (물론이지. 너의 오래된 아동용 책에서 하나 골라보자.)

① 문제없어. 너는 그 단체에서 다른 프로젝트를 찾을 수 있어.
✓물론이지. 너의 오래된 아동용 책에서 하나 골라보자.
③ 축하해. 마침내 너의 첫 오디오북을 만들었구나.
④ 그랬으면 좋겠구나. 너는 멋진 작가가 될 거야.
⑤ 맞아. 아이들은 네가 생각하는 것보다 더 빨리 자라.

문제 풀이
아이들을 위한 오디오북 녹음을 하는 남자는 자신의 도움이 필요한지 묻는 여자에게 좋은 책을 추천해 달라고 부탁한다. 이에 대한 여자의 응답은 ② 'Sure. Let's choose one from your old children's books.(물론이지. 너의 오래된 아동용 책에서 하나 골라보자.)'가 가장 적절하다.

14 여자의 마지막 말에 대한 남자의 응답

정답률 85% ▶ 정답 ①

W: Hi, Fred. What should we do for our history project?
역사 과제
M: Actually, I was thinking about it. Why don't we divide the roles for
나누다 역할들
the project?
W: Okay. Good idea. We have the research part, the visual material
조사 시각 자료
part, and the presentation part.
발표
M: Hmm, is there any part you want to take on?
맡다
W: Well, I would like to do the research. I've been collecting news
articles about history.
뉴스 기사들
M: Excellent. You are good at gathering necessary information.
모으는 것을 잘하다 필요한
(be good at V-ing: ~하는 것을 잘하다, gather: 모으다)
W: Thanks. Can you handle the visual material?
다루다
M: Okay. I'll take care of it. I have done it before.
~을 맡다
W: All right. Then, the only part left is the presentation.
남은(leave: 남기다)
M: (Well, let's do the presentation together.)

해석
여: 안녕, Fred. 우리의 역사 과제를 위해 우리는 무엇을 해야 할까?
남: 사실, 나는 그것에 대해 생각 중이었어. 과제를 위한 역할을 나누는 게 어떠니?
여: 알겠어. 좋은 생각이야. 우리에게는 조사 부분, 시각 자료 부분, 그리고 발표 부분이 있어.
남: 흠, 네가 맡고 싶은 부분이 있어?
여: 음, 나는 조사를 하고 싶어. 역사에 관한 뉴스 기사들을 수집해 왔거든.
남: 아주 좋아. 너는 필요한 정보를 모으는 것을 잘하잖아.
여: 고마워. 네가 시각 자료를 다룰 수 있겠니?
남: 그래. 내가 그것을 맡을게. 전에 해 본 적이 있어.
여: 알겠어. 그럼, 유일하게 남은 부분은 발표구나.
남: (음, 발표를 같이 하자.)
✓음, 발표를 같이 하자.
② 힘내! 나는 네가 최선을 다했다는 것을 알아.
③ 응, 나는 과학에서 좋은 점수를 받았어.
④ 와! 정말 훌륭한 발표였어.
⑤ 맞아. 나는 이미 과제를 끝냈어.

15 다음 상황에서 Robert가 Michelle에게 할 말

정답률 70% ▶ 정답 ①

W: Robert and Michelle are attending their high school orientation.
참석하고 있다(attend) 예비 교육
After short greetings, the teacher begins to explain student
간단한 인사 설명하기 시작하다
(begin to V: ~하기 시작하다, explain: 설명하다)
clubs, school activities, and school facilities. Robert is focusing
활동들 시설들
very carefully on the explanation. However, while writing down
~에 매우 주의 깊게 집중하고 있다 적는 도중에(while: ~하는 도중에,
(focus on: ~에 집중하다, carefully: 주의 깊게) write down: 적다)
important things about the school library, Robert drops his pen.
학교 도서관 떨어뜨리다

Trying to find his pen, Robert misses important information about
놓치다
the opening hours of the library, so now, Robert wants to ask
개방 시간
Michelle when the library is open. In this situation, what would
Robert most likely say to Michelle?
Robert: (When can I use the library?)

해석
여: Robert와 Michelle은 고등학교 예비 교육에 참석하고 있다. 간단한 인사 후에, 선생님은 학생 동아리, 학교 활동, 그리고 학교 시설에 대해 설명하기 시작한다. Robert는 설명에 매우 주의 깊게 집중하고 있다. 하지만 학교 도서관에 대한 중요한 사항들을 적는 도중에, Robert는 자신의 펜을 떨어뜨린다. 펜을 찾으려고 하다가, Robert는 도서관의 개방 시간에 대한 중요한 정보를 놓쳐서, 이제 Robert는 Michelle에게 언제 도서관이 문을 여는지 묻고 싶어 한다. 이러한 상황에서, Robert는 Michelle에게 뭐라고 말하겠는가?
Robert: (언제 도서관을 이용할 수 있니?)

☑①언제 도서관을 이용할 수 있니?
②어디에서 도서관을 찾을 수 있니?
③어떻게 독서 동아리에 가입할 수 있니?
④왜 너는 도서관에 가고 싶어 하니?
⑤분실물 보관소는 몇 시에 문을 여니?

16~17 1지문 2문항

M: Hello, listeners. Thank you for tuning in to our Happy Radio Show.
청취해
(tune in to: ~을 청취하다)
Are you taking good care of your health in the early spring? Today, I
~을 잘 돌보는   이른 봄
(take care of: ~을 돌보다)
want to recommend some foods that can reduce the symptoms of
추천하다   증상들
a cough. Ginger is a popular home remedy for coughs. A cup of hot
기침   생강   민간 요법(remedy: 치료법)
ginger tea can be helpful for reducing your cough. Lemon is a rich
도움이 되는   레몬
source of vitamin C. Lemon tea can help you relieve your cough.
공급원
Surprisingly, pineapple is another excellent food to help relieve a
놀랍게도   파인애플   완화하다
cough. When you are suffering from a cough, eating bananas also
~으로 고통을 받고 있다(suffer from)
helps to get rid of the symptoms more easily. These foods are rich
~을 없애다
in vitamins and they are recommended for people suffering from a
cough. I hope you have a healthy week.

해석
남: 안녕하세요, 청취자 여러분. Happy Radio Show를 청취해 주셔서 감사합니다. 여러분은 이른 봄에 건강 잘 돌보고 계신가요? 오늘, 저는 기침의 증상을 감소시킬 수 있는 몇 가지 음식들을 추천하고자 합니다. 생강은 기침에 대한 인기 있는 민간 요법입니다. 뜨거운 생강차 한 잔은 기침을 줄이는 데 도움이 될 수 있습니다. 레몬은 비타민 C의 풍부한 공급원입니다. 레몬차는 기침을 완화하는 데 도움을 줄 수 있습니다. 놀랍게도, 파인애플은 기침을 완화하는 데 도움을 주는 또 다른 훌륭한 음식입니다. 기침으로 고통을 받고 있을 때, 바나나를 먹는 것도 증상을 더 쉽게 없애는 데 도움이 됩니다. 이러한 음식들은 비타민이 풍부하고 기침으로 고통을 받는 사람들에게 추천됩니다. 여러분이 건강한 한 주를 보내시길 바랍니다.

16 남자가 하는 말의 주제   정답률 85%   ▶ 정답 ①

☑①기침을 완화하는 데 유용한 음식들
②적절한 음식 조리법의 중요성
③기침 증상의 다양한 원인들
④열에 대한 전통적인 민간 요법들
⑤날씨와 기침 사이의 연관성

17 언급된 음식 재료가 아닌 것   정답률 85%   ▶ 정답 ④

①생강   ②레몬
③파인애플   ☑④꿀
⑤바나나

---

23 2024년 6월 학력평가

01	③	02	①	03	③	04	⑤	05	④
06	③	07	⑤	08	②	09	⑤	10	④
11	①	12	③	13	⑤	14	②	15	③
16	③	17	④								

01 여자가 하는 말의 목적   정답률 90%   ▶ 정답 ③

[Chime bell rings.]
W: Attention, everyone! Our CEO, Mr. Wayne, has prepared a snack
스낵바
bar to celebrate our success on last month's project. Please come
축하하다   성공
down to the lobby and enjoy some delicious snacks. They'll be
로비   맛있는
available until 4 p.m. You'll be impressed by the amazing variety,
이용 가능한   ~에 감동하다   다양함
(impress: 감동을 주다)
from crispy fries and hot dogs to fresh lemonade and coffee. It'd
바삭바삭한   신선한
be great if you could bring your own personal cups for the drinks.
개인 컵들
See you there.

해석
[차임벨이 울린다.]
여: 주목해 주십시오, 여러분! 우리의 CEO인 Wayne 씨가 지난달 프로젝트의 성공을 축하하기 위해 스낵바를 준비했습니다. 로비로 내려오셔서 맛있는 간식을 즐기십시오. 오후 4시까지 이용 가능합니다. 여러분은 바삭바삭한 감자튀김과 핫도그부터 신선한 레모네이드와 커피까지 놀라울 정도의 다양함에 감동할 것입니다. 음료를 위해 자신의 개인 컵을 가지고 오시면 좋을 것 같습니다. 거기서 뵙겠습니다.

①친환경 제품 사용을 홍보하려고
②음식 대접에 대한 감사를 표하려고
☑③간식이 마련되어 있음을 안내하려고
④휴식 시간이 변경되었음을 공지하려고
⑤구내식당 메뉴에 관한 의견을 구하려고

02 남자의 의견   정답률 85%   ▶ 정답 ①

M: Hi, Pamela. Did you finish your history assignment?
역사 과제
W: Yes, Dad. I finished it quite easily with the help of AI.
쉽게   ~의 도움으로
M: Really? Do you mean you used an artificial-intelligence website?
인공 지능 웹 사이트
W: Yeah. I typed in the questions and AI gave me the answers right
~을 입력했다   질문들   답변들
away.
M: Well, is it a good idea to do your homework that way?
과제
W: Why not? It saves a lot of time and gives me just the information
절약하다   정보
I need.
M: I used to think so, too. But after trying it a couple of times, I found
예전에는 생각했다   두어 번
(used to V: 예전에는 ~했다)
out AI sometimes uses false information as well.
틀린
W: Really? I didn't know that.
M: Yeah, you shouldn't blindly trust the answers from AI.
맹목적으로 믿다
W: Okay. I'll keep that in mind next time.
그것을 명심하다(keep A in mind: A를 명심하다)

해석
남: 안녕, Pamela. 역사 과제는 다 했니?
여: 네, 아빠. AI의 도움으로 매우 쉽게 끝냈어요.
남: 정말? 인공 지능 웹 사이트를 이용했다는 말이니?
여: 네. 질문을 입력하니까 AI가 바로 답변을 해 줬어요.
남: 음, 과제를 그런 방식으로 하는 것이 좋은 생각일까?
여: 왜 안 돼요? 그것은 많은 시간을 절약하고 제가 필요로 하는 정보만 알려 주잖아요.

남: 나도 예전에는 그렇게 생각했어. 그런데 그것을 두어 번 사용해 본 후에, AI가 가끔 틀린 정보도 이용한다는 것을 알게 됐어.

여: 정말이에요? 저는 그것을 몰랐어요.

남: 그래, AI의 답변을 맹목적으로 믿으면 안돼.

여: 알겠어요. 다음에는 그것을 명심할게요.

☑① 인공 지능에서 얻은 정보를 맹목적으로 믿어서는 안 된다.
② 출처를 밝히지 않고 타인의 표현을 인용해서는 안 된다.
③ 인공 지능의 도움을 통해 과제물의 질을 높일 수 있다.
④ 과제를 할 때 본인의 생각이 들어가는 것이 중요하다.
⑤ 기술의 변화에 맞추어 작업 방식을 바꿀 필요가 있다.

문제 풀이

남자는 여자에게 AI를 사용해 본 자신의 경험을 말하며 AI가 잘못된 정보를 제공하는 경우도 있으므로 AI의 답변을 전적으로 신뢰해서는 안 된다고 조언하고 있다. 따라서 답은 ① '인공 지능에서 얻은 정보를 맹목적으로 믿어서는 안 된다.'이다.

---

03 여자가 하는 말의 요지

정답률 85%
▶ 정답 ③

W: Hello, listeners. This is Kelly Watson's *Love Yourself*. Have you ever thought about your social media use? Social media lets you stay connected with others easily. However, it can make you compare yourself with others, too. For example, a celebrity's post about going on a luxurious trip may make you jealous. Continuously making such comparisons stops you from looking at yourself the way you truly are. You might think, "Why can't I have a better life?" and feel small about yourself. As you can see, social media can have a negative effect on your self-esteem. I'll be right back with some tips for healthy social media use.

해석

여: 안녕하세요, 청취자 여러분. Kelly Watson의 'Love Yourself'입니다. 여러분은 소셜 미디어 사용에 대해 생각해 보신 적이 있나요? 소셜 미디어는 여러분이 다른 사람들과 쉽게 연결될 수 있게 해 줍니다. 하지만 그것은 여러분 자신과 다른 사람들을 비교하게 만들 수도 있습니다. 예를 들어, 호화로운 여행을 가는 것에 대한 유명인의 게시물은 여러분이 질투하게 만들지도 모릅니다. 끊임없이 그러한 비교를 하는 것은 여러분이 진정으로 있는 그대로의 자신을 바라보는 것을 막습니다. 여러분은 "왜 나는 더 나은 삶을 살 수 없을까?"라고 생각하고, 자신에 대해 초라한 기분이 들 수도 있습니다. 보시다시피, 소셜 미디어는 여러분의 자존감에 부정적인 영향을 미칠 수 있습니다. 저는 건강한 소셜 미디어 사용을 위한 몇 가지 조언을 가지고 바로 돌아오겠습니다.

① 소셜 미디어는 원만한 대인관계 유지에 도움이 된다.
② 온라인에서는 자아가 다양한 모습으로 표출될 수 있다.
☑③ 소셜 미디어는 자존감에 부정적인 영향을 줄 수 있다.
④ 친밀한 관계일수록 상대의 언행에 쉽게 영향을 받는다.
⑤ 유명인 사생활 보호의 중요성은 종종 간과된다.

---

04 그림에서 대화의 내용과 일치하지 않는 것

정답률 90%
▶ 정답 ⑤

W: Honey, I love this park!

M: Me, too. This park is so cool. But, oh, look! What's that in the tree?

W: It's just a kite stuck in the tree's branches.

M: I guess some kids went home without their kite.

W: By the same tree, a woman is walking her dog. They look so lovely.

M: What about the little girl beside her?

W: You mean the girl holding balloons in her hand?

M: Right. She's adorable. And look there! Did you notice a basket full of flowers on the picnic mat?

W: Yes, right. It adds a touch of romance to the scene.
(touch: 기운, romance: 설렘)

M: I think so, too. Oh, there's a fountain. Next to it, a man is playing the violin.

W: The melody is beautiful. I'm glad we came here.

해석

여: 여보, 저는 이 공원이 정말 좋아요!

남: 저도 그래요. 이 공원은 아주 멋져요. 그런데, 오, 봐요! 나무에 있는 저것은 뭐죠?

여: 그냥 나뭇가지에 낀 연이네요.

남: 몇몇 아이들이 연 없이 집에 갔나 봐요.

여: 같은 나무 옆에, 한 여자가 그녀의 개를 산책시키고 있네요. 그들은 정말 사랑스러워 보여요.

남: 그녀의 옆에 있는 여자아이는 어때요?

여: 손에 풍선들을 들고 있는 여자아이 말이에요?

남: 맞아요. 사랑스럽네요. 그리고 저기 봐요! 소풍용 돗자리 위에 있는 꽃이 가득 담긴 바구니를 봤어요?

여: 네, 그래요. 그것이 풍경에 설렘의 기운을 더해주네요.

남: 저도 그렇게 생각해요. 오, 분수대가 하나 있네요. 그 옆에서, 한 남자가 바이올린을 연주하고 있어요.

여: 멜로디가 아름답네요. 우리가 여기에 와서 기뻐요.

---

05 남자가 할 일

정답률 75%
▶ 정답 ④

M: Hey, Alice. I applied for the science camp next week. What about you?

W: Me, too. But I didn't know that there were so many things to do before the camp.

M: Right. Would you like to go over my checklist together?

W: Hmm, let's see. Did you upload your introduction video to the website?

M: Yes, I tried to show my interest in science. Oh, hey, have you picked which experiment to work on?

W: Yes. I decided to participate in a biology experiment.
(decide to V: ~하기로 결정하다, participate in: ~에 참가하다)

M: Me, too. Wasn't it difficult to make a plan for your experiment?

W: Actually, I haven't even started yet because I've never written a plan for a biology experiment before.

M: I'll show you mine after class. Maybe you can get some ideas.

W: Really? That'd be great. See you soon.

해석

남: 안녕, Alice. 나는 다음 주에 있을 과학 캠프에 지원했어. 너는 어때?

여: 나도 했어. 그런데 캠프 전에 해야 할 일이 정말 많다는 것을 몰랐어.

남: 맞아. 내 체크리스트를 함께 검토해 볼래?

여: 흠, 어디 보자. 웹 사이트에 자기 소개 영상을 업로드했니?

남: 응, 나는 과학에 대한 관심을 보여주려고 노력했어. 오, 얘, 너는 어떤 실험을 진행할지 결정했니?

여: 응. 나는 생물학 실험에 참가하기로 결정했어.

남: 나도 그래. 실험을 위한 계획서를 만드는 것이 어렵지 않았니?

여: 사실, 이전에 생물학 실험을 위한 계획서를 작성해 본 적이 한 번도 없어서 아직 시작도 못했어.

남: 수업 후에 내 것을 보여줄게. 어쩌면 아이디어를 좀 얻을 수 있을 거야.

여: 정말? 그러면 좋을 것 같아. 곧 보자.

① 과학 캠프 지원하기
② 참가 실험 결정하기
③ 체크리스트 작성하기
✔ 실험 계획서 보여주기
⑤ 자기 소개 영상 촬영하기

06 여자가 지불할 금액

정답률 50%

▶ 정답 ③

W: Hi, I'm looking for a backpack for my niece. She's going on a
　　　　　　　　　　　　배낭　　　　　(여자) 조카
camping trip this summer.
캠핑 여행

M: Great. We have this blue backpack that has multiple pockets.
　　　　　　　　　　　　　　　　　　　　　　많은　　　주머니들

W: It looks stylish and functional. How much is it?
　　　　　　멋진　　　실용적인

M: It's $50, but we have a special discount only on backpacks today.
　　　　　　　　　　　　　　　특별 할인
Every backpack is 10% off.

W: That's a great deal! I'll take it.

M: I'm sure your niece will love it. Do you need anything else?

W: Yes. I like this camping hat. How much is it?
　　　　　　　　　캠핑 모자

M: It's $10, not on sale, though.
　　　　　　　　할인 중인

W: That's okay. I'll take it as well.

M: Gift wrapping for them would be a total of $5. Would you like gift
　　선물 포장
wrapping?

W: Yes, please. Here's my credit card.

해석

여: 안녕하세요, 저는 조카를 위한 배낭을 찾고 있어요. 이번 여름에 캠핑 여행을 갈 예정이
거든요.
남: 멋지네요. 많은 주머니가 있는 이 파란색 배낭이 있습니다.
여: 멋지고 실용적인 것처럼 보이네요. 얼마인가요?
남: 50달러인데, 오늘은 배낭만 특별 할인을 해 드립니다. 모든 배낭이 10% 할인됩니다.
여: 잘됐네요! 그것을 살게요.
남: 조카분께서 분명 좋아하실 겁니다. 더 필요하신 것이 있습니까?
여: 네. 이 캠핑 모자가 마음에 드네요. 얼마인가요?
남: 10달러인데, 할인 중은 아닙니다.
여: 괜찮아요. 그것도 살게요.
남: 구매 상품에 대한 선물 포장 비용은 총 5달러입니다. 선물 포장을 해 드릴까요?
여: 네, 부탁드려요. 여기 제 신용카드가 있어요.

① $50　　　　　　　　　　　② $55
✔ $60　　　　　　　　　　　④ $65
⑤ $70

문제 풀이
파란색 배낭의 가격은 50달러인데 10% 할인을 받을 수 있다고 했으므로 실제 지불 가격은
45달러이다. 10달러인 캠핑 모자는 할인 중이 아니므로, 파란색 배낭과 캠핑 모자를 구매하
면 총액은 55달러이다. 여기에 선물 포장 비용 5달러를 포함하면 여자가 지불할 금액은 60달
러가 된다. 따라서 답은 ③ '$60'이다.

07 남자가 마술쇼에 갈 수 없는 이유

정답률 90%

▶ 정답 ⑤

W: Hi, Chris. How was your weekend?

M: Hello, Martha. I went to a rock concert and had fun. How about
　　　　　　　　　　　　　　　록 콘서트
you?

W: I've been preparing for tomorrow's club festival.
　　　　　　　　　　　　　　　　　동아리 축제

M: Oh, what kind of activity are you preparing for the festival?
　　　　　　　　　　활동

W: Our club members are presenting a magic show. Come and watch
　　　　　　　　　　보여줄 예정이다(present)　마술쇼
us at 4 p.m. tomorrow if you are available.
　　　　　　　　　　　　　　　　시간이 있는

M: I'd love to, but I can't make it.
　　　　　　　　　(모임 등에) 가다

W: Why? It'd be nice to have you there.

M: I'm sorry, but I have to attend my uncle's birthday party.
　　　　　　　　　　　　　　참석하다　　　　생일 파티

W: Oh, I understand. I hope you have a wonderful time with your
family.

M: Thank you, I will.

해석

여: 안녕, Chris. 주말은 어땠어?
남: 안녕, Martha. 나는 록 콘서트에 가서 재미있게 놀았어. 너는 어때?
여: 나는 내일 있을 동아리 축제를 준비하고 있었어.
남: 오, 축제를 위해 어떤 종류의 활동을 준비하고 있니?
여: 우리 동아리 회원들이 마술쇼를 보여줄 예정이야. 시간이 있으면 내일 오후 4시에 와서
봐.
남: 그러고 싶지만, 갈 수가 없어.
여: 왜? 네가 거기에 오면 좋을 텐데.
남: 미안하지만, 삼촌의 생일 파티에 참석해야 해.
여: 오, 이해해. 가족과 함께 즐거운 시간을 보내기를 바랄게.
남: 고마워, 그렇게.

① 록 콘서트에 가야 해서
② 다른 학교 축제에 가야 해서
③ 가족 중 아픈 사람이 있어서
④ 동아리 축제를 준비해야 해서
✔ 삼촌 생일 파티에 참석해야 해서

08 Victory Marathon에 관해 언급되지 않은 것

정답률 85%

▶ 정답 ②

W: Hey, Alex. Have you seen the announcement for the Victory
　　　　　　　　　　　　　　　　　　발표　　　　　승리 마라톤
Marathon?

M: Not yet, but I'm curious about it. When's the event?
　　　　　　　　궁금한　　　　　　　　　행사

W: It's on Saturday, July 13th.

M: Nice. Where will the race start?
　　　　　　　　경주

W: It will start at William Stadium.

M: Oh, great. How much does it cost to participate?
　　　　　　　　　　　(값·비용이) ~이다　　참가하다

W: It costs $30.

M: That's reasonable. How many participants are they expecting?
　　　합리적인　　　　　　　　참가자들

W: Last year, there were around 5,000. They say they expect about
　　　　　　　　　　　약　　　　　　　　　　　　거의 같은
the same this year.

M: I didn't know that many people love marathons. I'm in!

W: Great. I look forward to running with you.
　　　　　달리기를 기대하다
(look forward to V-ing: ~하기를 기대하다, run: 달리다)

해석

여: 안녕, Alex. Victory Marathon(승리 마라톤)에 대한 발표를 봤니?
남: 아직 못 봤지만, 나는 그것이 궁금해. 행사는 언제니?
여: 7월 13일 토요일이야.
남: 좋아. 경주는 어디에서 시작되니?
여: William Stadium에서 시작될 거야.
남: 오, 잘됐네. 참가비는 얼마야?
여: 30달러야.
남: 합리적이네. 얼마나 많은 참가자를 예상하고 있어?
여: 작년에는, 약 5,000명 정도였어. 올해도 거의 같을 것으로 예상한다고 해.
남: 많은 사람들이 마라톤을 좋아하는 줄 몰랐어. 나도 참여하게!
여: 좋아. 너와 함께 달리기를 기대할게.

① 행사 날짜　　　　　　　✔ 신청 방법
③ 출발 지점　　　　　　　④ 참가비
⑤ 예상 참가 인원

09 Violet Hill Mentorship에 관한 내용과 일치하지 않는 것

정답률 90%

▶ 정답 ⑤

M: Good morning, students of Violet Hill High School. This is
your principal speaking. I'm delighted to announce that the
　　　교장　　　　　　　　　　　　　　　　　　　알리다
annual Violet Hill Mentorship will be held next Friday. Our
매년 열리는　　　　　　　　　　　　　개최되다(hold: 개최하다)
school graduates who are now majoring in English literature,
　　　　　　　　　　　　현재 ~을 전공하고 있다　　영문학
(major in: ~을 전공하다)
bioengineering, and theater and film will be giving some tips on
생명 공학　　　　　　연극영화학　　　　　　　　　　　　　조언들
university life. To register for this event, visit our school website
대학 생활　　　등록하다

and submit two questions you would like to ask them in advance.
The deadline for registration is next Tuesday, so don't wait too
long. And remember, the maximum number of participants for
each major is 30 people. For more information, visit our school
website.

해석

남: 좋은 아침입니다, Violet Hill 고등학교 학생 여러분. 저는 교장입니다. 매년 열리는 Violet
Hill Mentorship이 다음 주 금요일에 개최될 예정이라는 것을 알려드리게 되어 기쁩니다.
현재 영문학, 생명 공학, 연극영화학을 전공하고 있는 우리 학교 졸업생들이 대학 생활에
대한 몇 가지 조언을 해 줄 것입니다. 이 행사에 등록하려면, 학교 웹 사이트를 방문하여
여러분이 그들에게 묻고 싶은 두 가지 질문을 미리 제출하십시오. 등록 마감일은 다음 주
화요일이므로, 너무 오래 기다리지 마십시오. 그리고 기억하십시오, 전공별 최대 참가 인
원은 30명입니다. 더 많은 정보를 원하시면, 학교 웹 사이트를 방문하십시오.

① 다음 주 금요일에 개최될 예정이다.
② 대학 생활에 관한 조언이 제공된다.
③ 신청 시 질문을 미리 제출해야 한다.
④ 신청 마감일은 다음 주 화요일이다.
☑ 전공별 참가 가능한 인원은 20명이다.

10 표에서 두 사람이 구입할 무선 진공청소기 ▶ 정답 ④ 〔정답률 80%〕

M: Honey, look. This website's Summer Sale has just begun.
W: Oh, great. Why don't we buy a new cordless vacuum cleaner?
M: Sure. There are five bestsellers shown here.
W: Let's check the battery life first.
M: I think it should be at least two hours so that we don't have to
charge it as often.
(don't have to V: ~할 필요가 없다, charge: 충전하다)
W: I agree. But let's not spend more than $400 on a vacuum cleaner.
M: Fine. Oh, some of these also have a wet cleaning function.
W: I'd love that. With that function, we can definitely save a lot of time.
M: Okay. What about the color? The white one looks better to me.
W: Right. It'll match the color tone of our living room.
M: Perfect. So, let's buy this one.
W: Great.

해석

남: 여보, 봐요. 이 웹 사이트의 여름 세일이 막 시작됐어요.
여: 오, 잘됐네요. 우리 새로운 무선 진공청소기를 사는 게 어때요?
남: 좋아요. 여기에 가장 잘 팔린 제품 5개가 나와 있어요.
여: 먼저 배터리 수명을 확인해 봐요.
남: 자주 충전할 필요가 없도록 최소한 2시간은 되어야 할 것 같아요.
여: 동의해요. 하지만 진공청소기에 400달러 이상은 쓰지 말아요.
남: 그래요. 오, 이것들 중에 일부는 습식 청소 기능도 있어요.
여: 그거 정말 좋네요. 그 기능을 사용하면, 분명 많은 시간을 절약할 수 있어요.
남: 알겠네요. 색상은 어때요? 흰색이 저는 더 좋아 보여요.
여: 그러네요. 우리 거실의 색조와 어울릴 거예요.
남: 완벽해요. 그럼, 이것을 삽시다.
여: 좋아요.

무선 진공청소기

	모델	배터리 수명	가격	습식 청소	색상
①	A	1시간	300달러	×	빨간색
②	B	2시간	330달러	×	흰색
③	C	2시간	370달러	○	빨간색
☑	D	3시간	390달러	○	흰색
⑤	E	3시간	410달러	○	검은색

11 남자의 마지막 말에 대한 여자의 응답 ▶ 정답 ① 〔정답률 65%〕

M: Mom, I want to have a cat. Have you ever thought about us
adopting a cat?
W: Sweetie, having a pet requires a lot of responsibility.
M: I'm totally ready for it. Mom, we could at least consider it.
W: (Fine. Let's talk about it over dinner.)

해석

남: 엄마, 저는 고양이를 키우고 싶어요. 우리가 고양이를 입양하는 것에 대해 생각해 보신 적
이 있나요?
여: 얘야, 반려동물을 키우는 것은 많은 책임감을 필요로 한단다.
남: 저는 그것에 대해 완전히 준비가 되어 있어요. 엄마, 우리는 적어도 그것을 고려해 볼 수
는 있어요.
여: (좋아. 저녁을 먹으면서 그것에 대해 얘기해 보자.)

☑ 좋아. 저녁을 먹으면서 그것에 대해 얘기해 보자.
② 알겠어. 다음에는 좀 더 책임감을 가지렴.
③ 좋아. 나는 이미 반려동물 사료를 좀 주문했어.
④ 안됐구나. 네 고양이가 빨리 나았으면 좋겠다.
⑤ 미안해. 나는 오늘 밤 네 고양이를 돌봐줄 수 없어.

12 여자의 마지막 말에 대한 남자의 응답 ▶ 정답 ③ 〔정답률 75%〕

W: Jake, I completely forgot about the math assignment. When's the
deadline?
M: You need to submit it by next Tuesday.
W: Phew, I still have some time. Where should I submit it?
M: (Upload your work to our school website.)

해석

여: Jake, 나는 수학 과제에 대해 완전히 잊어버렸어. 마감 기한이 언제야?
남: 다음 주 화요일까지 제출해야 해.
여: 휴, 아직 시간이 좀 있구나. 그것을 어디에 제출해야 하니?
남: (우리 학교 웹 사이트에 네 과제를 업로드해.)

① 나는 늦은 과제는 받아줄 수 없어.
② 너는 이번에 정말 잘했어.
☑ 우리 학교 웹 사이트에 네 과제를 업로드해.
④ 숙제를 스스로 하려고 노력해 봐.
⑤ 우리는 다음 수업 전에 그것을 끝낼 수 있어.

13 남자의 마지막 말에 대한 여자의 응답 ▶ 정답 ⑤ 〔정답률 80%〕

M: Hey, Cindy. Have you been playing a lot of badminton these days?
W: No, I've been experiencing some pain in my knee since a
badminton match last weekend.
M: I'm sorry to hear that. Did you go see a doctor?
W: Yes, I visited a local clinic yesterday.
M: I hope you feel better soon. By the way, have you ever taken a
badminton lesson?
W: No, I haven't. Why are you asking?
M: In my experience, that kind of injury can come from bad posture.
A lesson might reduce the risk of any further injury.
W: Well, I thought I didn't need those lessons.
M: Cindy, if you want to keep playing badminton without any injuries,
it's important to learn from an instructor to develop the right
posture.
W: (You're right. Maybe I should start taking badminton lessons.)

해석

남: 안녕, Cindy. 요즘에 배드민턴을 많이 치고 있니?

여: 아니, 지난 주말 배드민턴 경기 이후로 무릎에 통증을 좀 느끼고 있어.

남: 안됐구나. 병원에 다녀왔니?

여: 응, 어제 동네 병원에 갔었어.

남: 빨리 나았으면 좋겠다. 그런데, 너는 배드민턴 강습을 받은 적이 있니?

여: 아니, 없어. 왜 물어보는 거야?

남: 내 경험상, 그런 종류의 부상은 좋지 않은 자세에서 올 수 있어. 강습은 추가적인 부상 위험을 줄일 수도 있어.

여: 음, 나는 그런 강습이 필요하지 않다고 생각했어.

남: Cindy, 어떠한 부상도 없이 배드민턴을 계속 치고 싶다면, 올바른 자세를 익히기 위해 강사에게 배우는 것이 중요해.

여: (네 말이 맞아. 나는 배드민턴 강습을 받기 시작해야 할 것 같아.)

① 응. 내가 방문했던 병원의 전화번호를 알려줄 수 있어.

② 동의해. 어제 저녁 배드민턴 경기는 정말 멋졌어.

③ 문제없어. 이번에 내가 서브를 넣는 방법을 가르쳐 줄게.

④ 유감이야. 무릎 부상에서 빨리 회복하기를 바랄게.

☑네 말이 맞아. 나는 배드민턴 강습을 받기 시작해야 할 것 같아.

문제 풀이

남자는 배드민턴을 치다 무릎 부상을 당한 여자에게 좋지 않은 자세로 인한 부상 위험에 대해 설명하며 강사에 강습을 받아 올바른 자세를 익히라고 조언하고 있다. 이에 대한 여자의 응답으로 가장 적절한 것은 ⑤ 'You're right. Maybe I should start taking badminton lessons. (네 말이 맞아. 나는 배드민턴 강습을 받기 시작해야 할 것 같아.)'이다.

14 여자의 마지막 말에 대한 남자의 응답 ▶ 정답 ②

정답률 75%

W: Mike, don't you think climate change is kind of scary?
기후 변화 / 무서운

M: Right. The temperature seems higher than ever.
기온

W: I heard it's putting a number of animals in danger these days.
많은 동물들을 위험에 빠뜨리고 있다
(put A in danger: A를 위험에 빠뜨리다, a number of: 많은)

M: Right. Maybe one day we won't be able to see polar bears anymore.
볼 수 없을 것이다 / 북극곰들
(be able to V: ~할 수 있다)

W: That's not good. What can we do?

M: Use less plastic, plant more trees. Small things matter.
심다 / 중요하다

W: And maybe we can ride bikes instead of always asking for rides.
항상 차량을 요구하는 대신에
(instead of V-ing: ~하는 대신에, ask for: ~을 요구하다, ride: 차량)

M: Yeah. Making a Tree-Planting Day at school can also be helpful.
나무 심는 날 / 도움이 되는

W: Absolutely. Then, why don't we make our own school club to put it into action?
그것을 실행에 옮기다(put A into action: A를 실행에 옮기다)

M: (Great. Let's think about the club name first.)

해석

여: Mike, 기후 변화가 좀 무섭다고 생각하지 않니?

남: 맞아. 기온이 그 어느 때보다 높은 것 같아.

여: 그것이 요즘 많은 동물들을 위험에 빠뜨리고 있다고 들었어.

남: 맞아. 언젠가 우리가 북극곰을 더 이상 볼 수 없을지도 몰라.

여: 그럼 안 되는데. 우리가 무엇을 할 수 있을까?

남: 플라스틱을 덜 쓰고, 나무를 더 심어야지. 작은 것들이 중요해.

여: 그리고 항상 차량을 요구하는 대신에 자전거를 탈 수도 있어.

남: 그래. 학교에서 나무 심는 날을 정하는 것도 도움이 될 수 있어.

여: 당연하지. 그럼, 그것을 실행에 옮기기 위해 우리의 학교 동아리를 만드는 것은 어때?

남: (좋아. 일단 동아리 이름에 대해 생각해 보자.)

① 물론이지. 그것은 곰을 위한 완벽한 장소인 것 같아.

☑좋아. 일단 동아리 이름에 대해 생각해 보자.

③ 천만에. 나는 너를 언제든지 태워다 줄 수 있어.

④ 동의해. 플라스틱 사용을 포기하기는 힘들어.

⑤ 걱정하지 마. 나는 내 자전거를 수리 맡길 거야.

15 다음 상황에서 Laura가 Tony에게 할 말 ▶ 정답 ③

정답률 80%

W: Laura and Tony are close coworkers. Laura notices that Tony has
동료들
been looking unusually tired and pale recently. One day, she asks
매우 / 피곤한 / 창백한
Tony if he's not feeling well lately, but Tony says he's just a bit
건강 상태가 좋지 않다(feel well: 건강 상태가 좋다)

tired from work. Laura knows that Tony sometimes works even on
때때로
weekends without taking a break or getting any rest. However, this
휴식을 취하지 않거나 조금도 쉬지 않고
(without V-ing: ~하지 않고, take a break: 휴식을 취하다, get rest: 쉬다)
time, she is really worried about him and wants him to take at least
a couple of days off. In this situation, what would Laura most likely
최소한 이틀은 쉬다(take a day off: 하루 쉬다, at least: 최소한, a couple of: 둘의)
say to Tony?

Laura: (You'd better take a break for a few days.)

해석

여: Laura와 Tony는 가까운 동료이다. Laura는 Tony가 최근에 매우 피곤하고 창백해 보인다는 것을 알아차린다. 어느 날, 그녀는 Tony에게 요즘 건강 상태가 좋지 않은 것인지 물어보지만, Tony는 단지 일 때문에 조금 피곤할 뿐이라고 말한다. Laura는 Tony가 때때로 휴식을 취하지 않거나 조금도 쉬지 않고 주말에도 일한다는 것을 알고 있다. 하지만, 이번에, 그녀는 그가 정말 걱정되어 그가 최소한 이틀은 쉬기를 바란다. 이러한 상황에서, Laura는 Tony에게 뭐라고 말하겠는가?

Laura: (당신은 며칠 동안 휴식을 취하는 게 좋겠어요.)

① 저는 건강검진을 위해 병원에 방문하는 것을 좋아하지 않아요.

② 오늘 병원에 데려다 줘서 고마워요.

☑당신은 며칠 동안 휴식을 취하는 게 좋겠어요.

④ 당신은 마감일 전에 일을 끝내야 해요.

⑤ 미안하지만 지금은 당신의 업무량을 줄일 수 없어요.

16~17 1지문 2문항

M: Hello, Lincoln High School. This is David Newman, your current
현재의
student representative, and I'm speaking to you today to let
학생 대표
you know about the upcoming election for next year's student
다가오는 / 선거
representative. Candidates can now begin their campaigns,
후보자들 / 선거운동들
following these instructions. First, they can share short
지침들 / 공유하다
promotional video clips on their social media, but the video clips
홍보 동영상들 / 소셜 미디어
must not be longer than 3 minutes. Second, candidates can
display posters only in allowed areas, and it's important to keep
전시하다 / 포스터들 / 구역들
the size to A3 or smaller, as larger posters will be removed without
크기를 유지하다 / 제거되다(remove: 제거하다)
warning. Third, the use of pamphlets is allowed, but they must
팸플릿들
only be distributed within the school campus. Lastly, there will
배포되다(distribute: 배포하다)
be an online debate broadcast on our school website among the
온라인 토론 방송
candidates three days before the election. It's important to be
respectful toward the other candidates during the debate. Let's
존중하는
make this election a success.
성공

해석

남: 안녕하세요, Lincoln 고등학교 학생 여러분. 저는 현재 학생 대표인 David Newman이고, 다가오는 내년 학생 대표 선거에 대해 알려드리기 위해 오늘 여러분께 이야기하고 있습니다. 후보자들은 이제 이 지침들에 따라 선거운동을 시작할 수 있습니다. 첫째, 소셜 미디어에 짧은 홍보 동영상을 공유할 수 있지만, 동영상은 3분을 초과하면 안 됩니다. 둘째, 후보자들은 허용된 구역에만 포스터를 전시할 수 있으며, 크기를 A3 이하로 유지하는 것이 중요한데 더 큰 포스터는 경고 없이 제거될 것이기 때문입니다. 셋째, 팸플릿의 사용은 허용되지만, 학교 캠퍼스 내에서만 배포되어야 합니다. 마지막으로, 선거 3일 전에 학교 웹 사이트에서 후보자들 간의 온라인 토론 방송이 있을 예정입니다. 토론 중에는 다른 후보자들을 존중하는 것이 중요합니다. 이번 선거를 성공적으로 만들어 봅시다.

16 남자가 하는 말의 주제 ▶ 정답 ③

정답률 70%

① 언론과 유권자 사이의 관계들

② 학교 정책을 홍보하는 일반적인 방법들

☑학생 선거 캠페인에 관한 지침들

④ 후보자가 되기 위한 자격 요건들

⑤ 학교 토론에서 이기기 위한 유용한 조언들

17 언급된 매체가 아닌 것

정답률 90% ▶ 정답 ④

① 소셜 미디어
② 포스터
③ 팸플릿
④ 학교 신문 ✓
⑤ 학교 웹 사이트

---

24 2024년 9월 학력평가

01	③	02	③	03	⑤	04	④	05	②
06	③	07	④	08	③	09	④	10	④
11	①	12	②	13	①	14	①	15	①
16	⑤	17	③						

---

01 여자가 하는 말의 목적

정답률 85% ▶ 정답 ③

W: Hello! I'm Olivia Parker from Pineview City Subway. I have an announcement for this Saturday's fireworks festival. Many people are expected to visit and enjoy the festival late into the night. For smooth transportation and visitor safety, we're extending the operational hours of the subway on the day of the festival. The subway will run for an extra two hours after the regular last train from the festival area stations. For a comfortable and safe journey from the event, we encourage you to take advantage of our extended subway services. We hope you enjoy this fantastic festival with convenience. Thank you!

해석

여: 안녕하세요! 저는 Pineview 도시 지하철의 Olivia Parker입니다. 이번 주 토요일의 불꽃 축제에 대한 안내 말씀을 드립니다. 많은 사람들이 방문하여 밤늦게까지 축제를 즐길 것으로 예상됩니다. 원활한 교통과 방문객의 안전을 위해, 축제 당일에 지하철 운행 시간을 연장할 예정입니다. 지하철은 축제 지역 역에서 정규 막차 이후에 추가로 2시간 동안 운행될 것입니다. 행사로부터의 편안하고 안전한 이동을 위해, 연장된 지하철 서비스를 이용하실 것을 권장합니다. 이 환상적인 축제를 편리하게 즐기시길 바랍니다. 감사합니다!

① 축제 기간 연장을 요청하려고
② 신설된 지하철 노선을 홍보하려고
③ 축제 당일의 지하철 연장 운행을 안내하려고 ✓
④ 축제 방문객에게 안전 수칙 준수를 당부하려고
⑤ 축제 기간 중 도심 교통 통제 구간을 공지하려고

---

02 남자의 의견

정답률 90% ▶ 정답 ③

M: Hi, Emma. What's up? You look tired.

W: Hey, David. I always feel tired. Even though I sleep many hours, I guess I don't get any good sleep.

M: That's too bad. Is there anything you do before you go to bed?

W: I usually read webtoons on my smartphone for a few hours.

M: Ah, that's the problem. Having too much screen time right before bed is not good.

W: Really? But I'm so used to spending time on my phone at night!

M: Long exposure to the screen light can make your brain stay awake.

W: I never knew using smartphones had a negative impact on sleep.

M: Reducing your smartphone use before going to bed will increase the quality of your sleep.

W: Okay, I can give it a try.

해석

남: 안녕, Emma. 무슨 일 있니? 너 피곤해 보여.

여: 안녕, David. 나는 항상 피곤해. 많은 시간을 자지만, 잠을 잘 자지 못하는 것 같아.

남: 안타깝네. 잠자리에 들기 전에 하는 일이 있니?

여: 보통 몇 시간 동안 스마트폰으로 웹툰을 읽어.

남: 아, 그게 문제구나. 자기 직전에 너무 많은 화면 시청 시간을 갖는 것은 좋지 않아.

여: 정말? 하지만 나는 밤에 휴대폰으로 시간을 보내는 데 너무 익숙해!

남: 화면 불빛에의 장시간 노출은 뇌를 자지 않고 깨어 있게 만들 수 있어.

여: 나는 스마트폰 사용이 수면에 부정적인 영향을 미친다는 것을 전혀 몰랐어.

남: 잠자리에 들기 전에 스마트폰 사용을 줄이는 것은 수면의 질을 높일 거야.

여: 알겠어, 한번 해 볼게.

① 불규칙한 수면 습관은 청소년의 뇌 발달을 방해한다.
② 스마트폰의 화면 밝기를 조절하여 눈을 보호해야 한다.
③ 취침 전 스마트폰 사용을 줄여야 수면의 질이 높아진다. ✓
④ 집중력 향상을 위해 디지털 기기 사용을 최소화해야 한다.
⑤ 일정한 시간에 취침하는 것이 생체 리듬 유지에 도움을 준다.

---

03 남자가 하는 말의 요지

정답률 90% ▶ 정답 ⑤

M: Hello, listeners! Welcome to your *Daily Tips*. Today, I'll tell you a helpful way to relieve your stress. Recent research shows that having hobbies completely unrelated to your job can significantly reduce stress. For example, if you work in IT, consider exploring activities that are far from the digital field. Playing the guitar might be a good option rather than playing computer games. Let's enjoy hobbies that are different from our work! That'll be the best way to get a refreshing break. Remember, a well-chosen hobby can be a powerful tool for stress relief. Tune in tomorrow for more helpful daily tips!

해석

남: 안녕하세요, 청취자 여러분! 'Daily Tips(일일 정보)'에 오신 것을 환영합니다. 오늘, 저는 여러분께 스트레스를 완화할 수 있는 유용한 방법을 알려드릴 거예요. 최근 연구에 따르면 여러분의 직업과 전혀 관련 없는 취미를 갖는 것이 스트레스를 상당히 감소시킬 수 있다고 합니다. 예를 들어, 여러분이 IT 분야에서 일한다면, 디지털 분야와 거리가 먼 활동을 탐색하는 것을 고려해 보세요. 컴퓨터 게임을 하는 것보다는 기타를 연주하는 것이 좋은 선택이 될 수 있습니다. 업무와 다른 취미를 즐겨봅시다! 그것은 상쾌한 휴식을 취하는 가장 좋은 방법이 될 거예요. 기억하세요, 잘 선택한 취미는 스트레스 완화를 위한 강력한 도구가 될 수 있습니다. 더 유용한 일일 정보를 위해 내일도 청취해 주세요!

① 과도한 컴퓨터 사용은 스트레스 지수를 증가시킨다.
② 컴퓨터 관련 취미 활동은 IT 활용 능력을 향상시킨다.
③ 직업을 선택할 때 자신의 흥미와 적성을 고려해야 한다.
④ 다양한 악기 연주를 배우는 것은 인생을 풍요롭게 만든다.
⑤ 직업과 관련 없는 취미 활동이 스트레스 감소에 도움이 된다. ✓

---

04 그림에서 대화의 내용과 일치하지 않는 것

정답률 80% ▶ 정답 ④

M: Hey, Amy. Here is the new recording studio for our band. How do you like it?

W: Wow, these two speakers are impressive!

M: Yes, they are. The sound quality is excellent.

W: Also, the long desk between the speakers looks great.

M: Yeah. And on the desk, there is a microphone. We can use it to give recording directions.

W: Nice. Oh, this chair looks comfortable. It could be helpful for long
　recordings.
　　　　　　편한　　　　　　　도움이 되는
M: Agreed. And the rug under the chair gives the room a cozy feeling,
　doesn't it?
　　　　깔개　　　　　　　　　　　　　　　아늑한
W: Yes, and I like the flower patterns on the rug.
　　　　　　　　　　　꽃무늬
M: I like it, too. How about the poster on the wall?
　　　　　　　　　　　　　　포스터
W: It's cool. This studio feels like where music truly comes alive!
　　　　　　　　　　　　　　　　　　　　　　　활기를 띠다
M: I'm glad you like this place.
W: Absolutely. I can't wait to start recording here.
　　　　　　　　빨리 시작하고 싶다
　　　(can't wait to V: 빨리 ~하고 싶다, start: 시작하다)

해석

남: 안녕, Amy. 여기가 우리 밴드를 위한 새로운 녹음실이야. 어때?
여: 와, 이 두 개의 스피커가 인상적이야!
남: 응, 그렇지. 음질이 훌륭해.
여: 또한, 스피커 사이에 있는 긴 책상이 멋져 보여.
남: 그래. 그리고 책상 위에, 마이크가 있어. 우리는 녹음을 지시하는 데 그것을 사용할 수 있어.
여: 좋아. 오, 이 의자는 편해 보이네. 장시간 녹음에 도움이 될 수 있겠어.
남: 동의해. 그리고 의자 밑에 있는 깔개가 방에 아늑한 느낌을 줘, 그렇지 않니?
여: 응, 그리고 나는 깔개의 꽃무늬가 마음에 들어.
남: 나도 마음에 들어. 벽에 있는 포스터는 어때?
여: 멋지네. 이 녹음실은 음악이 정말 활기를 띠는 곳처럼 느껴져!
남: 이 장소가 마음에 든다니 다행이야.
여: 물론이지. 여기에서 빨리 녹음을 시작하고 싶어.

05 여자가 할 일

정답률 75%

▶ 정답 ②

W: Tony, I'm so excited for our Go-Green event!
M: Me, too. The event is almost here. Why don't we go over our
　　　　　　　　　　　　　　　　　　　　　　　　　　　　　검토하다
　preparations together?
　　준비 사항들
W: Okay. I think the exhibition booths are very important for our event.
　　　　　　　　　전시 부스들　　　　　　　　중요한
　How are they going?
M: Almost ready. I'm working on the booth setup this afternoon. What
　　　　　　　　　　　　　　　　　　　설치
　about the welcome gifts?
　　　　　환영 선물들
W: I've already prepared some eco-friendly bags.
　　　　　　　　　　　　　친환경적인
M: Perfect! What's next?
W: We need to confirm the list of guests for the ceremony.
　　　　　　　확인하다　　명단　　　　　　기념식
M: I double-checked the list. But I haven't sent the online invitation
　　재확인했다　　　　　　　　　　　　　　　　온라인 초대장들
　cards, yet.
W: No problem. I'll deal with it right away. How about the food and
　　　　　　　　~을 처리하다
　drinks?
M: I've scheduled food and drink services and I'll serve the guests
　with reusable dishes.
　　재사용 가능한 그릇들
W: Nice! I'm confident our event will be a great success.
　　　　　　확신하는　　　　　　　　　　성공

해석

여: Tony, 저는 우리의 Go-Green 행사가 정말 기대돼요!
남: 저도 그래요. 행사가 얼마 남지 않았어요. 준비 사항을 함께 검토해 보는 게 어때요?

여: 좋아요. 저는 전시 부스가 우리 행사에 있어서 매우 중요하다고 생각해요. 어떻게 되어 가
　고 있나요?
남: 거의 준비가 되었어요. 제가 오늘 오후에 부스 설치 작업을 할 거예요. 환영 선물은 어때요?
여: 제가 이미 친환경 가방을 준비했어요.
남: 완벽하네요! 다음은 무엇인가요?
여: 기념식을 위한 초대 손님 명단을 확인해야 해요.
남: 제가 명단을 재확인했어요. 그런데 아직 온라인 초대장을 보내지 않았어요.
여: 문제없어요. 제가 바로 그 일을 처리할게요. 음식과 음료는 어때요?
남: 식음료 서비스를 예약했는데 초대 손님들에게 재사용 가능한 그릇들을 제공할 거예요.
여: 좋아요! 저는 우리의 행사가 큰 성공을 거둘 것이라고 확신해요.

① 선물 준비하기
☑ 온라인 초대장 보내기
③ 음식 주문하기
④ 초대 손님 명단 확인하기
⑤ 전시 부스 설치하기

문제풀이

행사의 초대 손님 명단을 확인한 남자가 아직 온라인 초대장을 보내지 못했다고 말하자 여자
는 자신이 그 일을 바로 처리하겠다고 대답한다. 따라서 여자가 할 일은 ② '온라인 초대장 보
내기'이다.

06 남자가 지불할 금액

정답률 85%

▶ 정답 ③

W: Welcome to the Riverside Camping store. How can I help you?
M: I'm looking for a camping table for my family. Can you recommend
　　　　　　　　　　　캠핑 테이블　　　　　　　　　　　　　추천하다
　one?
W: Sure. How about this one? It's light and easy to fold, so it's our
　　　　　　　　　　　　　　　　　가벼운　　　　　접다
　best-selling product.
　　　　　　　제품
M: It looks good. How much is it?
W: It comes in two sizes. The small one is 30 dollars and the large one
　is 50 dollars.
M: I'll buy the large one. Are there folding chairs, too?
　　　　　　　　　　　　　　　　접이식 의자들
W: Yep. These folding chairs might go well with the table. They're 10
　　　　　　　　　　　　　　　~과 잘 어울리다
　dollars each.
M: Sounds good. I'll buy four of those chairs.
W: Okay. That's one large camping table and four chairs.
M: That's right. Can I use this discount coupon now?
　　　　　　　　　　　　　　　할인 쿠폰
W: Of course. You can get a 10% discount on the total price.
　　　　　　　　　　　10% 할인을 받다　　　　　총액
M: Perfect. Here's my credit card.

해석

여: Riverside 캠핑 매장에 오신 것을 환영합니다. 어떻게 도와드릴까요?
남: 저는 가족을 위한 캠핑 테이블을 찾고 있어요. 하나 추천해 주시겠어요?
여: 그럼요. 이것은 어떠신가요? 가볍고 접기 쉬워서, 가장 잘 팔리는 제품이에요.
남: 좋아 보이네요. 얼마인가요?
여: 그것은 두 가지 크기로 나와요. 작은 것은 30달러이고 큰 것은 50달러예요.
남: 큰 것을 살게요. 접이식 의자도 있나요?
여: 네. 이 접이식 의자가 그 테이블과 잘 어울릴 거예요. 개당 10달러예요.
남: 좋은 것 같네요. 그 의자 네 개를 살게요.
여: 알겠습니다. 큰 캠핑 테이블 한 개와 의자 네 개네요.
남: 맞아요. 지금 이 할인 쿠폰을 사용할 수 있나요?
여: 물론이죠. 총액에서 10% 할인을 받으실 수 있어요.
남: 완벽하네요. 여기 제 신용카드가 있어요.

① $63　　　　　　　　　　　　② $70
☑ $81　　　　　　　　　　　　④ $86
⑤ $90

문제풀이

가격이 50달러인 큰 캠핑 테이블 한 개와 10달러인 접이식 의자 네 개를 사면 총액은 90달러
이다. 쿠폰을 사용해서 10% 할인을 받을 수 있다고 했으므로, 남자가 지불할 금액은 9달러가
할인된 81달러이다. 따라서 답은 ③ '$81'이다.

07 여자가 이번 주말에 등산을 갈 수 없는 이유

정답률 90% ▶ 정답 ④

W: Lately, the weather has been lovely. This is a perfect time for climbing.
M: Indeed. Oh, would you like to go mountain climbing together?
W: Sounds awesome. I have all the climbing equipment.
M: Great. How about this upcoming weekend? I'll find a nice mountain for us.
W: Hold on, this weekend? I don't think I can make it then.
M: Really? All school tests are finally done, so I thought this weekend would be good for us.
W: Sorry, but I have something important to do this weekend.
M: Do you have a part-time job?
W: No. Actually, I need to practice dancing for the entire weekend.
M: Ah, for the dance competition you mentioned before?
W: Yes. Surprisingly, I made it through the first round, and it's the finals next Monday.
M: That's fantastic! I wish you the best of luck.

해석
여: 최근에, 날씨가 아주 좋았어. 지금이 등산하기에 완벽한 시기야.
남: 정말 그래. 오, 함께 등산을 갈까?
여: 너무 좋을 것 같아. 나는 모든 등산 장비를 가지고 있어.
남: 잘됐네. 다가오는 이번 주말은 어때? 내가 우리를 위한 멋진 산을 찾아볼게.
여: 잠깐, 이번 주말? 그때는 갈 수 없을 것 같아.
남: 정말? 드디어 모든 학교 시험이 끝나서, 나는 이번 주말이 우리에게 좋을 것이라고 생각했어.
여: 미안하지만, 이번 주말에 해야 할 중요한 일이 있어.
남: 아르바이트를 해야 하니?
여: 아니. 사실, 주말 내내 춤 연습을 해야 해.
남: 아, 전에 말했던 춤 경연 대회 때문에?
여: 응. 놀랍게도, 나는 1라운드를 통과했고, 다음 주 월요일이 결승전이야.
남: 환상적이다! 행운을 빌게.

① 아르바이트를 해야 해서
② 학교 시험공부를 해야 해서
③ 폭우로 인해 등산로가 폐쇄되어서
✔ 경연을 위한 춤 연습을 해야 해서
⑤ 주문한 등산 장비가 도착하지 않아서

08 Lakestate Apartment Yoga Program에 관해 언급되지 않은 것

정답률 85% ▶ 정답 ③

W: Grandpa, take a look at this. It's a Lakestate Apartment Yoga Program poster.
M: Wow, a new program for the residents. I've always wanted to join a yoga program.
W: I know, and this one is only for those aged 60 and above.
M: That's perfect for me. [Pause] Oh, it says it's held at 8 a.m. every Tuesday and Friday.
W: It'll be a good time for you. You're an early bird.
M: Yes, I am. How do I register?
W: You just need to fill out an application form at the apartment fitness center.
M: Okay, I think I'll go right now.
W: Good. But don't forget to take your ID card with you.
M: Oh, do I need that for the registration?
W: Yes. It says that on the poster. Would you like me to go with you?
M: That would be lovely.

해석
여: 할아버지, 이것 좀 보세요. Lakestate Apartment Yoga Program(Lakestate 아파트 요가 프로그램) 포스터예요.
남: 와, 주민들을 위한 새로운 프로그램이구나. 나는 항상 요가 프로그램에 참여하고 싶었단다.
여: 알아요, 그리고 이것은 60세 이상인 분들만을 위한 거예요.
남: 내게 안성맞춤이구나. [잠시 후] 오, 매주 화요일과 금요일 오전 8시에 진행된다고 나와 있어.
여: 할아버지께 좋은 시간이네요. 할아버지는 일찍 일어나시는 분이잖아요.
남: 응, 그렇지. 어떻게 등록하는 거니?
여: 아파트 헬스 클럽에서 신청서를 작성하시기만 하면 돼요.
남: 알겠어, 지금 바로 가야겠구나.
여: 좋아요. 그런데 신분증을 가져가시는 것을 잊지 마세요.
남: 오, 등록을 위해 그것이 필요하니?
여: 네. 포스터에 쓰여 있어요. 제가 함께 갈까요?
남: 그러면 정말 좋겠구나.

① 대상 연령
② 운영 요일
✔ 모집 인원
④ 등록 방법
⑤ 등록 준비물

09 Global Food Market에 관한 내용과 일치하지 않는 것

정답률 90% ▶ 정답 ④

W: Good morning! This is Allison from the student council. I'm happy to announce the Global Food Market right here at Westhill High School. Get ready for a delicious journey around the world in the school parking lot. Our Global Food Market will take place for two days, on September 25th and 26th. You can enjoy food from eight different countries, including Mexico and France. And there's no need to worry about prices. Every single dish is only five dollars. Wait! You don't eat meat? No problem! We also have menus for vegetarians. So, join us at the Global Food Market. It's not just about food, but a celebration of culture and diversity. Don't miss this chance to taste the world!

해석
여: 좋은 아침입니다! 저는 학생회의 Allison입니다. 바로 여기 Westhill 고등학교에서 Global Food Market에 대해 알려드리게 되어 기쁩니다. 학교 주차장에서 맛있는 세계 일주 여행을 준비하십시오. Global Food Market은 9월 25일과 26일 이틀간 열릴 것입니다. 여러분은 멕시코와 프랑스를 포함한 8개 국가의 음식을 즐길 수 있습니다. 그리고 가격에 대해 걱정할 필요는 없습니다. 모든 요리가 단돈 5달러입니다. 잠깐! 고기를 드시지 않습니까? 문제없습니다! 채식주의자를 위한 메뉴도 있습니다. 그러니 Global Food Market에서 저희와 함께 하십시오. 그것은 음식 뿐 아니라, 문화와 다양성을 축하하는 것입니다. 세계를 맛볼 수 있는 이 기회를 놓치지 마십시오!

① 학교 주차장에서 열린다.
② 이틀간 진행된다.
③ 8개 국가의 음식을 즐길 수 있다.
✔ 음식마다 가격이 다르다.
⑤ 채식주의자를 위한 메뉴가 있다.

10 표에서 남자가 주문할 디지털 텀블러

정답률 85% ▶ 정답 ④

W: Honey, what are you looking at?
M: I'm looking at digital tumblers. They show the temperature on an LED screen. Would you like to help me choose one?
W: Sure, let me see. [Pause] The price differs by model.
M: Hmm, I don't want to pay more than 60 dollars.
W: That sounds reasonable. Look, there are various sizes to choose from.
M: Less than 400ml would be too small for me.
W: Alright. Oh, there's a new function. Do you need the water intake display? It'll show you how much water you drink in a day.

M: That sounds smart. I'd love to have it. Then, I have just two options left.
W: What color do you like? You have too many black items and they're boring.
M: Okay. I'll go with the one that's not black. Then, I'll order this one.
W: Great idea!

해석
여: 여보, 무엇을 보고 있어요?
남: 디지털 텀블러를 보고 있어요. 그것들은 LED 화면에 온도를 보여주네요. 내가 하나 고르는 것을 도와줄래요?
여: 그럼요, 어디 봐요. [잠시 후] 모델마다 가격이 다르네요.
남: 흠, 저는 60달러 이상을 지불하고 싶지 않아요.
여: 합리적인 것 같아요. 봐요, 선택할 수 있는 다양한 크기가 있어요.
남: 400ml 미만은 저에게 너무 작을 거예요.
여: 좋아요. 오, 새로운 기능이 있네요. 수분 섭취량 표시 기능이 필요해요? 하루에 물을 얼마나 많이 마시는지 보여줄 거예요.
남: 멋진 것 같네요. 그 기능이 있으면 정말 좋겠어요. 그럼, 두 가지 선택지만 남았네요.
여: 어떤 색상이 마음에 들어요? 당신은 검은색 물건을 너무 많이 가지고 있고 그것들은 지루해요.
남: 알겠어요. 검은색이 아닌 것을 선택할게요. 그럼, 이것을 주문할게요.
여: 좋은 생각이에요!

디지털 텀블러

	모델	가격	크기	수분 섭취량 표시	색상
①	A	35달러	350ml	×	흰색
②	B	40달러	470ml	×	금색
③	C	45달러	470ml	○	검은색
✓④	D	55달러	550ml	○	흰색
⑤	E	65달러	550ml	○	금색

11
여자의 마지막 말에 대한 남자의 응답
정답률 55%
▶ 정답 ①

W: I easily catch a cold these days.
M: That's too bad. It's a good idea to keep some moisture in your room.
W: Oh, how does that relate to a cold?
M: (If it's too dry inside, you can easily get a cold.)

해석
여: 제가 요즘 감기에 쉽게 걸려요.
남: 유감이네요. 방에 습기를 좀 유지하는 것이 좋아요.
여: 오, 그것이 감기와 어떤 관계가 있나요?
남: (실내가 너무 건조하면, 감기에 쉽게 걸릴 수 있어요.)
✓① 실내가 너무 건조하면, 감기에 쉽게 걸릴 수 있어요.
② 기침을 할 때, 입을 가려야 해요.
③ 감기에 걸리지 않으려면 손을 씻어야 해요.
④ 몸을 따뜻하게 유지하는 것은 정말 중요해요.
⑤ 물을 마시는 것은 피부를 부드럽게 만들 수 있어요.

12
남자의 마지막 말에 대한 여자의 응답
정답률 70%
▶ 정답 ②

M: Mom, the bookshelf in my room is full of books. There's no space for new ones.
W: Well, how about throwing away the books you don't read anymore?
M: But some of them are in too good condition to throw away.
W: (Right. Then, shall we sell them at a used bookstore?)

해석
남: 엄마, 제 방의 책장이 책으로 가득 차 있어요. 새 책을 넣을 공간이 없어요.
여: 음, 더 이상 읽지 않는 책들을 버리는 것은 어떨까?
남: 하지만 그것들 중 일부는 버리기에는 너무 좋은 상태인데요.

여: (맞아. 그렇다면, 그것들을 중고 서점에 팔까?)
① 멋지구나. 새 책장이 네 방에 잘 어울려.
✓② 맞아. 그렇다면, 그것들을 중고 서점에 팔까?
③ 그렇구나. 그것들을 도서관에서 빌릴 수 있니?
④ 알겠어. 좋은 상태의 책을 사줄게.
⑤ 미안해. 아직 그 책을 다 읽지 못했어.

13
여자의 마지막 말에 대한 남자의 응답
정답률 55%
▶ 정답 ①

W: Hey, Peter. How's your group project going?
M: Hello, Ms. Adams. It's my first time as a leader, so it's quite challenging.
W: I thought your group was working well together.
M: Yes. We're all motivated and working hard, but progress is slow.
W: Well, what are you all working on at this moment?
M: Everyone is focusing on gathering data as much as possible.
W: Hmm, did you assign individual tasks to each member?
M: Oh, we haven't discussed it yet. We're not exactly sure who does what.
W: That's crucial. Otherwise, it can lead to overlapping tasks in a group project.
M: That makes sense. That's why our progress is not that fast.
W: Then, as the leader, what do you think you should do now?
M: (I'll clarify each group member's specific role.)

해석
여: 안녕, Peter. 조별 과제는 어떻게 되어 가고 있니?
남: 안녕하세요, Adams 선생님. 제가 처음으로 조장을 맡아서, 꽤 힘들어요.
여: 나는 너희 조가 잘 협력하고 있다고 생각했어.
남: 네. 저희는 모두 의욕적이고 열심히 노력하고 있지만, 진행이 느려요.
여: 음, 너희 모두 지금 무엇을 하고 있니?
남: 모두가 가능한 많은 자료를 모으는 것에 집중하고 있어요.
여: 흠, 너는 각 조원에게 개별 과업을 할당했니?
남: 오, 저희는 아직 그것을 논의하지 않았어요. 누가 무엇을 하는지 정확히 모르겠어요.
여: 그것은 매우 중요해. 그렇지 않으면, 그것이 조별 과제에서 서로 중복되는 과업으로 이어질 수 있어.
남: 일리가 있네요. 그래서 저희의 진행이 그렇게 빠르지 않은 거예요.
여: 그렇다면, 조장으로서 네가 지금 무엇을 해야 한다고 생각하니?
남: (저는 각 조원의 구체적인 역할을 명확하게 할 거예요.)
✓① 저는 각 조원의 구체적인 역할을 명확하게 할 거예요.
② 저는 저희 조의 연구를 위해 더 많은 자료를 수집할 거예요.
③ 제가 직접 그 대회에 도전해야겠어요.
④ 저는 조별 과제의 주제를 바꿔야 해요.
⑤ 제가 자료를 효과적으로 분석하는 방법을 알려드릴게요.

14
남자의 마지막 말에 대한 여자의 응답
정답률 60%
▶ 정답 ①

M: Hey, Emily! You're looking great these days.
W: Thanks, Isaac. I've been trying hard to get in better shape.
M: Good for you! I'm trying to get fit, too. But it's tough.
W: Haven't you been working out a lot lately?
M: Yeah, but I don't see a big difference. What's your secret?
W: Well, I started being careful about when I eat.
M: You mean like not eating right before bed?
W: Kind of. I noticed I was eating a lot at night. So now I don't eat after 7 p.m.
M: Hmm... I don't know if that's enough to get me in better shape.
W: (Trust me. When we eat makes a big difference.)

해석

남: 안녕, Emily! 너 요즘 정말 멋져 보여.

여: 고마워, Isaac. 나는 더 좋은 몸 상태가 되기 위해 열심히 노력하고 있어.

남: 대단하다! 나도 건강해지기 위해 노력하고 있어. 그런데 그것은 힘들어.

여: 너는 최근에 운동을 많이 하고 있지 않니?

남: 그래, 하지만 큰 차이는 보이지 않아. 네 비결은 뭐니?

여: 음, 나는 언제 먹는지에 대해 주의하기 시작했어.

남: 자기 직전에 먹지 않는 것처럼 말이니?

여: 비슷해. 나는 내가 밤에 많이 먹고 있다는 것을 알았어. 그래서 지금은 오후 7시 이후에는 먹지 않아.

남: 흠... 그것이 내가 더 좋은 상태가 되는 데 충분한지 모르겠어.

여: (나를 믿어. 우리가 언제 먹는지가 큰 차이를 만들어.)

☑ 나를 믿어. 우리가 언제 먹는지가 큰 차이를 만들어.

② 알겠어. 더 좋은 몸 상태가 되기 위해 내 식사를 점검할게.

③ 조언해 줘서 고마워. 하지만 나는 그것을 할 수 없을 것 같아.

④ 물론이지. 네 운동 루틴을 반드시 따르도록 할게.

⑤ 그래. 그런 이유로 나는 균형 잡힌 식단을 유지하는 데 성공하지 못했어.

문제 풀이

좋은 몸 상태를 유지하는 비결을 묻는 남자에게 여자는 음식을 먹는 시간에 대해 언급하며 오후 7시 이후에는 먹지 않는다고 대답한다. 그러한 방법이 충분한지 확신하지 못하는 남자의 말에 대한 여자의 응답으로 가장 적절한 것은 ① 'Trust me. When we eat makes a big difference.(나를 믿어. 우리가 언제 먹는지가 큰 차이를 만들어.)'이다.

15 다음 상황에서 Julia가 Sophie에게 할 말 [정답률 75%] ▶ 정답 ①

M: Julia is a college student, living in the dormitory. Recently, she ordered a new computer desk. Upon receiving the desk, she realized that the desk was a DIY product. It means she needs to put the pieces together to build the desk. However, it was complicated to assemble it by herself. Julia knows that Sophie, her best friend, is good at assembling DIY furniture and enjoys it. So, Julia wants to ask Sophie to help her with the desk. In this situation, what would Julia most likely say to Sophie?

Julia: (Could you help me assemble my desk?)

해석

남: Julia는 기숙사에 사는 대학생이다. 최근에, 그녀는 새 컴퓨터 책상을 주문했다. 책상을 받자마자, 그녀는 책상이 DIY 제품이라는 것을 깨달았다. 그것은 그녀가 부품들을 조립해서 책상을 만들어야 한다는 뜻이다. 하지만 그녀 혼자서 그것을 조립하는 것은 복잡했다. Julia는 가장 친한 친구인 Sophie가 DIY 가구 조립하는 것을 잘하고 그것을 즐긴다는 것을 알고 있다. 그래서 Julia는 Sophie에게 책상 조립을 도와달라고 부탁하고 싶다. 이러한 상황에서, Julia는 Sophie에게 뭐라고 말하겠는가?

Julia: (내가 책상 조립하는 것을 도와줄 수 있니?)

☑ 내가 책상 조립하는 것을 도와줄 수 있니?

② 네 책상을 어디에서 샀는지 알려줄 수 있니?

③ 새 컴퓨터를 함께 고르는 게 어떠니?

④ 가구를 스스로 수리하는 게 어떠니?

⑤ 내 방을 장식하기 위한 아이디어가 있니?

16~17 1지문 2문항

W: Hello, *Family-Life* subscribers! These days, many people are looking for clothes made from natural materials for their family. Today, I'd like to introduce some tips for how to properly wash natural material clothes. First, for cotton, like 100% cotton t-shirts,

you should hand-wash in cool water to avoid shrinking or wrinkling. Second, silk should be washed separately and quickly to keep its shape and color. Also, when you dry silk clothes such as blouses, avoid direct sunlight and dry them in the shade. Third, linen is a sensitive material to wash. For example, to wash linen jackets, use vinegar instead of fabric softener. Lastly, for wool, the best way is to wash as little as possible. If you have to wash wool sweaters, use special wool washing soap. Apply these tips so you can keep and enjoy natural clothes for a longer time!

해석

여: 안녕하세요, 'Family-Life' 구독자 여러분! 요즘, 많은 사람들이 가족을 위해 천연 소재로 만든 옷을 찾고 있습니다. 오늘, 저는 천연 소재의 옷을 올바르게 세탁하는 방법에 관한 몇 가지 정보를 소개하려고 합니다. 첫째, 100% 면직물 티셔츠와 같은 면직물은 줄어들거나 주름이 생기는 것을 피하기 위해 찬물에 손세탁해야 합니다. 둘째, 실크는 모양과 색상을 유지하기 위해 단독으로 빠르게 세탁해야 합니다. 또한, 블라우스처럼 실크로 만든 옷을 말릴 때는 직사광선을 피하고 그늘에서 말리세요. 셋째, 리넨은 세탁하기에 민감한 소재입니다. 예를 들어, 리넨 재킷을 세탁하려면, 섬유 유연제 대신에 식초를 사용하세요. 마지막으로, 울의 경우에는 가능한 한 적게 세탁하는 것이 가장 좋은 방법입니다. 울 스웨터를 세탁해야 한다면, 특수 울 세탁 비누를 사용하세요. 천연 소재의 옷을 더 오랫동안 보관하고 입을 수 있도록 이러한 정보를 활용하세요!

16 여자가 하는 말의 주제 [정답률 80%] ▶ 정답 ⑤

① 패션 업계의 소재 경향들

② 천연 소재의 옷을 만들면 얻을 수 있는 이점들

③ 천연 소재의 옷 구매에 대한 조언

④ 옷 세탁 방법의 발전

☑ 천연 소재의 옷을 세탁하는 올바른 방법들

17 언급된 소재가 아닌 것 [정답률 90%] ▶ 정답 ③

① 면직물   ② 실크

☑ 가죽   ④ 리넨

⑤ 울

딕테이션 정답

01 | 2018년 11월 학력평가   p.74

01. professional / forget to count / grateful / Write a gratitude journal / thankful

02. Walking to / tidying up / avoid distractions / Messy / organized study space

03. eyes are red / dry / rest / prescription

04. two laptop computers / microwave / photo on the bookshelf / round table

05. news to share / throw / missing / out of potatoes / No rush

06. experience / sheep feeding / cheese making / two adult / 10

07. adjusting / performance / I've been practicing / When exactly / meet my group members

08. starts at / historical tales / tasting / 100 people are accepted / register

09. legendary / free admission / not required / seeing it live

10. evenings / yoga by myself / doesn't work / 7 / 100

11. choose / What kind of club

12. local market / go and look around

13. impressed by / truly meaningful / how to paint / worried whether

14. rather disappointed / weren't elected / proved / become a better person

15. grades have not improved / easier / difficult ones / before going on to

16~17. While traveling / introduce / Scented / Paris / special moment of being / It'll remind / spirit

02 | 2019년 3월 학력평가   p.79

01. lockers / So we've decided to replace / leave them open / not removed

02. getting ready / hot and spicy / trying local food / culture

03. your store / prepare for / what kind of hat / suit / goes well

04. heart-shaped / banner / striped / school yearbook

05. assignment / due date / Take it easy / go to the beach

06. getting too tight / 30 / two kinds / you'll get

07. science / make some changes / correct / not clear

08. located in / four times larger / tree planting / open from

09. presenting / auditions / rehearsing for months / two days on March

10. exercise / should be at least / I don't want to spend / surface

11. started to learn / by yourself

12. looking for / check the gym

13. posters / make a new / start / using social media

14. write a review / choose / challenging / the use of reading

15. planning to join / sign up / during that period / look for another

16~17. Birds of a feather / animals appear / mice / guess / count your chickens / hasty / one with dogs

03 | 2019년 6월 학력평가   p.84

01. holding a charity event / a variety of / local / participate

02. allergy / positive effect / vitamins / helpful to

03. reservation online / a double room / available / buffet

04. wearing glasses / flower pot / comments / great scientists / star-shaped clock

05. within / finished decorating / What else / I'll write

06. 30 / 15 / light /off the total price

07. debate competition / I'd love to / speak / musical performance

08. search / recommend / no registration fee / December 14th / near

09. June / display / original prices / T-shirt as a gift

10. electric / can't spend / too short / waterproof / Which color

11. motor show / Are you free

12. raining / public transportation

13. meeting for our / take care of / delay / shall we make it

14. preparations / settled / haven't decided / look forward to

15. grew up / transfer to / such / remain in close touch

16~17. might disappear / coffee / has dropped / has resulted in / affect apple trees / lower / strawberry production

04 | 2019년 9월 학력평가   p.89

01. annual / how to prepare for / memorize / confident during the audition / shine

02. Storing / cool and dark / rot easily / keeps them from

03. voice / audio books we recorded / effects you added / script / recording booth

04. at the top between / the lock / two stereo speakers / round carpet

05. exchange / all set / haven't decided on / applications to compare / text

06. enjoys having / go out of / 30 / relaxation / 10

07. surfing / called / wait in / its long tradition / willing to

08. stressed out / various activities / in person / available anytime / refresh

09. upcoming / has been held / 90 minutes / taste and nutritional value

10. type / heavy / weighs less than / battery life / take up

11. reach you on / contact

12. join / choose from

13. video clip / counselor / practical experience / my uncle

14. weather / change the location / inform / broadcasting station / spread the news

15. hosting / take part in / items / permission

16~17. sharing it with / environment / materials / thrown away / financially / rent / bicycle

05 | 2019년 11월 학력평가   p.94

01. host and health expert / share some tips / eventually cause / keep your skin healthy

02. you'd better not / disturb / make you nervous / dependent on / careful not to

03. tickets here / show it / section for / goods / Enjoy your time

04. big round table / slide / see-saw / placed in the shape

05. about to check / sent text messages / participants / print out some materials

06. scented / 20 / any three / mobile coupon

07. I've been doing / available / applied for an overseas / I'll be abroad

08. November / participation fee / bring our own rackets / sign up online

09. sixth grade / different ages / movie showings / cartoon character bookmarks

10. art supplies / under / not very convenient / more than thirty / includes a sketchbook

11. umbrellas / Where can we

12. hand-out / afraid I lost

13. exhausted / made myself join / keep motivated / registration period / extended

14. bank account / I'll be broke / cut down on / consider / only where I need

15. forgets her appointments / responsible and reliable / remember / overcome

her habit of / remind her of

16~17. process of turning / plastic bottles / empty cans / wrap / an endless number of / planet

06 | 2020년 3월 학력평가   p.99

01. what you should do / keep out / clean / wear a mask

02. wrapping / filled it with / end up / simple for the environment

03. since your last visit / second / buy a wooden desk / downstairs

04. Unfortunately / left side / in a row / round table / rug

05. coming along / instruments / put the posters up / arranged

06. wireless earphones / two pairs / 80 / total price

07. reserved a campsite / finished / broke / take care of her

08. flyer / by selling bakery products / donated to / gym

09. head / includes music performances / range / The first 50 visitors

10. book a room / have in mind / mountain / breakfast / cheaper

11. This restaurant / recommend

12. forget to bring / it'd rain

13. to rent / get along well / bothers / Have you talked

14. scheduled for /needs repairing / date / text you

15. letters to parents / deliver / even missed / must give them to

16~17. where milk comes from / source / different animals / consumed / survive / twice the fat

07 | 2020년 6월 학력평가   p.104

01. busy preparing / move / where you are supposed / prearranged

02. sweating / look tired / eat something before / power for exercise

03. turn my novel into / if you directed / accepting / in person

04. set up / floor lamp / square table / fit well

05. Neither / plan to show / What else / I'll bake

06. I'd like to order / eight / newest item / Add / 10

07. outdoor swimming pool / even open / interview / start working

08. June / for teens like / nearby / World famous musicians

09. physics / present your projects / provide feedback and comments / the

first 100 visitors

10. thinking of / something different / Fridays / by six / considering

11. looking for / in your room

12. buy / What do you recommend

13. ask you a favor / look after my plants / water them every day

14. creative / several aspects / assigned / if it were shared

15. a pair of / delivered / explains / get her money back

16~17. suffer from back pain / useful types of exercise / decrease / yoga / walking / avoid

08 | 2020년 9월 학력평가   p.109

01. special musical performance / features / you'd like / nearby

02. choose for / important skills / chances of / improves

03. our company published / nicely expressed / will I translate / released

04. two birds / eye-catching / round table instead of / holding a magic stick

05. magazine / someone to take photos / presentation / call him to see

06. full-day / 30 / offer a discount / silver membership

07. I'm afraid I can't / science project / participate in / preparing for

08. Its purpose / activities to help relieve / Awesome / apply

09. upcoming / take place on / blind tea tasting / Reservations

10. don't want to spend / lasts / Three levels / foldable

11. book signing / want to come

12. setting up / Watching some video clips

13. competing / under construction / fully booked / would start

14. application letter / without being specific / opposite / it'll work

15. practicing / unable to concentrate / long periods of time / that he start

16~17. clear idea / make our lives better / lamps / low amounts / traffic lights

09 | 2020년 11월 학력평가   p.114

01. safety rules / in case of / out of the lane / while riding

02. having a hard time / almost midnight / stay awake / not a good idea

03. sunburn / almost gone / skin will completely recover / prescription

04. indoor bike / under the calendar / mat with the flower / matches well

05. fundraising / they worked fine / nicely

/ put the price tags

06. cushion for my dog / 40 / discount on / Each box / don't offer

07. call me earlier / schedule / being repaired / have dinner with

08. Where's / fun programs for children / runs / admission fee

09. began / continue for / related to / no parking lot nearby

10. particular drawing material / not pastel / in a group / Wednesday or Friday

11. smells / get the recipe

12. speakers / use them

13. old sweater / marketplace for used items / bought anything using / things to sell

14. movie streaming / fee has been charged / pay much attention / to end

15. Literature at university / how to improve / regularly / keep a diary

16~17. animals communicate / dogs mark their areas / convey certain messages / visual signals / make use of touch / contains

10 | 2021년 3월 학력평가   p.119

01. heavy rainstorm / slippery / be extra careful / slip on

02. having trouble sleeping / handled / Changing your pillow / works for

03. finally / holding a party / depend on a chef / from start

04. shoot online lectures / ring on the stand / round clock / in the corner

05. discount on / I've lost / get a new ID / I'll go there

06. 20 each / need four / knife / total purchase is over

07. borrow / due / experiment went well / all over again

08. upload their record / choose any place / registration fee / included

09. regular museum hours / models of planets / ages / not accepted

10. smart watch / one that's waterproof / longer than / cheaper

11. shopping / missing a button

12. where you bought / today after work

13. order / reusable / uses and throws away / What else can I

14. rode my bike / refreshing / good at biking / don't have

15. rock band / completely formed / Hearing / be the lead singer

16~17. animal companions love / keeping / cat's stress / run on a wheel / entertained / bored

11 | 2021년 6월 학력평가　p.124

01. lead to / get a flu vaccine / protect against / by the end

02. convenient / help bookstore owners / going out of business / local

03. locked out of / simple fix / pay extra / take you to finish

04. newly designed / microphone / star-shaped medal / practice

05. Smells / bit messy / pick up our daughter / instead

06. 30 dollars on sale / deal / charging port / first one

07. moving out / two tickets / turned me down / my niece

08. raise / walk / toilet train / takes responsibility

09. donate / encourage people to do / given to 100 students / make a difference

10. one on / don't recommend / extend up to / this cheaper one

11. packing / cold weather

12. can't eat out / an important business meeting

13. busy / Who's on / doing the research / what's your role

14. missed the deadline / forgetful / where I put / good about your app

15. talented and passionate / insists on / concerned / calm down and focus

16~17. light pollution / sea turtles / confuse / get disturbed / salmon migrate randomly / interrupts the mating calls / reproduce

12 | 2021년 9월 학력평가　p.129

01. ensure the safety / enforce / complaints / obey speed limits

02. mean / more careful / get hurt / apologize to

03. got through to / fan of the show / listening / calling us

04. answer correctly / round table / globe on the floor / crown

05. coming along / with decorating / grilled salmon sandwiches / order

06. 5 / two smalls / toppings / only on the medium

07. ended / feels completely fine / not enough space / probably

08. October 3rd / see the campus / admissions process / as a souvenir

09. By tagging / maximum number / will be delivered / end of this year

10. metal or wood / at least three / easier to control / 100

11. he's lost / looking for

12. kitchen closes / open

13. delayed / to stay / available / an additional charge

14. huge storm / scary / turn on any lights / basement is a mess

15. see a movie / has to watch / explains / look after

16~17. right time and place / lot to consider / bats sleep in caves / fly away / with one eye open / Giraffes / short intervals / dolphins / brain relax

13 | 2021년 11월 학력평가　p.134

01. international film / run till late / provide longer / extended service schedules

02. towel / even on a cloudy / harmful light / get a sunburn

03. All the dirt / while cleaning the inside / by / car wash center

04. decorating / striped curtains / round table / under the calendar

05. campaign / uploaded / reusable bag / bring them right away

06. best sellers / 50 / A pair of / off the total price

07. fantastic / booked it / pain in my ankle / completely fine

08. vacation / December 18th / an entrance fee / activities to enjoy

09. celebrate / related to / receive a team uniform / through active participation

10. Seaside / per night / camping car / kids' playground

11. moved / How long

12. nephew / loves seafood

13. reopening / favorite writers / in person / rescheduling

14. missed your call / replace / delay / at that time

15. in charge of / necessary information / larger / increase the size

16~17. gardening / grow even in shade / sunless / low-light conditions / partial / fascinating

14 | 2022년 3월 학력평가　p.139

01. lunch basketball league / sign-up sheet / change the registration method / fill out

02. skin problems / with your hands / spreading / Touching your face

03. speeches on climate change / an environmental activist / cartoonist / discuss

04. like a beach / recognize the boat / chair in the center / two surf boards

05. stuff to do / take the table / last

minute change / grab

06. eco-friendly / made from bamboo / 3 / off the total price

07. heading out to / message / suffering from / kit hasn't been delivered

08. another way of recycling / one man's garbage / living in / breakable items

09. Starting on / bring your own instrument / film our performance / limited to

10. No more than / working time / handle while cleaning / better choice

11. dust got in

12. mind / bothering

13. drop by / Come over any time / exciting / Maybe some snacks

14. talk about it / new year's resolutions / benefits / recommend you to join

15. reaches out to touch / concentrate / lose / without the permission

16~17. workshop / link bones / do certain exercises / supports your body weight / Horseback riding / unlike

15 | 2022년 6월 학력평가　p.144

01. have the walls painted / workers outside / might be some smell / cooperation

02. driver's license / while taking / speed limit signs / should follow

03. help me find / relationship / borrow at a time / return them on time

04. goes well with / striped curtains / star-shaped / warm

05. by myself / practiced / It's due / send the report

06. 20 / any discount / your ticket is free / at the original price

07. busy preparing / running / looking forward to / for a band audition

08. teenage / native speaker / cook traditional foods / class materials

09. head / parking lot / your own used items / get a shopping bag

10. what's your budget / prefer / waterproof / white ones

11. What kind of event

12. worried / take your mind off

13. thinking of / took the class together / offering / Where can I check

14. I've been working out / stretching / with other people / fitness course

15. planning to run for / an effective way / drawing / help him draw posters

16~17. listeners / healthy breakfast food list / Cheese / weight loss / Eating berries / lower in sugar

01. Director / form good reading habits / completely personalized / build

02. long face / missed the seller's note / much cheaper / read every detail

03. get a checkup / eyesight / blocks the light / use this frame

04. pond under the tree / painting of a bear / on the roof / ride the swings

05. ordered some groceries / should've taken / call the customer center / food in the fridge

06. 35 / a large one / message to say / off the total

07. bought it online / social media / too plain / made from recycled materials

08. looking at a poster / deadline for entry / winner gets / download the application

09. announce / picking up trash / need to bring any / first 30 participants

10. portable / its weight / an electric heater / customer rating

11. Where are you planning

12. Can I see / available

13. going to the gym / lots of other prizes / doubles / we partner up

14. traditional / shortening your explanation / True-or-False questions / have fun

15. career counselor / role model / book-signing / in person

16~17. take care of / air blown through / trumpets / away from direct / essential / guitars / lengthen the lifespan

01. heavy snow / we've closed / unavailable for / ready to be reopened

02. measuring spoons / as it is / too sweet / stick to

03. game scenario / inspired me to design / when I compose / background music

04. art assignment / light bulbs / square-shaped rug / nearby

05. set up a chair / draw / where's the sketchbook / I'll check

06. 15 / potato chips / One basket / grab any

07. missed / hurt my wrist / get injured / doctor told me

08. make his own / October 8th / costs only / register

09. competition / limited to / Winners will be decided / enthusiastic

10. should spend / machine washable / completely block sunlight / except for gray

11. ride / How long have you

12. wandering / if he's lost

13. I've come up with / good first impression / dress up / practice smiling

14. we're offering / a little tight / sold out / try them on

15. expert in the field / renowned / difficult to set up / reschedule

16~17. easily send messages / a few ways / special drum / smoke / reliable means / horse / delivered mail

01. As a big fan / first game / as possible to come / an incredible amount

02. I've caught / got prescribed / for others / could be dangerous

03. preparations / change the exhibition room / my works / main hall

04. flower pattern / two chairs for / heart-shaped leaves / butterfly on

05. busy helping / reserved a place / upload / post it online

06. now on sale for / red tumbler / 20 / carry around

07. drop by / brand name / all sold out / Thanks for checking

08. anyone aged / far from / an entry fee / fill out an application

09. happy to announce / note / special lecture / Registration begins

10. 50 / seems too small / heavier / need a lid

11. project / How did you learn

12. about to / give me a ride

13. harvested / almost ready / help you pick / need to prepare

14. had an argument / texted her saying / apology through / in person

15. college freshmen / relaxing / watch the sunrise / should wake up

16~17. enjoy sports / families can play / minimal equipment / table tennis / bowling

01. annual e-sports competition / need some volunteers / fill out / information

02. progress / take a walk / see things differently / come up with

03. breakable items / fastest way / an extra charge / do the express mail

04. wearing the hat / guitar next to / set up two speakers / poster on the wall

05. invitation / expecting / mean the smartphone / buy it now

06. for my sofa / 40 / go well with / It will give you

07. project for art class / I'm afraid / take care of / someone else

08. picking up trash / be held in / bring our own gloves / sign up for

09. we're hosting / All kinds of / vote for / receive a trophy

10. What's our budget / capacity / power-saving mode / warranties

11. So many people / in advance

12. grade / should go ask

13. secondhand bookstore / with a message / brings a smile / leave a note

14. planning / feel closer / helps me relieve / don't have any equipment

15. science group assignment / different sections / suddenly realizes / check out

16~17. introduce the best foods / high level of / calms the mind / nuts / sends signals / reduces

01. was supposed to hold / caused a leak / change the location / enjoy the performance

02. go for a run / in / get hurt / wear the right shoes

03. fan of your articles / start your costume designs / pick just one / our magazine

04. striped pattern / between two plants / round clock / two lamps

05. put them up around / terrific / lights / chairs for the audience

06. I'd like to order / large size is 50 / on all purchases / to be delivered

07. seem busy / has been booked / take care of / won't be back for

08. open to / This year's theme / deadline / winner will receive

09. opportunity to create / lecture about the history / register in advance / includes the cost

10. pay more than 300 / shouldn't get / less storage space / reviews are based on

11. bought / where you got

12. our food / less than 40

13. haven't seen you / important for my grade / Skipping meals / eat regularly

14. how to improve / repeatedly / put in more effort / over and over

15. passionate about environmental issues / careless / agrees / ask her to design

16~17. overtourism happens / deal with the problems / fewer / promote / limit access / docking on / car-restricted

21 | 2023년 11월 학력평가   p.173

01. wonderful experience / provides / Foreign languages / accompany you to where

02. translated text before copying / meanings different from / original writing / results

03. online marketplace / you've been using / want to sell / pick it up

04. hanging plant / dream big / square-shaped table / vending machine

05. did a survey / motivate / fewest leftovers / Could you prepare

06. service plans / 30 / I'd like that / promotion is over

07. chemistry project / book signing / all yours / attend my friend's wedding

08. December 23rd / medical check-up / a limit of / doing a good deed

09. one-day / is interested in / for a small fee / register in advance

10. not reasonable / standing desk / recyclable / doesn't match

11. real honor / mostly write about

12. to be in time / shuttle bus

13. opened a brand new / install / free trial period / it depends on you

14. with hearing difficulties / The more detailed / middle of the semester / position still

15. list of places / super delicious / reviews complaining / choose a better

16~17. avoid when feeding / single / cherries / large amounts / contains so much acid / harmful

22 | 2024년 3월 학력평가   p.178

01. heavy rain / make some rearrangements / delayed by / appreciate

02. thinking of buying / On my way here / basic traffic rules / stricter rules

03. worried about / tip about time management / miss the things

04. lockers on the left / trophy / right side / newspaper on the table

05. supplies / Anything else / chess set / take it with

06. fruit and vegetables / two bags of / five / get a discount

07. practice for / brought my soccer shoes / family dinner gathering / make up for

08. only for freshmen / materials / deadline for applying / giving out prizes

09. You're supposed to / such as / participate for two hours / application form

10. speed / more than / different / remaining battery

11. purse / last have

12. lunch / it's hard

13. get involved in / struggling with / right tone / recommend a good book

14. divide the roles / take on / necessary / only part left

15. attending / focusing very carefully / drops / opening hours

16~17. health / reduce the symptoms / rich source / pineapple / eating bananas / suffering from

23 | 2024년 6월 학력평가   p.183

01. snack bar to celebrate / lobby / impressed by / own personal cups

02. used an artificial-intelligence / saves / false / shouldn't blindly trust

03. stay connected with / Continuously making such comparisons / feel small / negative effect on

04. kite stuck / holding balloons / basket full of / playing the violin

05. applied for / upload your introduction / decided to participate in / I'll show you mine

06. stylish and functional / special discount only on / 10 / a total of

07. rock concert / kind of activity / Come and watch us / attend my uncle's birthday

08. announcement / July 13th / much does it cost / expect about the same

09. delighted to announce / bioengineering / deadline for registration / 30 people

10. battery life / charge it as often / wet cleaning / The white one

11. adopting / could at least consider

12. completely forgot / Where should I

13. pain in my knee / local clinic / bad posture / learn from an instructor

14. climate change / animals in danger / Small things matter / school club

15. unusually tired and pale / without taking a break / couple of days off

16~17. representative / upcoming election / following / social media / display posters / use of pamphlets / website among

24 | 2024년 9월 학력평가   p.188

01. fireworks / extending the operational hours / regular last train / convenience

02. right before bed / Long exposure to / negative impact / quality

03. completely unrelated to / exploring activities / different from / powerful tool

04. recording studio / long desk between / chair looks comfortable / flower patterns

05. exhibition booths / welcome gifts / online invitation / confident

06. light and easy / 50 / go well with / use this discount coupon

07. equipment / tests are finally / practice dancing / made it through

08. residents / aged 60 and above / How do I register / don't forget to take

09. delicious journey / September / Every single dish / celebration of culture

10. pay more than 60 / Less than / water intake / one that's not

11. how does that relate

12. throwing / good condition

13. motivated / assign individual tasks / lead to overlapping / you should do

14. hard to get in / careful about when / noticed / that's enough

15. Upon receiving / complicated / good at / help her with

16~17. made from natural materials / properly wash / avoid shrinking / its shape / sensitive / as little as

▶ **Don't hesitate to V :** 주저하지 마라

Please **don't hesitate to apply** for this volunteer work at our charity soccer match.

자선 축구 경기의 자원봉사 활동에 **지원하는 데 주저하지 마십시오.**

출처: 2024학년도 대학수학능력시험 01번

▶ **get into an argument :** 말다툼을 하게 되다

Tiffany and I **got into an argument** at school.

Tiffany와 제가 학교에서 **말다툼을 했어요.**

출처: 2024학년도 대학수학능력시험 02번

▶ **cut A off :** (말 등을) 끊다

That's why when somebody's talking, you shouldn't **cut them off**.

그래서 누군가 말할 때는 **그들의 말을 끊**지 말아야 한단다.

출처: 2024학년도 대학수학능력시험 02번

▶ **experience trouble V-ing :** ～하는 데 어려움을 겪다

But recently, more and more people are **experiencing trouble falling** asleep.

하지만 최근에 점점 더 많은 사람들이 잠드는 **데 어려움을 겪고 있습니다.**

출처: 2024학년도 대학수학능력시험 03번

▶ **eye-catching :** 눈길을 끄는

And isn't that striped tablecloth really **eye-catching**?

그리고 저 줄무늬 식탁보는 정말로 **눈길을 끌**지 않나요?

출처: 2024학년도 대학수학능력시험 04번

▶ **bother :** 괴롭히다, 귀찮게 하다

Then, are your allergy symptoms **bother**ing you again?

그럼, 알레르기 증상이 또 너를 **괴롭히는 거**야?

출처: 2024학년도 대학수학능력시험 07번

▶ **make it :** 성공하다, 도착하다

I'm afraid I can't **make it** this time.

미안하지만 이번에는 **갈 수** 없어.

출처: 2024학년도 대학수학능력시험 12번

▶ **look forward to V-ing :** ～하기를 기대하다

That's too bad. I was **look**ing **forward to seeing** you there.

아쉽다. 나는 거기서 너를 **보기를 기대하고** 있었어.

출처: 2024학년도 대학수학능력시험 12번

▶ **put A off :** 미루다, 연기하다

You make me think of my old passion to be a painter, but I **put it off** for too long.

당신은 화가가 되고 싶다는 저의 오랜 열정에 대해 생각하게 만드시지만, 저는 너무 오랫동안 **그것을 미뤘어요.**

출처: 2024학년도 대학수학능력시험 13번

▶ **hold :** 가지고 있다, 중단하다

Oh, there's one copy left there, but unfortunately we can't **hold** it for you.

오, 거기에 한 권이 남아 있는데 유감스럽게도 저희가 고객님을 위해 그것을 **예약해 드릴** 수는 없네요.

출처: 2024학년도 대학수학능력시험 14번

▶ **make sure :** 반드시 ~하다
make sure you visit our school library to submit your application.
신청서를 제출하기 위해 **반드시** 학교 도서관을 방문해 주십시오.
출처: 2023학년도 대학수학능력시험 01번

▶ **rich in :** ~이 풍부한
It said apple peels are **rich in** vitamins and minerals, so they moisturize our skin and enhance skin glow.
사과 껍질은 비타민과 미네랄**이 풍부해서**, 피부에 수분을 공급하고 피부 광채를 향상시킨다고 했어요.
출처: 2023학년도 대학수학능력시험 02번

▶ **It seems ~ :** ~인[한] 것 같다
It seems to include useful information.
유용한 정보를 포함하고 있는 **것 같아**.
출처: 2023학년도 대학수학능력시험 04번

▶ **remind A of B :** A에게 B에 대해 다시 한 번 알려주다
We need to **remind** our loyal customers **of** the event.
우리는 단골 고객들에게 행사에 대해 **다시 한 번 알려 줘야** 해요.
출처: 2023학년도 대학수학능력시험 05번

▶ **What about ~? :** ~은 어때?
What about the live music?
라이브 음악**은 어때요?**
출처: 2023학년도 대학수학능력시험 05번

▶ **be scheduled to V :** ~할 예정이다
I'm **scheduled to** shoot your school's graduation photos on Wednesday, November 23rd.
11월 23일 수요일에 선생님 학교의 졸업 사진을 촬영**할 예정이에요**.
출처: 2023학년도 대학수학능력시험 08번

▶ **in stock :** 재고가 있는
These are the ones we have **in stock**.
이것들은 **재고가 있는** 것들이에요.
출처: 2023학년도 대학수학능력시험 10번

▶ **be willing to V :** ~할 의향이 있는
How much **are** you **willing to** spend?
얼마를 쓰실 **의향이 있으신가요?**
출처: 2023학년도 대학수학능력시험 10번

▶ **fair :** 박람회; 공정한
Our son said he's going to a career **fair** and asked if we can come along.
우리 아들이 직업 **박람회**에 갈 거라고 우리가 함께 갈 수 있는지 물어봤어요.
출처: 2023학년도 대학수학능력시험 12번

▶ **have trouble with :** ~으로 곤란을 겪다
Is there anything specific you're **having trouble with**?
특별히 **곤란한 일이 있는** 거니?
출처: 2023학년도 대학수학능력시험 13번

▶ **for no reason :** 이유 없이, 공연히
Does your dog chew up your shoes or bark **for no reason** at times?
당신의 개가 당신의 신발을 씹거나 때때로 **이유 없이** 짖나요?
출처: 2022학년도 대학수학능력시험 01번

▶ **what do you think about[of]? :** ~에 대해 어떻게 생각해?
What do you think about the balloons next to the welcome banner**?**
환영 현수막 옆에 있는 풍선들**에 대해 어떻게 생각해?**
출처: 2022학년도 대학수학능력시험 04번

▶ **I guess (that) ~ :** ~이라고 생각하다
Oh, then **I guess** you have to study for the science quiz, right?
오, 그럼 과학 퀴즈를 위한 공부를 해야 **하는구나**, 그렇지?
출처: 2022학년도 대학수학능력시험 07번

▶ **on one's way to :** ~으로 가는 길[도중]에
Actually, I'm **on my way to** volunteer at the school library.
사실, 학교 도서관에 자원봉사를 하**러 가는 중**이야.
출처: 2022학년도 대학수학능력시험 07번

▶ **for free :** 무료로, 공짜로
We'll also give out a children's science magazine **for free**.
저희는 또한 어린이 과학 잡지를 **무료로** 나눠드릴 것입니다.
출처: 2022학년도 대학수학능력시험 09번

▶ **in advance :** 미리
There's no admission fee, but to participate, you must register **in advance**.
입장료는 없지만, 참가하시려면, **미리** 등록하셔야 합니다.
출처: 2022학년도 대학수학능력시험 09번

▶ **available :** 이용 가능한
Oh, only these rooms are **available**.
오, 이 룸들만 **이용 가능하**구나.
출처: 2022학년도 대학수학능력시험 10번

▶ **enough to V :** ~하기에 충분히 …한
We need a room big **enough to** accommodate six of us.
우리 6명을 수용**할 만큼 충분히** 큰 룸이 필요해.
출처: 2022학년도 대학수학능력시험 10번

▶ **since :** ~ 때문에, ~한 이래로
Since we're meeting for two hours, I don't think we can spend more than $20 per hour.
우리는 두 시간 동안 만나기로 했**기 때문에**, 시간당 20달러 이상은 쓸 수 없을 것 같아.
출처: 2022학년도 대학수학능력시험 10번

▶ **beyond :** ~을 초과한, ~을 뛰어넘는
It's **beyond** our budget.
그것은 우리의 예산을 **초과해**.
출처: 2022학년도 대학수학능력시험 10번

▶ **look up at :** ~을 올려다보다
Oh, so you went outdoors to **look up at** stars.
오, 그럼 별을 **올려다보**기 위해서 야외로 나갔겠구나.
출처: 2021학년도 대학수학능력시험 02번

▶ **become familiar with :** ~에 친숙해지다
And I think it helped my son **become familiar with** mathematical concepts.
그리고 그것은 내 아들이 수학 개념**에 친숙해지**도록 도와준 것 같아.
출처: 2021학년도 대학수학능력시험 02번

▶ **get used to N/V-ing :** ~에 익숙해지다
I think looking at stars is a good way for kids to **get used to** mathematical concepts.
별을 보는 것은 아이들이 수학 개념**에 익숙해지**는 좋은 방법인 것 같아.
출처: 2021학년도 대학수학능력시험 02번

▶ **be honored to V :** ~하게 되어 영광으로 생각하다
I'm **honored to** interview the person who designed the school I'm attending.
제가 다니는 학교를 설계하신 분을 인터뷰**하게 되어 영광으로 생각해요**.
출처: 2021학년도 대학수학능력시험 03번

▶ **fill A up with B :** A를 B로 가득 채우다
We're going to **fill** those **up with** donations of toys and books.
저희는 그것들**을** 장난감과 책 기증품들**로 가득 채울** 거예요.
출처: 2021학년도 대학수학능력시험 04번

▶ **need to V :** ~해야 한다
It was founded to deliver the message that we **need to** admit our failures to truly succeed.
그곳은 우리가 진정으로 성공하기 위해서는 우리의 실패를 인정**해야 한다**는 메시지를 전달하기 위해 설립되었어.
출처: 2021학년도 대학수학능력시험 08번

▶ **advance to :** ~에 진출하다
We had the most applicants in the history of this competition, and only 10 participants will **advance to** the final round.
이 대회의 역사상 가장 많은 지원자들이 있었으며, 오직 10명의 참가자들만 결선**에 진출할** 것입니다.
출처: 2021학년도 대학수학능력시험 09번

▶ **be about to V :** ~할 예정이다
You cannot park here because we**'re about to** close off this section of the parking lot.
저희가 주차장의 이 구획을 폐쇄**할 예정이**기 때문에 여기에 주차하실 수 없습니다.
출처: 2021학년도 대학수학능력시험 12번

▶ **be out of :** ~이 없다
We**'re out of** this model right now.
지금 당장은 이 모델**이 없어요**.
출처: 2021학년도 대학수학능력시험 13번

▶ **break down :** 고장 나다
My washing machine **broke down** yesterday.
제 세탁기가 어제 **고장 났어요**.
출처: 2021학년도 대학수학능력시험 13번

2025 마더텅 전국연합 학력평가 기출문제집 시리즈

학교 시험에 자주 출제되는 유형을 철저히 분석하여 적용한 유형별 기출문제집
중간·기말고사와 전국연합 학력평가 대비를 위한 기출문제집

NAME

book.toptutor.co.kr
구하기 어려운 교재는 마더텅
모바일(인터넷)을 이용하시면
즉시 배송해 드립니다.

고1 국어 영역 문학, 독서, 언어(문법) 수학 영역 공통수학1, 공통수학2 **영어 영역** 독해, 듣기, 어법·어휘 **탐구 영역** 통합사회1, 통합사회2 통합과학1, 통합과학2
고2 국어 영역 문학, 독서, 언어(문법) 수학 영역 수학Ⅰ, 수학Ⅱ **영어 영역** 독해, 듣기, 어법·어휘 **과학탐구** 물리학Ⅰ, 화학Ⅰ, 생명과학Ⅰ, 지구과학Ⅰ

9차 개정판 3쇄 2025년 3월 14일 (초판 1쇄 발행일 2015년 12월 15일) **발행처** (주)마더텅 **발행인** 문숙영
책임 편집 정다혜, 성현영
해설 집필 변선영, 신재진 **교정** 신재진, 조해라, 류도이, 한수연, 윤병철, 마혜진, 김보란, 윤은채, 손유민 / 이성수, 신종윤, 강희원, 김다현, 김미희, 오정문, 장영민, 신철현, 이은혜, 김민정, 한선영, 전진성, 김도현, 박소유, 박지연, 이용민, 심가원, 윤수빈, 전진리, 전도윤
해설 감수 김유경(올패스영어학원), 강산(EBS 영어)
디자인 김연실, 양은선 **인디자인 편집** 허문희 / 박수경 **컷** 박수빈 / 곽원영
제작 이주영 **홍보** 정반석 **주소** 서울시 금천구 가마산로 96, 708호 **등록번호** 제1-2423호(1999년 1월 8일)

*이 책의 내용은 (주)마더텅의 사전 동의 없이 어떠한 형태나 수단으로도 전재, 복사, 배포되거나 정보검색시스템에 저장될 수 없습니다.
*잘못 만들어진 책은 구입처에서 바꾸어 드립니다. *교재 및 기타 문의 사항은 이메일(mothert1004@toptutor.co.kr)로 보내 주시면 감사하겠습니다.
*이 책에는 네이버에서 제공한 나눔글꼴이 적용되어 있습니다. *교재 구입 시 온/오프라인 서점에 교재가 없는 경우 고객센터 전화 1661-1064(07:00~22:00)로 문의해 주시기 바랍니다.

마더텅 교재를 풀면서 궁금한 점이 생기셨나요? 교재 관련 내용 문의나 오류신고 사항이 있으면 아래 문의처로 보내 주세요!
문의하신 내용에 대해 성심성의껏 답변해 드리겠습니다. 또한 교재의 내용 오류 또는 오·탈자, 그 외 수정이 필요한 사항에 대해 가장 먼저
신고해 주신 분께는 감사의 마음을 담아 네이버페이 포인트 1천 원 을 보내 드립니다!

*기한: 2025년 12월 31일 *오류신고 이벤트는 당사 사정에 따라 조기 종료될 수 있습니다. *홈페이지에 게시된 정오표 기준으로 최초 신고된 오류에 한하여 상품권을 보내 드립니다.
🏠 홈페이지 www.toptutor.co.kr 🖥 교재Q&A게시판 ● 카카오톡 mothertongue ● 이메일 mothert1004@toptutor.co.kr
🎧 고객센터 전화 1661-1064(07:00~22:00) ✉ 문자 010-6640-1064(문자수신전용)

마더텅은 1999년 창업 이래 2024년까지 3,320만 부의 교재를 판매했습니다. 2024년 판매량은 309만 부로 자사 교재의 품질은 학원 강의와 온/오프라인 서점 판매량으로 검증받았습니다. [마더텅 수능기출문제집 시리즈]는 친절하고 자세한 해설로 수험생님들의 전폭적인 지지를 받으며 누적 판매 855만 부, 2024년 한 해에만 85만 부가 판매된 베스트셀러입니다. 또한 [중학 영문법 3800제]는 2007년부터 2024년까지 18년 동안 중학 영문법 부문 판매 1위를 지키며 명실공히 대한민국 최고의 영문법 교재로 자리매김했습니다. 그리고 2018년 출간된 [뿌리깊은 초등국어 독해력 시리즈]는 2024년까지 278만 부가 판매되면서 초등 국어 부문 판매 1위를 차지하였습니다.(교보문고/YES24 판매량 기준, EBS 제외) 이처럼 마더텅은 초·중·고 학습 참고서를 대표하는 대한민국 제일의 교육 브랜드로 자리잡게 되었습니다. 이와 같은 성원에 감사드리며, 앞으로도 효율적인 학습에 보탬이 되는 교재로 보답하겠습니다.

마더텅 학습 교재 이벤트에 참여해 주세요. 참여해 주신 분께 선물을 드립니다.

이벤트 1 1분 간단 교재 사용 후기 이벤트

마더텅은 고객님의 소중한 의견을 반영하여 보다 좋은 책을 만들고자 합니다. 교재 구매 후, <교재 사용 후기 이벤트>에 참여해 주신
모든 분께 감사의 마음을 담아 네이버페이 포인트 1천 원 을 보내 드립니다. 지금 **바로 QR 코드를 스캔**해 소중한 의견을 보내 주세요!

이벤트 2 마더텅 교재로 공부하는 인증샷 이벤트

필수 태그 #마더텅 #마더텅기출 #공스타그램
인스타그램에 <마더텅 교재로 공부하는 인증샷>을 올려 주시면 참여해 주신 모든 분께 감사의 마음을 담아
네이버페이 포인트 2천 원 을 보내 드립니다. 지금 **바로 QR 코드를 스캔**해 작성한 게시물의 URL을 입력해 주세요!

이벤트 3 딕테이션 이벤트

본 교재의 24회 딕테이션 페이지를 오려서 마더텅으로 보내 주세요! 추첨을 통해 소정의 상품을 보내 드립니다.

참여 방법 24회 딕테이션 (p.187~190) 풀이 및 채점 완료 → 해당 페이지를 모두 오려서 마더텅에 발송(우편, 택배 등)
→ QR 코드를 스캔하고 발송 인증

주소 (08501) 서울특별시 금천구 가마산로 96, 대륭테크노타운 8차 708호, 마더텅 이벤트 담당자 앞 / 010-6640-1064

※ 이벤트 기간: 2025년 12월 31일까지 (*해당 이벤트는 당사 사정에 따라 조기 종료될 수 있습니다.)

※ 자세한 사항은 해당 QR 코드를 스캔하거나 홈페이지 이벤트 공지 글을 참고해 주세요. ※ 당사 사정에 따라 이벤트의 내용이나 상품이 변경될 수 있으며 변경 시 홈페이지에 공지합니다.

※ 상품은 이벤트 참여일로부터 2~3일(영업일 기준) 내에 발송됩니다. (단, 이벤트 3은 예외) ※ 동일 교재로 세 가지 이벤트 모두 참여 가능합니다. (단, 같은 이벤트 중복 참여는 불가합니다.

01회
2018년 11월 학력평가   문제편 p.2 해설편 p.1

01 ②	02 ②	03 ①	04 ④	05 ①
06 ③	07 ⑤	08 ④	09 ④	10 ⑤
11 ④	12 ①	13 ④	14 ④	15 ⑤
16 ①	17 ③			

02회
2019년 3월 학력평가   문제편 p.5 해설편 p.6

01 ④	02 ⑤	03 ⑤	04 ④	05 ②
06 ①	07 ④	08 ④	09 ③	10 ②
11 ②	12 ①	13 ⑤	14 ②	15 ①
16 ①	17 ③			

03회
2019년 6월 학력평가   문제편 p.8 해설편 p.10

01 ①	02 ③	03 ①	04 ⑤	05 ①
06 ④	07 ②	08 ④	09 ①	10 ③
11 ②	12 ①	13 ②	14 ④	15 ③
16 ①	17 ⑤			

04회
2019년 9월 학력평가   문제편 p.11 해설편 p.15

01 ①	02 ③	03 ②	04 ④	05 ⑤
06 ④	07 ②	08 ④	09 ⑤	10 ⑤
11 ⑤	12 ①	13 ①	14 ①	15 ③
16 ①	17 ③			

05회
2019년 11월 학력평가   문제편 p.14 해설편 p.20

01 ③	02 ①	03 ④	04 ④	05 ⑤
06 ②	07 ④	08 ④	09 ⑤	10 ②
11 ②	12 ①	13 ④	14 ①	15 ①
16 ③	17 ③			

06회
2020년 3월 학력평가   문제편 p.17 해설편 p.25

01 ①	02 ⑤	03 ③	04 ④	05 ⑤
06 ②	07 ⑤	08 ⑤	09 ④	10 ②
11 ②	12 ①	13 ①	14 ③	15 ⑤
16 ⑤	17 ④			

07회
2020년 6월 학력평가   문제편 p.20 해설편 p.30

01 ②	02 ⑤	03 ②	04 ④	05 ⑤
06 ③	07 ⑤	08 ④	09 ⑤	10 ②
11 ①	12 ⑤	13 ①	14 ③	15 ①
16 ②	17 ④			

08회
2020년 9월 학력평가   문제편 p.23 해설편 p.34

01 ⑤	02 ①	03 ①	04 ④	05 ①
06 ⑤	07 ⑤	08 ⑤	09 ⑤	10 ②
11 ②	12 ④	13 ④	14 ②	15 ⑤
16 ①	17 ②			

09회
2020년 11월 학력평가   문제편 p.26 해설편 p.39

01 ②	02 ①	03 ②	04 ③	05 ③
06 ③	07 ②	08 ⑤	09 ⑤	10 ④
11 ⑤	12 ④	13 ①	14 ⑤	15 ③
16 ④	17 ④			

10회
2021년 3월 학력평가   문제편 p.29 해설편 p.44

01 ④	02 ④	03 ①	04 ③	05 ④
06 ③	07 ①	08 ②	09 ⑤	10 ②
11 ①	12 ①	13 ②	14 ③	15 ④
16 ②	17 ④			

11회
2021년 6월 학력평가   문제편 p.32 해설편 p.48

01 ②	02 ②	03 ②	04 ④	05 ④
06 ①	07 ③	08 ③	09 ④	10 ③
11 ②	12 ①	13 ①	14 ⑤	15 ③
16 ①	17 ④			

12회
2021년 9월 학력평가   문제편 p.35 해설편 p.53

01 ④	02 ②	03 ③	04 ③	05 ⑤
06 ③	07 ③	08 ③	09 ④	10 ②
11 ①	12 ①	13 ③	14 ①	15 ④
16 ②	17 ③			

13회
2021년 11월 학력평가   문제편 p.38 해설편 p.58

01 ②	02 ③	03 ①	04 ⑤	05 ②
06 ③	07 ①	08 ④	09 ④	10 ③
11 ①	12 ⑤	13 ⑤	14 ②	15 ③
16 ④	17 ⑤			

14회
2022년 3월 학력평가   문제편 p.41 해설편 p.62

01 ①	02 ③	03 ②	04 ④	05 ④
06 ③	07 ③	08 ③	09 ⑤	10 ③
11 ①	12 ⑤	13 ②	14 ②	15 ①
16 ④	17 ④			

15회
2022년 6월 학력평가   문제편 p.44 해설편 p.67

01 ②	02 ①	03 ⑤	04 ⑤	05 ①
06 ③	07 ①	08 ⑤	09 ⑤	10 ④
11 ①	12 ⑤	13 ③	14 ④	15 ④
16 ②	17 ④			

16회
2022년 9월 학력평가   문제편 p.47 해설편 p.71

01 ②	02 ⑤	03 ②	04 ④	05 ④
06 ③	07 ②	08 ②	09 ⑤	10 ④
11 ③	12 ④	13 ①	14 ③	15 ④
16 ①	17 ④			

17회
2022년 11월 학력평가   문제편 p.50 해설편 p.76

01 ①	02 ①	03 ①	04 ④	05 ⑤
06 ④	07 ①	08 ⑤	09 ④	10 ②
11 ②	12 ③	13 ③	14 ④	15 ②
16 ②	17 ④			

18회
2023년 3월 학력평가   문제편 p.53 해설편 p.81

01 ⑤	02 ②	03 ③	04 ⑤	05 ②
06 ②	07 ①	08 ③	09 ④	10 ②
11 ②	12 ①	13 ③	14 ④	15 ④
16 ③	17 ④			

19회
2023년 6월 학력평가   문제편 p.56 해설편 p.85

01 ②	02 ④	03 ①	04 ④	05 ⑤
06 ③	07 ④	08 ⑤	09 ③	10 ④
11 ①	12 ①	13 ②	14 ④	15 ⑤
16 ③	17 ④			

20회
2023년 9월 학력평가   문제편 p.59 해설편 p.89

01 ⑤	02 ①	03 ③	04 ⑤	05 ①
06 ⑤	07 ④	08 ⑤	09 ④	10 ④
11 ④	12 ④	13 ③	14 ④	15 ⑤
16 ③	17 ③			

21회
2023년 11월 학력평가   문제편 p.62 해설편 p.94

01 ②	02 ①	03 ⑤	04 ④	05 ①
06 ⑤	07 ⑤	08 ④	09 ④	10 ③
11 ①	12 ②	13 ④	14 ①	15 ④
16 ①	17 ⑤			

22회
2024년 3월 학력평가   문제편 p.65 해설편 p.99

01 ②	02 ②	03 ④	04 ④	05 ②
06 ③	07 ③	08 ④	09 ④	10 ⑤
11 ③	12 ⑤	13 ②	14 ②	15 ①
16 ①	17 ②			

23회
2024년 6월 학력평가   문제편 p.68 해설편 p.103

01 ②	02 ①	03 ③	04 ⑤	05 ④
06 ③	07 ③	08 ②	09 ④	10 ④
11 ③	12 ②	13 ⑤	14 ②	15 ②
16 ③	17 ③			

24회
2024년 9월 학력평가   문제편 p.71 해설편 p.108

01 ②	02 ②	03 ⑤	04 ④	05 ②
06 ④	07 ④	08 ⑤	09 ④	10 ④
11 ④	12 ②	13 ①	14 ①	15 ⑤
16 ⑤	17 ③			

영어 성적 향상 공부 방법

정서윤 님
서울 창덕여자고등학교
연세대학교 문화인류학과 합격
영어 영역 2등급 → 1등급
사용 교재 **까만책** 국어 언어와 매체, 한국지리, 정치와 법, 생활과 윤리, 윤리와 사상, 사회·문화
노란책 영어 영역

2023 마더텅 제7기 성적향상 장학생 은상

20분 제한 시간

시간을 20분 맞추어 놓고 문제를 풀었습니다. 문제를 풀며 모르는 단어를 미리 표시해 두었고, 채점 후에 모르는 단어들을 해설지에서 찾아 뜻을 적고 외웠습니다. 틀린 문제들은 시간 제한 없이 다시 풀었습니다.

단어 외우기

문제를 풀며 모르는 단어들을 꼭 체크해서 외워주는 게 매우 중요합니다. 특히 마더텅의 경우에는 해설지에 바로 단어의 뜻이 나와 있어 손쉽게 외울 수 있습니다.

손서영 님
경남 장유고등학교
부산대학교 간호학과 합격
영어 영역 3등급 → 2등급
사용 교재 **까만책** 국어 화법과 작문, 수학Ⅰ, 수학Ⅱ, 화학Ⅰ, 생명과학Ⅰ **빨간책** 영어 영역

2023 마더텅 제7기 성적향상 장학생 동상

영어 공부는 적은 양이라도 매일 푸는 것이 중요하다고 생각하여, 듣기와 독해 문제를 분리하여 매일 조금씩 풀었습니다. 특히 듣기 문제는 아침에 가볍게, 독해 문제는 점심 후에 집중해서 풀었으며, 특히 독해 문제는 40분 시간 제한 내에 풀고, 어려운 문제나 오래 걸린 문제는 색 있는 펜으로 다시 독해하여 학습했습니다.

모르는 단어나 헷갈리는 단어는 마더텅 교재의 단어장을 활용하여 지문에 기록해주었으며, 이를 통해 문맥에 맞는 단어 뜻을 이해하고, 실전에서 독해를 유연하게 풀 수 있었습니다.

최정우 님
강원 육민관고등학교
서울대학교 건축학과 합격
영어 영역 2등급 → 1등급
사용 교재 **까만책** 국어 문학, 물리학Ⅰ, 화학Ⅱ **빨간책** 영어 영역

2023 마더텅 제7기 성적향상 장학생 은상

1. 듣기

저는 듣기 부분과 독해 부분을 나누어서 풀이하였습니다. 평소 듣기에는 굉장히 자신이 있어서 듣기를 매번 풀지는 않았고, 가끔씩 감을 유지하기 위해 사용하였습니다.

2. 독해

독해 부분은 듣기 시간과 마킹 시간을 감안하여 18~45번 문제를 50분의 시간에 맞춰 풀이하는 것을 연습했습니다. 채점 뒤에 좀

더 학습이 필요한 유형을 파악하였고, 그 문제 유형에 대해서만 기출문제를 추가로 풀이한 뒤에 다시 틀린 문제를 풀어보는 방식으로 학습하였습니다. 추천을 하나 드리자면, 정해진 순서대로 푸는 것보다 3월에는 3월 모의고사를 풀고, 6월에는 6월 모의고사를 푸는 식으로 여러분의 타임라인에 맞춰 풀어가는 것이 모의고사, 그리고 수능을 준비하는 더 좋은 방법이라고 생각합니다.

김서영 님
부산 부산센텀여자고등학교
중앙대학교 독일어문학과 합격
영어 영역 2등급 → 1등급
사용 교재
까만책 국어 독서, 국어 문학, 국어 화법과 작문, 수학Ⅰ, 수학Ⅱ, 확률과 통계, 영어 독해

2023 마더텅 제7기 성적향상 장학생 동상

영어 성적 향상을 위해 매일 150개의 단어를 외우고, 마더텅 책을 통해 어려운 30번대 문항을 반복해서 풀이했습니다. 특별한 전략은 없었으며, 매주 적어도 3일 이상 공부하는 꾸준한 노력이 중요하다고 생각합니다.

김은채 님
강원 삼척여자고등학교
성균관대학교 생명과학과 합격
영어 영역 3등급 → 2등급
사용 교재 **까만책** 국어 독서, 영어 독해, 영어 듣기, 생명과학Ⅰ

2023 마더텅 제7기 성적향상 장학생 동상

1. 학습계획표 적극 활용 마더텅의 학습계획표는 영어 영역의 문항 배치를 따라 한 달 동안 한 권의 문제집을 완료할 수 있도록 도와주고, 자가 성취도를 평가하여 복습이 필요한 문제를 식별할 수 있습니다.

2. 동영상 강의 활용 유형별 tip 동영상을 활용하여 문제 해결 전에 유형에 대한 도움을 받고, 문제 풀이 시간을 효율적으로 관리하기 위해 쉬운 문제는 30초 내에, 어려운 문제는 최대 2분 내에 푸는 것을 목표로 합니다. 해설지를 통해 문제 해석을 하고, 색으로 문장의 구조와 모르는 단어의 뜻을 표시하여 이해를 도와주고, 동영상 강의를 통해 어려웠던 부분을 보완해줬습니다.

3. 많은 문제 풀기 영어 영역은 언어 공부의 일환으로, 많은 문장과 문제를 풀어야 합니다. 학습계획표에 명시된 분량을 최대한 따르고, 시간이 남으면 추가 문제도 도전했습니다. 듣기 능력 향상을 위해 처음에는 1배속으로 시작해 점차 속도를 높였으며, 모래 주머니 효과를 이용하여 더 어려운 속도를 연습했습니다. 듣기 대본의 빈칸을 채우고 문제를 풀고, 다시 들으면서 틀린 부분을 확인하고 모르는 단어를 학습했습니다.